A History of
MEDIEVAL
IRELAND

A History of
MEDIEVAL
IRELAND

A. J. OTWAY-RUTHVEN

Lecky Professor of History in the University of Dublin

With an Introduction by

KATHLEEN HUGHES

Fellow of Newnham College, Cambridge

LONDON · ERNEST BENN LIMITED
NEW YORK · BARNES & NOBLE INC

First Published *1968* by Ernest Benn Limited
Bouverie House · Fleet Street · London . EC4
and Barnes & Noble Inc. · *105* Fifth Avenue · New York *10003*

Distributed in Canada by
The General Publishing Company Limited · Toronto

© A. J. Otway-Ruthven *1968*

Printed in Great Britain

510-27801-9

Foreword

THIS book can be no more than an interim report: on almost every aspect of the middle ages in Ireland there is still an infinity of work to be done. I am painfully conscious of two major gaps, the economic history of the period, and the history of Gaelic Ireland, subjects which have hardly been touched by any writer and without which any account of the period is necessarily incomplete. But in the absence of any modern general work on medieval Ireland I have attempted to provide the synthesis which the student needs.

My debt to Miss K. Hughes for her introductory chapter is sufficiently obvious, but I have many others to thank. My colleague, Dr J. F. Lydon, read the whole book in typescript, saving me from many errors and making a number of valuable suggestions. My students, Miss Rosemary Fisher, Mr P. W. A. Asplin, and Mr C. A. Empey, allowed themselves to be used as guinea-pigs at an early stage. Mr E. G. Quin translated the fragment of Munster annals in University College, Oxford, MS 103 for me, and Mr K. W. Nicholls was unfailingly generous with references and transcripts. The Rev. P. Hiscock read my proofs. I have reason to be grateful to the staffs of all the libraries which I have used, to the patience and skill of the printers and publishers, and to Mrs K. M. Davies, who redrew my maps. To Trinity College, which has been the background of my whole working life, I owe more than I can ever express. But my primary debt is to my first teacher, the late Professor Edmund Curtis, to whose honoured memory this book is dedicated. I have differed from him on many points, as my own pupils will no doubt differ from me: I should be well content if I could think that they would remember me with as much gratitude and affection as I do him.

Trinity College, Dublin
August 1967   JOCELYN OTWAY-RUTHVEN

NOTE ON SPELLING

The spelling of Irish names presents certain difficulties. Where a generally accepted English form exists it has been used; where there is no such form, as in the case of a few place-names and the occasional personal name, I have used the Irish spelling.

ACKNOWLEDGEMENT

The maps in this book are based on the Ordnance Survey by permission of the Government of the Republic of Ireland (Permit No. 800).

Contents

vii

Maps

List of Abbreviations

AC	*The Annals of Connacht.*
A. Clon.	*The Annals of Clonmacnoise.*
Ad. Vit. Col.	*Adomnan's Life of Columba.*
AFM	*Annals of the Kingdom of Ireland by the Four Masters.*
AI	*The Annals of Innisfallen.*
ALC	*The Annals of Loch Cé.*
A.L.I.	*Ancient Laws of Ireland.*
A.P.C.	*Proceedings and Ordinances of the Privy Council of England.*
Arm.	*The Book of Armagh.*
A. Tig.	*Annals of Tigernach.*
AU	*Annals of Ulster.*
Betham, *Early Parliaments*	Betham, Sir W., *The Origin and History of the Constitution of England, and of the Early Parliaments of Ireland.*
B.M.	British Museum.
C.C.H.	*Rotulorum Patentium et Clausorum Cancellarie Hibernie Calendarium.*
C.C.R.	*Calendar of Close Rolls.*
C.D.I.	*Calendar of Documents Relating to Ireland.*
C.G.	*Críth Gablach.*
Clyn, *Annals*	*The Annals of Ireland by Friar John Clyn and Thady Dowling.*
Col.	*Collectio Canonum Hibernensis.*
Conf.	Confession of St Patrick.
Congress	*Proceedings of the International Congress of Celtic Studies, 1959.*
Council in Ireland	*A Roll of the Proceedings of the King's Council in Ireland.*
C.P.R.	*Calendar of Patent Rolls.*
C.S.	*Chronicon Scotorum.*
Dowling, *Annals*	See Clyn, *Annals.*
Early Statutes	*Statutes and Ordinances and Acts of the Parliament of Ireland, King John to Henry V.*
E.H.R.	*English Historical Review.*

Grace, *Annals*	*Jacobi Grace, Kilkenniensis, Annales Hiberniae.*
I.E.R.	*The Irish Ecclesiastical Record.*
I.H.S.	*Irish Historical Studies.*
Journ. C.H.A.S.	*Journal of the Cork Historical and Archaeological Society.*
Journ. R.S.A.I.	*Journal of the Royal Society of Antiquaries of Ireland.*
Llanthony Cartularies	*The Irish Cartularies of Llanthony Prima et Secunda.*
Lynch, *Feudal Dignities*	Lynch, W., *A View of the Legal Institutions, Honorary Hereditary Offices, and Feudal Baronies, Established in Ireland during the Reign of Henry the Second.*
MacFirbis, *Annals*	'Annals of Ireland . . . translated by Dudley Firbisse, or . . . Duald Mac Firbis . . .'
N.L.I.	National Library of Ireland.
Pa. I	Canons of the 'First Synod of St. Patrick'.
Pa. II.	Canons of the 'Second Synod of St. Patrick'.
Pipe Roll, *14 John*	The Irish Pipe Roll of 14 John.
Pipe Roll of Cloyne	*Rotulus Pipae Clonensis.*
P.L.	*Patrologia Latina.*
P.R.O.	Public Record Office.
Proc. R.I.A.	*Proceedings of the Royal Irish Academy.*
Reg. Alen	*Calendar of Archbishop Alen's Register.*
Reg. All Hallows	*Registrum Prioratus Omnium Sanctorum juxta Dublin.*
Reg. Fleming	Lawlor, H. J., 'A Calendar of the Register of Archbishop Fleming'.
Reg. Sweteman	Lawlor, H. J., 'A Calendar of the Register of Archbishop Sweteman'.
Rep. D.K.	*Reports of the Deputy Keeper of the Public Records of Ireland.*
T.C.D.	Trinity College, Dublin.
Thes. Pal.	*Thesaurus Palaeohibernicus.*
Trans. R. Hist. Soc.	*Transactions of the Royal Historical Society.*
U.J.A.	*Ulster Journal of Archaeology.*
Z.C.P.	*Zeitschrift für celtische Philologie.*

Introduction

GERALD of Wales tells us that he came to Ireland in 1183 partly to join in the Norman conquest, partly to see and explore the country, and to examine 'the primitive origin of its race'.[1] He returned in 1185 in the entourage of Prince John, and subsequently began his 'History'. It is generally recognized that his information was unsatisfactory and his point of view prejudiced: nevertheless his writings throw some light on an invader's attitude to the native Irish. Gerald stresses the primitive character of their way of life. They have rich pastures, good fishing and hunting, but poorly developed agriculture and 'little use for the money-making of towns'. They are lazy people, who think that 'the greatest pleasure is not to work and the greatest wealth is to enjoy liberty'. Their clothes and fashions are odd, their customs barbarous. The Normans had come as conquerors: in their military discipline, their castle-building, their financial organization and political administration their superiority to the Irish was immediately recognizable.

From Gerald's charge of barbarism the Irish may be defended. Much of his evidence would, however, support a just claim for the archaism of their civilization. During the millenium and more before the Normans arrived in Ireland, Britain and much of Europe had twice been fundamentally altered. Rome had re-formed in every aspect the lives of the Celtic peoples who came within her orbit, legal, administrative, linguistic, literary and artistic, and her influence endured to some extent long after her Empire fell. Then the Germanic barbarians had overrun the Empire. Ireland had missed the domination of Rome and had escaped the barbarian invasions, all save the very latest of them from Scandinavia. The Normans were the descendant of these most recent barbarian invaders, an energetic, ruthless, ambitious people, whereas Irish civilization in the tenth century probably still had much in common with that of the Gaulish Celts before the Romans arrived. The

---

[1] *Expugnatio*, ed. J. F. Dimock, *Opera* V (*Rolls S.* 1867), p. 351.

archaism of Irish civilization provides some explanation both of the success and of the difficulties of the Norman conquest and settlement, so it seems worth while to glance at its varied aspects.

The history of Ireland during the period immediately before the coming of Christianity has to be reconstructed partly from material evidence and partly from later literature. Of these two sources, material evidence might be expected to provide the more reliable authority. But although Ireland is exceptionally rich in antiquities, comparatively few sites have been properly excavated and most of these have revealed themselves as belonging to an earlier period or to Christian times, so that there is all too little detailed evidence about the settlements of the last few decades of paganism. Sites which have been competently excavated cannot always be precisely dated, because of the absence of dateable objects.[2]

Work on the material evidence has, however, made it very clear that the physical life of Ireland changed little during the first millenium A.D.[3] Throughout this period there was a settled population, living in fortified enclosures and in isolated huts, with private property in stock and at least private usufruct in land.[4] The chief wealth of the richer inhabitants was in stock, in particular, cattle: excavations of Early Christian sites have produced vast quantities of animal bones, which show that, after cattle, pigs formed the largest part of the farm stock, then sheep and horses.[5] The Two-mile Stone settlement provided evidence of large, irregularly shaped walls enclosing fields which must have been used as animal enclosures, and of terraces which may have been used for cultivation.[6] Corn was certainly grown in Ireland in the pre-Christian period, but throughout the first millennium tillage was decidedly subordinate to stock raising in Irish economy.[7] The excavation of Leacanabuaile (north of Caherciveen in co. Kerry) showed a site which may serve as indication of the life of a small community throughout

[2] For example St Gobnet's House, Ballyvourney. Report by Professor O'Kelly, *Journ.C.H.A.S.*, LVII (1952), pp. 18 ff.

[3] See V. B. Proudfoot, 'The Economy of the Irish Rath', *Mediaeval Archaeology*, V (1961), pp. 94–122.

[4] O. Davies, *Journ.R.S.A.I.*, LXXII (1942), pp. 98 ff., describing a settlement at Two Mile Stone in Co. Donegal.

[5] e.g. Ballinderry II, *Proc.R.I.A.*, XLVII (1941–2), p. 68; Lagore *Proc.R.I.A.*, LIII (1950), p. 225. For 'Cattle in Ancient and Mediaeval Irish Society', see A. T. Lucas, *O'Connell School Union Record, 1937–58*.

[6] see note (4) above.

[7] Duignan, 'Irish Agriculture in early historic times', *Journ.R.S.A.I.*, LXXIV (1944), pp. 124 ff.

the first millennium.[8] Here, although no fine ornaments were recovered, the people spun and wove cloth, had a plough and querns, and kept quite a well-stocked farm, mainly of cattle.

Archaeological evidence and literary evidence written down during the Christian period often support and complement each other, as Professor O'Kelly demonstrated when, after excavating some ancient Irish cooking places, he followed the practices related in the literary sources to boil and roast his joints at them, with outstanding success.[9] The most authoritative of the written information on early Irish society is to be found in the law tracts, generally recorded in the eighth century: here the work of the late Professor Thurneysen and of Professor Binchy has shown that the law tracts provide further information on Irish economy and social structure which can be fitted perfectly into the framework provided by the archaeologists. The heroic tales of the Ulster Cycle, however, provide one major problem of correlation with the material evidence. They were written down in the mid-seventh or early eighth century, at about the same time as the early law tracts, and they provide a self-consistent and circumstantial account of a pre-Christian society which seems to be similar to that which Roman occupation destroyed in Gaul and Britain.[10] But they depict a people among whom charioteering was one of the practices of the warrior aristocracy, whereas excavation has not brought to light any of the more important parts of chariots (as it has in Britain and Gaul).[11] Moreover the tales, though they provide vivid pictures of pre-Christian Irish society, show us an ideal life more or less confined to one class: they are what the pagan Irish aristocracy *ought* to have been like. Precisely how far back their tradition takes us is disputed, for while a generation ago scholars thought that their historical setting belonged to a period round about the time of the birth of Christ, there are now seen to be strong arguments in favour of a date considerably later.[12]

The La Tène civilization (which the tales depict) seems to have been established in Ireland at the end of the third century or in the

---

[8] Ó Ríordain and Foy, *Journ.C.H.A.S.*, XLVI (1941), pp. 85–99; see also L. and M. de Paor, *Early Christian Ireland*, p. 81. The excavators suggested a date during the Early Christian period for this site, possibly IX–X century. For a reappraisal of the dating see E. Rynne, *Proc.R.I.A.*, LXIII, C (1964), pp. 272–3.

[9] *Journ.R.S.A.I.*, LXXXIV (1954), pp. 105 ff.: the carbon dating techniques then employed suggested that these sites belonged to the Bronze Age.

[10] For a recent discussion see K. Jackson, *The Oldest Irish Tradition: a Window on the Iron Age*, Cambridge, 1964.

[11] E. M. Jope discusses the evidence for chariotry and paired draught in *U.J.A.*, XVII (1954), pp. 38 ff.

[12] Perhaps about the fourth century. See Jackson, op. cit.

second century B.C., but there is no reason to assume that it reached
its full flowering in Ireland and then died out at the same time as
it did in Britain. Ireland underwent no revolution in taste as Britain did, although in the first centuries A.D. Irish metalworkers
were in touch with British craftsmen, taking up the technical ac-
complishments of British workshops.[13] Fine objects, such as the
Keshcarrigan bowl, were imported.[14] With the weakening of Britain in the late fourth and early fifth centuries, Irish raiders went
over for loot, represented by the hoards from Balline and Ballin-
rees, and, most well known of all, illustrated by the career of St
Patrick. But in spite of such foreign contacts the designs of La
Tène art continued in Ireland until they were modified by the
new motifs introduced from Christian Europe, and even then they
are easily recognizable in the illumination and metalwork of the
Christian period.[15]

The early Irish law tracts, with their traditional corpus of law,
reveal a non-classical, heroic society which must go back in its
essentials to the pre-Christian period. At the head of it was an
aristocracy composed of the noble grades, whose status was measured partly by the number of their clients (céli). The clients
were of two classes, each having well defined rights and duties,
and beneath them were the tenants-at-will, people who might
be settled on a lord's land but whose condition was semi-
servile.[16]

The clients and their households were the people upon whom
Irish economy mainly rested. The law tracts indicate various grades
of commoner (boaire), men who belonged to the franchise-holding
classes of society, and who held from the lord a fief, usually of
stock, in return for rent.[17] Such a contract existed between the lord
and his free-client (soer-chéle). The lord might, however, give his
client not only a fief of stock but also a payment equal to the client's
honour price. When this occurred the commoner became the base-
client (doer-chéle or céle giallnai) of the lord and, in addition to the
food rent, provided an agreed amount of labour, for example in
building his fort and at harvest time. The lord had a share in the

---

[13] Jope and Wilson, *U.J.A.*, XX (1957), pp. 95–100. Cf. Jope, *U.J.A.*, XVII
(1954) pp. 81–91, for parallels of an earlier period.

[14] Jope, *U.J.A.*, XVII (1954), pp. 92 ff.

[15] F. Henry, *Irish Art* (London, 1965), opens with the statement: 'A remarkable continuity is one of the most striking aspects of Irish art.'

[16] One class of tenant-at-will was the *bothach*, 'cottier'. See G. MacNiocaill, 'The
Origins of the *Betagh*', *The Irish Jurist*, I (1966), pp. 292–98.

[17] The best brief account is by Professor Binchy, in *Early Irish Society*, ed. M.
Dillon, pp. 52–65. The notes to Professor Binchy's edition of *Críth Gablach* provide
an extremely valuable glossary of legal terms.

compensations due for certain injuries to his base client, but the client retained clearly defined legal rights.

Crith Gablach, compiled in the early eighth century, describes at some length a man of free-client status whom the tract regards as the typical free-commoner.[18] He is the *mruigfher*, or 'land-man'. He was a small farmer of some substance, for he was supposed to have land worth twenty-one *cumals*[19] stocked with twenty milch cows, two bulls, six oxen, twenty pigs, twenty sheep, four boars, two brood sows and a horse. He had adequate tools for farm work, icnluding his own plough, and his farm kitchen was well equipped. In the house he kept a supply of malt, salt and charcoal, and he had bacon, milk and ale always available. His own honour-price (*dire*) was six *sets* in value, and he could act in law on behalf of anyone up to that amount, while his property was protected from deliberate damage by definite amounts of compensation. The 'land-man' held a fief of stock from a lord of two *cumals* value (that is, twice the amount of his own honour-price) and paid on it quite a heavy annual rent of one milch cow with various accessories (vegetables and milk in summer, meat-products in winter). His rent was thus something like one sixth the value of his fief of stock, not counting the winter and summer food.

This represents a prosperous and independent class of commoners. Even the base client might terminate his contract with his lord under certain conditions and seek another lord. The client was able to improve his farm by his own work and build up his stock, and a commoner who became wealthy could rent out his stock to clients of his own, so that after three generations his grandson would be reckoned as a member of the noble grades. The structure of early Irish society, as it is described in the law tracts, provided opportunity for a considerable proportion of the population to reach a state of moderate plenty: the *mruigfher* described above must have lived almost as comfortably as the lord. What, then, were the rewards of nobility?

Honour was the noble's especial prerogative. This attribute was not estimated by physical amenities, though the noble afforded patronage to smiths and craftsmen, probably enjoyed richer clothing and certainly possessed finer horse-trappings, jewellery and personal possessions than the commoner. He was also accompanied by a larger retinue: the *aire tuise* (the fourth out of the seven grades

---

[18] ed. D. Binchy, Dublin, 1941. For the *mruigfher*, lines 171 ff.

[19] A *cumal* denotes a female slave, and is the highest unit of value. Six *sets* normally equals one *cumal*, and a *set* is usually calculated at one heifer or half a milch cow.

of nobility beginning with the king which are distinguished by *Críth Gablach*) had a retinue of eight men on public occasions, six when about his private affairs. But a man's status was measured chiefly by the amount of protection he could provide. In a society which had very little centralized authority and where law was privately executed, each class of society in effect controlled and protected its inferiors. In any contract sureties were taken for its performance, and a man could go surety only up to the value of his own honour-price; so the higher his status the more useful he could be. In certain legal cases oath helpers were required, and the oath of a man of superior rank had more weight than that of an inferior, so that he was said to 'over-swear'. By the time *Críth Gablach* was written down, a man could not offer eye-witness evidence (*fiadnaise*) or evidence as to character (*teist*) in cases involving an amount greater than his own honour-price. So in the actual execution of justice the man of high status had a wide competence.

The nobility as a class stood in close relationship to the king. The *aire túise* represented his kindred in dealings with the king, from whom he held a fief of stock and to whom he owed food rent and personal attendance. It was men like the *aire túise* who made up the petty king's retinue, and formed the core of the king's hostings. A man of the noble grades must on no account appear a coward and must be prepared to fight to defend his reputation: nevertheless the hero-tales give idealized portraits of the aristocracy, and the average noble must have been less proficient and less dangerous than the heroes of the epic tales.

The noble drew his income from the rents of his tenants. The *aire túise* had fifteen base clients who owed him labour services as well as rent, and twelve free clients from whom he drew his own retinue. The economy throughout the pre-Viking period must have been generally stable, for large parts of Ireland provide good land for pastoral farming, which could well bear the existing population, periodically reduced as it was by pestilence. Gerald complained that the Irish were lazy, but in the non-scientific, mainly pastoral farming of the Dark Ages there was little incentive to anything more than moderate physical effort. The noble classes seem to have done no manual work, and a considerable part of their time must have been spent in entertainment. In the weekly scheme of the king's business provided by *Críth Gablach*, only two days are spent on litigation and affairs of the kingdom, the rest of the week is taken up with domestic pleasures, chess playing and sport (in which horses and deer-hounds for hunting figure), and however unreal this schematization may be it shows what the lawyer thought to be the proper occupations of a king. In the king's hall there was a place not only for lawyers and the highest class of *filid*, but also for harpers, pipers, horn-players and jugglers. The quality of hospitality which a man could provide was one of the marks of his status.

The king's public business was, indeed, very limited. The petty king (or *rí tuaithe*, king of one *tuath*) had a higher honour-price than anyone except over-kings. *Críth Gablach* defines his *dire* as seven *cumals*: the noble grade next to him in rank has an honour-price of five *cumals*, the *aire tuise* (the fourth grade of nobility already mentioned) is worth between three and four (twenty *sets*), and the average free commoner one (the *mruigfher*, who has a *dire* of six *sets*). This means that in all legal proceedings within the kingdom the king had a wider competence than anyone else and could 'over-swear' all his fellows. The traditional common law was not generally executed by the king: nevertheless he had some responsibility for seeing that it was kept, for at the assembly (*oenach*) of his kingdom he had to take pledges for its performance. He had direct executive authority in domestic affairs only in certain defined crises, after his people had been defeated in battle or after pestilence. Under such circumstances he might be needed to protect them from each other, but the assumption is that normally the franchise-holding classes are themselves able to execute the common law. He represents his own kingdom in dealings with neighbouring *tuatha*, much as the *aire tuise* represents his kindred in dealings with the king. It is the king who is responsible for drawing up legal agreements with other kings, and taking pledges to see that they are kept. He also summons and leads his own host, both to protect his own kingdom and to make war against another king who refuses to come to terms or fails to keep agreements. The king, the lawyers say, ought to be just and fair-minded, ready to consult the learned, steady and patient. All the same, in domestic affairs he is merely the most important of the nobility: his functions are little different in kind from theirs, he merely enjoys a wider competence owing to his higher honour-price. It is as a war-leader that the king comes into his own. Normally only in leading his host to battle or in representing his kingdom in affairs with other kings has he special functions.

The Irish law of dynastic succession did not add to the security of the king's position, for every man whose father, grandfather or great-grandfather had held royal authority seems to have been himself 'the material of a king' and to have been eligible in theory for kingship. In practice one, the *tánaise ríg*, was probably designated as successor during the lifetime of the reigning king. All the same there were plenty of candidates, so that adversity or defeat in battle not infrequently ended in a change of ruler.

There were scores of petty kingdoms in early Ireland. They were loosely joined together in groups of three or four which recognized a royal overlord. These over-kings had no direct authority in the government of the petty kingdoms under their overlordship, but they could summon contingents from their sub-kingdoms to a larger host. Above them there was yet another class of over-king, the *rí ruirech* or 'king of over-kings', the highest class known to the law-tracts, with an honour-price of fourteen *cumals*, whose legal competence over-rode that of any other man and who therefore provided the highest executive authority in any case in which he was involved. *Críth Gablach* describes the king of Cashel as one of this class. It was not until much later that the *rí ruirech* secured anything like a universal overlordship. The legal evidence makes it clear that the overlordships were provincial, and the annals show that even the Fair of Tailtiu (which earlier Irish historians regarded as a national assembly) was regional in character.[20] The 'high-king', a title known to literature, has no constitutional significance at this period.[21]

The Irish legal and political system shared aspects in common with that of the Germanic barbarians, for example the importance of status, the idea that injuries must be paid for by compensation[22] and the inviolability of custom. But there are some marked differences. The political hierarchy in Ireland was more complicated, and lent itself less readily to the development of centralization. We shall see that the multitude of petty kingdoms made it comparatively easy to effect a landing, but very difficult to establish a permanent conquest. Moreover the function of the kindred in Irish society was not identical with that in the Teutonic. To the Irishman, as to the Anglo-Saxon, kin was of immense importance, for a man inherited his status from his forebears, as an adult often lived with the family group and could not dispose of the property he had inherited without the consent of his kin.[23] Yet, whereas in Irish

---

[20] The evidence is set out by D. A. Binchy, 'The Fair of Tailtiu and the Feast of Tara', *Ériu*, XVIII (1958), pp. 116 ff.

[21] Binchy, *Ériu*, XVIII (1958), pp. 44–54.

[22] In Germanic law compensation is calculated according to the *wergild* (the price paid if a man were killed) of the various classes.

[23] A man's immediate kin was a group of four generations, the *derbfhine*, consisting of persons related in the male line up to and including second cousins, who were the agnatic descendants of a common great-grandfather. The *derbfhine* was the normal property-holding unit. See D. Binchy in *Early Irish Society*, ed. M. Dillon, p. 58. There were also wider kin groups: see the text edited by M. Dillon, *Studies in Early Irish Law*, pp. 129 ff.

and Anglo-Saxon law the kindred was largely responsible for the liabilities and defaults of its members, Irish law apparently had a more highly developed surety system for which there is no close parallel in Anglo-Saxon society. When an Irishman made an important contract he gave a pledge and took sureties, which might be of three different kinds; one (the *ráth*) warrants with his property the performance of the obligation on which the principal had entered, another (the *aitire*) warrants it with his own person which may be imprisoned, and a third (the *naidm*) forces the *ráth*, by such means as distress, to fulfill his undertakings. No man could go surety for anyone with a higher honour-price than his own, but a man need not confine himself to his own kin in seeking sureties. There was no public authority in Ireland to execute the law, but the sureties, as well as the kin, played an important part in securing a man's rights.

Another considerable difference between Irish and Anglo-Saxon society rests in the relationship between a man and his lord, for Irish law lays much less emphasis on this than the English sources, which show that the association provided an important emotional, as well as legal, bond in England. Nor has England the highly developed fosterage system which is to be found in Ireland, where children were often sent away from their own homes for fosterage according to a system which is governed by detailed rules, concerning, for example, the fees required, what the child is to be taught, the fosterer's liability for the child's misdeeds and his responsibility for keeping him free from harm. This institution implies both legal and emotional ties beyond the immediate kindred, ties which might be continued in adult life when a man maintained a foster-parent in his old age. It adds to the complexity of Irish heroic society.

In this entirely de-centralized society, where no one public authority was finally responsible for the execution of the law, but where litigation was common, there was a special class of scholars who kept alive the knowledge of the law. Classical writers make it plain that the Celtic society of pre-Roman Gaul had had its learned class, composed of the *vates* who officiated at religious functions, the bards who were poets and singers, and the druids who were philosophers, teachers, lawyers and judges. The druids there were a highly respected, wealthy group who had submitted to a long process of oral education. We do not know exactly how the learned classes of pre-Christian Ireland functioned, but they certainly existed, and the lawyers and poets (*filid*) continued in the Christian period.

Secular law remained a distinct profession, with its technicalities and obscurities deliberately fostered by the archaic language in which it was repeated. Different law schools existed in Ireland where scholars received a long oral training, and where in the seventh and eighth centuries legal texts were written down and later received glosses and commentaries. At least one of these law schools, that in which the *Nemed* collection of texts was compiled, was closely associated with the poets, for the law was there learnt 'with a thread of poetry around it'.[24] Another school, belonging to the northern half, where the *Senchas Mar* was recorded about the beginning of the eighth century, seems to have been more specialized, a professional school of law.

There were many legal texts to be learned, and some scholars never proceeded beyond the lower grades of their profession. Such men were experts only in certain branches of the law, whereas the man who had reached its peak (the *ollam*) was universally competent: a tract on status, the *Miadslechta*, calls him 'an expert in every kind of knowledge in which his judgement is sought: he is consulted, he consults nobody'.[25] The juniors could plead cases or act as agents. It was not the jurist's business to execute the law, but to give advice when asked and to pass judgements on cases submitted to him for arbitration. The king had his own judge constantly in attendance, who stayed with him even when his normal retinue was reduced to three in the month of sowing (a ruling which has a very archaic sound), and on formal occasions sat in a place of honour very near the king.

The *filid*, whose training was also by memory, held a function in society as important as the jurists', for it was they who remembered genealogies and 'history'. Knowledge of a man's genealogy was necessary to establish his status and his claims to inheritance, so the king's *fili*, who knew the dynasty and origins of the royal house, was an essential part of his retinue. The lines on the fort of Rathangan and its seven generations of chiefs, though they are not in the old alliterative metre normally employed by the *filid*, record the kind of knowledge which the court poets of the kings of the Uí Berraidi must have possessed:

> The fort over against the oakwood,
> It was Bruigde's, it was Cathal's,
> It was Aed's, it was Ailill's,
> It was Conaing's, it was Cuiline's,
> And it was Mael Duin's.
> The fort remains after each king in turn
> And the hosts sleep in the ground.[26]

[24] Binchy, *Ériu*, XVII, p. 5.
[25] Binchy, *Ériu*, XVIII, p. 50.
[26] G. Murphy, *Early Irish Lyrics*, p. xvi.

What the *fili* held in his memory was information on genealogies and dynasties, tales of the heroic deeds of the past and the places with which they were associated. These formed his idea of 'history' (*senchas*), to be related at the *oenach* or to an aristocratic audience in the king's hall[27]; for the *fili* had a fund of such stories, so that he could relate a different one on each evening from the onset of winter (*Samain*, 1 November) to the coming of summer (*Beltaine*, 1 May), stories of cattle-raids, battles, sacks and sieges, feasts, wooings, elopements, adventure-journeys, deaths. The *filid* could not only recite such stories at length, but could expound them, using anecdotes for illustration,[28] and they were thus to a considerable degree the guardians of social morality for the aristocracy.

The saga of the Battle of Allen concerns a battle fought in 722 between the king of Leinster and the Uí Néill overlord, and exists in a text of the eleventh or twelfth century. It well demonstrates some of the qualities of the Irish 'historian'. The composer gives us the reason for the battle and the names of the Uí Néill kings who fell at the hands of the victorious Leinstermen: but the hero of the story is the story-teller and musician Donn Bo. It is he whose presence encourages men to join the northern host, he who is invited to provide entertainment before the battle and refuses, promising that the next night he will make music for king Fergal. So far the account is within the bounds of the possible, but the 'historian' also records the frenzy which seized nine kings at the battle, the shout of the minstrel Ua Maiglinni which remained in the air when his head was struck off, the singing of the severed head of Donn Bo, the joining of Donn Bo's head to his body and his resuscitation. All this was 'history' to the Irish story-teller, and by far the most moving part of the story is the singing of the lifeless Donn Bo, first with the other musicians on the battle field to his dead lord, then, his severed head set upon a pillar and his face to the wall, to the carousing Leinstermen until all the host wept at the sadness of his music. The learned class guarded the traditions of a people, and by reciting to an aristocratic audience trained to listen and appreciate, they maintained a common literary language and a common taste. Until the Norman conquest, which put an end to the *oenachs* and disturbed the patronage which the *filid* enjoyed, they maintained a continuous tradition intact from the pre-Christian past.

[27] G. Murphy, 'Bards and Filidh', *Éigse*, II (1940), pp. 200–207. Cf. Binchy, '*Filidecht* and *Coimgne*', *Ériu*, XVIII, pp. 139 ff.

[28] This is S. Mac Airt's suggestion, *Ériu*, XVIII (1958), p. 150. He considers the *fo-scéla* (anecdotes) may be a forerunner of hagiographical literature.

The *filid* were the most important of the men of letters; below them were other ranks, including the *baird* who composed panegyrics such as the ninth-century poem in praise of Aed, a north Leinster king. Such eulogies were rewarded with gifts and sung at feasts,[29] and the demand for them continued long after the Norman conquest.

In the pre-Christian period the *filid* may also have been seers and prophets. Our knowledge of the religious beliefs and practices of pagan Ireland is restricted by the nature of the sources, but studies in etymology and folk-lore are bringing to light traces of continuity with the pagan period. The major pagan festivals had been held at *Imbolc* (1 February), *Beltaine* (Mayday), *Lugnasad* (the beginning of harvest) and *Samain* (1 November): *Samain* was taken over by All Saints, *Imbolc* by St Brigid. According to Cormac's Glossary there were three sister-goddesses of this name worshipped by the *filid*, and Gerald tells of a sacred fire maintained at Kildare behind a hedge which no man must cross. The festival of *Lugnasad*, at the beginning of August, fell at a convenient time for public assemblies: Ulster seems to have held its fair at Emain then, Leinster at Carman, while the king of Tara convened the Uí Néill assembly at Tailtiu. These were the great provincial gatherings, opportunities for public business, judicial cases, the exchange of merchandise, games and sport; but less important assemblies of similar character also met for the sub-kingdoms, usually on the site of an ancient burial ground.[30]

There was still believed to be a definite connection in the historic period between the good king and the fertile land. The king was married to his land; and his union with her should bring forth a rich progeny, for at the inauguration rite of a king (his *banfheiss rigi*, or 'wife-feast of kingship') he was wedded to the goddess Ériu or to some other local goddess.[31] The annals say that the *cena* (alias *feis*) *Temro*, was held for Loegaire (*AU* 454) Ailill Molt (*AU* 470) and Diarmait (*AU* 560). These were presumably still pagan inauguration rites which ceased in the sixth century, for Diarmait's is the last in the series mentioned in the early annals; but the concept of the king's marriage to his land was preserved in the

[29] As the last stanza exclaims: 'Melodious praise songs modulate the name of Aed through pools of drink.' *Thes. Pal.*, II, p. 295. Flower, *Irish Tradition*, p. 28, Murphy 'Bards and Filidh,' *Éigse*, II (1940), p. 205.

[30] Máire Mac Neill has assembled the evidence for *The Festival of Lughnasa* in her book (Oxford, 1962). She points out that the major pilgrimages to the heights of Croagh Patrick, Slieve Donard and Mount Brandon were held on the last Sunday in July or the first Sunday in August.

[31] O'Rahilly, *Ériu*, XIV (1940), p. 14. *Feis* is the verbal noun of *foaid*, 'sleeps, spends the night'. On the *feis Temro* see J. Carney, *Studies in Irish Literature and History* (Dublin, 1955), pp. 334 ff.

literature,[32] and is most strikingly repeated in annal entries describing the inauguration of Felim O'Connor, king of Connacht, at Carnfree in 1310, a ceremony where Felim 'married the province of Connacht', which was considered to be 'the most splendid kingship-marriage ever celebrated in Connacht down to that day'.[33] Gerald's disgusted account of the inauguration rite of one of the Tirconnell kings, in which the king is joined to a mare upon which all the assembled company later feast, may have some foundation in twelfth-century folk-memory, if not in current practice.[34]

An early Irish king seems to have been limited by traditional prohibitions (gessa) and to have been compelled to follow certain traditional prescriptions (buadha). A tract edited by Professor Dillon describes the prescriptions of the king of Tara:

the fish of the Boyne, the deer of Luibnech, the mast of Mana, the bilberries of Bri Leith, the cress of Brossnach, water from the well of Tlachtga, the hares of Naas. All of these used to be brought to the king of Tara on the first of August (i.e. the feast of Lugnasad). And the year in which he used to consume them did not count against him as life spent, and he used to be victorious in battle on every side.

The tract names, in prose and verse, the gessa and buadha of the kings of Tara, Leinster, Munster, Connacht and Ulster, and concludes:

It is certain of the kings of Ireland, if they avoided their gessa and obtained their buadha, that they should suffer neither misfortune nor disturbance, and neither plague nor pestilence would come in their reign, and they would not fail with age before ninety years.[35]

Among the seven self-evident proofs giving superior testimony to the falsehood of a king which are named in one law tract are defeat in battle, dearth in his reign, dryness of cows, blight of fruit, scarcity of corn.[36] The lawful king must be accepted by the land, which manifests its pleasure in fertility. Success is the proof of his right. The king must protect his people, but he is more than the war-leader: he is mystically in union with the land.

The annals illustrate these attributes of the king. For example, they give in scattered sentences the career of Aed Alláin the son of that Fergal, overlord of the north, who had been killed at the battle of Allen. Aed was king of the Cenél Eóghain, one of the northern Uí Néill peoples, and in 732, 733 and 734 he fought with

<hr />

[32] See Binchy, Ériu, XVIII, p. 133 for references.
[33] AC, p. 323, ALC, I, p. 545.
[34] There is a Hindu ceremonial by which the king's wife enacts a symbolical union with a horse which is later killed and dismembered. Ireland and India, at the extreme ends of the Indo-European world, may both have preserved a similar archaic fertility rite. For Gerald's account, see Proc.R.I.A., LII, C, p. 168.
[35] Proc.R.I.A., LIV, C, pp. 8 ff.   [36] A.L.I., IV, 52.

Flaithbertach king of Cenél Conaill and overlord of the north. Flaithbertach was defeated and Aed finally took his place as overlord in 734. With it he seems to have assumed the protection of the *paruchia Patricii*, for in 735 (*AFM*) he went successfully to war with the Ulidians, incited by the abbot of Armagh in revenge for the profanation of a church. Two years later a meeting between Aed overlord of the northern half and Cathal king of Munster was held at Terryglass on the northern borders of Munster, and at this meeting the two over-kings agreed to impose the *Lex Patricii* throughout their realms.[37] Aed was now at the peak of his career. In the following year (738) he went to war with Leinster. The Annals of Ulster given an account of this battle in Latin, but in a style very unlike the usual laconic entries, as if the annalist were paraphrasing from a saga. The Leinstermen were completely routed. The two kings met in single combat, 'of whom one (that is Aed Alláin) survived though wounded, while the other had his head severed by the sword of battle'. But though Aed's army was undoubtedly victorious, the battle seems to have ended the distinguished years of his career, for the annals mention him no more until his overthrow. His victorious encounters now completely cease. In 742, moreover, there was disease[38] and the following year a rival, Domnall son of Murchad, defeated him in battle at Kells and took the overlordship from him. Aed's heroic period seems to have terminated with his wounding, and the season of disease must have further weakened his position, so that defeat and death followed. The warrior king who failed was rejected by land and people.

The structure of society described above, its economy, its legal and judicial system, its language and literature, retained a recognizable identity throughout the first half of Irish history up to the coming of the Normans. But during this period there were two major influences from without which substantially modified Irish life. The first in time, and the most far-reaching in its effect, was Christianity. Irish historians chose to record the speed with which Christianity had been accepted, and the cordial feelings which had always existed between the aristocracy and the clergy,[39] but closer

---

[37] *Lex Patricii tenuit Hiberniam.* For the 'laws' of saints, see below p. 27.
[38] *Lepra in Hibernia.*
[39] See the archbishop of Cashel's answer to his critic Gerald: 'Our people have always paid great honour and reverence to churchmen, and they have never put out their hands against the servants of God. But now a people has come to the kingdom (i.e. the Normans) which knows how, and is accustomed, to make martyrs.' Ed. J. J. O'Meara, *Proc.R.I.A.*, LII, C (1949), p. 171, and transl., *The Topography of Ireland*, Dundalk, 1951, p. 100.

examination of the sources suggests that the conversion was neither so quick nor so easy as later historians assumed, and that the seventh-century clergy whose writings form the basis for later accounts were consolidating a position which had been quite recently won.

Patrick leaves us in no doubt of the difficulties which he had to face in the first generation of the conversion: his imprisonment in fetters, his constant fear for his life and crucial danger on twelve different occasions, his anticipation of a martyr's death.[40] The canons attributed to Patricius, Auxilius and Iserninus (which I believe belong to the first half or middle of the sixth century[41]) show us a church not yet fully integrated with a society which was still predominantly pagan. The clergy had not yet taken their place alongside the *filid* in the legal structure, for a cleric might belong to the nobility or he might be detained *iugo servitutis*,[42] a man without the privileged status which Irish clerics had obtained by the time they appear in the seventh-century sources, when they had been assimilated to the noble grades. These canons imply that the jurists were still heathen, for they forbid Christians to take cases for trial to the secular courts.[43] We have already seen that king Diarmait celebrated the *feis Temro* in or about 560; this is the king who, according to a tradition reported in some versions of the annals,[44] had been fiercely opposed by Columcille at the battle of Culdrebene in 561, and for whom Fraechán made a 'druid's fence'. He may still have been a pagan.

Muirchú, writing his Life of Patrick towards the close of the seventh century, was rejoicing in the triumph of Christianity over paganism. The first chapters of the Life deal with Patrick's captivity in Ireland and escape (for which Muirchú was using a text of the Confession) and his training on the continent (for which he made use of material about Auxerre, possibly originally relating to Palladius). Then comes a long section dealing with the contest between Patrick and the pagan king Loegaire and his druids. This is without doubt the most dramatic part of the Life, where Muirchú's interest centred, and whereas much hagiography reads like a scrappy collection of anecdotes and information assembled from various different sources (indeed, Muirchú ends his Life with this

---

[40] *Conf.* cc. 15, 34, 52, 55, 59.
[41] For a discussion of their dating see Hughes, *The Church in Early Irish Society*, pp. 44 ff and Professor Binchy in the forthcoming number of *Studia Hibernica*.
[42] Ibid., pp. 46 ff on the cleric mentioned in *Pa.I.* 8 who is a *naidm* or enforcing surety and therefore a member of the noble grades. *Pa I.* 7 for the cleric held 'under the yoke of servitude'. See Binchy, *Studia Hibernica*, forthcoming number.
[43] *Pa I.* 21.   [44] *A. Tig.* in R.C. XVII, 143–4, *C.S.* 561.

kind of thing, and there is more appended in a further book) the
central part of Muirchú's Life has continuity and reads as if it were
a summary of some saga. Zimmer saw the most dramatic story in
it—that of the pagans' fury at Patrick's paschal fire which he had
lighted before the royal fire had been kindled on the pagan festival,
the subsequent encounter between Patrick and the *magi* and the
confusion of the pagan host—as reflecting the seventh-century ecclesiastical controversy on the date of Easter. The pagan fire ritual
to which Muirchú refers is to be associated with the festival of
Beltaine (Mayday),[45] so that Muirchú deliberately altered the
timing of his story, which certainly has undertones of the ecclesiastical controversies and political developments of the period.[46]
All the same, Muirchú's theme is the conquest of paganism, and
to it he constantly returns. He starts with the prophecy of the
pagan seers, couched in obscure verse, goes on to the first converts,
the opposition and death of Patrick's former pagan master. Then
comes the major encounter of the paschal and heathen fires on
Easter eve staged at the place 'which was the head of all heathenism
and idolatry, so that this unconquered wedge' (he means Christ's
resurrection) 'should be driven at the outset into the head of all
idolatry'. The king's seers know that, unless it is at once extinguished, Patrick's fire 'will never be put out'. On the following day,
when Patrick comes to the hall of Tara, Dubthach, one of the *filid*
(*poetam optimum*), rises to do him honour, and a series of contests
take place between Patrick and the king's *magi*. In the end the
king reluctantly submits to the Christian faith. This part of Muirchú's Life is a statement that Christianity had triumphed over the
strongholds of paganism, as by the later seventh century it had
certainly done: but Patrick's own Confession shows us 'a people
just coming to the faith' (c. 38), and the evidence suggests that
some of the most distinguished members of society, kings and men
of learning, clung to their paganism at least until well on in the
sixth century.

Christianity brought a new faith: as Patrick says, 'those wretches
who adore the sun' must give way to the true Sun, Christ (*Conf.*
60). It also brought a new learned class. By the seventh century the
filid as a class were Christian and the clerics had taken their place
alongside them. One law tract, *Uraicecht Bec*, probably drawn up
in the seventh or early eighth century, gives the priest an honour-
price equal to that of the petty king, and though there are differences between the tracts on the precise value accorded to the

---

[45] As Professor Binchy has clearly shown, *Ériu*, XVIII, p. 130.
[46] For a discussion of the various points of view, see Hughes, op. cit., pp. 116 ff.

various ecclesiastical grades, it is clear that bishops, priests, scribes and abbots are all in the top level of an aristocratic society. This means that the bishop can 'overswear' his inferiors; in *Críth Gablach* he is accompanied by a retinue of twelve like the petty king, and has similar rights to hospitality.[47] The early set of canons seems to forbid the cleric to act as an enforcing surety (*naidm*), a function which might have required him to take violent action,[48] but later the secular law recognizes that he may do so and the *Collectio Canonum Hibernensis*, compiled during the first half of the eighth century, makes detailed rulings about the various kinds of surety. When the early canons were drawn up, the leaders of the church had been unable (or possibly unwilling) to invoke any penalties other than penance and excommunication for what they condemn as misdeeds: but by the seventh century church legislators have the support of society for penalties which they assign for offences against the church.[49] The clergy are now part of the nobility and church property is protected by law.

But although the clergy had to be fitted into Irish society, Christianity made no fundamental changes in legal and administrative conceptions. There is evidence that some clerics tried to do so. The church introduced by the first missionaries had been divided into dioceses with a hierarchy of courts, a system based on classical conditions which had been evolved in the Roman Empire. The early canons insist on the bishop's authority within his own *paruchia*, which seems to be a territorial area coterminous with the *plebs*.[50] The canons passed in the seventh century by the adherents of the Roman Easter (the *Romani*) further elaborate these rulings, giving to the synod the final judicial authority in ecclesiastical affairs.[51] They attempt to introduce minor changes in administration. For example, in native law a man who contracted a debt needed witnesses and sureties, but the *Romani* say he must also get a written record, and they want to have business transactions confirmed 'by signature, in the manner of the Romans'.[52] The church of Armagh was glad to recognize Rome as the supreme ecclesiastical court of appeal, with Armagh immediately beneath, so that difficult cases which had no precedents and could not be settled 'by all the judges of the tribes of the Irish' could be referred to the successor of Patrick at Armagh.[53]

---

[47] *C.G.* 598–602.   [48] *Pa. I.* 8. For discussion see Hughes, op. cit., pp. 46 ff.
[49] Hughes, op. cit., pp. 131 ff.
[50] *Pa. I.* 24, 27, 30, 33. The *plebs* is probably the tuath (petty kingdom).
[51] *Col.* I, 8b, LVI, 4, XX, 3, 5, 6.   [52] *Col.* XXXIII. 4; *Pa. II.* 30.
[53] *ignota cunctis Scotorum gentium iudicibus.* Arm. 21. b. 2.

But in spite of the efforts of the Roman party, the ecclesiastical organization which eventually emerged was very unlike that of the continent. At Armagh in the late seventh century the *archiepiscopus* might be legal theory, but the *abbas* or *comarba* (the heir of the founder) was historic fact. A church of major importance needed a bishop: his position was of the highest dignity and he performed the functions of order connected with his office, but it was the abbot who controlled church property and jurisdiction. One story in Adamnán's Life of Columcille (written almost certainly between 688 and 692) shows that the abbot might even interfere in the bishop's functions, for Adamnán tells how one abbot persuaded a reluctant bishop to ordain a young favourite to the priesthood.[54] The bishop made the abbot lay his hand on the young man's head first, presumably in an attempt to shift some of the responsibility. Columcille and Adamnán both deplored this cowardly action, but it is easy to see that, in exceptional circumstances, such a case might arise.

Some of the legislation of the seventh century suggests that there were still churches administered by bishops, perhaps churches which had been founded in the early period of Christianity, but there is far more evidence to show that the abbot was now normally regarded as the chief administrator. Fairly frequently in the legislation and occasionally in the annals he is called *princeps*, indicating his executive authority. It is the *princeps* who receives bequests and burial fees on behalf of his church, and whose permission has to be sought before a body may be moved from the church's burial ground. Special regulations govern the division between the retiring abbot and the church of gifts made by outsiders during his tenure of office[55]; other rulings lay down the standard burial fees of a garment, horse and cow, or, for someone of the highest honour, two horses with a chariot and the bed-trappings and drinking vessel of the dead man.[56] The abbot has monastic clients who stand towards him in much the same contractual relationship as do clients to their secular lord. He acts as their lord (*dominus*) and they are under tribute (*sub censu*) to him. Canons passed in the seventh century by church lawyers who were regarded as belonging to the 'Irish' as distinct from the 'Roman' party, discuss the *monachi* as if they were the abbot's *doer-chéli*. The monk cannot act as surety or make bequests without his abbot's consent, but if he has made a bequest the abbot must repudiate it before a certain time has

[54] Ad. *Vit. Col.*, I. 36.
[55] *Col.* XLIII, 6. *omnes oblationes alienorum.*
[56] *Col.* XVIII, 6.

elapsed or it becomes legal.[57] The abbot was the administrative head of the church.

There is evidence in the legislation both for monks who were celibate and for monastic clients who were married. These clients are called *manaig* and formed part of the legal corporation of the church.[58] In some cases, eighth-century abbots seem themselves not to have been in major orders, and to have had sons, for the annals allow us to trace a family inheritance of abbatial office in certain monasteries. Two sons of abbot Crundmael of Lusk, who died in 736, were later in the century abbots of Lusk, while a third son was abbot of Duleek, and four sons of these three men all held monastic office at Lusk, the last one dying *infeliciter* in 805. At Slane during a period of four generations in the second half of the eighth century and the first half of the ninth century, two families provided ten abbots.[59] During the ninth century at Domnach Sechnaill three, or more probably four, generations of the same family reigned as abbots, of whom the last but one was 'secretly murdered' in 879, and the last 'killed by his brethren' in 886.[60] Thus one of the practices which caused the Norman prelates such disapproval seems to have been established by the eighth century.

Many of the abbots of the early Irish church were, however, celibate and in major orders as priests, like the abbots of Iona. Here the abbacy did not descend from father to son, and although all the abbots before the death of Adamnán in 704 except one were of the same tribe, some were only distantly related to their predecessors. A few Irish abbots were in episcopal orders, though this seems to have been rather rare. There were also clerics and celibates within the monastic communities practising a religious life, not following the farm-life of the *manaig*, and from the later eighth century onwards there were groups of ascetics founded under the inspiration of religious revival who were supported by the old churches, or who lived together in new monasteries under the rule of an abbot.

The Irish church had its periods of secularization and of spiritual revival, but the main lines of its organization remained constant from the seventh century until the twelfth. From the sixth century onwards some churches were ruled by abbots, and in the seventh century the judicial and administrative authority of the abbots became the norm, while the bishops were confined to spiritual

---

[57] For discussion and references see Hughes, op. cit., pp. 137-9.
[58] ibid., p. 140.
[59] ibid., pp. 162-3.
[60] ibid., p. 189.

functions only. Moreover, the territorial diocese under the bishop's
rule which had been introduced in the fifth century gave way during
the second half of the sixth century to confederations of monastic
houses all owing allegiance to a superior church (the *anoit* church)
whose abbot was head of the whole *paruchia*, in much the same way
as the over-king in secular life was acknowledged by the sub-kings.
Columcille, the most aristocratic of all the early abbots and probably the wealthiest, had founded a number of religious houses
before he left Ireland for Iona, houses which continued to acknowledge his overlordship: in the stories quoted by Adamnán he refers
to their inhabitants as 'my monks', and in the decades before the
Viking invasions the annals show us the abbots setting off from
Iona carrying the founder's relics to make a circuit of their Irish
possessions. The *paruchia Columbae* forms the example, *par excellence*,
of all the Irish confederations, but other founders were building
up groups of churches on similar, if less distinguished, lines.

The abbot of such a group had decided material advantages
over the bishop of a small territorial diocese. His field of expansion
was indefinite, for his disciples might travel widely and set up
houses which acknowledge his overlordship, not only in Ireland,
but in Scotland, England or on the continent, while the bishop, by
contrast, had been firmly told in the early canons not to invade
the jurisdiction of another bishop.

It would appear that in the seventh century some churches
which had originally been founded with a bishop having jurisdiction over a narrow territorial diocese were trying to claim *paruchiae*
of monastic type. The Book of the Angel, copied into the Book of
Armagh, provides a statement of Armagh's claim and rights, put
together by Armagh lawyers from information collected there in
the late seventh and early eighth century. In its opening section an
angel appears to Patrick and grants him a *terminus* and a *paruchia*.
The *terminus*, or *termonn*, was the area over which the abbot of
Armagh exercised direct authority, as the tribal king did over his
own kingdom; and, as the angel defined it, it covered the considerable area of Airgialla, Dal Araidhe and Ulaidh, but did not
include the kingdoms of Dal Riada or the northern and southern
Uí Néill.[61] This may be the area which formed the territorial diocese of early bishops of Armagh, for that *civitas*, founded so near
to the great fort of Emain, must once have been the ecclesiastical
capital of a large province. But by the seventh century this was not
sufficient for the heirs of Patrick. The angel explains that God has

[61] Binchy, *Studia Hibernica*, II (1962), pp. 60–61; MacNeill, *Journ.R.S.A.I.*,
XVIII (1928), p. 100.

given to Patrick and to his *civitas* 'all the tribes of the Irish'. In later sections of the text, the lawyers elaborate what jurisdiction over the *paruchia* means. All the existing churches which are free from tribute and were founded by episcopal order, and all the churches called *domnach* (a place name element which Professor Binchy has shown belongs to a very early stratum of loan words), are under the overlordship of the abbot of Armagh, whom they acknowledge as their superior, paying him a special tax (*peculiare censum*).[62] Patrick's heir is to be *dux principalis omnibus Hiberoniacum gentibus*, and like an over-king he travels with a larger retinue and 'overswears all churches and their rulers'.[63]

The evidence for Kildare is much less clear, for here we have no legal text, only a Life of St Brigid written by Cogitosus, probably in the 630s, but it suggests that Kildare may have been making a similar attempt to change from a territorial diocese to a confederation of churches. The Book of the Angel recognizes that central Leinster is exempt from Patrick's jurisdiction[64]: this may be the area which formed the original diocese of Kildare. In the 630s the church, which was wealthy, was ruled jointly by an abbess and a bishop who, in Cogitosus' day, was a son of the king of Leinster.[65] Cogitosus calls Conlaeth, the first bishop, *archiepiscopus*, 'high-bishop', the term which the Armagh lawyers apply to Patrick's heir, and the bishop of Kildare is 'chief bishop of the Irish bishops', that is, he is in the position of an overlord. As such he rules a *paruchia* which 'is diffused through all the Irish lands and extends from sea to sea', which has 'spread throughout the whole Irish island.'[66] If Kildare ever compiled a legal document analogous to the Book of the Angel, it has been lost, and Kildare's claims are consequently much vaguer than those of Armagh, whose overlordship became much more important than her own. Yet it seems that she attempted a claim similar to that made by Armagh and succeeded in establishing a *paruchia* of monastic churches.

We have comparatively little information about the early church in Munster, but an early law tract refers to the bishops of Cork and Emly as *uasal-epscop*, and gives them an honour-price equal to that of the king of Munster who was overlord of the southern half of Ireland,[67] so it would appear that ecclesiastical overlordships and their accompanying *paruchiae* were developing in the south as

[62] For discussion and references see Hughes, op. cit., pp. 86 ff., and pp. 275 ff. for translation of the *Liber Angeli*.
[63] *Arm.* 21 a. 2.
[64] *Arm.* 21 b. 2, 21 a. 1; Hughes, op. cit., p. 113.
[65] O'Briain, *Feil-sgribhinn Eoin Mhic Néill*, p. 460.
[66] *P.L.*, LXXII col. 778.   [67] *A.L.I.* V, 110-12.

elsewhere. None of these claims to overlordship formulated in the seventh century were necessarily exclusive of the rest. The bishops of Cork and Emly probably *were* the most eminent bishops in Munster, the bishop of Kildare was the chief bishop of Leinster, and the abbot of Armagh was probably by the eighth century the most important ecclesiastic in Ireland. Under the influence of the Roman party the abbot of Armagh was claiming some direct authority in the domestic affairs of other ecclesiastical overlords (a claim modelled on foreign not native institutions), for Armagh claimed to be an appeal court for Ireland; but whether she ever achieved this in the eighth century is very doubtful. Irish claims to archiepiscopacy in the pre-Viking age are analogous to the claims to secular overlordship.

The organization of the Christian church in Ireland was, then, deeply influenced by the non-classical legal and political system of the country. The Christian creed was accepted by pagan Ireland, but the alien institutions introduced with it were re-shaped along the lines of the country's own tradition of petty kings and overlords. As one early law tract points out, there were many things in the customary law which did not come into the canon of scripture, yet were not contrary to it. Dubthach, Patrick's first convert from among the learned class, was supposed to have shown all these to Patrick, and 'what did not disagree with the word of God in the written law, and with the conscience of the believers, was retained in the brehon code by the church and the *filid*'.[68] Among seventh-century canonists, who met in synods and passed legislation which has fortunately survived, there were two distinct groups, a 'Roman' party and an 'Irish' party. Their interests and sympathies were not identical. The 'Irish' party (were they descendants of the old men of learning?) worked hard to bring the church into line with the native law. They were almost completely successful.[69]

Whereas Christian institutions were remodelled to fit Irish society, the indirect effects of Christianity on art and learning were fundamental and far-reaching. The church became a great patron

[68] *A.L.I.*, III, 30, 2.
[69] The secular law of marriage recognized a chief wife (*cétmuinter*) and subsidiary wives, while divorce was permitted. Canons 18 and 19 of the 'Second Synod of Patrick' (ed. Bieler, *The Irish Penitentials*, Dublin 1963, pp. 196–7) which were probably formulated in the seventh century, suggest that, as administered by some clerics, the church's law of marriage had already been modified by Irish practice. See also Hughes, *The Church in Early Irish Society*, pp. 53, 131, for other early rulings. A canon of the Synod of Cashel (1101) and papal correspondence of the twelfth century (Sheehy, *Pont. Hib.*, I, p. 21) show that the later reformers found it very difficult to overthrow native marriage custom. For discussion see Gwynn, *I.E.R.*, LXVII, p. 110.

of the smiths and jewellers, for she needed altar-vessels and reliquaries. In the early seventh century the tombs of Brigid and
bishop Conlaeth on either side of the high altar in the church at
Kildare were decorated with gold, silver and many coloured precious stones and surmounted by crowns of gold and silver. The
churches needed liturgical books, some of which were ornamented
with paintings. Some seventh- and eighth-century monks travelled
widely, bringing home books with new motifs, so that the decora-
tive repertoire of the eighth-century craftsman was much wider
than that of his pre-Christian predecessor. Stone crosses were set
up, their ornament proceeding from the very simple incised designs
of the early period, through the elaborate abstract carving in relief
of the eighth-century high crosses to the panels of scripture scenes
on many of the monuments of the Viking age. The change in
patronage had brought a change in requirements and taste, and
Irish contacts with the Christian west brought a great expansion in
the artists' repertoire of motifs.

Christianity brought into Ireland a new language and a new
literature. The monastic schools applied themselves seriously to the
study of Latin grammar, sometimes glossing their manuscripts
with words and phrases in Irish and with a system of marks con-
necting one word with another.[70] They read and commented upon
the Scriptures. They introduced a new concept of history, for the
year-by-year annalistic record of the monastic chroniclers has little
in common with the ideas of the traditional *seanchas*. Yet they seem
to have been, in the main, sympathetic to secular learning. At
Iona it was customary to invite a visiting poet to entertain the
monks before his departure 'with a song of his own composition,
sung to a tune'.[71] Were such songs panegyrics of Columcille's
ancestors, songs of contests and battles? The oldest manuscript
containing tales of the Ulster cycle was written by a monk of Clonmacnoise about the year 1100, and towards the end of the twelfth
century Aed, abbot of Terryglass, copied a version of the *Tain Bo
Cuailnge* and transcribed at the end what seems to be a comment by
some earlier recorder: 'A blessing on everyone who will memorize
the *Tain* accurately in this form and will not put any other form
on it.' In Thurneysen's opinion the earliest version of the tale was
written down in the mid-seventh century by a *fili* trained in the
secular schools and familiar with Latin learning.[72] At about the

---

[70] M. Draak, *Mededelingen der Koninklijke Nederlandsche Akedemie van Wetenschap-
pen, aft Letterkunde*, Nierve Reeks , XX, No. 10, 1957, pp. 261–82.
[71] Ad. *Vit Col.*, I, 42.
[72] *Z.C.P.*, XIX, p. 209. Cf. Jackson, *The Oldest Irish Tradition*, p. 52.

same period ecclesiastical and secular lawyers must have been in friendly association, for then the canons of the 'Irish' synods were being drawn up by men familiar with traditional law, and the earliest secular law tracts seem to have been recorded in writing. Christianity gave to secular learning another medium, the written record, and at the same time enriched the intellectual life of Ireland with a new literature and new ideas.

In the ninth century, by which time Ireland had completely absorbed Christianity, she had to meet another and very different foreign invasion, for Scandinavian seafarers arrived, first to raid and after 830 to settle. They built fortifications on Irish bays and put their fleets on Irish lochs and rivers, so that few areas could be entirely free from their plunderings. According to the annals the monasteries found the violent raiding of most of the ninth century a devastating experience. This view is heightened and expanded in the twelfth-century saga of *The Wars of the Gaedhil with the Gaill*:

They made spoil-land and sword-land and conquered land of Ireland (says this story-teller). They ravaged her kingdoms and her privileged churches and her sacred places, and they rent her shrines and her reliquaries and her books. . . . In short, until the sand of the sea or the grass of the field or the stars of heaven are counted, it will not be easy to relate what the Gael all, without distinction, suffered from them. . . . In a word, they killed the kings and chieftains, the royal heirs and royal princes of Ireland. They killed the brave and valiant . . .

and so on.[73]

In the past, historians have usually accepted the effect of the Viking raids at the annalists' (and sometimes at the saga-writer's) evaluation, but Mr Peter Sawyer in a recent book on *The Age of the Vikings* has warned that 'the contemporary writings of the Christian west can hardly be expected to provide a balanced and impartial account of the Scandinavians', since the chroniclers were monks, whose abbeys were particularly vulnerable to Viking raids and a rich source of plunder. In his opinion the scale of Viking raids and density of the settlements have been exaggerated.[74] These conclusions are applied to evidence from several different areas, of which Ireland is only one and not the most important, so it may be worth while to re-examine the Irish sources.

It must first of all be understood that the picture provided by the annals is by no means identical with that in the second part of *Wars of the Gaedhil with the Gaill*. The first part of this work is closely related to a chronicle, but the second is a saga with Brian Boru as

[73] *Wars*, ed. Todd, pp. 41–3.
[74] *The Age of the Vikings*, p. 193. Cf. p. 136.

its hero. As its title states, it presents Irish history in the Viking age as a struggle of the Irish against the Foreigners, which reaches a triumphant apex with the rise of the royal house of Dál Cais and the career of Brian, and it has much the same disadvantages as other 'history' compiled by the Irish storytellers. The annals, on the other hand, provide a variety of entries for the Viking age— the deaths of kings, nobles and ecclesiastics, battles between the Irish themselves, Viking attacks, natural disasters and 'marvels'— and so give a much more balanced impression of events during the period. It is true that the annals do not provide equally good evidence for all areas of Ireland. Most of their references are to eastern and central districts, and even here the distribution of evidence is uneven. The east-central areas of Ireland now represented by Meath, Louth and co. Dublin, with Armagh to the north, the central-south which is now Offaly, Leix, north Leinster and Tipperary, with the monastery of Lismore to the south, are particularly well represented in the annals prior to 1000. The emphasis may shift with the years from one monastic house to another. The haphazard and fragmentary character of the evidence is only to be expected and must be recognized, but there seems no reason to doubt the substantial accuracy of the surviving entries which describe Hiberno-Norse relations.

Moreover, the annals show very clearly that Viking pressure was not consistently heavy from the time of the settlement until the Battle of Clontarf. From the 830s until towards the end of the century there are few years when Viking devastations are not recorded, but after 881 records of Viking attacks become fewer. In the 890s there were disagreements between different bands of Scandinavians, and no doubt some of the recruits who might have joined the Norse in Dublin were being diverted to war and settlement in England. In 902 the Dublin Gaill were heavily defeated by combined Irish armies from Brega (the kingdom near Dublin on the eastern seaboard) and Leinster; the annals note 'The expulsion of the Gentiles from Ireland . . . when they left a great number of their ships and escaped half dead, after having been wounded and broken.' The substantial accuracy of this entry is borne out by the absence of further Viking activity until 914 when a large new fleet of Scandinavians put in at Waterford. But from this time on the Gaill were back again in Ireland, plundering first in Munster and Leinster. In 917 a combined Irish army of the northern and southern Uí Néill and Munster failed to prevent Sitric's settlement in Dublin, and though Sitric left Dublin 'through the power of God' in 920, Godfrey arrived in 921. In the following decade there were fleets actively operating from Lough Foyle, Lough Ree, Lough Erne, Strangford Lough, Lough Neagh and Lough Corrib, and the coin evidence suggests that Scandinavians in Ireland were reinforced after the temporary expulsion of the Hiberno-Norse dynasty from York in 927.[75] The Irish kings, especially the Uí Néill, put up a strong resistance, sometimes winning substantial victories, and in the last four decades of the tenth century, with the rise of the Dál Cais in the south and the active Uí Néill in the north, the tide really began to turn against the Gaill.

The annals also show very clearly that the first century of Viking settlement was not a period of combined Irish opposition to the Vikings. Irish kings were used to encounters with each other, there were already scores of petty kingdoms, and at first the Vikings seemed to be yet another element in an already complex situation. They were excellent fighters, and Irish kings not infrequently allied with Viking contingents against each other.[76] Yet although at first sight the pattern seems to go on much as before, the scale of war was completely changed. Mr Sawyer maintains that what the Vikings most wanted was not only booty but also land for settlement; but in Ireland they occupied very little land, and it is difficult to believe that they met with fiercer resistance in ninth-century Ireland than in the comparatively well-organized kingdoms in England and the Carolingian empire. According to the Irish records, they sought plunder, and the annalists comment especially on their seizure of precious metals and slaves. Church property had been hedged around with legal protection for centuries, the persons of the clergy had a high honour-price and a Christian society had been accustomed to exact compensation for injuries against them. The Vikings cared nothing for these rights, they were ready to kill clerics, seize valuables and burn churches without fear of supernatural vengeance.[77] Once such practices began, it is easy to see that they would spread to Irish kings, as the annals record that they did, so that, by the tenth century, Irish kings were plundering and burning monastic property only less than the Norse. Thus the scale of war completely altered. The numbers engaged may not

[75] Dolley, *The Hiberno-Norse Coins in the British Museum* (1966), p. 28.

[76] e.g. *AU* 861 Aed, king of the northern Uí Néill, with the Gaill, plunders Meath. 868 Aed, with the Leinstermen and the Gaill, fights Brega. 881 Flann, king of Meath, with the Gaill, goes on a hosting to the north, in which Armagh is plundered.

[77] e.g. Blathmac was killed by Vikings on Iona on 24 July 825, because he refused to reveal the hiding-place in which the shrine ('the precious metals wherein lie the holy bones of S. Columba') had been secreted. The speech which Walafrid Strabo puts into the martyr's mouth may be a convention, but the manner of his death is probably not only true but typical.

have been large, for the Vikings settled in only a few coastal ports; but they put fleets on the great lakes of Ireland[78] and their unusual mobility meant that few areas were free from their depredations.

It is hard to see why the records of contemporary annalists should not be regarded as substantially true, for they are supported by the evidence of archaeology and institutions. Ninth-century Irish metalwork has been found in Scandinavian graves, much of it in the coastal areas of Rogaland, Sogn og Fjordane and Nord-Trundelag,[79] and Irish styles influenced Scandinavian artists. At home the superb metalwork and illumination of the pre-Viking age seems to have suffered a reverse, although workshops revived to some extent in the tenth century; for the security needed for craftsmen to produce such works as the Ardagh Chalice or the Book of Kells was no longer generally available. During the first century of Scandinavian settlement the most distinguished works of art produced for the church were the stone high crosses, now decorated with a complex iconography: Vikings were interested in precious metals, not in heavy sculpture. Churches of wood seem often to have been rebuilt in stone during this period, and towers were erected for watch and protection. Thus the material evidence bears out the annalists' account of Viking depredations.

The evidence of institutions points in the same direction. Schools of secular law had been active in recording legal texts during the late seventh and eighth centuries, but in the Viking age the texts become 'fossilized' and the lawyers turn their attention to gloss and commentary, which sometimes show a striking divorce from practical reality, for the conditions presupposed in the tracts had been considerably modified.[80] In the pre-Viking period, church lawyers, influenced by the brehons, had drawn up *cána* (*leges*) aimed both at protecting clerics, church property, women and children from violence, and at providing profits for the church from the legal penalties for contravention. The first *cáin* is recorded in the annals at 697 and the long series comes to an end in 842. The *cána* had been imposed by abbots and kings: after 842 abbots were no longer able to secure their performance, and perhaps kings were already realizing that plunder provided profits. Moreover, the destruction of the early Viking age widened the gap between the richer and less prosperous monasteries, for the richer houses were able to make

[78] e.g. *AU* 921, thirty-two ships on Lough Foyle.
[79] The evidence up to 1940 is set out in detail by Petersen in *Viking Antiquities in Gt. Britain and Ireland* Part V, ed. H. Shetelig. There is a more general statement in L. and M. de Paor, *Early Christian Ireland*, (1958), pp. 132 ff.
[80] Binchy, *Congress*, pp. 120 ff.

a better recovery, so that by the tenth century a few houses stand out from the rest in undisputed eminence.

Executive authority in Ireland had always been weak, and order in society had depended on a delicately adjusted balance, for the surety system rested on the conception of status, since no one could go surety for a man of higher status than his own. Status, in its turn, was conditioned partly by birth and partly by wealth. Consequently the troubles of the early Viking age must have severely shaken social security. It rapidly became evident that legal protection was unreliable and that force was the best defence. In the tenth century the churches were allying themselves to provincial kings, and sometimes local rulers become the abbots of monasteries. At this period the Irish church was probably more completely identified with secular life than ever before in its history.[81]

The most important governmental modification of the Viking age was in the growing power of overlordship, a development which has its roots in the pre-Viking period, but which expanded under the conditions created by the Viking swords. Petty kings could do very little to combat Viking attacks, but overlords could provide larger armies which might hope to gain substantial plunder from a successful encounter. When Dublin was sacked in 944 by the armies of the Uí Néill and the Leinstermen the profits must have been considerable, or when Mael Sechnaill II, overlord of the north, gained a great victory at Tara in 980, 'a measuring rod being required everywhere' (*AI*), the victors gained substantially: the Clonmacnoise annals (*Chronicon Scottorum*) say that on this occasion the Gaill paid a heavy tribute in cattle as well as jewels and goods beside.

Circumstances necessitated the growth of overlordships, and from the late ninth century onwards the Uí Néill overlords in the northern half were pursuing a consistently anti-Viking policy. The period of respite at the beginning of the tenth century seems to have encouraged some of the more important kings to attempt a solid defence, for in 917 there was a combined effort by the northern and southern Uí Néill, Munster and Leinster against the Vikings who were returning to Ireland.[82] The effort failed, and in 919 Niall Glundubh, overlord of the northern half, was killed in the third year of his reign when fighting the Vikings at Dublin. Donnchad of the southern Uí Néill and Muircertach son

---

[81] Hughes, op. cit., chap. 20.

[82] *AU* says that in one of these encounters, which seems to be an important one, on 22 August near Clonmel, the number of men killed in both armies was a hundred, most of them Gaill. This may be a rough estimate, but it can hardly be called an exaggerated figure. The annals do not usually give numbers of fallen.

of Niall of the northern Uí Néill both continued the fight against the Vikings. Ambitious overlords, however, had to deal not only with the Vikings but also with other Irish kings; so that Muircertach and Donnchad were mutual rivals, conducting hostings against each other. On one occasion (927) 'God separated them without any loss of life', and in 938 'God pacified them' so that they made a combined attack on Dublin, and the following year went together on a hosting to take pledges from Munster and Leinster. In 941 (*AU*) Muircertach seems to have been acting as Donnchad's ally in Munster, for 'he ravaged the Déisi and brought with him Cellachán king of Cashel in subjection to Donnchad',[83] but the brief period of united action came to an end with Muircertach's death at the hands of the Gaill in 943. Donnchad died the following year.

Even if the northern and southern branches of the Uí Néill could settle their differences, the provinces of Ulster and Leinster were a constant menace. Ulster allied with the Gaill in a plundering expedition in 933, though Muircertach defeated them and is said to have killed two hundred and forty men. The position of Leinster throughout the tenth century must have been particularly uncomfortable, for that province was especially vulnerable to raids from Dublin and to hostings from the Uí Néill and from Munster, so that the Leinstermen allied now with this power, now with that. In 944 (*AU*) the king of Leinster joined Congalach (successor of Donnchad as overlord of the north) in a successful raid on Dublin, when they carried off 'jewels, treasures and a great spoil', but Congalach was killed in 956 by Dublin Gaill and Leinstermen.[84]

The position of the Scandinavian colonists in the second half of the tenth century was very different from what it had been a hundred years earlier. The overlords of the Uí Néill were now very powerful. Domnall began his reign by securing recognition from Dal-Araidhe (960), Connacht (965) and Leinster (968), and Mael Sechnaill II, his successor as chief overlord in the north, was able to lead a strong army at the battle of Tara in 980. The sons of Cennétig took the lead against the Vikings in the south. Mathgamain defeated the Limerick Gaill in 967 and soon afterwards established himself as king of Munster, where later he was succeeded by his brother Brian. In 988 (*AU*) Mael Sechnaill and Brian, the two most powerful overlords in Ireland, made a joint hosting 'when they took the pledges of the Gaill for their submission to the Irish'.

---

[83] There is a highly elaborated account in *AFM*.
[84] The Four Masters say that Congalach went on a hosting into Leinster, and that the Leinstermen obtained help from the Dublin Gaill.

According to the Munster Annals of Inisfallen, Brian and Mael
Sechnaill divided the overlordship of Ireland between them, Brian
taking the hostages of Leinster and the Gaill, Mael Sechnaill taking
the hostages of Connacht. Meanwhile, though Irish authority was
less divided than ever before, struggles still went on among the
Scandinavian chieftains. By this time the initiative no longer lay
with the Gaill.

Though the colonists are still called *Gaill* in the annals, the term
no longer describes them very accurately, for they were intermarry-
ing with the Irish and were becoming Christian. Olaf son of Sitric,
ruler of Dublin, died in penance at Iona in 980 (*AFM*), and the
annals occasionally give names such as Gilla-Patraic son of Ivar
(*AU* 983) which suggest a Christian Irish mother. Moreover, Dublin
had become a great trading centre. The ninth-century Viking settlers had been coinless, but at the very end of the century a flood
of Cufic dirhams poured into the Scandianvian economy, to be
followed by Western pennies.[85] Coins were circulating among the
Hiberno-Norse in the tenth century: seven of the nine hoards deposited before the sack of Dublin in 944 are probably to be associated with the Dublin Gaill.[86] The distribution widens in the second
half of the century and there are outliers at Macroom and Mungret
in the west and at Burt and Derrykeighan near the northern coast,
but most of the tenth-century hoards are found in east central
Ireland between the Shannon and the Irish Sea, the Boyne valley
and Glendalough.[87] They are conclusive evidence that Dublin was
a commercial port. The merchants there would want freedom from
Irish raids and security in which to pursue their trade. All these
conditions supplied the Scandinavians with powerful incentives
towards peace.

It was in the interest of the Gaill and of the Irish that the colonies
should now be regarded as *tuatha* which accepted the overlordship
of a superior king. By the end of the century there were two con-
testants for the overlordship of all Ireland: Brian and Mael Sechnaill had divided the honours between them, but the situation
could not last. Brian had established royal government firmly in
Munster, had suppressed the Vikings of Limerick, had promptly
avenged any resistance to his authority within his overlordship,[88]
and had shown himself able to protect his own.[89] He had taken

---

[85] Dolley, *The Hiberno-Norse Coins in the British Museum* (1966), p. 25.
[86] Drogheda, Lugga co. Meath, Geashill co. Offaly, Glasnevin, Dublin,
Kildare, Glendalough. The other two are from co. Cork and Tipperary.
[87] Dolley, pp. 48 ff.   [88] e.g. *AI* 985.
[89] *AI* 990 Ros Ailithir was invaded by Gaill, the lector taken and later ransomed by Brian at Inis Cathiag.

hostages from the monastic houses of Lismore, Cork and Emly (all of which had previously provided candidates for the throne), and he had started building operations at Cashel and at other forts.[90] He took hostages from Osraige and Leinster, which acknowledged his overlordship, and harried the independent provinces on his borders, putting a fleet on Lough Ree to facilitate pressure on Meath and Connacht.[91]

This was Brian's situation when in 997–8 he and Mail Sechnaill had divided the overlordship of Ireland. In the next two years Brain made his overlordship of Dublin a reality. At Glen Mama in 999 he fought a great battle against the Gaill, and the following year besieged and burned Dublin. The 'king of the Gaill of Ath Cliath escaped from the battle to Ulaid, but found no protection for himself in Ireland until he handed over his hostages to Brian son of Cennétig; and Brian gave the fort to the Foreigners'. This means that Brian re-installed a Viking chief in Dublin to hold it as a sub-king acknowledging his overlordship.

But Mael Sechnaill and all the northern half including Connacht saw Brian's activities with alarm, and in 1001 built a boom across the Shannon at Athlone 'against the men of Munster'. The laconic entry of the annals for the following year reads: 'A hosting of the men of Munster into Connacht, and they took the hostages of Connacht at Athlone, and the hostages of Mael Sechnaill' (*AI*). Thereafter, Meath, the area under the immediate control of Mael Sechnaill, comes in with Brian, and, according to the facts reported in the annals, Mael Sechnaill, who until then had acted like an equal, after 1002 acted like a sub-king. There must have been more to the change-over than the annals tell us, and the saga on the *Wars of the Gaedhil with the Gaill* tells us a great deal more. This twelfth-century story-teller is writing long after the event and much of his detail may be fanciful, but he had a better sense of historical perspective in one particular than the contemporary annalists. He stresses the individualism of the sub-kingdoms, which had prevented united resistance again and again. According to his story, Brian demanded hostages (that is, submission) or battle, and Mael Sechnaill asked for a month's delay to consult his own sub-kings of the northern Uí Néill, Ulaid and Connacht, and if possible to muster his forces. The answer given by his uncle Aed of the northern Uí Néill was 'that he would not risk his life in battle against the Dál Cais in defence of sovereignty for any other man'.[92] The story-teller understood the moral.

[90] *AI* 995. Cf. 1012.   [91] *AI* 988, 993.   [92] *Wars*, p. 126.

With the submission of Mael Sechnaill and Connacht Brian was able to make a reality of the high-kingship, a title which, though used often enough in the literature, has little legal or historical significance until this period.[93] With a host composed of Munstermen and contingents from all his sub-kings—of Connacht, Meath, Leinster, the Gaill of Limerick and of Dublin—he moved against Ulster, which made submission and surrendered hostages. There remained the northern Uí Néill, and Brian took the hostages of Cenél Conaill and Cenél Eoghain in 1005. The next year, with representatives from all his sub-kings,[94] he made a circuit of the north, and at Armagh recognized the ecclesiastical overlordship of the heir of Patrick over the church of all Ireland. A scribe made a note to this effect in an empty half column of the Book of Armagh 'in the presence of Brian *imperator Scottorum*'.

Brian was in fact the first overlord of all Ireland. Although as overlord he had no direct authority in the domestic affairs of the kingdoms under his sovereignty, he seems to have kept in closer touch with his sub-kings than previous Irish overlords had done. They came to his new palace at Kincora on the Shannon (much as earlier the sub-kings of Athelstan the English overlord had attended his court), and their contingents joined in his hostings. But such union was so novel, and ran so completely against the Irish political tradition, that it could not last. The battle of Clontarf was fought in 1014 because Leinster and the Dublin Gaill defaulted, and with Brian's death the situation reverted to the norm.

By the eleventh century the Hiberno-Norse colonies were settling down alongside the other Irish *tuatha*. There were certain differences which marked them off from the Irish kingdoms. About 995 the Dublin kings had begun to strike their own currency, but most of Ireland seems to have remained coinless. The coin-hoards of the eleventh century are confined to the areas where the Hiberno-Norse were active, and are mainly concentrated in and near the Dublin kingdom.[95] Whereas Viking swords, brooches and other objects found their way through much of Ireland, the Irish were not interested in coins, and if they obtained them presumably they melted them down to make something more attractive. Ultimately Ireland gained a money economy, but not yet. The Dublin Gaill, the coin evidence proves, were more firmly established and more commercially active than the other colonies. As the century wore on, their

[93] See Binchy, *Ériu*, XVIII, pp. 113–38.
[94] *AI* including Airgialla, which was within the northern Uí Neill sphere.
[95] Dolley *Hiberno-Norse Coins*, map 4, opp. p. 44 and Dolley and Ingold, *Anglo-Saxon Coins*, p. 260.

contacts with Norway became less frequent, but they were in lively communication with England. Thus, when Dublin and the other Hiberno-Norse cities acquired bishops, they followed the English rather than the Irish pattern of church government, and the English archbishops of Canterbury made determined efforts to draw the new sees into their own primacy.

It is perhaps surprising that the Vikings did not have a more constructive influence on Irish history in the ninth and tenth centuries.[96] Although their numbers were not large, they were a people with wide contacts and, at least in the tenth century, a considerable commercial power. Their influence at first on Ireland was mainly destructive. As conditions became more settled their taste and styles influenced Irish artists, so that the addition to the craftsman's repertoire has to be set against the loss of treasures. Yet their first and continuing lesson to the Irish was in increased violence, so that the old restraints of society disappeared and the law atrophied. The more powerful Irish overlordships which developed were an answer to the new conditions, but the old tradition of decentralized independence was too pervasive to allow the growth of any direct government which could have met the Norman challenge.

[96] It will be evident that the quality of the Viking impact on Irish society is a matter of present controversy. Dr Lucas has very kindly allowed me to read, in proof, a paper of his on 'The Plundering and Burning of Churches in Ireland', now published in *Essays in Commemoration of Monsignor Michael Maloney*, ed. E. Rynne, pp. 172–229. The lists at the end of this paper, which assemble a great deal of most valuable evidence, seem to me to support the account which I have given above. I hope to discuss this question elsewhere.

CHAPTER I

The Coming of the Normans

AS WE HAVE seen, the Scandinavian raids of the ninth century affected Ireland as they did the rest of western Europe, but with markedly different results. In the Carolingian empire, once the over-ambitious attempt at a universal monarchy had collapsed in the ruin and chaos of the century, national monarchies emerged in France and Germany and, slowly in France but very rapidly in Germany, established a central government. In Anglo-Saxon England the kings of Wessex, after Alfred the Great had reduced the Danes to peace in a long series of campaigns, even though he had been unable to prevent a massive occupation of parts of eastern and northern England, had established a national monarchy which by the eleventh century had a highly sophisticated apparatus of government. It could be argued that the major contribution of the Norsemen to the development of western Europe had been to sweep away the debris of the past, whether the imperfectly understood remnants of Roman organization on the continent or the tribalism of the primitive Germanic peoples who had established themselves among the ruins of Rome, and force the development of new forms of organization out of which Europe as we know it eventually emerged.

In Ireland, however, things were different. In the first place, as we have seen, sovereignty was far more fragmented in ninth-century Ireland than was normal in western Europe; in the second place the traditions and institutions of the Celtic peoples differed considerably from those of the Germanic peoples who had occupied the greater part of western Europe after the collapse of the Roman empire in the west and, unlike them, had been very little, if at all, influenced by Roman institutions, since even the church, the only channel through which these could have reached them, had undergone a markedly insular development. The attacks of the Scandinavians produced dislocation and disorganization, but though they were contained, and Scandinavian settlement was less than in either France or England, being confined to the coastal strip from Dublin to Arklow, and the areas immediately surrounding

Wexford, Waterford, Cork and Limerick, no true national monarchy emerged, and when the Normans came in the later twelfth century Irish sovereignty was almost as fragmented as it had been three hundred years earlier, and forms of government had not changed. It was this, indeed, which made it impossible for the Normans to complete their conquest, for there was no single Irish ruler whose defeat meant the defeat and conquest of the country as a whole, as Harold's death at Hastings in 1066 had meant the conquest of Anglo-Saxon England, nor was there any established administrative machinery to be taken over. But equally it made it impossible for the Irish to resist them effectively.

This is not to say that the ninth and tenth centuries produced no changes in Ireland. It had been said that 'the coming of the Norsemen had a profound—one might even say a shattering—effect upon native Irish institutions'.[1] The old tribal dynasties were no longer sacred, but might be dethroned; the territory of an enemy, which had hitherto been inalienable, might be confiscated, becoming 'swordland'; the boundaries of the old territories began to shift as ambitious rulers seized opportunities of extending their power. And the fact that the Tara monarchy, though without any consistent success, was the main focus of resistance to the Scandinavians during the ninth and tenth centuries began to create the idea of an overlord who should be something more than a mere province king. But it was in fact an outsider, Brian Boruma, the king of the Dalcassians in what is now co. Clare, who at the end of the tenth century, having succeeded in making himself king of Cashel, seized also the monarchy of Tara and made himself the first effective High King. But this was not yet an effective national monarchy, but only 'a prize to be fought for by rival provincial kings'[2] and there was no development of such governmental institutions as would have given the High King any effective power outside his own province, or indeed outside his own tuath.[3] Moreover, though no rule of primogeniture was established in any monarchy of western Europe till a much later period,[4] the field of choice was wider among the Irish dynasties than was normal elsewhere, and the internal struggles which resulted were a grave source of weakness.

Many other changes, direct or indirect, followed from the Scandinavian invasions. A rural and pastoral society was introduced to

[1] D. Binchy, 'The Passing of the Old Order', *Congress*, p. 119.
[2] Ibid., p. 131.
[3] Ibid., *passim*.
[4] See e.g. J. M. Potter, 'The Development and Significance of the Salic Law of the Franks', *E.H.R.*, LII, pp. 235–53.

trade and to urban life, though the towns which the Northmen founded remained overwhelmingly Norse. The old kin organization seems to have been substantially modified, and in many other respects the pattern of Irish life seems to have been in course of rapid change in and after the eleventh century, though much work remains to be done before this can be traced in detail. But in one very important respect the twelfth century saw a revolution which brought Ireland into line with the rest of western Europe, and which was complete in outline, though not in detail, before the Normans came.

The old Celtic church organisation had been modified by the Scandinavian attacks. The great monasteries fell increasingly into the hands of lay dynasties of erenachs, and a growing secularization had developed, reaching its peak in the tenth century, which, though it could be parallelled on the continent,[5] was accentuated in Ireland by the fact that no organization other than that of the great monasteries existed. The first movement of change came from the Scandinavians themselves. In the early eleventh century Sitric king of Dublin, who had become a Christian, went on pilgrimage to Rome, and after his return founded a bishopric in Dublin of the normal territorial pattern, though it cannot have extended very far outside the walls of the city. When its first bishop, Dunan, died in 1074 his successor, Patrick, who had been trained as a monk at Worcester, was sent to Canterbury for consecration, as Dunan had probably been before him. When he returned to Ireland he brought with him letters from archbishop Lanfranc not only to the king of Dublin, but also to Turlough O'Brien, the grandson of Brian Boruma, king of Munster and High King 'with opposition',[6] in which Turlough was exhorted to reform abuses at a synod of the bishops and religious men of Ireland. Nothing came of this at the time, but by the end of the century the ideals of the continental reform movement, which had been given a central direction by the reform of the papacy itself in the middle of the century, and is inseparably connected with the career of pope Gregory VII (1073–85), were clearly influential in Ireland, though local circumstances gave them a special character. On the whole the evils principally attacked on the continent—the lay investiture of ecclesiastics, simony (the buying or selling of ecclesiastical office), and clerical marriage—do not seem to have been very prominent in Ireland, but the whole structure of the Irish church differed so

---

[5] See e.g. the case of the custodians of Arezzo, cited by R. W. Southern, *The Making of the Middle Ages*, pp. 128–30.

[6] He was recognized only by Munster and Leinster.

widely from the continental pattern that it was felt to be unsatisfactory because of this alone, while it is unlikely that it could really
have provided an adequate system of pastoral care. At any rate,
all the reformers, native or foreign, stress, often with somewhat
intemperate language, the vices of the Irish, which seem to have
consisted largely in observing not the canon law of marriage but
the Brehon law, which was indeed far removed from Christian
ideals, and seems to have been quite uninfluenced by their Christian profession. It was natural and inevitable that when the
movement became active in Ireland in the early twelfth century it
should be directed to the establishment of the normal system of
ecclesiastical organization.[7]

There was much contact with the continental church in the later
tenth and eleventh centuries, and towards the end of the eleventh
century the ideas of the reform movement seem to have been introduced in Ireland by the Hiberno-Norse bishops of Dublin and
Waterford,[8] trained as monks in England and consecrated by the
archbishops of Canterbury. They were associated with such men
as Mael-Maire Ua Dunain, bishop of Meath, and Domnall Ua
hEnna, bishop of Munster, and before the end of the century there
was in existence in Munster a group of reformers, led by Ua hEnna,
who died in 1098, when he was succeeded by Ua Dunain. The
group was protected and encouraged by Muirchertach O'Brien,
king of Munster, the great grandson of Brian Boruma, who in 1101
presided jointly with Ua Dunain over a meeting of the Irish bishops
at Cashel, first of the great reforming synods of the Irish church.

The synod of Cashel was not yet, however, concerned to revolu-
tionize the organization of the church. Its decrees were concerned
with the freeing of the church from secular tribute, the prohibition
of simony and the regulation of ecclesiastical appointments, demanding in particular that erenachs or abbots should be in orders
and unmarried, the exclusion from sanctuary of those guilty of the
gravest crimes, and the prohibition of marriage with very near
kindred. The attempt to forbid secular tribute was not new, and
was certainly not entirely successful: in the late thirteenth century
an Irish archbishop of Armagh was to use the bull *Clericis laicos* in
an attempt to prevent the exaction of 'secular tribute' from ecclesiastics and their tenants by the kinglets of Ulster.[9] Again, the

---

[7] For the history of the reform movement in Ireland, see the chapters contributed by the Rev. A. Gwynn, S. J., to D. Gleeson, *History of the Diocese of Killaloe*,
and his papers on this period, listed in *Medieval Studies presented to Aubrey Gwynn,
S.J.*, pp. 502–7; K. Hughes, *The Church in Early Irish Society*, chapters 23–24.

[8] The see of Waterford was founded in 1096.

[9] Hughes, loc. cit., pp. 263–4; below, p. 135–6.

attempt to regulate abuses of sanctuary was not new,[10] and the other decrees were perfectly consistent with a reform of the traditional organization. But by this time there must already have been a feeling that this was no longer satisfactory, and Gilbert, the first bishop of the Norse see of Limerick, who was consecrated *c.* 1107, wrote before 1111 a treatise *De statu ecclesiae* intended for the instruction of the Irish clergy, which set out the normal western structure of the territorial diocese, ruled by a bishop, and divided into parishes, with the dioceses grouped under the jurisdiction of archbishops. When in 1111 the next synod met at Rathbreasail, in the heart of Munster, presided over by Muirchertach O'Brien and by Gilbert of Limerick, now papal legate,[11] it effected a complete revolution by imposing this structure on the church in Ireland. Two provinces were created, Armagh and Cashel, the primacy being given to Armagh; there were to be twelve sees under Armagh, and eleven under Cashel. The existing territorial dioceses of Waterford and Limerick, but not yet Dublin, which was still subject to Canterbury, were fitted into the general framework, and though diocesan boundaries were as yet by no means finally fixed,[12] and were to be altered considerably during the century, often for political reasons, the church in Ireland had been set on the road to an organization of the normal western pattern. In 1152 at the synod of Kells, presided over by cardinal John Paparo as papal legate, *pallia* were given to four archbishops, Armagh, Cashel, Dublin and Tuam, and the Irish diocesan system as it was to endure was fully in being.

It must not be supposed that this revolution had been achieved without difficulty. The old ecclesiastical dynasties by no means always took their dispossession calmly: there were notable troubles at Armagh, and there must have been similar difficulties in many places. And even when this had been overcome, there remained the immensely complicated task of reorganizing property rights: as late as 1210 the clergy of Connacht assembled before the archbishop of Tuam to arrange for the transfer of the termon or coarb lands to the bishoprics in which they lay.[13] These were the lands of the Celtic monasteries, and the solution generally adopted was to leave the erenach families in possession as hereditary tenants of

---

[10] Hughes, loc. cit., p. 264.

[11] It is probable, though not certain, that Mael-Maire Ua Dunain had had legatine authority at Cashel in 1101. See ibid., pp. 256–7.

[12] Indeed in 1111 a synod at Uisneach in Meath, though accepting the principle of a diocesan hierarchy, made a different division of Meath.

[13] *A. Clon.*

the church. Before this was done there is nothing to suggest that any arrangements had been made for the support of the new bishoprics. Then there were cathedral chapters to be organized, a process certainly not completed till after the Norman conquest, and a division of property to be made between the bishop and the chapter.[14] Moreover, there was the immense task of carrying on that process of reform which had been begun in 1101 at Cashel and was certainly returned to in the other synods of the century, though the annals tell us nothing of its details. To judge by what such a native reformer as St Malachy of Armagh seems to have said this was a more than sufficient preoccupation for any bishop,[15] and the development of a parochial organization does not seem to have begun till after the Norman conquest.[16]

Side by side with all this, and an essential part of the process, was the introduction of the continental monastic orders. The earliest house seems to have been St Mary's, Dublin, founded from Savigny c. 1139, but far more influential were the foundation of the Cistercian house of Mellifont with monks from Clairvaux in 1142 and the introduction of Arroasian canons regular at some date before the middle of the twelfth century. By the 1160s a number of houses of both orders had already been founded in many parts of the country, and though the history of the Cistercians in particular was to be troubled,[17] they were immensely influential and completely superseded the older Celtic foundations.

Meanwhile, though the church in Ireland had been revolutionized during the first half of the twelfth century, there had been no corresponding change in political organization. The political overlordship which Brian Boruma had established by the beginning of the eleventh century, which might perhaps have been consolidated by his victory over the Danes at Clontarf in 1014, had come to nothing after his death during the battle.[18] Brian's descendants remained kings of Munster, and in the later eleventh century were still the most influential of the Irish rulers, but they were not supreme, and in the twelfth century the O'Connor kings of Connacht were the dominant power in the south. But after Turloch O'Connor died in 1156 Murchertach MacLochlainn, king of Tir

[14] The chapter of Down was created in 1180; that of Limerick in 1205; that of Cashel seems to have been still recent in 1224 (Reeves, *Ecclesiastical Antiquities*, pp. 163–4; *Black Book of Limerick*, no. CXLII; *Pontificia Hibernica*, I, no. 160; II, no. 388). Both Down and Limerick may earlier have had chapters differently constituted, but no chapter was ever created in Meath.

[15] *St. Bernard of Clairvaux's Life of St. Malachy of Armagh*, ed. H. J. Lawlor.

[16] See below, pp. 118–21, 126–7.

[17] See below, pp. 136–7, 141–2.

[18] See Curtis, *History of Medieval Ireland* (2nd edn.), pp. 4–12, 19–23, 27–34.

Eoghain, defeated Turloch's son, and by 1161 was described by the annals as 'king without opposition'. And in this year Mac-Lochlainn recognized Dermot MacMurrough as king of Leinster.

Dermot was the descendant of Dermot Mac Mael na mBo, who had died in battle in 1072 as king of Leinster and of the southern half. His immediate successors had also been kings of Leinster, but when Enna died in 1126 Turloch O'Connor gave the kingship of Leinster to his own son, Conor. In the next year a rising against this 'stranger in sovereignty' drove him out, but O'Connor replaced him by Donal MacFaelain, lord of the Ui Faelain of north Leinster. In 1134 Dermot MacMurrough, Enna's brother, who succeeded him as king of Ui Cennselaigh (Wexford and south Wicklow) in 1126, killed Donal, and was thereafter king of Leinster. In the ceaseless wars of the next thirty years he was sometimes in alliance with the O'Briens of Munster, sometimes with O'Melaghlin of Meath, sometimes with O'Connor, but with the rise of the power of Murchertach MacLochlainn towards the end of Turloch O'Connor's life he is found in alliance with MacLochlainn. And in 1152, in the course of a campaign between O'Connor and MacLochlainn, Dermot abducted Dervorgilla, the wife of O'Connor's ally, Tighernan O'Rourke of Breifne (Cavan and north Leitrim), who now became his mortal enemy. When in 1166 MacLochlainn by an act of treachery caused a rising against him which enabled Turloch O'Connor's son, Rory, to seize the high kingship the Dublin Danes and the Irish princes of north Leinster rose against MacMurrough, and Dermot was forced to submit to the new High King, who left him in possession of Ui Cennselaigh. But O'Rourke, still O'Connor's ally, seized the opportunity to take his revenge and marched on Ui Cennselaigh: on 1 August 1166 MacMurrough, seeing no hope of successful resistance, sailed for England.

Dermot's flight overseas is usually taken to mark the beginning of the Norman conquest of Ireland.[19] In fact, however, nothing was as yet changed. When he returned a year later with his Norman-Welsh mercenaries it was to continue the war to maintain his position as a province king as before: even when, flushed with victory, he proclaimed in 1170 that he was aiming at the high kingship the situation contained nothing essentially new. He had, indeed, offered to adopt Strongbow as his heir: a grave breach in

[19] The main sources for what follows are Giraldus Cambrensis, *Expugnatio Hibernica; The Song of Dermot and the Earl;* and the native Irish annals. They have been cited in detail by Orpen, *Normans*, I, and I have not in general given detailed references here. For the most recent criticism of the *Song*, see J. F. O'Doherty, 'Historical criticism of the Song of Dermot and the Earl', *I.H.S.*, I, pp. 4–20, and cf. ibid., pp. 294–6.

the fabric of native right and custom, though he probably saw it as analogous to the principle of swordland, but otherwise everything was within the framework of the native polity, and the struggle for supremacy might have continued substantially as before, with Strongbow as just another province king. It was with the intervention of Henry II in 1171 that the whole situation was revolutionized, and it is at that point that Norman conquest can really be said to have begun. Nevertheless, Dermot's action was of enormous importance in preparing the way for this. It was the success of his Norman allies which was, as we shall see, principally responsible for drawing Henry in to control them, and though had this not occurred Ireland would still no doubt have been colonized by Normans, drawing more and more of their kinsmen to themselves as had happened in southern Italy a century and a half earlier, it would have been a very different colony without the central control of the crown, and Norman lords would no doubt have been assimilated to Irish chieftains from a very early date.

It was natural that Dermot should seek refuge in Bristol, one of the principal ports trading with Ireland, where no doubt he had acquaintances. At any rate he was entertained by Robert fitz Harding, reeve of Bristol, and it was probably at his suggestion that he presently went in search of the king, whom after a long pursuit he found in Aquitaine. Henry was fully occupied in his own affairs, but he received Dermot kindly, took homage and fealty from him, promised him help, and gave him letters authorizing his subjects to give him aid as 'our vassal and liegeman' in recovering his kingdom. He sent orders to fitz Harding at Bristol to provide for Dermot, and then no doubt dismissed him from his mind.

Dermot, having gained as much as he could reasonably have hoped for, returned to Bristol and eventually made contact with one of the greatest of the Norman lords who enjoyed an almost independent power in the marches of south Wales, Richard fitz Gilbert de Clare, lord of Strigoil (Chepstow in Monmouthshire) and earl of Pembroke, the descendant of one of the companions of the conqueror, best known by the nickname of Strongbow.[20] He had been a supporter of Stephen, and was therefore out of favour with the king and not fully in possession of his inheritance, which must explain his readiness to contemplate so dubious an adventure. It was finally agreed between them that the earl should marry Dermot's eldest daughter, and should succeed him in Leinster, in

[20] The nickname seems really to have belonged to his father and was not applied to earl Richard by his contemporaries.

return for which he would assist in the recovery of the kingdom. This promise of the succession would of course have had no force in Irish law, but perhaps in Dermot's eyes Leinster was to be regarded as swordland, while to the Norman lord nothing would seem more natural. The earl was to come in the following spring (1168): in fact he seems to have been employed in the king's service shortly afterwards, and did not come till Dermot sent him urgent messages in 1170.

Fortified by this alliance, Dermot set out for Pembrokeshire, where he succeeded in enlisting the support of an important Norman-Welsh clan, the sons and grandsons of Nesta, daughter of Rhys ap Tewdwr, king of Deheubarth, by a variety of fathers. Maurice fitz Gerald, the son of Gerald of Windsor, castellan of Pembroke, and his half-brother, Robert fitz Stephen, the son of the constable of Aberteivi or Cardigan, were promised in fee the city of Wexford and two adjoining cantreds and undertook to come to Ireland in the spring of 1168. Then, early in August 1167, Dermot, who had perhaps had encouraging news from home, returned to Leinster, accompanied only by Richard fitz Godebert, a Pembrokeshire knight, with a small force—'only a few men, who crossed over in haste'[21] and did not long remain.

Dermot re-established himself in Ui Cennselaigh without apparent difficulty: O'Connor was preoccupied with the attempt to control Munster, and it may well have been some time before news of Dermot's return reached him. But, probably in the early winter, he advanced on Ui Cennselaigh with his allies, O'Rourke and O'Melaghlin. Dermot was defeated and forced to submit: O'Connor took hostages from him, O'Rourke accepted a compensation for the rape of Dervorgilla, and Dermot was left in possession of ten cantreds of Ui Cennselaigh, to which it was clearly hoped he would now be confined. O'Connor had other preoccupations and could hope that the threat from Leinster was now at an end. But Dermot's submission was only apparent: he sent messengers to Wales, and after the lapse of more than a year, about 1 May 1169, Robert fitz Stephen, with a force of thirty knights 'of his own kinsmen and retainers', sixty men at arms, and some three hundred archers and foot soldiers, 'the flower of the youth of Wales', landed at Bannow Bay on the south coast of Wexford, followed the next day by Maurice de Prendergast, a Fleming from Pembrokeshire, with ten men at arms and a body of archers in two ships.[22]

---

[21] *Song of Dermot and the Earl*, ll. 404–19.
[22] *Song of Dermot and the Earl*, ll. 441–62. Fitz Stephen brought at least three of his nephews, Robert de Barry, Meiler fitz Henry, and Miles fitz David.

The arrival of this body of professional soldiers revolutionized the situation. Dermot now had at his disposal a cavalry force of about one hundred, a substantial part of which was trained to act together, and what was perhaps even more important in the context of Irish warfare, a substantial force of archers. A hundred years earlier it had been these factors which largely secured the victory of the Normans over the Anglo-Saxon forces at Hastings. As a modern writer puts it, in describing the Norman conquest of England,

the individual knights must have known each other intimately and developed at least a rudimentary capacity for concerted action . . . Even in the eleventh century a Norman army was capable of something more than an unco-ordinated series of single combats.[23]

And the archers were probably even more important than the cavalry, for at this date the Irish had no missile weapon except stones thrown from slings. Giraldus stresses the importance of archers in Ireland,[24] though their usefulness must have been limited by the heavily wooded character of much of the country: even at the end of the fourteenth century it was desirable to time an expedition so that the leaves should have fallen.[25] But in fighting a people who took refuge in the woods and bogs the experience of Welsh warfare which the newcomers brought with them was of enormous importance, and must have been a major factor in their success.

The Normans were quickly joined by Dermot, and proceeded immediately to reduce Wexford, which was in due course handed over to fitz Stephen, while Hervey de Montmorency, Strongbow's uncle, who had accompanied the invaders to watch over his nephew's interests, was given two cantreds between Wexford and Waterford. They then proceeded to restore Dermot's supremacy in Leinster, raiding Ossory, Offelan and Omurethy, and then returning to raid Ossory again. But at this point the invaders quarrelled among themselves: Maurice de Prendergast wished to return to Wales, and when Dermot took steps to prevent this joined the king of Ossory. And it seems to have been at this point that O'Connor advanced with a great army against the new threat. He does not, indeed, seem to have attached very much importance to the Normans: the annals say that 'the fleet of the Flemings came to

[23] F. M. Stenton, *Anglo-Saxon England*, p. 585.
[24] *Expugnatio*, p. 397.
[25] J. F. Lydon, 'Richard II's Expeditions to Ireland', *Journ. R.S.A.I.*, XCIII, pp. 144-5. Some idea of the extent and distribution of medieval woodland can be obtained from E. McCracken, 'The woodlands of Ireland circa 1600', *I.H.S.*, XI, pp. 271-96.

Erin, they were ninety heroes dressed in mail and the Gaels put little store by them'.[26] But that Dermot should be asserting that supremacy over Leinster from which he had been driven in 1166 and again in 1167 was a serious matter which O'Connor could not afford to disregard. Dermot retreated before him, and, apparently without a battle, a treaty was entered into, by which Leinster was left to Dermot, who on his side recognized O'Connor as high king and gave his son as a hostage, secretly agreeing that he would bring in no more foreign mercenaries, and would send away fitz Stephen and his men as soon as Leinster was subdued.

Whether or not Dermot really intended to observe this treaty we cannot tell, but his hand was to some extent forced by the arrival shortly afterwards of Maurice fitz Gerald with ten knights, thirty men at arms, and about a hundred archers and foot soldiers. They landed at Wexford in two ships, and Dermot's forces were now restored to something near the level they had stood at before the desertion of Prendergast, who moreover after Dermot had come to the support of O'More of Leix against the king of Ossory decided to return to Wales. Next, apparently early in 1170, Dermot, with fitz Gerald, marched on Dublin and forced the Ostmen to submit, and then felt able to send a party under fitz Stephen to the assistance of his son-in-law, Donnell O'Brien, king of Limerick or north Munster, against O'Connor. It was after this, according to Giraldus, that he began to entertain designs of seizing the high kingship, and on the advice of fitz Stephen and fitz Gerald sent messages to Strongbow, urging him to come at once. Strongbow, encouraged by fitz Stephen's success, and having obtained leave from Henry II, though Giraldus says it was given in jest rather than in earnest, sent ahead at the beginning of May Raymond le Gros, another of the fitz Geralds, with ten knights and seventy archers, who entrenched themselves at Baginbun near Waterford, and having repulsed an attack from the Ostmen of Waterford awaited the earl's arrival.

Meanwhile Strongbow had been organizing his forces, and at last on 23 August landed near Waterford with a small army: about two hundred knights and some one thousand other troops. On 25 August, having been joined by Raymond, the army advanced to attack Waterford, which was taken by storm. Dermot Mac-Carthy is said to have attacked Strongbow's force after this, with all the Munstermen he could get, but evidently without success.[27] Dermot MacMurrough arrived shortly afterwards, with fitz

[26] A. Tig.
[27] Misc. Annals, p. 53.

Stephen and Maurice fitz Gerald, Eva was married to Strongbow, and the combined force then marched on Dublin, where the High King was assembling an army.

Strongbow's arrival, and the fact that it was being prepared had no doubt been known to the Irish for some time, was clearly recognized as opening a new phase in what were still, nevertheless, only the wars of province kings. But O'Connor had grave troubles in Munster, where the annals say the O'Briens had rebelled against him, so that there was great war between them[28]: he was not in a position to push matters too far. He guarded the passes to the south and west of Dublin, but when Dermot arrived before the city, having led the army over the mountains to avoid him, he did not prevent the Ostmen from negotiating. But Dublin was taken by storm on 21 September, while a large body of the citizens with their king, Asgall, fled by sea to their kinsmen in the islands. O'Connor withdrew his forces, and Dermot was left unhampered to reduce Offelan and Ossory, after which he invaded Meath, which was no part of his kingdom. When O'Connor protested that this was a breach of the treaty of 1169 he replied by claiming the high kingship. But Dermot's day was almost over: he died at Ferns at the beginning of May 1171, leaving Strongbow as his heir. Of his two legitimate sons, Connor, the hostage held by O'Connor, had been executed shortly before, while the other had been blinded by the king of Ossory, whose prisoner he was, in 1168, and so incapacitated from ruling. There remained the claims of his illegitimate son, Donell Kavanagh, and of his brother and other kinsmen, but Donell Kavanagh seems to have supported Strongbow, and it was Dermot's nephew, Murtough, who was supported by the Leinstermen.

Strongbow was now in a position of great difficulty. In Ireland he could expect the implacable hostility of all Dermot's enemies, and could hardly hope for any very solid support from his friends; in England he had the hostility of his own sovereign. Immediately before his embarkation in 1170, when it was already too late to draw back, messengers from Henry had arrived to forbid the expedition, and already before Dermot's death the king had ordered all his subjects in Ireland to return home before Easter on pain of forfeiture and perpetual banishment, and had forbidden exports to Ireland. The earl could thus get neither reinforcements nor supplies from England, and though he had sent Raymond le Gros to the king with a letter in which he said that he considered his acquisitions in Ireland as due to the king's favour, and held them

28 *A. Tig.*

at his disposition, Raymond had been received with great coldness, and had had no reply.

The immediate danger came, however, from the Irish. Those of Leinster are said to have risen against Strongbow,[29] while O'Connor was organizing a great army, and about the middle of May Asgall, the Danish king of Dublin, who had escaped in September, returned from the isles with a fleet and attacked the city, which was commanded by Miles de Cogan, fitz Stephen's son-in-law, in the absence of the earl. Asgall was defeated and executed after his capture, but soon afterwards O'Connor's army, which seems to have been drawn mainly from the northern half of Ireland, came up to surround the city, to which Strongbow had by now returned, while a fleet under Gottred king of Man blockaded the port. The siege continued for two months, and then, since supplies were running short and news had come that fitz Stephen was besieged at Carrick near Wexford and was in imminent danger, the Normans attempted to negotiate. Strongbow sent to O'Connor offering to become his man and hold Leinster of him, but O'Connor would offer him only the Norse cities of Dublin, Wexford and Waterford. And at this point the besiegers, who must have badly misjudged the temper of the Normans, drew off a great part of their forces, one body going south to raid Leinster and another north to cut the standing crop so that the garrison should not be able to provision itself from it. In a completely successful sortie the Normans defeated what remained, and the siege was raised.

Meanwhile, Henry II was preparing to intervene in person in Ireland. As a very young man he had once contemplated Irish conquests, as a provision for his brother William, but when at the Michaelmas council of 1155 the scheme was discussed, his mother, the empress Matilda, had strongly opposed it, and it was abandoned. But before this papal sanction for such a scheme had been obtained by an embassy of which John of Salisbury was a member. Writing in 1159 John tells us that

it was at my request that he [pope Adrian IV] granted to the illustrious king of the English, Henry II, the hereditary possession of Ireland, as his still extant letters attest; for all islands are reputed to belong by a long-established right to the church of Rome, to which they were granted by Constantine, who established and endowed it. He sent moreover by me to the king a golden ring, adorned by a fine emerald, in token of his investiture with the government of Ireland; and this ring is still, by the king's command, preserved in the public treasury.[30]

[29] *Song of Dermot and the Earl*, ll. 1734-45.
[30] *Metalogicon*, ed. G. C. Webb (Oxford, 1929), book IV, chapter 42.

John of Salisbury is an unimpeachable witness, and it is impossible to doubt that he obtained such a privilege as he describes. It had not been forgotten, and was to be produced at a later date, but for the moment Henry was on the worst of terms with the pope, who after the murder of Becket had imposed an interdict on his continental lands, and refused to receive his envoys. It was not till after Henry's reconciliation with the church in May 1172 that renewed sanction was sought. But the immediate occasion of Henry's intervention in 1171 is said to have been an appeal from the Irish themselves,[31] which must have been sent off shortly after Dermot's death at latest, for it was in a council held at Argentan in July that Henry decided to come himself to Ireland, and it may even belong to the preceding winter, when, after the fall of Dublin and the attack on Meath, exaggerated reports of these events are said to have been spread abroad, causing the king to issue his embargo.[32] Clearly Henry could not afford to let Strongbow establish himself as an independent ruler, and we need not suppose that he was unwilling to acquire fresh lands for himself, especially if he had been given reason to think that the Irish might welcome him.

Strongbow had been consolidating his success at Dublin. He was too late to relieve fitz Stephen, who had already been taken prisoner, but he persuaded his brother-in-law, the king of Limerick, to join him in an expedition against Ossory,[33] and after this Murtough MacMurrough came to terms with him, and was granted Ui Cennselaigh, while Donell Kavanagh was granted 'the pleas of Leinster', whatever that may mean—presumably, as Orpen suggested, some sort of jurisdiction over the Irish of the province.[34] The earl's immediate enemies in Leinster had thus been appeased, and it seems to have been at this point that Hervey de Montmorency returned from the embassy on which he had been sent to Henry II shortly after Dermot's death. Hervey had offered on behalf of the earl to surrender Dublin, Waterford, and other fortresses, and Henry, accepting this, promised to restore Strongbow's lands in Normandy, England and Wales, and to leave him in possession of the rest of Dermot's kingdom. He now brought letters summoning the earl to England, and the news of Henry's projected expedition.

Henry was preparing a very considerable army—five hundred

---

[31] Gervase of Canterbury, *Historical Works*, ed. W. Stubbs (Rolls Series, 1879–80), I, p. 235.
[32] *Expugnatio*, p. 259.
[33] *Song of Dermot and the Earl*, ll. 2033–54.
[34] *Normans*, I, p. 238.

knights and between three and four thousand archers—with an elaborate equipment of provisions, tools, portable wooden towers, horses, and in general everything necessary for an extensive campaign and siege warfare.[35] He must have been prepared for the possibility that he might have to fight Normans or Irish, or a combination of both, and it would obviously have been unsafe not to provide against it. But when Strongbow reached him, probably at Newent near Gloucester, where the army seems to have assembled, some time about the middle of September, he succeeded, not without difficulty, in persuading the king to accept the renewal of his oath of fealty, and to grant him Leinster, except for Dublin with the adjacent cantreds (that is, the modern co. Dublin and the coastal strip of the modern co. Wicklow), and the sea-coast towns and all the fortresses, to hold as a fief. Then or later he must have had a formal charter, laying down the service of one hundred knights by which we know Leinster was held, but it has not survived. This settled, Henry set out for Pembroke, from which he embarked on 16 October, landing next day at Crook near Waterford. The day after he entered Waterford and Strongbow formally surrendered the city to him and did homage for Leinster.

That there had in fact been negotiations between Henry and the Irish kings is strongly suggested by the events which followed. Before long Dermot king of Cork (Dermot MacCarthy of Desmond) came of his own free will and submitted to Henry, doing homage and swearing fealty, and giving hostages for the regular payment of a yearly tribute. Then Henry marched westwards, pausing first at Lismore, where he stayed for two days, and then going to Cashel, where Duvenald king of Limerick (Donnell O'Brien) met him by the river Suir, became tributary and did fealty. Others, who 'although not princes were men of consequence among their people',[36] also submitted voluntarily, and were sent home with gifts. Then Henry returned to Waterford and set out for Dublin through Ossory, receiving on the way the submission of the principal Leinster chieftains, and also of O'Carroll of Uriel (Louth) and O'Rourke of Breifne (Cavan and Leitrim), MacMurrough's old enemy. Giraldus alleges further that O'Connor met Henry's envoys at the Shannon and became tributary, binding himself by solemn oaths, but this is not supported by any other authority, and two English chronicles say that he held aloof, claiming that the whole of Ireland was rightly his. The annals say also that Henry received the

[35] *C.D.I.*, I, nos. 1–37.
[36] *Expugnatio*, p. 278. O'Brien is said to have been accompanied by Donnchadh Ó Mathghamhna, king of the Uí Eachach of Cork (*Misc. Annals*, p. 57).

pledges of Ulidia (Antrim and Down), but Giraldus says the Ulstermen did not submit.[37]

By this time it was near Christmas and Henry held his court in Dublin from 11 November to 2 February, entertaining many of the Irish princes. He must have attended to the organization of his new demesne during this period, but we have little evidence of what he did beyond the charter by which he granted to his men of Bristol the city of Dublin, to hold as they held Bristol.[38] He confirmed their lands to the monks of All Hallows,[39] and may well have given similar charters to other religious houses, but it is very likely that all the detailed work of organization was left to be performed by his representatives later.

Meanwhile, a church council was being held at Cashel, presided over by Christian, bishop of Lismore, the papal legate, with whom Henry had no doubt arranged this at Lismore in the autumn.[40] It is customary to write as if the Irish clergy of the twelfth century should have been imbued with the spirit and should have displayed the attitudes of modern Irish nationalism. But to suggest this is a gross distortion of historical possibilities. They were first of all churchmen, trained to a greater or less extent in the attitudes of an international body, and deeply influenced by new monastic orders of French origin. They had wholeheartedly accepted the Hildebrandine reform, which as we saw had begun to affect Ireland at the beginning of the century, and were struggling with the very difficult task of putting it fully into effect. They were clearly ready to welcome any secular support they could obtain in this, and though they can hardly have found Dermot MacMurrough's private life edifying, he had nevertheless been publicly a reformer, founding new monastic houses, and apparently securing the support of the clergy. Further, their secular loyalties will have been purely local—at most provincial: those of the men of Leinster or Munster, Meath or Connacht. Only the men of Connacht will have felt any great enthusiasm for O'Connor. To such men the Normans may well have seemed welcome allies in the task of establishing an ecclesiastical organization still very new in Ireland. Henry of Anjou might have quarrelled with the pope (they knew

---

[37] *Expugnatio*, pp. 278–9; Gervase of Canterbury, loc. cit., I, p. 235; *Gesta Henrici Secundi*, ed. W. Stubbs (Rolls Series, 1867), I, p. 25. MacDunlevy of Ulaidh is named by one annalist as having submitted (*Misc. Annals*, p. 57).

[38] *Historic and Municipal Documents*, p. 1. Dublin must of course have been largely denuded of citizens at this time, since many of the Ostmen had been killed at the taking of the city, and others had fled with Asgall. In spite of the charter the men of Bristol do not seem to have been specially prominent in Dublin.

[39] *Reg. All Hallows*, p. 20.

[40] Giraldus says it was held by Henry's command (*Expugnatio*, p. 281).

all about Becket, for Giraldus tells against himself the story of how
the archbishop of Cashel replied to the charge that there were no
Irish martyrs by saying, 'Now there is come into this land a people
who know how to make martyrs and have frequently done so'),[41]
but he was nevertheless a king who considered the organization
which they were seeking to impose the only right and proper one:
he would clearly have had a very short way with lay coarbs. Nothing could be more natural than that the bishops should support
him, particularly as the lay princes had submitted.

Christian O'Conarchy, bishop of Lismore and papal legate, had
been a monk at Clairvaux and had been sent by St Bernard as the
first abbot of Mellifont in 1142. There were also present at Cashel
the archbishops of Cashel, Dublin, and Tuam, and presumably
most or all of the other Irish bishops, together with a great number
of dignitaries. The archbishop of Armagh, who was more than
eighty years old, was unable to go to Cashel, but afterwards came
to Dublin and consented to all that had been done. The bishops
swore an oath of fealty to Henry, who was represented at the synod
by the abbot of the Cistercian house of Buildwas, to which St
Mary's abbey, Dublin, was subject, and the archdeacon of Llandaff, with other clerks. The synod enacted a set of constitutions,
condemning the marriage customs of the Brehon laws, requiring
the payment of tithes to the parish church, condemning the custom of the Irish kings of exacting hospitality from the churches,
enjoining the making of wills, and other matters, and finally enacted that divine offices should be henceforth celebrated in every
part of Ireland according to the forms and usages of the English
church. These constitutions were later confirmed and promulgated by the king. At Cashel the bishops also prepared a statement
of what Giraldus describes as 'the enormous offences and foul lives
of the people of that land', made under the seal of the legate—no
doubt it was much the same as what St Malachy had said to St
Bernard a generation earlier. Each bishop further gave Henry
letters under his seal confirming his submission, and these were
subsequently sent to the pope.[42]

Henry's new position had thus been accepted by both lay and
ecclesiastical authorities, and he is said to have intended to remain
in Ireland for the rest of the year, building castles and establishing
order.[43] He had had no news from England for some time, for the
winter had been one of exceptional storms, but he left Dublin at

[41] *Topographia*, pp. 178–9.
[42] *Pontificia Hibernica*, I, nos. 5–6.
[43] *Expugnatio*, pp. 285–6.

the beginning of February, and reached Wexford about the end of
the month. And here, late in March, he had at last news of a most
disquieting nature: the papal legates were threatening an interdict
unless he came at once to make reparation for Becket's murder,
and his eldest son, the young king Henry, was organizing a rebellion. Clearly he must return to England without avoidable delay.
He must still have had considerable suspicions of Strongbow, for
Giraldus says that he had been taking steps to strengthen his own
and weaken the earl's party,[44] and he had made certain that
Strongbow could assert no claim to Meath by granting it to Hugh
de Lacy, another marcher lord, to hold 'as Murrough O Melaghlin or any other before or after him best held it', by the service of
fifty knights.[45] Now de Lacy was appointed justiciar and constable
of Dublin, with a garrison which included fitz Stephen, Maurice
fitz Gerald, Meiler fitz Henry, and Miles fitz David, who were
thus kept apart from Strongbow, and garrisons were also placed in
Waterford and Wexford. Then on 17 April 1172 Henry sailed
from Wexford, never to return.[46]

Clearly much that Henry might have done had had to be left
undone. Presumably some sort of beginning had been made in
organizing what was to become the county of Dublin, the lands
reserved to the crown, but, as we shall see, the subinfeudation of
this area seems to have been in the first place the work of de Lacy.
Outside this area, everything was still vague and indefinite. Leinster was left to Strongbow, who had already successfully asserted
his possession of it, but de Lacy still had to make good his claim to
Meath. Elsewhere the submissions of the Irish chieftains still had
to be translated into fact, though the agreement with the kings of
Desmond and Thomond had enabled Henry to put garrisons in
the cities of Cork and Limerick. North of Dublin, O'Carroll of
Uriel seems to have remained on good terms with the Normans
for the rest of his life: after his death in 1188 or 1189 John spoke
of him as having held of him, and the initial Norman penetration
into co. Louth most probably took place by agreement with him.[47]
But otherwise outside Leinster nothing was secure, and no agreement had been come to with O'Connor, while the rulers of the
north-west had not been involved in anything that had happened.
On the other hand, the alliance of the clergy was a solid and important fact, and in September pope Alexander III, replying to

[44] Ibid., p. 284.
[45] Cal. Gormanston Reg., p. 177. For the de Lacys, see W. E. Wightman, The
Lacy Family in England and Normandy, 1066-1194.
[46] For the office of justiciar, see below, pp. 144-8.
[47] See below, pp. 70-72.

the letters of the prelates after the council of Cashel, addressed three letters to the archbishops and bishops of Ireland, to Henry himself, and to the kings and princes of Ireland. In the first two the pope referred to the enormities and crimes, the abominable foulness of the Irish, which he had learnt from the letters of the Irish prelates themselves, and from the verbal report of the archdeacon of Llandaff, who, as we saw, had been present at Cashel. The bishops were commanded to assist Henry in maintaining possession of the land, and in extirpating these abominations, visiting with the censures of the church any king, prince, or other person breaking his oath of fealty to Henry; Henry was congratulated and urged to show still greater energy in the reforming work so laudably begun. The kings and princes were commended for their voluntary submission, and admonished to maintain their oath and fealty inviolate. Henry was thus provided with the full support of the church, and these letters were most probably brought over by William fitz Audelm in March or April 1175, and published at the synod of Waterford.[48]

Meanwhile, Strongbow was consolidating his position in Leinster, and de Lacy was beginning to establish himself in Meath, which had been torn by wars since the death of Murrough O'Melaghlin in 1153. In 1169 O'Connor and O'Rourke had partitioned the kingdom between them; in 1170 the last of the O'Melaghlins had submitted to Dermot MacMurrough, who had thus had claims to it at his death, claims which Henry had prevented Strongbow from asserting for himself by granting it to de Lacy. De Lacy now advanced into Meath: he took Fore, and advanced as far as the Shannon, and in alliance with Donnell O'Rourke raided Muinter Anghaile, Muinter Ghiollagain, and the town of Ardagh, all now in co. Longford, but part of the ancient kingdom of Meath. At a meeting with Tighernan O'Rourke, one of the chieftains who had submitted to Henry, who claimed the eastern part of Meath for himself as a result of the partition of 1169, a dispute arose in the course of which O'Rourke was killed, each side subsequently accusing the other of treachery. But we cannot tell whether at this stage anything was done to make a permanent occupation of Meath, though it is likely that at least a beginning was made with that subinfeudation which was its necessary basis. But there was no opportunity to do very much, for in the spring of 1173 both Strongbow and de Lacy were summoned to serve in Henry's war in Normandy, and William fitz Audelm, Henry's dapifer, who had been with him in Ireland the year before, was sent over to take

[48] *Pontificia Hibernica*, I, nos. 5–7.

charge. This may, as has been suggested, have been due to the representations of Laurence O'Toole, the archbishop of Dublin, that the activities of Strongbow and de Lacy made the establishment of a settled peace in Ireland impossible,[49] but it is hard to think that Henry can ever have expected them to act otherwise: only by establishing their own followers in them could they hope to make their new lordships effective.

We know almost nothing of what fitz Audelm did in Ireland at this time. He seems to have published the pope's letters of the previous September, and he conducted an investigation of the lands held by St Mary's abbey, Dublin, so that Henry might issue a charter confirming its possessions.[50] There must have been more than this, but we know nothing of it. But in any case he seems to have returned to England in August or September, when Henry sent Strongbow back in sole charge of Ireland, with Raymond le Gros, for whom the earl had specially asked, as his assistant, and at the same time recalled from Ireland the troops he had left there.

Giraldus says that on his return Strongbow found most of the princes of the country in revolt against the king and against himself.[51] At any rate, he immediately sent an expedition against Offelan, which had constantly opposed MacMurrough, and seems now to have been finally reduced. Then, presumably in his capacity as the king's representative, he embarked on an attack on Munster, which if it were not quite unprovoked, as it may have been, must have been caused by some hostile action on the part of either Melaghlin O'Phelan, king of the Decies, the area immediately attacked, or Dermot MacCarthy, king of Desmond, both of whom had submitted to Henry in 1172. The Normans plundered Lismore, and defeating both an Ostman fleet from Cork and Dermot MacCarthy himself brought back a considerable prey to Waterford. But Donnell O'Brien, king of Thomond, Strongbow's brother-in-law, naturally took alarm at these proceedings: late in the year, with reinforcements under O'Connor's son, he led a force into Ossory, and seems to have met with no opposition, the Norman garrison of Kilkenny retreating on Waterford without attempting to defend the castle, which was destroyed. And at this point Strongbow lost his most capable military leader, for Raymond le Gros, who had quarrelled with the earl, returned to Wales on a pretext. It was thus Hervey de Montmorency who was

[49] J. F. O'Doherty, 'St. Laurence O'Toole and the Anglo-Norman Invasion', *Irish Ecclesiastical Record*, fifth series, L, pp. 614–16.
[50] *Chart. St. Mary's*, I, p. 138.
[51] *Expugnatio*, p. 308.

in command when, early in 1174, the attack on Munster was resumed, only to meet with complete defeat near Thurles. Strongbow retreated to Waterford, and, according to Giraldus, 'all the people of Ireland with one consent rose against the English'.[52]

O'Connor had been acting with O'Brien throughout: he now launched a great attack on the Normans in Meath, to the western part of which he had claims under the partition of 1169. Art O'Melaghlin had established himself there in 1170, and had just, in 1173, procured the murder of his rival, Donnell, who had submitted to MacMurrough in 1170: with Strongbow in retreat and de Lacy still on the continent there were clearly opportunities to be seized. It is unlikely that there had as yet been any Norman settlement in Meath: there were mote castles at Trim and Duleek, afterwards to be the centres of seigniorial manors, but though de Lacy may have made grants of land in Meath in 1172–3 it is likely that his followers had first occupied the lands he granted them in co. Dublin, in accordance with his charter of Meath which granted him also 'all the fees which he has granted or will grant round Dublin while he is my bailiff, doing me service at my city of Dublin'.[53] De Lacy clearly used this power to the full, for the majority of the tenants-in-chief of co. Dublin were also his tenants in Meath: Henry must have intended to strengthen de Lacy against Strongbow by enabling him to establish his followers in a dominant position, while the advantage for de Lacy of being able to establish his men in a relatively secure base from which they could advance into Meath is sufficiently obvious.

O'Connor seems to have met with no opposition when he crossed the Shannon. He had gathered a great army, drawn not only from Connacht, but also from the whole of Leth Cuinn, and they advanced on Trim. Hugh Tyrel, the constable, sent urgently to Strongbow for help, but though the earl summoned his men and marched northwards, accompanied by Raymond le Gros, whom he had induced to return with reinforcements by offering him his sister in marriage, O'Connor's advance was too rapid. Tyrel was forced to evacuate Trim, since the garrison was too small to make a stand, and O'Connor found the castle empty and destroyed it. Then, as Strongbow was coming up, the Irish retreated, closely pursued by the earl, who, however, only succeeded in cutting off part of the rearguard. The castle of Duleek had also been destroyed, but both it and Trim were now repaired, and in 1175 the Normans

[52] *Expugnatio*, p. 311.
[53] *Cal. Gormanston Register*, p. 177. See J. Otway-Ruthven, 'Knight Service in Ireland', *Journ. R.S.A.I.*, LXXXIX, pp. 7–9.

seem to have begun a systematic occupation of Meath. Manus O'Melaghlin was hanged at Trim, though Art O'Melaghlin seems to have been left undisturbed in west Meath, Clonard and Durrow were plundered, and the annals say that the whole country from Drogheda to Athlone was laid waste.[54]

By this time O'Connor must have given up hope of victory in the field, while from the Norman point of view some agreement with him was obviously desirable. The treaty made in 1175 must have been preceded by long negotiations, of which little trace has survived. Strongbow himself seems to have been with the king in the autumn, as was Laurence O'Toole, the archbishop of Dublin, who had been the intermediary between Strongbow and O'Connor during the siege of Dublin in 1171, and who can reasonably be supposed to have been concerned above all things to secure a settled peace. Meanwhile the archbishop of Armagh, according to the annals, had gone to Rome to confer with pope Alexander, and died there.[55] And a new attitude on the part of O'Connor is apparent at this time, for he invited the Normans to join him in an expedition against Donnell O'Brien of Thomond: Limerick was taken about the time the treaty was being drawn up, and a Norman garrison placed in the town.

O'Connor's envoys to Henry were the archbishop of Tuam, the abbot of St Brandon, and 'Master Laurence, my chancellor'. The treaty was concluded at Windsor on 6 October 1175. By it Henry granted that O'Connor, 'his liege king of Connacht', should be king under him, holding his land 'well and in peace, even as he held it before the king entered Ireland, but paying tribute for it'. The other Irish kings in possession were to hold in peace and render through O'Connor a tribute of one hide for every ten animals slain. Dublin, Meath as Murrough O'Melaghlin held it, Wexford with its appurtenances (i.e. Leinster), and Waterford as far as Dungarvan were reserved to the Normans. Fugitives were to return to the lands of the Normans, paying either the tribute or the ancient services due for their lands: if any (presumably of the unfree) refused to return, O'Connor was to force them to do so on request.[56] The treaty, in fact, recognized the existing political situation in Ireland: it was not really one that could last, but O'Connor may have hoped that it would, and was perfectly prepared to invoke the clause which entitled him to call on Norman assistance against rebels.

[54] *AFM, s.a* 1175, 1176; *ALC.*
[55] *AFM.*
[56] *Foedera*, I, p. 31.

Soon after this Raymond le Gros fell under suspicion. According to Giraldus, Hervey de Montmorency was in regular communication with Henry, and falsely represented to him that Raymond intended 'to secure to himself and his accomplices, not only Limerick, but the whole of Ireland'. That there was in fact some truth in this is strongly suggested by the curious letter in which at the end of May 1176 Raymond's wife, Strongbow's sister, sent him the news of her brother's death, as Giraldus himself tells us.[57] At any rate Henry believed the story, for early in 1176 he sent commissioners to recall Raymond. But before he could leave it was learnt that Donnell O'Brien was blockading Limerick, and he led a mixed force of cavalry and archers with an Irish contingent under MacMurrough and MacGilpatrick of Ossory to its relief. This was successfully achieved, and soon afterwards, at a meeting on the shores of Lough Derg, Raymond brought about an agreement between O'Connor and O'Brien, both of whom gave hostages and swore to preserve their allegiance to Henry. Then, at the request of Dermot MacCarthy of Desmond, he led an expedition to Cork, and recovered for MacCarthy his kingdom, of which his son had deprived him.

In all this Raymond had been acting more or less in accordance with the treaty of Windsor, but it was at this point that the whole situation was changed by the death of Strongbow, whose heir was his infant daughter. Raymond seems to have been in Cork when he received a letter from his wife, telling him that 'the great jaw tooth which used to give me so much trouble has fallen out', and urging him to return at once. When he reached Limerick it was decided that the town must be abandoned: it was entrusted to Donnell O'Brien, who swore to keep it safely and return it on demand, but broke the bridge and set fire to the town as soon as the garrison had marched out. It was to be twenty years before the Normans recovered it.

Strongbow's death had completely revolutionized the position, though Raymond did not in fact draw any advantage from it. Leinster seems, indeed, to have been fairly completely subinfeudated before the earl died, though MacGilpatrick seems to have been left in possession of the greater part of Ossory, and MacMurrough of the north and west of Wexford, while only the fringes of Leix had been touched.[58] But all this must now be taken into the

---

[57] *Expugnatio*, pp. 327, 332.
[58] The subinfeudation of Leinster has been fully described by Orpen, *Normans*, I, pp. 367–93. See also E. St J. Brooks, *Knights' Fees in Counties Wexford, Carlow* and *Kilkenny*, and J. Otway-Ruthven, 'Knights' Fees in Kildare, Leix and Offaly', *Journ. R.S.A.I.*, XCI, pp. 163–81.

king's hand during the minority of the heiress, and a new governor must be provided for the lordship of Ireland as a whole. De Lacy might have seemed an obvious choice, but while he and Strongbow had been used to counterbalance each other, to appoint de Lacy in the circumstances which now existed would have given him a practically uncontrolled power with which Henry was clearly not prepared to entrust him. The royal commissioners left Raymond temporarily in charge while they brought the news of Strongbow's death to the king, who appointed William fitz Audelm, who had already governed Ireland for some months in 1173, and sent with him John de Courcy, who seems never to have been in Ireland before, as well as Robert fitz Stephen and Miles de Cogan. According to Giraldus, fitz Audelm, whom he describes as

gentle to his enemies and severe to those who submitted . . . neither formidable to the one nor faithful to the other . . . full of guile, bland and deceitful, and much given to wine and women . . . covetous, crafty, and timid[59]

embarked on a persecution of the Geraldines, the most senior of whom, Maurice fitz Gerald, whose sons were the ancestors of the earls of Kildare and Desmond, died about 1 September.

Meanwhile de Courcy, who is said to have been granted Ulster by the king 'if he could conquer it',[60] had grown tired of his sub-ordination to fitz Audelm, and finding supporters among the Dublin garrison, whose pay seems to have been in arrears, he marched northwards with a force of twenty-two knights and about three hundred others, including some of the Irish. He passed rapidly through Meath and Uriel, and on the morning of the fourth day, about 1 February 1177, took Down completely by surprise, Rory MacDonlevy, its king, making no attempt to oppose him but flee-ing to collect an army. Cardinal Vivian, the papal legate, who had landed in Ulster from the Isle of Man and was on his way to Dublin, attempted to persuade de Courcy to abandon his conquest in return for an annual tribute, but without success, and at the end of a week MacDonlevy returned with a considerable force[61] to drive him out. But in spite of the disparity in numbers the Normans were victorious: Giraldus says there was an obstinate battle, but one set of native annals says that the Ulidians 'retreated without striking a blow when they saw the Englishmen with their horses in full battle-dress'. Both agree that there were heavy losses

---

[59] *Expugnatio*, p. 338.

[60] *Song of Dermot and the Earl*, ll. 2733–5. This is related in connection with Henry's visit to Ireland, but there is no evidence that de Courcy was in Ireland at the time: it is quite possible that Henry made such a half-jesting grant before de Courcy left England in 1176.

[61] Giraldus says 10,000 men, but this must be read simply as 'a large number'.

in the retreat.[62] There is no way of telling which account is correct, but even two generations later the sight of the Norman cavalry could still produce a panic-stricken flight, which well illustrates the military advantage which it gave them on suitable ground.[63]

MacDonlevy got away safe and returned in June, supported by the Cenel Eoghain and the clergy of the north with their most sacred relics as talismans to secure victory, but de Courcy was again successful, killing many of the chiefs of the Cenel Eoghain and taking the entire body of the clergy with their relics, most of which were subsequently restored. His position was now secured: with Down as his centre he could set about reducing the whole area east of the Bann. We have few details of the process, but after 1178, when he was defeated by Cumee O'Flynn, lord of Fir-Li (a district on the Bann in the north of co. Antrim), in the course of a cattle raid, we hear of no further fighting between the Normans and the Irish of eastern Ulster: instead Normans and Irish co-operate in raids west of the Bann, which do not seem to have met with any success, as was also the case with the raids which de Courcy made in Machaire Conaille and Cuailgne (the baronies of Upper and Lower Dundalk, co. Louth) in 1178 and 1180, when Murrough O'Carroll, king of Uriel, in conjunction with MacDonlevy on the first occasion, defeated him without apparent difficulty. Within Ulidia active opposition does not seem to have existed: the Irish were left in possession of the inland and more mountainous parts of the country, while elsewhere Norman settlers were widely spread, as is clearly shown by the distribution of mote castles, most of which had probably been erected by *c.* 1200.[64] Giraldus says of de Courcy that

after the many conflicts of a long war, and severe struggles on every side, being raised by his victories to the summit of power, he erected castles throughout Ulster in suitable places, and established it in a most firm peace, not without the greatest labour and privation and many perils.[65]

Meanwhile, after the failure of his mediation at Down, cardinal Vivian had continued to Dublin, where according to Giraldus a synod was held at which

he made a public declaration of the right of the king of England to Ireland, and the confirmation of the pope; and strictly commanded and enjoined both the clergy and people, under pain of excommunication, on no rash pretence to presume to forfeit their allegiance.[66]

[62] *Expugnatio*, pp. 338–41; *Misc. Annals*, p. 65 (*s.a.* 1178).
[63] See below, p. 193.
[64] For the mote castles of co. Down see *The Archaeological Survey of Northern Ireland: County Down*, pp. 116–19, 122, 185–206.
[65] *Expugnatio*, p. 345.   [66] Ibid., pp. 345–6.

It was perhaps on this occasion that the bull *Laudabiliter* was actually published. Its authenticity has been shown to be unquestionable, and it was to have an interesting later history in the thirteenth and fourteenth centuries as an instrument of propaganda used against the government by both English and native Irish.[67]

Soon after this synod there occurred the first Norman incursion into Connacht, assisted, perhaps invited, by Rory O'Connor's son, Murrough. It was led by Miles de Cogan, constable of the Dublin garrison, and *custos* of that area: it would seem that it was intended as a raid rather than as an attempt at occupation, and it may have been due to factors in the internal politics of the province which are unknown to us. In any case it was completely unsuccessful: the Connachtmen laid waste the country before the Normans, who though they reached Roscommon and Tuam were forced by hunger to retreat across the Shannon, fighting their way through the army which Rory O'Connor had by now brought up.

The only positive achievement of fitz Audelm during his stay in Ireland seems to have been the foundation of St Thomas's abbey, Dublin,[68] and he was clearly not a man to succeed in a country in which he had no personal interest. It is likely that from the beginning Henry had intended his appointment only as an interim measure till more permanent arrangements could be made, and by this time he had decided what these should be. He recalled fitz Audelm, fitz Stephen and de Cogan, and the affairs of Ireland were settled at a council held at Oxford in May 1177. It does not seem that he regarded the treaty of Windsor as abrogated, or even as unworkable,[69] but clearly the arrangements for the administration of Ireland needed elaboration. But that the general principles of the arrangements made with O'Connor in 1175 were regarded by both sides as still in operation is shown by the facts that in 1180 O'Connor sent his son to Henry as a hostage 'upon the agreements made between them concerning the payment of the tribute of Ireland', and that the annals, recording the death of Hugh de Lacy in 1186, say 'he was king of Meath and Breffny and Uriel, and it was to him that the tribute of Connacht was paid'.[70]

It is clear then that the arrangements made at Oxford in May

[67] J. F. O'Doherty, 'Rome and the Anglo-Norman Invasion of Ireland', *I.E.R.*, XLII, pp. 131–45; J. Watt, 'Laudabiliter in Medieval Diplomacy and Propaganda', ibid., LXXXVII, pp. 420–32; M. P. Sheehy, 'The Bull *Laudabiliter*', *Journal of the Galway Archaeological and Historical Society*, XXIX, pp. 45–70.
[68] T. Leland, *History of Ireland*, I, p. 127.
[69] See J. F. O'Doherty, 'St. Laurence O'Toole and the Anglo-Norman Invasion', *I.E.R.*, LI, pp. 136–8.
[70] *ALC*.

1177 still accepted the general principle of a division of Ireland between Norman and Irish lordship, with O'Connor as the dominant Irish ruler. The weakness of the Irish position was, of course, that O'Connor was really interested only in his own kingdom: so long as he was not threatened there, he would not seriously resist Norman advances, and would indeed be quite ready to invite Norman action against his under-kings elsewhere, as had been shown in Munster in 1175, and ready to accept that the Normans should replace an under-king who had shown himself rebellious. The under-kings themselves were ready to assist the Normans against each other, and piecemeal Norman expansion was thus facilitated.

The arrangements made in 1177 were clearly dominated by the desire to make certain that no single great vassal should be able to establish an overwhelming power in Ireland. In the first place, with papal approval, Henry made his son, John, lord of Ireland. It is likely that he intended by this not only to provide for his favourite son, but also to provide a resident ruler to curb the ambitions of the Norman barons, but since John was only ten years old the fruition of any such plan was still some years in the future, solving no immediate problem. To deal with this, the first step was the division of Strongbow's lordship of Leinster. Wexford, its *caput*, with the modern co. Carlow, the southern part of co. Kildare, and Leix, was given into the custody of William fitz Audelm; Ossory was separated from Leinster and attached to the royal demesne lands of Waterford, now defined as extending to the Blackwater beyond Lismore and given into the custody of Robert le Poer, the marshal; the lands of north Kildare were attached to the service of Dublin, as was Meath, and the whole was given into the custody of Hugh de Lacy, who was given a new charter for Meath, requiring the service of one hundred knights.[71] Giraldus says that de Lacy was appointed procurator-general of Ireland with Robert le Poer joined in the commission with him: in fact it was probably shared with fitz Audelm, whom Giraldus ignores, but de Lacy's central position will have given him the advantage. In addition, speculative grants were made of the kingdoms of Cork and Limerick: Cork from the Blackwater to Brandon Head in Kerry to Robert fitz Stephen and Miles de Cogan, who were to hold it between them by the service of sixty knights, and Limerick to three courtiers, none of whom had any previous connection with Ireland, and who surrendered the grant later in the year on the grounds that

[71] Meath was later held by the old service of fifty knights: the service of one hundred may have been meant to include Dublin and north Kildare.

the land had still to be conquered, when it was granted to Philip de Braose.[72]

As far as our evidence goes, O'Connor accepted these grants without protest. As we have seen, he had had trouble with the O'Briens in Limerick, and had invoked Norman assistance there in 1175; O'Brien's re-establishment in the troubles which followed Strongbow's death must have been most unwelcome to the High King, who saw himself threatened by a dangerous opponent whose removal he would welcome. We have less information about the position in Cork, but there had been troubles and Norman intervention there already in 1176. Nothing is said by our sources about Ulster, where de Courcy was in the early stages of establishing himself, but O'Connor is most unlikely to have been interested in what was happening there, and while we are told that de Courcy began the conquest against fitz Audelm's prohibition this does not necessarily imply royal disapproval of the conquest itself: it might mean only that fitz Audelm was unwilling to have the Dublin garrison weakened. It is true that no royal grant to de Courcy has survived, but it is impossible to believe that he would have been appointed to govern Ireland for John, as he was in 1185, unless his position in Ireland had been regularized.

The grant of Limerick led to no immediate occupation, for when de Braose, accompanied by fitz Stephen and de Cogan, advanced on the town the citizens set fire to it, and de Braose decided to abandon all attempt at conquest. According to Giraldus

it is no wonder that this expedition turned out so unfortunately, considering the number of cut-throats, and murderers, and lewd fellows, whom Philip de Braose had, by his own special choice, got together from South Wales and its marches, to accompany him.[73]

But though Limerick was left for the time being, Cork was successfully occupied, the Normans being assisted by Murtough O'Brien, son of Donnell. The city itself was already held by a Norman governor, Richard of London (it had been expressly reserved to the king at Oxford, but there seems to be no evidence as to how or when it had been occupied), and the Normans thus had a secure base from which to operate. They seem to have come to an agreement with Dermot MacCarthy after a conflict of which we have no details, and obtained seven cantreds, which they divided by lot, while, according to Giraldus, the remaining twenty-four cantreds of the kingdom, evidently left in MacCarthy's possession, were to

---

[72] Ware, *Antiquities of Ireland*, ed. Harris, p. 194; *Gesta Henrici*, loc. cit., I, p. 172; Hoveden, *Chronica*, ed. W. Stubbs (Rolls Series, 1868–71), II, pp. 133–6.
[73] *Expugnatio*, p. 349.

pay a tribute which was to be divided between them, while they acted jointly as the king's representatives in his city of Cork and its cantred. Fitz Stephen took the area east of the city, where considerable progress seems to have been made with Norman settlement in the next few years; de Cogan had the cantreds west of it. but we have little evidence as to the occupation of this area.[74] De Cogan himself was assassinated in 1182, and a general rising of the Irish under Dermot MacCarthy followed, but fitz Stephen, who was besieged in Cork, was relieved by Raymond le Gros, and the position was restored.

Meanwhile we must suppose that fitz Audelm was consolidating the occupation of Waterford, though we hear nothing of the process, and de Lacy, who was now first in Ireland for any considerable period, was certainly active in Dublin, Meath, and north Leinster, where Giraldus says that he was building strong castles throughout Leinster and Meath.[75] De Lacy, whom Giraldus describes with an enthusiasm which he otherwise reserves for the Geraldines, seems to have been the ablest of the first conquerors, except perhaps for Strongbow, and, according to Giraldus, made it his first care to restore peace and order, restoring confidence by his mild administration and firm adherence to treaties. But by the beginning of 1179 the Irish were complaining to Henry that de Lacy, fitz Audelm, and others whom he had set over them were treating them violently and unjustly, while Giraldus says that, probably after his second marriage to the daughter of Rory O'Connor, a marriage contracted 'after the manner of the country' in 1180, without Henry's leave, suspicions arose that de Lacy intended to throw off his allegiance and be crowned king of Ireland.[76] Whether this were so or not (it should be remembered that he had great estates on the borders of Wales, which he is unlikely to have been willing to see confiscated), it would seem to have been generally believed, and he was certainly achieving that predominant power in Ireland which it seems to have been Henry's consistent policy to prevent from falling into the hands of any single subject.

---

[74] *Expugnatio*, p. 348. The twenty-four cantreds of course included south Kerry. Orpen collects the evidence as to the early sub-infeudation of Cork and the later descent of the lands of fitz Stephen and de Cogan (*Normans*, II, pp. 43–50, and see *Pipe Roll, 14 John*, p. 48). Giraldus' account of the conquest of Cork has particular authority, since on his first visit to Ireland in 1183 he was in Cork and must have had a first-hand account from his uncle, fitz Stephen.

[75] The annals say that in 1176 castles had been built at Dunshaughlin, Trim, Skreen, Navan, Knowth and Slane, all in co. Meath (*Misc. Annals*, pp. 61, 63).

[76] *Expugnatio*, p. 353; William of Newburgh, *Historia rerum Anglicarum*, ed. R. Howlett, *Chronicles of the Reigns of Stephen, etc.* (Rolls Series, 1884–5), I, pp. 239–40.

In the late spring of 1181 Henry sent John de Lacy, constable of Chester, and Richard de Pec, an itinerant justice, to supersede Hugh, recalling him to England. In the winter of 1181–2, however, he was sent back as governor, and by this time Laurence O'Toole, the last of the Celtic archbishops of Dublin, who had died in Normandy on 14 November 1180 on his way to a meeting with Henry, had been replaced by a man of a very different type, John Comyn, a monk of Evesham in Worcestershire, an experienced royal official, who was consecrated at Velletri by the pope on 21 March 1182, and on whom Henry may well have relied to curb de Lacy's ambitions. At any rate, a royal clerk, Robert of Shrewsbury, had been associated with him.

But in any case, by this time the lord of Ireland, John, was coming to the age where he might reasonably be expected to take up his inheritance. In the summer of 1184 Henry sent archbishop Comyn to Ireland to prepare for John's coming, and in September sent Philip of Worcester to replace de Lacy, who seems, however, to have retained the office of constable. Then, on Mid-Lent Sunday 1185, Henry knighted John at Windsor, and sent him to govern the lordship of Ireland with an army of about three hundred knights and a considerable body of horsemen and archers. A new epoch in the history of the Norman colony in Ireland was about to begin.

It is fair to assume that the lands so far occupied by the Normans had been more or less thoroughly subinfeudated by this time, though the process of forming the new manors and attracting settlers from England can only have been in its very early stages.[77] But it is clear that the preliminary work of providing fortified centres at the principal manorial sites was well advanced, and this was the first essential which made effective settlement possible. The annals tell us that when de Lacy was killed in 1186 Meath from the Shannon to the sea was full of castles and of foreigners,[78] and though expansion into the southern half of the modern co. Longford came later, there is plenty of evidence that the statement is substantially true, so that a wedge of Norman occupation had been driven right across the centre of Ireland. On the coast, from Drogheda south and west to beyond Cork, everything was in the hands of the Normans, and in Leinster the settlement extended far inland. North Munster was still outside the sphere of occupation, and Connacht was untouched, though the tribute due under the treaty of Windsor was still a mark of subordination. To the north, Uriel still remained untouched under O'Carroll, and no Norman grants were to be

[77] See below, pp. 108–17.
[78] ALC.

made there till after his death in 1188 or 1189,[79] but beyond it the eastern part of Ulster, the modern counties of Antrim and Down, had been occupied by de Courcy. The rest of Ulster, however, was unaffected, and much of it was to remain so throughout the middle ages. And everywhere we can be sure, though we hear of it only occasionally, arrangements were being made with native rulers, by which they retained a part of their territories on condition of paying tribute, as MacCarthy did in Cork, as O'Hanlon and others did in Ulidia, and as O'Farrell did in Conmaicne.[80] It was only exceptionally that a native king was turned into a pure feudal tenant, as Macgillamocholmog was in Dublin.[81]

The lands retained in the king's hand, Dublin and Waterford, seem also to have been very extensively granted out on feudal terms by this time. The remarkable thing about the settlement of Dublin is the extent to which lands here were given to men who also appear as tenants in Meath: there can be no doubt that this was done by Hugh de Lacy under the terms of his charter, so that these grants must have been made before September 1184 at latest,[82] while in the south of the county there was a group of Leinster tenants whose lands in Dublin had been granted to them by Strongbow on behalf of the king, so that this area had been settled by the Normans before 1176. Some of the grants made by de Lacy in 'Ocadhesi'—i.e. north-western Dublin—were revoked by Philip of Worcester, and the lands restored as royal mensal lands[83] (an arrangement which had perhaps been made when Henry II was in Ireland): these must have been the manors which we find being granted out piecemeal early in the next century. There remained a solid block of demesne manors—the modern parishes of Newcastle, Esker, Saggart, and Crumlin—in the south of the county, which were retained as royal demesne throughout the middle ages.

[79] J. Otway-Ruthven, 'The Partition of the de Verdon Lands', *Proc. R.I.A.*, LXVI C.

[80] Ibid.; Orpen, *Normans*, IV, pp. 148–9; below, pp. 215–6.

[81] See J. Mills, 'Norman Settlement in Leinster: the Cantreds near Dublin', *Journ. R.S.A.I.*, XXIV, pp. 161–3.

[82] Many of these appear first in royal grants which ignore de Lacy's original charters. Cf. that of Castleknock, E. St J. Brooks, 'The Grant of Castleknock to Hugh Tyrel', *Journ. R.S.A.I.*, LXIII, pp. 206–20.

[83] *Expugnatio*, pp. 359–60.

The Consolidation of the Conquest

JOHN'S expedition was prepared with great care, but though it may well have resulted in the introduction of the elements of an organized central government which, in the absence of records, we cannot now trace, the character of the new lord of Ireland ensured that its purely political effects should be unfortunate. John landed at Waterford on 25 April 1185, and as Giraldus, who had been sent with him by the king and was therefore an eyewitness, tells us

> there met him at Waterford a great many of the Irish of the better class in those parts; men who, having been hitherto loyal to the English and disposed to be peaceable, came to congratulate him as their new lord, and receive him with the kiss of peace. But our new-comers and Normans not only treated them with contempt and derision, but even rudely pulled them by their beards, which the Irishmen wore full and long, according to the custom of their country.

It is not surprising that these men immediately betook themselves to O'Connor, O'Brien and MacCarthy, who were, according to Giraldus, at that time the main stay of Ireland, telling them that their new lord was an ill-mannered child, surrounded by other children, from whom no good could be hoped. The kings of Connacht, Thomond and Desmond had been preparing to come in to John: they now resolved to resist the English to the death, entering into an association for the purpose and abandoning old enmities. Giraldus says also that 'our own Irishmen, who had faithfully stood by us from the first coming over of fitz Stephen and the earl' were deprived of their lands, which were given to the newcomers, and naturally betook themselves to the enemy. And not only were the Irish wantonly alienated in this way, but the older settlers were out of favour and were 'more harassed by their enemies within than by the enemy without the walls'. At the same time, Giraldus complains that John's favourites were militarily incompetent, and that 'we even rob the church of its lands and possessions, and strive to

---

[1] Detailed references to the sources for the period covered in this chapter are given by Orpen, *Normans*.

abridge or annul its ancient rights and privileges'.[2] There may well be some exaggeration in all this, for Giraldus was naturally prejudiced in favour of his kinsmen, the first settlers, but it is quite clear that John's expedition was not a success.

John returned to England on 17 December, after being in Ireland for nearly eight months. We cannot trace his movements in detail, but he seems to have made a progress from Waterford through south Munster, where he tested charters at Lismore in west Waterford and Ardfinnan in south Tipperary, erecting castles at both places. From Ardfinnan he went perhaps to Tipperaghny in south-west Kilkenny where he tested another charter and again built a castle. Then we hear of him at Kildare, where he tested several charters, and he finally appeared in Dublin, where he probably spent the autumn and early winter. It does not seem that he attempted any serious military operations, but we hear of skirmishes between the garrisons of the new castles and the forces of O'Brien. But that the extension of the conquest into the kingdom of Limerick which had been contemplated in the abortive grant to Philip de Braose in 1177 was now to be seriously undertaken is shown by the grant which John made to Theobald Walter at Waterford.

Theobald Walter, the founder of the great Butler family, which was to dominate so much of the later history of Ireland, was the son and eventual heir of Hervey Walter of Amounderness in Lancashire, hereditary Butler of England, and nephew by marriage of Ranulf Glanville, the great justiciar, who had been John's tutor. His brother, Hubert, was archbishop of Canterbury, and he himself was granted the office of hereditary butler of Ireland by John, probably at this time. At Waterford John granted him five and a half cantreds in the land of Limerick: a grant defined as the borough of Killaloe and the half cantred of Trucheked Maleth in which it lay, and the cantreds of Elykarvel, Elyochgardi, Euermond, Aros and Wedene, and Woedeneoccadelon and Wodeneoidernan. These territories are now the baronies of Tullagh, co. Clare; Clonlisk and Ballybritt in co. Offaly; Eliogarty, Upper and Lower Ormond, and Owney and Arra, co. Tipperary; and Owneybeg, Clanwilliam, and Coonagh, co. Limerick.[3] The whole north-eastern part of the kingdom of Limerick had thus been granted to a man who would be prepared to put his grant into effect, and, probably at the same time, Philip of Worcester seems to have been made

---

[2] *Expugnatio*, pp. 389–93.
[3] These territories are identified by D. Gleeson, *A History of the Diocese of Killaloe*, pp. 176–7.

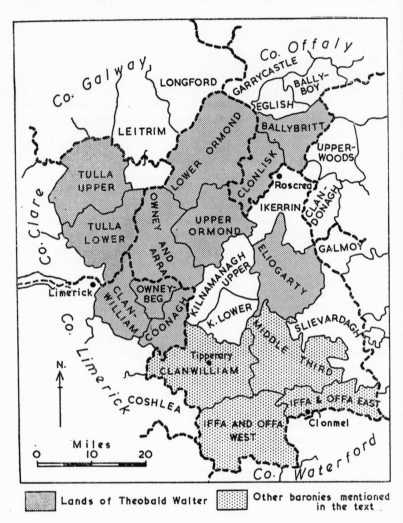

Grants in northern Munster in 1185

a grant including at least part of the barony of Middlethird in south Tipperary, while then or a little later William de Burgo, brother of Hubert de Burgo the later justiciar of England, who also came with John and founded another family of the first importance in Ireland, had grants in the baronies of Clanwilliam and Iffa and Offa, co. Tipperary. De Burgo secured his position by a marriage to the daughter of Donnell O'Brien.

The western boundary of the Norman colony had thus been extended in theory to the Shannon near Limerick, and even beyond it at Killaloe, though the Butlers never seem to have made any attempt to colonize co. Clare, contenting themselves with an agreement with the MacNamaras.[4] But that Theobald Walter was active in the area east of the Shannon from 1185 on is suggested by the statement that in 1185 Dermot MacCarthy and others were killed by the men of Cork and the forces of Theobald Walter in a parley near Cork.[5] No reaction seems to have been provoked from O'Connor by all this: as we have seen, he had apparently acquiesced in the grants of Cork and Limerick made in 1177, but the league of which Giraldus tells us might lead one to suppose that he would now have acted in support of O'Brien. In fact, however, internal disturbances in Connacht largely neutralized it during these years. Rory O'Connor, who had in 1183 given up his kingship to his son, Conor Maenmoy, and retired to a monastery, was now attempting to recover the kingdom, and a confused war was in progress in which Rory was supported by Donnell O'Brien and by some of the Munster settlers, while Conor also secured the assistance of the foreigners, and an English chronicler tells us that a great part of John's forces deserted to the Irish.[6] Conor, no more than his father, was anxious to strengthen the O'Briens, and can be supposed to have seen a potential rival to the high kingship weakened with complete indifference.

John de Courcy, who seems to have been in England in this year, was appointed as justiciar on John's departure, and Giraldus says that 'under his rule the kingdom speedily began to enjoy more tranquillity'. And in the next year, in July 1186, while Hugh de Lacy was supervising the building of a castle at Durrow, the site of a Columban abbey, he was assassinated 'by direction of the Sinnach Ua Catharnaigh in reparation to Colmcille while building a castle in his church in Durmagh'.[7] The lordship of Leinster was already

[4] Cal. Ormond Deeds, II, no. 36.
[5] Expugnatio, p. 386; ALC, AFM.
[6] Gesta Henrici Secundi, loc. cit., I, p. 339.
[7] AU, and cf. ALC. The Sinnach was the chief of Teffia in Westmeath.

in John's hands; now de Lacy's land of Meath fell also to be governed by his officials, for though Hugh left sons to succeed him they seem all to have been minors at his death, and the eldest probably did not get possession of Meath till 1194. Henry, who is said to have rejoiced openly on hearing of de Lacy's death, intended that John should return to Ireland to take possession of his lands, but was induced to recall him by the death of his son, Geoffrey of Brittany, and sent Philip of Worcester to Ireland instead, presumably to govern Meath as its *custos*.

Almost all the leaders of the first conquest were now dead. Robert fitz Stephen's death is not recorded,[8] but we hear nothing more of him: he seems to have been succeeded in Cork by his nephew, Raymond le Gros, who died at some time in the 1190s. Meiler fitz Henry, indeed, was left, and was to have a turbulent career at the beginning of the next century, but he was almost alone. And with the exception of Maurice fitz Gerald, whose descendants were not really prominent till later, and Hugh de Lacy, whose sons were minors, these men left no sons to succeed them: the way was clear for the new men who had come with John, the Butlers, de Burgos, de Verdons and Pipards.

We have already seen how Theobald Walter and William de Burgo had been established in Tipperary and Limerick. Bertram de Verdon, John's seneschal, and Gilbert Pipard, both experienced officials, were left in Ireland when John returned to England: we must suppose that they had been granted lands, but we have no indication of what they may have held at this time. But in 1188 or 1189 Murrough O'Carroll, king of Uriel, died, and in 1189 or 1190 John granted to de Verdon four cantreds in Uriel and a half cantred in Louth, lands which included the modern baronies of Upper and Lower Dundalk, and the eastern part of the barony of Louth, as well as lands stretching far north into co. Armagh, though no attempt seems to have been made to occupy these, de Verdon contenting himself with drawing rents from the Irish kings. Peter Pipard was granted at the same time the barony of Ardee, co. Louth, and lands which seem to have included the baronies of Farney, Cremorne, and Dartry, co. Monaghan, and part of the barony of Upper Fews, co. Armagh, though here again occupation does not seem to have gone beyond the barony of Farney. It would seem that occupation had begun some years earlier, probably by agreement with O'Carroll, and that the position already reached was now being confirmed by John. The western half of the barony

---

[8] It has been suggested that he was killed with Miles de Cogan in 1182 (*Misc. Annals*, p. 71), but he was certainly living later than this.

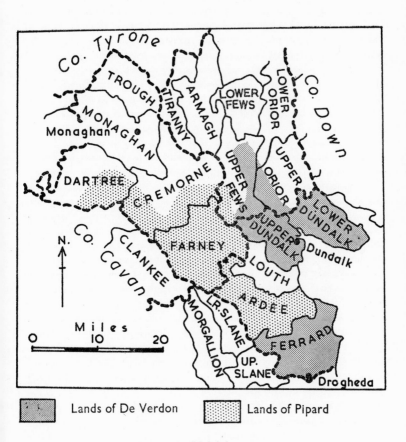

Lands of De Verdon   Lands of Pipard

Grants in Uriel in 1190

of Louth was retained as royal demesne; so perhaps was the barony of Ferrard, though the de Verdons held it by the end of the century.[9]

The whole coast from north Antrim to beyond Cork was now controlled by the settlers. We have very little evidence as to the activities of de Courcy as justiciar. In 1187 Conor Maenmoy O'Connor raided Meath and burnt the castle of Killare, and in 1188 de Courcy made a retaliatory expedition to Connacht in the company of a rival O'Connor, and was completely unsuccessful. In Ulster he was actively consolidating his lordship, but presumably most of his time had to be devoted to the administration of the colony as a whole, and it is not till after he had ceased to be justiciar that the annals show him attempting to expand beyond the Bann. But by 1192 at latest he had been replaced as justiciar by Peter Pipard and William le Petit, and in that year we find a systematic advance beginning in Munster. The Normans advanced as far as Killaloe, and though they were checked by Donnell O'Brien castles were erected at Kilfeacle, held by William de Burgo, who married O'Brien's daughter, probably in 1193, and Knockgraffon, held by Philip of Worcester. In 1193 O'Brien is said to have consented to the erection of the castle of Briginis 'for the purpose of distressing MacCarthy'.[10] Donnell O'Brien died in the next year, and rivalries for the kingdom seem to have induced his sons to act in agreement with their brother-in-law, William de Burgo, so that the consolidation of Norman settlement was facilitated. Philip of Worcester came to Ireland in 1195 'to reinforce the English of Munster', presumably in organizing what was later to be the barony of Knockgraffon. No doubt as a reaction to all this, Cathal Crovderg O'Connor, Rory's younger brother, who was now disputing Connacht with him, invaded Munster, reaching Cashel and destroying a number of castles. A principal motive in this raid had no doubt been the speculative grant of Connacht which seems to have been made to de Burgo at this time. Meanwhile there was 'a hosting by John de Courcy and the son of Hugh de Lacy to gain supremacy over the foreigners of Leinster and Munster',[11] which

---

[9] See D. MacIomhair, 'The Boundaries of Fir Rois', *County Louth Archaeological Journal*, XV, pp. 144–79; J. Otway-Ruthven, 'The Partition of the de Verdon Lands', *Proc. R.I.A.*, LXVI. Pipard's grant is said to be of the lands which he got from his brother Gilbert of the latter's acquisition. Both Bertram de Verdon and Gilbert Pipard were now in England; both accompanied Richard I on his crusade and died on it. De Verdon was succeeded by his sons Thomas and Nicholas successively.

[10] *AI; Misc. Annals*, p. 75.

[11] *ALC*.

should probably be connected with de Burgo's grant to de Lacy of ten cantreds in Connacht, comprising approximately the modern co. Sligo. At Athlone Cathal Crovderg met de Courcy and de Lacy, and a peace was made by which the Normans clearly recognized Crovderg as king of Connacht.

Meanwhile, during the period in 1193-4 when John was in rebellion against his brother, there seem to have been considerable disturbances among the Normans. After his accession in 1199 John wrote to the justiciar saying that John de Courcy and W. de Lacy had destroyed his land of Ireland, and it seems that de Courcy and de Lacy had been the heads of the party in Ireland which supported the king against John, thus securing the bitter enmity of a very dangerous man. Apparently after the surrender of Nottingham in 1194, which marked the final collapse of John's rebellion, Walter de Lacy did homage to the king for his lands in Ireland, and we are told that he received the lordship of Meath and apprehended Peter Pipard, John's justiciar, and his knights. In 1195 there was a hosting by de Courcy and de Lacy 'to assume power over the Foreigners of Leinster and Munster', and in 1196 de Courcy and MacMahon are said to have plundered Louth and burned its castle.[12] But by this time John had been reinstated, and had appointed Hamo de Valognes as justiciar, biding his time to revenge himself on de Courcy and de Lacy.

By this time the Normans were in occupation of the city of Limerick, apparently with the consent of the O'Briens, and, probably in 1197, John gave the city a charter, granting it all the liberties of Dublin. At the same time he granted Hamo de Valognes two cantreds in Hochenil—the baronies of Upper and Lower Connello, co. Limerick. The sons of Maurice fitz Gerald all had grants in the county, as had William de Burgo, but the general pattern was one of relatively small grants, with no single great predominant interest. The O'Briens seem to have offered no opposition, probably seeing in all this a welcome check on MacCarthy, and O'Connor's acquiescence had evidently been secured at Athlone in 1195. By the end of the century the Norman occupation of Munster was well on the way to consolidation, for in north Tipperary we find Theobald Walter active round Nenagh, granting lands in Elyocarroll and Eliogarty and founding the abbey of Woney (Abington) in co. Limerick. But Theobald Walter died in 1205, and it is likely that much of the organization of this area was undertaken when it was in the king's hand during the long minority

---

[12] *C.D.I.*, I, no. 90; *Histoire de Guillaume le Maréchal*, ed. P. Meyer (Paris, 1891-1901), ll. 10289-304; *ALC; Misc. Annals*, p. 77; T.C.D., MS E. 3. 20, p. 135.

of his son, Theobald Walter II.[13] Meanwhile, in 1201, John had revived the grant of 1177 to Philip de Braose in favour of his nephew, William de Braose, to whom he granted the honour of Limerick, retaining only the city and the cantred of the Ostmen, the crosses,[14] and the service of William de Burgo, to hold by the service of sixty knights. All the other grantees in this area thus became sub-tenants of de Braose, but the grant of course lapsed with his fall in 1208–9.

Meanwhile, in the north John de Courcy seems to have begun in 1197 a planned expansion along the northern coast, actuated, according to an English chronicler, by the desire to revenge the murder of his brother, Jordan, by an Irishman of his household. He erected a castle—evidently the mote at Mount Sandal on the Bann south of Coleraine—and from this base laid waste the cantred of Keenaght, subjugating territories of which he gave a great part to Duncan, son of Gilbert of Galloway, his wife's cousin[15] (de Courcy had married in 1180 Affreca, daughter of the king of Man). These lands must have been in Keenaght, for there is nothing to suggest that there was any occupation of the country round Derry itself, though de Courcy raided as far west as Derry and Inishowen both then and in 1199. But by this time John had become king, and was only waiting for an opportunity to avenge himself on de Courcy and de Lacy, an opportunity which came when in 1201 de Courcy allowed himself to become entangled in the affairs of Connacht.

Cathal Crovderg O'Connor was still the dominant power in Connacht, and in 1199, perhaps alarmed by the fresh grants which were being made in Limerick, or possibly by unrecorded activities of Walter de Lacy, he raided Athlone and burned the castle, and in the next year attacked both the king's castle at Limerick and de Burgo's at Castleconnell, and made a great raid into Westmeath, though he was defeated and driven back. Next, evidently in fear that his internal enemies might seize this opportunity, he proceeded to attack his rival, Cathal Carrach, who defeated him and called on de Burgo, who seems to have been acting as the royal governor in Munster. De Burgo came to his assistance, and Cathal Crovderg fled to the north to seek allies. In 1201 he came back, supported by

[13] The wardship must have belonged to de Braose till his fall (below, pp. 79–81). For the grants made by Theobald Walter I see Cal. Ormond Deeds, I, nos. 10, 23, 32–4. The hospital of St John Baptist (Tyone) at Nenagh was founded by Theobald Walter II (ibid., no. 22, which is misplaced in the calendar, and should be dated c. 1224).

[14] i.e. the churchlands (see below, pp. 175, 182–3).

[15] Hoveden, Chronica, ed. W. Stubbs (Rolls Series, 1868–71), IV, p. 25.

O'Neill and others of the Irish rulers of the north, but was defeated, and a second attempt in company with John de Courcy and Hugh de Lacy, Walter's younger brother, again met with a complete defeat from Cathal Carrach, supported by de Burgo. The defeated armies escaped to Meath, and de Lacy now arrested both de Courcy and Cathal Crovderg. O'Connor seems to have been forced to agree to the surrender of some lands in Connacht, apparently those west of the Shannon near Athlone which had been granted to Geoffrey de Costentin, an important tenant in both Westmeath and north co. Dublin, in return for which he was now supported against Cathal Carrach by the royal government. As for de Courcy, de Lacy threatened to hand him over to the king, 'who had long wished to take him', but finally released him as the result of a private bargain. But in 1203 de Lacy, who had important interests on the borders of Ulster, since at some time between 1191 and 1199 he had married the sister of Thomas de Verdon, obtaining with her half de Verdon's land of Uriel,[16] took the offensive against de Courcy, invading Ulster and defeating him at Down. In 1204 he again invaded Ulster, and this time he not only defeated de Courcy, but took him prisoner, though he was afterwards released. In all this de Lacy was clearly acting with the approval of the king, who during this period repeatedly summoned de Courcy to come to his service, a summons which de Courcy very naturally disregarded. Finally, on 29 May 1205, Hugh de Lacy, who, with his elder brother Walter, the lord of Meath, had had in the previous November what was apparently a provisional grant of eight cantreds in Ulster, was granted all the land of Ulster, whereof the king belted him earl, to hold of the king in fee as John de Courcy held it on the day when Hugh defeated and took him prisoner. The crosses were reserved to the king, but otherwise Hugh's power was not restricted in any way.[17] It is not clear what happened to de Courcy, but he must have been reconciled to the king before 1210, when he seems to have accompanied him to Ireland, and was certainly dead by September 1219, when the justiciar was ordered to give his widow her dower.[18] As for Hugh de Lacy, whose ambition John had used to pull down de Courcy, in due course John was to pull him down too.

Meanwhile, in Connacht the position of Cathal Crovderg had been firmly established with Norman assistance. In November 1201

---

[16] J. Otway-Ruthven, 'The Partition of the de Verdon Lands', loc. cit.

[17] *C.D.I.*, I, nos. 240, 263. For the crosses, see below, pp. 175, 182–3.

[18] *C.D.I.*, I, no. 901. For the dower, see J. Otway-Ruthven, 'The Dower Charter of John de Courcy's Wife', *U.J.A.*, third series, XII, pp. 77–81.

the king had given a commission, the terms of which are not stated, to Meiler fitz Henry, who was now justiciar, William de Burgo, and Geoffrey de Costentin: the barons of Meath were ordered to have faith in what these commissioners told them on behalf of the king.[19] At this time de Burgo, together with the O'Briens, seems to have been conducting an expedition into Desmond, whose hostages he obtained,[20] but the commission must have had to do with the affairs of Connacht, for any attack on which Meath was of course a natural base. At any rate, Cathal Crovderg, who was now released, joined de Burgo, and early in 1202 they marched into Connacht as far as Boyle, co. Roscommon, where de Burgo proceeded to fortify himself. But a massacre of his men on a mistaken report of his death caused a rupture, since de Burgo blamed Cathal Crovderg, and the Normans withdrew to Limerick: the only result of the expedition had been the almost accidental death of Cathal Carrach in a skirmish, leaving Cathal Crovderg without a serious native rival. Early in 1203 de Burgo attacked him, in alliance with the sons of Conor Maenmoy, building himself a castle at Meelick, co. Galway, and raiding the country from this base: he was apparently trying to put into effect the speculative grant of Connacht which seems to have been made to him some years earlier. But the justiciar was not prepared to countenance these proceedings; he summoned de Burgo to Limerick, and forced him to surrender Limerick, of which he was the royal keeper, and his Munster lands to the king. He then reported to the king, making complaints against de Burgo which he was summoned to the king's court to answer, while the custody of Limerick was given to de Braose. Negotiations were opened with Cathal Crovderg on behalf of John; de Burgo seems to have been restored to favour, but died in the winter of 1205–6, leaving a son who was still a minor. His lands were taken into the king's hand, and in December 1205 an agreement had been made with Cathal Crovderg, who was to hold a third of Connacht in fee as a barony, paying an annual tribute for the rest. His position as a vassal king was thus established much as Rory O'Connor's had been after 1177, but it was clearly a precarious one which could hardly be maintained for long. It was not, however, till after his death in 1224 that Norman occupation of the province was to begin.

With the death of William de Burgo so soon after that of Theobald Walter the ablest of the Norman leaders in Munster had disappeared. William de Braose had indeed, as we saw, been granted

[19] *C.D.I.*, I, no. 157.
[20] *AI; Misc. Annals*, p. 81.

the 'honour of Limerick' in 1201, the king retaining only the lands of William de Burgo and the city of Limerick with its cantred. The effect of this had been to make the other grantees in the area sub-tenants of de Braose, and Theobald Walter, and no doubt others, had had to get his confirmation of John's grants to them.[21] Now, presumably, Theobald's lands were in his custody, and Philip of Worcester, who had resisted him in arms, had been ordered to give up to him all his lands and castles in 1202. In 1203 John had given the custody of Limerick itself to William, and though a year later it was surrendered to the justiciar, it was regranted to William in 1205. But de Braose was an absentee: his deputy in Limerick was his son-in-law, Walter de Lacy, lord of Meath, and in the winter of 1206–7 de Lacy was involved in a violent quarrel with the justiciar, who was his tenant for lands in Meath.

By this time a new figure had appeared on the Irish scene: perhaps the ablest and most remarkable of all the Norman leaders of this period. William Marshal, the hereditary marshal of England, now a man past sixty, had been given Strongbow's heiress, Isabel de Clare, in marriage by Henry II in 1189, and had thus become lord of all Strongbow's lands in England, Wales and Ireland, an inheritance which put him among the very greatest of the English barons. He had difficulty in obtaining seisin of the Irish lands from John, who is said to have given them up only when Richard I intervened,[22] but he does not seem to have visited them in person till the beginning of 1207, when he obtained a reluctant consent from John to go to Ireland. Three years earlier his nephew, John Marshal, had been sent to Ireland as his seneschal, and there must of course have been a regular succession of seneschals responsible for the administration of his lands ever since he got seisin of them, but it is probable that the rapid development in the organization of Leinster which clearly took place in the early years of the thirteenth century was largely due to the earl himself, for he remained in Ireland almost continuously from 1207 to 1213. But in 1207 it is clear that there may have been more immediate reasons for his anxiety to go to Ireland, for the activities of Meiler fitz Henry as justiciar were clearly causing unrest. He was already on bad terms with Walter de Lacy after the seizure of Limerick, and what concerned the Marshal more immediately, he had taken Offaly, which was of course part of the lordship of Leinster, into the king's hand. This must have been in the exercise of the king's right of prerogative wardship, by which he claimed the custody of all the lands of a

[21] Gilbert, *Facsimiles*, part II, pl. lxvii, lxviii; *Cal. Ormond Deeds*, I, nos. 25–7.
[22] *Histoire de Guillaume le Maréchal*, ll. 9581–618.

tenant-in-chief, no matter of whom they were held. The tenant of Offaly had been Gerald fitz Maurice, who had married one of the daughters and heiresses of Robert de Bermingham, the first feoffee,[23] and had died in 1203. It was evidently considered at the time that Leinster was in the same position as Durham and certain other English and Welsh lands, where the king did not claim this right,[24] for in January 1204 the justiciar was ordered to deliver the lands and castles, with the heir, to the Marshal. But there were evidently second thoughts, for before May 1207 Offaly had been taken into the king's hand, and the barons of both Leinster and Meath were moved to protest to the king, and were well snubbed for their pains, John saying that it had been done by his order.[25] It is clear, though we know nothing of the details, that conflict between the Marshal and the justiciar continued to develop throughout the summer and autumn: finally, probably in October, the king summoned both to his presence, and also, apparently, a number of other Anglo-Irish magnates, for we find royal charters witnessed in November by the bishops of Waterford and Meath, John Marshal, and others.[26] Walter de Lacy too was in England, but he had certainly been there for some months, having been summoned in April.[27] It looks as if the occasion were being taken to have a general review of the position in Ireland. Meanwhile, in Ireland the Marshal had left his wife and lands in the keeping of his most trusted followers, and no sooner had he left the country than the justiciar's followers began a series of raids. Meiler himself seems to have been allowed to return to Ireland before the end of the year, and got royal letters ordering the Marshal's principal followers to return to England. They, however, refused to do so, and obtained the assistance of Hugh de Lacy, the earl of Ulster, who brought a considerable force against Meiler's lands in Meath, successfully besieging his castle of Ardnurcher. Meiler was later taken prisoner and obliged to give the countess Isabel hostages. In March 1208 John restored both the Marshal and Walter de Lacy to favour, giving them new charters for their lands, in which he expressly renounced the right of prerogative wardship, though he reserved to the crown the four pleas of arson, rape, treasure trove and forstal, with pleas of appeal of felonious breach of the peace, and provided for appeals to

[23] There were certainly at least two daughters. See J. Otway-Ruthven, 'Knights' Fees in Kildare, Leix and Offaly', *Journ. R.S.A.I.*, XCI, p. 178.
[24] See below, p. 186, n. 184.
[25] *C.D.I.*, I, nos. 195, 329. Orpen, *Normans*, II, pp. 36–7, 210, completely misunderstood the background to this.
[26] *Rotuli Chartarum, passim.*
[27] *C.D.I.*, I, nos. 324–5.

the royal courts in case of default of justice or injuries done by the lord himself, and reserved the crosses.[28]

The Marshal and de Lacy now returned to Ireland, and fitz Henry was soon superseded: he does not appear as justiciar after June 1208, and Walter de Lacy may have acted for a time. But John's favourite, John de Grey, bishop of Norwich, almost the only man whom he consistently trusted, was justiciar by the end of the year,[29] and was to remain so till 1213: an experienced royal administrator and a man of remarkable ability, under whom considerable advances were made. But John's quarrel with William de Braose was to convulse Ireland before anything else could happen. The origins of the quarrel belong to the history of England and need not be discussed here, but de Braose was not only the lord of Limerick, but was also the father-in-law of Walter de Lacy, while the Marshal was apparently his feudal tenant, and all three men were closely connected by their position in the marches of Wales. It was natural that when William fled in the autumn of 1208 he should go to Ireland, where he took refuge with the Marshal. The justiciar, John de Grey, ordered the Marshal to hand him over: the Marshal said that he was only doing his feudal duty in sheltering his lord, and, rather disingenuously, that he knew nothing of any quarrel between de Braose and the king. After they had been with him for three weeks, he escorted de Braose and his family into Meath, where they were welcomed by de Lacy. For the time being there was nothing that the justiciar could do against the combination of the lords of Leinster, Meath and Ulster, and the king had enough to preoccupy him in England, where there was trouble on the borders of Wales, and the possibility that the discontented northern barons might ally themselves with Scotland: it was not till the summer of 1209 that this possibility was removed by the treaty which he forced on William of Scotland, and he was free to act in Ireland.

In May 1210 John prepared his expedition to Ireland: the feudal levy, with Flemish mercenaries in addition. The Marshal was with him, for however reluctant he might be to join an expedition clearly directed against the de Lacys he could not disobey the king's summons. On 20 June John landed at Crook, near Waterford, where he was joined by the justiciar, with Irish troops from Munster and Desmond,[30] and immediately set out for Dublin,

[28] For a discussion of this, see below. pp. 182–3.
[29] The *Annals of Dunstable* (*Annales Monastici*, ed. R. Luard, III, p. 30) say he was sent in Feb. 1208. See also *Curia Regis Rolls*, V, p. 200; *Rotuli Litterarum Patentium*, p. 79.
[30] *C.D.I.*, I, p. 61.

making a progress through the Marshal's lordship of Leinster. In Dublin, which he reached on 27 or 28 June, he was approached by five of the principal tenants of Meath, acting as messengers of Walter de Lacy: Walter, they said, placed all his castles and lands in the king's hand, to retain or restore as he pleased, and left his brother Hugh, through whom he had incurred great loss, to the king's pleasure.[31] John was not appeased: he proceeded to march through eastern Meath, taking possession of the castles, and then turned northwards into Louth on his way to attack Hugh de Lacy, reaching Louth itself on 7 July. About this time he was joined by four hundred soldiers who had been with Walter de Lacy: clearly the de Lacys could not count on their followers against the king, and several of Walter's principal tenants had been among those who witnessed John's grant of Ratoath to Philip of Worcester.[32]

John was now approaching the baronies of Upper and Lower Dundalk, where Hugh de Lacy held lands which cannot be very precisely identified, but which amounted to about half the total area, as the marriage portion of his wife, Lecelina de Verdon.[33] Here Hugh de Lacy was burning his own castles, 'and he himself fled to Carrickfergus, leaving the chiefs of his people burning and destroying the castles of the country'.[34] But no active opposition seems to have been offered to John, who proceeded along the coast to Carlingford, where he occupied the castle, and then northwards into Ulster, where the de Lacys were making a stand at Carrickfergus, the strongest castle of the lordship. It surrendered after a short siege, but the de Lacys escaped by sea, though a number of their followers were taken in the castle. As for de Braose, he himself had been in Wales since early in the summer, but though his wife and sons were among those who escaped from the castle, Matilda de Braose and her son William were taken by Duncan of Carrick, one of the Galloway Scots to whom John was shortly to grant so much of Ulster, and handed over to John to die miserably of starvation.

John remained at Carrickfergus for some days, and then turned southwards, reaching Drogheda on 8 August. From Drogheda he struck westwards through Meath, going as far as Granard and returning through Rathwire. Then on 18 August he was back in Dublin, and on 24 or 25 August left Ireland. He had been in the country for just over nine weeks, and in that short time had driven

---

[31] Ibid., no. 402.
[32] Ibid., p. 62; *Cal. Gormanston Reg.*, pp. 179–80.
[33] J. Otway-Ruthven, 'The Partition of the de Verdon Lands', loc. cit.
[34] *AI*, Dublin MS, 1211, cited by Orpen, *Normans*, II, p. 251.

the de Lacys out of both Meath and Ulster, taking both lordships
into his own hand, while the de Braose lordship in Limerick, which
the justiciar had probably occupied some time earlier, had naturally come to an end. The Marshal was the only magnate of the
first rank left in the country. And in addition to this triumph over
the Norman magnates, John had established relationships with a
number of the Irish kings. At his first arrival Donough Cairbrech
O'Brien had met him at Waterford and got a grant of the castle
and lordship of Carrickogunnell, co. Limerick, to hold at a yearly
rent of 60 marks.[35] His elder brother, Mortough Finn, accompanied John on his march into Ulster, appearing as 'Mariadac, king of
Limerick'. Aedh O'Neill of Tir Eoghain also seems to have joined
John in Ulster, and Cathal Crovderg O'Connor was with him with
a large force, but their relations ended in a quarrel. It seems that
Cathal, in the natural anxiety to secure the succession of his son
after him, had induced John to promise him a charter of the third
part of Connacht which should include Aedh, who was to be given
as a hostage. When after Carrickfergus he went home to fetch the
boy his wife refused to let him go, and when he met John at Rathwire without him, John in a fury seized four leading members of
O'Connor's court as hostages in his place. It was left to the justiciar
to make a settlement with O'Connor after John had gone. But according to an English chronicler twenty Irish kings did homage to
John in Dublin, and though we do not know who they were, it is
clear that there was a general readiness among the Irish to accept
him.[36]

All this adds up to a considerable achievement, but it was to be
suggested in the next reign that John had done a good deal more.
According to Henry III

he caused to be made and to be sworn to by the magnates of Ireland [a charter]
concerning the observance of the laws and customs of England in Ireland . . .
the laws and customs of the realm of England which the lord king John our father
of happy memory with the common consent of all men of Ireland ordained to
be kept in that land.[37]

No such charter as this writ refers to has survived,[38] but the statement is so precise that it is impossible to doubt that one existed.
On the other hand, there is ample proof that English law, and

35 *Misc. Annals*, p. 87. This must have been a grant for as long as it was in the
king's hand, for it had belonged to William de Burgo, whose lands and heir were
still in the king's wardship.
36 *C.D.I.*, I, p. 62; *ALC*; Roger of Wendover, *Flores Historiarum*, ed. H. O.
Coxe (English Historical Society, 1841–4), III, p. 233.
37 *Early Statutes*, pp. 23, 24.
38 The English chancery rolls are missing at this date.

much of the normal machinery of English administration, had been in existence in the colony at a considerably earlier date.[39] What probably lies behind this is that John held a council during the week which he spent in Dublin before returning to England, made such a formal declaration as to the force of English law in Ireland as is suggested by a charter, and made formal arrangements for the royal administration of Meath, Ulster and Munster. The ultimate restoration of Meath and Ulster to the de Lacys would seem to have been contemplated, for in 1212–13 both were administered by seneschals, but Munster—i.e. Limerick and Tipperary, the lordship of de Braose—was a county governed by a royal sheriff, and it is likely that this arrangement dates from John's visit.[40]

On John's departure John de Grey was left behind as justiciar, and his first action seems to have been to settle the dispute with O'Connor. He secured the approach to Connacht by building a bridge and castle at Athlone, and at the same time an expedition was led into Connacht by Geoffrey de Marisco, the nephew of John Comyn, archbishop of Dublin, and Thomas fitz Maurice, the ancestor of the earls of Desmond, with the English of Munster and Donough Cairbrech O'Brien. O'Connor showed himself ready to come to terms: he met the justiciar at Athlone, gave hostages including one of his sons, and acknowledged his obligation to pay tribute. Till his death he remained undisturbed in Connacht, and in 1215 had a charter of the province to hold in fee, in return for a large payment.

The next step was a concerted action against the northern chieftains in 1212. From the south-west they were attacked, presumably with the approval of Cathal Crovderg, by a force of Connachtmen, led by Gilbert MacCostello, who built a castle at Cael Uisce, somewhere near Assaroe. To the north an attack was made by the Galloway Scots, who had been granted a great part of the earldom of Ulster—apparently the whole coast from the Foyle to the Glens of Antrim—in the spring of this year.[41] The grant had been made to Alan fitz Roland, lord of Galloway, but it was his brother, Thomas, earl of Athol, who came by sea to Derry, and, supported by O'Donnell, raided Inishowen. Meanwhile the justiciar himself led a force to Clones, co. Monaghan, which had been included in Peter Pipard's grant of c. 1190, and built a castle there. The de Lacys already had a castle at Kilmore, co. Cavan, and there also

---

[39] See below, chapter V, passim.

[40] Pipe Roll, 14 John. Wendover asserts that John established 'the laws and customs of England, appointing sheriffs and other officers to administer justice' (loc. cit., pp. 233–4), and this must be what he meant.

[41] C.D.I., I, no. 427.

seems to have been one in existence at Belturbet, co. Cavan[42]: these formed a natural base for an advance into the Clones area. But though the expedition, which seems to have been based on the feudal service, was clearly on a considerable scale,[43] the advance into Tir Eoghan was checked by MacMahon and Aedh O'Neill, and the garrison left at Clones was unable to hold the castle, which was burned by O'Neill in the next year, while about the same time his father-in-law, O'Hegney of Fermanagh, burned the castle of Caoluisce and killed its garrison.

Meanwhile, the justiciar's attention had been claimed by disturbances on the borders of Meath and Munster. The whole area concerned was of course in the king's hand, since Meath had not been restored to Walter de Lacy, and Theobald Walter's son was still a minor. The disturbances seem to have arisen largely from the ambitions of members of the Irish kingly families, and to have been directed as much against the ruling chiefs as against the Norman settlers, and we find Murtough O'Brien opposed to his first cousin, Donough Cairbrech, the reigning king of Thomond, and Cormac O'Melaghlin opposing Melaghlin Beg. In 1208 Murtough had destroyed the castles of Kinnity, Birr and Lorrha, as well as the castle of Athronny in Leix, while O'Melaghlin had been raiding the barony of Clonlonan, opposed by Melaghlin Beg as well as the English. Then in 1212 he took Delvin MacCoghlan[44] (the barony of Garrycastle, co. Offaly), and the justiciar led an expedition against him, probably after the expedition to Clones, in alliance with Donough Cairbrech O'Brien, but was defeated at a battle in Fircal. Though in the next year Cormac was defeated by a purely Irish combination, an expedition of the English of Meath against him was defeated with considerable losses.

By this time John de Grey had returned to England bringing with him a considerable force to support the king, whose quarrel with his barons was increasingly acute, and seems to have been temporarily replaced as justiciar by Geoffrey de Marisco, archbishop Comyn's nephew, who had had important grants of land in Limerick. Then in July 1213 Henry of London, the new archbishop of Dublin, another experienced royal administrator, who had already been employed in Ireland on a number of special missions, was sent to take the place of the bishop of Norwich. His first task seems to have been to deal with the disturbances in south-west Meath and northern Munster: he first built a castle at Roscrea,

---

[42] *Pipe Roll, 14 John*, pp. 22–4, 32, 36–8.
[43] Ibid., *passim*.
[44] This was 'Macart's war', *Pipe Roll, 14 John, passim*.

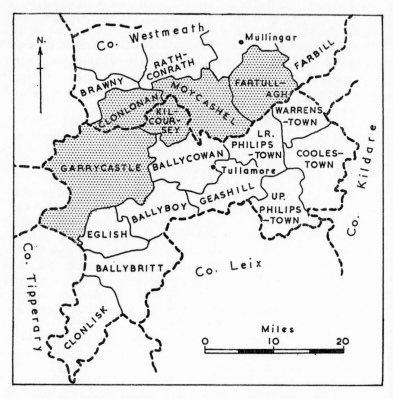

The south-western baronies of the lordship of Meath

where the king's force and council assembled,[45] and from this base defeated Murtough O'Brien. In the next year (1214) the attack was on Cormac Mac Art O'Melaghlin, whose raids had continued. He was defeated by

all the forces of the English of Ulster, Mounster, Lynster, and Meath, together with all the Irish forces that owed service to the king of England throughout all the provinces and parts of Ireland:[46]

clearly a full muster of the feudal host, together with Irish auxiliaries. A castle was built at Clonmacnoise, and the castles of Durrow, Birr and Kinnitty were rebuilt, forming a continuous chain of strong-points in this whole area, and we hear no more of Cormac Mac Art.

By this time the troubles between John and his barons in England were reaching their climax. It is remarkable that there seems to have been no corresponding movement in Ireland, but presumably the expulsion of the de Lacys had removed the only possible leaders of opposition, for the Marshal was consistently loyal to John, and was one of the small group of magnates who acted as mediators. Probably about October 1212 he had at John's instigation been the chief of a group of Irish barons, many of whom were his own tenants, though some held in Meath, while others, like Nicholas de Verdon, were tenants-in-chief, which made a declaration of support for John in the quarrel with the pope over the church of Canterbury—'with the king they are prepared to live or die; and to the last they will faithfully and inseparably adhere to the king'— though a little earlier the Marshal had urged the king to make peace with the church.[47] When, early in 1213, John summoned his army to resist the threatened invasion of the king of France, the Marshal and the bishop of Norwich, neither of whom ever returned to Ireland, brought a force from Ireland alleged by a chronicler to consist of five hundred knights and many other horsemen.[48] In the summer John was reconciled with the church, and not only the bishop of Norwich, and the new archbishop of Dublin, who was about to succeed him as justiciar, but also the Marshal were among the witnesses to the instrument by which John surrendered both England and Ireland to the pope, receiving them back to hold of the Roman church. The rapid development of the baronial movement which resulted in the wringing of the Great Charter from a reluctant king in June 1215 followed, but the Irish baronage had

[45] *C.D.I.*, I, no. 2760.
[46] *A. Clon*, pp. 226–7, *s.a.* 1213, but the other annals place these events in 1214.
[47] *C.D.I.*, I, nos. 444, 448.
[48] Wendover, loc. cit., III, pp. 245–6. The numbers are probably exaggerated.

no part in this, and it is clear that John was making every effort to secure their continued support. Thus in February the justiciar was ordered to buy scarlet cloth for robes to be given to 'the kings of Ireland and other faithful subjects of the king', and negotiations began for the restoration of Meath to Walter de Lacy, while after the sealing of the Great Charter there was a series of grants to Irish towns and to individuals. Among others, the service due from Meiler fitz Henry for his land in Leinster, which the king had kept in his hand in 1208, was restored to the Marshal, though not till just after John's death, and Meath was restored to Walter de Lacy, though no settlement was made with his brother Hugh.[49] In the civil war which followed the granting of the charter Ireland was in no way involved, and only one Irish tenant-in-chief, Nicholas de Verdon.[50]

Meanwhile, in July 1215, John had replaced the archbishop as justiciar by Geoffrey de Marisco. Geoffrey, a member of an important Somersetshire family, who was later to be involved in ruinous scandals, was now at the height of his power, for with both the Marshal and Walter de Lacy still in England, he was probably the most powerful magnate actually in Ireland. He was a tenant-in-chief in Limerick and in Kerry, where expansion was going on just at this moment; he held part of Offaly in right of his wife, Eva de Bermingham, whom he had married after the death of her first husband, Gerald fitz Maurice, in 1203. His relative, Joan de Marisco, was married to Theobald Walter II, who was still a minor, and he had thus a special interest in the great Butler property in Munster, which was still in wardship, and therefore under the justiciar's control.

A westward expansion in Desmond seems to have been going on for some years before this, facilitated by quarrels between the sons of Donnell MacCarthy, who died in 1206. The actual course of the movement is by no means clear, but by about 1214 it seems that a string of castles had been erected along the line of the river Maine, and at Killorglin near the mouth of the Laune, protecting a settlement in the lands in north Kerry which had been granted to Meiler fitz Henry in 1200, while two more were erected in the neighbourhood of Killarney, and a further group along the coast from Kenmare to Galley Head. An Irish annalist, listing the castles, says that it was during the wars of the rival MacCarthys in 1214 that 'the Galls overran the whole of Munster in every direction,

<hr />

[49] *C.D.I.*, I, nos. 531, 542, 544, 550, 563, 573, 576, 577–8, 587–99, 601, 607, 612–3, 621, 628, 631–2, 725. For Meiler's lands in Leinster, see *Pipe Roll, 14 John,* p. 16.
[50] *C.D.I.*, I, no. 727.

from the Shannon to the sea'.[51] About 1216 Meiler fitz Henry entered a religious order, leaving no son to succeed him, and his lands
escheated to the crown[52]: those in Kerry seem to have been granted
mainly to John fitz Thomas fitz Gerald, the son of Thomas fitz
Gerald of Shanid, ancestor of the earls of Desmond; but some
grants, such as that to John de Clahull of Offerba (the eastern part
of the barony of Corcaguiny), which had been made by Meiler
were now confirmed by the crown, while the justiciar gave Ossurys
(western Corcaguiny) to his son, Robert, and retained the castle of
Killorglin for himself.[53] Meanwhile, on 3 July 1215, John had
granted to Thomas fitz Anthony, a tenant of the earl Marshal in
Kilkenny, and his seneschal in Leinster, the hereditary shrievalty
of the counties of Waterford and Desmond, with the king's escheats
in Desmond, the issues of which were to provide for the safe keeping
of bailiwicks and castles.[54] The forward movement of the years
which followed must have been under the immediate direction of
fitz Anthony, and seems to have been made with the agreement of
MacCarthy: at any rate, in 1221 Dermot MacCarthy was one of
the Irish rulers to whom the replacement of Geoffrey de Marisco
by Henry of London was announced, and there is no trace of any
fighting beyond the statement of the annals that in 1220 or 1221
there was 'a hosting by Geoffrey Marisco into Desmumu', which
seems to have been confined to west Cork.[55]

At the same time there was a forward movement along the north
coast of the Shannon estuary, in south co. Clare, where the justiciar's own interests seem chiefly to have lain. At the time when
Limerick had been occupied, in 1197, this area, the modern baronies of Bunratty, Clonderlaw, Moyarta, Ibrickane and Islands, seems
to have been included in the agreement made with O'Brien. At
least one grant had been made in the area before John's accession
in 1199, and others followed,[56] though there is nothing to show that
there was any effective occupation till much later in the century.
But in north Munster de Marisco was certainly active during his
justiciarship: the Butler lordship in Ormond was still in the king's
hand, and it seems that it was during this period that the castle at
Nenagh was constructed. Moreover in 1217 de Marisco built a
castle at Killaloe, where, according to the annals, 'the English of

[51] *Misc. Annals*, p. 91.
[52] That is, those held in chief: his lands in Leinster and Meath reverted to the
Marshal and de Lacy.
[53] Orpen, *Normans, III*, pp. 133–4.
[54] *C.D.I.*, I, no. 576. For the descent of this grant, which was to be important
in the foundation of the power of the earls of Desmond, see *I.H.S.*, V, pp. 2–3.
[55] *Misc. Annals*, p. 93; *s.a.* 1220; *AI*, *s.a.* 1221.
[56] Orpen, *Normans*, IV, pp. 53–5.

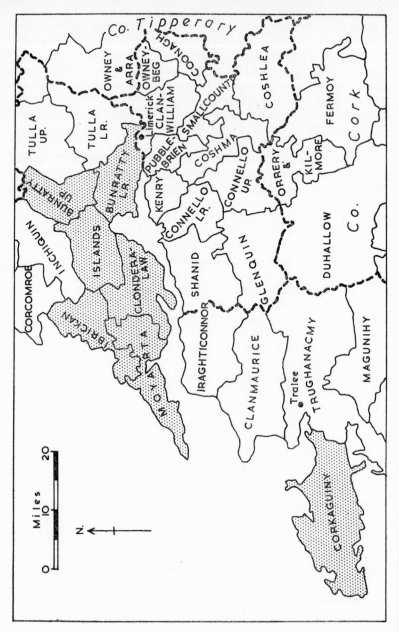

Counties Clare and Kerry

Meath and Leinster' had made an unsuccessful attempt to build one in 1207.[57] This was a natural move in the expansion of the settlement, but that it was done in 1217 is certainly connected with the attempt to secure the diocese of Killaloe for Robert Travers, the justiciar's nephew, who seems to have been a member of a family which held Ballinaclogh, just south of Nenagh, from the Butlers. Travers was accepted by the king as having been canonically elected in January 1217, and was consecrated by the bishops of Waterford, Limerick and Emly; the chapter of Killaloe protested to the pope that they had canonically and unanimously elected the archdeacon of Killaloe. A long dispute followed, and when James the penitentiary arrived in Ireland as papal legate in 1221 he formally deposed Travers and the archdeacon was duly consecrated. The dispute was not yet ended, but we need not pursue it: the attempt to extend Norman influence had failed for the time being, and no further attempts to expand beyond the Shannon seem to have been made till the middle of the century.[58]

Meanwhile, it is clear that there had been disturbances in the de Lacy lands, but we know nothing of them in detail. Walter de Lacy was still in England, and does not seem to have come to take possession of Meath till 1220, but the annals say that in 1215 William de Lacy, his half-brother, who had been released on the surety of Walter and others on 10 February 1215,[59]

came from England and tooke upon him the kingdome of Meath and government thereof. Whereupon there arose great contention and warrs between the English of the south of Ireland in generall and him, whereby many damages and losses of preys and spoyles were sustained by either party.[60]

There is no other evidence of this, but there is nothing improbable in William's having been sent over to govern Meath for his brother. We next hear of him at the beginning of 1217, when he was ordered to deliver to the justiciar the castles of Rath and Carlingford which he had taken, and to satisfy him for the damage done to the king and country by the taking of these castles, while by July Walter de Lacy had given security that he would make amends for William's excesses towards the king.[61] It would seem that William had been trying to assert the de Lacy rights in Ulster. After this we hear nothing more of him for a time, but Walter returned to Meath in 1220, and embarked on what was clearly a planned expansion in Breifne—Cavan and Leitrim—where early in the century he had

[57] *A. Clon.*, p. 222.
[58] For Travers, see D. Gleeson, *A History of the Diocese of Killaloe*, pp. 223–35.
[59] *C.D.I.*, I, no. 536.
[60] *A. Clon.*, p. 228.
[61] *C.D.I.*, I, nos. 755, 791.

already had castles at Kilmore and Belturbet, while the de Angulos, his tenants in Navan, seem to have had enfeoffments which they had actually settled in south Leitrim. Now, in 1220, Walter 'performed a great hosting to the crannog of O'Reilly. He went upon it and obtained hostages and great power'.[62] In the next year he made what must have been a confirmatory grant to de Angulo of south Leitrim and south-west Cavan. By 1224 Cathal Crovderg O'Connor was complaining to the king that William de Lacy, 'Cathal's enemy and kinsman of the king's enemy', detained 'Ubrim, Conmacin, and Caled'—that is, Breifne and Conmaicne, now counties Cavan, Leitrim and Longford, claimed as part of Connacht. Clearly William de Lacy was in charge in this area, and in 1223 the annals say that he and the English of Meath with their forces founded a castle at Loghloygeachan, soon broken down by the Connachtmen, as had happened to the castle which Walter de Lacy began at Athleague (Lanesborough) in co. Longford in 1221.[63]

For some time before this Geoffrey de Marisco had clearly been proving unsatisfactory as justiciar. In April 1217 it had been ordered that the rents and fines of Ireland should be received only at the Dublin exchequer before the barons, and the archbishop of Dublin had been sent back to Ireland, the justiciar being ordered to spend the money coming into the exchequer by his advice, and to do nothing without his assent. In February 1218 we hear that though ordered to come to England to do homage and report on the state of Ireland Geoffrey had not done so. It was not till August 1220 that he appeared before the council at Oxford and entered into an elaborate agreement, designed primarily to control him in matters of finance. But even the giving of his sons as hostages and his lands as security did not restrain him, and on 17 July 1221 he was replaced by archbishop Henry of London in terms which suggest that he had systematically turned the king's revenues and rights in Ireland to his own profit. On 1 November the royal castles in Ireland were formally surrendered to the king in Geoffrey's name, and he was released from 'all account, question and quest' concerning the office of justiciar.[64]

By this time the problem of Hugh de Lacy and Ulster was becoming acute. Negotiations seem to have gone on throughout 1222, but came to nothing, and by June 1223 Hugh was plotting to invade Ireland, and the justiciar was ordered to garrison the Irish castles, while in October the custody of Ulster and its castles

---

[62] *ALC.* O'Reilly's crannog was in Lough Oughter, co. Cavan.
[63] See J. Otway-Ruthven, 'The Partition of the de Verdon Lands', loc. cit.
[64] *C.D.I.*, I, nos. 777, 780, 815, 949, 1001, 1015.

was given to John Marshal.[65] But it would seem that before this
became effective de Lacy had reached Ireland, for the archbishop, reporting to the king in the next summer, after he had
ceased to be justiciar, wrote that he had placed 'a good and sufficient *familia*' in the castles of Ulster with knights and foot soldiers
to keep the extern lands and the coasts when he heard of Hugh's
coming, and had had to spend in the stipends of horsemen and
foot serjeants and in gifts to the barons £500 of what had come
into the exchequer in Easter term, as soon as Hugh arrived. After
that he was forced to spend, in order to pay 'the *familia* of your
army'—that is, presumably, the household knights who appear in
accounts later in the century—[66] all he could have of the king's or
his own, and to borrow a great sum from Dublin and other cities
and towns to maintain the expenses of the army before he could
persuade the barons to serve.[67]

Hugh de Lacy had on his arrival gone not to Ulster, but to
Meath, where his half-brother William welcomed him, and proceeded to make war, 'pillaging and burning the king's land, killing
and holding his men to ransom'.[68] In March 1224 it was agreed
that Walter de Lacy, who had been in England for some time,
should go to Ireland to reduce his men of Meath to order, and in
May William Marshal the younger (his father had died in 1219)
was appointed justiciar and landed at Waterford on 19 June. On
28 June the archbishop handed over to him the office of justiciar,
the royal castles, and the whole land of Meath except the castle of
Trim, which Walter de Lacy was to use as his headquarters.[69]
Meath was by this time disturbed not only by the adherents of
Hugh de Lacy, but also by Aedh, the son of Cathal Crovderg
O'Connor, one of whose first actions after his father's death on 28
May had been to raid Annaly, taking and burning de Lacy's
castle of Lissardowlan and killing 'every one whom he found in it,
both Foreigners and Gael'.[70] The Marshal, as soon as he had taken
office, went straight to Trim, where he and Walter de Lacy be-
sieged the castle, and were joined by a body of barons, including
Geoffrey de Marisco who had been holding a parley with Aedh
O'Connor. A party was detached to relieve Carrickfergus, which
was being besieged by Hugh de Lacy, and another was sent against

[65] *C.D.I.*, I, nos. 1110, 1114, 1140.
[66] See e.g. ibid., II, pp. 148, 150, 178–80, 237–9.
[67] P.R.O. London, S.C. 1/60/120. Cf. *C.D.I.*, I, nos. 1265, 1463.
[68] *C.D.I.*, I, no. 1180.
[69] Ibid., nos. 1180, 1185, 1203; P.R.O., London, S.C. 1/60/120. The liberty
of Meath had been taken into the king's hand in 1223; see below, p. 159, 185.
[70] *ALC; AC.*

William de Lacy, who was defeated and fled to the Irish, while
O'Reilly, who had just come to the king's peace, besieged the
castle of 'Cronoc Orauly' in Lough Oughter, where William had
left the women of his family, and took it with the assistance of a
force sent by the Marshal, which also took the castle of Kilmore,
held by one of William's half-brothers, Sir Henry Blund. Trim was
obliged to surrender on 11 August, after a siege of seven weeks.[71]
Meath had been reduced to order, but Hugh de Lacy was still at
large in Ulster, and so presumably was William, of whom we hear
little more: he seems to have been reconciled to the king, for in
1227 he had a grant of £20 a year to maintain him on the king's
service, and in 1230 he was on the king's service beyond the sea.
Then in 1233

William Delacy, chiefest champion in these parts of Europe, and the hardiest
and strongest hand of any Englishman from the Nicene seas to this place, or
Irishman, was hurt in a skirmish in the Brenie, came to his house, and there
died of the wounde.[72]

With him died that expansion in Cavan which he seems to have
led, for we hear nothing more of the Normans in this area.

Meanwhile, in the summer of 1224 Hugh de Lacy, with Aedh
O'Neill, had attacked the lands which the Galloway Scots had
been granted by John in Ulster, demolishing the castle of Coleraine,
and seems then to have moved south-eastwards to Dundalk, where
he laid waste the lands of his brother-in-law, Nicholas de Verdon.
Here the Marshal came up to meet him with an army reinforced
by O'Connor, who had come to the peace, MacCarthy and O'Brien,
and, apparently without any fighting, Hugh surrendered to the
Marshal and was sent to the king. In May 1225 Walter de Lacy
made a fine with the king to recover the lands of those of his tenants
who had supported Hugh, and the castles of Trim and Kilmore[73]
were returned to him, though Drogheda, with Hugh's castles of
Nobber and Ratoath, was retained by the crown. Ulster was not
restored to Hugh till 1227, and then with elaborate precautions
of sureties and hostages, and, it seems, for his life only.[74]

By this time the affairs of Connacht had become the predominant interest in Irish affairs. Cathal Crovderg had died in May
1224, and his son Aedh succeeded him. But the same ruinous dispute about the succession that had occurred in all the Irish kingdoms arose here too: the sons of Rory O'Connor, the last ard-ri, in

[71] C.D.I., I, nos. 1203, 1204.
[72] Ibid., nos. 1520, 1833; A. Clon., p. 234.
[73] Kilmore was burnt by Cathal O'Reilly in 1226 (AC), and we hear no more
of it.
[74] C.D.I., I, nos. 1210, 1218-19, 1289, 1371-4, 1498.

alliance with Aedh O'Neill, rose against him in 1225, supported, and according to the annals invited, by the whole of Connacht except MacDermot. The rebellion was completely successful: O'Neill made Turlough O'Connor king, and Aedh went to Athlone, where he seems to have found Geoffrey de Marisco, who was acting as deputy justiciar since the Marshal was in England. He returned with Norman reinforcements, led by de Marisco, as well as O'Brien and O'Melaghlin, while another Norman force, apparently acting quite independently, came up from the south under the sheriff of Cork—no doubt Thomas fitz Anthony—with Murrough O'Brien. Confused operations followed, and eventually, after the land had been extensively plundered, the sons of Rory O'Connor were driven out. But by now Richard de Burgo had returned to Ireland; in May 1225 he had been appointed seneschal of Munster (Tipperary and Limerick), where his lands lay, and constable of the castle of Limerick, with 250 marks a year for his support on the king's service. Then in June 1226 the Marshal, who was still in England, was superseded as justiciar by Geoffrey de Marisco, and, completely reversing the policy of supporting Aedh O'Connor which had hitherto been followed, the new justiciar was ordered to summon Aedh before the king's court in Dublin 'to surrender the land of Connacht, which he ought no longer to hold on account of his father's and his own forfeiture'. Richard de Burgo, who had had in 1215 a charter, never put into effect, of 'all the land of Connacht which William his father held of the king', was to be given seisin of Connacht to hold at a rent, five of the best cantreds nearest the castle of Athlone being reserved for the king's use.[75]

The reasons for this change of policy are not clear. Presumably the favour shown to Richard de Burgo must be attributed to the fact that his uncle, Hubert de Burgh, was justiciar of England, and, since the king was still a minor, had practically supreme control of the government, but it is clear that Aedh O'Connor had no support from his own people, and it may well have seemed in every way the proper course to abandon the attempt to impose him on Connacht: in the next few years we find the sons of Rory O'Connor acting in concert with de Burgo and the Normans. But it is quite clear that the new policy was bitterly opposed by the Marshal, and that he was supported in this by his leading tenants. According to de Marisco, writing to the king some time after his landing at Waterford in August,

all the Irish are so banded together and so wheedled by William Crassus [the Marshal's seneschal in Leinster] that they cannot be recalled from their conspir-

[75] *C.D.I.*, I, nos. 653, 1395, 1402–03.

acy . . . the justiciar cannot obtain from the earl's bailiffs the delivery of the king's castles . . . all the castles of Ireland are fortified against the king, except the castle of Limerick in the custody of Richard de Burgo, who always assists the justiciar in the king's affairs . . . he advises the king to take into his hand the castle of Roscrea, committed during pleasure to Theobald Walter, who had so misconducted himself in regard to the king that though he has married the justiciar's daughter, and has by her a son, the justiciar would, if it is the king's will, deprive him of all the land which he holds of the king in Ireland . . . he has fortified the castle of Dublin . . . against the king.

But the Marshal was not prepared to push his opposition to the point of active resistance to the king: he submitted in August and returned to Ireland on the king's service, no doubt to see that the royal castles held by his bailiffs were delivered to the new justiciar.[76]

As for Aedh O'Connor, he refused to come to the meeting at Dublin to which he had been summoned by de Marisco, and a meeting near Athlone was arranged instead. The justiciar was represented by his son, William de Marisco, and Aedh came in person. But unfortunately Aedh, 'remembering the treachery and deceit practised on him in Dublin', attacked the Normans, who seem to have been taken completely by surprise, and were either killed or taken prisoner, a success which Aedh followed up by plundering and burning Athlone. The inevitable reaction followed: on 21 May 1227 Richard de Burgo was granted in fee the whole land of Connacht, to hold at an annual rent of 500 marks (300 for the first five years) and the service of ten knights, the king reserving to himself the five cantreds as before, and the crosses. This was followed by a hosting led by the justiciar in which he took the hostages of the Sil Murray and built castles at Randown and Athleague,[77] so that there was now a chain of castles from Lanesborough to the mouth of the Shannon. Further south de Burgo led a force which plundered the country round Inishmaine in Lough Mask, while a third expedition, from Meath, attacked west Connacht. All these expeditions were accompanied by one or other of the sons of Rory O'Connor, and Aedh son of Cathal O'Connor seems to have been unable to offer any effective resistance, but fled to O'Donnell. He returned later in the year and seems to have been engaged in negotiations with Geoffrey de Marisco when he was killed almost accidentally in the latter's house.[78]

Meanwhile, on 13 February 1228, de Burgo's power had been consolidated by his appointment as justiciar to replace de Marisco,

---

[76] *C.D.I.*, I, nos. 1440, 1443.
[77] See above, p. 90.
[78] *AC; ALC; AU; A. Clon.; C.D.I.*, I, nos. 1518, 1581.

who is said to have asked to be released from office. And now one of the sons of Rory O'Connor was inaugurated as king. According to the annals

a great assembly was convened by the Galls of Ireland and the Gaels, including the kings and chieftains of Ireland, in Connacht about the two sons of Ruaidri, Toirrdelbach and Aed . . . All the Connachtmen elected Aed son of Ruaidri in the presence of Galls and Gaels; and when they had reached the assembly he and the men of Connacht made for Carnfree, where he was installed as was customary.[79]

This did not prevent wars between the O'Connors continuing, and in 1230 'Aed son of Ruaidri and the men of Connacht turned against Mac William Burke and the Galls of Ireland', persuaded, we are told, by Mageraghty and MacDermot, who swore that they 'would never own a lord who should bring them into the house of the Galls'[80]—a new and ominous sign for the future of the colony, for hitherto kings supported by the Normans had shown themselves perfectly ready to co-operate with them. De Burgo now chose Felim, a younger son of Cathal Crovderg, to supplant Aedh, and marched into Connacht with the English forces and also O'Brien and MacCarthy. Felim was established as king, and Aedh was obliged to flee to O'Neill. In the next year, however, Felim was deposed by de Burgo and Aedh was restored. And in the same year the incastellation of Connacht was actively commenced, de Burgo building a castle at Galway, while Adam de Stanton, a tenant of the Marshal in Leinster,[81] who had been granted five knights' fees round Dunamon in the modern co. Roscommon, began a castle there.[82]

Since 1225 the affairs of Connacht had dominated Irish politics, but now a quarrel which had begun in England was about to take pride of place. Henry III, who was only nine when his father died, had declared himself to be of full age in January 1227, when he was nineteen, but Hubert de Burgh, who had been justiciar since shortly before John's death, continued to hold office, and in effect directed the government. But by the end of 1231 he was no longer trusted by the king, who seems to have found him overbearing and was resentful of recent failures in Wales, while the magnates had always disliked and distrusted him as an upstart. It was easy for

[79] *AC.*
[80] *AC; ALC.*
[81] Orpen makes him tenant of Moone, co. Kildare (*Normans*, III, pp. 176, 215), but in fact he held Dunlost and part of the barony of Clane (J. Otway-Ruthven, 'Knights' Fees in Kildare, Leix and Offaly', *Journ. R.S.A.I.*, XCI, pp. 168–70).
[82] *C.D.I.*, I, no. 1715; *AC; ALC.*

Peter des Roches, bishop of Winchester, one of Henry's Poitevin favourites who had formerly been his tutor, to secure Hubert's downfall. He was dismissed from office in July 1232, and after a trial before his peers in November was imprisoned and stripped of all his offices. The bishop of Winchester and Peter des Rivaux, his son or nephew, were to be in complete control of English affairs till 1234.

The immediate consequence of all this in Ireland was the fall of Richard de Burgo, Hubert's nephew. On 16 June 1232 Hubert had, indeed, been appointed as justiciar of Ireland with Richard as his deputy, but in fact nothing came of this. On 28 July Peter des Rivaux was granted for life an assemblage of offices which gave him complete control of the royal finances in Ireland, as well as the custody of the castles of Drogheda, Athlone, Randown and Limerick, of Decies and Desmond, the cities of Limerick and Cork, and of Dungarvan. On 2 September Maurice fitz Gerald was appointed justiciar during pleasure, and on 4 February 1233 a commission was appointed to audit de Burgo's accounts as justiciar, and to require him to make amends for 'all the trespasses he has committed against the king'.[83]

Meanwhile, all the progress the Normans had made in Connacht had been undone. In August 1232 the king, saying that he had been informed that de Burgo had seized 'Frethelin', son of a former king of Connacht, imprisoned him, and treated him grievously and shamefully, had ordered Felim's release, and in 1233 Felim set about asserting his own supremacy. In alliance with MacDermot, king of Moylurg, he defeated Aedh O'Connor in a battle in which Aedh himself and many of his kindred were killed and the sovereignty of that branch of the O'Connors was finally ended. Then Felim proceeded to destroy all the castles which had been built in the last few years and 'assumed the kingship and sovereignty'. In April or May 1233 he seems to have been negotiating directly with the king, proposing to visit him in England, and Henry seems to have imagined that a *modus vivendi* could be established, instructing him that before he came he should take the castle of Meelick, still held by de Burgo, quiet Connacht, and deliver both to the justiciar, who at the same time was being urged to subject the whole of Connacht to the king. By the middle of July Henry was preparing an expedition to Ireland, to take place in the early autumn, but before that time a violent quarrel with the earl Marshal caused its abandonment.[84]

William Marshal the younger had died childless in April 1231

[83] *C.D.I.*, I, nos. 1969, 1977, 2012.
[84] *C.D.I.*, I, nos. 1975, 2032, 2039, 2046, 2049–50, 2052–4, 2058–9; *AC*; *ALC*.

and was succeeded by his brother Richard, after some difficulties caused by the fact that Richard held his father's lands in Normandy, and was thus a vassal of the king of France. He rapidly became the leader of the opposition which was growing against Peter des Rivaux by the spring of 1233, and by the end of August Henry had determined to attack him. By October war was raging in south Wales and the march, and by February 1234 it was clear that the Marshal and his allies were winning. At the end of December a naval patrol had been established in the Irish sea,[85] no doubt to intercept him if he crossed to Ireland, but early in February he landed, and after some initial successes met his enemies at the Curragh on 1 April for discussions preliminary to a truce, but was attacked, receiving wounds of which he died a fortnight later. The English chroniclers say that he was betrayed by his own vassals, but there is no other evidence for this, or for the charges of treachery in this affair which they make against Geoffrey de Marisco, who was himself, with two sons and three nephews, taken prisoner by the justiciar, and released only for a heavy fine.[86] In the next year Geoffrey was suspected of complicity in the murder of Henry Clement, a messenger from the justiciar, who had boasted that he had brought about the Marshal's death, and was murdered in his London lodgings. The murder was said to have been committed by Geoffrey's son, William, who escaped to Lundy island, where he had a colourful career as a pirate before he was taken and executed in 1242. Geoffrey himself was eventually cleared, but was again discredited after 1238, when he seems to have been suspected of complicity in the attempted murder of the king himself, and died miserably in exile in 1245.[87]

Meanwhile, in Ireland troubles had by no means ceased with the death of the Marshal, whose brother, Gilbert, was allowed to succeed him. In the south-west the MacCarthys attacked the Norman settlement in north Kerry, but were defeated with heavy losses at Tralee; Felim O'Connor raided Meath, burning Ballyloughloe, Ardnurcher and other places; and Donough Cairbrech O'Brien, who had up to this point steadily co-operated with the Normans, attacked the city of Limerick. More generalized disturbances are suggested by the order of November that 'bands of malefactors who rode through Ireland to perpetrate fire, robberies, and other injuries' should be arrested and brought to trial.[88] It is

---

[85] *C.D.I.*, I, no. 2080.
[86] The story is fully discussed by Orpen, *Normans*, III, pp. 61–72.
[87] See Powicke, *King Henry III and the Lord Edward*, II, pp. 740–59.
[88] *Misc. Annals*, p. 99; *AI*; *A. Clon.*, p. 234; *35th Rep. D.K.*, p. 35; *C.D.I.*, I, no. 2229.

not surprising that the policy of the last year was reversed. Richard de Burgo had co-operated in the attack on the Marshal, and his uncle's enemies in England had fallen, the movement which Richard Marshal had led having in the end been completely successful. Peter des Rivaux was dismissed from all his offices in April 1234, and already there had been comings and goings of messengers between England and Ireland, while by May the justiciar and Richard de Burgo and other magnates had sent petitions to the king which Henry said he was unwilling to answer till he had conferred with the justiciar, the bishops of Ferns and Meath, and Hugh de Lacy, earl of Ulster, who were summoned to him.[89] When they went we do not know: the justiciar was still being summoned to come in July; most probably he was with the king by the last week in August, when the affairs of Ireland were clearly being considered, and in particular a new treasurer and a new chamberlain of the exchequer were appointed. Then in the last week of September 'Duncan de Carbrac'—Donough Cairbrech O'Brien—made his peace with Henry, making a fine of 400 marks for remission of the king's ire because he had opposed him in the war with Richard Marshal. On 7 October, no doubt after protracted negotiations, Richard de Burgo, in return for the enormous fine of 3,000 marks, was restored to

such seisin of the land of Connacht as he had when the king disseised him owing to his account at the time when he was justiciar of Ireland, and the strife with Hubert de Burgh, earl of Kent, his uncle,

to hold in fee by the service of twenty knights and an annual rent of 500 marks, retaining to the king the five cantreds, the crosses, royal dignities, and the office of justice. The justiciar must have remained with the king till the end of the year, for in February 1235 Henry wrote to him that he rejoiced to learn that he had safely arrived in Ireland.[90]

The grant of Connacht was all very well, but the work of conquest had of course to be begun again. In the early summer of 1235 what seems to have been a full muster of the Norman forces of Ireland, led by the justiciar, with de Burgo, Hugh de Lacy, Walter de Ridelisford, who commanded the Leinstermen, and John Cogan, who led a Munster contingent, and 'the bands of all Ireland along with them', entered Connacht. The campaign which followed is described in unusual detail by the annals: they marched north from Athlone to Boyle, co. Roscommon, reaching it on the vigil of

[89] C.D.I., I, nos. 2102, 2104–05, 2112–14.
[90] C.D.I., I, nos. 2156, 2158, 2202, 2217–19, 2250.

Trinity (2 June), and then turned south against O'Brien of Thomond, who had presumably failed to observe the settlement made with the king in the previous year. O'Connor, who had so far evaded them, now joined O'Brien, and both were defeated: O'Brien made peace, and Felim O'Connor escaped to O'Donnell. The Normans now returned northwards to Connacht, which they occupied without much opposition, the most dramatic incidents being a successful attack by sea on the islands in Clew Bay, and the reduction of MacDermot's island fortress in Lough Ce with the aid of siege-engines. The conquest was no doubt complete by August, when the king, 'for his grievances and expenses this year in the war of Connacht', granted de Burgo easier terms for the payment of his fine for Connacht.[91]

According to the annals the Normans

bore away no pledge or hostage at that time, nor did they leave peace or settlement in the country, for the Gaels were killing and robbing each other to obtain what little the Galls had left behind them.[92]

In fact, however, the campaign resulted in a division of Connacht between Irish and Normans. Felim O'Connor finally agreed to hold the 'king's cantreds' in the modern co. Roscommon at a rent, and seems to have paid £300 a year with some regularity till his death in 1265.[93] The rest of Connacht comprised the fee of Richard de Burgo, and he built a castle at Loughrea, which was to be his principal demesne manor in Connacht, in 1236. This area seems to have been strongly settled with relatively small tenants, but a large part of Galway and the whole of Sligo and Mayo were granted in large fiefs to men who were already important tenants elsewhere in Ireland, and though we hear of a good many burgage settlements, it seems that in general Norman settlement was slight, and in most areas the Irish chiefs must have been comparatively undisturbed, for the majority of the grantees were fully occupied in the development of their other lands.[94]

The major preoccupation of 1235 was certainly the conquest of Connacht, and that of the next few years the making it effective, but there were other anxieties. In August 1235 it seems to have been feared that Gilbert Marshal was about to renew his brother's war: writing to the justiciar in terms which suggest that a state of near panic existed in Ireland, the king assured him that if anyone

[91] *AC*; *ALC*; *C.D.I.*, I, no. 2283.
[92] *AC*; *ALC*.
[93] *AC*; *ALC*; *35th Rep. D.K.*, p. 44. Cf. Orpen, *Normans*, III, pp. 185, n. 2, 240, n. 2.
[94] The subinfeudation of Connacht is fully described by Orpen, *Normans*, III, pp. 190–224.

sought to disturb Ireland or to wage war neither he nor the king's subjects should be anxious; the king will never be wanting to them; they should cast aside all fear; the magnates were to be assembled and exhorted to remain firm in their wonted fidelity. Similar letters were sent to all the principal magnates, but nothing more appears as to the whole affair.[95] Otherwise, apart from an unexplained quarrel between the justiciar and Felim O'Connor in 1236, which had no permanent results, the chief interest of the next few years was in Ulster. Here, after the death of Aedh O'Neill in 1230, the O'Loughlins and O'Neills disputed the kingship, and in 1238 an expedition led by the justiciar and Hugh de Lacy expelled O'Loughlin and set up O'Neill, obtaining the hostages of the Cenel Conaill and Cenel Eoghain. It was no doubt, as Orpen suggested, at this time that de Lacy made Maurice fitz Gerald, the justiciar, a grant of Tir Conaill 'by the right metes and bounds between Keneleon and Tyrconyll', to hold by the service of four knights, a speculative grant which he seems to have attempted to make good. In 1242 he led an expedition to Cenel Conaill and obtained hostages, and that these submissions were not merely nominal is suggested by the letters in which Henry III in 1244 asked not only the southern kings and the chieftains east of the Bann, but also the kings of Tir Conaill and Tir Eoghain, to join in an expedition against the Scots.[96]

The Ulster chiefs had been directly subordinate to de Lacy, but he died before February 1243, and his earldom reverted to the crown, presumably because of the unrecorded terms on which it had been restored to him, for he left at least one daughter, the wife of David fitz William, baron of Naas. In Meath Walter de Lacy had died early in 1241, and since both Gilbert, his eldest son, and Gilbert's son Walter, whom he had recognized as his heir in May 1238, were already dead, his whole inheritance fell to be divided between his grand-daughters, producing fundamental changes in the great lordship of Meath.[97] Richard de Burgo accompanied the king on his expedition to Poitou in the winter of 1242–3, and died on it as the result of hardships endured at sea: his sons were minors, and all his lands in Munster and Connacht were thus in the king's wardship. Finally, in December 1245, Anselm, the fifth and last son of the first William Marshal, died childless like his brothers, and the whole of the Marshal inheritance fell to be divided among his five sisters or their representatives. The division of the lordship

[95] C.D.I., I, nos. 2284–5.
[96] Red Book of Kildare, no. 21; C.D.I., I, no. 2716. For the position of O'Donnell, see below, p. 216.
[97] See below, p. 187.

of Leinster into five parts again produced fundamental changes,[98] but though in the fourteenth century the marked tendency of the first settlers to die out in a series of daughters was to produce a sub-division of lordships which was certainly a cause of weakness, this process had not yet reached a point which was really damaging. Nevertheless, in the few years after 1240 a quite remarkable trans-formation of the Anglo-Irish scene had taken place, and at the same time, with the conquest of Connacht, the territorial expansion of the Normans in Ireland had practically reached its peak. It is time for us to review the character of the society which had been established.

[98] See below, pp. 186–7.

CHAPTER III

The Structure of Norman-Irish Society

THE CONQUEST which has just been described presented immense problems of organization. In England a hundred years before the time of Strongbow and Henry II the Normans had been confronted by not dissimilar difficulties, and had dealt with them by a largely military occupation retaining much of Anglo-Saxon law, custom and institutions, and superimposing their own developed system of feudalism. But the Norman conquest of England had been much more rapid and more complete than that of Ireland, and in other respects the position in Ireland was very different from that which had existed in England in 1066, for the structure of Celtic society differed far more widely from the general continental pattern than had that of Anglo-Saxon England, while by the later twelfth century the new Anglo-Norman society was already setting on lines which precluded that ready adoption of alien custom which had been so marked a feature of Norman conquest in both Wales and Italy. The institutions which developed in Norman Ireland were therefore of purely Anglo-Norman type, and there was, at least theoretically, no divergence between the law of England and that of the Norman colony in Ireland.

The development of the elements of the central governmental system began when Henry II appointed Hugh de Lacy as justiciar in 1172; that of the local organization of counties had already begun before John became king in 1199. The whole structure of central and local government will be considered later,[1] but its basis was the occupation of the land, and this was provided for on the standard lines of Norman feudalism.[2] Henry granted Meath to Hugh de Lacy to hold by the service of fifty knights; the grant of Leinster to Strongbow required the service of a hundred. Later grants, all made before John's death in 1216, brought the total up

[1] See below, chapter V.
[2] For the organization of feudalism in Ireland, see J. Otway-Ruthven, 'Knight Service in Ireland', *Journ. R.S.A.I.*, LXXXIX, pp. 1–15.

to a maximum of 427 knights, in units ranging from the large contingents of Leinster or Meath to the service of a single foot serjeant from an eighth of a knight's fee, as in some holdings in co. Dublin. It is clear that the original intention was that these contingents should actually serve in the field, but the feudal host was already an archaic form of military organization, and scutage, the money equivalent for personal service, which is invariably called royal service in Ireland, had appeared in England as early as 1100. It was entirely in the king's discretion whether money or actual personal service should be required on any given occasion, and in 1222 a general direction was issued that tenants-in-chief in Munster (Tipperary and Limerick), Des (Waterford), Desmond (Cork), and the vale of Dublin should pay scutage when the justiciar went with an armed force to Ulster and Keneleon or other remote parts.[3] The position of Desmond at this date is not clear, but the others were all areas with a comparatively large number of small tenants-in-chief, and it seems to have been contemplated that large contingents, such as that of Leinster, would come in person. Even after this we find individual tenants serving in person on occasion: Hugh Tyrel of Castleknock, co. Dublin, served in person in 1253, 1254, and 1262, though he paid scutage for an expedition to Keneleon in 1258; in 1261 William de Valence, lord of Wexford, accounting for a scutage, was excused the service of three knights which had been performed by his tenants 'as testified by letters from Richard son of John, then marshal of the army'. As late as 1332 Geoffrey le Bret, tenant of Rathfarnham, co. Dublin, was exempted from a scutage

in respect of a service and a half and the fifth part of a service . . . because . . . he was in his proper person in the company of said justiciar at Limerick when the service was proclaimed . . . in the king's service at his own expense prepared as was becoming with a man at arms and a hobeler.

Sometimes too a seneschal would bring the forces of a liberty to perform the service due from it: in 1332 the service of a third part of one hundred services due from the liberty of Kilkenny was performed by the seneschal, who

at the time said service was proclaimed . . . was at Limerick prompt and ready to perform said service . . . with 25 men at arms and 80 hobelers.[4]

Such instances are, however, exceptional. Whatever the original intention had been, scutage rather than personal service seems to have been the general rule in Ireland from early in the thirteenth

---

[3] *C.D.I.*, I, no. 1048.
[4] P.R.O., London, C47/10/15, no. 5; *35th Rep. D.K.*, p. 38; *43rd Rep. D.K.*, pp. 45–46; *44th Rep. D.K.*, p. 21.

century, partly because of the general tendencies of the age, and partly, no doubt, because of the particular situation, which will have made it undesirable to deplete the country as a whole of its fighting men. The occasion for its levy arose more frequently in Ireland than in England. Not only have we a definite statement in 1281 that the king's service is often proclaimed in Ireland, but we have records of some twenty scutages during the thirty-five years of the reign of Edward I.[5] Moreover, from time to time, particularly under Henry III, the royal service either of the whole country or of a particular area might be granted to a subject to aid him in constructing a castle or for some other military purpose. By the end of the thirteenth century the assent of the magnates to a grant to a subject was considered necessary, but this does not seem to have been so earlier.[6] Since the military tenant in Ireland was in many parts of the country exposed to constant attacks on his lands it is not surprising that various devices to lighten the burden in one way or other were resorted to, but we will return to these later. In certain areas, as in co. Dublin and in the de Verdon lands in co. Louth, the original organization seems to have been directed towards reinforcing the garrisons of castles in time of war rather than serving in the field, but before the end of the thirteenth century this had been turned into an obligation to pay scutage.[7] When we get detailed records the rate of scutage had been fixed at 40 shillings for a knight's fee, in Ireland as in England, but under Henry III a service was sometimes taken at half this rate.[8] The lands of the church were not included in the system: whereas the ecclesiastical tenants-in-chief in England all owed quotas of knights, in Ireland not only was no attempt made to impose them, but in 1218 there was a definite order that ecclesiastics should not render service to the king or anyone else for their possessions.[9]

Particularly in the larger tenancies in chief there was, of course, extensive sub-infeudation, and all the great tenants-in-chief, in Ireland as in England, enfeoffed considerably more than the number of knights needed to fulfil their bare quotas. Thus Leinster, the sub-infeudation of which we know in detail, had about 180 knight's fees, though it owed only the service of a hundred; Meath, which

---

[5] For scutage as a tax, see below, pp. 163–4.

[6] C.D.I., II, no. 1801; Cal. Justic. Rolls, I, p. 362; C.C.R., 1318–24, pp. 55, 90.

[7] J. Otway-Ruthven, 'Knight Service in Ireland', loc. cit., pp. 7–9; 'The Partition of the de Verdon Lands', Proc. R.I.A., LXVI C. For castle guard in England, see C. Warren Hollister, The Military Organization of Norman England, pp. 140–61.

[8] Cal. Gormanston Reg., p. 13.

[9] C.D.I., I, no. 849.

owed fifty, had some 120.[10] And many of these sub-tenants had military sub-tenants of their own, though only the greater ones were in a position to provide by sub-infeudation for more service than they themselves owed their immediate lords.[11] Moreover, though the immediate tenants of a great lord, holding a complete knight's fee or some manageable fraction of it,[12] might be incorporated in a feudal army, their own sub-tenants, holding perhaps sixty acres, for which they might owe the service of anything from a twentieth to a sixtieth of a knight's fee,[13] must have been on a basis of scutage from the first, for though it was certainly possible for such small tenants to be grouped so that one of their number served while the rest contributed to his expenses, as was done in England though we have no evidence for it in Ireland, the tenant of a single knight's fee would not normally have a sufficient number of tenants of his own for this to be done. The motive behind the creation of these very small military tenancies cannot therefore have been a military, nor even a financial one, for a greater income could have been obtained by leasing the land than was provided by scutages and the other feudal incidents: it seems most likely that the aim was to attract the smaller tenant by giving him a superior status.

All these military tenancies were held by exactly the same rules of law as applied in England.[14] In Norman Wales there were beside English fees Welsh ones, held by the rules of Welsh customary law; in Norman Italy fees held by Lombard law. But nothing of this developed in Ireland: even where a military tenant was of native Irish descent, as a few were, the ordinary legal rules of Norman feudalism as developed in England applied. The tenant, though he had that absolute right of inheritance which had by this time been established, paid a relief on his succession, the recognition of the lord's original right to regrant the fee as he pleased on the death of a tenant; at his death, his minor heir and lands were in the wardship of the lord, who, subject only to the obligation of maintaining the heir and other children, and to the rules as to waste laid down in the Great Charter and subsequent legislation, might enjoy the profits, including the marriage of the heir, himself, or grant them

[10] See E. St J. Brooks, *Knights' Fees in Counties Wexford, Carlow and Kilkenny*; J. Otway-Ruthven, 'Knights' Fees in Kildare, Leix and Offaly', *Journ. R.S.A.I.*, XCI, pp. 163–81; 'The Partition of the de Verdon Lands', *Proc. R.I.A.*, LXVI C; *Cal. Gormanston Reg.*, pp. 10–13.
[11] 'Knight Service in Ireland', loc. cit., p. 6.
[12] An eighth of a fee sent a foot serjeant (ibid., p. 3).
[13] See below, p. 107.
[14] For Norman feudalism in England, see Sir Frank Stenton, *The First Century of English Feudalism*.

away as he pleased. As in England the king enjoyed the right of prerogative wardship: that is, he had the wardship of all the lands of a tenant-in-chief, even though some of them were held immediately of other lords. This rule was not really of very great importance in Ireland, since the right was waived for lands in the great lordships of Leinster and Meath, a distinction they shared with the English palatinates, the marcher lordships of Wales, and the lands of the archbishop of Canterbury.[15] If the tenant died without heirs, or if he committed a felony, his land would escheat to the lord: in the case of a felony the king had the right of year, day and waste, might, that is, enter on the land and extract every possible profit from it, regardless of any rules as to waste, for a year and a day, after which it was handed over to the immediate lord. The tenant's widow, who had a right to be dowered with a third of her husband's lands for life, must obtain the lord's leave for her marriage, since her new husband would be the tenant of her dower lands. A widower, on the other hand, provided that a living child had been born to them (the formal proof required was that it should have been heard to cry within the four walls), continued, by the custom known as the courtesy of England, to hold all his late wife's lands for life, to the exclusion of her heirs. Finally, and most important of all in the special circumstances of Ireland, though the tenant's eldest son was the sole heir to his lands to the exclusion of all others, should he leave no son but several daughters his lands must be divided equally between the daughters.[16] Since many of the first conquerors and their descendants showed a marked tendency to produce female heirs in successive generations the repeated partitions which resulted reduced lordships to unmanageable fractions, gravely weakening the position of the colony in some important districts, and producing a sometimes dangerous unrest among the junior branches of the family concerned. It was not till the fourteenth century that this really became a serious problem, but already in 1287 Thomas fitz Leones, finding himself dying childless, had endeavoured to disinherit his sister by granting away his manor of Coulmolyn, co. Meath, to his uncle, so that the banner of his kindred might be maintained, and in 1299 a very remarkable settlement of the barony of Ikeathy, co. Kildare, provided that it should pass, in the absence of male heirs, to

the most noble, worthy, strong, and praiseworthy of the pure blood and name of Rochefordeyns, issued from the blood of Sir Walter de Rupeforti and Lady

[15] See below, p. 186, n. 184.
[16] The English law as to certain aspects of this was expressly stated for the benefit of Ireland in 1236 (*Early Statutes*, p. 30).

Eva de Herford his wife . . . chosen by the four nearest of our blood and name
. . . to whom the whole barony of Okethy with all appurtenances indivisible shall
remain: so that the inheritance shall never pass to daughters.

This attempt to defeat the ordinary law of inheritance was, however, soon abandoned, for early in the fourteenth century Henry
de Rocheford sold the barony to Edward I.[17]

The knight's fee in Ireland seems to have been a considerably
more precise unit than it was in England. It is clear that at the
time of the Norman conquest of England Norman feudalism had
not yet evolved any conception of a standard knight's fee, but by
the middle of the twelfth century standards of size or value, which
might differ widely as between one honour and another, were already developing.[18] It was these standards which the Normans
brought with them to Ireland, for the language of royal charters
under Henry II and John clearly implies that the area of a knight's
fee was fixed and known, though not necessarily everywhere the
same, while we can trace the same conception in much sub-infeudation. In co. Dublin a knight's fee of about ten ploughlands seems
to have been usual; in the sub-infeudation of the lordship of Meath
twenty ploughlands was the area considered appropriate in what
corresponded to the modern co. Meath, but further west it was
thirty, reflecting, no doubt, the more disturbed conditions of this
area. But whatever pattern of fee a particular lord adopted seems
to have been applied with great consistency, and the fact that two
distinct patterns are apparent in the sub-infeudation of the de
Verdon lands in Louth can only be explained by the fact that much
of this property was held for a time by Hugh de Lacy, earl of Ulster,
as his wife's *maritagium*, and he must have conducted its sub-
infeudation on a pattern distinct from that of de Verdon.[19]

A not uncommon device in royal charters was to lighten the
burden of service by granting several fees to be held by the service
of one: it was much used for areas in which war with the Irish was
likely to be constant. The same device must have been used for
sub-tenants, but what the records show is the sub-tenant in many
cases owing scutage at rates less than the standard 40 shillings
for a knight's fee. It was not, however, uncommon for the sub-
tenant in Ireland to owe an annual rent in addition to his military
obligations. Normally the knight's fee was coincident with the ecclesiastical parish, which still survives as the civil parish: the

[17] *C.D.I.*, III, no. 525; *Cal. Justic. Rolls*, I, p. 326.
[18] See Stenton, *First Century of English Feudalism*, pp. 163–8.
[19] J. Otway-Ruthven, 'Knight Service in Ireland', loc. cit., pp. 9–11; 'The
Partition of the de Verdon Lands', *Proc. R.I.A.*, LXVI C.

reasons for this will be considered later.[20] It should of course be remembered that by no means everyone who held a knight's fee, much less those who held only fractional fees, was necessarily a knight, and though this did not matter for military purposes, for certain legal purposes the verdicts of juries of knights were essential. In the fourteenth century, therefore, we find in Ireland, as in England, distraint of knighthood: all those holding lands of a certain value were required under penalties to take upon themselves the order of knighthood. Finally we should note that the military tenant was normally required to do suit at his lord's court,[21] to give counsel when called upon, and to aid him with money grants when required, though except on certain specified occasions his consent must be obtained to this.[22]

The work of settlement had, of course, only begun with the creation of these military tenancies, which was probably not completed till the second generation of the conquest. There remained the task of making an effective occupation of the new manors. The first step must have been to provide for their defence by the erection of some sort of strong point, usually, though by no means always, a mote castle. These great earthen mounds, originally crowned by stockades, with the fortified baileys or courtyards at their base, were secure against any sudden attack in the absence of artillery, and are still familiar objects of the Irish countryside. Occasionally the Normans may have adapted a pre-existing earthwork; occasionally, as at Fore in Westmeath, they used a natural feature, but in general the motes seem to have been constructed from the ground up. They could be rapidly constructed, and could be later replaced, when time and means allowed, by a stone castle, as at Trim, co. Meath.[23] But this was possible only for the greatest lords in the thirteenth century, and even the erection of a mote seems to have required greater resources than were normally available to the lord of a single manor: many had to content themselves with a house and courtyard, presumably surrounded by a wooden stockade.[24] But many motes were erected, and their distribution is a good index to the extent of Norman settlement.[25]

[20] Below, pp. 119-20.
[21] For the small tenant-in-chief this was interpreted as suit at the county court (see e.g. *Cal. Pembroke Deeds*, no. 4; *C.D.I.*, IV, no. 605; *Cal. Justic. Rolls*, I, p. 246; N.L.I., Harris Collectanea, I, p. 288).
[22] See below, pp. 166, 169-70.
[23] See *The Archaeological Survey of Northern Ireland: County Down*, pp. 116-19, 122, 185-206; H. G. Leask, *Irish Castles*.
[24] J. Otway-Ruthven, 'The Character of Norman Settlement in Ireland', *Historical Studies*, V, p. 76.
[25] See the map in Orpen, *Normans*, II, though there are many more than it shows.

The next step must have been to provide for the peopling of the manor. Without tenants it was useless to its lord, and he seldom seems to have had more than two or three hundred acres in his demesne.[26] And it is here that we come to the crucial point, for the effectiveness of the Norman conquest of Ireland depended ultimately on the effective occupation of their lands by the military tenants of every degree. Who were their tenants, what was their standing, where did they come from, how were they recruited?

We have, unfortunately, very little evidence for the first period of the Norman colony, but with the reign of Edward I records become comparatively abundant, and they make it plain that, seen in its proper perspective, the Norman settlement of Ireland was no mere military occupation supported by the settlement of English and French burgesses in a few towns, but a part of that great movement of peasant colonization which dominates so much of the economic history of Europe from the eleventh to the fourteenth century, arising out of what can only have been a spontaneous growth of population, and slackening as that growth slackens with the troubles of the fourteenth century. The decline which was already apparent in the early fourteenth century, though it seems to have become acute only after the Black Death, and the failure to recover quickly from the Bruce invasion suggested by the statement to be found in so many extents of the 1320s and 1330s and later that in outlying districts lands 'lie waste and uncultivated for lack of tenants', may well be explained in terms of the general European experience.[27]

There were six classes of tenants to be found on Norman-Irish manors[28]: free tenants, farmers, gavillers, cottiers, betaghs, and burgesses. Not every manor had all of these, but all had most of them. The free tenants fall into two sub-groups: the strictly military tenants, who owed personal service in war, or scutage in lieu of it, and were liable to all the incidents of feudal tenure; and others who held in fee-farm, who held, that is, in perpetually heritable dependent tenure, like the military tenants, but owed instead of military service a money rent, fixed for ever by the charter of first

[26] The acre here and throughout, unless otherwise stated, is not the statute acre but that of the medieval extents, which was certainly much larger. Mills thought that round Dublin it was 2½ statute acres ('Notices of the Manor of St. Sepulchre', *Journ. R.S.A.I.*, series 4, IX, pp. 35–36), and this equation seems reasonably accurate in many parts of the country.

[27] See J. Otway-Ruthven, 'The Character of Norman Settlement', loc. cit.; below, pp. 252–3.

[28] For tenants and agriculture generally, see J. Otway-Ruthven, 'The Organization of Anglo-Irish Agriculture in the Middle Ages', *Journ. R.S.A.I.*, LXXXI, pp. 1–13.

enfeoffment of their ancestors. Strictly speaking, the rule of English law, which treated such tenures as socage, giving the lord no right of wardship or marriage, should have applied to fee-farm tenants, and it was ruled that it did in 1285 and 1331, but local custom seems here to have prevailed, and by the fifteenth century these tenancies had been assimilated to military tenancies in this respect.[29] Normally all free tenants owed suit to the court of the fee, usually once a fortnight, but sometimes only twice a year, while some were altogether exempt.

Below the free tenants came the farmers: men holding their land on lease for a term of years at a money rent, usually related precisely to the acreage which they held. They were clearly of exactly the same class as the smaller free tenants, who indeed not uncommonly augmented their inherited holdings by taking some additional land at farm. They seem normally to have owed suit of court, and they often owed labour services in addition to their money rent: on the Christ Church manors in co. Dublin in 1326 each farmer having a full plough ploughed two days in winter and two in spring, did two days hoeing, hay-making, two days reaping, two carting corn (he was given his food for this), and rendered a hen at Christmas.[30]

The gavillers were tenants-at-will, whose holdings seem in practice to have descended from father to son, and who by the sixteenth century were being equated with the English copy-holder. They seem, however, to have been personally free, whereas the medieval ancestors of the English copy-holder had been villeins. There can be no doubt that they too owed labour services and did suit at the lord's court, as well as paying a money rent, but no detailed account of their position seems to have survived. Cottiers held only their cottages and crofts, and paid a money rent and labour services—two days reaping, two days hoeing and two days haymaking on the Christ Church manors[31]—and a hen at Christmas. On the Christ Church manors, and presumably everywhere, the majority of them were the permanently employed farm servants, who were paid a small money wage, plus substantial allowances of grain. They too seem to have been personally free.

The betaghs were an important element in the population of many manors, though in some, for example Moycarkey, co. Tipperary,[32] they do not seem to have existed at all. They were in

29 J. Otway-Ruthven, 'Knight Service in Ireland', *Journ. R.S.A.I.*, LXXXIX, p. 2, n. 4.
30 *Account Roll of Holy Trinity*, pp. 189–91.
31 Ibid., pp. 191–2, 193–4, 195–6.
32 *Red Book of Ormond*, pp. 56–60

approximately the same position as the English villein, and the essential feature of this tenure is expressed in a papal letter of 1261 which describes them as 'laymen attached to the soil, commonly called Betagii'.[33] We normally find them living in what seem to have been family groups in distinct townlands. Like the English villein they owed labour services rather than rent: at Lisronagh, co. Tipperary, in 1333 each betagh plough must plough an acre for wheat and an acre for oats, receiving from each *seisona* two shillings from the lord. Each betagh holding thirty acres must find three men in autumn for one day to reap wheat, and for two days for oats; all other betaghs must reap wheat for one day and oats for one day. Every betagh with a farm beast must cart the lord's wheat to the haggard with the lord's wagons or carts till all is in, and was given food and drink once a day. They must spread the lord's meadow and make hay and stack it and cart it to the haggard. Those who had horses must do carriage for the lord at their own expense, unless they must be away for a night, when it was at the lord's expense. They must carry the lord's letters or those of his ministers concerning the affairs of the manor at their own expense within the county. They must find fuel for the lord or his chief ministers when they were resident in the manor. The lord or his chief ministers might take prisage of their victuals for cash at a reasonable valuation. They must do service at the lord's will. From those who had three animals the lord had the best beast as a heriot at their death; from those who had fewer, twelve pence. They must come to the lord's court. Each acre of betagh land paid $\frac{1}{2}$d. a year for handmills: for exemption, that is, from the obligation to grind their grain at the lord's mill.[34]

All this is very similar to English villein tenures, though the labour services of the English villein were very much heavier, and very similar conditions obtained on the estates of the bishops of Cloyne: ploughing, weeding, reaping, and carting services; suit of court and mill; turf; renders of hens at Christmas; heriots. But at Cloyne there was a further class, clans of whom it could be said

The men of the nation of Omcgane are pure men of St. Colman and belong to the church . . . The lord can take all of them, and their sons and daughters, in all places, and seize their goods and sell them, and likewise he can make them stay on his land in whatever place he wishes, and they give the lord a heriot, and after their death all their goods are at the lord's will, and they ought not to make a will unless by his leave . . . John called Lowys is a pure Irishman and of the family of Okarny, and they say that all his goods, lands and tenements belong to

[33] *C.D.I.*, II, no. 717.
[34] E. Curtis, 'Rental of the Manor of Lisronagh, 1333, and Notes on 'Betagh' Tenure in Medieval Ireland', *Proc. R.I.A.*, XLIII C, pp. 41–76.

the lord bishop of Cloyne, because all of the family of Okarny are Irish of the church of St. Colman, and *nativi*.[35]

This was equivalent to the villeinage in gross of English law, but must represent a pre-conquest position, for till 1284 the bishops of Cloyne had all been Irishmen, and it is most improbable that they would have imposed on their tenants a state of servitude borrowed from England, or that it would have been introduced in the late thirteenth century. Clearly the betaghs everywhere originated in the servile clans of Celtic Ireland, and it had been a Celtic king who *c.* 1166 granted to his new priory of All Hallows Baldoyle, co. Dublin, with its men, to wit Melisus Macfeilecan with his sons and nephews.[36] The average betagh holding seems to have been from seven to ten acres (*i.e.* some seventeen to twenty-five statute acres), and by the end of the thirteenth century their labour services had often been commuted for a money rent.[37]

Finally we come to the burgesses, who, though they did not, of course, exist on every manor, are found in a great many, and sometimes formed practically the entire recorded population, as at Moyaliff and Ardmail, co. Tipperary.[38] They held their burgages at a low fixed rent, and they owed suit not to the court of the manor, but to their own court, the hundred, whose judgement was the judgement of their fellow burgesses. But though they had the elements of an urban constitution, and many of them were no doubt artisans and petty merchants, they not uncommonly owed labour services, ranging from carting iron and salt from Cashel for payment when directed to do so by the bailiff at Moyaliff, to drawing hay, reaping and drawing corn, and repairing the mill-pond at Swords, co. Dublin, and four days ploughing, hoeing and reaping, two days carting grain, and carting iron, wine and salt at Kilmaclennan, co. Cork.[39] Clearly these were primarily agricultural communities, and indeed the burgesses of Kilmaclennan are said to be betaghs, for they cannot go outside the town except to pasture on the bishop's demesne lands.[40] The average burgage holding consisted of only some three acres in the fields, besides the burgage plot itself, but it is very probable that in many cases the burgesses also rented some of the demesne lands, for in extents these are

[35] *Pipe Roll of Cloyne*, pp. 8, 38. John called Lowys was nevertheless a man of some substance (ibid., pp. 38–39).
[36] *Reg. All Hallows*, pp. 50–51. But see G. MacNiocaill, 'The Origins of the *Betagh*', *The Irish Jurist*, new series, I, pp. 292–98.
[37] J. Otway-Ruthven, 'The Organization of Anglo-Irish Agriculture in the Middle Ages', *Journ. R.S.A.I.*, LXXXI, p. 12.
[38] *Red Book of Ormond*, pp. 62–67.
[39] Ibid., p. 66; *Reg. Alen*, p. 177; *Pipe Roll of Cloyne*, pp. 15–16.
[40] Ibid., p. 18.

usually valued at so much an acre in a way which suggests that what lies behind the valuation is not the crops which the lord could obtain, but the rent which he might expect, and the commutation of betagh services by the later thirteenth century suggests that many lords were not cultivating their demesnes themselves.

Who were the tenants in these different classes, and where did they come from? To answer these questions we are driven back almost entirely on the evidence of surnames. True hereditary surnames were still of course in an early stage of development in twelfth-century England, and were by no means fixed even in the thirteenth century. Irish surnames probably became fixed rather earlier than English ones, though Welsh surnames did not really become fixed till modern times. But apart from surnames, there is also the evidence of Christian names, and though as time went on the Irish began to use names of the Norman type, such as Thomas or William, in the thirteenth century, particularly in its first half, they still used Celtic names. It is, however, clear that Anglicized Celts sometimes adopted English surnames as well as English Christian names, so that though we can accept an Irish patronymic as certain evidence of Irish descent, we cannot be sure that an English name invariably proves English descent. But in an overwhelming majority of cases it is safe enough to accept the name as evidence, and though intermarriages certainly occurred, they will have been least frequent in the areas of heaviest English settlement. And though the great majority of the substantial military tenants can be traced to their origins in England or Wales, for the lesser men we have no evidence but their surnames.[41]

Given these premises, an analysis of the evidence of the surviving manorial extents and inquisitions post mortem, which, though hardly any are earlier than the reign of Edward I, certainly reflect the position reached quite early in the thirteenth century, yields some very interesting results. We cannot, of course, arrive at anything like a complete picture, for none of the extents gives full details of more than single manors, and even there there will have been at least cottier holdings under the larger sub-tenants which are not enumerated in the extents. Nevertheless, it is possible to form a picture of the population structure of a number of manors which, though certainly distorted, may be assumed to be within measureable distance of historical truth, while the manors in question are sufficiently scattered to form a reasonable sample. And the surprising fact is the high proportion of tenants of English origin

[41] J. Otway-Ruthven, 'The Character of Norman Settlement', loc. cit., pp 77-78.

in a number of manors who held either freely, or on leases for a term of years, or as burgesses, sometimes as gavillers, or even as cottagers, holdings small enough to make it a reasonable certainty that they were cultivating them themselves. At Cloncurry, co. Kildare, in 1304 there was a total recorded population of 191 English and 111 Irish, all presumably heads of households. Of the English, 112 were burgesses, and fifteen free tenants with 20 acres or less, while there were in addition thirty-six English farmers and nine gavillers. At Moycarkey, co. Tipperary, in the same year there were thirty-nine English tenants and only nine Irish (this was a manor where there were no betaghs); twenty-nine of the English tenants held 20 acres or less. At Moyaliff, co. Tipperary, which was almost entirely a burgess settlement, there were c. 1305 fifty-nine English and three Irish burgesses. In north Tipperary, on the other hand, though here and there there had been a little English settlement, the Irish were predominant. In parts of co. Limerick the picture is again one of a substantial settlement of small English tenants, still persisting as late as 1341.[42] At Dowth, co. Meath, there were in 1253 nine fee farm tenants, six English and three Irish, of whom the English had holdings ranging from 21 acres to two ploughlands. There was one English and one Irish free tenant, each of whom owed work for his holding. The only other tenants on this small manor (it was estimated at five ploughlands, and the acreage of the modern civil parish is 1,463 statute acres) were an unspecified number of cottiers, whose labour services had been commuted. In the same year at Lynn, co. Westmeath, there were six English fee farm tenants, one of whom held only 13 acres, one English tenant-at-will, holding only 20 acres, ten unnamed cottiers, and an unspecified number of betaghs.[43] It is reasonably certain that at Lynn the population was predominantly Irish, but at Dowth it may well have been half English, and in such manors as Moycarkey it was clearly overwhelmingly English. Examples might be multiplied, and it is clear that over wide areas along the east and south coasts, and far inland, there had been, probably in the first two generations after the conquest, a substantial immigration of a genuinely peasant population of English, or sometimes Welsh, origin. Everywhere the majority, though not all, of the free tenants are English; so are the farmers; almost all the burgesses, where they are named, are English; sometimes a fair proportion of the gavillers and cottiers; surprisingly, there are sometimes a few English or Welsh names among the betaghs. It is not necessary to suppose that this

[42] Ibid., pp. 79–83.
[43] C.D.I., II, no. 179. Dowth (Duuethe) is incorrectly printed as Dunethe.

immigration inevitably produced any considerable displacement of population; the population of England at the time of Domesday Book (1086) has been estimated at some 1,375,000, and the population of Ireland two or three generations later may reasonably be supposed to have been of much the same order. Certainly charters of the early thirteenth century suggest that there was a lack of men, both English and Irish, rather than a lack of land, and it seems that the small tenant had no difficulty in finding land.[44] But by the end of the thirteenth century, as the evidence already cited shows, in many areas settlers of English descent formed at least half the population, and sometimes considerably more, and all along the east coast, in the inland counties of Leinster, in south Tipperary, Waterford, and parts of Cork and Limerick there had been a relatively heavy immigration. This settlement was in general limited to the lowland areas: above the 600-foot contour we find few signs of Norman occupation, and, for instance, in Imaal, co. Wicklow, then part of Kildare, we find c. 1300 that a burgage settlement has failed, and that a number of Irishmen hold the higher levels as substantial free tenants.[45] Elsewhere, as in much of the area north of Nenagh, in parts of inland Ulster, and in most, though not all, of south Longford, no real attempt at settlement seems to have been made: Irish chieftains continued undisturbed, owing, and sometimes even paying, to the newcomers the tributes they had formerly paid to Irish overlords.

Where did the settlers come from? Many of the greatest men, Strongbow himself, the de Lacys, and others, came from the marcher lordships of south Wales. It has always been assumed that Strongbow's followers came largely from Pembrokeshire, and much has been said of his Flemings. But though Fleming is a well-known name in Norman Ireland, an examination of other names, such as Lawless (still common in parts of Leinster), shows clearly that many of his followers came from Monmouthshire, where he was lord of Strigoil (Chepstow), from Glamorgan, and in general from the whole of south Wales. Most of these were Normans, but there were native Welsh among them.[46] Other settlers came from Devon and Cornwall (Deveneys and Cornwaleys are both names commonly found); from Lancashire, like the de Samlesburys of Moycarkey, who must have come with the Butlers from their Lancashire lands;

[44] J. Otway-Ruthven, 'The Character of Norman Settlement', loc. cit., p. 77. J. C. Russell suggests that the population of Ireland in the later thirteenth century may have been about 675,000 ('Late Thirteenth-Century Ireland as a Region', *Demography*, III, pp. 500–12).
[45] *Red Book of Ormond*, pp. 19–20.
[46] 'The Character of Norman Settlement', loc. cit., p. 78.

from Derbyshire, like the Dowdalls of co. Louth, whose name was
originally Douedale. But most of the lesser men have unrevealing
surnames, of the type which start as nick-names or trade names:
Belejaumbe, Proudfoot, Tanner, Lorimer. Clearly most, though
not all, came from western England or Wales, and presumably
many were recruited in the districts from which their lords came.

And here we come to the question of the inducements offered to
settlers. It has already been suggested that one was the status of a
military tenant: there can be no doubt that burgage tenure was
another and very powerful one. Quite apart from the true towns
which developed along the coast and at certain inland centres there
was a very large number of pseudo-boroughs widely scattered
through the country, places which can never have been more than
nucleated villages in any real sense, but which had been given the
elements of an urban constitution. We know of fourteen or fifteen
in medieval Kildare,[47] as many in Tipperary, eleven on the lands
of the archbishop of Dublin alone, and there were certainly many
more than we know of, for lords of every degree created them freely.
By the fifteenth century it was held that a royal grant was necessary
to authorize them, but earlier not only the lords of great liberties
with almost palatine rights freely gave them grants of the law of
Breteuil, but also their sub-tenants, and even the sub-tenants of
those sub-tenants. Clearly, whatever the original intention of the
grantors, the great majority of these places can never have been
more than specially privileged villages, and the conclusion is irre-
sistible that, as on the continent, the grant of the elements of an
urban constitution was a bait widely used to attract settlers.[48] The
general pattern used seems to have been the custom of Breteuil,
a Norman town extensively used as an exemplar in south-western
England and the Welsh marches, so that the transmission of its
custom to Norman Ireland was natural and easy. The original
custom has not survived, but a reconstruction shows that among
its principal features were a fixed annual rent of twelve pence for
each burgage, freedom of alienation of burgages, a low fixed
amercement[49] for all except the gravest offences, the limitation of
the period for which the lord might have credit, denial to the lord
of any rights of wardship or marriage, and restrictions on the imprisonment of burgesses.[50] The affairs of the borough were managed not in the manor court, but in its own hundred, of which the
burgesses were the only suitors. It was, indeed, the lord's court,

[47] See the map facing *I.H.S.*, XI, p. 196.
[48] 'The Character of Norman Settlement', loc. cit., p. 79.
[49] The equivalent of the modern fine.
[50] M. Bateson, 'The Laws of Breteuil', *E.H.R.*, XV, pp. 754-7.

but since its judgement was the judgement of the suitors their interests were reasonably safeguarded.

These were clearly very considerable inducements, drawing men to Ireland as they had drawn them to Welsh boroughs. But most of these settlements were unmistakably of a purely agricultural character, and only a very local trade can have been done in them. As we have seen, the burgesses not uncommonly owed labour services on the demesne, and though their burgage holdings were small, it is very likely that they supplemented them by renting part of the demesne. It is interesting that Irish lords too seem to have felt the need to attract settlers in this way: *c.* 1238 bishop David O'Kelly of Cloyne founded a borough at Kilmaclennan, co. Cork, and in 1251 his successor, bishop Daniel, gave it the laws of Breteuil. We cannot tell who bishop David's burgesses were, but in the middle of the fourteenth century out of some twenty-seven burgesses, who owed quite heavy labour services and were said to be in the position of betaghs, only four or five had Irish names.[51] And everywhere we find that where the names of burgesses are given, almost all are English.

The agricultural structure of the new manors was clearly modelled on English practice. The betaghs no doubt cultivated their own lands on the native system, but there is adequate evidence of the dispersed strip holdings of the English open field system all over the area which, as we have seen, was populated by English settlers: indeed on the archbishop's lands in co. Dublin strips and furlongs persisted in some places till the early nineteenth century, though elsewhere they seem to have disappeared much earlier. But the lord's lands seem usually to have been separate from those of the tenants, and there is evidence that a good deal of consolidation of strips was going on in the fourteenth century. A three course rotation was that commonly used, as in England: winter corn (wheat or rye); spring corn (oats); fallow.[52] There is evidence that the eight ox plough was that commonly used.[53] There was a good deal of sheep farming, and the custom on the export of wool, woolfells and hides yielded considerable sums under Edward I, while in the same period large quantities of grain were exported to supply the king's armies in Scotland.[54] The lord's demesne seems to have averaged about 300 acres, perhaps some 750 statute acres, of which not more than about two-thirds would be under cultivation in any

[51] *Pipe Roll of Cloyne*, pp. 15–22; above, p. 112.
[52] J. Otway-Ruthven, 'The Organization of Anglo-Irish Agriculture in the Middle Ages', *Journ. R.S.A.I.*, LXXXI, pp. 1–13.
[53] *Pipe Roll 14 John*, pp. 38, 40; *Red Book of Ormond*, p. 28.
[54] See below, pp. 218, 224.

given year. It is clear that labour services played a comparatively small part in its cultivation. The labour services owed by tenants nowhere approached the hundred days work or more in the year which the English villein commonly owed his lord. The heaviest recorded are those of the betaghs of Lisronagh, or the tenants of Ballyboe, co. Tipperary, who in 1415–16 each owed the lord a total of fifteen days work in the year.[55] Where the lord cultivated his demesne himself, as on the Christ Church manors in co. Dublin, the only ones for which we have really detailed accounts, the bulk of the labour needed was hired: at Clonkeen (Kill of the Grange) in 1344, out of a total of 562 days' work reaping, 471 were done by labourers hired by the day and only ninety-one by customary tenants.[56] The cottiers and other small tenants no doubt provided the hired labourers, and the cottiers will also have provided the regular staff of paid labourers, carters, ploughmen, herds and others, employed throughout the year. But as has been said, it seems likely that in many places lords were no longer cultivating their demesnes themselves by the later thirteenth century.

Side by side with this secular organization of the manor went its ecclesiastical organization. As we have seen, the organization of the new territorial dioceses initiated at the beginning of the twelfth century was substantially complete before the Normans came. But parochial organization was another matter, and it seems probable that no more than a bare beginning had been made in this, and that almost everywhere the defined, organized territorial parish was still unknown. The synod of Cashel of 1171–2 decreed that every man should pay tithe to his parish church, and it seems reasonably clear that this marks the real starting point of parochial organization, for tithes are of cardinal importance in the formation of the territorial parish: arising out of the produce of the land, and forming the inalienable property of the rector of the parish, they ensure that the land in question cannot be detached from one parish and attached to another, for this would be to deprive the rector of his property. Thus, once the tithe-supported parish had been formed, its outline became a permanent feature of ecclesiastical geography, and the ecclesiastical parishes which slowly developed during the middle ages still exist as civil parishes, though these have no longer any function.[57]

[55] Above, p. 111; *Red Book of Ormond*, p. 123.
[56] *Account Roll of Holy Trinity*, pp. 64–67.
[57] The ecclesiastical parishes of the Church of Ireland, though many have been amalgamated, correspond closely to the medieval parishes; the Roman Catholic parishes, which, because of the break in continuity caused by the Reformation, were organized afresh in the eighteenth century, and not, of course, on a basis of tithe, show considerable divergences from them.

An early stage in the organization of a lordship was, in many cases, the granting of 'the ecclesiastical benefices (i.e. the tithes) of all my men and tenants' to a religious house, either one of those like St Mary's, Dublin, which had been founded with the first introduction of monasticism of the continental type before the Norman conquest, or the new ones, like Tristernagh in Westmeath or Abbeylara near Granard, co. Longford, founded by the settlers. We are fortunate in being able to trace the development of one such grant in detail. Before 1175 Adam de Feypo, lord of Skreen, co. Meath, founded a chapel of St Nicholas in his castle of Skreen, and assigned to it the tithes of all his lands in the bishopric of Clonard (later Meath). He said later that he was the first to give tithes in the bishopric; all others were then usurped by the lay hand. Clearly at this date there was no organized parish of Skreen, or the tithes would have belonged to it. About 1180 the chapel with its tithes was granted to St Mary's, Dublin, and before 1186 we hear of the church of Skreen, which must mean that the monks had organized the whole area as a parish. But since they were the rector, they could subdivide it as they saw fit without injury to anyone's rights, and by 1231 there were, besides the church of St Columba of Skreen, with its chapel of St Nicholas, five other churches and five chapels. By the early fourteenth century two of these chapelries had been formed into a parish, and by 1540, when the extents of monastic property made at the dissolution next give us a full view of the area, there were nine rectories: the full modern total but for one interesting exception. The modern parish of Lismullen is composed of the lands of the nunnery of Lismullen, founded by bishop Richard de la Cornere for his sister Avice c. 1240. But at this date the lands concerned were already involved in St Mary's parish of Skreen, and their tithe could not be subtracted from it to endow a separate parish belonging to the nuns. Only the clean sweep of monastic property made it possible, exceptionally, to do this, but in an overwhelming majority of cases the old parishes were continued unaltered: that it was not so in this case was due to the fact that the lands of the nunnery went intact to a grantee who also got a grant of the tithes.[58]

Nothing is clearer than the identification of manor and parish. The subdivisions of the original undivided parish of Skreen correspond very closely to the list of de Feypo's principal tenants c. 1200; the chapelries of Galtrim in 1540 (they had become separate parishes by the time Ussher, as bishop of Meath, listed the parishes of

[58] A. J. Otway-Ruthven, 'Parochial Development in the Rural Deanery of Skreen', *Journ. R.S.A.I.*, XCIV, pp. 111–22.

his diocese in 1622) correspond to the holdings of the principal sub-tenants of the Husseys of Galtrim in the fourteenth century.[59] Where we have a continuous series of deeds relating to the same place, early deeds will commonly describe the land as being in such a tenement, later ones as being in the parish of that name. The detached portions of so many parishes seem all to be explicable in terms of the accidents of tenure. Thus in co. Dublin a townland in the geographical centre of the parish of Holmpatrick belongs not to it, but to the parish of Lusk, while another, physically within Lusk, nevertheless belongs to Holmpatrick. The explanation seems to be simply that the first did not belong to the priory of Holm-patrick and that the second did, for the parish of Holmpatrick consists exclusively of lands which belonged to the priory. More-over, they must have belonged to it at the time of the formation of the parochial system in this area, for one townland, which is not detached, but which was not granted to the priory till 1367, is part of the parish of Lusk, of whose revenues its tithes formed a part, and from which it could not therefore be separated.[60]

Of course, not all parishes belonged to monastic houses. Some-times the bishop of the diocese obtained their advowsons, and in any case he had the advowsons of the parishes formed out of his own lands; sometimes a secular lord retained an advowson as his own property. There was a very scandalous quarrel between the bishop of Meath and the lord of Galtrim as to the advowson of that church in the thirteenth century.[61] But a great many were granted to monastic houses, and the monasteries were probably the most powerful influence in the development of the parochial system over the whole area of Norman settlement. The organization and the size of parishes must have depended partly on the policy of parti-cular monastic houses, which, as we have seen, could, since they were the rectors, divide up their parishes as they liked without in-fringing the rights of anyone, and partly on the willingness of the laity to build churches. In general, however, it seems clear that even comparatively small tenants were anxious to have their lands an independent parish: some of them consist of only a single town-land, with an area of no more than some six or seven hundred statute acres, like Follistown and Staffordstown, two of the parishes which were formed out of the grant of Skreen. It is of course only in the areas of Norman settlement that this general picture is true: the development of parishes in the areas which remained purely

[59] Ibid.
[60] J. Otway-Ruthven, 'The Medieval Church Lands of County Dublin', *Medieval Studies Presented to Aubrey Gwynn, S.J.*, p. 68.
[61] *C.D.I.*, III, no. 503.

Irish followed rather different lines, and is harder to trace in the absence of record material.[62] But, at least in certain areas, the parishes which can be shown to have been held by abbeys of Norman foundation are a valuable index of the extent of Norman domination, though not necessarily of solid settlement, and of the possessions of particular grantors. Thus at the dissolution the Cistercian house of Abbeylara or Granard, co. Longford, founded by Richard de Tuit in 1210, had the rectories not only of south-western Cavan (the baronies of Clonmahon and Tullyhunco) which were adjacent to Granard, and may be supposed to have formed part of Tuit's territory, but also 'all the parish churches in Clyncolman, Bravyn Obroyn, Calry and Delvyn McCoghlan', that is, in the baronies of Clonlonan and Brawney, co. Westmeath, and Garrycastle, co. Offaly. We know that the Tuits held Ballyloughloe in the barony of Clonlonan by the service of five knights, and it is highly probable that this whole group of parishes represents an original grant by Richard de Tuit of the tithes of all his lands, some of which will certainly have continued to be held by Irish chieftains. Again, at the dissolution the Gilbertine priory of Loughsewdy, co. Westmeath, the western *caput* of the de Verdon half of the lordship of Meath, had all those parishes in co. Longford which we know to have been part of the de Verdon share, representing almost certainly an original grant by the de Lacys.[63]

An important part of the Norman organization of their conquests was the foundation of new monastic houses, and both the greatest men, such as the Marshals and de Lacys, and their more important sub-tenants, such as Richard de Tuit at Granard and Geoffrey de Costentin at Tristernagh,[64] established new foundations and endowed them richly with both lands and tithes. These houses were certainly intended to be centres of Norman influence, and they managed their lands much as the lay magnates did, but as the colony contracted in the fourteenth century and later they inevitably tended to become purely Irish. Of the new orders which were introduced, the most important in the organization of the colony were the military orders, the Templars and Hospitallers. Both orders, based in co. Dublin, acquired extensive lands throughout the country: the Templars in counties Wexford, Carlow, Louth, Waterford and Tipperary (these went to the Hospitallers after the suppression of the Templars at the beginning of the fourteenth century); the Hospitallers in counties Kildare, Wexford, Meath,

[62] See below, pp. 126–7.
[63] *Extents of Monastic Possessions*, pp. 281–2, 285; J. Otway-Ruthven, 'The Partition of the de Verdon Lands', *Proc. R.I.A.*, LXVI C.
[64] See *Reg. Tristernagh*.

Down, Waterford, Cork and Limerick. These great estates were important centres of English influence, while in the fourteenth century the prior of the Hospital begins to appear as an important figure in the central governmental organization of the country.[65]

So far nothing has been said of the demesne manors retained in the king's hand. In the early days of the colony the intention seems to have been to retain a good deal permanently in demesne, but this was evidently found unsatisfactory, and by the middle of the thirteenth century there were only five demesne manors: Crumlin, near Dublin; Newcastle Lyons, Esker and Saggart, south-west of the city in an area much exposed to the attacks of the Irish of the mountains; and Newcastle Mackinegan, co. Wicklow, also in what was really a border district, where there was an important royal castle. Newcastle Mackinegan is the only one of the demesne manors of which we have a detailed extent: in 1305 there were two free tenants, holding three ploughlands and half a ploughland respectively, and 191 burgages; no other tenants are mentioned.[66] There were also the lands of Othe, Obrun and Okelli, all in co. Wicklow, which are often accounted for together with Newcastle Mackinegan, but we do not hear of them after 1301. At the beginning of the thirteenth century all three had been farmed by betaghs, and this probably remained the position throughout.[67]

All the demesne lands showed a considerable increase in farm rents during the thirteenth century, the most spectacular cases being Saggart, which went up from £30 to £112 18s. 4d., and Newcastle Lyons, which increased from £40 to £147 5s. 8d. This increase seems to have been achieved by a change from a policy of leasing the manor as a whole to one of allowing the actual occupying tenants to lease the lands directly from the crown. It seems also that the new rents in these two manors were heavier than the lands could bear, for under Edward I heavy arrears accumulated, particularly in Saggart. Early in the reign of Edward III, after the tenants had petitioned that

their lands and possession have long been destroyed by reason of the wars and disturbances by the invasions of the Scots and Irish in those parts, their houses burned and their goods plundered, and they are reduced to such want and misery that they can in no way pay the said arrears; and yet they are so oppressed by reason of the said arrears, both by arrest of their bodies, and by divers distraints, that many have become vagrants, begging their bread

[65] See below, pp. 127–8, 136–8, 141–3, for the orders in general.
[66] *Cal. Justic. Rolls*, II, p. 28. There were also burgesses at Saggart.
[67] *Pipe Roll, 14 John*, p. 10; *36th Rep. D.K.*, p. 59; *37th Rep. D.K.*, p. 26; *38th Rep. D.K.*, p. 55; *C.D.I.*, II, no. 2329.

the arrears were remitted, and the farm rents reduced.[68]

So far we have been concerned entirely with the character of rural settlement, but the establishment of towns was also of great importance. Reference has already been made to the many villages which had the elements of an urban constitution, but towns proper were a very different matter, and were to be one of the main bastions of Norman power. In Celtic Ireland no true towns had existed, apart from the Norse settlements of Dublin, Wexford, Waterford, Cork and Limerick: these continued, newly chartered by the king except for Wexford, the first centre of the lordship of Leinster, and a number of new urban settlements which were to become true towns were established, either by the king or by the greatest lords. There were several in Ulster, of which the most important was Carrickfergus; then, going south, Dundalk, founded by Bertram de Verdon in the time of John; Drogheda, originally two separate towns, Drogheda on the side of Louth, founded by Bertram de Verdon and given a charter of the laws of Breteuil by the king in 1213, and Drogheda on the side of Meath, founded by Walter de Lacy in 1194, but taken into the hand of the crown under John and never restored. Then came Dublin, given a charter in 1171–2; Wexford, another Ostman town continued under the Normans; New Ross, founded by the Marshals and already a port at the beginning of Henry III's reign; Waterford, given a charter by John in 1215[69]; Youghal; Cork, which certainly had charters from Henry II and John, and was called a city in 1215; Limerick, granted the liberties of the citizens of Dublin by John, probably in 1197; Galway.[70] These were all ports, and there were others, such as Wicklow or Dungarvan, which never became really important. Those important enough to be centres in which customs were collected under Edward I were, in order of the magnitude of the sums collected, New Ross, Waterford, Cork, Drogheda, Dublin, Youghal, Galway, Limerick, the Ulster ports (probably Carrickfergus and Coleraine), and the Kerry ports (presumably Dingle and Tralee). New Ross and Waterford each regularly produced more than twice as much as any other port, but this concentration of export through the ports of the south-east declined in Edward's later years.[71]

---

[68] *Cat. Pipe Rolls, passim*; *C.P.R., 1330–34*, p. 551; *C.C.R., 1333–7*, p. 343; P.R.O. London, S.C. 8/197/9811.

[69] Orpen pointed out that the date given in the text of the charter as we have it (vii John) must have been xvii in the original. (*Normans*, II, p. 314). The text is certainly corrupt in other respects: no doubt the original had been damaged, and was misread when copied.

[70] Irish borough charters are conveniently collected in G. MacNiocaill, *Na Buirgéist*.

[71] *Cat. Pipe Rolls, passim*.

Inland, towns developed round castles, whether founded by royal charter at such places as Athlone, or by such lords as the Marshals at Kilkenny or Kildare. All the towns which became of real commercial importance were situated on navigable waterways, and clearly these were, as everywhere in Europe, of paramount importance in the transport conditions of the age. Many other places in the course of the thirteenth and fourteenth centuries were granted the right to hold fairs and markets, and though such grants no doubt often express pious hopes rather than any correspondence to commercial fact, there must have been a brisk and lively trade in the hey-day of the colony. Some idea of its staples can be formed from the lists of commodities on which towns were from time to time granted the right to levy tolls in order to raise funds to build a bridge or wall themselves: wine, salt, and foodstuffs; horses and cattle; hides, wool, woolfells; cloth of all kinds; iron, lead, tin, dyestuffs, timber, fuel, millstones, nails, horseshoes, cordwain, wax.[72] Dublin is the only town of which we have an early roll of citizens, possibly belonging to the first generation of the conquest.[73] It lists some 1,600 names, including goldsmiths, tailors, shoemakers, weavers, mercers, cordwainers, tanners, saddlers, lorimers, smiths, carpenters, masons, fishermen, bakers, vintners, butchers and millers. As far as their surnames indicate their origins, they came from all over England, though predominantly from the south-west; from south Wales; and from a handful of Scottish and French towns. Henry II had granted the men of Bristol his city of Dublin to be inhabited, with all the liberties and free customs which they had at home, but clearly many besides the men of Bristol had taken the opportunity to start again in a new country.

In the thirteenth century and later there was a steady development of urban privilege in Ireland as elsewhere and one of the most important stages in this was the grant to the citizens of the right to farm their city: that is, to discharge their obligations to the crown by a fixed annual payment, for which they were themselves responsible, to the exclusion of the officers of the crown. Dublin obtained this right in 1215, Waterford in 1232, and Cork ten years later. Limerick and the two Droghedas had been added to the list by the reign of Edward I. And though in the later middle ages the more distant towns tended to be cut off from the government in Dublin, failing to pay their farm rents, and behaving almost as autonomous institutions,[74] they were and remained important centres of English influence.

[72] *C.D.I.*, passim.
[73] *Historic and Municipal Documents*, pp. 3–48.
[74] See below, pp. 370, 373.

The native Irish were never excluded from the towns, but since they had no urban tradition it was in the countryside that they played their major part in this society. It is quite clear that it was everywhere interpenetrated by them, though mainly among the smaller tenants. But there seems to have been a large class of free Irish resident among the English, and in the advowson of some lord, who were distinct from and superior to the betaghs and could change from one lord to another.[75] Unless they or their ancestors had obtained a grant of English law, they had access to the king's courts only through their lords, but otherwise their position can have differed little from that of the small tenant or artisan of English descent, and as time went on there must have been more and more assimilation.[76] The nature of the surviving records ensures that we hear of them largely through their crimes, but these are very commonly committed in association with men of English origin.[77] And the story of the party in MacGilpatrick's house on Shrove Tuesday in 1417 which ended in the death of a son of the earl of Ormond, killed by MacGilpatrick's blacksmith while they were dancing, suggests a whole world of friendly intercourse which must have been a more common pattern of life than is usually supposed.[78]

All this shaded imperceptibly into the purely Irish world which still remained in large parts of the country. The earls of Desmond became as much Irish as English during the fourteenth century; the earls of Ormond, though remaining English, retained Irish chiefs by indentures, and led forces largely composed of Irishmen to fight under the justiciar.[79] The Irish of Munster and even of Connacht were necessarily affected by these contacts, and in Leinster O'Toole was to write to Richard II in 1395, 'without buying and selling I can in no way live . . . I would that you send me your letters patent so that for the future I may enjoy free buying and selling in your fairs and towns'.[80] Only in the north-west, where the advance that the earls of Ulster had led had collapsed after the murder of the Brown Earl in 1333, did the archaic world that the Normans had found in the twelfth century remain almost unaltered into the early modern period.

[75] *Cal. Justic. Rolls*, I, p. 162; ibid., II, pp. 326–7; ibid., III, pp. 230–31.

[76] See below, pp. 188–90. It has generally been supposed that in the records *Hibernicus* is equivalent to betagh or *nativus* (the equivalent of the English villein), and writing in 1950 I accepted this view (*I.H.S.*, VII, pp. 1–16). But I now think that when the records say that a man is the *Hibernicus* of a lord they mean that he is in his advowson, not that he is his betagh tenant. Betaghs, like the English villeins, were, of course, excluded from the royal courts.

[77] *Cal. Justic. Rolls, passim*.

[78] *AC*.

[79] See below, pp. 273–5.

[80] Curtis, *Richard II in Ireland*, pp. 125–6.

The Medieval Irish Church

A S WE SAW, the reorganization of the church in Ireland on the basis of the territorial diocese had been completed before the Normans came. Some readjustments were subsequently made, of which the union of the see of Glendalough with that of Dublin in 1216 may serve as an example,[2] but in essentials the structure was complete. At a lower level, however, it does not seem that even a beginning had been made with the organization of parishes: the essential basis of the parochial system as it developed in western Europe was the system of tithes, payable by particular lands to a particular church for its support, and both Norman and Irish sources agree that tithes were not paid in Ireland before the later twelfth century.[3] We need not be surprised at this: the work of creating the new diocesan system must have fully engaged the attention and energies of the reformers of the first half of the century. And here the coming of the Normans accelerated a development which would have occurred in any case, as part of the process of bringing the church in Ireland into line with the general pattern of western Christendom, for to them the parish was as natural and normal a part of life as the knight's fee or the manor. As we have seen, the creation of parishes seems everywhere to have accompanied the creation of manors, and areas where there are a number of small parishes correspond very closely to areas of Norman settlement.[4] And during the late twelfth and thirteenth centuries the creation of parishes must also have proceeded in the parts of the country dominated by the Irish. By the early fourteenth century, and probably well before this, Ireland was covered by a network of parishes, with the solitary exception of the diocese of Ardagh in the counties of Longford and Leitrim, where no such

---

[1] The only general account of the church in this period is in *History of the Church of Ireland*, ed. W. Alison Phillips, II, chapters 2 and 3.

[2] For details and references see Orpen, *Normans*, II, pp. 71–73.

[3] *Chart. St. Mary's*, II, p. 22; *AC, s.a.* 1224. The decree of the synod of Cashel in 1171–2 seems to be the real starting point of parochial organization in Ireland. (See above, p. 118.)

[4] Above, pp. 118–21; D. F. Gleeson, 'The Coarbs of Killaloe Diocese', *Journ. R.S.A.I.*, LXXIX, pp. 160–69.

development seems yet to have taken place.[5] The development was uneven: in some parts of the country there was already something near the final total of parishes; in others, as for instance the rural deanery of Ardnurcher, there might be only a single parish in an area where there were finally to be fourteen.[6] Outside the area of Norman settlement parishes seem to have been formed from the old monastic termons, from the lands of new monastic houses where these were not identical with the old termons, or from the lands of ancient family population groups.[7] Everywhere they were grouped by the early fourteenth century into rural deaneries which seem to have been based on old Irish territories.

While in the twelfth century the organization of the secular clergy in Ireland had been transformed, so was that of the monasteries. The principal influence, as we have seen, had been that of the Cistercians, but it was not the only one: there had been houses under the influence of both Tiron and Savigny before the Cistercians came, while it is probable that there were houses of Augustinian canons by the middle of the twelfth century.[8] The Normans added considerably to the number of foundations: nine new Cistercian houses; nine new Benedictine establishments[9]; some sixteen houses of Augustinian canons, with four houses of canonesses. In addition they introduced new orders: the Crutched Friars, who were in fact regular canons under the rule of St Augustine whose houses were also hospitals for the sick, seem to have been introduced in Dublin in 1188, and a number of other houses of the order were founded in urban centres during the next thirty years, while the Hospitallers of St Thomas of Acon had two houses, and the Trinitarians one.[10] Then there were the Victorine canons, whose most important house was St Thomas's abbey, Dublin, founded by William fitz Audelm on behalf of Henry II in 1178. A solitary Gilbertine house was established at Loughsewdy in Westmeath. And finally there were the military orders: the Templars, estab-

[5] See the ecclesiastical taxation printed in *C.D.I.*, V, nos. 693–729. See also G. J. Hand, 'The Dating of the Early Fourteenth-Century Ecclesiastical Valuations of Ireland', *Irish Theological Quarterly*, XXIV, pp. 271–4.

[6] Ardnurcher included most of the barony of Moycashel in Westmeath and four baronies in Offaly (*Ussher's Works*, I, pp. liii–cxxv).

[7] Gleeson, loc. cit., p. 160.

[8] H. G. Richardson, 'Some Norman Monastic Foundations in Ireland', *Medieval Studies Presented to Aubrey Gwynn, S.J.*, pp. 29–43; A. Gwynn, S.J., 'The Origins of St. Mary's Abbey, Dublin', *Journ. R.S.A.I.*, LXXIX, pp. 110–25; P. J. Dunning, 'The Arroasian Order in Medieval Ireland', *I.H.S.*, IV, pp. 297–315.

[9] There was one pre-Norman Benedictine house.

[10] R. N. Hadcock, 'The Order of the Holy Cross in Ireland', *Medieval Studies Presented to Aubrey Gwynn, S.J.*, pp. 44–53.

lished in Ireland when they were granted Clontarf, co. Dublin, by Henry II in 1172, and the Hospitallers who were granted Kilmainham by Strongbow, presumably on behalf of the king.[11]

Both the bishoprics and the monastic houses were endowed with landed property, while the monasteries also drew a considerable income from the tithes of the parishes whose advowsons they owned.[12] But it was landed property which provided the major part of the income of almost all, and some bishops and abbeys were very great landowners indeed. The archbishops of Dublin held nearly a quarter of the modern co. Dublin, as well as a great extent of land in the modern co. Wicklow, formerly the property of Glendalough, while other church property in co. Dublin came to as much again.[13] This concentration of land in the hands of the church was unusual,[14] but an abbey such as the Cistercian house of Mellifont, which held an enormous block of land along the Boyne in cos. Meath and Louth, as well as much more scattered land, was a far greater landowner than many a lay tenant-in-chief.[15] Much of this land had everywhere been held before the conquest, but substantial grants were made by the Normans, not only to the new houses which they founded, but also to the older ones.[16] Inevitably there were disputes about particular lands claimed by the church on one hand and by a new Norman grantee on the other,[17] but in general it is clear that pains were taken to ascertain the rights of the church, and these were confirmed by royal charters, though usually for a fine, which might be substantial.[18] And unlike the lands of the church in England, no doubt because of the development of canon law between 1066 and the later twelfth century, church lands in Ireland were held of the

[11] T. Leland, *History of Ireland*, I, p. 127; *Historic and Municipal Documents*, pp. 495–9.

[12] There is no study of this, but the monastic rectories were listed at the dissolution: see *Extents of Monastic Possessions*. There is an interesting list of tithes due from a number of rectories in Meath in *Llanthony Cartularies*, pp. 180–91.

[13] J. Otway-Ruthven, 'The Medieval Church Lands of County Dublin', *Medieval Studies Presented to Aubrey Gwynn, S.J.*, pp. 54–73.

[14] No study has been published for any other area, but church lands are shown on the maps in J. Otway-Ruthven, 'The Medieval County of Kildare', *I.H.S.*, XI, pp. 181–99, and 'The Partition of the de Verdon Lands', *Proc. R.I.A.*, LXVI C.

[15] Father Colmcille, O.C.S.O., *The Story of Mellifont*. For all the lands of St Mary's, Dublin, see C. Ó Conbhuí, 'The Lands of St. Mary's Abbey, Dublin', *Proc. R.I.A.*, LXII C, pp. 21–84.

[16] J. Otway-Ruthven, 'The Medieval Church Lands of County Dublin', loc. cit.

[17] See e.g. *Chart. St. Mary's*, I, pp. 29–30; *Reg. All Hallows*, pp. 51–52.

[18] See *Chart. St. Mary's*, I, pp. 81–82, 138; *Reg. All Hallows*, pp. 11–20; *Crede Mihi*, nos. XXXIII, XXXIV, XLIV; *C.D.I.*, I, nos. 50, 335.

crown without any obligation of military service.[19] But it should be noted that though the church held a great deal of land in Ireland, individual churches were much poorer than comparable English churches: there were a great many Irish bishoprics, so that there was necessarily less for each one, and incomes from land in Ireland were certainly less than in England.

By the early thirteenth century the church in Ireland was thus organized much as it was elsewhere in western Europe. There were of course some survivals from the older order: in the north and west there were still coarbs and erenachs, who in Ulster survived into the seventeenth century. But on the whole these survivals were unimportant. And in the early thirteenth century the organization of Irish cathedrals on the lines then fashionable in England had begun, with no longer the monastic chapters of an earlier age, but secular ones in which each canon had his own prebend as a separate source of income. In Dublin archbishop John Comyn established St Patrick's with a secular chapter, apparently because he was unable to dislodge the Arroasian canons of Christ Church: in Limerick an Irishman, bishop Donatus O'Brien, established a secular chapter in his cathedral in 1205, 'considering English custom', a striking example of the persistence of the spirit which had been manifested at the synod of Cashel.[20]

There is, indeed, much evidence to show that at this period Norman and Irish churchmen were still co-operating more or less happily with each other and with the settlers. Malachy, bishop of Down, joined with John de Courcy in founding or re-founding monasteries; the Irishman, archbishop Felix of Tuam, powerfully supported the claim of the Norman archbishop of Dublin to the see of Glendalough at the fourth Lateran Council (1215–16). Norman settlers adopted the cults of Celtic saints. There is at this period no evidence of racial conflict in the church, but rather of co-operation in the working out of the twelfth-century programme of reform.[21] And though in the course of the thirteenth century an unbroken succession of English bishops was established in all the dioceses of the province of Dublin, as well as Meath, Limerick and Waterford, most of the dioceses of Cashel had more Irish bishops

[19] See J. Otway-Ruthven, 'Knight Service in Ireland', *Journ. R.S.A.I.*, LXXXIX, pp. 1–2.

[20] G. J. Hand, 'The Medieval Chapter of St. Mary's Cathedral, Limerick', *Medieval Studies Presented to Aubrey Gwynn, S.J.*, pp. 74–89.

[21] H. G. Richardson, 'Some Norman Monastic Foundations in Ireland', ibid., pp. 29–43; P. J. Dunning, 'Irish Representatives and Irish Ecclesiastical Affairs at the Fourth Lateran Council', ibid., pp. 90–113; K. Hughes, 'The Offices of S. Finnian of Clonard and S. Cianan of Duleek', *Analecta Bollandiana*, LXXIII, pp. 342–72; ibid., LXXV, pp. 337–9.

than English during the century, and all the archbishops of Cashel were Irish. In the province of Tuam, though there were Norman archbishops from 1286 to 1312, all the other bishops were Irish, and in Armagh only the dioceses of Down and Connor had an unbroken succession of Norman bishops, and most of the other bishops of the province during the thirteenth century were Irish, while Armagh itself had a Norman, a German, an Italian, and four Irish archbishops.[22] But this racial mixture did not necessarily mean racial conflict. Racial conflicts did, as we shall see, undoubtedly arise, but it is reading history backwards to suppose that in the twelfth and thirteenth centuries members of an international, and indeed supranational, body such as the church displayed the attitudes of nineteenth- and twentieth-century nationalism. Given the relations between church and state which existed everywhere during the middle ages it was essential for the proper functioning of both that there should be co-operation between them, and the medieval Irish bishop, whatever his racial origins, was normally prepared to co-operate with the state as long as the rights of his see were respected. The bishops who in the late thirteenth century sought to secure the abandonment of Brehon law for the common law were all native Irishmen[23]; Stephen O'Brogan, archbishop of Cashel, was warmly commended in 1291 for his 'immense fealty and affection to the king'; the archbishop of Cashel who represented in 1353 that he was involved in almost continuous wars against the Irish enemy was an O'Kelly; the archbishop of Tuam, again an O'Kelly, was active in procuring submissions to Richard II in 1395.[24] The quarrels of such men as Nicholas Mac Maol Íosa, archbishop of Armagh 1272–1303, with the crown were over matters of jurisdiction and rights which were unconnected with racial issues and might have arisen anywhere, and Mac Maol Íosa maintained an alliance with the justiciar, Stephen de Fulbourne, archbishop of Tuam, during the 1280's, while his English successors maintained against the crown those rights for which he had been contending, and in 1291 a number of his English contemporaries in Irish sees entered into a joint undertaking with him to resist secular encroachments.[25] It is difficult to see that things would

[22] J. A. Watt, 'English Law and the Irish Church: the Reign of Edward I', *Medieval Studies Presented to Aubrey Gwynn, S.J.*, pp. 133–67; succession lists in *Handbook of British Chronology* (1961).

[23] Below, p. 189.

[24] *Parliaments and Councils*, p. 199; P.R.O. Dublin, Mem. Rolls, vol. 26, pp. 310–12; below, p. 332.

[25] A. Gwynn, 'Nicholas Mac Maol Íosa, Archbishop of Armagh, 1272–1303', *Feil-Sgríbhinn Eóin Mhic Néill*, pp. 394–405; J. A. Watt, 'English Law and the Irish Church: the Reign of Edward I,', loc. cit.

have been very different if Mac Maol Íosa had been an Englishman, and it has been justly pointed out that the attitude of bishops depended more on their proximity to the centre of royal government than on their racial origins.[26]

On the other hand, while bishops were properly concerned to defend the rights of their churches against secular encroachments, it was not necessarily improper for the crown to seek to ensure that bishops should be such men as it could work with. It is not clear exactly what lay behind the mandate of 1217 to the justiciar that as 'the peace of Ireland has been frequently disturbed by elections of Irishmen' none should in future be elected or promoted in any cathedral.[27] It does not correspond with the facts as known to us, and has been attributed with great probability to Henry of London, archbishop of Dublin, who had been justiciar from 1213 to 1215, but archbishop Henry had just been in friendly co-operation with such Irishmen as the archbishop of Tuam at the Lateran Council from which he had just returned,[28] and perhaps we should think rather of Geoffrey de Marisco, the justiciar. It must certainly be connected with the disputed elections of this date in Killaloe and Ardfert, where the chapters had elected Irishmen and the elections were set aside as invalid because the king's licence had not been obtained and the election of Norman candidates secured: in each case the papal court ultimately decided in favour of the Irishman. In Armagh, also vacant in 1217, the chapter freely elected the only Englishman to rule there during the century, though again the king's licence had not been obtained, and the election had to be repeated. But Henry of London, who had been appointed papal legate in April 1217, when the pope spoke of the flame of revolt against the king's authority which had now broken out in Ireland as well as England, was a man who provoked quarrels, and so was the justiciar, Geoffrey de Marisco. By the end of 1218 there was a dispute between the archbishop of Cashel and the justiciar over the archbishop's lands in Cashel. By the end of 1219 the archbishop of Cashel was on his way to Rome to complain to the pope in person. In July 1220 Henry of London was abruptly deprived of his legatine authority; a new legate was appointed at the end of the month; in August the exclusion of Irishmen from the cathedrals was expressly denounced by the pope as 'unheard of audacity . . . so bold and wicked an abuse', and other complaints of the archbishop of

[26] Ibid., p. 163.
[27] C.D.I., I, nos. 736, 739.
[28] A. Gwynn, 'Henry of London, Archbishop of Dublin', Studies, XXXVIII, pp. 295–306, 389–402; P. J. Dunning, 'Irish Representatives and Irish Ecclesiastical Affairs at the Fourth Lateran Council', loc. cit.

Cashel were to be redressed, including the complaint that church lands had been seized for the building of castles.[29]

The policy inaugurated in 1217 was abandoned after this, but in 1250 Henry III had occasion to complain to the pope that the Irish prelates and their chapters had decreed that no Englishman should be received as a canon in any cathedral church. The pope ordered that the ordinance should be revoked: we have no evidence as to which dioceses had been involved.[30] Again in 1284 it was alleged that Irish bishops always provided Irishmen only to their churches.[31] But in fact the composition of a chapter inevitably reflected the situation in the diocese: apart from the special case of St Patrick's, Dublin, where many of the canons were royal officials, chapters tended to be filled by members of the leading local families, and while in some dioceses such as Limerick, the only one whose chapter has been studied in detail, this would produce a racially mixed chapter, in others the natural processes of selection would produce one predominantly or entirely of one or other race.[32] But during the early thirteenth century a very important part of the custom of the English church, which gave the crown effective supervision of episcopal elections, had been successfully established: the common law procedure, approved by the papacy, by which the king must be informed by the chapter of a vacancy, and his licence to elect obtained. The bishop-elect must then obtain the royal approval and take an oath of fealty before he could recover his temporalities from the escheator.[33] Chapters were often negligent in observing this procedure, and here those dominated by Normans were as remiss as the Irish, and metropolitans, both Norman and Irish, might admit bishops without insisting that these formalities should be observed, but in the course of the thirteenth century the due observance of the procedure became very general throughout the country.

The right of the crown to the custody of the temporalities during

29 A. Gwynn, 'Henry of London', loc. cit. A number of Irish castles were built on church land: Roscrea, Roscommon, Trim, Kildare and others, while at Kilkenny land was taken to enlarge the town, and compensation was normally given (C.D.I., II, no. 861; Reg. Swayne, p. 39; P.R.O. London, S.C. 8/55/2720; below, pp. 199, 202–3).
30 C.D.I., I, no. 3084; Pontificia Hibernica, II, no. 326,
31 C.D.I., III, p. 10.
32 G. J. Hand, 'The Medieval Chapter of St. Mary's Cathedral, Limerick', loc. cit.; J. A. Watt, 'English Law and the Irish Church', loc. cit., pp. 140–41, 143.
33 The procedure is fully explained by J. A. Watt, 'English Law and the Irish Church: the Reign of Edward I', loc. cit., pp. 137–9, 163–7. Only four dioceses never sought licence to elect during the thirteenth century. For the escheator, see below, pp. 161–2. The temporalities included the great bulk of church lands, though not those specially dedicated to God at the foundation of the church and not, of course, such spiritual rights as tithes.

a vacancy was certainly a powerful factor in this: there were, of course, parts of the country in which it was impossible to assert it, as in much of the province of Tuam, and a good deal of that of Armagh, but by the end of the thirteenth century twenty-two of the thirty-four Irish bishoprics were figuring in the escheator's accounts when the occasion arose. Earlier in the century both Norman and Irish bishops seem to have united in an attempt to shake off this control, but in vain. The province of Armagh was a special case: archbishop Mac Maol Íosa was to claim that the church of Armagh had the right to custody of the temporalities of all the dioceses of the province during vacancy, a right which had been lost in some places through the negligence of his predecessors, but which he asked the king to restore. It was however adjudged in 1279 that the archbishop had no such special right, and that the custody of temporalities in his province, as elsewhere in England and Ireland, belonged to the king. Soon after this, one of his suffragans, Hugh of Taghmon, bishop of Meath, died, and as Hugh had in the 1250s made a determined attempt to remove his diocese from subjection to Armagh the archbishop must have been particularly interested in the succession. He set aside the elected candidate, claimed that the appointment had lapsed to him, and nominated the justiciar's brother. Disputes followed, and there was an official inquiry into the whole conduct of the Irish administration, which condemned the justiciar and his brother and found that the archbishop had appropriated to himself the custody of temporalities during vacancies and requests for licence to elect in his province, 'against the royal dignity, and to the great damage of the king, and against the king's liberties'. It was recommended that no Irishman should ever be archbishop [or bishop] because

they always preach against the king . . . and always provide Irishmen in their churches . . . so that the election of bishops can be made by Irishmen to maintain their race (linguam).[34]

But in fact, though after this the crown did for the first time succeed in getting custody of the temporalities of Derry, the other disputed bishoprics, Clogher, Dromore, Kilmore and Raphoe, remained outside the control of the escheator.[35]

During the thirteenth and early fourteenth centuries it was in fact the local forces represented in the chapters which determined the composition of the episcopate. The king might on occasion

[34] *Medieval Studies Presented to Aubrey Gwynn, S.J.*, pp. 150–51, n. 71.
[35] This dispute has been discussed by A. Gwynn, 'Nicholas Mac Maol Íosa', loc. cit., and J. A. Watt, 'English Law and the Irish Church', loc. cit., pp. 145–53. The escheator's success in Derry must have been due to the contemporary advance of the power of the earl of Ulster (see below, pp. 214–6).

object to a candidate, as when Henry III protested to the pope
that David MacCarwell, archbishop elect of Cashel, was suspect
as being bound by ties of friendship and kindred with men who
had plotted against the king's majesty,[36] but in fact none was ever
refused, and there was no conflict with the papacy, which in this
period exercised its right to provide only in cases of appeal. In
practice, though the king's advisers might fulminate against the
native Irish, as in 1284, or as the justiciar did in 1277,[37] 'Edward
I had a genuine *modus vivendi* with the Irish church'.[38]

In other matters concerning the relations of church and state
the general principle that 'the law of England and of Ireland is,
and ought to be, the same'[39] also held good. There is ample proof
that the common law principle that the clerk had the same status
before the courts as the layman, unless he was accused of a felony,
when he had the 'benefit of clergy', which entitled him to be tried
and punished only by the ecclesiastical courts, held good in Ireland
as in England. The conditions under which it might be claimed,
and the manner of its exercise, seem to have been exactly the same
in both countries. And in other matters the relations of lay and
ecclesiastical courts seem to have been exactly the same: disputes
about details, and allegations that one or other side had usurped
jurisdiction, were frequent, but the underlying principles were not
questioned.[40] But in 1291, evidently as the result of pressure on
them to make a grant of taxation to the king, the bishops of Ireland
showed a remarkable tendency to combine in a joint protest
against secular encroachments on ecclesiastical liberties. They had
presented a number of complaints in May, when the request for
taxation had been made, dealing with clerical privilege, writs of
prohibition forbidding the ecclesiastical courts to entertain matters
claimed for the secular courts, the claims of the ecclesiastical courts
in certain property matters, the law of sanctuary, and kindred
matters. Only one clause was concerned with the specifically Irish
situation, complaining that clergy ministering to outlaws and felons
were arrested as if they were accomplices. The king replied tartly
that certain Irish prelates tended to make such duties a cover for
evil: they should not be undertaken without previous consultation
with the justiciar. Favourable replies were given to most of the

[36] *Pontificia Hibernica*, II, no. 388. MacCarwell was also opposed, on other
grounds, by the bishops of the province.
[37] Above, p. 133; *I.H.S.*, VI, p. 267.
[38] J. A. Watt, 'English Law and the Irish Church', loc. cit., p. 144.
[39] See below, p. 188.
[40] See J. A. Watt, loc. cit., pp. 153-6. For the relationship of ecclesiastical
courts to the common law in England, see Z. N. Brooke, *The English Church and
the Papacy*.

other complaints, though everywhere the king took his stand firmly on the common law position.[41] Negotiations about the tax followed in local assemblies of the clergy, without apparently much success, and in September the archbishop of Armagh, with all his suffragans, entered into a solemn undertaking at Trim, sealed and sworn to, by which they bound themselves to resist in common any secular encroachment on ecclesiastical rights. It was intended to involve all the bishops of Ireland in this, but we hear nothing more of it.[42]

Meanwhile, it should be remembered that bishops in the purely Irish parts of Ireland had to deal with Irish rulers as well as with the king of England. We have not a great deal of evidence as to the position here, but it is interesting that in 1216 Innocent III wrote to the king of Connacht (Cathal Crovderg O'Connor), requiring him to permit freedom of episcopal and abbatial elections.[43] But the most remarkable evidence comes from a lost register of the diocese of Clogher, which shows us Nicholas Mac Maol Íosa, archbishop of Armagh, publishing Boniface VIII's bull *Clericis laicos*, which forbade lay rulers to exact or ecclesiastics to pay taxation without papal consent, to the Irish rulers of his province. The bull was published in Rome in February 1296: on receiving it, apparently late in 1297, the archbishop summoned O'Neill and the other lords of Tir Eoghain before him, and had the bull read aloud to them, and explained it. They formally accepted it, and sealed an undertaking to this effect. Mac Maol Íosa then went in procession, with the relics of saints and the bishop of Clogher and his clergy, to the land of MacMahon, where he published it to the Irish lords of Oriel. On 27 November 1297 MacMahon and the other lords of his territory swore a corporal oath to abandon all 'thefts, rapines, arsons and whatsoever violences and injuries' against ecclesiastics and their tenants, and artisans employed by them. They swore to abandon the quartering of troops, horses and dogs on them, and they promised to prevent attacks on them by their kernes and galloglasses (*satellites et scotici*). A scale of penalties to be paid in cows to the bishop of Clogher was laid down for breach of these undertakings: if they were not paid, they undertook to deliver the offenders to the bishop's prison for punishment by him. Finally they undertook to leave various matters to ecclesiastical jurisdiction, and to recognize the rights of the church in intestacy. Maguire of Fermanagh and his lords then entered into a like undertaking.[44]

[41] *Early Statutes*, pp. 178–91.　　[42] *Reg. Swayne*, p. 3.
[43] P. J. Dunning, 'Letters of Pope Innocent III to Ireland', *Archivium Hibernicum*, XIII, p. 42; *Pontificia Hibernica*, I, no. 92.
[44] H. J. Lawlor, 'Fragments of a Lost Register of the Diocese of Clogher', *Louth Archaeological Journal*, IV, pp. 226–57. This fragment is on pp. 248–53.

We must suppose that similar steps were taken in other dioceses of the province, but as far as our evidence goes, these proceedings were confined to the Irish. It is most suggestive to find the bull, designed to prevent the exaction of extraordinary taxation from ecclesiastics by the national monarchies of western Europe, being used by the archbishop against the 'Irish exactions' of the kinglets of Ulster, and it is clear that they were a continuing problem, for the surviving registers of Armagh are full of complaints of injuries done to ecclesiastics and their property by O'Neill and others.[45] Similar problems no doubt existed in the province of Tuam, and in parts of that of Cashel, but there is no evidence for these areas.

Meanwhile, the monastic orders had been developing, not always happily, for it was here that racial conflict was to be really acute. The Cistercians particularly fell on evil days early in the thirteenth century, probably because of an over-rapid development. The Irish houses fell into two groups, those which had been founded from Mellifont or its daughter houses, and those founded from St Mary's abbey, Dublin.[46] The *filiatio Mellifontis* was predominantly Irish in character, and the general chapter of the order which met annually at Cîteaux and was ultimately responsible for all houses had difficulties with it early in the thirteenth century. In 1216 the statutes of the general chapter speak of the many enormities which had grown up in Mellifont, and in the next year the abbot was deposed: among other offences he had refused to receive the visitors sent by the abbot of Clairvaux, to whom the reformation of the daughter house of Mellifont had been entrusted. We hear also of a serious decay of discipline in other Irish houses of the order, and complaints recur at each general chapter. Then in 1227 at a visitation carried out by two French abbots the cellarer of Mellifont and the abbot of Baltinglass, who was deposed, were charged with conspiracy against the order. The monks of Baltinglass violently expelled their new abbot, and the general chapter took vigorous action on receiving the report of the visitors. Five abbots were deposed as leaders of the conspiracy[47]; and a number of houses were transferred from their dependence on Mellifont to new mother houses in England and Wales. In the next year Stephen de Lexington, abbot of Stanley, commissioned by the abbot of Clairvaux, to whom the task of reforming the order in Ireland had been entrusted, carried out a general visitation of the Irish houses. The abbot

---

[45] See *Reg. Fleming, Reg. Swayne, Reg. Sweteman, passim.*

[46] See Fr. Colmcille, *The Story of Mellifont* and A. Gwynn, 'The Origins of St. Mary's Abbey, Dublin', *Journ. R.S.A.I.*, LXXIX, pp. 110–25.

[47] These were the abbots of Assaroe, co. Donegal; Boyle, co. Roscommon; Fermoy, co. Cork; Odorney, co. Kerry; and Newry, co. Down.

of Mellifont, whose life had been threatened by his monks, resigned, and was replaced by a Frenchman, the prior of Beaubec; a number of monks had already fled from the house, taking with them the cross, the chalices, the charters, and some books. Most of the fugitives were eventually reconciled to the order, and were transferred to other houses, while new monks and lay brothers were introduced. In general, the visitor reported that there had been dilapidation and alienation of monastic property in the Irish houses of the order, and grave breaches of monastic discipline, including murder and association with robbers and plunderers. Racial conflicts seem to have been behind many of the disorders, and the visitor ordered that in future no one should be admitted to the order in Ireland unless he could confess his faults in either French or Latin: the Irish language had been used to cloak conspiracies, and the rule was in future to be expounded only in French, so that when the abbot of Clairvaux made his visitation in person or by deputy he could understand and make himself understood. He had, he said, no intention of excluding any man because of his race, but was anxious to ensure that only suitable persons were admitted. Further steps were taken to complete the dispersal of the *filiatio Mellifontis*, but disorders were not entirely ended: in 1231 the monks of Suir, co. Tipperary, Fermoy, co. Cork, and Corcumroe, co. Clare, refused to admit the visitors sent by their new mother house, and there were disturbances in which the abbot of Fermoy and a monk of Suir were murdered. After this, however, though there were repeated complaints that the Irish abbots were lax in attendance at the general chapters of the order, things seem to have settled down. Finally in 1274, at the instance, or so it was believed, of David MacCarwell, archbishop of Cashel, who had become a Cistercian and had founded a new house near Cashel in 1272, the general chapter restored its former daughter houses to Mellifont. At this time it was alleged that Mellifont was exclusively Irish, and in 1275 the general chapter forbade the exclusion of anyone on grounds of race, but by 1321 it could be said that it had become the practice in Mellifont and 'other houses of that order in Ireland' to admit no one who could not swear that he was not of English race and was not related to the English. The general chapter's answer was to command all abbots, and especially those of Ireland, to admit indifferently suitable persons of all races.[48]

Meanwhile, the new mendicant orders had appeared in Ireland

[48] *The Story of Mellifont*, chapters 4–5; A. Gwynn, 'Edward I and the Proposed Purchase of English Law for the Irish', *Trans. R. Hist. Soc.*, 5th series, 10, pp. 117–23; *I.H.S.*, VI, p. 267; *C.C.R., 1318–23*, p. 404.

very shortly after their foundation, the Dominicans as early as 1224, and the Franciscans in 1231 or 1232. The Augustinian friars seem to have reached Ireland in the middle of the thirteenth century, and the Carmelites a little later. Traditionally the first Franciscan house was at Youghal, and by the middle of the century they were widely spread in the sea-port towns, as well as inland at such places as Athlone, Kilkenny and Castledermot. The early houses were all in English-dominated areas, but by 1284 the official report on the administration of the Fulbournes, after recommending that no Irishman should be a bishop because they always maintain their own race (*linguam*), continued that the Franciscans and Dominicans also made much of that race.[49] And in 1291 there was a general chapter of the Franciscans in Cork in connection with a visitation of the order by the Minister General when racial animosities led to actual violence between English and Irish friars, in the course of which sixteen are said to have been killed. About the same time the bishop of Kildare, himself a Franciscan, was warning Edward I of the seditious correspondence of certain friars with Irish rulers.[50] It is against this background that we should set the Irish parliament's enactment of 1310 that no Irishman should be admitted to any religious house 'in a territory at peace, or in English land', which was, however, repealed a few months later at the instance of the archbishop of Armagh, Walter Jorz.[51]

During the Bruce invasion many clergy, and particularly the Franciscans, were active in Bruce's support, both in their preaching and in giving him material assistance. But this was not necessarily a matter of race: Adam of Northampton, bishop of Ferns, was suspected of adherence to the Scots; a Franciscan who seems to have adhered to Bruce expressed extreme anti-Irish sentiments in his presence, or so O'Neill said; a number of Anglo-Irish magnates either adhered to Bruce or were suspected of having done so.[52] Religious houses suffered a good deal from the raids of the Scots, and in the middle of the century they suffered, like the rest of the country, from the Black Death, mortality being perhaps particularly high among the friars, most of whose houses were in the towns.[53] And in the second half of the century the friars, and

[49] *C.D.I.*, III, p. 10; above, p. 133.
[50] E. B. FitzMaurice and A. G. Little, *Materials for the History of the Franciscan Province of Ireland*, pp. 52–53, 63–64.
[51] *Early Statutes*, p. 272; *Transactions of the Kilkenny Archaeological Society*, I, pp. 509–10.
[52] J. F. Lydon, 'The Bruce Invasion of Ireland', *Historical Studies*, IV, p. 115; below, pp. 228, 230, 233.
[53] Below, pp. 267–70.

particularly the Franciscans, were being attacked on general grounds both by certain bishops, including Richard fitz Ralph, archbishop of Armagh, and by some of the regular clergy.[54]

With the decline of English power in Ireland which became apparent in the second half of the fourteenth century, though in fact it had begun earlier, the problem of the two races in the church seems to have become more pressing. The statutes of Kilkenny in 1366 enacted that beneficed clergy living among the English should learn English; that no Irishman 'of the nations of the Irish' should be admitted by provision, collation, or presentation into any cathedral, collegiate church, or benefice among the English of the land; and that no religious house among the English should in future admit Irishmen. Among the bishops who approved the statutes were the archbishops of Cashel and Tuam and the bishop of Killaloe, all Irishmen, and in fact the statute established a system of control rather than an absolute prohibition, for at this time, and for long afterwards, the king had the unquestioned prerogative right of dispensing individuals from conforming to the requirements of a statute, and this power was in fact widely used to permit Irishmen to hold benefices.[55] The desirability of a knowledge of English was returned to by Richard II's government in 1381, when the ambassadors who were being sent to Rome were instructed to ask the pope to provide no prelates in Ireland without the king's consent, and only such as were faithful to him, asking also that the prelates of Ireland should be instructed to cause their subjects to learn English, and to provide no one to any dignity or benefice unless he could speak and understand it, 'since experience teaches that of the diversity of tongues in that land wars and divers tribulations have arisen'. This was later limited to a request that prelates should know English, which was not entirely unreasonable if they were to co-operate with an English-speaking government.[56]

By this time the great schism which divided western Christendom from 1378 to 1417 was making its effects felt in Ireland as elsewhere. England had adhered to the Roman pope and France to the anti-pope at Avignon: it was natural that the enemies of the English government in Ireland should look to Avignon. By May 1380 Urban, the pope of Rome, was anxious because he had heard nothing from his collector in Ireland, the bishop of Emly: the

[54] History of the Church of Ireland, II, pp. 106–09.

[55] Early Statutes, pp. 434, 444–6, 466–8; below, pp. 292–3.

[56] E. Perroy, L'Angleterre et le Grand Schisme D'Occident (Paris, 1933), pp. 394–5, 399, 403. Many of the Irish clergy had in fact been educated abroad, and must have been bi-lingual, or even tri-lingual, while many of the Anglo-Irish magnates certainly spoke Irish. See below, pp. 143, 293.

collector in England was ordered to make discreet inquiries as to the position in Ireland. In 1381 the archbishop of Cashel and the wardens of the Franciscan houses of Cashel and Galway were ordered to pursue the anti-pope's supporters in Ireland. Already Avignon had supporters in the dioceses of Clonfert and Elphin in Tuam, and was in correspondence with the bishops of Killaloe in Cashel and Raphoe in Armagh. And the anti-pope was given an opportunity by the death of three of the Irish archbishops at this time: he provided Thomas O'Colman to Armagh, a certain Michael to Cashel, and Gregory O'Mochain to Tuam. None of the three was able to establish himself permanently, though it is possible that all had some influence for a time, but the supporters of the anti-pope had a considerable success in Tuam. Here O'Mochain's predecessor and namesake had also adhered to Avignon, and not later than 1383 the prior of the Augustinian house of St Coman of Roscommon, commissioned by the anti-pope to convoke an assembly of the clergy and laity of Ireland to explain the origins of the schism and denounce his rival, was able to organize a synod at Roscommon under the archbishop's protection. The bishops of Kilmacduagh, Clonfert and Achonry were ready to accept the propaganda of the anti-pope, but the bishops of Killala and Elphin, both Englishmen, vigorously opposed it. They proclaimed their archbishop schismatic, and paid the papal taxes collected in their dioceses to the Urbanist collector. But the province of Tuam adhered obstinately to the anti-pope for at least ten years, though the attitude of archbishop O'Kelly, elected in the summer of 1392 (he had been bishop of Clonfert since 1378), who was certainly a supporter of Richard II in 1394-5, was perhaps ambiguous. But though Rome seems to have secured control of the archbishopric during the 1390s, none of the bishops provided by it to the other dioceses of the province during the last twenty years of the fourteenth century seems to have been able to get possession. We have no such detailed information for Armagh, but there is reason to suppose that in the purely Irish parts of this province too the adherents of the anti-pope were dominant.[57]

As in other parts of Europe these dissensions must have produced a considerable decline in the church. The development of the system of papal provisions, which had first become really important in the second quarter of the fourteenth century, had been one of the features of papal government against which many reformers

[57] E. Perroy, loc. cit., pp. 96–103; A. Gwynn, 'Ireland and the English Nation at the Council of Constance', *Proc. R.I.A.*, XLV C, pp. 183–233; *History of the Church of Ireland*, II, pp. 117–22; succession lists in *Handbook of British Chronology*.

had campaigned, though without success, during the conciliar movement which ended the schism.[58] The English Statute of Provisors of 1351, followed by the Statute of Praemunire in 1353, enacted that election to bishoprics and other elective dignities and benefices should be free, and made papal provisions void, while persons were forbidden to sue in a foreign realm for matters cognizable in the king's court. These statutes were not formally extended to Ireland, though they were certainly regarded as applicable, till in 1411 it was ordered that the statute against provisors should be enrolled and proclaimed. This was, however, largely ineffective: the area in which the Dublin government could act effectively was steadily shrinking, and the activities of 'Rome-runners', who secured from the papacy provision to some benefice which they coveted by denouncing the occupant, became one of the worst abuses of clerical life in fifteenth-century Ireland. Octavian del Palatio, archbishop of Armagh 1479–1513, had some success in checking it in his own diocese, but it was rampant everywhere.[59] This Italian archbishop finding himself in a diocese which had been divided for centuries between Armagh *inter Anglicos*, that is, approximately co. Louth, and Armagh *inter Hibernicos*, the rest of the diocese, set himself to bring about some measure of reform, and was not entirely unsuccessful.[60] It should be remembered, however, that though the fourteenth- and fifteenth-century archbishops had confined themselves largely to co. Louth, and had gone little outside their own province because of the dispute about the primacy and their claim to have the primatial cross carried before them wherever they went,[61] in fact, as their registers show, there was friendly co-operation between them and the clergy *inter Hibernicos*, presided over by the dean of Armagh. And in 1397 archbishop John Colton had carried out a detailed visitation of the diocese of Derry during its vacancy.[62]

There is only too much evidence in the registers of Armagh and elsewhere of laxity among the secular clergy in the fifteenth century, nor were matters better among the religious orders. The general chapter of the Cistercians made repeated attempts to enforce reform throughout its jurisdiction in the second half of the fifteenth century, but largely in vain. In 1472 it said that it learnt

---

[58] G. Barraclough, *Papal Provisions*.
[59] *History of the Church of Ireland*, pp. 122–6; R. D. Edwards, 'Papal Provisions in Fifteenth Century Ireland', *Medieval Studies Presented to Aubrey Gwynn, S.J.*, pp. 265–80; A. Gwynn, *The Medieval Province of Armagh*, pp. 13–15.
[60] Ibid., *passim*.
[61] *History of the Church of Ireland*, pp. 92–93.
[62] *Acts of Archbishop Colton*.

that Mellifont, the fount of honey, had been changed into a fount of poison, though there are no details beyond evidence of grave dilapidation of the property of the house. And by this time the abbeys of the west seem to have ceased to have any connection with the rest of the order, probably because of the disruption which had been caused by the schism. Reporting to the abbot of either Cîteaux or Clairvaux c. 1498 the abbot of Mellifont, which had been predominantly Anglo-Irish since the middle of the fourteenth century, wrote of the ruin and desolation of the order in Ireland, partly, he thought, because of the ceaseless wars between the two races; partly because of commendations and provisions from Rome, so that many had been made abbots who had no experience of the order; partly because laymen had in many cases taken over the revenues of houses. There were only two houses in Ireland, Dublin and Mellifont, where the rule was observed, and the Cistercian habit was still worn. For the last hundred years those of the more remote districts had not visited their father abbot,[63] and many of them, being without a visitor and recognizing no superior, had become rebels. He begged to be excused from making another visitation of the houses in the Irish parts of the country: lately the provisors and commendatories who occupied these houses had manned the battlements and belfries of the churches on his approach, threatening him with showers of javelins, stones and arrows, and expelling him violently and by force of arms.[64]

Among the mendicant orders, the Observant movement which had appeared on the continent in the fourteenth century, aiming at reform by a stricter observance of the rule, reached Ireland in the fifteenth century, and showed a remarkable development, principally in Connacht. The first Franciscan house of the Observant movement in Ireland was Quin, co. Clare, founded before 1433, but it was in the second half of the century that the movement really developed, and there was a remarkable proliferation of houses in the west.[65] There was a similar movement among the Dominicans, and eight new houses of Augustinian friars were founded between the end of the fourteenth century and 1461, all but one of them in Connacht, and all ultimately centres of the Observant movement.[66] There seems to have been an element of

[63] This would bring it back to the time of the Schism (above, pp. 139–40), and is probable enough on general grounds.

[64] *The Story of Mellifont*, chapters 7 and 8. The report of 1498 is from the register of archbishop Octavian of Armagh.

[65] FitzMaurice and Little, *Materials*, pp. xxx–xxxii.

[66] F. X. Martin, 'The Irish Augustinian Reform Movement in the Fifteenth Century,' *Medieval Studies Presented to Aubrey Gwynn, S.J.*, pp. 230–64.

proprietorship by the families, Irish and Anglo-Irish, by whom these houses were founded, but some element of reform must have been involved. And as elsewhere during this period, a number of chantries were founded in Ireland during the fifteenth century, while architectural evidence makes it plain that a number of parish churches were built or rebuilt.

Such education as was available in Ireland in the middle ages must have been provided by the church. There is evidence of schools in a few towns,[67] but it was clearly expected that chantry priests should keep schools, for in 1305 a jury said that this would be the great advantage of a chantry which the earl of Ulster proposed to found at Loughrea or Ballintubber.[68] But though the religious orders provided for their own education up to a point, at any higher level it had to be sought abroad, the attempt made by archbishop Bicknor to found a university at Dublin after the Bruce invasion having come to nothing. Both Anglo-Irish and native Irish went abroad to study in considerable numbers, and we find for instance that Thomas O'Colman, lector of the Franciscans at Armagh in 1375, had studied at Paris, Oxford and Cambridge,[69] while in the later middle ages the Anglo-Irish layman often studied at the Inns of Court in London.

---

[67] There was a 'house of scholars' in Drogheda in the mid-fifteenth century (*Reg. Swayne*, p. 199), and an acre of meadow called the 'scole akir' near Dundalk in 1336 (*Dowdall Deeds*, nos. 124, 180).
[68] *Cal. Justic. Rolls*, II, p. 142.
[69] *Cal. Papal Letters*, IV, p. 206.

The Government of the
Norman-Irish State

GOVERNMENTAL institutions in Norman Ireland were inevitably modelled on those of England, and as the middle ages progressed developed along the same lines. But in twelfth-century England central government was still the affair of the king and his unspecialized *curia*, dealing with a range of business within the competence of any man of normal ability and average experience of affairs. During the century the development of specialized techniques for particular classes of business, the first of which was that of the exchequer which appeared as early as the reign of Henry I, began to produce specialized departments, which in time split off from the parent *curia*, but at the time of the Norman conquest of Ireland all this was still in its infancy, and the central government of the new colony was to begin with organized very much as that of England had been in the early twelfth century, developing the newer institutions as they developed in England, though usually rather later.[1]

There was of course one major difference between the two governments: the king was almost never in Ireland, and never for more than a few months. But in the twelfth century the kings of England, who were also dukes of Normandy and from Henry II on dukes of Aquitaine, had been much out of England, and to meet this position there had been developed the office of the justiciar, who was the permanent head of the administration and governed for the king during his frequent absences on the continent.[2] The office was ready made to be imported into Ireland, and the chief governor of Ireland normally had the title of chief justiciar or justiciar of Ireland till the later fourteenth century, when that

---

[1] The only modern textbook is J. E. A. Jolliffe, *The Constitutional History of Medieval England*. See also H. G. Richardson and G. O. Sayles, *The Governance of Mediaeval England from the Conquest to Magna Carta*, which expresses views many of which are controversial. S. B. Chrimes, *An Introduction to the Administrative History of Mediaeval England* is a valuable survey.
[2] See F. J. West, *The Justiciarship in England, 1066–1232.*

of the king's lieutenant became usual. The justiciar was an omni-competent official in an age when specialization of function was still in its infancy, and government was still the direct and personal affair of the king: he was at one and the same time the military chief of the colony, the head of its civil administration, and its supreme judge, subject always, of course, to the over-riding power of the king, whose deputy he was.[3]

The chief governor, whatever his title, was normally, of course, appointed by the king, but there was a long-established and obvi-ously necessary tradition, supposed in the fifteenth century to have been established by Henry II (the 'statute of fitz Empress'), by which should a chief governor die in office, leave the country without appointing a deputy, or be suddenly incapacitated from acting, the Irish council should appoint a successor till the king made other arrangements. We have a detailed account of the pro-cedure in the emergency created by the sudden death of the earl of March, the king's lieutenant, in December 1381,[4] but there are many similar cases throughout the middle ages. Finally in 1479, 'as there has been great ambiguity and doubt among the judges' as to the manner of election, it was declared that it should be done by the whole council, together with the archbishops of Dublin and Armagh, the bishops of Meath and Kildare, the mayors of Dublin and Drogheda, and the lords of parliament of the pale, the limited area in which Anglo-Irish government was now fully operative.[5]

The powers of the justiciar are implicit in the oath prescribed for Maurice fitz Gerald in 1232: he was to swear to be faithful to the king; to render justice to everyone according to his lawful power, legal knowledge, and the custom of the kingdom; faithfully to preserve the rights, liberties and dignities of the king. It was not in the thirteenth century thought necessary to spell out the powers required to perform these duties, but the age was one of increasing definition,[6] and in the fourteenth century the powers of chief gov-ernors began to be expressly listed in their commissions, though it was not till the fifteenth century that many powers which had cer-tainly been exercised since the earliest times were formally conveyed to them. It will sufficiently illustrate the development to point out that the power to make war on the king's enemies and rebels, which justiciars had certainly exercised from the beginning, was first ex-pressly mentioned in a commission in 1396, and did not become a

[3] Detailed references for what follows will be found in A. J. Otway-Ruthven, 'The Chief Governors of Mediaeval Ireland', *Journ. R.S.A.I.*, XCV, pp. 227–36.
[4] *Parliaments and Councils*, no. 66; below, pp. 315–16.
[5] *Statute Rolls, Edward IV*, pt. 2, pp. 660–62.
[6] Cf. T. F. T. Plucknett, *Legislation of Edward I*, pp. 41–43.

regular feature till 1428. But on occasion in the fourteenth century a justiciar might be gravely embarrassed by the failure of his commission to specify a particular power. Thus in January 1351 the new chancellor, John of St Paul, archbishop of Dublin, a former official of the English chancery, believing that the justiciar had no power to grant charters of pardon for homicides, felonies and trespasses committed in Ireland unless it had been specially granted by his commission, refused to seal such charters. The council, considering the matter, and that time out of mind justiciars had of their own authority and by right of their office, without other warrant or power from the king, granted such charters of pardon, and that the continuous state of war in Ireland made it essential that they should be able to do so, agreed that such pardons should continue to be issued till the king signified his will, but Thomas de Rokeby, the justiciar, with the treasurer and other exchequer officials, the judges, and the rest of the council had to guarantee to indemnify the chancellor.[7]

Of the powers exercised by chief governors, the most important were the power to make war, and the associated right to proclaim the royal service—that is, to summon the tenants-in-chief either to serve in person or to pay scutage; to issue pardons; to control the royal officials in general, with power to dismiss all except the most important—usually the chancellor, treasurer, and chief justices; to do justice to all according to the laws and customs of Ireland; and in general to provide for the administration and safety of the country. They exercised the royal rights of patronage in the church, though the more valuable benefices were usually reserved to the king, and they had the rights of purveyance and prisage—that is, of taking goods whether the seller were willing or not, at a price which was often below the market rate, and was not always promptly paid—rights which, though necessary for the efficiency of government in the conditions of the middle ages, were a major grievance in both England and Ireland,[8] as well as the associated right of carriage, or compelling the provision of transport. Finally, they had the right to summon parliaments and councils and to make statutes and ordinances in them, first expressly mentioned in 1420, though it certainly existed much earlier. And all had the right to appoint deputies to exercise their functions during their absence from the country, a power extensively used by the fifteenth-century lieutenants, many of whom acted almost entirely by deputy.

[7] P.R.O. Dublin, Mem. Rolls, vol. 25, pp. 230–34. In 1377 the Irish council, noting that Ormond's commission as justiciar made no mention of charters of pardon, agreed that he should have this power (*C.C.H.*, p. 103, no. 21).

[8] See below, pp. 299, 304, 350–51.

By 1228 the justiciar's salary had been fixed at £500 a year, out of which he was obliged to maintain a force of twenty men-at-arms, and as many armoured horses. This remained the standard sum for the rest of the middle ages, but though the original theory seems to have been that this, together with the royal service due to the king, should provide for all military expenses, it was of course quite insufficient for the purpose, as was recognized by 1285 when the appointment of Stephen de Fulbourne provided that when necessary for the defence of the country money should be paid out of the exchequer to a clerk appointed by the treasurer and barons as paymaster, an arrangement which became the permanent one. By the second half of the fourteenth century the continuous state of warfare into which the country had fallen made the maintenance of a substantial standing force necessary, and chief governors were often granted the whole revenue of the country, as well as substantial sums from the English revenue, though, particularly in the fifteenth century, they found it always difficult and often impossible to obtain payment. The constant complaints that the people are ruined by their failure to pay their just debts vividly illustrate the financial difficulties in which they found themselves.[9]

From the beginning many chief governors were Anglo-Irish magnates, though from time to time, and particularly in the early fourteenth century, English administrators were sent over. But from the middle of the fourteenth century on, there was an increasing demand from the Anglo-Irish, magnates and commons alike, that the king should come to Ireland in person, or at least send some great lord of the blood royal, well provided with men and money, as his lieutenant.[10] But though serious attempts were made under both Edward III and Richard II to restore the position of the colony in this way, in the fifteenth century, though a similar policy was superficially attempted from time to time, the decadence of the English as well as the Irish revenue by this time made its total failure inevitable. Not only was Henry IV's son, Thomas of Lancaster, a mere child when appointed as lieutenant, but he was left in actual destitution for lack of payment from England: he does not seem to have possessed any marked ability, but it is hardly surprising that he governed almost entirely as an absentee by deputies.[11] Richard, duke of York, though lieutenant from 1447 to 1460, was in Ireland for less than two years during this period, and again had great difficulty in securing any payment[12]; George, duke of Clarence, lieutenant from 1462 to 1470 and from 1470 to

[9] See below, pp. 347, 351, 359, 365. [10] See below, pp. 284–5, 318, 369, 396.
[11] See below, pp. 342–7. [12] See below, pp. 318–2.

1477, never visited the country at all. It was inevitable in the circumstances that for long periods the government should be conducted by Anglo-Irish magnates acting as the deputies of absentee lieutenants, and in the Yorkist period the political circumstances which had eclipsed the Butlers left the earls of Kildare the only possible candidates.

In the performance of his functions the chief governor was from the first assisted by a council,[13] modelled on the king's council in England, but relatively more important, since the authority of justiciar or lieutenant was only a delegated one. In its early days this was inevitably, as in every feudal state, primarily of baronial composition: thus in 1205 the justiciar was ordered to wage no war against the marchers unless by advice of the subjects of the king whose fidelity and service were necessary to maintain war.[14] Some of the magnates, both lay and ecclesiastical, must always have been about the justiciar's court: should it be necessary to enlarge this nucleus, others could be summoned. Such a council varied enormously in both personnel and size, but the justiciar will never have been without counsel, which it was part of the feudal duty of a tenant-in-chief to provide when required. But in the thirteenth century the growing specialization and sophistication of Angevin government was transforming the king's council in England. The heads of the specialized governmental departments which were developing became a dominant factor and the idea of a body of defined and limited membership, the continual council which supervised all the day to day business of government, appeared, while the occasional large assemblies of tenants-in-chief were something separate, and in the course of the century became part of the new court of parliament.

The Irish council inevitably followed the same development. In Ireland as in England the council became a primarily official body, afforced from time to time by the presence of certain magnates, but necessarily dominated by the officials who had to carry out the day to day business of government. We cannot trace the early stages of this development in Ireland very fully, but from time to time in the early years of Henry III the justiciar was ordered to admit to his councils persons whom we know to have been justices or exchequer officials,[15] and before the end of the reign it was clearly assumed that the principal officials were by virtue of their office

---

[13] For the Irish council, see Richardson and Sayles, *The Irish Parliament in the Middle Ages*, chapters 3 and 12.

[14] *C.D.I.*, I, no. 268.

[15] Ibid., nos. 893, 1067, 2044 and cf. ibid., no. 1599.

members of the council without further order. The treasurer,[16] chancellor and escheator were normally present; the itinerant justices attended when available; the first known justice of the common bench was receiving an annual fee of 20 marks 'that he may be of the justiciar's council' in 1275. This must mean that he was not yet recognized as a member by right of office, but by 1302 a plea before the justices of the bench was interrupted because 'the justices left the bench and went to the council of the king as they were summoned, and they were there a long time'. By the second half of the fourteenth century it seems that not only the chancellor, treasurer, chief justices and chief baron of the exchequer were members of the council, but also the other judges, the keeper of the rolls of chancery, and sometimes other officials of less importance.[17]

From time to time other persons were appointed as members of the council and specially sworn. Thus in April 1234 Master Thomas de Craville was appointed to the council, and was to swear that he would faithfully serve the justiciar and not reveal his secrets, a development of particular interest as it coincides with the first reference to a councillor's oath in England. There seems to be no further reference to the development of the sworn council in Ireland till 1297, when two persons were described as sworn of the council; then in 1319 Philip de Slane of the order of Friars Preachers was sworn of the king's council of Ireland with an annual fee of 5 marks for life. But most of the persons specially appointed to the council had been, or would be in future, prominent officials, like Stephen, bishop of Meath, a former treasurer, appointed in 1374 as one of the king's council in Ireland with an annual fee of 100 marks during pleasure.[18]

It does not seem that anyone had a right to attend council meetings, though obviously the chancellor and treasurer, with whom the justiciar was constantly directed to act, could not well be excluded. But otherwise it seems to have been a matter for the chief governor's discretion who should be summoned to any particular meeting or to deal with any particular matter. Thus in 1317 Roger Mortimer was to consult with those of the king's council and others whom he thought fit as to the allegations against the earl of Ulster;

16 Till the end of the thirteenth century the treasurer had precedence, but after that the chancellor (Richardson and Sayles, *The Irish Parliament in the Middle Ages*, p. 28).

17 *C.D.I.*, II, p. 238; ibid., III, no. 891; *Cal. Justic. Rolls*, I, p. 417; Richardson and Sayles, loc. cit., pp. 31–33.

18 *C.D.I.*, I, no. 2105; ibid., IV, no. 441; *C.C.R., 1318–23*, p. 161; ibid., *1374–7*, p. 5; *C.C.H.*, p. 23, no. 104; *C.P.R., 1370–74*, p. 413.

in 1319 the justiciar was to assemble such as he saw fit of the king's council to discuss the request of the earl of Kildare for the grant of the king's service (i.e. for a scutage[19]); in 1338 the justiciar and chancellor were to call together those of the council whom they wished to enquire into allegations that royal rights had been improvidently alienated. It was only very occasionally that a chief governor was ordered not to act without the assent of the whole council, though this was required in 1327 for the grant of pardons for felonies and for the release of prisoners or hostages taken in the time of the late justiciar. From time to time the official council was afforced by magnates: thus in April 1294 a number were present at a council meeting in Dublin where William de Vescy, lord of Kildare, the ex-justiciar, accused John fitz Thomas of defamation, and from time to time we find individual magnates present, as were bishops, but there is no evidence that they concerned themselves with normal routine business.[20]

Since almost everything the justiciar did was in fact done in collaboration with the council, it was like him endlessly itinerant, just as the English council itinerated in attendance on the king. It had thus no fixed centre, even though in 1299 a long seat of straw was bought for the council house, presumably in Dublin castle. In 1427 and 1430 we hear of a chamber by the exchequer called 'le counsel chaumbre', and in 1431 of the council room within the castle of Dublin; ten years later it is defined as being in the king's chapel in Dublin castle. But even when the council met in Dublin, it might hold its meetings elsewhere: in Christ Church, at the archbishop's palace of St Sepulchre, in St Thomas's abbey, or in the chapter house of the friars preachers. Outside Dublin, it had of course not even the shadow of a fixed centre, but met in the most convenient church or chapter house.[21]

The clerical work of the council was probably first done by the clerks directly attached to the justiciar of whom we hear from time to time,[22] and later by chancery clerks. But in the middle of the fourteenth century we begin to find traces of a specialized clerk of

[19] Kildare had petitioned for this to finance an expedition to avenge the death of Richard de Clare (P.R.O. London, S.C. 8/119/5946; *C.C.R., 1318-23*, pp. 80, 90). See below, pp. 236-7.

[20] *C.C.R., 1313-18*, p. 469; ibid., *1318-23*, p. 90; ibid., *1327-30*, p. 134; *C.D.I.*, IV, no. 147; *Cal. Justic. Rolls*, III, pp. 238-9; Richardson and Sayles, loc. cit., pp. 25-27, 33-35.

[21] *C.D.I.*, IV, no. 589; *C.C.H.*, p. 85, no. 149; p. 148, no. 42; p. 181, no. 41; p. 205, no. 86; p. 225, no. 28; p. 243, no. 30; p. 246, no. 31; p. 252, nos. 38, 40; p. 253, no. 18; p. 260, no. 26; p. 261, no. 3; p. 262, nos. 24, 27; p. 263, no. 25; *Cal. Ormond Deeds*, III, no. 159; *Statutes, Henry VI*, p. 34.

[22] See below, pp. 155, 157.

the council. Thomas de Wodehouse, clerk, had 50 shillings in 1344 'for gratuitous service rendered to the king in his secret council', and in 1374 royal letters were read to the council by Thomas de Thelwall, clerk. It is probable that these men were already acting as clerks of the council, but the office does not seem to be mentioned by name till 1450, when Thomas Walshe, who seems to have been clerk of the council for at least eight years, was granted 10 marks yearly towards the fee of his office.[23]

The council thus constituted exercised all the powers of government in conjunction with the chief governor. No detail was too small for it; nothing not expressly reserved to the king was too great. And like the king and council in England the justiciar and council in Ireland exercised judicial functions which were clearly of great importance, though here perhaps more than anywhere else there were, as we shall see, a number of matters which could not be finally determined without reference to the king himself—to take only one example, only the king could adjudicate on matters arising out of a charter granted by himself or his ancestors. With the development of a specialized judiciary most judicial business became a matter for the professional courts of justice, but there remained always a number of cases best dealt with by the justiciar and council, whether because they concerned the quarrels of men too great to be easily dealt with elsewhere, or because they were matters for which the common law did not provide a remedy. About the middle of the fourteenth century we find that cases of this kind were beginning to be attracted to the chancery, but in Ireland it does not seem to have developed an equitable jurisdiction till the end of the middle ages. Such cases had of course usually been brought before the council by way of petition, and there were also many petitions from those aggrieved by the actions of exchequer officials, which were referred to the treasurer and barons of the exchequer with appropriate directions.[24] It was by way of petition too that such council actions as the grant of lands or the increase of official salaries were usually initiated. But it should be remembered that it was also always possible to petition the king directly, and such petitions can be shown to be the basis of most, if not all, of the grants relating to Ireland made under the English great seal, while others were referred to the appropriate authorities in Ireland.[25]

[23] *C.C.H.*, p. 44, no. 52; p. 85, no. 149; *Statutes, Henry VI*, p. 278.
[24] A large number of such petitions were enrolled on the Irish Memoranda Rolls, and survive in transcripts in the P.R.O., Dublin.
[25] A mass of such petitions survives in the series of Ancient Petitions (S.C.8) in the P.R.O., London.

In everything that they did, the chief governor and council in Ireland were of course subject to the over-riding control of the king. It is clear that close contact was kept, the usual method being for the justiciar, or the justiciar and council, to send messengers to the king, usually with reports in writing setting forth the state of the country, while the king in turn sent emissaries 'to survey the state of Ireland' or to deal with specific matters. The more important of these emissaries sat with the council while in Ireland.[26] From time to time the justiciar was summoned to England 'to certify regarding the state of Ireland', and, particularly in the thirteenth century, a constant stream of directions on specific points was sent to him under the English great seal. This appears to slacken in the fourteenth century and later, but in fact the directions continued, though now under the small seals, the privy seal, developed in the course of the thirteenth century, and the signet, developed during the later fourteenth century, the records of which have not survived.[27] There was no doubt some slackening of direct royal control in the later middle ages, but we need not suppose that it was as great as the surviving records would suggest.

It does not seem that the specialized organs of government began to develop out of the council in Ireland, the equivalent of the royal *curia* in England, till after the first generation of the conquest. Even in England only the exchequer was at all fully developed at the time, and it was natural that the exchequer should be the first to appear in Ireland. Some sort of financial organization must have been developed at an early stage, and by 1200 it was being described as the exchequer, with no suggestion that this was an innovation. But though this must mean that the characteristic exchequer system of accounting had been introduced, and there were rolls which must have been pipe rolls, and probably also memoranda rolls, there was as yet no treasurer: the justiciar seems to have been directly responsible for the revenue, with under him a clerk who was the effective head of the machinery of collection and account. It was not till 1217 that this clerk was given the title of treasurer: there was a chamberlain *eo nomine* at least two years earlier. No doubt each kept rolls of issues and receipts, for each acted as a check upon the other, and they were jointly responsible for all issues of money.

An essential feature of the exchequer organization was a court

[26] See Richardson and Sayles, loc. cit., pp. 35–36.
[27] A number of such letters which would in the thirteenth century have been under the great seal can be traced. See e.g. *Council in Ireland*, pp. xvi, 255–60, 304–5; *Grants of King Edward the Fifth*, ed. J. G. Nichols (Camden Society, 1854) pp. 71–73.

which could determine financial disputes, and we find the barons of the exchequer, who were the judges of this court, mentioned as early as 1207. But these were not as yet the class of specialized exchequer officials they were later to become: they were high officials, the treasurer and chamberlain, the chancellor when his office was developed, judges—in fact, the leading members of the council. The appointment of a special class of barons to hold the pleas of the exchequer did not begin in England till 1234; they do not appear in Ireland till 1277, and soon after this the exchequer court, originally the court in which judgements were passed on the debts of subjects to the crown, developed, as in England, a court of common law, resorted to particularly by merchants. Meanwhile, other features of the English exchequer had been added: in 1232 the chancellor's clerk who represented his master in the exchequer, keeping a roll which was a check on the pipe roll (the treasurer's roll), and also the exchequer seal, and who finally became a purely exchequer official, the chancellor of the exchequer. From 1291 there were two chamberlains, who acted as a check on each other, and, jointly, on the treasurer. By 1285 and no doubt much earlier there was a whole series of subordinate officials, corresponding to those of the English exchequer, and thereafter development continued along parallel lines.[28]

It was inevitable that the development of the second great department, the chancery, should be later. In England it was the secretarial department of the king's household, and only began to 'go out of court'—to be separated, that is, from the old undifferentiated *curia*—in the reign of Henry III. The justiciar had, of course, his own household, and his own seal, but as long as the king's chancery was as much a part of his household as were the purely domestic departments it could not be expected that he would establish a separate sealing department for Ireland, while no permanent Irish governmental institution could arise out of the households of the justiciars. It is clear, however, that in the early days the seal used in the day to day government of the country was the justiciar's own, and writs were in his name. Thus in 1204 the justiciar was granted that his writ should run throughout Ireland, and in 1207 the king in a letter to 'all of Ireland' ordered

---

[28] See H. G. Richardson and G. O. Sayles, *The Administration of Ireland, 1172–1377*, pp. 21–22, 24–27, 46–47; H. G. Richardson, 'Norman Ireland in 1212', *I.H.S.*, III, pp. 144–58. No complete study of the Irish exchequer has yet been attempted. For the revenue see below, pp. 162–8. From the reign of Edward I till the end of that of Edward III the Irish treasurer periodically accounted at the English exchequer, and this has ensured the survival of a mass of financial records.

them not to answer in any court for their free tenements except by writ of the king [i.e. from the English chancery] or the justiciar,[29] and a grant to the bishop of Limerick in 1216 is in the form of latters patent of Geoffrey de Marisco, the justiciar. In 1220 de Marisco, making an agreement with the king at Oxford, cannot put his own seal to it because 'the justiciar has committed his seal in Ireland for purposes of justice'.[30] There must, of course, have been some sort of organized writing office, though perhaps only that of the exchequer, but certainly nothing which could be called a chancery.

The separate Irish chancery began in 1232, when Henry III granted the English chancellor, Ralph Neville, bishop of Chichester, the chancery of Ireland to hold for life, with all the liberties and free customs thereto belonging. Neville nominated a deputy to execute the office in his place: having taken oath, he was to have free administration of the office of chancery and the seal; he was to be present at the justiciar's councils; he was to have a clerk at the exchequer to keep a counter-roll, and a clerk at the assizes before the justiciar to keep a roll and writs of pleas, as the chancellor had in England.[31] The writ speaks as if the chancery were already in existence, but it is most unlikely that it was, and it is fair to assume that it had to be created by Geoffrey de Turville, Neville's deputy. After Neville's death in 1244 his deputy, then Robert Luttrell, was continued as chancellor of Ireland, and from this date the office had a continuous independent existence.

The creation of an Irish chancery did not mean that the English great seal ceased to have validity in Ireland: as a seal in direct contact with the king it had exactly the same validity in Ireland as in England. In 1339 the king addressed letters close to the escheator of Kilkenny ordering him to deliver to the bishop of Ossory the temporalities of his see: the sheriff had been ordered to do so by English writ, but had refused to receive or execute it,

asserting that he will not execute it unless it comes from the chancery of Ireland under the seal used there, at which the king is much angered, chiefly because all his subjects are bound by their allegiance to obey his orders under the great seal of England.[32]

Attempts were, indeed, made in the fifteenth century to assert that men should not be summoned out of Ireland (i.e. to answer before

[29] This was directed against writs issued by lords of liberties. See below, pp. 181–7.
[30] *Early Statutes*, pp. 3–4; *The Black Book of Limerick*, pp. 57, 126; C.D.I., I, no. 949.
[31] *Close Rolls, 1231–4*, pp. 112–13.
[32] C.C.R., *1339–41*, p. 259.

the king's courts in England) by English writs,[33] but without success, and the general validity of the English great seal in Ireland was not challenged. But by the beginning of the fourteenth century it does seem to have been felt that at any rate writs of course (the writs in standard form initiating legal proceedings which could be obtained by anyone on payment of a fee) should issue from the Irish chancery. Twenty years earlier it seems, however, that such writs were still being issued by the justiciar's clerks, presumably under his seal and in his name.[34]

The organization of the Irish chancery in the thirteenth century is very obscure, since none of the rolls which were certainly compiled in this period survived the middle ages. It is clear that there was a good deal of exchequer influence, and that clerks could easily pass from one department to the other even as late as the second half of the fourteenth century. But at all stages it seems to have been under-staffed, with too few clerks, of inadequate qualifications. By the sixteenth century the Irish chancery establishment was modelled on that of England, but this seems to have been a Tudor innovation: in the earlier period there was a much less elaborate organization. About 1285 it was alleged that there was only one clerk in the chancery, who knew little of its business; some fifty years later there was only one clerk and a clerklet (*clerionnet*), who knew nothing of any business that was not of course.[35] The office of keeper of the rolls certainly existed by the second decade of the fourteenth century, though the Irish chancery rolls of the middle ages never developed the elaborate sub-divisions of the English chancery: as far as we know there were only patent and close rolls. By the end of the reign of Edward III there was a clerk of the hanaper[36] (the department which received and accounted for the fees paid for sealing), and he had presumably existed earlier, though during the thirteenth and fourteenth centuries the issues of the seal normally went to the chancellor, who was presumably expected to maintain the chancery clerks out of this income, as had been the case when a similar arrangement existed in England. Beyond these officials we know almost nothing of the organization of the chancery clerks: there seem to have been perhaps normally four senior clerks, though they do not seem to have been competent to do much more than routine work, and the Irish chancery clearly

---

[33] See below, pp. 370, 387. The motive of the parliament of 1460 was of course purely political, but such writs might be used to harass a man by his private enemies.
[34] See Richardson and Sayles, *The Administration of Ireland*, p. 16, n. 7.
[35] *C.D.I.*, III, p. 10; *Council in Ireland*, p. 320.
[36] Richardson and Sayles, *The Administration of Ireland*, p. 18, n. 3.

did not offer the dignified and progressive career that the English chancery did. English chancery clerks were sent over from time to time, particularly in the fourteenth century to serve as keepers of the rolls, but we cannot tell how far they succeeded in influencing the development of the office.[37]

Richard II's visit to Ireland in 1394–5 produced an attempt to reorganize the Irish chancery, bringing it more into line with that of England. When a new chancellor, the bishop of Meath, was appointed in June 1395, his patent reserved to the king 'all issues and profits of the great seal there, usually received heretofore by the chancellor', and granted him instead, in addition to his regular salary of £40, an annual sum of £80 for the expenses of the chancery establishment: he was required

by ordinance of the king and council to find a keeper of the rolls of chancery, and other clerks for the said chancery, and to have them at his table, and whilst they are on eyre to find the cost of their horses, one clerk being assigned by the chancellor as keeper of the hanaper.

At the same time it was ordered that he should normally remain in Dublin: if he were obliged to leave it to attend on the lieutenant or justiciar he might, if prevented from doing so by infirmity or other cause, send the great seal to them by 'some sufficient person for whom he will answer for doing and executing what he himself would do if personally present'.[38] The arrangement as to the expenses of the chancery establishment was continued throughout the fifteenth century, with variations in the sums granted, but the chancellor seems to have been no more fixed in Dublin than before, though as the area directly controlled by the Dublin government shrank his journeyings were progressively limited.

It is hard to say how far the chancery had any fixed headquarters during the middle ages. We hear that in the early fourteenth century there was a place near Dublin castle where the pleas of all the king's courts, including the chancery, were accustomed to be held,[39] but in fact the chancery was endlessly itinerant, usually in attendance on the chief governor.[40] Even during a campaign the chancellor was often in attendance on the justiciar or lieutenant, and there are several fourteenth-century grants empowering him to maintain soldiers at the king's wages for the purpose. But they were of course sometimes separated, and such separations had in

---

[37] Ibid., pp. 14–21; J. Otway-Ruthven, 'The Mediaeval Irish Chancery', *Album Helen Maud Cam* (Louvain-Paris, 1961), II, pp. 119–38.

[38] *C.P.R., 1391–6*, pp. 602, 607.

[39] P.R.O. London, S.C. 8/118/5881. See below, p. 238.

[40] The printed calendar often omits the place at which letters were dated (it is of course possible that the original rolls did not always give the place).

England brought about the development first of the privy seal, and then when it too followed the chancery out of court, the signet, as instruments which remained part of the household and were always immediately available to the king. Letters under these small seals might have original force, conveying the king's orders directly to officials or others, or they might be warrants for the issue of instruments under the great seal, or for payments out of the exchequer.

No precisely parallel development could take place in Ireland, for no permanent official sealing department could be evolved from the households of constantly changing chief governors. But the same necessity existed, and in any case chancellors no doubt wanted warrants which they could show if necessary. By the early fourteenth century, and no doubt earlier, chancery instruments were being warranted by bill of the justiciar, and in 1351 the council stated that time out of mind charters of pardon had been sealed in the chancery by bills of justiciars sealed with their seals, while in 1343 Christ Church had paid 2 shillings to 'the justiciar's privy clerk for a bill of *supersedeas* directed to the clerks of the chancery'.[41] We can reasonably suppose that letters with original force were also issued under the private seals of chief governors, but there is no evidence of this in surviving records.[42] The problem of judicial writs—those which the courts of law needed to issue during the progress of a case—was a little different, since apart from the court attendant on the justiciar they were either fixed in Dublin, or if those of the itinerant justices might be fixed elsewhere for a long time. In August 1344 it was ordered that judicial seals should be made, and their custody was granted to Robert de Scardeburgh, just appointed chief justice of the justiciar's bench, but seven years later the seals had neither been made nor delivered to him.[43] It seems that the difficulty was met by the use of the exchequer seal, for in 1351 the treasurer and chancellor of the exchequer were forbidden to seal any judicial writs except those concerning the pleas of the exchequer as long as the great seal of the chancery was within twenty miles of the exchequer; the chancellor was to have the sealing of such writs as was customary in England. Finally, from 1375 on the judges were authorized to issue such writs without

[41] P.R.O. Dublin, Mem. Rolls, vol. 25, pp. 230–34 (see above, p. 146); *Account Roll of Holy Trinity*, p. 44. C. 1285 it was alleged that 'not only clerks of chancery but clerks of the justiciar take excessive fines for writing writs' (*C.D.I.*, III, p. 10), and in 1393 a clerk speaks of his service with the bishop of Meath, justiciar, as keeper of his privy seal (*Council in Ireland*, p. 113).

[42] In 1423 the council was hesitant about accepting Edmund Mortimer's appointment of a deputy under his own seal (*C.C.H.*, p. 232, no. 1).

[43] *Cal. Fine Rolls*, 1337–47, p. 387; *C.C.R., 1343–6*, pp. 455, 461; P.R.O. Dublin, Mem. Rolls, vol. 25, pp. 591–2.

seals, reserving the fee for the seal to the chancellor or the hanaper.[44]

It would seem that in the early days of the colony the justiciar's *curia* was the sole source of centralized justice, and probably the main bulk of judicial work was done in the county courts, which will be described later.[45] On occasion the justiciar presided over a county court: thus, probably in 1199, the enemies of William le Brun were bound to keep the peace to him in the county court of Dublin before the justiciar. This simple structure was inevitable, since at the time of the Norman conquest of Ireland judicial specialization was only just beginning within the *curia regis* in England. The references to the king's court in Ireland which occur from time to time during the reign of John are no doubt to the court held before the justiciar. But from time to time justices were appointed, perhaps only to deal with a single case: thus in 1204 four persons, one a magnate and the others royal administrators, were appointed to deal with the quarrels between Meiler fitz Henry and William de Burgo, and in 1207 reference is made to the justices whom the king or the justiciar may send to administer law.[46]

The establishment of a continuous specialized judiciary in Ireland has been attributed with a certain plausibility to John's visit to Ireland in 1210, since later tradition said that John enjoined the laws and customs of England to be kept in Ireland 'when he was last in that land'.[47] It is possible that during his short stay in Ireland John did appoint itinerant justices: at all events what seems to be the first reference to them in Ireland occurs in the pipe roll of 1212, though this solitary reference to an eyre may well mean that it had taken place a number of years earlier, for had it been very recent one would expect many amercements to have been still due.[48] Between 1217 and 1221 we hear of the king's court at Limerick; in 1218 justices itinerant seem to have been working in Ulster, and in 1221 the institution was finally organized: we hear that there was only one justice itinerant in Ireland, and that this was the custom of the country, an unsatisfactory one, for it was not the custom for a single justice to keep a record, and in any case duplicate rolls were desirable. Two more justices were therefore to be associated with the existing justice itinerant, a knight

---

[44] *C.C.R., 1349–54*, p. 293; *C.C.H.*, p. 94, no. 154; p. 137, no. 230; p. 141, nos. 208–9; p. 176, no. 160; p. 203, no. 38. For the judicial aspect of the chancery, see below, p. 172. For the late medieval chancery in general, see J. Otway-Ruthven, 'The Mediaeval Irish Chancery', loc. cit. To the list of chancellors on p. 134 add: 1441, 27 February, Richard Wogan (*C.P.R., 1436–41*, p. 514).

[45] See below, pp. 173–4, 177.

[46] *C.D.I.*, I, nos. 101, 116, 126, 209, 352.

[47] Elrington Ball, *The Judges in Ireland*, I, pp. 3–4; *Early Statutes*, p. 21.

[48] *Pipe Roll, 14 John*, p. 18.

and a clerk, Thomas fitz Adam and Bartholomew of the chamber, both of whom had been much engaged in administration in Ireland since the time of John. This was not really the appointment of new justices, for fitz Adam had certainly been acting as a justice earlier, but rather a reform of procedure, and thereafter an establishment of three justices sitting together seems to be normal.[49]

The itinerant justices are the only kind of which we hear during the first half of the thirteenth century. They held their eyres throughout the country, presumably functioning much as in England, till the early fourteenth century, when, as in England, the eyre of justices commissioned to hold all pleas, the characteristic feature of the general eyre, faded out.[50] At the beginning of the period they tended to be royal administrators rather than professional lawyers, but by the second half of the thirteenth century, as in England, the judges had become professionals. In the intervals between eyres they sat at Dublin, and from 1248 we hear frequently of the king's justices in the bench at Dublin, but this is not yet a separate court: as far as our evidence goes there is only one body of judges, and the sessions of the court at Dublin must have been suspended when they went on eyre elsewhere in the country. It is not till 1274 that we find the bench at Dublin with a distinct body of judges of its own, and throughout the reign of Edward I there is still no clear-cut division between justices itinerant and justices of the bench, the same men serving indifferently in one or other capacity.[51] Nevertheless the bench, the court of common pleas, was now in existence as a distinct court.

Meanwhile, the justiciar's court, which was later to develop into the chief place, the equivalent of the English king's bench, had of course had a continuous existence, and itinerated with the justiciar. In December 1222 Roger Huscarl, a judge of the English bench, was sent to Ireland 'to attend with the justiciar to the king's affairs and pleas', and the justiciar was ordered to admit him to his councils. He sat with the justiciar in the trial which deprived Walter de Lacy of his right to try the pleas of the crown in Meath, probably in 1223,[52] and he appears presiding over assizes at Drogheda in an undated deed. In 1225 he had a grant of 20 librates of land in Ireland during pleasure, to maintain him in the king's service, and later a grant of £20 a year at the exchequer. He had returned to

---

[49] *Monastic and Episcopal Deeds*, p. 226; *C.D.I.*, I, nos. 833, 985; Richardson and Sayles, loc. cit., p. 30.
[50] See the lists in Richardson and Sayles, loc. cit., pp. 132–47. In 1246–7 the eyre was in Ulster (*Cal. Gormanston Register*, p. 160).
[51] Richardson and Sayles, loc. cit., pp. 31–33, 34–35.
[52] For the liberty of Meath, see below, pp. 181–2, 185–6, 187.

England by 1227, and we do not know what was done to provide professional advice for the justiciar's court after this, but it would seem that it was supplied by the itinerant justices, and from at least 1270 one of them in particular was closely associated with the justiciar. It was not however till 1286 that any judge was specifically named and paid to hear the pleas which follow the justiciar, and thereafter there was a regular succession, though it is not till 1324 that we find a second justice of the justiciar's bench.[53]

Meanwhile, as in England, much justice was done locally by persons working under more limited commissions. We cannot trace them before the reign of Edward I, but they cannot then have been an innovation, and from the 1270s on there are constant references to commissions of gaol delivery and commissions of assize, sometimes held by the professional judges, either alone or in association with others, and sometimes by persons who were not professional judges at all. Regular circuits of justices of assize seem to have been organized as in England, though we also find commissions to take a single assize even in the fifteenth century. But long before this the commissions of oyer and terminer which can be traced in Ireland to the beginning of the fourteenth century and had no doubt been issued earlier had become the most usual form.[54]

It will be apparent from all this that the activity of officials of the central government permeated the whole area controlled by it. Apart from the exchequer and the common bench, which were normally at Dublin, though they were removed to Carlow in 1361 and remained there till 1394,[55] there was no fixed centre of government. The chief governor, though he might remain fixed at Dublin for considerable periods, was constantly journeying through the country, attended by the council, by the 'court which followed the justiciar', the later chief place or court of king's bench, and often by the chancery. Justices acting under the various commissions held sessions throughout the country. Though the exchequer was fixed, its officials were not, and were constantly being sent out 'to hasten the levy of the king's debts', or on other exchequer business:

[53] C.D.I., I, nos. 1065–7, 1271–2, 1295; Chart. St. Mary's, I, p. 64; Richardson and Sayles, loc. cit., pp. 33–38.
[54] For the various commissions, see W. S. Holdsworth, A History of English Law, I (7th edn., ed. A. L. Goodhart and H. G. Hanbury), pp. 265–76. The commission of assize gave only a very limited civil jurisdiction, to try the actions concerning land covered by the assizes introduced under Henry II; the commission of gaol delivery empowered the commissioners to try the persons confined in a certain gaol; the commission of oyer and terminer gave power to try either all crimes committed in a specified area, or certain classes of crime only. The evidence for these commissions in Ireland has not been dealt with in print: much of it will be found in C.C.H., Cal. Justic. Rolls, and Cat. Pipe Rolls.
[55] See below, pp. 287, 327.

thus on 15 October 1352 one of the barons and the second chamberlain were appointed with William de Barton, the chief engrosser, to 'supervise the levy of arrears of debts throughout Ireland', and Barton was continuously so engaged till 18 April 1353.[56] And there was the constant activity of one important member of the central government not so far mentioned, the escheator.

The escheator was the official who had charge of all lands temporarily in the king's hand, whether through forfeiture (such lands were usually speedily regranted), because of the minority of the heir of a tenant-in-chief, or because of the vacancy of a bishopric or abbey. The income from these sources naturally varied considerably from year to year, but in the thirteenth century it formed a substantial part of the revenue, and the escheator was, after the treasurer and chancellor, a leading member of the council. Till the middle of the century escheats seem to have been normally in the custody of the justiciar, but from 1250 there is a regular succession of escheators, who during the period when the future Edward I was lord of Ireland during his father's lifetime answered directly to the king for the temporalities of vacant bishoprics and abbeys, which he had reserved to himself.[57]

The kind of activity in which the escheator was involved is well suggested by a writ of 1290 which speaks of his expenses in

the custody of castles, manors, and heirs in the king's hand, difficult marches, fighting against rebels, proceeding to and remaining in the said marches, castles, manors and lands with an armed force, loss of horses . . .[58]

It was his duty to take possession of the land on behalf of the king, and to hold what might be a whole series of inquisitions to establish its exact value (the widow's dower would be based on this, and also the division of the estate if it passed to co-heiresses) and the identity and age of the next heir. If the heir were of full age he would be ordered to give him seisin of the land, and his duties ended there; if not, until the heir came of age or the wardship was granted to someone else the escheator was responsible for the maintenance and defence of the property and the maintenance of the heir in a manner fitted to his position.[59] He was frequently ordered to hold inquisitions *ad quod damnum*, usually to ascertain if it would be prejudicial to the king if land were granted to a religious house; he was often an itinerant justice; and he might attend the justiciar or

---

[56] P.R.O. Dublin, Mem. Rolls, vol. 26, pp. 602-3, 605.
[57] See Richardson and Sayles, *The Administration of Ireland*, pp. 27-29.
[58] *C.D.I.*, III, no. 730.
[59] In the case of a bishopric or abbey the escheator had custody till the successor was accepted by the king, when he was directed to restore the temporalities.

the treasurer in his progresses. Thus in 1276 the escheator was allowed the expenses incurred in accompanying the bishop of Waterford, then treasurer, in Ulster, 'to see the state of the land and hold assizes there'.[60] He had an annual fee of £40, with 40s. a year for robes, but might make a good deal in addition to this: in 1346 the subprior of Christ Church brought a writ of *supersedeas* to the escheator, and paid him 20s. for executing it, with 4s. to two of his clerks *ex curialitate*.[61] By the end of the reign of Edward III, when the prestige of the office was clearly declining, it was regularly combined with that of clerk of the markets and keeper of weights and measures, whose duty it was to enforce all regulations about weights and measures, and whose activities led to such complaints that in 1363 they were suspended for a year,

as the king has learned that the people of Ireland suffer much hurt by the frequent visits of the inspectors there deputed, who more for gain and extortion than for the advantage of the king and people come in divers parts divers times in the year at will, and commit divers extortions, hardships, grievances and excesses.[62]

In the performance of these functions, spread all over the country, the escheator employed deputies, or sub-escheators, and must have done so from the first, though the state of the records does not allow us to trace them beyond the 1270s. In 1344 it was ordered that each sheriff should exercise the office of escheator in his county, and this arrangement, which must have deprived the escheator of effective control, was continued for some years, but was abandoned later in the century.[63]

By the second half of the fourteenth century the revenue from the escheatry was unimportant, but in the thirteenth century it had been an important, though fluctuating, part of the total income. The Irish revenue, like the English, can be described under six main heads: the income from the king's feudal rights, much, but not all, of which was collected and accounted for by the escheator; 'rents of assize'—fixed annual payments of various kinds, principally the rents of the demesne lands and the farm rents of the towns; the profits of the county courts; the profits of justice; the customs, in and after the reign of Edward I; and finally general taxation.[64]

We have nothing which would enable us to form any estimate of the average Irish revenue before the reign of Edward I: the only

[60] *36th Rep. D.K.*, p. 33, and see ibid., pp. 61–62.
[61] *38th Rep. D.K.*, p. 82; *53rd Rep. D.K.*, p. 43; *Account Roll of Holy Trinity*, pp. 110–11.
[62] *C.C.R., 1360–64*, p. 488.
[63] *C.C.R., 1343–6*, p. 455.
[64] See *Cat. Pipe Rolls, passim*.

thing of which we can be certain is that during this period it was possible for the crown to draw very substantial sums from Ireland.[65] In the reign of Edward I the records become more informative, and an analysis of the sums received by the treasurer shows that between 1278 and 1299 they amounted to an annual average of £6,300, which between 1299 and 1315 fell to £4,190, a figure which conceals a fairly steady decline throughout the period. Thereafter the decline was continuous, though in the 1360s a recovery began, which produced a slight but significant increase in the annual average, which was, however, still less than half of what it had been in the later thirteenth century.[66]

Much detailed work remains to be done before we can arrive at the reality which lies behind such figures. But one late thirteenth-century analysis of the sources of Irish revenue has survived,[67] though it deals with only a part of them: the profits of the counties, rents of assize, royal service, the prisage of wines, and the customs. The profits of the counties amounted c. 1284 to £265 7s. 6d.: they represent the profits of justice in the county courts, and no more need be said of them. The rents of assize, which included the fee farm rents of the cities—Dublin, Waterford, Cork, Limerick and Drogheda—as well as the demesne manors and the rents of certain other lands, were estimated at the very substantial sum of £2,476; a scutage at £837. The prisage of wines was not estimated in money, but the customs were valued at 2,000 marks (£1,333 6s. 8d.).

To take first the strictly feudal rights, those which arose from the king's position as overlord of feudal tenants, a great part of the income which arose was dealt with, as we have seen, by the escheator. The reliefs paid by heirs who were of full age when they succeeded were paid directly into the exchequer (in most cases having been collected by the sheriffs): the total amount obviously fluctuated greatly from year to year, but can never have been very large.[68] The aids, assistance in money given by the tenant to his lord, are best considered in connection with taxation in general.[69] But scutages, the commutation paid by a military tenant instead of service in person, were of very considerable importance in Ireland. About 1284 they were, as we have seen, estimated at £837, which 'the king can have whenever there is war': a little later it would have

---

[65] J. F. Lydon, 'Edward II and the Revenues of Ireland in 1311–12', *I.H.S.*, XIV, pp. 39–57.
[66] H. G. Richardson and G. O. Sayles, 'Irish Revenue, 1278–1384', *Proc. R.I.A.*, LXII C, pp. 87–100.
[67] *C.D.I.*, II, no. 2329.
[68] The amounts had been fixed by the Great Charter at 40s. for a knight's fee and £100 for a barony.   [69] See below, pp. 166–8.

amounted to about £850. Usually, of course, some of the lands owing these services will have been in the king's hand because of minorities, but in such a case the exchequer demanded the payment of scutage from all the military sub-tenants, which in the case of one of the great liberties would substantially increase the total received by the crown, since they had many more knight's fees than were required to perform their bare quota of service.[70] On the other hand, this revenue was not always easy to collect, and clearly declined considerably from the later fourteenth century on: in 1372 the exchequer was ordered not to enforce the payment of scutage for lands 'now by the Irish rebels wasted and occupied'.[71] But a sum of not far short of £1,000 was a substantial item in the Irish revenue, and scutages were levied with great frequency: the evidence for the first half of the thirteenth century is inadequate, but we know of at least six between 1254 and 1272, while Edward I was only lord of Ireland; there were eighteen between 1272 and 1307; five under Edward II; twelve between 1327 and 1377; five under Richard II; twelve at least during the fifteenth century.[72] It is clear that scutages were a more important feature of the Irish revenue than has been generally realized.

We have nowhere any estimate of the profits of justice: they included not only the fees payable for writs, the amercements (the equivalent of the modern fine) imposed in the course of legal proceedings, and the chattels of felons confiscated to the crown—sums which, though usually individually small, might amount to a considerable total—but also fines, theoretically voluntary payments made to secure some favour, such as a charter of pardon. That they were at any rate believed to be of very considerable potential value is shown by fourteenth-century statements that the justiciar was no longer able to hold his sessions, 'by the profits of which the wars used to be maintained'.[73] The 'rents of assize' need no particular comment; the customs—the 'great and ancient custom' levied on the export of wool, wool-fells and hides from all the ports of Ireland, including those within liberties, which had its basis in the right of the king to control movement into and out of the land, but was first put on a regularly profitable basis under Edward I—were clearly of great importance in this reign, but declined in the fourteenth century.[74]

[70] See J. Otway-Ruthven, 'Knight Service in Ireland', *Journ. R.S.A.I.*, LXXXIX, pp. 5–6.
[71] *C.C.R., 1369–74*, pp. 380–81.
[72] In the thirteenth century a 'half service'—i.e. a scutage at 20s. a fee instead of 40s.—was sometimes taken (*Cal. Gormanston Reg.*, p. 13).
[73] See below, p. 284.   [74] For the customs revenue, see *Cat. Pipe Rolls, passim.*

These were the main sources of the ordinary revenue (general taxation, which was of course only occasional, will be considered later), and as we have seen, in the thirteenth century, and even in the early fourteenth, they brought in substantial sums, which left a surplus to be sent to the king. But already in the reign of Edward II it was becoming apparent that the Irish government was being starved of the financial resources which it needed,[75] and after this period the revenue, already declining at the beginning of the century, fell steadily, apart from a slight improvement in the 1360s, to an annual average of just under £2,500 between 1368 and 1384.[76] We must suppose that the decline continued as the area in which Anglo-Irish government was effective shrank, and at just this time a new factor further reduced the amounts actually received by the treasurer. From the reign of Richard II onwards there was a growing tendency to intercept revenue at its source by granting items of the ordinary revenue either to officials in payment or part payment of their salaries, to cities for the repair and maintenance of their walls, or simply to favoured individuals. A statement of the sources of Irish revenue prepared c. 1406, of which only fragments have survived, shows almost everything it lists as either granted away, or else unobtainable because of rebellion[77]; the process seems to have been greatly accelerated while Talbot was lieutenant under Henry V[78]; and in 1485 the first detailed statement of the Irish revenue to survive shows a total revenue of just under £2,000, of which only £185 12s. 8d. had not been intercepted at its source.[79] It seems clear that this had in fact been the position throughout the fifteenth century, and the grants to chief governors of all the revenues of Ireland thus meant in practice little more than the proceeds of scutages, with such grants of extraordinary taxation as they could secure.

It is instructive to compare the revenue of 1485 with that of two hundred years earlier.[80] The fee farm rents of the cities were unchanged, but had all been granted away. Other 'rents of assize' had not only been granted away, but in spite of the addition to the royal manors of the Mortimer lands of the house of York showed a catastrophic decline, amounting to only £532 as against £2,082 in 1284. This was due partly to heavy reductions in the sums at which manors were assessed, and partly to the disappearance from

[75] See below, pp. 220–21.
[76] Richardson and Sayles, 'Irish Revenue, 1278–1384', loc. cit.
[77] Trinity College, Cambridge, MS O. 8. 13. See below, p. 343.
[78] See *Rotuli Selecti, passim.*
[79] *Analecta Hibernica*, X, pp. 17–28.
[80] See above, p. 163.

the list of lands in Munster and Connacht, and even of the demesne lands in the modern co. Wicklow. The customs revenue had all been granted away, and amounted to no more than £500 as against the earlier 2,000 marks. The profits of the counties have disappeared; the king's feudal rights are not mentioned, and there was no scutage in this year. The profits of the courts amounted to £152, all granted to officials towards their fees; £26 13s. 4d. from the hanaper went to the chancellor. There was left to the lieutenant only £5 from the lordship of Meath; £94 15s. 9½d. from the mint; and £80 16s. 10½d. from the Dublin and Meath lands of the absentee earl of Ormond.[81] The account goes on to relate that a total of £1,064 was formerly receivable from Connacht, Munster and Ulster, besides £21,333 which it alleges was formerly received by the earl of Ulster from Ulster and Connacht.

All this meant that in the fourteenth and fifteenth centuries extraordinary taxation became of increasing importance. As in every feudal state, it originated in the obligation of the vassal to assist his lord when the lord could show that a state of necessity existed. Added to this was the right of a lord to exact tallages, payments originally arbitrarily taken by the lord without any basis of consent from his demesne lands, including the chartered towns on those lands. By the later thirteenth century the towns were, however, being included in the general aid-paying, consenting community. And finally, by the thirteenth century old clerical immunities from secular taxation were being eroded all over western Europe, and very early in the century we find some at least of the Irish clergy contributing to aids.[82]

The known history of extraordinary taxation in Ireland begins in 1204, when John appealed to both clergy and laity for an aid to recover his duchy of Normandy. It seems that he obtained one, though we do not know what form it took. In 1207 there was a further general tax, a levy of a thirteenth on personal property, assessed by itinerant justices, in both England and Ireland: it seems that this must have been consented to by the Anglo-Irish barons present at the council at Oxford which granted it for England. In 1210 there was again an aid in both England and Ireland, this time based on land, to meet the expenses of John's expedition to Ireland, and there was a second aid in Ireland, apparently in 1211. The first seems to have been levied as a carucage; the second perhaps

---

[81] There must have been a regular income from the lands of absentees (see below, p. 296), but so many exemptions were granted that its total must usually have been small.

[82] Richardson and Sayles, *The Irish Parliament in the Middle Ages*, pp. 45–46, 48–49.

as a scutage.[83] It is impossible to tell what the total yield of any of these levies was, but no doubt much if not all of it was remitted to the king.[84] We need not trace the taxes which were levied on a number of occasions during the reign of Henry III: with the exception of the taxation of the clergy by means of grants from the pope in 1226, 1254, and 1266 they were of the same general type and clearly sanctioned by feudal custom. But during the century, starting at least as early as 1207, there was developed in Ireland a system of levying royal subsidies locally for local purposes which was not found in England, and which was to be of great importance in the later financial history of Ireland: many of the campaigns of the fourteenth century and later were at least partly financed by these local subsidies, presumably granted in the county courts.[85]

In the reign of Edward I subsidies continued to be granted to the king for his general purposes, in 1292 and 1300, the reluctance of the clergy being overcome by enlisting the aid of the papacy.[86] Even as late as the 1330s the community of the land of Ireland was granting subsidies for the king's Scottish war.[87] After this, however, the necessities of the country swallowed up all that could be obtained in this way, and after the middle of the fourteenth century substantial contributions from the English exchequer were required.[88] A general pattern of taxation in Ireland for Irish purposes was very slowly worked out: in the fourteenth century there is a strong tendency for different communities to make grants at different rates in the same assembly, and even a parliamentary grant may be limited to certain parts of the country only. As late as 1346 the collection of a subsidy from the clergy of the province of Cashel was strenuously opposed on the grounds that no prelate of the province had consented. Under William of Windsor relatively very heavy taxation was attempted, provoking a storm of opposition,[89] and no further attempt was made to obtain general taxation till 1380, after which a regular pattern of parliamentary subsidies was

---

[83] Richardson and Sayles, loc. cit., pp. 48–50. I am not entirely convinced by their argument as to the basis of the second aid: the evidence is slight and seems susceptible of other explanations. In any case there were in Leinster not the 125 fees they suggest, but about 180 (see J. Otway-Ruthven, 'Knights' Fees in Kildare, Leix and Offaly', *Journ. R.S.A.I.*, XCI, p. 164).

[84] See J. F. Lydon, 'Edward II and the Revenues of Ireland in 1311–12', *I.H.S.*, XIV, p. 41.

[85] See Richardson and Sayles, *The Irish Parliament in the Middle Ages*, pp. 51, 115–18, 238–43.

[86] Ibid., p. 67. For the clergy in 1291 see also J. A. Watt, 'English Law and the Irish Church: the Reign of Edward I', *Medieval Studies Presented to Aubrey Gwynn, S.J.*, pp. 157–8.

[87] Richardson and Sayles, *The Irish Parliament in the Middle Ages*, p. 67.

[88] Ibid., p. 111.   [89] See below, pp. 299–300

established. By the end of Henry V's reign it seems that the tradition that subsidies should not exceed 700 marks (£466 13s. 4d.) in any one year, the sum which was certainly customary later in the fifteenth century, was already established, as well as an elaborate system of dividing this total among the counties, and between the clergy, laity and towns of each county.[90] It was no doubt the continuance of local taxation which made the sum obtainable by general taxation so small.

By the later fourteenth century general taxation had become a parliamentary matter, but as we have seen this had not always been so, nor had parliament any necessary connection with taxation, or with representation, in its origins. In the thirteenth century rulers all over western Europe had begun to hold special formal sessions of their courts, to which the name *parliamentum*, originally a colloquialism, was eventually applied.[91] In England at any rate these sessions seem originally to have had a judicial purpose, developing, it has been suggested, out of the mass of financial cases arising from the anarchy of the war at the end of John's reign, which needed some tribunal of general authority to deal with them.[92] In 1258 the Provisions of Oxford, the result of the triumph of the English barons in their struggle with Henry III, which were to be applied also to Ireland,[93] laid down that there were to be three parliaments a year, to be attended by the councillors, 'to treat of the common business of the realm and of the king'. Though the Provisions were swept away with the final defeat of the baronial party at Evesham in 1265, it can hardly be coincidence that the first parliament we hear of in Ireland met in 1264, and though we cannot tell if they were regularly organized at this time, twenty-one can be traced during the reign of Edward I.[94]

The essential element in these early parliaments was the council, normally strengthened by the summons of magnates, both lay and ecclesiastical. It was no doubt the very small number of really great lay tenants in Ireland that led to the summons of some quite minor tenants-in-chief as well as some of the greater sub-tenants. So constituted Irish parliaments dealt with judicial matters, and occasionally produced legislation,[95] while much administrative

[90] Richardson and Sayles, loc. cit., pp. 234–8.

[91] H. G. Richardson, 'The Origins of Parliament', *Trans. R. Hist. Soc.*, Series IV, XI, pp. 137–83.

[92] J. E. A. Jolliffe, 'Some Factors in the Beginnings of Parliament', ibid., XXII, pp. 101–39.

[93] Proclamation of the king's adhesion to the Provisions was to be made in Ireland as well as England (*Foedera*, I, p. 378).

[94] Richardson and Sayles, loc. cit., pp. 333–4.

[95] Ibid., pp. 58, 60, 63–66, 290–93.

business was discussed by the council in parliament. But it was not till 1300 that a demand for taxation was made in an assembly which we know to have been a parliament, and this inaugurated a far-reaching change in the composition of Irish parliaments, though it was long before it was completed.

Apart from the obligatory aids which the feudal tenant must pay when the occasion arose,[96] no freeman could be taxed without his consent. This was simple enough where the magnates were concerned: there were not so many in either England or Ireland that they could not be assembled, presented with a statement of the king's necessity, and induced to make a grant, while during the first half of the thirteenth century the principle that, provided all had been duly summoned, both the absent and a dissenting minority at the assembly were bound by the consent of the majority had been securely established. But though at the beginning of the century it seems to have been held that the sub-tenant was sufficiently bound by the consent of his lord, who was assumed to represent him, this no longer held good in the second half of the century, while the position of the towns, which were everywhere growing in wealth and importance, was a further difficulty. Everywhere in western Europe rulers whose financial needs were steadily growing faced the problem of gaining the assent of new classes of society to taxation, and everywhere the problem was finally solved in the same way. It was of course possible to approach communities individually, and indeed this was what was ultimately done in Ireland in 1300.[97] But it was more satisfactory for the ruler to obtain consent in a central assembly, and the general western European solution, pioneered by pope Innocent III at the beginning of the thirteenth century,[98] was to require communities to send proctors or representatives, with full power to assent on their behalf to whatever was decided by the assembly. By the end of the century the procedure had been fully worked out, and when taxation was to be asked for, communities in many parts of western Europe were being required to send to central assemblies proctors equipped with *plena potestas* to assent on their behalf.[99]

[96] In England, and consequently in Ireland, these were, in addition to scutage, the knighting of the lord's eldest son, the first marriage of his eldest daughter, and his own ransom.　　　　[97] Richardson and Sayles, loc. cit., pp. 67–68.

[98] See Gaines Post, *Studies in Medieval Legal Thought* (Princeton University Press, 1964), pp. 85–88. For the very important part played by the church in the dissemination of representative theory, see also M. V. Clarke, *Medieval Representation and Consent*, chapter xiii.

[99] See Gaines Post, loc. cit., pp. 91–162. For England, see J. G. Edwards, 'The *Plena Potestas* of English Parliamentary Representatives', *Oxford Essays in Medieval History presented to H. E. Salter*; for Ireland, J. F. Lydon, 'William of Windsor and the Irish Parliament', *E.H.R.*, LXXX, pp. 252–67.

Communities might of course be summoned to send representatives on occasions when taxation was not required, and might be summoned to assemblies which were not formally parliaments. Thus in Ireland in 1254 representatives of towns, shires and liberties seem to have been summoned with the magnates to a meeting which was not a parliament to have the king's request for an aid expounded to them. In 1297 representatives of the counties and liberties were summoned to the Irish parliament, and in 1299 representatives of the towns[100] : on neither occasion was there any question of taxation. The king, or his representative, was entitled to seek counsel from anyone he liked, whenever he liked. But it was the necessity of gaining consent to taxation, and the fact that this was most conveniently obtained in parliaments, that in the long run, rather later in Ireland than in England, made the commons first a normal and then a necessary part of every parliament.

It does not appear that the summons of the commons to Irish parliaments became invariable till after the middle of the fourteenth century (in England they were summoned to every parliament after 1330), but by the end of the reign of Edward III they had an established place, and had been joined by the clerical proctors, representatives of the lower clergy, who had been summoned to English parliaments till 1341, but had in England succeeded in asserting a right to tax themselves separately in their own assemblies. In Ireland it seems that the consent of the prelates had been considered to bind their clergy, whom they had perhaps consulted in diocesan assemblies, but in 1371 proctors of the lower clergy were summoned to a parliament, for the first time, so far as we know, and thereafter they became a regular part of Irish parliaments.[101]

By this time the medieval Irish parliament was taking on its final form, which differed in some respects from that of the English parliament. By the reign of Richard II the notion of a defined and limited class of peers of parliament had appeared in Ireland, with the result that far fewer lay magnates were summoned by individual writ, while the number of heads of religious houses summoned also tended to shrink steadily, largely as a result of claims for exemption by abbots and priors themselves. Lay magnates, on the other hand, were by the fifteenth century eagerly seeking parliamentary peerages and jealous of their precedence.[102] And long before this, by the reign of Richard II, the peers had become integrated with

[100] See Richardson and Sayles, loc. cit., pp. 53, 61.
[101] See M. V. Clarke, loc. cit., chapter iv; J. F. Lydon, 'The Irish Church and Taxation in the Fourteenth Century', *I.E.R.*, CIII, pp. 158–65.
[102] See Richardson and Sayles, loc. cit., chapter 9.

the council in parliament, a development which had taken place in England in the second decade of the fourteenth century, and were recognizably the later house of lords. A peculiar feature of the Irish system, not found in England, was the practice of amercing those who absented themselves from parliaments when summoned, applied intermittently to all classes summoned throughout the period.[103] Below the peers were the representatives of the commons: shires, liberties,[104] and towns, who had by the reign of Richard II become a regular part of parliaments, and who had from the later thirteenth century been summoned to come with *plena potestas* from their constituents.[105] To these we must add from 1371 on the clerical proctors, who did not coalesce with the commons, but formed a separate 'house' of their own, and were also required to come with *plena potestas*. The numbers summoned steadily shrank during the middle ages: in the early fourteenth century as many as ninety laymen might be summoned by individual writ, but by the end of the fifteenth century there were only fifteen temporal peers. The majority of the thirty-two Irish bishops seem usually to have been summoned, but by no means all of them attended; something under twenty heads of religious houses seem to have been summoned in the 1370s, but by the middle of the fifteenth century this had been reduced to six. As for the commons, the maximum number of counties and liberties was fourteen,[106] and the maximum number of towns twelve. As the area controlled by the central government shrank so, inevitably, did their numbers. As for the clerical proctors, there should theoretically have been two from each diocese, with two for the cathedral clergy in some places: in fact in the fifteenth century there seems to have been something under thirty.

As we have seen, in the course of the fourteenth century parliamentary taxation had become an established institution, though side by side with it local taxation continued. Legislation became more frequent in the later middle ages, but it was 'with rare exceptions . . . unimportant and ephemeral, designed to solve an im-

[103] Richardson and Sayles, loc. cit., chapter 10. Their argument for the Irish origin of the *Modus Tenendi Parliamentum* is based partly on this sytem of amercements, which is one of its features, and for its late fourteenth-century date on the presence of the clerical proctors, who had disappeared in England early in the century. See below, pp. 354–5.

[104] In England the liberties of Chester and Durham were not represented in parliaments during the middle ages.

[105] See J. F. Lydon, 'William of Windsor and the Irish Parliament', *E.H.R.*, LXXX, pp. 252–67.

[106] The crosslands (see below, pp. 175, 182–3) were summoned separately, but seem in practice to have shared their representation with the liberties within which they lay.

mediate problem and not to inaugurate a new policy.'[107] No separate statute rolls, distinct from the parliament rolls, were compiled, and apart from the Statutes of Kilkenny,[108] few Irish statutes seem to have been of any great importance. Much English legislation applied also to Ireland, for till very late in the middle ages the authority of a statute was that of the king, not that of the parliament in which it was promulgated, and in the fourteenth century he could still issue ordinances binding in Ireland without reference to any parliament at all.[109] But it was largely in parliaments that the immediate problems of the Irish administration were discussed, and the messages relating to the state of the country which had earlier been addressed to the king by the justiciar and council were by the later fourteenth century being sent by the lords and commons of Ireland, assembled in parliaments or great councils.[110] But though the commons were clearly growing in importance in the fifteenth century, and it was possible to accuse Ormond of having improperly secured the return of members of his household,[111] while by the middle of the century all parliamentary petitions were referred to them and their support was clearly regarded as important by petitioners, it is nevertheless certain that parliaments were dominated by the ministerial council and the peers. The commons were, however, much involved in the matter of petitions, and this was an all-important stage in the evolution of the legislative process. In England by the fifteenth century the development of the equitable jurisdiction of the chancery had deflected many petitions that would earlier have gone to the council in parliament. In Ireland, though the chancery had certainly had some judicial functions by the end of the thirteenth century, and continued to exercise them in the fifteenth,[112] it was in parliament that equitable remedies were sought, though there may have been some attempt to develop an equitable jurisdiction in chancery before the end of the century.[113] Another factor in bringing petitions to the Irish parliament was the decay of the courts of common law, whose business shrank steadily during the fifteenth century as disorder mounted.

Side by side with parliaments in Ireland in the later middle ages were assemblies described as great councils which do not differ

[107] Richardson and Sayles, *Parliaments in Medieval Ireland*, p. 23.
[108] See below, pp. 291–4.
[109] See below, p. 256.
[110] For great councils, see below, pp. 172–3.
[111] See below, p. 371.
[112] J. Otway-Ruthven, 'The Mediaeval Irish Chancery', loc. cit., p. 130; *A.P.C.*, II, p. 43.
[113] Richardson and Sayles, *The Irish Parliament in the Middle Ages*, pp. 215–19.

very perceptibly from them and seem to have had exactly the same composition, functions and powers. The only obvious difference is that for a parliament the period of summons must be at least forty days, while the period of summons for a great council was sometimes, though not always, or even often, less. There must have been some real difference behind the difference of terminology, but it seems impossible to discover what it was.

In continental countries the representation of the commons had taken a rather different form to that of England and Ireland. In the Spanish kingdoms, in France, in Italy, and in the German principalities, the third estate consisted with rare exceptions only of the representatives of the towns. That the commons in England and Ireland consisted not only of the townsmen but also of representatives of the countryside, the knights of the shires, was the result of the form taken by the organization of local government, to which we must now turn.

When the Normans conquered England in 1066 they had found a well organized system of local government, which they had retained intact. Except in the extreme north the whole country had already been divided into shires, which were themselves divided into hundreds. Each shire and each hundred had its own court, the shire court meeting twice a year and the hundred every month. The shire court was presided over by the sheriff, the principal local agent of the crown, but he was a president, not a judge: it was the suitors of the court—that is, the free community of the shire—who declared the customary law. Nor were there trials as we understand them: the accused must clear himself by oath or ordeal, which revealed the judgement of God. And not only were civil and criminal disputes settled in these courts, but administrative business of all kinds was dealt with, the king's commands were published, and private grants of all kinds were made known. In the course of the twelfth century the shire courts came to be held monthly, and the hundred court at intervals of three weeks, and the burdensome duty of suit of court came to be attached to particular holdings of land, to be, that is, an incident of tenure rather than of free status.[114]

It was inevitably this system that the Normans introduced into Ireland, using on the whole not pre-existing divisions but those which they created for themselves in the course of settlement. The creation of shires was gradual: Dublin is the only one that can be traced back to the twelfth century, and even then does not appear in the records till the 1190s, though it must have existed earlier.

[114] Pollock and Maitland, *History of English Law*, 2nd edition, I, pp. 537-41.

Waterford and Cork, administered together, had a sheriff by
1207–8, and Munster (the later counties of Tipperary and Limerick) was organized as a shire by 1211–12, though probably this had
not been done till 1210. The liberties, Leinster, Ulster and Meath,
were of course outside the shire organization (though they had one
of their own)[115]: Ulster and Meath were in the king's hand from
1210 to 1227 for Ulster and 1215 for Meath,[116] and were administered by royal officials who were described as seneschals, not sheriffs. Uriel or Louth was administered with Ulster during this period,
but was a shire with its own sheriff by 1233, this organization
having presumably been created after Ulster was restored to Hugh
de Lacy. Kerry (the north of the modern county, round Tralee)
was a shire by 1233; Tipperary and Limerick, which seem to have
had separate shire courts by 1235, became completely separate
shires, each with its own sheriff, between 1251 and 1254; Connacht
was a shire by 1247; the sheriff of Roscommon appears in 1292.[117]
Meanwhile, the liberties of Leinster and Meath had been partitioned by subdivision among co-heiresses: Leinster had become
four liberties, based on its previous division into shires[118]; Meath,
which had never been shired, had been divided between the liberty
of Trim and the lands of de Verdon, which were administered as
part of the county of Dublin since he had been refused his claim to
a liberty. In 1297 Kildare, one of the Leinster liberties, which had
just been obtained by the king from its lord, William de Vescy,
became a royal shire like another, while the lands of de Verdon
were made into the shire of Meath, with its county court at Kells.
In 1306 a second Leinster liberty, Carlow, reverted to the crown,
and became a royal shire. By the death of Edward I there were
thus twelve shires, Dublin, Waterford, Cork, Kerry, Louth, Limerick, Tipperary, Connacht, Roscommon, Kildare, Meath and Carlow, as well as the liberties of Kilkenny, Wexford, Trim and Ulster.

After the Bruce invasion a new wave of liberty creation removed
some of these from the list. Kildare was restored as a liberty for
Thomas fitz John, the second earl of Kildare, in 1317, but this was
short-lived: in 1345 it was taken into the king's hand by a judgement in the justiciar's court, and was never recovered in spite of
repeated petitions.[119] Carlow had already, in 1312, been granted

115 See below, pp. 186–7.
116 See above, pp. 79–81, 82, 86, 92.
117 J. Otway-Ruthven, 'Anglo-Irish Shire Government in the Thirteenth Century', I.H.S., V, pp. 1–28.
118 See below, pp. 186–7.
119 J. Otway-Ruthven, 'The Medieval County of Kildare', I.H.S., XI, pp. 181–
99.

as a liberty by Edward II to his half-brother, Thomas of Brotherton, duke of Norfolk, who granted it in 1333 to his son-in-law, William de Montacute, for life. The liberty eventually passed to Margaret, the eldest daughter and heiress of Thomas of Brotherton, and to her heirs, but during the fourteenth century was much in the king's hand 'because Margaret dwelt continually in England so that no one came to Ireland to defend the lands', and because she alienated it without licence to the earl of Pembroke, lord of Wexford.[120]

Outside Leinster, Louth was erected into a liberty for John de Bermingham, who had finally defeated Edward Bruce at Faughart,[121] in 1318, but for his life only, and the grant lapsed when he was murdered in 1328. Roger Mortimer had it regranted to himself in 1331, but this too lapsed with his fall and execution in that year. But more lasting liberties were created by the grant of Tipperary to James le Botiller, first earl of Ormond, in 1328, and Kerry to Maurice fitz Thomas, first earl of Desmond, in 1329.[123] The liberty of Kerry lasted until the ruin of the Desmonds in the sixteenth century, but that of Tipperary was not finally extinguished till the forfeiture of the second duke of Ormond in 1716.[124] The organization of the liberties and their relation to the royal government will be considered later, but it should be pointed out here that there were enclaves of territory within all of them which formed no part of the liberty, but were directly subject to royal sheriffs, the lands of the church or crosslands, which were reserved to the crown in all the Irish liberties. In the thirteenth century all were administered by the sheriff of Dublin, but this can never have been a satisfactory arrangement, and when the county of Meath was created in 1297 the crosslands within the liberty of Trim were attached to it, while at the same time the opportunity was taken to create a sheriff of the crosses of Ulster.[125] By the reign of Edward III we find that all the crosslands had been organized as separate counties, each with its own sheriff.[126]

[120] W. F. Nugent, 'Carlow in the Middle Ages', *Journ. R.S.A.I.*, LXXXV, pp. 62–76; *C.P.R., 1330–34*, p. 402; *C.C.R., 1333–7*, p. 264; *Cal. Inq. P.M.*, XIV, p. 152.

[121] See below, p. 237.

[122] J. Otway-Ruthven, 'The Partition of the de Verdon Lands', *Proc. R.I.A.*, LXVI C.

[123] *Cal. Chart. Rolls, 1327–41*, p. 123; *C.P.R., 1327–30*, p. 336; ibid., *1330–34*, pp. 336, 564.

[124] The original grant of Tipperary was for the life of the first earl. It was regranted for life to the second earl, and finally, in 1372, to him and his heirs male (*C.P.R., 1494–1509*, p. 26, and see *Complete Peerage*, X, p. 120).

[125] *Early Statutes*, pp. 196–8.

[126] For the crosses, see below, pp. 182–3.

The subdivision of the Irish county was the cantred, later the barony, which corresponded to the English hundred.[127] As the conquest progressed cantreds seem to have been formed, occasionally by taking a pre-existing Irish territory, such as Ely O'Carroll, but more often by grouping several *tuatha*. The records nowhere speak of any court comparable to the English hundred court, but that such courts existed is certainly implied by the corporate responsibility of the cantreds for amercements, and their separate representation in the eyre.[128] It was presumably in them that the sheriff held his tourn.

At the head of the shire organization was the sheriff, the principal local representative of the royal government. During the thirteenth century he might be appointed either under the English great seal or by the Irish justiciar or treasurer, but in 1293 it was laid down that sheriffs and other bailiffs who answered at the exchequer should be appointed by the treasurer and barons of the exchequer and removed by them. This arrangement was on the whole adhered to for fifty years, but in 1341 the treasurer was forbidden to appoint sheriffs or other officers without the advice and assent of the justiciar, chancellor and others of the council, as he was alleged to have appointed them arbitrarily, nominating some so that he might extort money from them to be released from office, and proposing unqualified persons.[129] Then, in 1355, the king and council in England ordered that in each county in Ireland a sheriff should be elected annually by the community of the county in the full court, holding office for one year only, after which he should not be re-admitted to office till he had accounted for the issues in the exchequer.[130] This order was immediately acted on: on 5 September the keepers of the peace and coroners in all the Irish counties were ordered to assemble twenty-four of the best men of the county, either separately or in the next full county, and with them to choose one of the twenty-four as sheriff. We know that this was actually done in Dublin, Kildare, Louth and Meath, and presumably in the other counties. In the 1360s sheriffs were still being elected, though usually by a smaller number, and usually either

127 The first conquerors seem to have adapted the Welsh *cantref*, a territorial unit of the same type, with which many of them were of course familiar, to Irish conditions. See J. Hogan, 'The tricha cét and related land measures', *Proc. R.I.A.*, XXXVIII C, pp. 148–235.

128 J. Otway-Ruthven, 'Anglo-Irish Shire Government in the Thirteenth Century', loc. cit., p. 9.

129 *C.C.R., 1341–3*, pp. 308, 309, 356–7. An ordinance of 1331 had directed that sheriffs should be elected in the counties, but it does not seem to have been effective (*Early Statutes*, p. 324).

130 *C.C.R., 1354–60*, pp. 144–5.

in the exchequer, or before the chief governor and council when they were in the county. In January 1369 the archbishop of Tuam was ordered to cause a sheriff of Connacht to be elected by the oath of good and law-worthy men, *minus suspectorum*.[131]

The Anglo-Irish sheriff's functions seem to have been identical with those of his English counterpart.[132] He might or might not in the thirteenth century hold his shire at farm; after this the practice of farming seems to have been abandoned. But in any case the profits of the county which were included in his farm were unimportant[133]: it was as the agent responsible for the collection of the bulk of the ordinary revenue of the crown that the sheriff was really important at the exchequer, where he had to account, receiving due allowance for the sums he had been ordered to spend locally, whether for the repair of the king's castles, the purchase of provisions for the king's French, Welsh or Scottish wars, the expenses of the emissaries of the central government, or a host of other purposes.

But the sheriff was not only indispensable in the collection of revenue; he was also an essential officer of the royal courts. When the justiciar or the justices in eyre held their sessions it was the sheriff who was responsible for bringing before them all pleas and all persons who should be present. He was responsible for the custody of prisoners, and it was he who was ordered to levy debts recovered by judgement of the court and to execute royal writs of all kinds. He had also judicial functions of his own. In the county court he was, of course, only a president, but he was responsible for the conduct of its business, both the judicial business which steadily declined in the thirteenth century and afterwards as legislation removed matters of various kinds to the royal courts, and the administrative business which remained important throughout the middle ages. But it was in the court known as the sheriff's tourn, held twice yearly, presumably in each cantred or barony, that he exercised real judicial power, enquiring on oath as to a wide variety of administrative and judicial matters, and deciding the lesser offences himself though the more serious were reserved for the royal judges.[134] But the English frankpledge, a compulsory association of neighbours who were collectively responsible for producing each other in court when required, which it was one of the chief functions of the English sheriff's tourn to enforce, does not seem to have been introduced into Ireland: instead, in the absence of any

---

[131] *C.C.H.*, p. 64, nos. 146–7; P.R.O., Dublin, Mem. Rolls, vol. 27, pp. 24–25, 27; vol. 28, *passim*; vol. 29, *passim*; vol. 30, pp. 14–15, 22, 28–29.
[132] See W. A. Morris, *The Medieval English Sheriff to 1300*.
[133] See above, p. 163.
[134] See J. Otway-Ruthven, 'Anglo-Irish Shire Government', loc. cit.

police organization, Irish administration tended to revert to the older principle of making the kin responsible.[135] But the sheriff had of course to attach those indicted before him, and this was frequently resisted by force, which might necessitate the calling out of the *posse comitatus*. And given the constant state of warfare in Ireland, particularly in the fourteenth century and later, his military functions were far more important than they were in England. Thus in 1349 the sheriff of Cork was unable to appear before the barons of the exchequer in July because 'the county of Cork rose in war between English and English, and English and Irish', and the bishops of Cloyne and Lismore and the keepers of the peace had required him to remain to maintain the peace of the county. In the same year the sheriff of the cross of Tipperary was assigned by the king's court to defend the liberty of Tipperary as the seneschal had been killed by the king's Irish enemies. In 1368 the sheriff of Waterford had been killed by 'les Poers' before he could account, while the sheriff of Meath had been imprisoned by 'the malefactors of Carbry'. In 1374 an ex-sheriff of Louth petitioned for the remission of an amercement: he had not appeared in the exchequer because he was keeping the marches of Uriel against 'McGynouse' and other Irish of Ulster.[136]

Besides all this, the sheriff might be directed by the central government to do anything that needed to be done in the county. To assist him he seems normally to have had a sub-sheriff, appointed by himself; one or more clerks; sometimes, perhaps always, a receiver, who took charge of the moneys collected. In addition he had a body of serjeants, who did most of the actual routine work of serving writs, collecting debts, and so on. But the sheriff had little effective control over the serjeants, for in most, if not all, counties there was an hereditary chief serjeant, the chief serjeant of fee, who held his office as a fief from the king, and does not seem to have been in practice subject to any real control by the sheriff, though he could be, and frequently was, removed from office for misconduct by the exchequer or the judges, only to recover it by making fine with the king. Under him were the serjeants of cantreds, whom he appointed, and who in turn had their own sub-serjeants.[137]

---

[135] *Early Statutes*, pp. 266, 306, 312, 378, 448.

[136] P.R.O. Dublin, Mem. Rolls, vol. 25, pp. 241–2; 247–8; vol. 30, pp. 1, 7; *Dowdall Deeds*, no. 257. The sheriffs of Cork and Limerick tried to escape amercements for non-appearance in 1374 by alleging that 'fervent war' existed in their counties, but a jury denied this (P.R.O. Dublin, Mem. Rolls, vol. 30, pp. 322–4).

[137] J. Otway-Ruthven, loc. cit., and 'The Medieval County of Kildare', loc. cit., pp. 193–4.

In the thirteenth century the offices of sheriff and serjeant were profitable ones, and the office of sheriff seems to have been eagerly sought. This was perhaps a matter of prestige as much as anything else, for though the sheriff was entitled to certain customary fees, it is unlikely that the total sums involved were very great, and the office entailed considerable risks as well as heavy responsibilities. In the thirteenth century it was often an important stage in the career of professional administrators; later most sheriffs seem to have been country gentlemen. But it must be remembered that the office gave great opportunities for extortion, and this was also the case with the serjeants. This must always have been an attraction for the more unscrupulous, but the number of people who in the fourteenth century and later in Ireland, as in England, obtained charters exempting them from undertaking this or any other office against their will suggests that the burden of responsibility and the risk of heavy amercement at the exchequer, or in the chancery for undue return of a writ, was making men increasingly unwilling to undertake it.[138]

The sheriff and his serjeants, though the most prominent, were not the only officers of local government. The office of coroner, or keeper of the pleas of the crown, was established in England in 1194[139]: it is first mentioned in Ireland in 1264, but was not then new, and it may have existed in the time of John Comyn, archbishop of Dublin, who died in 1212.[140] The coroner's special duties were to hold inquests on dead bodies[141]; to receive abjurations of the land made by felons in sanctuary[142]; to hear appeals, confessions of felons, and appeals of approvers; and to attend or organize exactions and outlawries in the county court.[143] All these might, of course, involve the forfeiture of lands or goods to the crown, and these he was obliged to secure, as well as securing the appearance of witnesses and keeping a record of what had happened.[144] He might in addition be required, either alone or with the sheriff, to perform any other administrative duties, and he must have enough land in the county to answer the king.[145] He was elected by the oath of twelve men in the county court.[146]

---

[138] See e.g. *C.P.R., 1354–8*, pp. 563–4.
[139] R. F. Hunnisett, *The Medieval English Coroner*.
[140] *C.D.I.*, II, pp. 206–7; *Reg. Alen*, pp. 104, 101–14, *passim*.
[141] *Cal. Justic. Rolls, passim*.
[142] Ibid., I, pp. 34, 45, 405–6; ibid., II, p. 513; ibid., III, pp. 227, 304; *C.C.H.*, p. 134, no. 141.
[143] *Cal. Justic. Rolls*, I, p. 60.
[144] Ibid., pp. 167–76, *passim*.
[145] *C.C.H.*, p. 7, nos. 28–30; p. 9, no. 102; p. 71, no. 97.
[146] *Cal. Justic. Rolls*, I, pp. 60, 71, 411.

The office of coroner, though important, had a fixed and limited place in the scheme of administration, and shows no significant development after its first appearance. Far more important for the future was the office of the keepers of the peace. Its origins go back to the same date as that of the coroner: in 1195 in England knights were to be appointed as keepers of the peace to assist the sheriff to maintain order. No regular system appears till much later, but similar appointments were made from time to time during the thirteenth century, and by the 1320s keepers of the peace were being regularly appointed in each county of England. In Ireland the first trace of the office seems to be in 1277, when payments were made for guarding the march of the vale of Dublin; in 1283 a conservator of the king's peace in the vale of Dublin is named; in 1295 we hear of those assigned 'to keep the country' in Limerick.[147] It is improbable that a permanent office already existed, but in 1297 it was enacted that in every county and liberty where the Irish dwell two magnates should be assigned, who when the justiciar was in remote parts might lawfully treat for peace with the Irish putting themselves at war.[148] From this date keepers of the peace appear regularly, and in 1308 it was ordered that the English statute of Winchester (1285), which was concerned with police matters, and also repeated the provisions of Henry II's assize of arms, requiring every free man to equip himself with arms according to the amount of his property, should be proclaimed and observed in Ireland, while in each county the justiciar was to appoint two of the 'most approved, lawful and discreet knights of that county' to enforce it.[149] In fact the numbers of keepers of the peace were often much greater, several in each cantred, with a chief keeper of the peace for the whole county. Their commissions required them to

assess and array all men of those parts between the ages of 60 and 16 to horse and arms, hobelars and footmen, so that they be ready and prepared to set out in the king's service, whenever and wherever necessary, to fight felons and rebels, as well English as Irish, invading those parts.

They had power to follow, arrest, and commit to prison all disobedient to the assessment and array, as well as idle hobelars or footmen, wandering through the country and destroying the faithful people. They had power to amerce those who were defaulters at the array.[150] They might also be given other powers: to treat

---

[147] *C.D.I.*, II, nos. 1496, 2241, 2310; ibid., III, p. 73; *Cal. Justic. Rolls*, I, p. 40.
[148] *Early Statutes*, p. 212.
[149] Ibid., pp. 244–52.
[150] *C.C.H.*, p. 50, no. 21; p. 51, no. 29; p. 52, nos. 50–52; p. 71, no. 102; p. 105, no. 99; p. 121, no. 84.

with the rebel Irish in order to reform them to the peace; to make diligent scrutiny lest any sold provisions, horses or arms to the Irish.[151] They were in general to enforce the statute of Winchester. In 1387 they were to enquire concerning felonies and to commit felons, sending the indictments before the lieutenant, while they themselves were to amerce those who did not rise to the hue and cry.[152] By the beginning of the fifteenth century they are beginning to be commissioned as justices and keepers of the peace, though the old type of appointment as keepers of the peace only continues.[153] We have no evidence that they ever exercised judicial functions during the middle ages in Ireland, and it is clear that it was their military functions which were all-important. They seem to have exercised these functions in co-operation with the sheriff, though they were not subordinate to him.

With the keepers of the peace local organization in the shires is complete, and we must now turn to the liberties, which in the thirteenth and fourteenth centuries particularly were quite as important in the organization of local government in Ireland as were the shires. The liberties in Ireland go back to the beginnings of the Norman conquest, when in 1172 Henry II granted to Hugh de Lacy the land of Meath, to hold as Murrough O'Melaghlin or any other before or after him best held it, with all liberties and free customs which Henry himself had or could have there.[154] He must have given a similar charter to Strongbow for Leinster, and at some later date de Courcy must have had one for Ulster. These charters, though lacking the precision which the next century would have required, were certainly intended to convey the fullest liberties, giving their holders almost royal rights, with complete control of all administration and all jurisdiction, to the exclusion of royal officials. The reference to O'Melaghlin must have been intended to convey the rights over the native Irish which a native king would have, while to the Normans the rights which were being conveyed were those of the English king over them. And both Strongbow and de Lacy must have interpreted their grants in the light of practice in the marcher lordships of Wales, even though the constitutional position there was not identical.[155]

With the thirteenth century a process of definition began. The

---

[151] Ibid., p. 50, no. 3; p. 99, nos. 275, 277; p. 136-7, nos. 213-16.
[152] Ibid., p. 136, no. 213.   [153] Ibid., p. 160a, no. 19, and *passim*.
[154] *Cal. Gormanston Reg.*, p. 177.
[155] See A. J. Otway-Ruthven, 'The Constitutional Position of the Great Lord-'ships of South Wales', *Trans. R. Hist. Soc.*, 5th series, 8, pp. 1-20; J. G. Edwards, The Normans and the Welsh March', *Proceedings of the British Academy*, XLII, pp. 155-77.

grant of Ulster to Hugh de Lacy the younger in 1205 was as de Courcy held it, saving the crosses to the king,[156] and the dispute with Meiler fitz Henry[157] resulted in 1208 in the grant of fresh charters for Meath and Leinster in which the king expressly reserved to himself the pleas of the crown, jurisdiction in error, and the crosses, the church lands within the liberty.[158] The pleas of the crown were evidently only the four pleas of arson, rape, treasure trove and forestall which were reserved to the crown in all the Irish liberties,[159] but this reservation seems to have been new, for when in 1252 Geoffrey de Geneville, who had married one of Walter de Lacy's co-heiresses, was granted all liberties and free customs in Meath as Walter had best had them he succeeded in obtaining jurisdiction over these four pleas, and had thus a more completely exclusive jurisdiction than the lord of any other Irish liberty.[160] But the same argument proves that the royal writ of error had always run in Meath, and so presumably in Leinster, and that the crosses had always been reserved to the crown. These were very important differences from the position in Wales: there the royal writ of error did not run, so that in the marcher lordships law and custom could diverge widely from the common law, as it could not in the English palatinate or the Irish liberty; and up to the later thirteenth century the lords of south Wales had claimed to have the custody of all church lands within their lordships during vacancies.[161] But in Ireland, as in England, the action of any liberty court could be brought before the royal courts by writ of error, so that no divergent legal development was possible; and church lands were no part of the liberty in which they were geographically situated, but were held directly of the crown. Strictly speaking, this applied only to land which had been held by the church when the liberty was created: land granted to it later could be subtracted from the liberty only with the consent of the lord, who might otherwise have seen his rights gradually whittled away without his consent, and even without his knowledge. Thus, not all church land

---

[156] *C.D.I.*, I, no. 263.

[157] See above, pp. 77–9.

[158] *C.D.I.*, I, nos. 381–2.

[159] They were reserved in the grant of Ulster to Walter de Burgo in 1263, and in the charters of Tipperary and Kerry (above, p. 175). For these pleas, see N. Hurnard, 'The Anglo-Norman Franchises', *E.H.R.*, LXIV, pp. 289–327, 433–60. Miss Hurnard minimizes the importance of forestall (an assault on the king's highway: cf. *Cal. Justic. Rolls*, I, p. 171), but it was clearly of great importance in the thirteenth century. Cf. 'The Constitutional Position of the Great Lordships of South Wales', loc. cit., p. 10.

[160] *Cal. Gormanston Reg.*, p. 178.

[161] 'The Constitutional Position of the Great Lordships of South Wales', loc. cit., pp. 10–12, 17–18.

was necessarily cross land, and endless opportunities for dispute existed, since a zealous escheator might occupy such land during a vacancy, claiming that it was part of the cross.[162]

The theory of the liberties as it developed in the thirteenth century was stated by Bracton: those things which belong to jurisdiction and peace pertain only to the crown and the royal dignity, and cannot be separated from the crown since they constitute it. Such jurisdictions or rights could only be possessed by private persons if they had been given to them as delegated jurisdiction.[163] The corollary of this was that the franchise holder was in effect a royal official, though a hereditary one to whom the profits of justice went, and could be deprived of his franchise unless he exercised it in accordance with law.[164] He must execute royal writs within his lordship, for though all actions arising within the liberty must be tried in its courts, there were matters affecting residents within the liberty which arose elsewhere, and the resulting writs must be sent directly to the lord or his seneschal for execution[165]: the liberty is 'exempt and separate from any of the king's counties',[166] and must not be entered by the king's officers. Only if the lord has failed to execute such a writ can the king's sheriff be specially authorized to enter the liberty to execute it.[167] The liberties of England had begun in the attempts of Anglo-Saxon kings to enlist their magnates in the preservation of order by giving them a share of the profits, the royal dues arising in the courts of shire and hundred. Where the lands in which this right to take the royal dues had been granted were sufficiently extensive, they were often by the eleventh century being administered by hundred courts presided over no longer by royal officials, but by the officials of the grantee. After the Norman conquest of 1066 there was added to this the right of every feudal lord to hold a court for his tenants which was concerned with matters arising out of the feudal relationship, and at the same time, with the growing power of the crown and of its agent, the sheriff, the lords of liberties, whether ecclesiastics or the Norman laymen who had succeeded to the rights of Anglo-Saxon predecessors, began to secure grants excluding royal officials, both sheriffs and justices, from their privileged lands. In the later twelfth and early thirteenth centuries the very greatest franchises, Chester

---

[162] J. Otway-Ruthven, 'Anglo-Irish Shire Government in the Thirteenth Century', *I.H.S.*, V, pp. 7–8. For the administration of the crosses, see above, p. 175.

[163] *De Legibus et Consuetudinibus Angliae*, Bk. 2, c. 24.

[164] See H. M. Cam, *Liberties and Communities in Medieval England*, pp. 183–4.

[165] *Cal. Justic. Rolls*, II, p. 241.

[166] B. M. MS Add. 4790, ff. 92d–93.   [167] *Cal. Justic. Rolls*, *passim*.

and Durham, developed those rights which were later to be called palatine.[168] Meanwhile, in the marches of Wales, lords who had conquered for themselves lands which had never been governed by the English crown had established lordships which were almost entirely independent of it. But in spite of the strong Welsh marcher connections of the Norman conquerors of Ireland it was the English tradition of liberties which prevailed, no doubt because of the very early date at which the crown intervened in the conquest of Ireland. The lord of an Irish liberty was thus an agent of the royal government, with which he must co-operate, though enjoying a position of great power and prestige and privileged to receive those dues which would otherwise have gone to the king. The only important exception was that, unlike the greatest English franchises, the Irish liberties were from the first subject to general taxation, and it must have been for this reason that they were represented in the Irish parliament.[169]

Within these liberties it was the lord's writ, not the king's, which ran, and the lord's peace which prevailed. This necessarily involved the erection of a system of central government paralleling that of the king, though inevitably on a smaller scale. All the Irish liberties had very similar institutions, which were apparently developed gradually during the first half of the thirteenth century. The first official to appear in all of them must have been the seneschal, who occupied the same place in the government of the liberty that the justiciar did in the country as a whole. He represented his lord, and was, like the justiciar, an omnicompetent official with functions at once military, administrative, judicial and financial. He was the person primarily responsible for the defence of the liberty, and it was he who led its knight service to the royal host.[170] He presided over the liberty court, which dealt with those cases which would elsewhere have gone before either the itinerant justices or the bench at Dublin.[171] It was he who accounted for his lord at the exchequer of Dublin, dealing not only with the lord's own liability for scutages, reliefs, fines, or anything else of the kind, but also with any debts owed to the crown by others within the liberty which he had been ordered by royal writ to collect.[172] It was for this reason that his appointment must be notified to the exchequer, and that he must take oath to the king in it.[173]

---

[168] See H. M. Cam, *Law-finders and Law-makers in Medieval England*, pp. 22–43.
[169] See above, p. 171.
[170] *C.D.I.*, III, pp. 265–6; *43rd Rep. D.K.*, p. 46.
[171] See e.g. *C.D.I.*, II, no. 1647.
[172] See *Cat. Pipe Rolls*, *passim*.
[173] See P.R.O. Dublin, Mem. Rolls, *passim*.

Other officers seem to have developed more slowly. In the early thirteenth century the Marshals seem to have had a single household chancery for all their scattered lands in England, Ireland and Wales, but after the partition of the Marshal inheritance in 1247 we hear of a chancellor in each of the four liberties into which Leinster had been divided.[174] In 1309–10 it was alleged that Hugh de Lacy had had his own chancellor in Ulster before 1220, and this is likely enough, though the first certain evidence of a chancellor in Ulster comes from 1276.[175] We first hear of one in Trim in 1299, but he must have existed earlier.[176] As for financial organization, there must have been receivers or treasurers in each liberty from the first, and there is a reference to an exchequer at Kilkenny under the Marshals[177]; by the late thirteenth century every liberty had its exchequer. In judicial matters the seneschal was often assisted by regular justices by the same period.[178] And during the thirteenth century all the liberties took a decisive step in their development, in obtaining the right to use the new judicial procedure introduced by Henry II in his assizes, by which a case relating to land held by free tenure could be decided by the verdict of a jury, instead of by trial by battle.[179] This procedure had been adopted in Leinster before 1224[180]; in Meath it was delayed because the liberty was in the king's hand from 1210 till 1215, and again from c. 1223 till Walter de Lacy's death in 1241, during which period Walter acted as the king's sheriff in his own land,[181] but in 1257 de Geneville, the husband of one of de Lacy's co-heiresses, was granted that he might use by his writs those liberties which Walter de Lacy had been accustomed to use without writs, and the adoption of the new procedure must date from this.[182] We have no means of dating it in Ulster, but it had certainly happened before the end of the century.

Little more need be said about the central government of the liberties. They seem also to have had escheators,[183] and we should notice that in Leinster and Meath the king expressly abandoned his right of prerogative wardship: the right, that is, to have the

[174] C.D.I., II, no. 1096.
[175] B.M. MS Add. 4790, ff. 92d–93; C.D.I., II, no. 1219.
[176] Cal. Justic. Rolls, I, p. 293.
[177] C.D.I., II, no. 861.
[178] See e.g. Cal. Justic. Rolls, II, p. 63.
[179] This had been introduced in Durham c. 1208, and about the same time in Chester: in general only the king could compel a man to swear as a juror. But see J. Scammell, 'The Origin and Limitations of the Liberty of Durham', E.H.R., LXXXI, pp. 449–73.
[180] Cal. Gormanston Reg., pp. 201–2.
[181] C.D.I., II, nos. 810, 1645.
[182] Cal. Gormanston Reg., p. 179. Suis brevibus should read sine brevibus.
[183] Cal. Ormond Deeds, III, no. 342 (6).

wardship of all the lands of any tenant-in-chief during a minority, no matter of whom they were held. Since most of the more important sub-tenants in the liberties also held of the king elsewhere, this right if enforced would have meant that the lords of the liberties would have lost an important part of their feudal revenue.[184] And finally, the lord had, like the king, his council, with which we find seneschals acting in the absence of the lord.[185]

The local government of the liberties need not detain us for long. They were organized on exactly the same lines as the royal shires, with sheriffs, who must have been much overshadowed by the seneschal, chief serjeants and serjeants of cantreds or baronies, often holding in fee.[186] The chief peculiarity was that in two cases, Meath after the partition and Tipperary, a liberty shared a hereditary chief serjeant with a royal county, which could be embarrassing.[187] The county courts were organized like those of the royal counties, and had exactly the same jurisdiction and functions: no attempt was made to follow the Welsh marcher pattern of an omnicompetent county court.[188]

The liberties of Leinster and Ulster were each divided into several shires: the area involved would otherwise have been unmanageably large. Those of Ulster existed in embryo by 1226,[189] though the boundaries had changed a good deal before the end of the century. Leinster was divided into Wexford, Carlow, Kilkenny and Kildare, the shires which existed at the time of the partition of 1247 and determined the form it took. The liberty had to be divided into five: this was done by giving each of the four senior co-heiresses an existing county, with its court and the profits attached, which included the suit of all the lands included in the county; the fifth share was formed from the lands in the modern counties of Leix and Offaly which were then part of Kildare. There could be no question of forming this area into a new county, for its lands, with the profits arising from their suit to the county court, were part of

---

[184] *C.D.I.*, I, nos. 381, 382. In England the king had this right everywhere except in Durham, the marches of Wales, and the lands of the archbishop of Canterbury (*Statutes of the Realm*, I, p. 80). The bishop himself had it in Durham (*Registrum Palatinum Dunelmense*, ed. T. D. Hardy (Rolls Series, 1873–8), III, p. 62): it does not appear whether the lords of Leinster and Meath enjoyed it. See also above, pp. 77–8.   [185] See e.g. *Reg. Fleming*, no. 260.

[186] See J. Otway-Ruthven, 'The Medieval County of Kildare', *I.H.S.*, XI, pp. 181–99; W. F. Nugent, 'Carlow in the Middle Ages', *Journ. R.S.A.I.*, LXXXV, pp. 62–76.

[187] J. Otway-Ruthven, 'Anglo-Irish Shire Government in the Thirteenth Century', *I.H.S.*, V, p. 22.

[188] J. Otway-Ruthven, 'The Constitutional Position of the Great Lordships of South Wales', *Trans. R. Hist. Soc.*, 5th series, 8, pp. 5–6.

[189] *C.D.I.*, I, no. 1468.

Kildare, and continued to be administered by its officials.[190] The single liberty of Leinster was thus divided into four liberties, each with its separate governmental structure. The partition of Meath followed a different pattern: as there was no pre-existing division into shires, it was divided so as to give each of the co-heiresses lands scattered fairly evenly through the whole area, with the demesne manors of Trim and Fore assigned to de Geneville, and Kells, Duleek, Loughsewdy and most of the demesne lands in Longford to de Verdon.[191] De Geneville obtained the renewal of de Lacy's liberties in their fullest extent for his lordship of Trim[192]; de Verdon, in spite of repeated attempts, got only the very restricted liberty which de Lacy had held at his death, and finally had to submit to seeing his lands made first part of co. Dublin, and then the royal county of Meath.[193] As for the later liberties, Kerry and Tipperary, they were organized on the same lines as the older ones, and need no separate description.

As we have seen, the lord of a liberty was a royal agent. The law which he must execute within his liberty was the law of the land, and the royal writ of error would ensure that he did so. But unless and until he failed to execute justice, all matters other than the reserved pleas arising in the liberty, even if he were himself a party to the action, were for his court alone,[194] and none of the king's officials might enter the liberty unless he had failed to execute a royal writ. The only exceptions to the competence of his court were cases in which a royal charter, on which only the king or his court could adjudicate, was pleaded,[195] and cases in which his court could not compel the appearance of some party, as when in an action concerning land a warrantor had no lands within the liberty.[196] The sanction by which the way in which the lord exercised his liberty could be controlled was of course the taking of the liberty into the king's hand, and though this seldom entailed final forfeiture, it sometimes did, as in the case of Kildare.[197]

It remains for us to consider the legal system which underlay the whole structure of central and local government which has been

[190] See 'The Medieval County of Kildare', loc. cit. The same problems were produced by the partition of the Welsh lands: see 'The Constitutional Position of the Great Lordships of South Wales', loc. cit.

[191] See J. Otway-Ruthven, 'The Partition of the de Verdon Lands'. Proc. R.I.A., LXVI C.

[192] See above, p. 182.

[193] C.D.I., II, nos. 810, 1645, 1670, 1673; above, p. 174.

[194] C.D.I., III, no. 525.

[195] Cal. Justic. Rolls, 1305-7, pp. 63-64.

[196] Ibid., 1295-1303, p. 214. In making a grant of land the grantor must give a warranty to give proof of his title if it were challenged.

[197] See above, p. 174.

described, and here the situation is perfectly clear. The constant assumption is that the law of Ireland is, and ought to be, the same as that of England,[198] and though there were some divergences,[199] this assumption was substantially justified in practice. The Norman conquests in Wales had been made at the beginning of the twelfth century, when a wide variety of legal custom was accepted as a matter of course and the common law, the law of the king's court, had barely begun to emerge. In Wales, therefore, it had been possible for each lordship to develop its own amalgam of archaic feudal law, Welsh customary law, and parts of the common law, and to maintain it, thanks to their peculiar constitutional position. In Ireland the conquest, begun two generations later, came at the point when the common law under the influence of perhaps the ablest and most remarkable of the medieval kings of England was already rapidly developing, and since the crown took control in the very early stages the common law was inevitably imposed. But it was imposed on a personal basis: while, inevitably, the Irish in the unconquered areas were left to their own customary legal system, the Brehon law, the free Irish in the conquered areas had no access to the courts of common law unless they had been expressly granted the right to use English law. They were not, indeed, either rightless or deprived of legal protection, but action in the courts could only be taken on their behalf by their lord, and it seems to have been usual for them to put themselves in the advowry of a lord, to whom they paid a small annual fee. An Irishman seeking to take action in his own person could be answered simply that he was an Irishman, and the action failed, though the courts regarded this defence with disfavour, and required strict proof of it. As a defendant the Irishman seems to have been under no disadvantage.[200]

The position had clearly many practical inconveniences, but they could be obviated by the grant of a charter of English law, which seems to have been easily obtainable. We have no means of telling how many such charters were in fact granted, for apart from the loss of records it is clear that many chancery instruments of all kinds were never enrolled,[201] but in the later thirteenth century an attempt was made to secure the general extension of Eng-

[198] *Early Statutes*, pp. 20, 21, 23–4, 30, 31–32, 33, 35; *C.D.I.*, I, nos. 1430, 1458, 1481, 1679; ibid., II, no. 318.

[199] See e.g. *Journ. R.S.A.I.*, LXXXIX, p. 2, n. 4.

[200] See G. J. Hand, 'The Status of the Native Irish in the Lordship of Ireland, 1272–1331', *The Irish Jurist*, new series, I, pp. 93–115, which discusses and adds to earlier work. See also his forthcoming book, *English Law in Ireland, 1290–1324*, and above, p. 125.

[201] See below, p. 334, n. 50.

lish law to the Irish. The negotiations are first mentioned in a letter written by the justiciar, probably late in 1276, and continued till 1280 when they seem to have broken down. But the movement seems to have been an entirely ecclesiastical one, led by the arch-bishop of Cashel and the bishops of Killaloe and Emly. David MacCarwell, archbishop of Cashel 1254–89, was a Cistercian, and evidently a reformer: it seems more than likely that the aim of the bishops was to stamp out the Brehon law, certain aspects of which, and particularly the law of marriage, which the common law left entirely to the church courts, had been attacked by reformers from the twelfth century on.[202] Certainly no Irish layman was involved in the leadership of the movement, though it was said that the laity supported it.[203] It has been suggested that the first move came from Edward I himself, whom the archbishop may well have met in France in the summer of 1274, but it is perhaps more likely that if this meeting took place the archbishop raised the subject, and found such proposals welcomed by a king who in relation to the problem of the two laws in Wales was to hold strongly that 'by his coronation oath he is bound to root out from the boundaries of his kingdom all bad laws and customs'.[204] When he wrote in 1277 that 'the laws which the Irish use are detestable to God and so contrary to all laws that they ought not to be called laws'[205] he may well have been echoing what he had heard from the archbishop, who was certainly in England in that year.[206]

Whatever the motives behind the approach may have been, it came to nothing in the end, and no further demand for a general enfranchisement seems to have been made. In any case, with the progressive decline in the area effectively controlled by the Anglo-Irish government in the fourteenth and fifteenth centuries there was less and less motive for desiring it. In the early fourteenth century opinion among the Anglo-Irish seems to have swung towards a general extension of English law to the Irish, and in 1331 it was ordered that 'one and the same law be made as well for the Irish as for the English, except the service of betaghs in the power of their lords'.[207] This was successfully pleaded in the Anglo-Irish courts in the same year,[208] but it is hard to tell how far it was

---

[202] See above, pp. 37–8.
[203] *C.D.I.*, II, no. 1400; *I.H.S.*, VI, pp. 267–8.
[204] J. C. Davies, *The Welsh Assize Roll*, p. 60. Also *Registrum Epistolarum Fratris Johannis Peckham*, ed. C. T. Martin (Rolls Series 1882–5), I, pp. 135–7.
[205] *C.D.I.*, II, no. 1408.
[206] See A. Gwynn, 'Edward I and the Proposed Purchase of English Law for the Irish, c. 1276–80', *Trans. R. Hist. Soc.*, fifth series, 10, pp. 111–27.
[207] *Early Statutes*, p. 324.
[208] Betham, *Early Parliaments*, p. 292.

effective: certainly charters of English law continued to be issued during the rest of the middle ages.[209]

Behind all this lay the relation of the Anglo-Irish administration to the English crown. The common law, as we have seen, ran in Ireland, and English statutes were part of it. It did not matter that they had been promulgated in an English parliament, for their authority was that of the king and it was only late in the middle ages that it came to be that of the king in parliament. Much English legislation was of course irrelevant to Irish conditions, and such statutes were ignored, but this does not affect the general principle, while the king could and did legislate specifically for Ireland. The action of the Irish courts of justice was controlled by the possibility of appeal to the English court of king's bench by writ of error or *certiorari*; many grievances came from Ireland to the king in England by way of petitions to the English parliament, though the stream lessened markedly after the reign of Edward I. Complaints against ministers continued, of course, but were now more likely to come before the king and council, outside parliament. Moreover, the Irish exchequer was subject to that of Westminster, the Irish treasurer being required to account there periodically from 1293 on. This control, however, lapsed when in the later fourteenth century it became normal to grant the chief governor the whole revenue of Ireland.[210] And though in general direct control seems to have slackened in the fifteenth century, there was certainly a constant stream of directions from England to the Irish administration, no longer under the great seal, but under the privy seal or the signet, the records of which have not survived, while the greater Irish officials were still appointed by the king under the English great seal. The claim of the parliament held by York at Drogheda in 1460 that Ireland was 'a separate body corporate' subject only to the laws approved in its own parliament, and that writs under English seals summoning residents in Ireland to answer outside it were invalid was made in a revolutionary situation, and was totally unhistorical. The Yorkist monarchy, once established, felt itself in no way bound by it, and it must be regarded as a mere aberration, not corresponding to any constitutional fact.[211]

[209] *C.C.H.*, passim. For the whole subject, see J. Otway-Ruthven, 'The Request of the Irish for English Law, 1277–80', *I.H.S.*, VI, pp. 261–9, and 'The Native Irish and English Law in Medieval Ireland', ibid., VII, pp. 1–16; A. Gwynn, loc. cit.; G. J. Hand, loc. cit. For the betaghs, see above, pp. 110–12.

[210] See above, p. 147.

[211] See Richardson and Sayles, *The Irish Parliament in the Middle Ages*, chapter 16.

The Later Thirteenth Century:
the Colony at its Peak

AT THE beginning of November 1245 Maurice fitz Gerald, who had been justiciar for thirteen years, was replaced by John fitz Geoffrey, a son of Geoffrey fitz Peter, earl of Essex. John had married Isabel, widow of Gilbert son of Walter de Lacy, and daughter of Matilda Marshal and Hugh Bigod earl of Norfolk, and thus had, through her, interests in Ireland. He was to remain justiciar for ten years, but did not arrive in Ireland till the next summer: in the interval the bishop of Ossory, an experienced official, was appointed by the king as his deputy.

The new justiciar was for the time being in immediate control of the greater part of the colony. After the death of Hugh de Lacy the earldom of Ulster had, as we saw, come into the king's hand, and the whole north-east was now governed from Dublin. Leinster passed to the Marshal heiresses after the death of Anselm Marshal in December 1245, but was necessarily taken into the king's hand till the immensely complicated task of dividing it into five precisely equal shares could be completed. This was not done till May 1247, and till then it was governed by a royal seneschal, and the royal liberties which the earls marshal had had were in abeyance.[2] Richard de Burgo's heir, Walter, was still a minor and did not obtain seisin of his father's lands till 1250: the whole of Connacht, as well as his lands in Tipperary, was thus in the king's hand. A number of minor tenants-in-chief were also in wardship, and to modern eyes it may appear that a great opportunity to extend royal control on a permanent basis was lost when all these lands were restored to the heirs with their liberties intact, or when, as in the case of half of Meath, the heirs were allowed to have liberties which at an earlier date had been partially resumed.[3] But it is wholly unrealistic to think that in the circumstances of the age it

[1] Detailed references for the basic narrative of this chapter will be found in Orpen, *Normans*.
[2] *C.D.I.*, I, no. 2836; above, pp. 181–3, 186–7.
[3] See above, pp. 182, 187.

would have been possible to do anything else. In the thirteenth century, even in England and to a much greater extent in the Norman lordship of Ireland, efficient government was still very largely conditional on co-operation between the king and his magnates, and this would not have been secured by denying to an heir the rights which his predecessor had enjoyed, and to which he had a clear hereditary title as a matter of law. In the second place, the resources available to any government were necessarily limited— it is difficult for us to realize how limited—and given the accepted theory that the franchise holder enjoyed his rights as a royal deputy, and was in effect a royal official, though a hereditary one who could not be removed unless he had in some way failed to perform his duty to the king,[4] it is difficult to suppose that remote control by the justiciar, who was necessarily preoccupied with a great mass of other matters, would have been locally as effective as control exercised on the spot by the franchise-holder through his own officials, who could be made to answer to the crown when necessary. In the next century excessive division among co-heiresses who were usually married to absentees damaged the efficiency of the system: in the thirteenth century it was probably on balance beneficial.

The fact that Ulster and, for the time being, Connacht were in the king's hand naturally concentrated attention on them. The justiciar held an eyre in Ulster, probably in 1247–8, in the course of which he must have surveyed and reorganized the whole administration of the province,[5] and in 1248 built a bridge across the Bann at Coleraine and erected a castle on the west bank of the river. From this base he seems to have attacked the Cenel Eoghain, who gave him hostages and made peace. To the west royal activity had begun rather earlier, since Maurice fitz Gerald, the previous justiciar, was directly interested as feoffee of the manor of Sligo, where he built a castle in 1245. In 1246, apparently after he had ceased to be justiciar, he raided from this base into Tir Conaill, and in the summer of 1247 with a 'great army of Galls' he again attacked Tir Conaill and had a considerable success, repeated in 1248, though it did not involve more than the establishment of a sphere of influence. It was after this that, as we have seen, the Cenel Eoghain decided to make peace with the justiciar. But throughout Ireland there were troubles at this time: in Munster, apparently as the result of disputes about the succession to Cormac MacCarthy, who

---

[4] See above, p. 183–4.
[5] This eyre is not listed in *The Administration of Medieval Ireland*, but is clearly proved by *Cal. Gormanston Register*, p. 160.

died in 1247, in which the settlers had taken part, 'a great war was
waged against the Galls of Desmond, and great harm inflicted on
them' in 1249. In the same year there were disturbances in Leinster which caused the justiciar to lead an army into the country:
the Marshal partition was still being put into effect, and no doubt
there was a certain lack of governance. The major disturbance of
1249 was however in Connacht: Felim O'Connor's son, Aedh,
attacked the settlers: his father fled to them, and a major expedition, 'the Galls of Meath and Leinster, a great host', was led by the
justiciar to join Maurice fitz Gerald and his forces. They converged
on each other in Roscommon and set up one of Felim's nephews as
king, and though others of the O'Connors attacked the settlers at
Athenry in September they were decisively defeated, fleeing in
terror at the sight of the Norman cavalry. But in 1250 Felim returned with the Cenel Eoghain as his allies, and having expelled
his nephew was restored by the justiciar, though with diminished
lands, for the king now began to make grants to Normans in the
barony of Roscommon.

All this must have reinforced the determination of the justiciar
to subdue the Cenel Eoghain. In 1250 Maurice fitz Gerald, in
alliance with the O'Reillys of Breifne, invaded Cenel Eoghain without much success, but in 1252 the justiciar launched a major attack,
leading an army north by way of Dundalk, where the annals say
the contingents from Meath and Munster quarrelled among themselves. This must have been the 'army of Maincoue' which appears
in the exchequer accounts of the period,[6] for the castle of Moy
Cova (Dromore, co. Down) was built, or rather rebuilt, in this
year, while to the west Maurice fitz Gerald rebuilt the castle of
Cael Uisce, at or near Belleek, co. Fermanagh. Brian O'Neill submitted and gave hostages, but in the next year Maurice fitz Gerald
again raided Cenel Eoghain, and O'Neill retaliated by raiding
south Down, burning towns and destroying Moy Cova and other
castles. In 1254, after the king had granted Ireland as an appanage
to Edward, his eldest son, the new justiciar was ordered to direct
his attention to the pacification of Ulster, 'where some Irishmen
have risen against the lord Edward'.

Meanwhile, in the west Connacht continued in a state of confusion, with wars between the Irish kings in which the Norman
settlers participated. In and after 1253 Felim O'Connor's son, Aedh,
conducted operations across the Shannon against the O'Reillys of
Breifne, an area in which the Normans of Meath had made some
settlement, led by the Nangles of Navan, though it does not seem

[6] Gilbert, *Facsimiles*, part II, plate lxxiii; *Analecta Hibernica*, II, pp. 262–5.

to have lasted beyond the middle of the century.[7] The O'Reillys had been in alliance with Maurice fitz Gerald when he attacked Cenel Eoghain in 1250; in 1253 they invaded Muinter Eoluis in co. Leitrim to attack the MacRannells, but Aedh O'Connor came to the assistance of the MacRannells and utterly routed the O'Reillys. Then in 1255 some attempt at a general pacification of the area seems to have been made: Felim O'Connor sent envoys to the king in England; the archbishop of Tuam and Maurice fitz Gerald went to him in person. The archbishop's business was no doubt primarily ecclesiastical,[8] but he may well have been concerned also with the secular affairs of the province, which must have been the sole concern of the others. Then there was a meeting between O'Connor and Walter de Burgo, who had had seisin of his lands in 1250, 'where they made peace and where everything for which Felim was contending was conceded'. But this peace did not last: in the next year de Burgo, in alliance with the O'Reillys, attacked the O'Connors and O'Rourkes, who in September 1256 decisively defeated the O'Reillys before they had effected a junction with de Burgo.

By this time a new justiciar, Alan de la Zouche, had been appointed. He met Aedh O'Connor at Randown on the Shannon and made peace with him, and in 1256 O'Connor also met John de Verdon, the husband of one of the de Lacy co-heiresses, whose share of Meath included nearly all the lordship's lands and claims in Longford and Leitrim, thus impinging directly on the O'Connor position.[9] It was perhaps in connection with all this that the archbishop of Tuam returned to England, where he died in the summer of 1256. Then in 1257 Felim O'Connor himself met the justiciar and Walter de Burgo and 'the chief Galls of Connacht and the rest of Ireland' at Athlone, and an agreement was made, the terms of which we do not know. It was in any case to be made ineffective by Aedh O'Connor, who in 1258, together with Teig O'Brien, son of the king of Thomond, who had defeated the Munster settlers in the previous year, met Brian O'Neill at Cael Uisce on the Erne, where the castle built by Maurice fitz Gerald had been destroyed by O'Donnell, and made an alliance with him.

It was not the first time that the sons of Irish rulers had attacked the settlers although their fathers supported them, but the appearance of a general confederacy was a new and ominous sign. We hear that O'Connor and O'Brien gave the kingship of the Gaels of

---

[7] See Orpen, *Normans*, vol. III, pp. 32–36; J. Otway–Ruthven, 'The Partition of the de Verdon Lands', *Proc. R.I.A.*, LXVI C.

[8] *C.D.I.*, II, nos. 460, 503.

[9] 'The Partition of the de Verdon Lands', loc. cit.

Ireland to Brian O'Neill, and in 1260 the alliance came to fruition. Teig O'Brien had died in 1259, but Aedh O'Connor with the chief men of Connacht joined O'Neill, and in May their joint armies attacked the settlers at Down, and were heavily defeated by the local levies. Brian himself was killed, with many other leading men of both Ulster and Connacht, though Aedh O'Connor escaped. The movement had been a complete failure.

In the south, however, things were different. No doubt because of the death of Teig O'Brien in 1259 Thomond was relatively quiet, but Desmond had been disturbed for several years by succession disputes among the MacCarthys, in which the settlers had supported one or other side, and great damage had been done. It does not seem that Fineen MacCarthy had been involved in the confederacy with O'Neill, but in 1261, after he had destroyed a number of the settlers' castles, action was taken against him. The 'half service of Desmond' was proclaimed,[10] and William de Dene, who had become justiciar in the previous year, led the king's army into Desmond, partly financed by loans from merchants which the barons of Desmond undertook to repay. On 24 July he engaged MacCarthy at Callann in the mountainous country near Kenmare, and was utterly defeated with heavy losses, which included John fitz Thomas, the ancestor of the earls of Desmond, and his son, Maurice. It was more than twenty years before John's grandson and heir came of age, and the inquisition taken in 1282 as to his lands says repeatedly that they are 'waste by the war of the Irish', 'destroyed by the war of the Irish', vividly suggesting the erosion of the Norman position in the south-west since 1261.[11] The battle seems, indeed, to have been a real turning-point in this area.

But though things went badly in the south-west, the victory of 1260 at Down was followed by renewed action against O'Connor in Connacht. Late in 1260 John de Verdon, lord of half Meath in right of his wife, came to Ireland, and in 1261 was active in Longford, marking out the site of a castle at Moydow. Then in 1262 the 'army of Roscommon' was proclaimed,[12] and an 'immense army', a 'great host', was led by the justiciar and John de Verdon to join Walter de Burgo in Connacht, while Aedh O'Connor also assembled a great host and attacked the settlers. But no battle took place: Aedh met de Burgo, and presumably the justiciar, and a peace was concluded, Felim O'Connor apparently undertaking to pay a considerable fine (which remained as a debt on the pipe rolls for

[10] *35th Rep. D.K.*, p. 42. This was a service at half the standard rate of scutage: cf. *Cal. Gormanston Reg.*, p. 13.

[11] *C.D.I.*, II, no. 1912.

[12] *35th Rep. D.K.*, p. 42.

years) in order to obtain it. But there were further hostilities in 1263, and in 1264 another meeting at Athlone made another short-lived peace. And meanwhile Walter de Burgo had greatly increased his power, for on 15 July 1263 he had been granted the land of Ulster, to hold as Hugh de Lacy had held it, and must have been formally created earl of Ulster about the same time.[13]

Soon after this disputes between de Burgo and Maurice fitz Maurice, the son of the late justiciar, caused widespread disturbances, as to the details of which we know very little, but which must have paralysed the government of the country for some time. On 6 December 1264 Maurice and his nephew, Maurice fitz Gerald, seized Richard de la Rochelle, who had become justiciar on the death of William de Dene in 1261, Theobald Butler and John de Cogan, and imprisoned them. Walter de Burgo in retaliation seized Maurice fitz Maurice's castles in Connacht, and each side proceeded to plunder the other's lands. We nowhere learn what lay behind this, but it is impossible not to suppose that the dispute was connected with the Barons' War in England, which was by this time in its last and most acute stage. Prolonged quarrels between the king and the barons had led in 1258 to the Provisions of Oxford (which were to be applied to Ireland too) which, in effect, put the royal government in commission. It is impossible now to trace the effect of this in Ireland, but it is reasonable to suppose that one of its fruits was the appearance of organized parliaments in Ireland, the first of which we know having been held in the summer of 1264.[14] Disputes inevitably arose about the Provisions, and late in 1263 it was agreed to submit them to the arbitration of King Louis of France: in January 1264, in the Mise of Amiens, he annulled the Provisions, depriving the barons of all control over a king who had shown himself increasingly incompetent. War had been made inevitable: in May the royalist army was completely defeated at Lewes, and Henry and his son Edward, the lord of Ireland, were taken prisoner. Simon de Montfort, earl of Leicester, and his associates regained control of the government, but it still remained to reach a satisfactory settlement which could unite the country, and there was the threat of invasion organized from France by Henry's queen, the French king's sister-in-law, and the exiles from England, while the papal legate formally excommunicated the upholders of the Provisions in October. And the marcher

[13] B.M. MS Add. 4790, f. 104d and Add. 6041, f. 100d. The order for livery is dated 3 September 1263 (B.M. MS Lansdowne 229, f. 98d). The grant was in exchange for lands in south Tipperary which were subsequently granted to Otho de Grandison.
[14] See above, p. 168.

lords of the west, who had been captured at Lewes but released so that the defence of the marches of Wales could be maintained, were an element of extreme danger to de Montfort, who by the end of November was preparing to take military action against them, and on 12 December forced them to agree to terms which put the west under his control. In the parliament which met at London in January 1265 a form of peace was prepared and finally agreed to in March: one of its conditions was that Henry and Edward should secure the adherence to it of Ireland and 'other lands subject to the king of England'. But defections from the baronial party were already beginning; at the end of May Edward escaped and sought refuge with Roger Mortimer, lord of Wigmore, and the marchers; on 4 August de Montfort was defeated and killed at Evesham, and the baronial movement was effectively at an end.

It is against this background that one must set the events of 1264–5 in Ireland, for it is impossible to believe that they were unconnected. The great Irish lords were all involved on one or other side in England. Most of them seem to have been royalists: John de Verdon, who was taken prisoner with the king at Lewes; Roger Mortimer, who held lands in Leinster in right of his wife, one of the Marshal co-heiresses; William de Valence, lord of Pembroke and Wexford in right of his wife; the earl of Norfolk, lord of Carlow; Geoffrey de Geneville, whose wife was one of the de Lacy co-heiresses, and at whose castle of Ludlow Edward took refuge after his escape in May 1265. On the other side, Simon de Montfort's wife, Eleanor, the widow of William Marshal the younger, had rights of dower in Leinster, though these had been commuted for a cash annuity. Much more important was the position of Gilbert de Clare, earl of Gloucester and lord of Kilkenny, who succeeded his father in 1262 and was one of de Montfort's leading supporters till March 1265, when he deserted the baronial party.[15] Most of these were, of course, absentees, but their agents in Ireland must have reflected the political attitudes of their lords. And there can be no doubt that these political divisions will have been reflected in the attitudes of many lesser men, as well as some great ones whose position is not clear because they were not substantial landowners in England and the Irish records are particularly imperfect at this period.

Seen in the light of all this, the seizure of the justiciar and his associates by the fitz Geralds in December 1264 inevitably appears

---

[15] A recent study of the de Clares and their estates is M. Altschul, *A Baronial Family in Medieval England: the Clares, 1217–1314*. (Baltimore: The Johns Hopkins Press, 1965).

as a move in the great political struggle that was going on in England, though it must be admitted that there is no other trace of a connection between them and the Montfortian party. It is clear, however, that there had been earlier disturbances in Ireland, for in May 1262, when Henry had been in process of recovering his authority for a time, he had summoned the justiciar, with Geoffrey de Geneville, Walter de Burgo, and Maurice fitz Maurice, to come to England to certify concerning the state of the country 'on account of the discords lately stirred up there'.[16]

The capture of the justiciar gave the signal for the outbreak of civil war in Ireland. Geoffrey de Geneville, acting as deputy justiciar, put Dublin castle in a state of defence,[17] and led a force against the fitz Geralds; Walter de Burgo, now earl of Ulster, made war against them in Connacht. In February de Montfort's government, omitting all reference to either de la Rochelle or de Geneville, asked the archbishop of Dublin to take upon himself the office of justiciar, as Ireland was 'likely to be disturbed by discord prevailing among the great men and magnates'. Nothing seems to have come of this: probably the archbishop prudently declined an office certain to be thankless, though he seems to have sent messengers describing the state of the country.[18] Then in May de la Rochelle was ordered to come to England to report. But before this, on 15 April 1265, de Geneville had summoned an assembly of magnates to Dublin, where a series of ordinances was produced which the magnates swore to observe. They were presumably concerned with ending the disturbances: the only one whose terms we know provided that all who had been disseised without legal process should recover the estate they had had when the disturbances began.[19] In June, in letters denouncing Edward's adherence to the marchers, and appointing the bishop of Meath as justiciar, de Montfort wrote in the king's name that he rejoiced to hear that the discord between Maurice fitz Gerald and Walter de Burgo had been appeased, and begged them to cultivate a feeling of mutual charity.[20] In fact Richard de la Rochelle remained justiciar, and de Montfort's power was soon utterly destroyed at Evesham.

Though the disturbances had affected practically the whole of the country the Irish seem to have taken surprisingly little advantrage of this opportunity. The absence of John de Verdon, and his capture with the royalists at Lewes in May 1264, was probably

[16] *C.D.I.*, II, no. 727.
[17] *35th Rep. D.K.*, p. 47.
[18] *C.D.I.*, II, nos. 758, 766.
[19] Richardson and Sayles, *The Irish Parliament in the Middle Ages*, p. 59.
[20] *C.D.I.*, II, no. 776.

what gave the signal for the attacks made by O'Melaghlin on the western baronies of Westmeath, in the course of which he burnt Ballyloughloe, held of de Verdon by the Tuits. In 1265 Aedh O'Connor burnt three of the Geraldine castles, but Ulster under de Burgo seems to have been perfectly quiet, and we hear of no trouble with the Irish of Munster.

Meanwhile, in 1265 Felim O'Connor died, and was succeeded by Aedh, who had, as we have seen, exercised a predominant influence in Connacht for some years, and had been consistently hostile to the English. He made his 'royal raid' into Offaly, a Geraldine district, and the Annals of Connacht are full of burnings in Sligo in 1266, though O'Connor himself appears only as attacking the O'Rourkes of Breifne. De Burgo seems to have ignored all this, trying only, though without success, to repress O'Melaghlin, who was perhaps raiding westwards across the Shannon; it was not till 1267 that he raided O'Connor's lands in Roscommon. In 1268 there was again fighting between O'Connor and the Normans, in which O'Connor was victorious, and we hear of troubles all along the Shannon frontier of Meath. And in 1269, under a new justiciar, Robert de Ufford, it seems that a definite decision to deal with the problem of Connacht was taken.

Richard de la Rochelle is said to have marked out the site of a castle at Roscommon in 1262, but nothing had then been done. Now, in 1269, Ufford went to Connacht, and, according to the prior and convent of St Coman of Roscommon, on whose lands the castle was built, perambulated the whole cantred of Roscommon together with the greater men of the council and found no place 'so suitable, firm and worthy as in the tenement of our church of Roscommon near the lake vulgarly called Lochnanen', where he proceeded to build a castle without their consent or that of the bishop.[21] In the same year Maurice fitz Maurice rebuilt the castle of Sligo, though the town was burnt by O'Donnell in 1270. In 1270 there was a full scale campaign, de Burgo and the deputy justiciar, Richard de Exeter, combining in an attack on O'Connor, who routed them and destroyed several castles. And in the same year Brian Roe O'Brien, who had succeeded his father in Thomond in 1268, rose against the Normans and took Clare castle, near Ennis. Then in 1271 Walter de Burgo, who had been the leading spirit among the Normans for twenty years, died prematurely at Galway after a short illness, and the way was open for further successes by

[21] P.R.O., London, S.C. 1/20/45. The royal service seems to have been proclaimed for this: there was an army of Dunmore in Ufford's time (P.R.O., London, S.C. 1/17/185).

Aedh O'Connor. In 1272 he 'burnt Meath as far as Granard', John de Verdon's eldest son having been killed in a battle with the O'Farrells in Annaly (south Longford) the year before, and destroyed Roscommon castle.

James de Audeley had been appointed as justiciar after Ufford's return to England in 1270 and found himself in 1271 faced with grave problems of defence: in Connacht, now in the king's hand, for de Burgo's heir was still a minor; in Ulster, also of course in the king's hand, where the new seneschal, William fitz Warin, was opposed by some of the English settlers; and in Thomond, where Brian O'Brien was still in open rebellion. The justiciar's accounts show the royal service summoned to Athlone[22]; the army 'proceeding to and remaining to succour' the castles of Athlone, Randown and Roscommon; horse and foot soldiers coming from various parts of Ireland; 'Breynroth'—Brian O'Brien—forced to give hostages (it must have been in the course of this campaign that the justiciar borrowed 100 marks from the community of Clonmel)[23]; O'Neill, MacCahan, and other Irishmen coming to the king's peace; activity in co. Wicklow against the O'Byrnes and O'Tooles.[24] Clearly de Audeley entered upon his office with great enthusiasm and energy, but in 1272 he too died, by an accidental fall from his horse.

Soon after this Henry III was dead, on 16 November 1272, and his son Edward, who had been lord of Ireland since 1254, succeeded him. In practice, of course, this made no real difference to Ireland. None of the annals mentions the grant of Ireland to Edward, nor do they mention Henry's death. As lord Edward had never visited Ireland, though it was from time to time proposed that he should, and he did not visit it as king either. One very marked feature of the period of his lordship is the frequent change of justiciar: from 1232 to 1256 there had been only two justiciars, but from 1256 to 1272 there were eight, of whom only Richard de la Rochelle held office for more than two years, while three died in office. Most of them were strangers to Ireland, and it must thus have been possible for the great Norman-Irish lords to establish a predominant position in the running of the colony. But since few of Edward's writs found their way into the rolls of his father's chancery, and almost nothing has survived from the Irish chancery for any part of the thirteenth century, we are dependent very largely on the annals for the history of the whole period, and this means that its detail is

[22] C.D.I., II, no. 889. Elsewhere this service is called the army of Dunmore (P.R.O., London, S.C. 1/17/185).

[23] P.R.O., London, S.C. 1/16/49.

[24] C.D.I., II, nos. 889–91.

almost unknown to us. The fact that with the accession of Edward I Ireland once more figures prominently in the English public records gives an impression of a new energy and vigour which is certainly misleading. Edward's accession marked no significant change in development, and the Irish resurgence so prominent in the early years of his reign had, as we have seen, been a dominant factor in Norman-Irish affairs for most of the period of his lordship.

Connacht was still a grave problem in 1272, but in 1274 Aedh O'Connor died, and for many years the energies of the Connacht-men were to be distracted by disputes as to the succession. The most urgent problem in 1272 seems to have been that of Thomond, and in 1273 Maurice fitz Maurice, who had become justiciar, pre-sumably by the appointment of the Irish council, on de Audeley's death, led an expedition against O'Brien,[25] obtaining hostages from him. Then in 1276 the problem of this area was dealt with by granting it to Thomas de Clare, the younger brother of the earl of Gloucester, who had for some ten years been one of Edward's most intimate advisers, and had come to Ireland late in 1274 and in the next year married the daughter and eventual co-heiress of Maurice fitz Maurice. On 26 January 1276 he was granted the whole land of Thomond to hold in fee tail, with all liberties which the earls Marshal had had in their lands, though the grant of liberties was for his life only, and the existing tenants-in-chief were not included in it. The most important of them, Robert de Muscegros, was how-ever eliminated within a few weeks when the king gave him an exchange in England for his castle of Bunratty, with the cantred of Tradry and the tuath of Ocormok, which were regranted to de Clare.[26]

Meanwhile in the autumn of 1273 Geoffrey de Geneville, lord of Trim in right of his wife, one of the de Lacy co-heiresses, had come to Ireland as justiciar. The most immediate problem was that of the mountain areas of the modern co. Wicklow, then part of co. Dublin, which were for the most part included in the lands of the archbishop of Dublin and were in the king's hand during a vacancy from 1271 to 1279. The Irish clans of the mountains continually raided the king's demesne manors in south co. Dublin: about this time the burgesses and farmers of Saggart represented that in late June, while they were working in the fields, their stock had been driven off by Irish thieves, and forty of their men had been killed in following the raiders and two taken prisoner.[27] It was found

[25] A service was proclaimed at Athenry in Maurice's time, probably for this expedition (P.R.O., London, S.C. 1/17/185).
[26] For Thomas de Clare see Altschul, *The Clares*, pp. 187–97.
[27] P.R.O., London, S.C. 1/20/200.

necessary to conduct operations against the Irish of the mountains in a terrain which deprived the Norman forces of all the advantages which cavalry gave them elsewhere. In 1274 a force under de Geneville was defeated at Glenmalure with heavy losses in both slain and prisoners; by the next year the MacMurroughs seem to have joined the rising, and there was an 'army of Tristeldermot',[28] and apparently another expedition to Glenmalure. Then in 1276 a great effort was made: another army, led by Thomas de Clare and de Geneville, who brought 2,000 men from Meath, and including a contingent from Connacht under Maurice fitz Maurice, attacked Glenmalure, but again the Norman forces were defeated with heavy losses. And throughout the period we hear of guards being maintained in the 'vale of Dublin'—south co. Dublin, under the mountains, where the king's demesne manors lay[29]—and of expenditure on the New Castle of Mackinegan (Newcastle, co. Wicklow) which was the principal base of operations. But the army led against Glenmalure in 1277, by which time de Geneville, at his own urgent request,[30] had been replaced as justiciar by Robert de Ufford, seems to have been more successful than any of the earlier expeditions, and Ufford was able to report to the king that affairs were much improved and that 'the thieves who were in Glyndelory had departed'.[31]

Throughout this period it had been necessary to pay a good deal of attention to the affairs of Connacht. Probably in the summer of 1274 there was an expedition to Roscommon, for which the royal service was proclaimed, with the purpose of rebuilding the castle. The justiciar was joined by Peter de Bermingham 'with a good power', and Jordan de Exeter, the sheriff of Connacht, and some of the Irish of Connacht came to the peace, though a detached party going towards Randown was attacked by 'Tatheg Occonchor who calls himself king of Connacht', who was however routed. De Geneville, 'a man of great condition and discretion', wrote the monks of Roscommon, having obtained the agreement of the bishop and chapter and of the monks, rebuilt the castle, and in the course of this expedition also paid a great deal of attention to the castles along the Shannon. Roscommon castle was again thrown down by Aedh O'Connor in 1277, and was rebuilt by the justiciar in 1278,

[28] *36th Rep. D.K.*, p. 46. The Leinster liberties seem to have granted aids towards some of these expeditions (ibid., pp. 72, 74). Tristeldermot is the modern Castledermot.

[29] In addition the tenants of these manors maintained their own guards (P.R.O., London, S.C. 1/20/200).

[30] P.R.O., London, S.C. 1/18/12.

[31] There is said to have been a summons of the royal service to Castledermot about this time (P.R.O., London, S.C. 1/17/185).

when there seems to have been a summons of the royal service to Athenry. And at this time the monks give him their demesne lands to construct a town in exchange for other lands two miles away, for which reason, they wrote ruefully, they had sustained *minas mortalles et jacturas non modicas* from the greater Irish of the whole country, and Ufford was not paying them the fifteen marks a year de Geneville had promised them for the site of the castle.[32] It was at the same time that the O'Connor lands were reduced to the northern half of Roscommon, and it is probable that the organization of the southern half as a royal county belongs to this period, though the sheriff of Roscommon first appears in the records in 1292.[33]

During this period Thomas de Clare was establishing himself in his lordship of Thomond. It appears that the O'Briens were divided into two main factions, contending for the kingship, one of which allied itself with de Clare. In 1277, however, de Clare executed Brian O'Brien, king of Thomond, his former ally, for reasons which are not made clear: the alliance was renewed with the dead king's son, Donough O'Brien, within the year. In 1278 or 1279 de Clare began to build a castle at Quin and was heavily defeated by the O'Briens, but in 1281 the royal forces came to his assistance, and though the wars between O'Brien factions continued his position seems to have been securely established after this time, and at his death in 1287 there was a flourishing Norman settlement round Bunratty and Quin.

In January 1280 Richard de Burgo, earl of Ulster, had livery of his inheritance, and Ulster and to some extent Connacht, apart from Roscommon, were no longer the direct concern of the royal government. For more than forty years the 'Red Earl' was to be the most important of the Norman-Irish magnates, and it is clear that considerable advances in Norman colonization in Ulster were made in his time. There had been troubles in Ulster during his minority, not only with the Irish (we hear in 1276 of 'the war of Ulster' and fighting with O'Hanlon) but also between the king's seneschal, William fitz Warin, and the de Mandevilles, who were powerful in north Antrim and made war in alliance with O'Neill and O'Cahan, while the Irish chiefs of Antrim and Down, as well as O'Neill of Inishowen, sided with fitz Warin. The Mandevilles were defeated, but the personal quarrel between them and fitz Warin was to be long-lived. These disturbances, however, were less important than the quantity of surviving records of them would

[32] *36th Rep. D.K.*, p. 26; P.R.O., London, S.C. 1/18/15; S.C. 1/20/45.
[33] *C.D.I.*, III, pp. 510, 520.

suggest, and the prosperity of the earldom does not seem to have been much affected. But de Burgo did not come himself to Ireland till 1286.

Meanwhile Robert de Ufford, who had been justiciar since 1276, had gone to England before the middle of April 1280, leaving Stephen de Fulbourne, bishop of Waterford, the treasurer, as his deputy.[34] Ufford returned to Ireland before the end of the year, but on 21 November 1281, as he was 'so affected by infirmity that he cannot attend to the office', it was committed to Fulbourne, who held it till his death in July 1288.[35] There was a good deal of disturbance in the country: we hear that there was in 1281 'great and general warfare between the foreigners and Gaedil, so that many people were slain and many depredations committed'.[36] In west Connacht the Barretts and Cusacks had a quarrel which ended in a battle that found its way into all the annals,[37] and behind all this there was the constant dispute among the O'Connors as to the kingship which had led to five kings in the six years before 1280. In 1281 Ufford was in Connacht in July and in November, and Fulbourne went there in 1282.[38] In 1283 he seems to have been occupied in Leinster: at least we hear that there was 'great warfare in Laigin, and the castle of Lege was burnt by the Gaedil of Laigin and Mide'.[39] Then in 1284 there was a full scale expedition to Connacht, which lasted from late July to the end of August.[40] Its occasion is given by the annals as the killing of Simon de Exeter, and operations seem to have been in northern Roscommon. But Connacht remained disturbed, and in 1285 there were troubles in Meath, where O'Melaghlin twice defeated Norman armies.

Meanwhile the activities of the justiciar seem to have been provoking great discontent. He had been treasurer since Michaelmas 1274, and had retained the office on becoming justiciar, though acting by deputies, of whom the chief was his brother, Walter de Fulbourne. An investigation of the whole administration in 1284 gave an opportunity for these discontents to find expression. There was a violent dispute as to the liability of certain tenants-in-chief in co. Dublin to pay scutage[41]; there were assertions that the justi-

---

[34] A major preoccupation of his justiciarship had been the request of the Irish for English law: see above, pp. 188–9.
[35] He continued to be treasurer till 1285, exercising the office by deputy.
[36] AI.
[37] The royal government was strong enough to take William Barrett's lands into the king's hand (Cal. Justic. Rolls, I, pp. 227–8, 312).
[38] C.D.I., II, no. 2291, pp. 535, 537.
[39] AI.   [40] C.D.I., II, pp. 539–40.
[41] J. Otway-Ruthven, 'Knight Service in Ireland', Journ. R.S.A.I., LXXXIX, pp. 7–9.

ciar had used his position to enrich himself at the expense of the revenue, and that he had corruptly extorted payments of all kinds from individuals; while it was alleged that 'little wars had been caused in the land by the Irish because they had no confidence in the justiciar'.[42] It is impossible to tell what justification there was for all this, but at any rate, though great irregularities were found in his account he was pardoned all arrears above £4,000 and continued in the office of justiciar at a fixed salary of £500, holding it till his death in July 1288, though the office of treasurer was given to Nicholas de Clere.

Before this, in 1286, Richard de Burgo had come to Ireland for the first time. His first attention seems to have been given to Connacht, which was, as we have seen, considerably disturbed, while in this year his principal tenant there, Maurice fitz Maurice, died, leaving only daughters to succeed him. It is true that they were in theory sub-tenants, holding of Gerald fitz Maurice, the fourth baron of Offaly, but their possessions were too great a part of the province for the earl to ignore them. Maurice fitz Gerald had acquired from Hugh de Lacy Carbury and the northern half of Luighne, as well as his theoretical claim to Tir Conaill; from Jordan de Exeter the southern half of Luighne; his son got Corran from the Prendergasts. These great territories formed the Geraldine manor of Sligo. In addition they claimed Fermanagh. To the south, in Galway, they had the manors of Ardrahan and Kilcolgan, while in Mayo they held most of the barony of Kilmaine, Conmaicne Cuile. De Burgo could not but be interested in the succession, and the annals say he made a great hosting into Connacht, obtaining ascendancy wherever he came and taking hostages of the whole province; then, with the forces of Connacht, he turned northwards against Tir Conaill and Tir Eoghain, taking hostages from each, and deposing Donnell, son of Brian O'Neill, in favour of Nial Culanach O'Neill.

So far John fitz Thomas, who was to be second only to de Burgo for the rest of the century, held only a minor place as tenant of Banada in Sligo, which had been granted to his father by Maurice fitz Maurice. But the disappearance of his uncle left him a dominant position in Connacht, immensely strengthened when in 1287 his cousin, Gerald fitz Maurice, fourth baron of Offaly, died childless, leaving John the head of the Leinster Geraldines and baron of Offaly, though it was not till 1293 that he obtained from Gerald's aunt, Juliana, the wife of John de Cogan, a quitclaim of all her rights to the Geraldine lands. The Connacht lands had been divi-

[42] *C.D.I.*, III, p. 15.

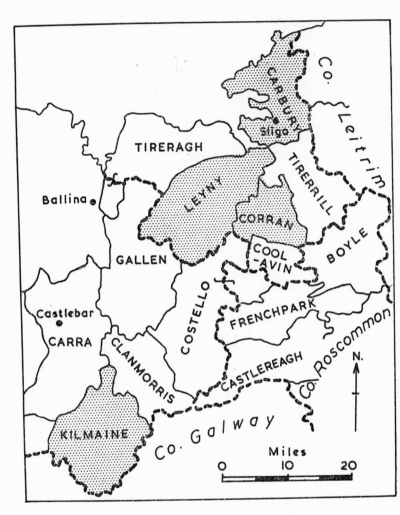

The Geraldine Lands in Connacht

ded in 1289 between the daughters of Maurice fitz Maurice: Amabil, and Juliana, the widow of Thomas de Clare. John acquired
Amabil's share in 1288, though the final formal quitclaim was not
made till 1293. This included the manor of Sligo, which in 1289
included four cantreds in Tir Conaill: the coast up to Donegal
town, and part at least of the barony of Raphoe. These lands, which
were evidently in the occupation of the Irish, for we are told only
that they were accustomed to pay a rent, were no doubt the con-
crete result of the expeditions against Tir Conaill of which we hear
repeatedly in the 1240s and 50s, and may well have been a bone of
contention between de Burgo and fitz Thomas, for the original
grant of Tir Conaill had been made by Hugh de Lacy, earl of
Ulster, and it is not impossible that de Burgo thought that it was
held of him, and fitz Thomas that it was held directly of the king,
while in any case de Burgo had claims and interests in Tir Conaill.
When de Burgo next led an army into Connacht in 1288 fitz
Thomas was not yet in occupation of Amabil's inheritance but it
had been made over to him, and he was now baron of Offaly, a
great man in his own right.[43] The occasion of this expedition seems
to have been the renewal of the civil wars of the O'Connors: de
Burgo backed one candidate and found fitz Thomas backing another,
upon which he withdrew.

By this time there was a new justiciar, John de Sandford, archbishop of Dublin, who had been appointed by the council on the
death of Fulbourne in July 1288. We are fortunate in having an
unusually full account of the activities of the central authority in
this period in the detailed account of Sandford's expenses while he
was justiciar.[44] He was elected by the council on 7 July, and on 20
July, having summoned the royal service to Kildare for 9 September against the Irish of Offaly and Leix, he set out for Connacht
'to survey the king's castles and pacify that land'. By 23 August he
had returned from Connacht, and was at Reban, co. Kildare. On
9 September the service of Leinster—one hundred knights—came
in person to Kildare, led by the four seneschals: the rest of the
country seems to have paid scutage. Having reviewed the army
and posted it to guard the marches of Offaly and Leix, Sandford
set off for the south, having had news that the Irish of Desmond
had become unsettled. He reached Cork on 24 September and was
there for a few days; on 1 October he was at Limerick, and after
three days came back by way of Clonmel and Waterford, reaching
Kildare in the middle of October in the comfortable knowledge

[43] Red Book of Kildare, nos. 30, 32–34, 85–94, 129.
[44] C.D.I., III, no. 559.

that he had induced the Irish of Desmond to come to the king's peace. But the war in Offaly still continued, and the service ended on 18 October: he had to arrange for Geoffrey de Geneville, Peter de Bermingham, lord of Tethmoy, and John fitz Thomas to guard the northern marches, being paid out of the money received for scutage[45]: he himself arranged guards for the southern march. Presumably he then returned to Dublin, but he arranged for an eyre to be held at Clonmel in January 1289, and was there himself to supervise its opening on 14 January, after which he went on to Desmond. He was back at Carlow on 30 January, and presumably went on to Dublin. On 13 March he was at Drogheda, and went west from it through Theobald de Verdon's lands in Meath 'to inspect the state of those parts', and then on to Connacht 'to survey and supply the king's castles there'. He was at Roscommon and Randown from 23 March to 18 April, and then went on to Dunmore and Tuam

to provide a force to make war against Omalethel and other Irish being at war and against the king's peace in the marches of Meath, and to cut a pass in the parts of Meath and Connacht.

He seems to have raised an army of one hundred horse and 4,500 foot, as well as Magnus O'Connor with all his force: the annals say that they were heavily defeated by O'Melaghlin, who 'behaved himself with such Lyonlike force, valour, and courage that he might be well compared to Hector'.[46] But in the next year this Carbry MacArt O'Melaghlin, who had been one of the most successful of the Irish leaders of his time, was treacherously killed by MacCochlan of Delvin MacCochlan, and we hear that 'for this cause the earle of Ulster spoyled and destroyed the said McCoghlan and his country', which may suggest an alliance of which we have no other knowledge.[47]

Meanwhile, at the end of April 1289, the justiciar had returned from Connacht to Leinster, but by the middle of June he was again on his way to Clonmel, where the eyre was still in progress, and went on from there to Limerick and Cork, being concerned with 'arduous affairs touching the king and the earl of Connacht (i.e. de Burgo) and the state of Desmond and Thomond': Thomas de Clare had died in 1287, when his heir was only six. In the autumn Sandford was again concerned with the disturbances in Leix and Offaly, where 'the king's lieges were daily killed, their houses

---

[45] Cf. Cal. Justic. Rolls, II, pp. 74, 83; P.R.O., London, C 47/10/17, no. 5.
[46] A. Clon.
[47] AC; A. Clon. In 1292 MacCochlan was killed in his own country by one of the Berminghams at the earl's instigation (AC).

burned, and intolerable depredations made'. All attempts to induce the Irish to come to the peace having failed, it was decided that an army must be raised, and 'all men of good will to the king', Irish as well as English, throughout Leinster and Munster were summoned to Buttevant in Leix, and a ten days expedition from 26 September to 4 October reduced the Irish to peace, in spite of the defeat of fitz Thomas and Peter de Bermingham.[48] And by this time Sandford had begun a series of parliaments: one at Dublin after Michaelmas, another at Dublin in January 1290, and a third at Kilkenny in April, at which time the justiciar's deputies were engaged in organizing an expedition with O'Connor against O'Melaghlin and 'other enemies of the king then at war in the marches of Meath, and to cut the pass of Delvin'.[49] Then in May there was news of trouble at Athlone, and the justiciar went there himself, starting on 6 May and returning on 14 May.[50] Finally on 14 June he set out on a tour of the south and west to inspect officials, proclaiming that complaints of them might be made to him. He went through Meath and on to Connacht, Tipperary, Limerick, Cork and Waterford, spending two months on the whole tour. Sandford was perhaps an exceptionally conscientious official, but activity of this kind was nevertheless the normal pattern of a justiciar's life. We know that John Wogan was as energetic; that we do not know it certainly of others must be ascribed to the deficiency of records.

Sandford was succeeded in November 1290 by a very different man, William de Vescy, lord of Kildare, whose activities produced a greater surviving volume of complaint than those of any other chief governor of the middle ages. De Vescy's mother had been the eldest of the seven daughters of Sybil Marshal, to whom Kildare had been assigned in the partition of 1247, and though a careful division had been made between them, Agnes de Vescy had succeeded in asserting herself as, in practice, the sole ruler of the liberty, subject only to cash payments to her sisters. When Agnes died in 1290 this position was inherited by her son, William. But Kildare included not only the modern county, but also the territories of Offaly and Leix. In the partition Leix had been assigned to the fifth of the Marshal co-heiresses, Eva de Braose. Her heirs were, of course, tenants-in-chief, but Leix remained administratively part of the liberty of Kildare, owing suit to the county court of Kildare, and subject to the administrative attentions of the

[48] *AC*. The justiciar's account shows expenses for the rescue of fitz Thomas.
[49] This may have been the 'army of Roscrea' proclaimed in Sandford's time (*37th Rep.D.K.*, p. 43; *C.D.I.*, IV, nos. 23, 86, 129).
[50] Cf. *C.D.I.*, III, no. 653.

officials of the liberty.[51] Moreover, the baron of Offaly, John fitz Thomas, was de Vescy's tenant, though the knight service he owed for the manors of Lea and Geashill had been assigned to Mortimer, lord of Dunamase, one of the heirs of Eva de Braose.[52] To a man as ambitious as fitz Thomas undoubtedly was, the position must have been galling in the extreme, and de Vescy's rights seem to have been exercised in a high-handed and tactless way, while if all the complaints made against de Vescy in the English parliament were true he was clearly unhampered by any undue scrupulousness.[53]

By 1289, when Peter de Bermingham of Tethmoy entered into one of the earliest known indentures of service with him,[54] fitz Thomas was clearly building up his power. But de Burgo was of course dominant in Connacht: in 1291, after a successful piece of king-making in Tir Eoghain, he raided Tir Conaill, and then entered Connacht, where he obtained what the annals say was a pretended submission, presumably from the Irish chieftains.[55] After this there was war between the O'Connor factions, with the settlers taking part on both sides. Then in 1292 the earl launched an expedition against Magnus, the successful claimant, who seems to have submitted to him unequivocally. But Magnus died in 1293 and the justiciar made Aedh O'Connor king in succession to him: ten days later fitz Thomas took Aedh prisoner, though he was presently released and restored to power by the justiciar.[56] In the summer de Vescy summoned the royal service of Ireland to Kildare to proceed against Offaly: this was possibly to attack fitz Thomas, for the king, asserting that this tended to his injury and that of the people of Ireland, took the unprecedented step of cancelling the summons.[57] It is clear that feeling was building up against de Vescy: in the English parliament of Michaelmas 1293 a whole series of complaints was made against him by John fitz Thomas and others. Then, on 1 April 1294, what must have been a very sensational case began, when before the council at Dublin in the presence of the earls of Gloucester and Ulster and other magnates de Vescy accused fitz Thomas of having defamed him to the king

[51] J. Otway-Ruthven, 'The Medieval County of Kildare', *I.H.S.*, XI, pp. 181–99.
[52] J. Otway-Ruthven, 'Knights' Fees in Kildare, Leix and Offaly', *Journ. R.S.A.I.*, XCI, pp. 178–9.
[53] *C.D.I.*, IV, no. 106; H. G. Richardson and G. O. Sayles, *Rotuli Parliamentorum Anglie Hactenus Inediti*, pp. 30–45.
[54] *Red Book of Kildare*, no. 11.
[55] De Burgo and the justiciar are said to have gone to Ulster with an army against O'Hanlon and other kinglets (Grace, *Annals*, p. 40).
[56] Cf. *Rotuli Parliamentorum Hactenus Inediti*, pp. 41–42.
[57] *C.D.I.*, IV, nos. 62–64.

and council in England, and fitz Thomas retorted that de Vescy had said to him that the king was the most perverse and dastardly knight of his kingdom, with other things 'against our lord the king and his state'. A wager of battle followed; the parties were summoned before the king at Westminster; on 24 July de Vescy appeared ready to give battle, but fitz Thomas did not. De Vescy thus won his case by default, and nothing more is heard of the affair. But he had been removed from office before 4 June, when the Irish council appointed William fitz Roger, prior of Kilmainham, to act till the king provided a justiciar.

Meanwhile, though fitz Thomas had freed himself of de Vescy, his quarrel with de Burgo remained. Fighting continued among the O'Connor factions in Connacht, and presently Aedh O'Connor broke down fitz Thomas's castle of Sligo. Fitz Thomas and Bermingham retaliated by an attempt to depose Aedh, but though they devastated the country they had no permanent success. Then, on 11 December 1294, fitz Thomas took de Burgo prisoner, and held him in his castle of Lea till he was released by the council in parliament at Kilkenny on 12 March 1295. It was time, for the annals tell us that the whole country had been disturbed by the quarrel. The justiciar was absent, and the treasury seems to have been empty, for the chancellor, who seems to have taken charge, represented that he took his own money to keep the land.[58] Fitz Thomas's motive is strongly suggested by the only condition of the release of which we know, for on 13 March de Burgo set his seal to a release to him of all his lordship of all the lands which fitz Thomas had in Connacht.[59] But this could not be a final settlement. By August 1295 fitz Thomas had been impleaded by the king in his court at Westminster for this and other offences, and had submitted to the king's will. On 15 November 1296, for good service in the war in Scotland, he had a general pardon for all offences in Ireland except those against de Burgo, and finally, by agreements made in 1298 and 1299, he gave de Burgo all his lands in Connacht, so that the rivalry was at last ended.[60]

Thomas fitz Maurice, the head of the Desmond Geraldines, had been appointed by the Irish council to succeed Dodingeseles, and seems to have been chiefly engaged in the war in Leinster which had been sparked off by the events of 1294 and continued all

---

[58] P.R.O., London, S.C. 8/100/4960. William Dodingeseles had been appointed as justiciar on 18 October 1294, and was paid from 19 October to 19 April 1295, but had certainly died some time before this.

[59] *Red Book of Kildare*, no. 9.

[60] *C.D.I.*, IV, nos. 246, 344; *Cal. Justic. Rolls*, I, pp. 234–6; *Red Book of Kildare*, no. 192.

through the first half of 1295, after which fitz Maurice received to the king's peace 'Maurice Macmuryarthi Macmurchoth with all his nation and following', on condition that they kept the peace, gave hostages for the MacMurroughs, O'Byrnes and O'Tooles, and gave pledges for the payment of six hundred cows for depredations done by them. They were also to make satisfaction for damage done to betaghs or other tenants of the king or others, who were to make like satisfaction to MacMurrough. MacMurrough further swore to make war against any of his following who infringed the covenant or made war against the king. The royal service had been summoned to Castledermot for this war; nothing appears as to O'Connor Faly, who had certainly taken the opportunity to rise in 1294, when he took de Vescy's castle of Kildare and destroyed the records of the lordship.

On 18 October 1295 John Wogan, lord of Picton in Pembrokeshire, who seems to have had no previous connection with Ireland, was appointed as justiciar, and held the office till June 1308, and again from May 1309, till August 1312. Wogan, who founded in Ireland a family which remained important in north Kildare till it died out in co-heiresses in the early eighteenth century, is perhaps the best documented justiciar of the middle ages, thanks to the fact that the Justiciary Rolls for his period of office had been calendared before their destruction in 1922, and this has given what is probably a misleading impression of him as the ablest and most energetic of chief governors. He was, however, certainly favoured by his long, continuous period of office, and during it the area subject to direct royal government was substantially increased by what seems to have been a deliberate royal policy, showing itself also in other parts of Edward's dominions.[61] In 1297 William de Vescy surrendered to the crown the liberty of Kildare, while that of Carlow fell in to the crown on the death of Roger Bigod in 1306. Other important accessions of territory had been the surrender to the crown in 1281 of her lands in Connacht, south Kildare, and co. Dublin by Christina de Mariscis, one of the co-heiresses of the de Ridelisfords; of lands in Kildare by John de Mohun, one of the Marshal co-heirs, in 1299; and of all his lands in Ireland—principally the baronies of Ardee, co. Louth, and Ikeathy, co. Kildare— by Ralph Pipard in 1302.[62] Moreover, more important than all, half the liberty of Meath had been firmly incorporated in the royal counties. When Meath had been divided between the co-heiresses

[61] See J. Otway-Ruthven, 'The Constitutional Position of the Great Lordships of South Wales', *Trans. R. Hist. Soc.*, fifth series, VIII, pp. 15–16.

[62] For references, see J. Otway-Ruthven, 'The Medieval County of Kildare', loc. cit., p. 196.

of Walter de Lacy, Matilda, wife of Geoffrey de Geneville, had received her share as fully as de Lacy had best held it, but Margery, wife of John de Verdon, seems to have got only the restricted liberties which her grandfather had held at his death.[63] In practice, however, her half seems to have been treated as a liberty till *c.* 1280, after which it was incorporated in the royal county of Dublin and was in 1297 created a separate county, with its own county court at Kells. The area of direct royal government had thus been greatly increased during Edward's reign: by its end only Wexford and Kilkenny remained as liberties in Leinster, and only half of Meath. But it is by no means certain that this added to the efficiency of a government the resources of which were strictly limited: it is perhaps not altogether surprising that under Edward II both Carlow and Kildare were reconstituted as liberties, while under Edward III new liberties were created in Tipperary and Kerry, and, for a short time, Louth.

Wogan found the feud between de Burgo and fitz Thomas ended, and the country more or less at peace when he reached Ireland in December 1295, and fitz Maurice, the *custos*, had just completed an eyre in the south-west, in the course of which he had heard pleas in Tipperary, Limerick, Cork and Kerry. There were, of course, occasional disturbances: in the midlands O'Farrell had been making war against the settlers, razing de Verdon's castle of Moydow, and the neighbouring castle of Newtown, as well as the castle of Moybreakry, now Street, co. Westmeath. It is not surprising that the earl of Ulster's men had stopped the ferries of Connacht.[64] In Ulster and Connacht the civil wars of the Irish, in which the settlers often took part, continued, but though in 1297 the Irish of Slievemargy burnt Leighlin, and the 'service of Cumber' (Castlecomer) was summoned, and early in 1298 an expedition was necessary to relieve Bunratty, still in the king's hand because of minority, which was being besieged by Turlough O'Brien,[65] these were the only major incidents of these years. In the summer of 1297 it was possible for the justiciar and other officials to write to the king that the country was 'at peace according to its manner', though there were too many, English and Irish, who wished to do evil, and they feared that there might be trouble in Munster over the death of Sir Richard Harold, of which some of the 'Borgheyns' (the de Burgos) were accused.[66]

[63] See above, pp. 182, 187.
[64] *Cal. Justic. Rolls*, I, p. 73. These must have been the ferries across the Shannon.
[65] Grace, *Annals*, p. 44; *C.D.I.*, IV, nos. 442, 454, 521; *38th Rep. D.K.*, pp. 42, 45.
[66] P.R.O., London, S.C. 1/16/132. Cf. *Cal. Justic. Rolls*, I, pp. 120–21. Harold had been with John fitz Thomas in Scotland.

These were conditions in which peaceful development could take place. In 1297 the justiciar held an eyre at Kildare, where, as we saw, de Vescy had just surrendered the liberty to the king, and surveyed its whole organization, reorganizing it as a royal county, a subject which had already been dealt with in the parliament held at Dublin in the Easter term of that year.[67] But it was in Ulster and Connacht that expansion really seems to have been going on at the end of Edward's reign. After the final settlement of his quarrel with fitz Thomas in 1298, which, as we have seen, eliminated the Geraldines from Connacht, the Red Earl devoted his energies to the consolidation and extension of his lands. There had certainly been a considerable expansion of settlement beyond the Bann, in the modern co. Derry, since the middle of the century: we cannot trace its stages, but by 1296 the north of the county had clearly been settled. As early as 1300 there was some occupation of Inishowen, and in 1305 the earl built a castle at Northburgh (Greencastle, co. Donegal), and had leave from the bishop of Derry to set up a parish church there. In the same year he had from the king a grant of free chase in all his demesne lands of 'Torterye, Kenath, Kenalowen, Inchyven, Menkeue, and Matherne': that is, in districts which included the whole coast as far as Lough Swilly, and which were all in the immediate occupation of the Irish.[68] In April 1307 he obtained from the bishop of Raphoe all his land in Derry, and had probably already obtained from the bishop of Derry the city of Derry, together with lands in Inishowen. In 1312 the earl was petitioning the king that

a land which is called Derecolmkyll in Ulster which is *en Iricherie* which the said earl has purchased in the king's fee and by his leave should be enfranchised as his other lands of Ulster are.

In 1322, when de Burgo was an old man, and the position in Ulster had been much weakened by the results of the Bruce invasion, half the town of Derry was leased to the bishop of Raphoe, to hold at the earl's will, and in 1327 a new bishop of Derry complained to pope John XXII that the earl, 'supported by the favour of the temporal power', had compelled his predecessor to agree unwillingly to an arrangement by which the earl and his heirs had for twenty years held at a small annual rent a certain part of the city of Derry, the temporal jurisdiction there, and other rights of the

[67] *Early Statutes*, pp. 196–8.
[68] *C.D.I.*, IV, no. 338; ibid., V. no. 304; British Museum MS Add. 6041, f. 102. The lands in which free chase was granted are Tuirtre, co. Antrim; Cianacht, or south co. Derry; Cenel Eoghain (approximately co. Tyrone); Inishowen, co. Donegal; Moy Cova, round Dromore, co. Down; and Mourne, co. Down.

church of Derry. The archbishop of Armagh was ordered to hold an inquiry, but nothing further appears as to it.[69]

It is clear, then, that from the end of the thirteenth century de Burgo was vigorously extending the area of his lordship in Ulster. Much of this expansion, of course, rested on his relationships with the native Irish. These must have originated under Hugh de Lacy, if not, indeed, under John de Courcy: in no other way can we account for the division of the services owed by O'Hanlon for Orior between de Burgo and de Verdon.[70] And it is clear enough that in the time of Henry III the chiefs of the Irish of Ulster were regarded as being in some sort of tenurial relationship to the crown, which it must be remembered held the earldom from Hugh de Lacy's death in 1241 till 1263. Thus in 1244 a number of Irish rulers, including O'Neill, O'Donnell, and other Ulster chiefs, had been requested to join in person and with a force the justiciar and other subjects about to undertake an expedition to Scotland,[71] and similar letters occur as late as the reign of Edward III. The pipe rolls show O'Neill owing cows for rent, and he and O'Flynn of Tuirtre owed money aids for the king's wars.[72] Aedh Buidhe O'Neill, who succeeded Brian of the battle of Down as king of the Cenel Eoghain, appears in 1261–2 as 'retained with his fellows in the service of the lord Edward for keeping peace in the marches of Ulster' at a regular salary. In 1269 he acknowledged his subordination to de Burgo with remarkable explicitness, acknowledging that he ought to hold his regality from him, and if he fails to observe his undertakings the earl may eject him from it and give it to whomsoever he pleases.[73] When in the early 1270s Aedh Buidhe and O'Cahan joined with the Mandevilles in a war against the king's seneschal, who was governing Ulster during the Red Earl's minority, the other Ulster chiefs wrote to the king saying that they were ready to obey the seneschal as the king himself.[74]

We need not, of course, suppose that this subordination was necessarily a very close one. In Tir Eoghain the earl frequently intervened as a king-maker, but otherwise the Irish must have been

[69] British Museum MS Add. 6041, f. 101d; *C.P.R., 1307–13*, p. 292; *C.C.H.*, p. 18, no. 128; British Museum MS Cotton Titus B. XI, f. 2; Theiner, *Vetera Monumenta*, p. 237; *Cal. Papal Letters*, II, p. 256. *Iricherie* seems to be intended as the name of a district: cf. *Cal. Justic. Rolls*, II, p. 134: land towards *magna Irecheria*.

[70] J. Otway-Ruthven, 'The Partition of the de Verdon Lands', loc. cit.

[71] *C.D.I.*, I, no. 2716. This expedition never took place.

[72] Davies, *Discovery of the True Causes why Ireland was never Entirely Subdued* (1747), p. 20; Gilbert, *Facsimiles*, part II, plate lxxiii.

[73] E. Curtis, 'Sheriffs' Accounts of the Honor of Dungarvan, of Tweskard in Ulster, and of County Waterford, 1261–3', *Proc. R.I.A.*, XXXIX C, pp. 1–17; *3rd Report of the Historical MSS Commission*, p. 231.

[74] *C.D.I.*, II, no. 953.

left to conduct their affairs unhindered. More control must have been exercised over the Irish east of the Bann, but we have no detailed information. But all the Irish of Ulster, apparently including even O'Donnell, held their lands of the earl by the service of maintaining 'satellites' or kerne to serve the earl in his wars, and most of them also paid, or perhaps only owed, rents in cows.[75] These satellites were the 'bonnaght of Ulster' of later documents, and indeed already had that name in 1323, when the Red Earl granted to Henry de Mandeville 'the intendance of all satellites of our bonhaght in Ulster . . . as at any time they did to William Mchulyn'. In November 1331, after de Mandeville had been imprisoned for his share in the earl of Desmond's conspiracies, Stephen McHoulyn bound himself in £200 to the new earl for the *constablerie de bonnaght*, but the earl's murder in 1333 meant that in future the service, though never forgotten, was unenforceable.[76] This service, nothing quite parallel to which can be traced in any of the other lordships,[77] no doubt had its origins in Irish custom. It was perhaps from its exercise that O'Hanlon and MacMahon and others were returning in 1297 when they were killed by the English of Dundalk 'as they returned from the earl'.[78]

While this extension of power and influence was going on in Ulster, de Burgo was also active in Connacht. In 1300, two years after he had acquired the manor of Sligo from John fitz Thomas, he built a great castle at Ballymote to strengthen its defences. In 1305 he petitioned the king that

whereas Oconoghur an Irishman, who has perpetrated many homicides and robberies in the earl's land of Connacht, and continues to do so in hurt of the king's peace, holds in farm land of the king in Connacht called Scilmorthy, it might be granted to the earl or another Englishman, for as much yearly rent as the said Irishman has hitherto been accustomed to render, or in exchange for lands of the same value in the land of peace.[79]

[75] The inquisition of 1333 (*Cal. Inq. P.M.*, VII, p. 378) gives a total of 345 satellites, and does not mention O'Donnell; one of 1342 adds O'Donnell with 80 satellites, O'Reilly with 120 and O'Garvagh with 40: it also records that rents of cows were due from the Irish of eastern Ulster, except MacMahon and O'Hanlon, who paid rent to de Verdon (P.R.O., London, C 47/10/20/14; J. Otway-Ruthven, 'The Partition of the de Verdon Lands', *Proc. R.I.A.*, LXVI C). The Cenel Conaill had given hostages in 1238 (above, p. 100), and it would seem that the belief that O'Donnell was totally independent throughout the middle ages needs re-examination.

[76] *C.P.R., 1385-9*, p. 308; B.M. MS Add. 6041, f. 104; E. Curtis, 'The "Bonnaght" of Ulster', *Hermathena*, XXI, pp. 87–105; 'The MacQuillan or Mandeville Lords of the Route', *Proc. R.I.A.*, XLIV C, pp. 99–113; below, pp. 329, 364, 380.

[77] Elsewhere the Irish chiefs might be bound to assist a Norman overlord in war with all their power, but that is not the same thing. See e.g. *Cal. Ormond Deeds*, II, no. 46.

[78] *ALC.*   [79] *C.D.I.*, V, no. 437; *Cal. Justic. Rolls*, II, pp. 133–4.

It does not appear that anything came of this, and the civil wars of the O'Connors continued, while in 1307 'the Galls of Roscommon' were defeated with heavy losses in dead and prisoners by O'Kelly of Ui Maine at Ahascragh, the sheriff of Roscommon, Jordan de Exeter, being among the prisoners.[80] By 1308 the English of the Sligo area were acting in concert with MacDermot, the most powerful of the *irrachts*, against one of the factions and were defeated. Then, in 1309, MacDermot, acting in support of his foster son, Felim O'Connor, invited the intervention of the English, who were led by William de Burgo, the earl's first cousin, who seems to have been governing Connacht for him. A campaign followed, and eventually, in 1310, the rival claimant was assassinated by one Seonac Mac Uighilin (i.e. MacQuillan), a mercenary captain, at the instigation, it was alleged, of William de Burgo, who now billetted Mac Uighilin and his mercenaries on Sil Murray. But MacDermot,

much resenting the action of the Galls in restricting and diminishing his power—for the Galls felt sure that if this one man were weak the whole province of Connacht would be in their own hands,

took his foster son and inaugurated him at Carnfree with all the traditional ceremonies.[81]

In all this activity in Ulster and Connacht the only real interruption, as far as we know, had been in 1303. The earl had indeed taken part, with John Wogan, the justiciar, John fitz Thomas, Theobald Butler, and others in the campaign in Scotland against Balliol.[82] He was summoned, with John fitz Thomas, Geoffrey de Geneville, Theobald de Verdon, and a number of others to the expedition to Flanders in the late summer of 1297, the king promising that they should remain with him in person: an obvious reference to the violent quarrel which had broken out in England when Roger Bigod, earl marshal, the lord of Carlow, had refused to serve abroad in this campaign except with the king himself. In fact, however, only John fitz Thomas seems to have gone, and on 23 October, by which time a truce had already been made with France, the justiciar was ordered to withdraw from the agreements with the Irish magnates, as some of their articles seemed very hard. In 1301 the Irish magnates were again summoned, this time to an expedition to Scotland, but though every effort was made to persuade de Burgo to come, he refused. In 1303, however, he seems to

[80] *ALC.*

[81] *AC.*

[82] See J. F. Lydon, 'An Irish Army in Scotland, 1296', *The Irish Sword*, V, pp. 184–90. It was on this occasion that de Burgo renewed his acquaintance with Robert Bruce, and the marriage of his sister to James the Stewart of Scotland was arranged (*C.D.I.*, IV, no. 338; below, pp. 224–5).

have been given his own terms, and took an important part in the Scottish campaign of that year.[83]

It was, of course, nothing new for Irish resources to be used in wars outside Ireland. At least one of the Irish tenants-in-chief had served in person in Gascony in 1254[84]; Irish troops had been employed in Edward's wars in Wales in 1256–7. Provisions of all kinds were sent throughout the century to armies in France, Wales and Scotland; brattices (wooden breastworks) were prefabricated in Ireland and shipped to Wales; timber, cloth and other things were all bought by the Irish exchequer to supply the king's armies. It is quite impossible to estimate what the total cost of all this may have been, nor did the drain on the Irish revenue end there. The expedition to Scotland in 1296 cost the Irish exchequer more than £5,500. And throughout the thirteenth century there had been a steady flow of payments from Ireland to the king's wardrobe in England, amounting between 1203 and 1307 to a minimum of nearly £90,000, and probably very much more, while in addition substantial sums were from time to time paid out in settlement of the king's debts outside Ireland. Since the average annual revenue under Edward I seems to have been no more than £6,300 it is not surprising that by the reign of Edward II the justiciar was representing that what was left of the Irish revenue did not suffice for the preservation of the peace. But by this time it was too late: the Irish revenue was already declining, no doubt largely as a result of increasing lawlessness, and though in 1311 a change of policy, almost certainly connected with the movement of the Ordainers in England which sought to control the king and to cut off the flow of revenues into the wardrobe for that purpose, was announced, it was very shortly abandoned.[85]

With the beginning of the fourteenth century the state of Leinster seems to have deteriorated abruptly. In 1301, no doubt as a result of the departure of the justiciar for the expedition to Scotland, the Irish of the mountains rose: the royal service was proclaimed at Newcastle McKynegan, and Wogan's deputy led an expedition based on Newcastle from 18 January 1302 to 12 March, while in the same period Walter Wogan had a small force in north Wexford 'to repress the rebellion of the MacMurroughs and O'Byrnes',

[83] J. F. Lydon, 'Irish Levies in the Scottish Wars, 1296–1302', *The Irish Sword*, V, pp. 207–17.

[84] P.R.O., London, C 47/10/15/5.

[85] J. F. Lydon, 'Three Exchequer Documents from the Reign of Henry III', *Proc. R.I.A.*, LXV C, pp. 1–27; 'Edward II and the Revenues of Ireland in 1311–12,' *I.H.S.*, XIV, pp. 39–57; 'An Irish Army in Scotland in 1296', loc. cit., p. 188; H. G. Richardson and G. O. Sayles, 'Irish Revenue, 1278–1384', *Proc. R.I.A.*, LXII C, pp. 87–100.

and in the late summer or autumn another expedition against the O'Nolans in Carlow was necessary.[86] Another service seems to have been proclaimed in 1302, and there was certainly one at Kilkenny in 1303.[87] In 1305 a service was summoned to Kildare, which must have been due to the disturbances which can reasonably be supposed to have been produced by the atrocious murder in Peter de Bermingham's castle of Carbury of O'Connor Faly and some thirty of his family and following: there was 'great warfare in the above year between the foreigners and Gaedil in Leinster and Desmond'.[88] In the summer of 1306 the justiciar was leading an expedition against the 'Irish felons of the mountains of Leinster' which cost £1,800 in wages alone, and his deputy was engaged in a similar expedition with two hundred hobelars and five hundred footmen from 23 October 1308 to 18 November.[89] In 1309 the service of Castlekevin was proclaimed, and Peter de Gaveston, Edward II's favourite, who had been sent to Ireland as the king's lieutenant in the previous summer as the result of baronial opposition to him in England, led a force to restore the position in the neighbourhood of Glendalough, where the Irish had burnt the archbishop's castle of Castlekevin a year earlier: he is alleged before he left Ireland in June to have subdued the O'Byrnes, rebuilt Newcastle and Castlekevin, and cut a pass between Castlekevin and Glendalough.[90]

And while war continued in the Wicklow mountains (in 1311 the Irish rose again, burning and robbing the king's manor of Saggart, and a force was led against them by the justiciar), there were other disturbances in these years. In 1305 the seneschal of Wexford had been killed by the Irish; in 1306 'Peter Bermingham lost many men in the borders of Meath'. In 1307 the Irish of Offaly burned the castle of Geashill and besieged that of Lea, and in this year a royal service was proclaimed at Loughsewdy. In 1308 Athy was burned by the Irish.[91] In 1309 Maurice de Canteton raised a war in Wexford: he

slew Richard Talun, and afterwards . . . having combined with Dounlyng Obryn and other Irishmen from the mountains of Leinster, openly put themselves at

---

[86] *38th Rep. D.K.*, p. 87; *Cal. Justic. Rolls*, I, pp. 382–3; ibid., III, pp. 19–20; *Report of the Commissioners respecting the Public Records of Ireland, 1810–15*, p. 167.
[87] *Cal. Justic. Rolls*, II, p. 296.
[88] *AI*; *Cal. Justic. Rolls*, II, pp. 215, 242, 296.
[89] *C.D.I.*, V, nos. 549, 556, 561, 567; *39th Rep. D.K.*, p. 34.
[90] *39th Rep. D.K.*, p. 34; *C.C.H.*, p. 9, no. 77; Grace, *Annals*, p. 55. Castlekevin was certainly rebuilt, the archbishop of Dublin, its lord, contributing £100 to the cost (*39th Rep. D.K.*, p. 34).
[91] *C.C.H.*, p. 19, nos. 14, 29; *Chart. St. Mary's*, II, pp. 291, 332, 335–6, 338; *Cal. Justic. Rolls*, III, pp. 3–4.

war against the king with standards displayed, doing many murders, robberies and other evils.

Wogan led a force against them in September, and long lists of persons, Irish as well as English, were pardoned all offences in return for their good service in fighting them.[92] In February 1310 John Boneville, the king's seneschal of the former liberties of Carlow and Kildare, was killed, allegedly by Arnald le Poer, who was said to be in alliance with the Irish of the mountains of Leinster, and to have been besieging Boneville. He and various members of his household were acquitted of the murder by a jury of knights in July—it was said to have been committed by David de Offyntoun —but were convicted of having carried away Boneville's goods after his death, and admitted to make fine. In Lent of this year the justiciar went with a force to Munster, to settle disputes and bring rebels to justice, and early in the year there was also a dispute between the de Lacys in Meath on one side, and John fitz Thomas and John son of Peter de Bermingham of Tethmoy on the other.[93] In the autumn there was trouble of a different kind: MacMahon and O'Reilly 'openly put themselves at war against the king on account of divers dissensions between the English and Irish of their marches'. One of the justices of the bench was sent to treat with them, and an agreement was concluded by which in return for a fine they received charters of pardon, and complaints were to be settled by arbitration, but unfortunately a few days before the peace was proclaimed some of the settlers of co. Louth raided one of the O'Reillys, who retaliated by robbing and burning Robertstown in the barony of Kells, co. Meath, 'so that the whole peace of those marches is destroyed'.[94]

The history of these years will have made it abundantly plain that there was little ground for Orpen's assertion that during Wogan's long term of office there was 'but little disturbance on the Irish marches and no conflict between the Irish magnates and the Government, or between the Irish magnates themselves'.[95] But the demands of the king on the Irish revenue continued, and nearly one half of the recorded expenditure of Irish treasurers during this period went on the Scottish war, while Edward II continued, as

[92] C.C.H., p. 12, no. 9; p. 14, no. 222; 39th Rep. D.K., p. 31; Cal. Justic. Rolls, III, pp. 145–6, 159–61, 199–200, 237, 247; C.C.R., 1307–13, pp. 181, 413, 422; Cal. Fine Rolls, 1307–19, p. 185.
[93] C.C.H., p. 13, nos. 49, 58–59; 39th Rep. D.K., pp. 45, 46; Cal. Justic. Rolls, III, pp. 156, 163–4, 217, 247.
[94] Cal. Justic. Rolls, III, pp. 161, 209–10, 211, 213, and cf. ibid., pp. 170–71, 173–4; C.C.H., p. 15, no. 12.
[95] Normans, IV, p. 39.

his father had done, to demand remittances of cash. By the summer of 1311 the Irish government was acutely conscious of financial difficulty, and in this year a combination of its representations, and the determination of the Ordainers in England to deprive the crown of free revenue, produced a very temporary reversal of the policy of the previous century. On 9 October the king ordered the justiciar and treasurer to cause all debts due to the crown to be levied with all speed, and to apply this and all other revenue 'to the reformation of the estate of the land and its salvation'. Strenuous attempts were now made to levy outstanding debts, but it seems unlikely that this substantially increased the revenue. And in any case, before very long the king reverted to ordering the payment of his debts from the issues of Ireland, and the supply of provisions for the war in Scotland, to be paid for by the Irish revenue, while in April 1314 he ordered the handing over for the purposes of the war of all the cash then in the Irish exchequer, as well as everything received in the next three months. The Irish administration was thus financially crippled before Bruce's invasion began in 1315, and by the second half of the fourteenth century Ireland had become a permanent financial liability to the English crown.[96]

Meanwhile, a full-scale war had developed in south-western Ireland. Things had been relatively quiet in Thomond for some time, but after the death of Turlough O'Brien in 1306 war broke out between rival branches of the O'Briens. In 1308 Wogan while in Limerick had effected an amicable agreement between 'Doneghugh Obrien, chief of the Irish of Thomond' and the city of Limerick, which provided that 'the subjects of the one chief of Thomond or his tenants be not distrained or attached by the occasion of the debts or trespasses of the other chief or his tenants'.[97] In 1311 matters entered a new phase, when the war became one which involved not only the Irish of co. Clare, but also the de Burgos, who supported Donough O'Brien, and de Clare, who supported Dermot. In May 1311 a royal writ ordered Edmund le Botiller and others to forbid Richard de Clare and Donough O'Brien, 'who calls himself king of the Irish of Thomond', to continue to make war against each other. But Donough and the de Burgos invaded Tradry, William de Burgo having with him many of the Connacht men and the Normans of Meath, and on 20 May at Bunratty there was

---

[96] Lydon, 'Edward II and the Revenues of Ireland in 1311–12', loc. cit. The Ordinances applied also to Ireland, and in pursuance of them a general resumption of grants made since 16 March 1310, and the abolition of new customs and maltotes were ordered (ibid., p. 39; C.C.R., 1307–13, p. 411; Cal. Fine Rolls, 1307–19, p. 108).

[97] Cal. Justic. Rolls, III, p. 2.

a pitched battle between them and de Clare, who was supported by a few of the Normans of Desmond and a few Irish. De Burgo and others were taken prisoner, and both sides seem to have had considerable losses.[98] Donough O'Brien retreated, and was killed later in the year by some of his own clan. Dermot O'Brien, de Clare's ally, now became king—he 'was made full king by the foreigners and the Gaedil'—and William de Burgo was released by de Clare on conditions which he broke, returning to Thomond to make war on de Clare and Dermot. Before the end of the year there had been another battle at Bunratty in which de Clare was defeated, and after this the earl of Ulster intervened, holding a conference with de Clare at which a partition of Thomond between the rival O'Briens was arranged.[99] Fighting continued, but in 1313 the partition was actually made, and peace established, and in 1314 Richard de Clare went to England. But immediately afterwards the O'Brien wars broke out again, with the Normans on opposite sides as before, and the de Clare party ultimately victorious.

Meanwhile, in the east there had been serious and unexplained disturbances in co. Louth, where Robert de Verdon and others rose in rebellion in Lent 1312,

appropriating to themselves as if by conquest the demesne lands of the king, administering the oath of fealty as well to free tenants and betaghs of the king as to other inhabitants of the said county and taking homage.

There appears to have been no local resistance: the lands of Drew de Merlon, who held the barony of Louth of the king, were taken into the king's hand by the justiciar and council on account of the weakness of his bailiffs, who were unable to resist them.[100] They seem to have plundered much of the baronies of Ferrard and Ardee, and the justiciar collected a force at Dublin, and, sending a party to occupy Ardee, went himself to Drogheda, where the community of the county asked that 'to avoid the injury that might come to the country by the coming of the army' they might guard it themselves, led by Nicholas and Milo de Verdon, Robert's brothers.[101] The justiciar, allowing this, disbanded his force, but Nicholas and Milo proceeded to join their brother at Louth, and then fought and

---

[98] C.C.H., p. 17, no. 84; AI; Misc. Annals, p. 109.

[99] The earl was certainly associated with the whole war by public opinion, for in October of this year the keeper of the customs explained the decline of revenue from Galway by the 'war recently developed between Richard de Burgh and Richard de Clare in the parts of Thomond' (Lydon, 'Edward II and the Revenues of Ireland', loc. cit., p. 45, n. 20).

[100] C.C.R., 1307-13, p. 531.

[101] They were the younger brothers of Theobald de Verdon.

defeated the royal force from Ardee, alleging later that it had been feloniously burning the towns of the countryside, and

such felons ought not to have been spared because they carried as a banner the standard of the king, inasmuch as it is not to be presumed that it is a true standard of the king, with the carrying of which were done arson and robbery upon the loyal people of the king and those who were at peace.

Robert de Verdon and others subsequently surrendered to Roger Mortimer on the promise of safety of life and limb, and finally, in April 1313, the entire community of free tenants and others of the whole county of Louth, except the men of Drogheda, were allowed to make fine with the king in the sum of 500 marks, to be assessed on individuals according to their guilt and ability to pay by men elected by the community.[102]

Before this Wogan had ceased to be justiciar, on 6 August 1312, and Edmund le Botiller acted till 18 June 1314, when he was replaced by Theobald de Verdon. De Verdon, however, left office in February 1315, when Edmund le Botiller was appointed and thus had to meet the Bruce invasion at the end of May, showing himself possessed of little ability. But in any case the financial difficulties which have been outlined, and the growing state of lawlessness which had been apparent since the beginning of the century, the most alarming feature of which was the quarrels between the Anglo-Irish themselves, immensely complicated the task. There was clearly a general malaise, and an alarming number of the Anglo-Irish in Ulster and elsewhere were to show themselves ready to support Bruce.

---

[102] To the sources given by Orpen, add *Cal. Justic. Rolls.*, III, pp. 191, 237–9, 265–6, 275–8; *C.C.R.*, *1307–13*, pp. 525–6; ibid., *1313–18*, p. 36.

CHAPTER VII

The Bruce Invasion and its Aftermath

THROUGHOUT Edward I's Scottish wars Ireland had been a source of both men and supplies for the English crown, and continued to be so under Edward II.[1] But Edward II had had little interest in the war, and none of his father's ability: Bruce had had success after success, and when at last in the summer of 1314 Edward led a great army against the Scots, he was decisively defeated at Bannockburn on 24 June. Among those killed was the earl of Gloucester, whose great inheritance, which included the liberty of Kilkenny in Ireland, now fell to be divided among his sisters.

After Bannockburn Bruce clearly had the initiative, and an attack on the English position in Ireland offered many advantages. It would cut off a source of supply from England, it would provide her with yet another preoccupation, and it could be made to provide a settlement for his brother Edward, who might well become an embarrassment in Scotland. Moreover, there were many connections between Scotland and Ulster. It will be remembered that John had granted lands in Antrim to Alan of Galloway and Duncan of Carrick, and though these grants seem to have lapsed, Bruce's mother, from whom he inherited the earldom of Carrick, was Duncan's grand-daughter and the claim may well have been remembered. In addition certain of the Ulster settlers, notably the Bissets in the Glens of Antrim, seem to have been of Scottish origin and may have begun as Duncan's tenants. And there were more recent connections. In 1286 in the unexplained agreement known as the Turnberry Band the Bruces, with James the Stewart of Scotland, one of the Guardians of the realm after the death of Alexander III, and others undertook to support the earl of Ulster and Thomas de Clare against their adversaries. This can hardly refer to anything but some enterprise in Ireland, where Richard

---

[1] *C.C.H.*, p. 18, no. 147; p. 19, no. 7; *Cal. Justic. Rolls*, III, pp. 56, 77, 116, 163, 209; *C.C.R., 1307–13*, pp. 316, 413, 422, 525–6; ibid., *1313–18*, p. 36; Bain, *Calendar of Documents relating to Scotland*, III, pp. 395–6.

de Burgo had appeared for the first time in this year,[2] but we hear
of nothing more. But it is clear that a connection existed, and in
1296 James the Stewart married Egidia or Gelis de Burgo, the
earl's sister, acquiring with her lands about the river Roe in co.
Derry. Later, in 1302, Robert Bruce himself married as his second
wife the earl's daughter, Elizabeth, whose son, David II, succeeded
him. And there were connections at a lower level, for in the late
thirteenth century the galloglasses, professional mercenary soldiers
drawn from the Hebrides, had begun to appear in Ireland, where
they were employed by the native Irish rulers.[3] And at all times
geographical conditions ensured that there should be coming and
going between two countries separated by no more than thirteen
miles of sea, while the extent of Scottish influence in Ulster is indi-
cated by the fact that the dates of payment usual there were the
Martinmas and Pentecost of Scotland, not the Michaelmas and
Easter of England and the rest of Ireland. Robert Bruce himself,
when driven from Scotland by his enemies in 1294, seems to have
gone to Ireland, and almost certainly fled to Rathlin Island, of
which the Bissets were lords, after the rout of Methven in 1306.[4]

It is likely that plans for the invasion of Ireland began soon after
Bannockburn, and there must have been negotiations with the
Irish chiefs of Ulster. An undated letter from Robert Bruce to 'all
the kings of Ireland, to the prelates and clergy, and to the inhabitants of all Ireland, his friends', in which he refers to the common
ancestry, language and customs of Irish and Scots, and speaks of
negotiations to strengthen their friendship, 'so that with God's
will your nation may be able to recover her ancient liberty', must
certainly belong to this period.[5] But the mission of John de Hotham,
whose connection with Ireland had begun at least as early as 1301,
and who was sent from England at the end of August 1314 'to explain certain matters concerning the king' with letters of credence
to a long list of magnates, including the earl of Ulster, probably
reflected the quarrels of England rather than any fear of Scottish
intervention in Ireland.[6]

---

[2] See above, p. 205.

[3] A. McKerral, 'West Highland Mercenaries in Ireland', *Scottish Historical
Review*, XXX, pp. 1–14. It is not impossible that some galloglasses were employed by the earl of Ulster himself.

[4] For Scottish affairs in this period, see G. W. S. Barrow, *Robert Bruce*. For
the attitude of the Bissets, see ibid., pp. 238–9.

[5] Ibid., p. 434, and *Scottish Historical Review*, XLII, pp. 38–39.

[6] *C.C.R., 1313–18*, p. 193. Hotham, who was later to be bishop of Ely and
treasurer and chancellor of England, was in Ireland from 5 September to 30
November (*Analecta Hibernica*, II, p. 203). For his earlier connections with Ireland, see *38th Rep. D.K.*, p. 54; *Cal. Justic. Rolls*, II, p. 290; ibid., III, p. 86;
C.C.H., p. 8, no. 75.

Edward Bruce landed, probably at Larne, on 25 May 1315. It does not seem that the colonists had expected a landing, for the earl was in Connacht, and it was left to the local levies to meet a force of experienced veterans, who inevitably defeated them. Bruce was now joined by Donnell O'Neill, king of Tir Eoghain, O'Cahan, O'Hanlon, MacGilmurry, MacCartan and O'Hagan: the other chiefs of Ulster held off, hoping each 'to retain the chief power over his own district and hold it free from tribute and taxation'.[7] He then marched southwards, defeated the local Irish chiefs in the Moyry pass, and on 29 June took and burned Dundalk, and then plundered its neighbourhood.[8]

Meanwhile the earl of Ulster was assembling his forces in Connacht, and Edmund le Botiller, who had succeeded Theobald de Verdon as justiciar when he left office on 27 February, seems to have proclaimed the 'army of Greencastle'[9] and marched northwards. The earl, with Felim O'Connor, assembled his forces at Roscommon, and he and the justiciar met south of Ardee, co. Louth, on 22 July. But now it was decided that the Connacht force alone should advance against Bruce, and the annalists agree in saying that this was at the earl's insistence:

I have here a force of 36,000 or more, and it is large enough to expel an equal number from the country, or to kill them in it. And since they have invaded my territory, I deem it preferable to proceed against them at my own expense, and to employ my own force.[10]

The most probable explanation of this is that he feared that if Ulster were recovered by the royal forces it might be treated as an escheat. At any rate, he advanced alone against Bruce, who retreated northwards, and presently the two armies were facing each other across the Bann at Coleraine, where Bruce had broken down the bridge. The earl's forces were now gravely weakened by the defection of Felim O'Connor, whose forces must have constituted a major part of the Connacht army, for Bruce

sent men to seek him out covertly and to offer him the possession of Connacht without partition, if he would desert the earl and maintain his right to that

---

[7] *County Louth Archaeological Journal*, I, p. 81.

[8] The only monograph on the Bruce invasion is O. Armstrong, *Edward Bruce's Invasion of Ireland*, but there is an important paper, J. F. Lydon 'The Bruce invasion of Ireland,' *Historical Studies*, IV, pp. 111–25.

[9] *Analecta Hibernica*, II, p. 266. Clyn (*Annals*, pp. 11–12) says there was a parliament of magnates at Kilkenny at the beginning of June 'to have aid and council against the Scots', but a valid parliament required forty days notice, and Bruce had only landed on 25 May. Perhaps the parliament, which is mentioned nowhere else, was really held at the beginning of July, or perhaps Clyn confused it with the parliament which was certainly held at Kilkenny in July 1316, which he does not mention.   [10] *AI*. The numbers must be regarded as pictorial.

province. And Feidlim listened tolerantly to these proposals and agreed with Edward.[11]

And meanwhile Felim's rival, Rory O'Connor, had visited Bruce at Coleraine and

promised to banish the Galls from the lordship of Connacht. And Edward consented after that to his making war on the Galls, provided that he did not commit depredation on Feidlim or trespass on his territory.[12]

The net result of all this was chaos in Connacht: Rory, assembling the men of Connacht and Breifne, burned all the principal towns of Connacht, was recognized as king by all the Irish chiefs except MacDermot, and was inaugurated at Carnfree. So far, Felim had still been with de Burgo, but on hearing of Rory's successes, he told the earl he must return to Connacht, and having fought his way through Ulster and Oriel reached his uncle, Sean O'Farrell, in Longford, where he suffered a final defeat after which he gave leave to his *irrachts* to accept Rory's lordship for the time being.

The earl, seeing his army so reduced, had fallen back from Coleraine to Connor, co. Antrim, where on 10 September he was defeated by the Scots with considerable loss, including the capture of his cousin William de Burgo. The Ulster English fled to Carrickfergus, where they were presently besieged; the earl fled to Connacht, where he was joined by the English settlers, and certain Irish chiefs: Felim O'Connor, Murrough O'Brien of Thomond,[13] MacDermot, and Gilbert O'Kelly of Ui Maine, 'who had all been expelled from the country'. MacDermot's pride was offended by this 'throng of deposed kings and exiles' and he withdrew and submitted to Rory, but soon returned to Felim. After this Connacht was entirely occupied by war between Rory O'Connor on one side and Felim, supported by the settlers, on the other, while the earl was 'a wanderer up and down Ireland, with no power or lordship', and O'Donnell raided Carbury and destroyed Sligo castle. In 1316 Rory was defeated and killed at Templetogher, co. Galway, and Felim, restored to the kingship, 'set out to banish the Galls of West Connacht'. But by this time William de Burgo had been released by the Scots, and on 10 August Felim met him in battle at Athenry and was utterly defeated and killed, with very many of his followers. But though after this 'all the Sil Murray except MacDermot' made peace with de Burgo, the country remained disturbed, and had of course been extensively wasted in the course of all this fighting:

[11] *AC.*
[12] *AC.*
[13] This was the O'Brien who had been supported by the de Burgos in Thomond and had been driven into Connacht in 1314 (*AI*).

after the battle of Connor the forces of Connacht, both English
and Irish, were in effect eliminated from the struggle with
Bruce.[14]

Meanwhile, in the east of the country Bruce had been going
from success to success. By the end of August 1315 the English
government had taken alarm, and was preparing to send John de
Hotham back to Ireland to co-ordinate measures against the Scots,
and on 1 September the justiciar and chancellor were ordered to
cause the magnates of Ireland to be convoked so that he might explain certain matters to them.[15] No doubt this was the parliament
held at Dublin on 27 October. But whatever was decided on at it,
nothing effective resulted, and in November Bruce was able to
advance into Meath, where about 6 December he met and defeated
Roger Mortimer, lord of Trim in right of his wife. Mortimer had
to flee to Dublin, and though the castle of Trim was held for him,
the other half of Meath lay open to Bruce, for de Verdon, its lord,
was in England where he died in July 1316, and no attempt seems
to have been made to co-ordinate its defence. Bruce marched westwards to Granard, and then south to Loughsewdy, plundering and
burning as he went. He spent Christmas at Loughsewdy and then,
burning the place behind him, marched on, guided by Mortimer's
tenants the de Lacys, who had joined him, through Irish territories,
into Leinster. Passing through Tethmoy he reached Kildare, where
he remained before the castle for three days. But the constable had
provisioned and garrisoned the castle, at a cost, as he alleged, of
more than £200, so that he was not taken by surprise, and though
he lost two of his kindred in the assault, the Scots were driven off,[16]
and went on south to Castledermot.

Meanwhile the English had been trying to reorganize themselves
after the disasters in Ulster and Meath. Mortimer had left the
country, and the justiciar and council, with Hotham, had summoned all the magnates to come to resist the Scots. John fitz
Thomas and his son Thomas, Maurice fitz Thomas, John le Poer,
baron of Dunoyl, Arnald le Poer, Maurice de Rocheford, and
David and Miles de la Roche, with their retinues of men-at-arms,
hobelers[17] and footmen, had responded, and when the Scots moved
out of Castledermot they found them waiting for them near Ard-

---

[14] For all these events see *AC.*

[15] *C.P.R., 1313–17*, pp. 346, 347; *C.C.R., 1313–18*, pp. 246, 308. The justiciar
and treasurer were in Munster in September (Bain, *Calendar of Documents relating
to Scotland*, III, no. 447).

[16] P.R.O., London, S.C. 8/4/183, 184; *Rotuli Parliamentorum*, I, p. 385.

[17] Light cavalry. See J. F. Lydon, 'The Hobelar: an Irish Contribution to
Mediaeval Warfare', *The Irish Sword*, II, pp. 12–16.

scull. But though Hotham wrote that the force was quite large
enough to have defeated the Scots, the annals say that the English
leaders quarrelled among themselves, and Bruce, though he had
losses, was left in possession of the field, which Hotham tactfully
explained to the king as due to mischance. The justiciar retreated
to Dublin, and it was perhaps at this time that Hotham, acting on
an earlier decision of the council, ordered the bell-tower of the
church of St Mary del Dam, from which Dame Street takes its
name, to be pulled down and the stones used for the repair of the
castle 'against certain perils that were feared'. Meanwhile the
Scots had established themselves in fortalices in Leix among the
Irish where cavalry could not be used against them. On 4 February
at Dublin the magnates who had been at Ardscull (at Hotham's
request they had left their troops in the Castledermot area), together with Richard de Clare, who had just arrived, swore to defend the king's rights in Ireland, and that their bodies, lands and
chattels should be forfeit if they failed in their loyalty. On the same
day the justices of the bench were ordered to postpone pleas till
after Easter because of the Scots. The treasury was empty; there
had been great expenses for the maintenance of the war, and nothing could be got because of the state of the country: Hotham
asked for £500 in haste.[18]

When Hotham wrote, on 15 February, the Scots were preparing
to attack John fitz Thomas's castle of Geashill in Offaly, but the
difficulties of provisioning an army in a countryside wasted by war
and suffering from a severe famine after a disastrous harvest seem
to have led to the abandonment of this plan: they suddenly retreated northwards through Fore, and so back to Ulster, which
they reached before the end of the month. No attempt to pursue
them was made, and indeed the attention of the authorities in the
south was sufficiently engaged by repeated sporadic risings of the
Irish of Leinster, against whom an expedition was sent in July,
while a subsidy for local defence was granted by the men of Fingal
and Leinster. It is clear that financial difficulties were acute: the
Irish revenue was in any case already declining during Edward's
reign, and Hotham had been obliged to borrow during the spring
for 'the prosecution of certain of the king's affairs'.[19]

[18] P.R.O., London, C 81/93/3594ᶜ (briefly calendared in Bain, *Calendar of
Documents relating to Scotland*, III, no. 469); *C.C.R., 1313–18*, p. 333; ibid., *1318–23*,
p. 90; *Cal. Chancery Warrants*, I, p. 436; *Historic and Municipal Documents*, pp.
405–6, and cf. ibid., p. 373; Gilbert, *Viceroys*, p. 527.

[19] *C.C.R., 1313–18*, pp. 289, 346; *Historic and Municipal Documents*, pp. 355–7,
375–83; J. F. Lydon, 'The Bruce Invasion', *Historical Studies*, IV, pp. 119–20;
above, p. 163.

In Ulster Bruce was holding a parliament, where we are told he hanged many, and about 1 May he had himself crowned as king of Ireland near Dundalk—at Faughart, according to Irish tradition. He took de Burgo's castle of Northburgh in Inishowen, and also succeeded in taking Greencastle, opposite Carlingford, though it was soon recaptured. Carrickfergus, the principal castle of Ulster, held out against him till September 1316, when the defenders were forced by hunger to surrender on terms of safety to life and limb.[20] The local settlers had occasional successes against raiding parties of Scots, and clearly Bruce's rule was not completely effective, but some of the settlers, including the Bissets, adhered to him, perhaps because of Scottish sympathies, or perhaps simply despairing of any effective action from Dublin. In the autumn he returned to Scotland, and succeeded in persuading his brother to intervene in Ireland: about Christmas Robert Bruce himself landed at Carrickfergus with an important force of galloglasses, and a new attack on the south was about to begin.

It was believed at the time that Robert Bruce had in mind a possible descent on the Welsh coast. It is certain that he was conscious of the importance to his kingdom of the western islands, and of the connections with north-eastern Ireland which geographical conditions made inevitable, and which were in any case the tradition of his mother's family. But in fact, given Edward Bruce's character, the attempt to make him the effective ruler of Ireland never had any real chance of success, and though it gravely embarrassed the English government in Ireland, it also drained away men and resources which the king of Scotland might more profitably have employed elsewhere. The native Irish seem to have been quickly disillusioned; only O'Neill remained an enthusiastic supporter, and the expedition which left Ulster early in February 1317 can never have had any real chance of permanent success.[21]

By 16 February the Scots had reached Slane, co. Meath, from which they advanced southwards to Skreen, and then on towards Dublin. The earl of Ulster, who was at his manor of Ratoath, ambushed them, but after hard fighting had to flee to Dublin, while Bruce advanced to Castleknock, within sight of the city, on 23 February. Meanwhile, on 21 February, the mayor of Dublin had seized and imprisoned the earl, apparently on suspicion that he had been in complicity with the Scots: a suspicion which was not unnatural, since his daughter was Robert Bruce's wife, and since his action against the Scots had been ineffective at all stages, but

20 G. O. Sayles, 'The Siege of Carrickfergus Castle', *I.H.S.*, X, pp. 94–100.
21 See Barrow, *Robert Bruce*, pp. 339–40, 441–3.

which there is no evidence to prove or disprove.[22] At the same time the citizens pulled down the buildings outside the north wall of the city, and hurriedly built a new wall along the quay, and on the night of the 23rd they set fire to the western suburb about Thomas Street to prevent the Scots from using it as a base from which to assault the city. But Bruce did not attempt an assault: instead he turned southwards into Kildare, and then into Kilkenny and west to Tipperary, burning and plundering everywhere, and on to Limerick, 'proposing to effect a junction with the whole Irish army at Saingel' (Singland, near Limerick).[23] Clearly the Scots had been in communication with Donough O'Brien, who had recently been expelled from Thomond. But all this time the justiciar's army had been hanging about their rear, and now, while Bruce was at Castleconnell on the Shannon, early in April, the magnates were near Caherconlish, one of the justiciar's manors, a little to the south, also living off the countryside,[24] and accompanied by Murrough, the reigning O'Brien, who had been supported by de Clare. About the middle of April, having learnt that reinforcements were arriving from England, Bruce retreated in the night, and passing through much the same country reached Kildare, and then went northwards through Trim, reaching Ulster at the beginning of May. Robert Bruce had returned to Scotland before the end of the month, and nothing more is heard of Edward for over a year, though he continued to dominate Ulster.

Meanwhile, the English government had at last brought itself to pay some attention to the problems of Ireland. The defeat at Bannockburn had put the king at the mercy of his domestic enemies, and Thomas of Lancaster, the chief of the Ordainers, in effect controlled the country. But Lancaster's abilities were by no means equal to the demands which this position made on them, and, alleging that the plots of the courtiers made it dangerous for him to approach the court, he tended simply to abstain from meetings of council and parliament. The *Vita Edwardi* says that 'whatever pleases the king the earl's servants try to upset; and whatever pleases the earl the king's servants call treachery'. All effective government was paralysed as a result, and there was much unrest throughout England, while from 1315 to 1317 there was a general

[22] See Lydon, 'The Bruce Invasion', loc. cit., pp. 116–19.
[23] *AI.*
[24] Robert Bagod petitioned that when Robert Bruce and the Scots came to the neighbourhood of Limerick, a great part of the justiciar's army remained for a fortnight on his lands, and since the council had ordered that in such a case men should take their provisions wherever they were, they took his grain, cattle, sheep and pigs to the value of 400 marks (P.R.O., London, S.C. 8/92/4560).

European famine. By the end of 1316 a middle party was emerging, led by the earl of Pembroke (who, it should be remembered, had interests in Ireland, since he was lord of Wexford), and including Roger Mortimer, lord of Trim, among its members, as well as the husbands of the Gloucester co-heiresses, Hugh le Despenser, Roger Damory, and Hugh D'Audeley, joint lords of Kilkenny. There was a large official and courtier element in the group, and though it did not triumph till the summer of 1318, we may probably regard the decision to pay some effective attention to the affairs of Ireland which was obviously taken at the end of 1316 as one of the first-fruits of an alliance so many of the members of which had a direct and personal interest in the country's prosperity.

Already in the summer of 1316 the king had begun to restore some of the officials whom the earlier baronial purge had removed, and we find the first signs of some attention to Irish affairs in the creation of the earldom of Kildare for John fitz Thomas in May. He was dead in the following September, and was succeeded by his son, Thomas fitz John, for whom the liberty of Kildare was restored in August 1317.[25] In October 1316 the Irish treasurer was authorized to promise £100 for 'any deed committed against Edward de Brus, a rebel, being in the land of Ireland, by which he may lose life or limb'.[26] But it was not till the end of November that anything really effective was done, in the appointment of Roger Mortimer as the king's lieutenant. In December arrangements were being made for 1,000 Genoese soldiers, armed with plate, to be landed in Dublin in July 1317, and in January 1317 all except Pembroke who had lands in Ireland were ordered to go themselves or send others for them to defend their lands, while a number of individuals were ordered to be at Haverford at the Purification (2 February) ready to set out for Ireland and stay there for its defence,

the king having ordained by himself and the council that Roger de Mortimer of Wyggemore shall be at Haverford at the above feast with a multitude of men for the purpose of proceeding to Ireland to repel the invasion of that country by Edward de Brus and his accomplices, Scotch rebels.[27]

It was not, however, till 7 April that Mortimer actually landed at Youghal and set out for Limerick, having sent word to Edmund le Botiller to do nothing till he arrived, but, as we have seen, Bruce had left the area before Mortimer reached it.

[25] See J. Otway-Ruthven, 'The Medieval County of Kildare', *I.H.S.*, XI, pp. 197–8.
[26] *C.P.R., 1313–17*, p. 551.
[27] *Calendar of Documents relating to Scotland*, III, no. 519; *Cal. Chancery Warrants*, p. 455; *C.C.R., 1313–18*, pp. 450–51.

Mortimer seems to have been content to see the Scots retreat, and made no attempt to follow them up: it would, indeed, probably have been impossible to provide for his forces in a countryside ruined by war and famine, while in any case, since the English were now beginning to recover control of the Irish Sea, which the Scots had had for a time at the beginning of the invasion, Bruce's ultimate defeat was now clearly inevitable.[28] Instead the lieutenant concerned himself with the affairs of the south, which were sufficiently pressing. The first problem was that of the earl of Ulster, who was still being held a prisoner by the Dubliners, in spite of royal orders that there should be an enquiry into the causes of his imprisonment, and that he should be sent under safe-conduct to England. The Dubliners had a series of grievances at this time, concerning the billeting of troops, purveyance, and similar matters, and there was ill-feeling between them and the magnates, and some open violence.[29] Nor was the earl the only person to come under suspicion: it must have been about this time that it was represented to the king that Richard de Exeter, chief justice of the common bench, was greatly suspected by the lords and others because of the alliance between him and Walter de Lacy, his father-in-law, the king's enemy, and other *malueises alliances* with other enemies, while Hugh Canon, another judge, who was a protégé of the earl of Ulster, was said to have ordered his brother-in-law to guide Bruce through Kildare.[30] On 8 May the earl was released by the council, undertaking to take no action against the citizens except by legal process, and finally at the parliament held in June he took oath and found sureties that he would obey the law and repel the king's enemies.

Meanwhile, Mortimer had been dealing with the de Lacys, who were his own tenants. In January 1317 before the justiciar they had been accused of inviting Bruce to Ireland, and a jury composed of the leading tenants of Meath had cleared them of this charge, saying that they had never treated with Bruce till after Mortimer's defeat, when, at Mortimer's request, they had treated with him, and had led him among the Irish towards Leinster, saving the English land of the liberty of Trim, and so doing more good than harm to the king and his people. With a number of others, including some Irishmen, they were therefore admitted to make fine with the king.[31] But this cannot have been the whole story, for by the end

[28] See Lydon, 'The Bruce Invasion', loc. cit., p. 121.
[29] Ibid., pp. 118–19.
[30] P.R.O., London, S.C. 8/118/5886; S.C. 1/35/91; *Chart. St. Mary's*, II, p. 299.
[31] Ibid., pp. 407–9 (from the justiciary roll).

of February they were leading Bruce into Kildare, and now, at Whitsuntide, Mortimer went to Trim and sent letters to them to appear before him, which they ignored, and then sent a knight to treat with them, whom they killed. Mortimer then led an army against them, and in two engagements they were defeated: some fled to Connacht, and Walter de Lacy was said to have gone to Bruce in Ulster. Mortimer summoned the whole council before him on 18 July and recorded these felonies: they had not only refused to come to the king's peace, but had risen with banners displayed against the king's banner. They were convicted by his record, and their property forfeited to the king, though the lands were later regranted to Mortimer, of whom they had been held.[32]

But Meath was not the only part of the south where order had to be restored. Having secured the western flank of his lordship by forcing O'Farrell of Annaly to come to the peace and give hostages, Mortimer proceeded against the Irish of the Wicklow mountains with some success. Then he turned to Munster: the government was at Cork by the end of November, and seems to have remained there till January 1318, when it appears at Clonmel. In February it returned to Dublin through Kilkenny, and was at Drogheda in March.[33] The administration, both central and local, must have needed a good deal of attention, and there were the problems presented by the necessity of providing for the defence and administration of the great de Verdon inheritance—half Meath and a great part of co. Louth—in the king's hand because of de Verdon's death in the summer of 1316 and the minority of his four daughters, the co-heiresses.[34] The liberty of Kilkenny too was still in the king's hand: in May 1316 its custody had been granted to Richard de Clare of Thomond, 'in consideration of his great labours in repelling the Scots', to hold 'during pleasure and the continuance of the disturbance by the Scots', and, probably late in 1317, it was ordained by Mortimer and the council that it should remain undivided among Gloucester's three sisters, who were his co-heiresses, until further orders.[35]

[32] Ibid., pp. 355–6, 409–16 (from the *coram rege* roll, viii Edward III); *Proc. R.I.A.*, XL, C, p. 333. The proceedings before the Irish council were being challenged in 1334 on the grounds that they had not been condemned by due process of law: for conviction by record, used against Thomas of Lancaster in 1322 and successfully challenged by his brother in 1327, see T. F. T. Plucknett, 'The Origin of Impeachment', *Trans. R. Hist. Soc.*, series 4, XXIV, pp. 56–64.

[33] *C.C.H.*, pp. 21–6, *passim*.

[34] See J. Otway-Ruthven, 'The Partition of the de Verdon Lands', *Proc. R.I.A.*, LXVI C; *42nd Rep. D.K.*, pp. 24, 26.

[35] *C.P.R., 1313–17*, p. 459; *C.C.H.*, p. 25, no. 187.

Meanwhile, the English government had been negotiating with the papacy. A number of the Irish prelates were known or suspected to have collaborated with the Scots,[36] and the king was particularly anxious that the archiepiscopal sees of Cashel and Dublin, which were both vacant, should be filled by men who would support his government in Ireland. Late in 1316 a mission was sent to the papacy at Avignon, where John XXII had been pope since August. In the event Edward got all he could have hoped for from the papacy: the vacancies were filled by men acceptable to him, who were enjoined by the pope to restrain their clergy from inciting the people to rebellion, while the supporters of the Bruces were excommunicated, as were those friars who were preaching rebellion.[37] And in March 1317 the pope warned Robert Bruce to desist from invading and occupying the lands of England, Wales and Ireland, while in the summer two cardinals were sent to England to endeavour to arrange a peace. They were rebuffed by Bruce, because the letters were not addressed to him as king, and the mission had little effect, though the cardinals remained in England till August 1318. It was apparently during this period that Donnell O'Neill addressed his remonstrance to the pope, styling himself 'king of Ulster and true heir by hereditary right of all Ireland'. He listed in rather general terms his grievances against the colonists, whom he accused of having disregarded the conditions of the bull *Laudabiliter*, a copy of which he enclosed. He alleged that the churches had been deprived of half their possessions[38]; he complained bitterly that the Irish were not allowed the benefits of English law[39]; he complained of the statute 'lately made in the city of St Canice' (Kilkenny) that no mere Irishman should be admitted into a religious order among the English in the land of peace.[40] He listed the murders of Brian O'Brien by Thomas de Clare in 1277, of the MacMurroughs at Arklow in 1282, and of the O'Connors by Peter de Bermingham in 1305, and alleged that the English said it was no worse to kill an Irishman than a brute beast: Friar Simon, brother of the bishop of Connor, had expressly said before Edward Bruce that it was no sin to kill an Irishman, and if he did so himself he would nonetheless celebrate mass. Two

[36] See Lydon, 'The Bruce Invasion', loc. cit., p. 115.

[37] See J. A. Watt, 'Negotiations between Edward II and John XXII concerning Ireland', *I.H.S.*, X, pp. 1–20.

[38] There is nothing to suggest that this was true: perhaps he was referring to the special case of the church of Derry (above, pp. 214–5), and O'Neill himself had taken lands from the archbishop of Armagh (*Reg. Fleming*, no. 170).

[39] See above, pp. 188–9.

[40] In February 1310, but the statute was revoked in May of the same year. See above, p. 138.

years earlier many of the Irish had sent letters to the king by John de Hotham, offering to hold their lands immediately of him, but had had no reply: they had called on Bruce to aid them, and O'Neill had granted him all his right in the kingdom by his letters patent [41]

This statement of the Irish case was a little disingenuous. It ignored the fact that the northern chiefs, to whom it must be taken to relate, held of de Burgo and had risen against him with Bruce in 1315, while O'Neill's claim to be high king by hereditary right would certainly not have been generally accepted by the Irish outside Ulster.[42] No doubt the settlers could have compiled a list of Irish atrocities to set against it. It was undoubtedly motivated largely by the ambitions of O'Neill, who had twice been deposed by de Burgo, in 1286 and 1291, and was clearly on bad terms with the earl. But much in it was justified, and though the pope had good reasons of general policy for supporting Edward, he sent it to him in May 1318, urging him to consult with his council as to the correction of these grievances.

By 1318 the affairs of the west were again receiving attention. On 8 March, after discussion between Mortimer, Richard de Bermingham, lord of Athenry, and others of the council, O'Connor, 'prince of the Irish of Connacht', was granted the lands of Shilmorthy, Fethys and Tyrmany, saving the lands of the English and lands granted in burgage, to hold during pleasure at the due and accustomed rent.[43] This must have been Cathal O'Connor, who in this year 'seized the kingship of Connacht . . . and placed himself under the protection of William Burke and all the Connacht Galls'.[44] The settlement of Connacht after the disturbances which had been going on since 1315 was thus sealed, though at the price of the virtual abandonment of the royal county of Roscommon, an ominous retreat. And in May the English position in the southwest received a disastrous blow. The Irish of Thomond had been conducting a civil war, and a meeting which seems to have been called at Limerick to settle the dispute came to nothing. Richard de Clare took up arms to defend his protegé, Mahon O'Brien, and on 10 May 1318 was killed in a skirmish at Disert O'Dea. His heir

[41] Fordun, *Scotichronicon*, ed. W. Goodall (Edinburgh, 1759), II, pp. 259–68. For the invitation to Bruce, cf. *County Louth Archaeological Journal*, I, pp. 79–81.

[42] A letter from O'Neill to Fineen MacCarthy of Desmond, apparently written on 25 March 1317, urged him to put his name to letters to the pope which must have been the Remonstrance, but it is evident that he refused (H. Wood, 'Letter from Domnal O'Neill to Fineen MacCarthy, 1317', *Proc. R.I.A.*, XXXVII C, pp. 141–8).

[43] *C.C.H.*, p. 23, no. 103.

[44] *AC*.

was a minor, and died three years later leaving as his heirs only his aunts, the wives of Robert de Welles and Bartholomew de Baddlesmere. Though the escheator acted energetically on Richard's death, garrisoning his castle of Bunratty,[45] there was little hope of maintaining the position, and with the division of the inheritance after 1321 the English foothold in co. Clare was effectively lost.

Mortimer had no part in this, for he was recalled to England on 5 May 1318, when the archbishop of Cashel was appointed as *custos* by the council. In August the king appointed as justiciar Alexander de Bicknor, the archbishop of Dublin, who took up office just in time for the long-delayed defeat of Bruce. We know nothing of what Bruce had done since the retreat from Limerick, but now, in October, he advanced south from Ulster, openly supported by the de Lacys, and with a considerable force of Irish as well as his Scots. An English force was hurriedly collected at Dundalk under the command of John de Bermingham of Tethmoy,[46] who was accompanied by the local gentry and the sheriff of Louth, with some of the townsmen of Drogheda. Bruce made a stand on the hill of Faughart, just north of Dundalk—the place where he is said to have been crowned in 1316—and the English, advancing from the south-west, at last, for the first time in all these campaigns, defeated Bruce, whose body was found on the field after the fight.

To judge from the language of the annals, a long nightmare was removed, not only from the English, but also from the Irish. The Irish annals said, with striking unanimity, that Bruce

was the common ruin of the Gaels and Galls of Ireland . . . never was there a better deed done for the Irish than this, since the beginning of the world and the banishing of the Fomorians from Ireland. For in this Bruce's time, for three years and a half, falsehood and famine and homicide filled the country, and undoubtedly men ate each other in Ireland.

A contemporary Connacht tract blames those who called in 'Scottish foreigners less noble than our own foreigners'.[47] And enormous damage had been done, which gravely weakened the English interest. In all the outlying districts a retreat is evident, and though in fact a decline seems to have begun before the end of the thirteenth century, the Bruce invasion, combined with the general European slackening of colonization at this period, and the special

[45] *42nd Rep. D.K.*, p. 21.
[46] Proof that he was of Tethmoy, not Athenry, is supplied by T.C.D. MS E. 3. 4, p. 59 and *44th Rep. D.K.*, p. 32; *47th Rep. D.K.*, pp. 66–67.
[47] *AC*; *AU*; *A. Clon.*; *Tribes and Customs of Hy Many*, ed. J. O'Donovan (Irish Archaeological Society, 1843), pp. 136–7.

circumstances which in early fourteenth-century Ireland resulted in an excessive fractioning of a number of great inheritances among co-heiresses who were married to absentees, certainly accelerated it. The abandonment of the county of Roscommon was only the first sign of what was to come, and a new attitude is apparent in dealings with the Irish after this period.[48]

Meanwhile there was much which needed to be done. In 1319 there was no proffer at the exchequer from the county of Roscommon because there was no sheriff there, nor had been since the coming of the Scots to Ireland, and Ulster was of course in the same position.[49] Even in Dublin, the burning of the suburbs in 1317 had left the administration partly homeless: a petition from 'the ministers of Ireland' complains that the community of Dublin

by their own hastiness, for fear of the Scots, burnt the king's manor near the castle of Dublin outside the walls, where the pleas of the whole land had always been held, as well the pleas of the justiciar and the bench as of the exchequer, and of the county court, and the place of the chancery, so that the pleas of every place of the said land are held in divers places in the said town of Dublin, so that no minister can come or consult with others as business requires, as they were accustomed and ought to do, to the king's great damage and loss, and the great grievance, damage and loss of the people of the said land, and to the damage and grievance and great inconvenience of all the ministers of the land.[50]

The revenue had been reduced, and was difficult to collect. Dublin had to be allowed a considerable sum in compensation for the damage done in preparing to resist the Scots; in 1316 the men of Drogheda had hurriedly repaired their walls, which had been in a ruinous state, and provisioned the town, and later had corresponding allowances; in the same year the citizens of Cork had been put to great expense 'in erecting anew a wall around the city', and they too had to be pardoned some of their farm. By 1320 the citizens of Limerick were so impoverished that they could scarcely keep the city from Irish felons or repair the walls, and were pardoned their farm indefinitely.[51] Sheriffs and lords of liberties had to be allowed sums which could not be levied on account of the disturbance; the king's demesne lands in south co. Dublin had been 'robbed, burned and destroyed by Scots and Irish rebels and enemies', 'invaded, burned and totally devastated by the Irish of the mountains, who rose in war immediately on the arrival of the

[48] See below, pp. 272–6.
[49] P.R.O., Dublin, Memorandum Roll, 13–14 Edward II, m. 2.
[50] P.R.O., London, S.C. 8/118/5881.
[51] *C.C.R.*, *1313–18*, p. 396; ibid., *1318–23*, p. 87; *C.P.R.*, *1313–17*, pp. 471, 509; ibid., *1317–21*, p. 204; *C.C.H.*, p. 21, no. 20; *39th Rep. D.K.*, p. 71; *Parliaments and Councils*, pp. 5–6.

Scots in Ireland'.[52] Moreover there were long lists of persons who had to be rewarded or compensated, ranging from John de Bermingham, the victor of Dundalk, or the Hospitallers, who maintained that they had been robbed of goods to the value of £1,000 in Ulster, to John Cadel who asked for the office of porter of Dublin castle for good service, and because he had lost his brother and cousin by the Scots in Ireland.[53] Bermingham was created earl of Louth on 12 May 1319, and was later granted Louth to hold as a liberty for life, so that he was interposed as lord between the king and the de Verdon co-heiresses and other tenants-in-chief.[54] For lesser men, the forfeited lands of those who had adhered to the Scots provided a useful pool of rewards, though some had to be pardoned debts due to the king.[55] It was necessary to grant the treasurer an indemnity,

as during the time the Scots were in Ireland many deeds were done by the king's ministers in Ireland as well on account of the urgent necessity for defending the land as for the sustenance of his lieges on his service there, for which such ministers may be harassed.

The justiciar and chancellor were ordered in February 1319 not to make any charters of pardon for adherence to the Scots without the king's special order, and in May orders were given for an inquiry into Bruce's adherents, though this was cancelled in the following February.[56]

Meanwhile, Roger Mortimer had been appointed as justiciar in March 1319 and arrived in Ireland in June. By this time the Middle Party, of which he was a prominent member, had triumphed in England. Led by Pembroke, it included a number of men with important interests in Ireland; Pembroke himself, as lord of Wexford, Mortimer, lord of Trim in right of his wife, and himself one of the Marshal co-heirs, Damory, Despenser and Audeley, the husbands of the Gloucester co-heiresses, lords of Kilkenny. Among the ecclesiastics there was Hotham, now bishop of Ely, treasurer from 1317 to 1318 and then chancellor till 1320, who had at any rate an intimate knowledge of Irish affairs, and may be supposed to have retained some interest in them. The earl marshal, Thomas of Brotherton, the king's half brother, to whom the liberty of Carlow had been granted in 1312, was also a member of the group. By

---

[52] P.R.O., London, S.C. 8/118/5888; *39th Rep. D.K.*, pp. 67, 70; *C.C.R., 1318–23*, p. 80; Gilbert, *Historic and Municipal Documents*, pp. 456–62; *C.P.R., 1330–34*, p. 551.
[53] P.R.O., London, S.C. 8/4/151; S.C. 8/118/5887.
[54] J. Otway-Ruthven, 'The Partition of the de Verdon Lands', loc. cit.
[55] See e.g. *C.C.R., 1318–23*, p. 2.
[56] *C.P.R., 1317–21*, pp. 269, 371; *C.C.R., 1318–23*, pp. 55, 175–6.

August 1318 it had succeeded in obtaining control of the English government, and though its main interest was the continuing war with Scotland, it is clear that it was not unconcerned with Ireland. Mortimer's appointment as justiciar may be taken as a sign of this, but in September 1319 the attempt to recover Berwick from the Scots was disastrously defeated, and the break-up of the party began in 1320, when the ambitions of the Despensers, who were endeavouring to obtain the whole of the de Clare property in Wales and the title of earl of Gloucester, alienated the other marcher lords. Pembroke continued to stand by the king, but the others formed a confederation which by the spring of 1321 had led to open war in the marches of Wales and the defeat of Despenser. It was no doubt the growing tension in the marches that led Mortimer to appoint Thomas fitz John, earl of Kildare, as his deputy in September 1320, and return to England.

While in Ireland he seems to have been active in the restoration of order. The mayor and community of Dublin, writing to the king on 7 October 1320, said that he had 'thought much of saving and keeping the peace of your land'.[57] At the end of April 1320 the affairs of Ulster were considered in a parliament at Dublin, and it was decided 'by the common council of Ireland' that Richard de Burgo might hold, by himself and his ministers, all pleas and other business in the court of his liberty of Ulster as fully as before the coming of the Scots to Ireland.[58] In May he led an expedition to Munster against English rebels, 'especially of the names of Burkeyn and Barry'.[59] But a genuine attempt seems to have been made to deal with the Irish by conciliation. On 7 June 1319 Mortimer was given power to receive into English law all Irishmen who wished to come to it, and on the same day, on their petition, the earls of Kildare and Louth had power, during pleasure, to receive into English law all their men and tenants, being Irish, who wished to come in. They were to notify the king immediately of the names of such Irishmen so that letters patent might be issued. At the instance of de Burgo, a charter of English law was granted to the O'Maddens of Ui Maine in June 1320, when the justiciar seems to have been at Athlone.[60] And apart from an expedition against the Irish of Slievemargy, we hear of no military action against them. There was, indeed, the question of the grant of the king's service (i.e. a

---

[57] *Historic and Municipal Documents*, pp. 391–2. Since it mentions Kildare as Mortimer's deputy, this letter can only belong to 1320.

[58] *C.C.H.*, p. 27, no. 46.

[59] Ibid., p. 28, no. 11.

[60] *C.P.R., 1317–21*, pp. 339, 342, 563; *C.C.H.*, p. 28, no. 93. For the O'Maddens, cf. *Cal. Ormond Deeds*, II, no. 427 (22).

scutage) to Richard de Burgo for Ulster, and to Thomas fitz John to avenge the death of Richard de Clare, but nothing seems to have come of it: it was held that the consent of the magnates would be necessary, and probably this could not be obtained.[61]

Thomas fitz John was appointed as justiciar to succeed Mortimer in April 1321, though the earl of Louth was appointed a month later. He does not seem, however, to have returned to Ireland till the end of August, and Kildare acted till then. And by this time the Middle Party in England was fast breaking up. The Despensers had been banished in the summer of 1321, but by the end of the year the king was strong enough to recall them, and the waning of Mortimer's power was shown when in December the justiciar was empowered to remove the judges appointed by him and commissioned to correct errors in pleas held before him.[62] In January 1322 the king was able to occupy the main strongholds of his enemies in the Welsh marches; in March, at Boroughbridge, he defeated Lancaster, who was sentenced to death and executed as a traitor and rebel. In May at the parliament of York the Ordinances were revoked, and the Despensers were now in complete control of the government. Mortimer and Audeley were in prison; Baddlesmere was hanged; Damory had been killed when the king seized Tutbury in March, and his lands were forfeit. Pembroke was the only one of the group connected with Ireland to escape: he had associated himself with the judgement on Lancaster, but even so he was obliged to pledge his body, lands and goods to obey and aid the king. The Irish lands of Despenser, Damory and Audeley—that is, the liberty of Kilkenny—had perhaps never yet been delivered to them, and the treasurer was now appointed as 'surveyor and chief keeper'[63]; those of Mortimer—Trim, and his lands in Leix—were of course taken into the king's hand, though he held Trim only in right of his wife. In an eyre held at Drogheda in 1321-2 the liberties of Trim were forfeited, since he did not appear to defend them against a writ of *quo warranto*.[64] And at the same time, a very important wardship had fallen into the king's hand when Edmund le Botiller died in 1321, leaving a minor heir, while the heir of Richard de Clare had died in the same year, leaving his aunts, one of whom was Baddlesmere's widow, to succeed him. Richard de Bermingham, lord of Athenry, died in 1322, William de Burgo and Pembroke, whose heir was still a minor, in 1324, and finally

[61] *42nd Rep. D.K.*, p. 49; *C.C.R., 1318–23*, pp. 55, 80, 90.
[62] *C.P.R., 1321–4*, pp. 40, 43.
[63] *Cal. Fine Rolls, 1319–27*, pp. 121, 410; *C.C.H.*, p. 30, no. 29.
[64] H. Wood, 'The Muniments of Edmund de Mortimer', *Proc. R.I.A.*, XL C. pp. 337–47.

in 1326 the earl of Ulster himself. The face of Irish politics had been dramatically changed.

The Despensers found themselves, of course, faced with the endless problems of the Scottish war, and already in April 1322 the king was sending orders that Ireland should supply a force of 300 men-at-arms, 1,000 hobelers, and 6,000 footmen, to be paid by the Irish treasury, while the earl of Ulster was asked to come with as many horse and foot as possible at his own expense. In the end, however, a truce was made with the Scots in March 1323, and the expedition never took place.[65] In the summer of 1323 Mortimer escaped, and it was feared that he might take refuge in Ireland: the magnates and towns were strictly ordered to arrest him and bring him to the king,[66] but in fact he escaped to France, where he was to ally himself with Edward's wife and in due course bring about his downfall. But though in August 1324 there were fears of a French invasion, and the king wrote to a number of Irish lords, commending them for their faithful conduct, of which he said the justiciar had informed him verbally, and urging them to continue it, and to give credence to what the justiciar explained on his behalf, and later ordered the preparation of all ships in Irish ports for war, and the arrest of all subjects of the king of France,[67] nothing came of all this, and it was not till the end of September 1326 that Isabella and Mortimer actually invaded England.

Meanwhile in Ireland a major preoccupation of the justiciar continued to be the now endemic warfare with the Irish of the Leinster mountains. In 1324 there was an expedition against 'the king's enemies of the mountains of Leinster, and especially the McMurghuthys and Obrynnes', for which the 'army of Tylagh' was proclaimed, the first scutage, as far as we know, since 1315. In the next summer it was still necessary to set guards against them at Baltinglass and Dunlavan,[68] though the Anglo-Irish annals tell us nothing of this, being pre-occupied with the scandal of the first Irish witchcraft trial, that of Dame Alice Kyteler of Kilkenny.[69] And by this time there was already in existence a feud among the Anglo-Irish barons, for Arnald le Poer, seneschal of Kilkenny and therefore probably an adherent of the Despensers, whose own lands were in Tipperary and Waterford, and Maurice fitz Thomas, the head of the Munster Geraldines, were ordered in the summer of

---

[65] *C.C.R., 1318–23*, pp. 529–30, 556–7, 690, 719–20; *C.P.R., 1321–4*, pp. 97, 205.
[66] *C.C.R., 1323–7*, pp. 133–4.
[67] *C.C.R., 1323–7*, p. 308; *C.C.H.*, p. 30, nos. 10–11.
[68] *C.C.H.*, p. 31, nos. 80, 83; p. 32, no. 103; *43rd Rep. D.K.*, p. 33.
[69] See *The Proceedings against Dame Alice Kyteler*, ed. T. Wright (Camden Society, 1843).

1325 to desist from assembling troops to attack each other. A year later Maurice fitz Thomas and John le Poer of Dunoyl had leave to treat with felons of their names, families and following up to the end of November, and the sheriffs of Munster were forbidden to arrest such felons. In December the same sheriffs were ordered to issue proclamations forbidding confederacies, and not only Maurice fitz Thomas and Arnald le Poer, but also John de Bermingham and others, were forbidden to join them. The dispute must have been spreading, and in 1327, as we shall see, it was to break into open war.[70]

By this time there had been a revolution in England. The victory of Isabella and Mortimer, the deposition and later the murder of Edward II, and his replacement by his son, Edward III, in January 1327, meant that for the next few years the English government was dominated by Mortimer. The lordship of Trim was of course restored to him, and in 1330 he was granted royal jurisdiction over the de Verdon half of Meath, which once more became a single undivided liberty, and further succeeded in obtaining the liberty of Louth, which had lapsed on the death of John de Bermingham in 1328, as well as the custody of the liberty of Kildare during the minority of the heir of Thomas fitz John.[71] He had thus created for himself an enormous territorial power in the very heart of Ireland, though of course all these grants lapsed within a few months with his disgrace and execution on 29 November. His widow succeeded in recovering her inheritance, the lordship of Trim, but the rest was gone.[72]

Edward II's last justiciar had been John Darcy, an unimportant household knight, who was replaced after Edward's deposition by the earl of Kildare. Kildare took up office on 12 May, and held it for less than a year, dying on 5 April 1328. He was immediately confronted by a very difficult situation in Ulster. The earl had died shortly before 25 June 1326; his grandson and heir was a minor, and in August Darcy had led an armed force to Ulster to take it into the king's hands. But in the late spring or early summer of 1327[73] Robert Bruce descended on Ulster, landing at Larne, intending, it was later alleged, to proceed, with the connivance of certain Irish, to Wales with an army and thence to invade England.

[70] For the documentation of this dispute, see Orpen, *Normans*, IV, pp. 221–6. For the career of Maurice fitz Thomas, see G. O. Sayles, 'The Rebellious First Earl of Desmond', *Medieval Studies Presented to Aubrey Gwynn, S.J.*, pp. 203–29; and 'The Legal Proceedings against the First Earl of Desmond', *Analecta Hibernica*, XXIII, pp. 3–47.
[71] See J. Otway-Ruthven, 'The Partition of the de Verdon Lands', loc. cit.
[72] Ibid.
[73] *Circa Pascha*. Easter in 1327 was on 12 April. This date, given by the Irish government in 1331, seems very early since Bruce was still in Ulster on 12 July.

The justiciar sent an emissary, one John, son of William Jordan, to persuade him to withdraw, and according to the Irish government in 1331 his 'subtlety, industry and labour' effected this. But before Bruce's departure, the seneschal of Ulster, Henry de Mandeville, had, on 12 July, concluded an agreement with him by which, in return for a year's truce, the Ulstermen undertook to deliver to the Scots at Larne 100 *cendres* of wheat and 100 *cendres* of barley, half at Martinmas and half at Pentecost, and Bruce expressly included in the truce 'all the Irish of Ulster who wish to be his men'. On 23 July the Irish government was writing to the king of the 'frightful news that Sir Robert de Brus your enemy' was proposing a conquest, but he seems to have returned to Scotland soon after this. A copy of the agreement with Mandeville was sent to England by one of the late earl's officials with an alarming account of the disorders of Ulster: the only reassuring factor he could find was that Bruce was gravely ill.[74] The part played by Henry de Mandeville in all this is certainly ambiguous, and before long he was to be found in alliance with the earl of Desmond in clearly treasonable activities.[75]

The failure of the Irish government to take positive action in Ulster at this time is easily understood when we consider the troubles of the south. The dispute between Arnald le Poer and Maurice fitz Thomas which had already been in existence in 1325 flared up into open war in 1327, involving a number of other magnates. The timing suggests that the original dispute, which may have been a relatively simple one over land-holding, had been caught up into one between the adherents of Edward II and the Despensers and those of Mortimer. Certainly we cannot suppose that the Irish magnates were either unaware of or indifferent to the revolution which had taken place in England, and they were well acquainted with Mortimer, whose territorial ambitions were presently to show themselves to be no less unbridled than those of the Despensers had been in Wales.[76] In July the king, or rather Mortimer, wrote that Maurice fitz Thomas, John de Bermingham, James le Botiller, Maurice de Rocheford, and John le Poer, baron of Dunoyl, had hitherto refused to be intendant to or obey the

74 R. Nicholson, 'A Sequel to Edward Bruce's Invasion of Ireland', *Scottish Historical Review*, XLII, pp. 30–40; P.R.O., London, S.C. 1/38/76.
75 For the Mandevilles, see E. Curtis, 'The MacQuillan or Mandeville Lords of the Route', *Proc. R.I.A.*, XLIV C, pp. 99–113; J. H. R. Greeves, 'Robert I and the de Mandevilles of Ulster', *Transactions of the Dumfriesshire and Galloway Natural History and Antiquarian Society*, 3rd series, XXXIV, pp. 59–73. Henry de Mandeville had been appointed as hereditary constable of the bonnacht of Ulster in 1323 (*C.P.R., 1385–9*, p. 308. See above, p. 216).
76 See above, p. 243.

justiciar, and it seems likely that they were maintaining, no doubt
for their own purposes, an allegiance to Edward II, who was not
murdered till September.[77]

In the war which began in 1327 Maurice fitz Thomas was supported by the Butlers and the Berminghams; Arnald le Poer by the
de Burgos.[78] Maurice was successful, and the justiciar, towards the
end of the year, named a day for the parties to appear, but Arnald
le Poer went to England in February 1328, while his opponents
continued to harry his lands with so great an army that the ministers feared they would next attack the towns. Maurice fitz Thomas
and his allies now sent messengers to the council to say that they
would come to Kilkenny and clear themselves before it: they had
no intention of doing any harm to the king's lands, but only of
avenging themselves on their enemies. When they appeared, the
council postponed the matter till the month after Easter, by which
time Kildare, the justiciar, was dead, and Roger Outlaw, prior of
the Hospitallers, the chancellor, was acting in his place. The dispute continued, for in June John de Bermingham, earl of Louth,
Arnald le Poer, Walter son of William le Botiller, Maurice fitz
Thomas, and John son of Robert Poer were all forbidden to make
assemblies of men-at-arms because of the disputes between them
and other magnates, to war on the said magnates, to invade their
lands, or to disturb the king's peace in any way. But a number of
the leaders were about to disappear. About 25 November 1328
the bishop of Ossory reported to the council that Arnald le Poer
had been convicted before him of heresy: the council was obliged
to arrest and imprison Arnald, while the bishop was given a day
to prosecute the case. He did not, however, appear, alleging that
his enemies made the ways unsafe for him, and adding that the
acting justiciar was a supporter of heresy, and had abetted Arnald
le Poer in it. Outlaw triumphantly cleared himself in a parliament
at Dublin, probably that of January 1329; Arnald's case was referred to the next parliament in April, before which he had died
in prison. In June 1329 John de Bermingham, with a number of
his kindred and others, was killed at Braganstown, co. Louth, by
the local gentry, apparently constituting the *posse comitatus*.[79] And

[77] *C.C.R.*, *1327–30*, pp. 206–7. There had clearly been hesitations, for the
king was told in July that the bishop of Meath had been the first of the clergy
to be intendant to him (P.R.O., London, S.C. 1/38/76).
[78] The earl of Ulster was still a minor in England, but his mother, Elizabeth
de Clare, was one of the co-heiresses of Gloucester, and so had a third of the
liberty of Kilkenny.
[79] This does not seem to have been connected with the quarrels of the magnates: contemporary opinion, as reported by Clyn, says it was because the
Louth men were unwilling that he should rule over them (*Annals*, p. 20).

in the April parliament a solemn peace had been made between Maurice fitz Thomas and the earl of Ulster, whose Irish lands the escheator had been ordered to restore in October 1327 (he had been escorted to them in the autumn of 1328 by Robert Bruce himself, making a last appearance in Ulster[80]). The bishop of Ossory, clearly a difficult and unsatisfactory man, was charged with fomenting feuds among the magnates and on 18 June 1329, when an inquiry was about to be held, fled to England, and, when summoned before the king, to Rome. The king warned the pope against him: ten years later he was himself accused of heresy.[81] The details of the peace between de Burgo and Maurice fitz Thomas were worked out before the new justiciar, John Darcy, who took up office in May 1329. In July he went to Kilkenny to establish peace between de Burgo and the Poers and Barrys on one side, and James le Botiller, created earl of Ormond in the previous October, fitz Thomas, and William de Bermingham on the other. Fitz Thomas was created earl of Desmond in August, and was also granted in tail male the county of Kerry as a royal liberty, there being reserved to the crown only the usual four pleas and the crosses. As he was already hereditary chief serjeant of counties Waterford, Cork and Kerry, this meant that all royal power in Kerry was effectively in his hands. After a further session of the justiciar at Kilkenny in September and October a final settlement seems to have been reached, for on 14 October Desmond was given a general pardon, and on 1 November the justiciar was given power to admit to the king's peace those of his men who were charged with felonies or trespasses committed between Michaelmas 1327 and 10 October 1329.[82]

The Irish had not been slow to take advantage of the opportunities offered by these discords. Early in 1328 the Irish of Leinster had met together and chosen a king, Donnell son of Art Mac-Murrough, who raised his banner near Dublin and proposed to pass through all the lands of Ireland, but he was immediately captured, and so, soon after, was the leader of the O'Tooles.[83] In April 1329 the O'Brennans and MacGilpatricks were burning and raiding in Kilkenny; at the beginning of August Brian O'Brien

[80] Nicholson, 'A Sequel to Edward Bruce's Invasion of Ireland', loc. cit.

[81] *Foedera*, II, pp. 767, 810, 1082. Cf. *C.P.R., 1350–54*, p. 55; *Cal. Fine Rolls, 1347–56*, p. 292.

[82] *43rd Rep. D.K.*, pp. 28, 65; N.L.I., MS 761, p. 56; *C.P.R., 1327–30*, p. 457; *Cal. Chart. Rolls, 1327–41*, p. 123; J. Otway-Ruthven, 'Anglo-Irish Shire Government in the Thirteenth Century', *I.H.S.*, V, pp. 22–23. Ormond had had a similar grant of liberties in Tipperary, though for life only, nine months earlier: Tipperary was not granted in tail male till 1372. See above, p. 175, n. 124.

[83] O'Toole was executed, but MacMurrough escaped in January 1330.

burnt the towns of Athassel and Tipperary; a little later the Mac-
Geoghegans, associated with some of the de Lacys, killed Sir Thomas
le Botiller and a number of others near Mullingar, while in November the O'Nolans were up in co. Carlow, taking prisoners who
included the earl of Ormond's brother, and had their lands wasted
by the earl in revenge. In August, and again in December, the
justiciar led an expedition against the O'Byrnes, which seems to
have been based on Wicklow and supplied by sea; at the end of
October he was fighting the O'Mores and O'Dempseys; in November the MacGeoghegans and de Lacys. But disturbances continued,
and in February 1330 O'Dempsey took the castle of Lea. By this
time the justiciar and council had summoned Desmond to bring
an army at the king's wages, and he came with a force which included Brian O'Brien, who had raided Tipperary the year before.
This was the O'Brien who had been supported by Richard de
Clare in Thomond, and was now supported by Desmond: since
Brian was establishing himself in north Tipperary, where there
were important de Burgo lands, this was no doubt one of the causes
of the dispute between the earls of Desmond and Ulster. Desmond
defeated first the O'Nolans and then the O'Mores, taking hostages
from each, and then recovered the castle of Lea.[84] But before the
end of April Desmond was having it proclaimed that no one should
obey either the sheriff of Limerick or any other servant of the king,
and in May Brian O'Brien defeated and killed James de Beaufo,
sheriff of Limerick, with many others, laid waste the whole countryside, and was subsequently harboured by Desmond.[85] A great
force was now led against him, the 'army of Athissel', for which a
scutage was proclaimed. The expedition occupied the whole of
July, but does not seem to have achieved very much. And though
Desmond and others were arrested and charged with aiding and
abetting O'Brien, and were committed to gaol, they soon escaped.[86]
But in the same year there were some minor successes against the
Irish of Leinster, and in Meath the MacGeoghegans were defeated
by the local landowners.

By the end of 1330 the whole political situation in both England
and Ireland had been revolutionized by the fall of Mortimer, who
was executed as a traitor at the end of November. Since his interests in Ireland had been so great, the attention of the new government was inevitably drawn to it, and the whole position seems to

[84] *Chart. St. Mary's*, II, pp. 370–72; Clyn, *Annals*, p. 21; *43rd Rep. D.K.*, pp.
28, 42; N.L.I., MS 761, p. 56.
[85] *Analecta Hibernica*, XXIII, pp. 9, 14.
[86] *43rd Rep. D.K.*, pp. 43–44, 45, 47; Sayles, 'The Rebellious First Earl of
Desmond', loc. cit., p. 211.

have been reviewed in a parliament held at Westminster in March 1331, when an important series of ordinances dealing with Ireland was produced.[87] Clearly based on local information, they were concerned mainly with local government and the preservation of the peace. The justiciar was forbidden to grant pardons for homicides or for robberies and arson committed in future, without referring them to the king; no one was to maintain Irishmen or any others against the king's peace (this was perhaps directed primarily against Desmond); truces between English and Irish were to be carefully observed; landowners were to be required to provide for the defence of their lands, whether in the marches or not; there was to be one and the same law for English and Irish.[88] There was very little in all this that was new, but it was followed by other measures: a general resumption of all grants made since Edward III's accession—that is, the grants made by Mortimer; the appointment of the justiciar, chancellor and treasurer to hear and determine complaints of oppressions by the king's ministers in Ireland; and in October an order to twenty-five English magnates, headed by the earl marshal, lord of Carlow, to provide for the recovery and safe-custody of their lands in Ireland occupied by rebels, coupled with an announcement that it had been agreed in the present parliament that the king should go to Ireland in person 'to refrain his said enemies and their malice'. On 5 November the earl of Ulster and the archbishop of Dublin were ordered to come at once to the king in England 'to treat with him secretly concerning his passage to Ireland'.[89]

Meanwhile, in February Sir Anthony Lucy had been appointed justiciar, and a few days later the earl of Ulster was appointed as lieutenant with special responsibility for the maintenance of the peace. Neither reached Ireland till the summer (the earl was sworn *in pleno consilio* on 17 July), and the parliament summoned to Dublin for 1 July was adjourned to Kilkenny on 1 August, as some of the magnates had not appeared. At Kilkenny Desmond and others appeared, submitted to the king's grace, and were pardoned, but Desmond then persuaded Brian O'Brien not to meet the justiciar at Limerick, where it had been arranged that negotiations should take place, and Lucy arrested him and confined him in Dublin castle, where he remained till 1333. A jury subsequently alleged that he had intended to kill not only the justiciar, but also the

---

[87] *Early Statutes*, pp. 322–8.
[88] See above, p. 189.
[89] *Cal. Fine Rolls, 1327–37*, p. 241; *C.P.R., 1330–34*, p. 135; *C.C.R., 1330–33*, pp. 400–01. The whole project of the king's visit was eventually abandoned: see below, p. 253.

chancellor, treasurer, escheator and the whole council. In November the justiciar was ordered to take into the king's hand half the land of Desmond, which it was alleged the earl had obtained from Thomas de Carew, who had no title to it. Then, at the end of January 1332, Lucy led a force into Munster, where he remained till 2 May. He captured William de Bermingham and his son Walter, two of Desmond's principal supporters, at Clonmel in February,[90] and he took a series of inquisitions between August 1331 and August 1332, which provide a mass of information as to Desmond's activities.[91] It seems that well before 1320 he had taken advantage of the breakdown of government brought about by the Bruce invasion to adapt to his own use the ancient custom of *cain*, which entitled a chieftain to claim sustenance for himself and his retinue on his journeys among his people.[92] He used this to maintain a retinue of kerns, and it was alleged that wrongdoers, both English and Irish, came to him from all over the south and west, 'and he received them and avowed them as his men . . . they were known as MacThomas's Rout throughout Ireland'.[93] Throughout the 1320s he had used this force to ravage the counties of Limerick, Cork and Waterford, allying himself with the Cantetons, and with Brian O'Brien of Thomond and Dermot MacCarthy of Desmond.[94]

In 1326, if the jurors of 1332 are to be believed, Desmond's ambitions had carried him a stage further. On 7 July, at Kilkenny, Thomas fitz John, John de Bermingham, James le Botiller, William de Bermingham, the bishop of Ossory, Brian O'Brien and others had met him and formed a sworn confederacy to establish an independent kingdom in Ireland with Desmond as king.[95] It is really impossible to believe this story as it stands. That there was a confederacy, and that it included just these men, except perhaps Thomas fitz John, there is every reason to suppose,[96] and Desmond may conceivably have hoped to make himself king—it was clearly widely believed that he did—but it is difficult to imagine that either Thomas fitz John, John de Bermingham, or James le Botiller, the earls of Kildare, Louth and Ormond, would have been

[90] William de Bermingham was hanged at Dublin in July; his son was eventually released, and was justiciar in 1346–9.

[91] Sayles, 'The Legal Proceedings against the First Earl of Desmond', *Anallecta Hibernica*, XXIII, pp. 1–47 *passim* and pp. 8, 14–15; *Cal. Fine Rolls, 1327–37*, pp. 286–7; *43rd Rep. D.K.*, pp. 53–4; Sayles, 'The Rebellious First Earl of Desmond', loc. cit.

[92] This is the 'coign' of later medieval Ireland, which was to be so universal a grievance.

[93] *Analecta Hibernica*, XXIII, p. 8.

[94] Ibid., *passim*.

[95] Ibid., p. 6.

[96] See above, pp. 244–6.

willing to expose themselves to the risk of condemnation as traitors for his sake. But however this may be, it would appear that early in 1331 another conspiracy was formed, by which, it was alleged, Desmond, William de Bermingham, Walter de Burgo, O'Brien and MacNamara agreed on a general rising with the object of making Desmond king and establishing four province kingdoms: Munster and Meath for Desmond, Connacht for de Burgo, Leinster for Bermingham, and Ulster for Henry de Mandeville.[97] It is not surprising that William de Bermingham was executed: it was presumably felt to be unsafe to proceed to extremes against Desmond, and on 4 August 1332 Roger Outlaw, prior of the Hospital, who had often been deputy justiciar and till very recently chancellor, was given power to treat and agree with those at war against the king in Ireland, and the justiciar was ordered to stay execution against any magnates imprisoned for felonies till the king came to Ireland or further order.[98]

Meanwhile, from May to August the justiciar was occupied in Leinster, where he recovered and rebuilt the castles of Clonmore and Arklow, but in July Bunratty castle was taken by the Irish of Thomond. At the parliament which met at Dublin on 17 August it was decided to summon the royal service to Limerick for 5 October. Maurice de Rocheford had already been ordered to stay on the custody of Any, to fight 'Breen O Breen, our enemy and rebel', and the justiciar seems to have gone on ahead, for wages were paid to a force accompanying him to Thomond on the king's service from 9 September to 15 November. It must have been after this expedition that

after All Saints the earl of Ormond and the Geraldines and the Burkes with the common people warred against Bren O Bren, and killed many of his people, and took great preys from them.[99]

On 30 September 1332 John Darcy was reappointed to succeed Lucy, though Lucy continued to act till 3 December and Darcy did not arrive till February 1333, Thomas de Burgh, the treasurer, acting in the interval. The main task was, of course, to complete the settlement of the problems presented by Desmond. Desmond himself was still a prisoner in Dublin castle; so were Henry de Mandeville, who had been arrested at some time in 1331,[100] and Walter de Bermingham. Walter de Burgo had been arrested in

[97] *Analecta Hibernica*, XXIII, pp. 12–14.
[98] *C.P.R., 1330–34*, p. 325; *C.C.R., 1330–33*, pp. 484–5.
[99] *43rd Rep. D.K.*, pp. 54–5, 56; *Parliaments and Councils*, nos. 9, 11; Clyn, *Annals*, p. 24. This army was one of the occasions on which a few tenants-in-chief served in person (*44th Rep. D.K.*, p. 21).
[100] *C.C.R., 1330–33*, p. 410.

November 1331 by the order of the earl of Ulster, and imprisoned in the castle of Northburgh, where he died in 1332. It must have been felt that it would be unsafe to proceed to extremes against Desmond: apart from any other consideration, his execution would have left a vacuum of power in the south-west from which only the MacCarthys, O'Briens and MacNamaras would have profited. Finally, early in June 1333, 'at the request of the whole clergy of the land of Ireland, and of others, as well magnates as others of the community of the said land', by the king's special grace, and with the assent of his council, as well in England as in Ireland, Desmond was released, on the mainprise of the earls of Ulster and Ormond, sixteen knights, and eight other magnates, who guaranteed his future good behaviour, and that he would never again raise war in Ireland or be of *mala couina* against the king or his ministers. The earl, who had sworn to observe all this before the high altar of Christ Church cathedral on 17 May, in the presence of the justiciar and other officials, the mayor of Dublin, and many of the people, clerks and laymen, gave hostages for the observance of the agreement. His liberty of Kerry, which had of course been taken into the king's hand after the edict of resumption of 1331, was restored to him in July 1334.[101] It was to be some ten years before he gave trouble again.

Meanwhile, events in the north had illustrated only too vividly what might have happened in Desmond if Maurice had been executed. On 6 June 1333, the day before Desmond was released, the earl of Ulster was treacherously murdered at Le Ford, the modern Belfast, by his own men, John de Logan and two of the Mandevilles, who are said to have been incited to the murder by Walter de Burgo's widow. The earl's widow fled by sea with her infant daughter, the heiress of Ulster and Connacht, and considerable disturbances followed, quelled by the justiciar, who in July brought the army which had been prepared to join the king in Scotland to Ulster. But the murderers had fled to the Irish, and the inquisitions post mortem taken later in the year show that within six months of the earl's death the whole position west of the Bann had been lost, never to be recovered during the middle ages, while Ulster east of the Bann was never again to be ruled by a resident lord. As much as anything else, the passing of so much authority all over Ireland into the hands of absentee lords in this century, and the fragmentation of lordships by division among co-heiresses, was to bring about the decline of the colony.

[101] *Parliaments and Councils*, no. 12; *C.P.R.*, *1330–34*, p. 564. For Bermingham and de Mandeville, see below, p. 252, n. 1.

CHAPTER VIII

The Ebbing Tide: From the Murder of the Earl of Ulster to the Black Death

WITH THE murder of William de Burgo the disturbances which had torn Ireland ever since the Bruce invasion began ceased for the time, the magnates being perhaps shocked by their own excesses, and quelled by the new vigour which had been shown in the last two years. Desmond, as we have seen, had just been released; Walter de Bermingham and Henry de Mandeville were still in jail[1]; the new earl of Kildare was a minor who did not get livery of his lands till 1342; John de Bermingham, Arnald le Poer, Walter de Burgo and William de Bermingham were all dead. But the damage which had been done, whether by Bruce's raids, by the feuds of the Anglo-Irish, or by the seizing of the opportunities thus presented by the native Irish, remained. In 1323 an inquisition as to the lands of Roger de Mortimer had found the castle of Dunamase burnt by the Irish, and the whole of what had been a great and flourishing manor, full of free tenants, farmers and burgesses, waste, with nothing left of its former prosperity but a handful of burgesses in the New Town of Leix. In 1324 the burgages of Ferns, co. Wexford, 'render nothing on account of the war'; in 1334 the priory of Selskar in the same county alleged that all its lands and rents were destroyed by the war of 'McMurhuth' and other Irish: the monks were, they said, about to abandon their house and dwell in the countryside with their friends. The inquisition post mortem taken as to the lands of the earl of Kildare in 1329 had found that his manor of Geashill in Leix was worth nothing because in the hands of the Irish, while

1 De Bermingham's release after trial and suitable punishment was ordered in November 1333, and de Mandeville's 'as Maurice fitz Thomas, earl of Desmond . . . was released' in March 1334. Bermingham subsequently served in Scotland, and his father's forfeited lands were restored to him for good service in Scotland and Ireland in 1337. He was justiciar from 1348 to 1349. Mandeville seems to have been employed in Ulster (*C.C.R., 1333–7*, pp. 187, 209; *Cal. Fine Rolls, 1337–47*, pp. 10–11; *C.C.H.*, p. 38, no. 58; p. 41, no. 35).

in 1331 his demesne lands in co. Limerick were largely waste, 'because of the wars and for lack of tenants', the manor of Grean was worth nothing because occupied by the Irish, and the value of his lands in the county had fallen by as much as two-thirds in some places. In 1331 the de Verdon castle of Roche, co. Louth, was still a ruin, burnt by the Irish, and the demesne lands in co. Longford lay waste for lack of tenants. Even within a few miles of Dublin the manor of Bray was 'in the march, so that scarcely anything can be received therefrom'.[2]

In these circumstances it was not of much avail that a number of lordships, notably Kildare and an Ulster in which everything beyond the Bann had been lost within a few months of the Brown Earl's murder, were in the king's hand because of minorities. Only vigorous reinforcement from England could have saved the situation for the colonists, and the expedition which the king had announced in 1331, and for which preparations had continued all through 1332, had been abandoned in September 1332, after Edward Balliol had invaded Scotland with remarkable initial success, completely routing the forces of the earl of Mar, the regent for Bruce's infant son, at Dupplin Moor in August. It was not to be expected that Edward III should neglect the opportunities which this offered for intervention in Scotland, or indeed the not impossible danger of Scottish attacks on the north of England: at the parliament of September it was decided that the king (who should have crossed to Ireland at the end of the month) should remain in England, though men and money should be sent to Ireland. In the early summer of 1333 Edward led an expedition against the Scots, defeating them at Halidon Hill and taking Berwick, but the Irish forces which had been preparing to join him had been diverted to Ulster to quell the disturbances arising out of the earl's murder, though the justiciar later led a small expedition towards Dumbarton, the chief of the few strongholds in which Bruce's supporters still held out. But in the spring of 1335 preparations were begun for a considerable expedition from Ireland in aid of a fresh campaign in Scotland, where there had been a widespread rising against Balliol, who had suggested to Edward that a force should be made ready in Ireland to co-operate with the men of the western isles, whom he alleged to be his supporters.

It was hoped that a very large force could be raised in Ireland for this expedition: 600 men-at-arms, 1,500 hobelers, and 6,000

[2] P.R.O., London, C 47/10/18, no. 17 (cf. *C.D.I.*, II, no. 2028); S.C. 8/242/12054; *C.C.R.*, *1323–7*, p. 363; *Red Book of Kildare*, nos. 126–8, 132, 133; J. Otway-Ruthven, 'The Partition of the de Verdon Lands', *Proc. R.I.A.*, LXVI C; *C.C.H.*, p. 39, no. 79.

footmen. Letters were addressed to all the bishops, to the mayor of Dublin, to the earls of Ormond and Desmond, to fifty-five knights, more than a hundred esquires, and fourteen Irish chiefs.[3] The justiciar was empowered to issue pardons to both English and Irish, excepting only those concerned in the murder of the earl of Ulster. Meanwhile ships were being requisitioned and fitted up, provisions and military stores of all kinds were being prepared, and a great catapult in Dublin castle was being repaired. But when the expedition finally sailed under the command of the justiciar it consisted only of the earls of Desmond and Ormond, fourteen bannerets (of whom Walter de Bermingham, no doubt, like Desmond, earnestly giving proof of his reformation, was one), 472 men-at-arms (the only contingent which approached the hoped-for numbers), 291 hobelers, and 805 footmen, of whom many were archers.[4] It was not till near the end of August that the expedition actually sailed. It seems that it besieged Rothesay castle, though without success, and the bulk of the troops went home after little more than three weeks, though Desmond, with thirty men-at-arms, and the retinues of the justiciar, Walter de Bermingham, and Thomas Wogan, a total of some 150 men-at-arms, forty hobelers, and 200 footmen, with the great engine, remained till 15 October, when the king disbanded his own army. He had had encouraging successes in this campaign, to which the presence of the Irish forces in Bute may have contributed, but these had been undone by the end of the year, and before long he was to be totally preoccupied by war with France.[5]

Meanwhile, Ireland seems to have been almost orderly. In 1334 there were indeed expeditions against the Irish of Cork, Thomond, and Leinster, but in 1335 attempts seem to have been made to treat with the Irish, no doubt in the hope of persuading them to join the expedition against Scotland. At any rate an emissary was sent to Connacht, to O'Connor and Edmund son of Richard de Burgo, and Roger Outlaw, the chancellor, who was acting as deputy justiciar, was treating with the Irish in Ulster, and with those of

[3] There were six from the borders of Meath; two O'Neills, O'Hanlon and MacCartan from Ulster; O'Connor, O'Brien, and 'MacDermot', and MacMurrough. The list was presumably based on information supplied by the Irish government, but only MacMurrough responded.
[4] Much the largest contingent was brought by Desmond who had his troops at Drogheda on 30 July. Thomas Wogan's wages for this expedition from 7 June to 15 October were still in arrears in 1352 (*C.C.R., 1349–54*, p. 451). It is interesting to compare this force of just under 1,600 men with the armies of about 1,000 which were being used in Ireland twenty years later.
[5] R. Nicholson, 'An Irish expedition to Scotland in 1335', *I.H.S.*, XIII, pp. 197–211.

the midlands and Leinster.[6] But the main interest of the period seems to have been in Connacht, where a confused struggle seems to have been going on between Edmund de Burgo, the younger son of the Red Earl,[7] and the sons of William 'Liath' de Burgo, the Red Earl's first cousin, of whom the Walter de Burgo who died in the castle of Northburgh had been one. His brothers remained: William or Ulick, and Edmund 'Albanach', who had accompanied his father to Scotland when he was taken prisoner by Bruce at Connor, and had, according to later tradition, remained there for many years, till, seeing his opportunity after the murder of the Brown Earl, he landed in the Owles of Mayo, and married O'Malley's daughter.[8] In 1335 we are told that he despoiled all west Connacht: 'he slew many people and executed raids, burnings, and untold damage against the Earl's son and the posterity of Richard Burke in the same year'. In 1336 he was raiding the O'Flanagans round Elphin, co. Roscommon, and in 1337 Turlough O'Connor was building a stronghold against him at Athleague, co. Roscommon. Then, in 1338, 'Edmund Burke, son of the earl of Ulster, was taken prisoner by Edmund (Albanach) Burke, and afterwards a stone was tied about his neck, and he was cast into Loch Mask'.[9] The annals go on to say that after this Turlough O'Connor obtained the ascendancy in Connacht and Edmund Albanach was driven out and took to the islands, while the colonists were expelled from Leyney and Corann, 'and their lordship was assumed by their native Gaels'. But before long Edmund Albanach had returned,[10] and succeeded in establishing himself firmly in the de Burgo lands in northern Connacht, while his brother William took possession of the Galway lands, disregarding the rights of the murdered earl's daughter, which no great effort seems to have been made to enforce.

Meanwhile, there had been the usual troubles in the rest of the country. Even in 1335 the O'Mores, O'Byrnes, and O'Carrolls had all been in arms, and at the end of the year Maurice fitz Thomas was leading an expedition against Brian O'Brien. In June 1336 O'Brien burnt the town of Tipperary, and O'More had induced all the Irish of all Leinster and Munster to rise in war.[11] This must have been the cause of the 'army of Kilkenny' proclaimed in this

---

[6] *C.C.H.*, p. 37, no. 8; p. 38, nos. 21, 47; p. 39, nos. 65, 70, 93; p. 41, nos. 22, 38–39, 42; *44th Rep. D.K.*, p. 21.

[7] i.e. Edmund son of Richard de Burgo.

[8] See *Galway Arch. Soc.*, XIII, p. 57 (*recte* 121).

[9] *AC.*

[10] In 1340 he and his brother Reymund, 'for good service in Ireland', were pardoned for the murder and all other offences (*C.P.R., 1338–40*, p. 440).

[11] Clyn, *Annals*, pp. 26–27.

year, and we find the justiciar going with an army to Connacht
and Uriel to parley with O'Connor and MacGeoghegan, and to
Offaly and Leinster to parley with and fight O'Connor Faly,
O'Dempsey, the O'Tooles and the O'Byrnes, who had risen in
war, while Ormond led 'a multitude of men-at-arms' from Munster
against the O'Mores, O'Nolans, O'Byrnes and MacMurroughs,
and Edmund de Burgo remained in Munster to fight Brian O'Brien.
The justiciar himself led an expedition to Munster against O'Brien
and MacNamara in the autumn.[12]

In 1335 a subsidy had been granted by the community of the
land of Ireland for the Scottish war, and at the same time petitions
had probably been sent to the king, for in May 1336 he sent the
justiciar, chancellor and treasurer 'certain things ordained by him
and his council for the reformation of the state of Ireland, and the
direction of the king's affairs there, and for the confirmation of the
king's peace and the punishment of malefactors and delinquents'.
There seems to be no trace of these articles, but in June an order
which certainly proceeded from a petition required the Irish government to treat 'all who ought to be ruled by English law' equally,
because it has been shown to the king by 'honest men of those parts
and public fame proclaims' that all the king's ministers in Ireland
'show too great favour to the powerful, permitting them to oppress
the poor, to invade the king's rights, to usurp the royal power, to
detain the king's debts, to institute novelties and perpetrate various crimes'. In July a proclamation was ordered that no royal
official in Ireland should have the wardship of the liberties or lands
of others, or hold another office (presumably within a liberty) on
pain of loss of office, according to an order made by the king and
council in England, and early in 1337 we hear that it had lately
been ordered in the English parliament that lords holding lands in
Ireland should pay a subsidy for the defence of their marches.[13]
But complaints must have continued: in July 1337 the king ordered
the archbishop of Dublin, Alexander de Bicknor, an experienced
official, to come without delay to inform him and the council
touching the state of Ireland,[14] and on the next day John de
Charlton, one of the lords of the Welsh marches, a former courtier
of Edward II, was appointed as justiciar, though it was not till the
middle of October that he reached Ireland. At the same time a new
chancellor, Thomas de Charlton, bishop of Hereford, the justiciar's
brother, a new treasurer, and new justices of the justiciar's bench

[12] *45th Rep. D.K.*, pp. 32, 35, 39; *C.C.H.*, p. 20, nos. 3–11, 17, 21–22, 27. This
roll, calendared as the Close Roll of 10 Edward II, is really that of 10 Edward III.
[13] *C.C.R., 1333–7*, pp. 579, 679, 689–90; ibid., *1337–9*, p.12.
[14] Ibid., p. 150.

were appointed, though the appointment of the justices did not take effect. The justiciar was to have a force of two hundred Welsh footmen, and no doubt it was hoped that this ministerial revolution would solve the problems of Ireland by applying to them the experience gained in the Welsh marches.

Meanwhile in England interest had shifted from the continuing quarrel with Scotland (though in September 1337 Richard de Mandeville with 'a multitude of Scottish felons' had invaded the Isle of Man, and an expedition was being prepared in Ireland to recover it[15]) to the outbreak of hostilities with France. Philip of France had declared Gascony confiscated in May 1337; all through the summer diplomatic preparations went on; in October Edward formally laid claim to the crown of France, though it was to be two years before an organized campaign began. Every effort was made during this period to secure the maximum revenue from Ireland, while in April 1340 Reymund de Burgo, Edmund Albanach's brother, who had just been pardoned for all offences,[16] was preparing a force of men-at-arms and hobelers to go to France for the war there: the Irish treasurer was ordered to provide shipping and pay for the voyage. A little later Reymund appears supplying horses for the king's service.[17] But at this stage Edward's campaign was meeting with little success: in September 1340 he was obliged to agree to a truce with the French to last till midsummer; in November, in grave straits for money, he returned hurriedly from the Low Countries to revenge himself on his ministers, against whom he charged an incompetence amounting to treason which had left him without means to pursue the war. In the course of the crisis which followed he removed all his ministers in England, and all the sheriffs, and set up a commission in each county to enquire into the behaviour of all officials, commissions which proceeded 'so sternly and arbitrarily that none escaped unpunished whether he had conducted the king's business well or ill'.[18]

The crisis did not directly concern Ireland, but it must have been in connection with it that certain changes were made. John de Charlton had been removed as the result of complaints against him in May 1338, and his brother, the bishop, had been *custos* till March 1340, when Darcy had been reappointed, though he acted entirely by deputy. Now, in March 1341, John Morice, who had

[15] *C.C.H.*, p. 42, nos. 7–8. [16] See above, p. 255, n. 10.
[17] *C.C.R.*, *1337–9*, p. 423; ibid., *1339–41*, pp. 98–99, 397, 547; *Cal. Fine Rolls, 1337–47*, pp. 91, 122; *47th Rep. D.K.*, p. 60; *C.P.R.*, *1338–40*, p. 440; ibid., *1340–43*, p. 49.
[18] Murimuth, *Continuatio Chronicarum*, ed. E. M. Thompson (Rolls Series, 1889), pp. 116–20.

been escheator in Ireland from 1329 to 1336, and had just been acting as one of the special commissioners in Oxfordshire, Berkshire, and Buckinghamshire, was appointed as Darcy's deputy, and sent over with instructions to conduct a general inquiry into the central administration: the numbers, fees, wages, and duties of royal officials; whether their offices were necessary or not; the conduct of officials since 1330; and 'all other matters affecting the state of the land and the king's profit'. In addition, all debts due to the king were to be levied without delay, in consideration of his needs for the French war. In July a general resumption of all grants made since the death of Edward I was ordered, though with a promise that those made for 'true, just and reasonable causes' should be renewed. Three days later it was ordered that all officials who were beneficed, married, and held property in Ireland, and had nothing in England, should be removed and replaced by fit Englishmen, having lands and benefices in England, who alone were to be employed in future, as the king and council considered that such men would serve him better: a policy first adumbrated in 1338, when the king and council had ordered that the justices of both benches in Ireland should be English.[19]

We cannot tell how much of this wholly unrealistic and largely impracticable programme, calculated to cause the maximum resentment, was in fact put into effect: there were at any rate no spectacular changes in the personnel of the central government. But there was enough to occupy the new deputy. Immediately before his arrival the archbishop of Dublin, who had been acting justiciar since 22 February, had been engaged in Munster; Morice on taking up office on 16 May seems to have gone northwards to Dundalk. From 2 August to 2 October he was leading an army against MacMurrough—presumably the 'army of Tristeldermot' for which a scutage was levied in this year—while from 16 January 1342 to 16 May he was in the neighbourhood of Mullingar, conducting a campaign against the Irish on the borders of Meath, who 'waged war against the king and his faithful people'. At the same time some of the settlers were disaffected, for in May the justiciar was ordered to detain in safe custody Sir Richard de Tuit of Ballyloughloe, arrested for certain treasons committed by him in warring against the king and his lieges.[20] And meanwhile the king, who

---

[19] *C.C.R.*, *1337–9*, p. 392; ibid., *1341–3*, pp. 30, 39, 184–5; *C.P.R.*, *1340–43*, p. 207; *Cal. Fine Rolls, 1337–47*, p. 234.

[20] *Analecta Hibernica*, II, pp. 226–7; *47th Rep. D.K.*, pp. 49, 64; *53rd Rep. D.K.*, pp. 45–46; *C.C.R.*, *1341–3*, p. 441; *C.C.H.*, p. 45, no. 78. There was a campaign against the O'Byrnes in co. Wicklow from 16 July to 4 September 1342 (*53rd Rep. D.K.*, pp. 44–45).

was preparing to lead an army to Brittany in the autumn of 1342, had ordered a force of 120 men-at-arms and 900 hobelers to be prepared in Ireland and sent to him to serve beyond seas.[21]

Long before this, the order for a general resumption of grants had provoked a considerable storm. A parliament was held at Dublin in October 1341, and adjourned to Kilkenny in November. Desmond had failed to attend it at Dublin: according to the chronicler, the deputy and other officials dared not attend at Kilkenny. Certainly the magnates and townsmen alike were angry: the chronicle says that never before had such notable wrath and manifest division arisen between the English of England and the English of Ireland, and a set of petitions sharply critical of the administration was prepared and messengers appointed by the 'prelates, earls, barons and community of Ireland' to bring them to the king.[22] The neglect of ministers, they said, had caused the destruction of wardships, especially Connacht and Ulster, as well as the king's demesne manors and castles: more than a third of the land of Ireland, conquered in the time of the king's ancestors, had come into the hands of his Irish enemies, and the English lieges were so impoverished that they could scarcely live. The king's castles, of which they listed Roscommon, Randown and Athlone, together with Bunratty and others which should be in his hands, had been lost because the treasurer corruptly appropriated the greater part of the fees for their keeping to himself; no payment had been made for prises of foodstuffs taken for the war in Scotland and elsewhere, though the treasurer had had full allowance. Ministers who should account at the exchequer were heavily in debt: some could not pay, and others had gone to England, so that sums already levied from the people were still demanded from them. Ministers held several offices at once in order to receive the fees. Ministers had allowed separate truces or peaces to be made with the Irish, and after a peace or truce made with the Irish by the king's ministers any of the lieges who attempted to recover their lands occupied by the Irish were punished, so that the lands were permanently lost. They complained of a variety of official oppressions; they said that whereas no land could be well governed without law and arms, the king's ministers in Ireland often failed in both, for where, as in Connacht and elsewhere, there was continual war between the English 'linages' the ministers neither came to execute the law against the malefactors nor to restrain them by force of arms: instead they rode in arms where there was no need in order to receive

---

[21] Cal. Fine Rolls, 1337–47, p. 278.
[22] Grace, Annals, pp. 132–4; Chart. St. Mary's, II, pp. 383–4.

wages. They complained that ministers levied scutages without
necessity and without the consent of the magnates, and levied
money for services which should be rendered in person[23] (the king
pointed out sharply that it was for the justiciar to summon the
royal service when he saw fit). They alleged that persons indicted
in Ireland had been unreasonably summoned by English writs to
answer in England for felonies and trespasses supposed to have
been committed in Ireland; they complained that peers of the land,
ministers and others, were taken and imprisoned without indictment, and were detained in prison at the will of the king's ministers.
And above all they complained of the resumption, saying with a
certain disingenuity that, unlike those of the king's allegiance in
Scotland, Gascony, and Wales, they had never behaved other than
well and loyally towards their liege lord, and complaining of those
sent to govern them from England, who knew nothing of Ireland,
and had nothing of their own of which to live till they had obtained
it by extortion from the people of Ireland.[24]

The petitions must have reached the king early in 1342, and
after deliberation with the council he returned them on 14 April
with a favourable reply on almost every point, though this was of
course no guarantee that the administrative abuses complained of
would not continue. A new chancellor had however been appointed: John Larcher, prior of the Hospital, one of the messengers
sent to the king with the petition, and this must have had a reassuring effect. In any case, the policy which Morice had been sent to
enforce was abandoned, though he remained deputy till 1344,
when Ralph de Ufford was appointed as justiciar in February,
reaching Ireland in June.

Ufford, who was the grandson of Robert de Ufford, justiciar
under Edward I, had married Maud, daughter of Henry earl of
Lancaster and widow of the earl of Ulster, and had therefore important interests in Ireland in her right. It was clearly contemplated that he should make a general inquiry into the conduct of
ministers in Ireland, for a week before his appointment proclamation had been ordered that no one who had been a minister in
Ireland should leave the country until the arrival of the justices
whom the king had appointed to enquire into the behaviour of
ministers, and until such enquiry had been made. In June Ufford
was ordered to seize into the king's hand all lands in Ireland laid
waste by war and abandoned and to regrant them for a term, and

---

[23] It is interesting to find the claim that tenants-in-chief were entitled to serve
in person at their election still persisting. See above, p. 204.
[24] *Early Statutes*, pp. 332–63; *C.C.R.*, *1341–3*, pp. 508–16.

also to enquire into lands granted for the defence of the marches which had been occupied by the Irish because the tenants failed to defend them. In November a general enquiry was ordered into all lands and other rights granted by the king since 1330; those extended by favour and fraud, or not extended at all, were to be extended without delay.[25] It is possible that the zeal with which Ufford executed these instructions contributed to the violent animosity which the Dublin annalist displays against him: a man who deprived clergy and laity, rich and poor, of their goods, neither observing the rights of the church nor the law of the kingdom, led by the counsel of his wife. At his death the intemperate weather which had persisted ever since his arrival suddenly ceased, and clergy and people celebrated Easter with especial joy.[26] In estimating the accuracy of this we may remember that this annalist had shown some sympathy towards Desmond's accomplices twelve years earlier, and towards Desmond himself now, and Desmond was once more a major preoccupation of the Irish government.

It is clear that Desmond had long been acting with a certain disregard for the niceties of the law, but it was not till towards the end of 1343 that he conspicuously clashed with the royal authorities, when he forcibly took possession of the barony of Inchiquin (Imokilly, co. Cork), in the king's wardship because of the death of Sir Giles Baddlesmere. Early in 1344 he was involved in a feud of the Barrys in co. Cork, which led to war and the killing of a number of royal officials, and it was later alleged that in the spring he was once more aiming at the crown, and wrote to the Irish of all four provinces urging them to unite in rebellion, and to the kings of France and Scotland urging them to make war on Edward as he would himself in Ireland. He was further thought to have sent an embassy to the pope denouncing Edward's rule in Ireland, and offering an annual payment of 3,000 marks if he were allowed to be the pope's representative in Ireland. In July he had a force of 1,000 men—'a great army of armed men, as well Irish as outlaws' —which attempted to conquer the king's town of Youghal for him, and was harbouring 'MacDermot'—Dermot MacCarthy lord of Duhallow and Muskerry—and others, the king's enemies and outlaws.[27]

---

[25] *C.C.R., 1343–6*, pp. 341, 375, 478; *Cal. Fine Rolls, 1337–47*, pp. 380, 402; *C.P.R., 1343–5*, p. 417.

[26] *Chart. St. Mary's*, II, pp. 385, 388.

[27] G. O. Sayles, 'The rebellious first earl of Desmond', *Medieval Studies presented to Aubrey Gwynn, S.J.*, pp. 203–29; 'The Legal Proceedings against the first earl of Desmond', *Analecta Hibernica*, XXIII, pp. 3–47, especially pp. 20–21, 29–30, 32–36.

It was into this situation that Ufford came when he reached Ireland on 13 July, and he acted with promptitude. Writing to the king on 24 October he excuses himself for not having reported earlier: on his arrival he found the land so troubled as well by the outrages of the English who would not obey the court as by the war of the Irish who hope to drive the English from the country that within eight days he had gone by advice of the council to Munster, where insufferable grievances had been committed in the county of Cork and its neighbourhood. He had reached Cork before 2 August, when an inquisition was taken there before him; on 4 August he was at Youghal, then returned to Cork, and by 2 September was at Clonmel, co. Tipperary. After this, he told the king, he returned through Leinster among the Irish, who were much inclined to do ill, and did it from day to day, but 'they do not bear themselves so high now as they did'. The 'riots' in Munster are, he says optimistically, at an end.[28]

It is hard to see why he thought so, but perhaps he had discounted some of the statements made by the jurors, such as the allegation that at the end of July Desmond had formed a sworn confederacy with, among others, various de Mandevilles, Barrys, Cantetons and MacCarthys to form a single 'covin' against the king of England, maintaining each other against the king and rising together in war.[29] Though Desmond, who had bought the marriage of the heir of the first earl of Ormond and was withholding the payment, was negotiating with the king,[30] outrages continued. In February 1345 Desmond summoned an assembly of magnates at Callan, to which he came with a large force, but the other magnates, having been forbidden by royal writs to attend such 'suspect conventicles', stayed at home. He did not attend the parliament held at Dublin in June, but instead rode as if at war against the king's land of Ely and Ormond, attacking, though without success, the castle of Nenagh.[31] On 7 July, and not before it was time, Ufford proclaimed the royal service.[32] In September and October Desmond's castles of Askeaton, co. Limerick, and Castle Island in Kerry were taken, and though Desmond himself

---

[28] Ibid.; P.R.O., London, S.C. 1/56/7.

[29] *Analecta Hibernica*, XXIII, pp. 37–38.

[30] *C.C.R.*, *1343–6*, pp. 328–392.

[31] The damage done is illustrated by the rental made in August 1345 (*Cal. Ormond Deeds*, II, no. 316. This has been misplaced in the calendar: it certainly belongs to 1345). Ely and Ormond were still in wardship: the second earl of Ormond did not get livery of his inheritance till February 1347.

[32] The inquisition printed by Professor Sayles (loc. cit., p. 26) says this was at Cashel; the Pipe Rolls spoke of the army of Moydesshell (*54th Rep. D.K.*, pp. 23, 49).

escaped to the Irish, his supporters were taken and executed or forced to give hostages and pay heavy fines, while those who had been mainpernors for him in 1333 were obliged to seek formal pardons.[33]

Ufford's main achievement had been the reduction of Desmond, and when he died prematurely on 9 April 1346, after an illness long enough for news of it to have reached the king in England,[34] the Irish council wrote that had he lived the conflict would have been completely ended, for it remained only to capture Desmond, who remained resolutely among the Irish enemies.[35] But he had also led an expedition to Ulster, where of course his wife's interests lay, apparently early in 1345, and had defeated and driven out Thomas MacCartan and deposed Henry O'Neill, replacing him by Aedh O'Neill, *et sic cum laude et triumpho revertitur*, while earlier he had forced MacMurrough to give hostages to keep the peace.[36] And he had shown himself ready to act with firmness against the Anglo-Irish magnates: it is not clear what we should make of the Dublin annalist's story that in the autumn of 1345 he sent two writs, one ordering the earl of Kildare to come with all his force to assist him and the king, and another ordering that he should be arrested and imprisoned, and that Kildare was treacherously taken while he was sitting in the exchequer with the council, but in 1346 Kildare, being a prisoner in the castle of Dublin, was released on the surety of twenty-four gentlemen of his county.[37] And at Naas early in December 1345 Ufford took the liberty of Kildare into the king's hand on the grounds that the earl had claimed to have before his seneschal cognizance of pleas by his own writs issuing from his chancery, though the charter of Edward II granting him the liberty had not expressly conferred any such power.[38]

Roger Darcy was appointed as justiciar by the Irish council on the day after Ufford's death, and served till 14 May, when John Morice came from England with a commission dated just before Ufford's death in anticipation of it. But by this time Walter de Bermingham had been appointed in England, and took up office

<hr />

[33] Sayles, loc. cit.; *Cal. Gormanston Reg.*, p. 127; *C.P.R., 1348–50*, p. 49.

[34] *C.C.H.*, p. 49, no. 62.

[35] Sayles, loc. cit., p. 223.

[36] *Chart. St. Mary's*, II, p. 385; Clyn, *Annals*, p. 30. According to *AU* Mac-Cartan was hanged by the English in 1347.

[37] *Chart. St. Mary's*, II, pp. 386, 389; Genealogical Office, MS 192, pp. 52–53. The Dublin annals say Kildare was released on 23 May 1346.

[38] P.R.O., London, C 47/87/2, no. 11. In spite of repeated attempts neither Kildare nor his descendants ever recovered the liberty. See above p. 174.

on 29 June.[39] Before this Desmond had surrendered on condition that he was given special protection and allowed to go to England to answer the charges brought against him: in September he sailed from Youghal with his wife and sons. Eventually, in February 1348, he was released on bail, and in November 1349 he was formally pardoned for his treason and restored to his dignities and estates. He returned to Ireland about May 1350; in Michaelmas term 1351 the outlawries proclaimed against him in Ireland in 1345 were annulled, and before he died in January 1356 he had been justiciar for several months.[40]

The major preoccupation of the English government in appointing Bermingham was clearly the continuing state of war in Ireland. He was given full power to treat with the 'captains of the Irish' to bring them into the king's peace; to receive into the king's peace and fealty both English and Irish now in rebellion, and to grant them pardons by the advice of the chancellor and treasurer. The instructions which had been given to Ufford as to lands wasted by war and abandoned, and as to lands granted for the defence of the marches, were substantially repeated.[41] Three weeks after his arrival, when he had no doubt reported to England on the conditions he found, he was given leave to retain at the king's wages a standing force of ten men-at-arms and fifty archers in addition to his normal retinue 'so long as he shall be justiciar and the war there endure'.[42]

He had indeed found the country still greatly disturbed. Ufford's illness and death must have severely weakened the governmental effort, and Clyn says that soon afterwards 'all the Irish of Leinster universally put themselves at war against the English and the men of peace, burning, spoiling and killing whom they could'. O'More, O'Connor Faly and O'Dempsey destroyed Lea and other castles; MacGilpatrick burnt the town of Aghabo; in June the Irish of Ulster killed several hundred of the English of Louth.[43] But the ending of the troubles in Munster must have been the most pressing need, and by 3 August Bermingham was at Clonmel, where

[39] Morice was appointed as chancellor on 20 May. He wrote plaintively in July that when he arrived in May he had found the peace troubled and grain very dear; things had then improved, but on the news that another justiciar was coming the people's mood changed greatly and they were less obedient to the peace. His commission as chancellor had not arrived: what should he do? (P.R.O., London, S.C. 1/38/109).
[40] Sayles, loc. cit.; below, p. 281.
[41] See above, pp. 260–61.
[42] *C.P.R., 1345–8*, pp. 88, 119, 156; *Cal. Fine Rolls, 1337–47*, p. 470; *C.C.R., 1346–9*, p. 77. The power to pardon excluded Desmond, Thomas fitz John, and Walter de Mandeville.
[43] Clyn, *Annals*, pp. 32–33.

yet another inquisition denounced Desmond. At Cashel on 6 August John Morice was appointed seneschal of Desmond's forfeited lands in Tipperary and Waterford, and on 20 August at Kilmallock he was ordered to take inquisitions as to felonies and transgressions committed against the inhabitants of these lands after they had come to the king's hand. On 1 September Richard son of Edmund de Burgo was appointed to arrest all 'malefactors and disturbers of the peace of the name and kindred of the Burkeyns' in Waterford, Tipperary, and elsewhere in Munster, and by this time the justiciar was already in Kerry, where he took an inquisition at Tralee on 26 August.[44]

Meanwhile the defence of Leinster seems to have been entrusted to the local authorities, not without success: at least Clyn tells us that the sheriff of Kilkenny 'took a great prey upon Carwyl McGillepatricke and upon his men'. In September Sir Fulk de la Frene took O'More's son and killed the son of Roderick O'Carroll, prince of Ely O'Carroll, who had 'killed, exiled and ejected from their lands of Elycarwyl those of the nations of Barry, Milleborne, Bret, and other English of the country, and held and occupied their lands and castles'. Then, in November, the justiciar, together with the earl of Kildare, proceeded against O'More and O'Dempsey and completely defeated them, forcing them to submit to the king's grace. O'More gave hostages, undertook to pay a heavy fine of cows, and recognized that he held his land of Bellet of the manor of Dunamase.[45]

Meanwhile the war in France continued, and in late August Edward had won the great victory of Crecy, after which he settled down to besiege Calais, while in October the Scots, invading England partly in response to an appeal from France, were heavily defeated at Neville's Cross near Durham, and king David taken prisoner. In May 1347 Kildare, Fulk de la Frene, and others, summoned by the king, joined the army besieging Calais,[46] which finally surrendered in August. In Ireland the south-west, in spite of being visited by the justiciar in two successive years, was clearly still disturbed, and indeed the jurors at Tralee in August had said that, in spite of his surrender, Desmond had written only four days earlier to MacCarthy and other Irish urging them to rise in war against the English and continue in it until he returned to Ireland.

[44] *Analecta Hibernica*, XXIII, pp. 43–46; *C.C.H.*, p. 51, nos. 32, 38; p. 53, no. 108.
[45] Clyn, *Annals*, p. 33; *Chart. St. Mary's*, II, pp. 389–90; Genealogical Office, MS 192, pp. 53–55.
[46] *Chart. St. Mary's*, II, p. 390; Clyn, *Annals*, p. 34; *Analecta Hibernica*, II, pp. 225–6.

It was perhaps not unconnected with Desmond's intrigues that in January 1347 the archbishop of Cashel and the bishops of Emly, Limerick and Lismore, on the ground that no bishop of the province had assented, hindered the collection of the subsidy which had been granted for the wars by the parliament which met at Kilkenny in October 1346, and ordered that any clerk who paid it should be deprived of his benefice and unfrocked, and any layman, and his children to the third generation, should be excommunicated.[47] But in the west there were encouraging developments: for the last time the English of Connacht, where of course Bermingham had powerful connections, were showing some deference to the king's government. When the justiciar was holding his sessions at Trim in May fourteen of the Connacht tenants, de Burgos, Prendergasts, de Angulo, Butler, Stanton, Barrett, Lawless, appeared before him, made their submission, and gave hostages. And in the autumn he went himself to Connacht, where the chancellor with the great seal was in attendance on him from 26 August to 25 October, and a seneschal and coroners were elected and took oath before him.[48]

By this time there had again been complaints about the behaviour of the king's ministers. In September a commission of oyer and terminer had been issued to deal with official oppressions committed by Hugh de Burgh, who had been treasurer from 1339 to 1343 and a baron of the exchequer both earlier and later, and in November this was extended to cover oppressions by all the king's ministers in Ireland except the justiciar and chancellor. Three days later Bermingham himself was summoned to attend the parliament to be held at Westminster in January 1348 to give his counsel.[49] He was absent from Ireland from the end of November till the end of April, and it was perhaps as a result of this that late in December O'Kennedy, having according to Clyn made a conspiracy of the Irish of all four provinces, burned the town of Nenagh, and the whole country and all the castles of Ormond, except that of Nenagh itself. In the spring he was captured by the Purcells, and afterwards hanged at Thurles.[50] The king's wardship of Ormond had come to an end in the previous February, when the new earl had livery

---

[47] *Analecta Hibernica*, XXIII, p. 46; N. L. I., Harris Collectanea, II, pp. 208–9; Genealogical Office, MS 192, pp. 34–35; Betham, *Early Parliaments*, pp. 292–3. Early in February the bishop of Lismore came to Clonmel, and *in media ville* solemnly excommunicated all who paid the subsidy or had anything to do with its levy.

[48] Genealogical Office, MS 192, pp. 11–12, 27, 28; *Analecta Hibernica*, II, pp. 215–16. On 14 July he had been at Clonmel (*C.P.R., 1348–50*, p. 84).

[49] *C.P.R., 1345–8*, pp. 399, 464; *C.C.R., 1346–9*, p. 413.

[50] Clyn, *Annals*, p. 34.

of his lands: long afterwards it was said that the loss of the earl's lands in Ormond had taken place when they were in the king's wardship in the time of Edward III, and it is clear enough that though there had evidently been some retreat earlier they had been substantially reduced during this period. When in November 1347 the king granted to Ormond the liberty of Tipperary, which his father had held for life only, it involved in practice a considerably smaller area.

Bermingham returned to Ireland on 26 April 1348, and seems to have been immediately engaged in a campaign against the O'Kennedys and O'Carrolls in Ormond and Ely O'Carroll, and 'Breen O'Breen' in Arra. The justiciar's campaign seems to have continued till 27 July, and in July and August Clyn tells us that Fulk de la Frene, who was seneschal of Ormond's lands, the earl himself being still in England, held a great guard at Nenagh, recalled the faithful men who had been driven out to their own lands, had the walls broken down by the Irish rebuilt, and with heavy fines of cows and delivery of hostages forced the Irish to return to their due submission, which no one had thought possible. After this, the justiciar, who was still in Tipperary on 19 August, seems to have conducted a campaign in Munster, for which the army of Mallow had been proclaimed, and was in Cork in November.[51]

So far the justiciar could be well satisfied. With the defeat of Desmond Kerry had been brought effectively within the sphere of royal government: sheriffs were accounting at the exchequer, and officials were being regularly appointed. His tour in Connacht in 1347 had been at least encouraging. The situation in the midlands seemed to have been restored, and the Irish of Leinster seem to have been quiet. It might have seemed that the position had been stabilized, and that further recovery would be possible. But in the early autumn of 1348 the Black Death had reached Ireland, and the colony was weakened to an extent from which it never really recovered during the middle ages.

This, the second great pandemic of bubonic plague in historical times, appeared in western Europe in 1347, spreading along the lines of communication, and reached England in July 1348, first, apparently, in Dorsetshire, spreading westwards through Somerset and Devon and north-eastwards to London, and then throughout the country. It was most probably from Bristol, one of the main

---

[51] *Analecta Hibernica*, II, pp. 210–11, 228–9; *Ormond Deeds*, III, p. 342; *54th Rep. D.K.*, p. 50; *C.C.R. 1346–9*, p. 580; *C.P.R.*, *1391–6*, p. 205; Clyn, *Annals*, p. 35.

centres of Anglo-Irish trade in this period, that the plague reached
Ireland, appearing at Howth and Drogheda at the beginning of
August, though the timing is so close that it may possibly have come
direct from the continent. Clyn, whose account of it is particularly
vivid, tells us that the cities of Dublin and Drogheda were 'almost
destroyed and wasted of men, so that in Dublin alone from the
beginning of August to Christmas fourteen thousand men died'.
We cannot, of course, take this figure as anything more than pictorial, but clearly the mortality in the towns was very great, and in
1351 the jurors of an inquisition said that 'in the time of the said
pestilence the greater part of the citizens of Cork and other faithful
men of the king dwelling there went the way of all flesh'.[52] In Lent
1349 the plague reached Kilkenny: on 6 March eight of the Friars
Preachers were already dead, and

'hardly in any house did one only die, but commonly man and wife, with their
children and household, went one way, that of death. And I, Friar John Clyn,
of the order of Minors and the convent of Kilkenny, have written those notable
facts which happened in my time in this book, as I have learned them as an eye-
witness, or from trustworthy accounts, and lest notable deeds should perish with
time and recede from the memory of those to come, seeing so many evils and the
whole world as it were in evil plight, I, awaiting death among the dead, have set
them down in writing . . . and lest the writing should perish with the writer . . .
I leave parchment to continue the work, if perchance any man survive, or any
of the race of Adam may escape this pestilence and continue the work so
begun.'

It would seem, indeed, that the chronicler did die of the plague in
this year, for only a few short notes follow.[53]

It is clear that the plague was widespread in Ireland. In the
course of the next few years not only Dublin, but also Cork, Clonmel, and New Ross petitioned successfully for assistance in view of
impoverishment caused by the plague; in 1351 the dean and chapter of Cashel said that their lands and rents had been 'all but
totally destroyed by the king's Irish enemies and by the mortality
of their tenants in the last plague'; in 1354 the tenants of the king's
demesne manors in co. Dublin say they are entirely impoverished
by the late pestilence and the excessive prises of the king's ministers.[54] The ravages of the plague were presumably greatest in the
towns, where conditions were most favourable for the spread of
the infection, but it must also have been widespread in the countryside, and had reached the west by 1349, when the Irish annals

[52] Genealogical Office, MS 192, pp. 93–94.
[53] Clyn, *Annals*, pp. 35–38.
[54] *C.C.R.*, *1349–54*, p. 376; *C.P.R.*, *1354–8*, p. 91; P.R.O., Dublin, Mem.
Rolls, vol. 26, pp. 17–19.

refer to it in Moylurg, co. Roscommon.[55] There is no indication in the annals of the period of the year in which the plague reached Connacht, but Richard fitzRalph, archbishop of Armagh, preaching before the pope at Avignon in August 1349, said that it was believed to have destroyed more than two-thirds of the English nation, but had not yet, he was credibly assured, done any notable harm to either the Irish or the Scottish nation. The plague, he added, had fallen most heavily on those who lived near the sea, and there had been a greater number of deaths among fishermen and sailors than in any other class. It does not seem that there was any unusual mortality among officials in this period, but the prior of the hospital, John Larcher, died suddenly in 1349, possibly of the plague.[56]

We have no way of estimating the total mortality in Ireland, but there is no reason to suppose that it was significantly different from that in other European countries. In England it is possible that about half the clergy died; the death-rate in Bristol has been estimated at between 35 and 40 per cent of the total population; in the hundred of Farnham in Surrey mortality was fifteen times greater than normal in 1348-9 and ten times greater in 1349-50; in some English manors as many as two-thirds of the tenants died.[57] The incidence of plague must, of course, have been greatest where the rat population was highest: round the ports, and in the towns, and in the corn-growing areas; it is likely to have been least in the largely pastoral districts of the west. But the mortality was not merely that of one or two terrible years: in Ireland, as elsewhere, a permanent focus of infection remained. We hear in Ireland, as elsewhere, of a second outbreak in 1361, and again in 1370—'the third and greatest plague, in which many nobles, citizens, and innumerable children died'.[58] Nor did the infection then die out: in 1384 we hear that John Burke died of the plague; in 1398 'a great plague this year'; in January 1425 Edmund Mortimer died of the plague at Trim. Even in the sixteenth century the commissioners extending the possessions of monastic houses were unable to approach Kells

---

[55] 'A great plague in Moylurg and all Ireland this year. Matha son of Cathal O Ruairc died of the plague. The Earl's grandson died. Risderd O Raigillig, king of East Brefne, died.' (AC). The O'Rourke territory was in co. Leitrim, and O'Reilly's in co. Cavan. The earl's grandson was Richard son of Edmund de Burgo, who had been taken prisoner by the de Burgos of Connacht earlier in the year.

[56] A. Gwynn, 'The Black Death in Ireland', Studies, XXIV, pp. 25–42.

[57] See M. McKisack, The Fourteenth Century, 1307–1399, pp. 331–5, for references.

[58] Chart. St. Mary's, II, pp. 395, 397. For the outbreak of 1361, see below, p. 288.

in the autumn of 1540 because of the plague there.[59] It has been
estimated that in England the Black Death, followed by the later
outbreaks, may have reduced the population by half by the end
of the fourteenth century[60]: it is not improbable that the effect on
the Anglo-Irish population was the same. Since the complaint in
so many parts of the colony from the time of the Bruce invasion on
had been of a lack of tenants we need not be surprised that its
history for the rest of the middle ages is one of steadily accelerating
decline. And though it is clear that the Irish too suffered, it is
probable that, since they were not town-dwellers, their losses of
population were considerably smaller in proportion. Certainly in
1360 a petition sent to the king by a great council spoke of the
enfeeblement of the lieges by the plague, 'which was so great
and so hideous among the English lieges and not among the
Irish'.[61]

At the end of forty years of almost continuous misfortune the
colony had changed greatly since the time of Edward I, when it
had reached its greatest extension and prosperity. After Bermingham's visitation in 1347 Connacht seems to have been effectively
outside the sphere of the Dublin government: in the second half of
the century seneschals or sheriffs continued to be appointed, but
there is nothing to suggest that the government could in fact control them, and in 1393 the bishop of Clonmacnoise complained
that when, having been appointed as a justice in Connacht, he
went there Walter Bermingham, lord of Athenry, then sheriff, refused to escort him, and he had to give one of O'Kelly's sons £20
to do so.[62] In the middle of the century the castles of Roscommon
and Randown were still held precariously, but both had been lost
before the end of Edward III's reign.[63] And certainly the annals
show no trace of governmental action beyond the Shannon: royal
authority, as far as it was represented at all, seems to have been
exercised chiefly by the Berminghams of Athenry, but the annals
tell us only of the endless wars between the rival branches of the
O'Connors, MacDermot and O'Kelly, and between the clans of

[59] AC; Extents of Irish Monastic Possessions, pp. 253, 264. Fragmentary annals
which seem to be from Lough Ree, co. Longford, show a widespread epidemic
with heavy mortality in 1392–3, but this was not necessarily the plague (Misc.
Annals, pp. 145–9).
[60] J. C. Russell, British Medieval Population, pp. 229–35, 367, cited by M.
McKisack, The Fourteenth Century, p. 332.
[61] Parliaments and Councils, no. 16.
[62] Council in Ireland, pp. 230–31.
[63] AC; ALC; A. Clon.; AU; C.P.R., 1340–43, p. 475; C.C.H., p. 43b, no. 9; p.
45, no. 58; p. 46, no. 99; 54th Rep. D.K., p. 47. Turlough O'Connor took Roscommon in 1341 and held it for a year or two, but it had been recovered before
1344.

the Anglo-Norman settlers, de Burgos, de Exeters, Mac Costellos (once de Angulos), and others, rapidly becoming half Irish.

In the north, Ulster beyond the Bann was irretrievably lost; so too in the south-west was Thomond. In Desmond governmental activity was still powerful, and in the 1350s there was even to be a recovery in this area[64]: it was not till later in the century that it ceased to be within the ambit of the central government. But much land on the fringes of Westmeath which had been occupied, however thinly, by the tenants of de Verdon or de Geneville at the end of Edward I's reign was lost, and in Ormond, though the castle of Nenagh was still held by the earl, and he still held the manor of Nenagh, and Ballinaclogh or Weyperous just south of it, the Irish were clearly dominant north of Nenagh. And perhaps most ominous of all, the Irish of Leinster, O'Tooles, O'Byrnes and Mac-Murroughs in the modern counties of Wicklow and Wexford, and even in the mountains of south co. Dublin, O'Mores and O'Connors in Leix and Offaly, as well as other lesser clans, were by now in a practically continuous state of insurrection, providing a constant preoccupation for the government at Dublin.

Nor were the Irish the only danger: one of the major factors weakening the colony from the early fourteenth century was certainly the constant state of warfare among themselves into which certain of the settlers had fallen, for reasons which are not altogether clear. It must, of course, be remembered that in medieval societies throughout Europe a far higher degree of disorder was normal than would have been regarded as tolerable at any later period, but the disorders of sections of Anglo-Irish society went beyond this. It has been generally assumed that much of it can be explained as due to the unwillingness of the junior branches of a family to see the lands of their ancestors pass through heiresses to strangers who were often absentees, but though there was certainly a strong feeling that the lands of a family should be kept within it,[65] the cases usually cited to prove the general contention that this was the primary cause of rebellion and lawlessness are far from convincing. It has, for instance, been alleged that the rebellion of the de Verdons in 1312 was an early instance,[66] but this does not really stand up to examination. The de Verdons who rebelled were the brothers of the head of the family, Theobald de Verdon, who was still a comparatively young man: his children, it is true, were

[64] See below, pp. 279–80.

[65] See *C.D.I.*, III, no. 453, and M. Devitt, 'The Barony of Okethy', *Kildare Archaeological Society Journal*, VIII, pp. 276–301, 388–98, 464–88.

[66] Curtis, *History of Mediaeval Ireland* (2nd edn.), pp. 179, 181–2, 184. See above, pp. 222–3.

all daughters, but there was no reason why he should not still leave a son to succeed him. Moreover, the list of lands which they attacked does not suggest that they were attempting to seize the de Verdon inheritance: they operated mainly against the crown lands in the barony of Louth; the lands of Ardee, lately acquired by the crown from the Pipards; and against church lands in the barony of Ferrard.[67] It is unlikely that we shall ever know what the real causes of the rebellion were, but they can hardly have been what Curtis suggested. Again, there seems to be no reason to suppose that the constant disorders associated with the de Cantetons and Roches in Wexford and Cork, or with the le Poers in Waterford, really arose from discontents of this kind. The clearest case would seem to be that of the de Burgos in Connacht: they certainly occupied lands which were the inheritance of the Brown Earl's infant daughter. But it is clear that there was a general malaise, which is probably to be explained largely by the weakness of a government which was no longer able to act promptly for the repression of malefactors in the outlying districts, as it had still been able to do in the early years of the century, together with that weakening of defence by the failure of absentees to take an active interest in their lands of which there were so many complaints during the period, and a certain collapse of morale which would naturally have been produced by successive disasters.

Faced by the new situation, the principal Anglo-Irish magnates were resorting more and more to agreements with the Irish in which they cut their losses by recognizing the Irish reoccupation of reconquered lands in return for an overlordship which must often have been only nominal. Arrangements of this kind were not, of course, new. The arrangements under which the Irish chiefs of Ulster owed services to the earls of Ulster and those on the borders of de Verdon's lands owed him rents were certainly early,[68] and there must have been other unrecorded services of the same kind. But these do not in most cases represent retreats by the colonists[69]: it is in the fourteenth century that a new attitude is clear. In 1318 the earl of Kildare grants to Hugh O'Toole lands which seem to have been waste, stipulating that Hugh shall rise with the men of the county against any malefactors of his 'nation'.[70] In 1337

---

[67] *Cal. Justic. Rolls*, III, pp. 237–9, 265.

[68] *Calendar of Inquisitions Post Mortem*, VIII, p. 378; J. Otway-Ruthven, 'The Partition of the de Verdon Lands', *Proc. R.I.A.*, LXVI C.

[69] A retreat may lie behind the late thirteenth-century grant by Ralph Pipard to 'Enegus Macmahan' of lands in the modern co. Monaghan (*Cal. Ormond Deeds*, I, no. 268).

[70] *Red Book of Kildare*, no. 139.

Edmund de Burgo 'accorded and made peace with Bryan Bane o'Bryan: where it was agreed of both sides that as much lands as Bryan Bane wasted of the Demeasne of William Burkes should be held by Bryan Bane for the valuable rent thereof'.[71] And the year before Ormond had made what was practically a treaty with O'Kennedy, 'concerning all arsons, preys, homicides, and whatsoever transgressions committed up to this date'. O'Kennedy was granted what seems to have been the northern part of the barony of Lower Ormond 'as far as was in the earl' (some of these lands belonged to de Burgo), and the western part of Upper Ormond, lands which he no doubt already occupied, to hold at a rent. The Irish were to be exempt from suit at the county court, but were to do suit at the court of Nenagh for four years till they were fully agreed with the men of the marches. Careful arrangements were made for the settlement of disputes: injuries done to the earl or his betaghs by the O'Kennedys were to be paid for triply; injuries to any of the earl's English tenants shall be paid for twice, half to the earl and half to the injured party. Injuries to the O'Kennedys are to be paid for in the same way. In the case of a treacherous killing by either side, the manslayer is to be handed over, if he can be found: if not, his lord is to levy the price and pay it twice to the kin and once to the lord. O'Kennedy agrees that he will answer the earl in his army as he should, and as he was accustomed to answer to him and his ancestors, and should any, English or Irish, rise against the earl, O'Kennedy with his men will rise against them in his aid. The parties found guarantors: the archbishop of Cashel and the bishop of Killaloe; the leading de Burgos; various O'Briens, MacGilpatrick, MacLoughlin, MacNamara and others, sworn to enforce the observance of the treaty.[72]

How far this remarkable agreement was effective it is hard to tell. The inquisitions post mortem taken after Ormond's death in 1338 show that the O'Kennedys were nominally the earl's tenants, and their services were assigned in dower to his widow, though it is unlikely that she was able to enforce them.[73] In 1347, as we have seen, O'Kennedy was at war against the new earl, and had considerable successes, though the lost ground was at least partially recovered in the next year. Then in 1356 a new agreement between

---

[71] *A. Clon.*; *AC.* For William we should certainly read Edmund: the lands concerned were pretty certainly in Arra, where this branch of the O'Briens had established itself. Clyn's *Annals* show Brian Bán continuously raiding Eliogarty from 1325 to 1336.

[72] *Cal. Ormond Deeds*, I, no. 682. Cf. ibid., no. 700.

[73] *Cal. Inquisitions Post Mortem*, VIII, pp. 123, 126-7; *C.C.R., 1339-41*, pp. 152-3.

the earl and 'Rotheric' O'Kennedy, principal of his nation, confirms the peace made between them before the earl went to England and makes arrangements for satisfying complaints against O'Kennedy by the judgement of arbitrators chosen by each side. But though the agreement binds O'Kennedy to be 'obedient and respondent' to the earl, he appears, even more clearly than had his predecessor in 1336, as an independent power. That there had already been a retreat before the Irish in other parts of the county is clearly shown by the statements of the inquisition of 1338 about the manor of Moyaliff, where land had been granted to the Irish by the lord's charter. In 1358 Ormond granted to Brian O'Kennedy, captain of his nation, land actually in the manor of Nenagh, and in 1354 he had made a grant of land, possibly near Toomevara, to O'Meara.[74]

At the same time, both Ormond and Kildare, and no doubt other lords whose archives have not survived, were building up not only among the Anglo-Irish, but also among the Irish themselves, a system of indentured retainers, of which John fitz Thomas, Kildare's ancestor, had perhaps been the pioneer in Ireland.[75] Now in the mid-fourteenth century Kildare made an agreement in 1350 with Maurice Schynnach, king of Fertewac and Monthyrcagan and Fergal MacGeoghegan, duke of Keneraliagh, by which they became his men for their lives, undertaking to give him counsel and aid against all except the king and Mortimer, and to follow Kildare's banner, voyages, and wars throughout Ireland at his expense. In 1368 he retained two of the O'Dempseys and Sheyn son of Art, who undertook to stay with him in peace and war against 'Odymescy and his sons with all his *irraght*', and against all others, English or Irish, except the king, while Kildare undertook to support them, and to include them in any peace with O'Dempsey.[76] In the same way, in 1356 Ormond agreed with Mahon O'Kennedy that Mahon has 'made his retinue with the earl for all his life, to serve him in all matters against all whomsoever, for his life and at his own costs in the marches of Ormond and Ely, and elsewhere at the earl's cost', receiving in return a grant

---

[74] *Cal Ormond Deeds*, II, nos. 22, 34, 48; ibid., III, no. 347. *Cal. Inquisitions Post Mortem*, VIII, p. 120 omits the statement about Moyaliff.

[75] An indenture between him and Peter de Bermingham, dated 26 April 1289, is one of the earliest known in the British Isles (*Red Book of Kildare*, no. 11).

[76] *Red Book of Kildare*, nos. 168, 169. Fertewac and Monthyrcagan are Fartullagh, co. Westmeath, and Muinter Thadhgain, now the barony of Kilcoursey in cos. Westmeath and Offaly; Keneraliagh is Cineal Fhiachach, now the barony of Moycashel, co. Westmeath. Mortimer was lord of Trim, and this is interesting evidence that these men were in some sort of tenurial relationship to him. See above, p. 65.

of lands for life, and the reversion of the lands held for life by his
father. In the same year, Donough MacNamara made a similar
agreement to serve 'at his own cost in his marches where he can
return home, and elsewhere in Ireland at the earl's cost', and was
granted the reversion of the lands which his father held of the earl
in Thomond. In 1358 Edmund O'Kennedy, who seems to have
been Ormond's prisoner in England, obtained his release for a
cash payment and the delivery of hostages, and undertook to pay
rent for the lands which he held in Ormond,

'and he shall come to the courts of the earl as in ancient times was the custom,
and he shall be respondent and attendant on the earl in war with all his power
in his marches at his own cost; and if he go outside his own marches he shall be
with 100 horses and 60 men on foot everywhere with the earl at the latter's cost.
And in case he has otherwise the 15 ploughlands aforesaid, he shall account to
the earl for 40 horses and 120 men on foot.'

Each was to make good damage done to the other by his men, and
O'Kennedy undertook to keep his idlemen so that they should not
quarter themselves on the earl's tenants, unless it be in aid of the
country for one night only.[77]

These agreements, which we must suppose to represent a great
body of others, now lost, vividly illustrate the constant complaints
about 'kernes and idlemen' kept in the land of peace, and it was no
doubt by such agreements that Desmond had maintained his 'satellites who are called Rout', quartering them on the king's lieges of
Kerry, whose ancestors had never been burdened by such servitude.[78] It must have been by such agreements that Ormond obtained the bulk of the troops whom he brought to serve under
Rokeby in the 1350s, and the Berminghams and others will have
been in the same position. On a smaller scale, Irish troops were
employed as local guards: already before 1360 a 'kethern' of
twenty-four foot soldiers, finding their viands at the cost of the
country and paid £8 a year, was being employed for the safeguard
of the manor of Rathwire, and a similar body to guard the tenants
of the manor of Trim against 'the hostile incursions of the malefactors of Carbry and Offaly'.[79]

It would clearly be an over-simplification to think of the position
as purely a matter of racial conflict. If we are to believe what the
inquisitions said about Desmond, the Irish chieftains were ready
to make alliances with him which were intended to put him in a

[77] *Cal. Ormond Deeds*, II, nos. 35, 36, 46.
[78] *Analecta Hibernica*, XXIII, p. 43.
[79] P.R.O., Dublin, Mem. Rolls, vol. 28, pp. 495–9, vol. 29, pp. 465–8; vol.
30, pp. 25–26.

position of sovereignty[80]; they were certainly ready, as we have seen, to be retained by Kildare, Ormond, and others, and fight against other Irishmen under the English king's banner. From their point of view this was no doubt largely a matter of securing advantages in the constant internecine struggles within each Irish 'nation', but there is no reason to suppose that genuinely friendly relations never existed. And it is interesting to find in 1355 that the late captain of the O'Mores, having taken hostages from his brother and having no safe place in his country in which to keep them, had sent them to the king's prison in Dublin castle: they were now restored to his brother, the new captain, at his request.[81] And while the O'Mores were much more often at war with the colonists than not, some clans, conspicuously the MacCarthys of Muskerry,[82] were normally on the side of the crown.

[80] Above, pp. 249–50, 261.
[81] Genealogical Office, MS 192, p. 112.
[82] See below, pp. 279–80.

CHAPTER IX

The Attempt at Recovery: Lionel of Clarence and William of Windsor

TWO HUNDRED years later the Irish chancellor, Gerrard, after intensive study of the records saw the 1350s as the turning point of the English colony in Ireland, the period in which 'the estate became thus tattered'.[1] And clearly the Black Death and its *sequelae* greatly accelerated the decline which as we have seen had begun perhaps two generations earlier, and made any recovery of the thirteenth-century position finally impossible. When in July 1349, while the plague was still raging, Sir Thomas Rokeby, a veteran of the Scottish wars, was appointed to succeed Walter de Bermingham as justiciar the English government must have recognized that the position had deteriorated, for 'because the land of Ireland is not in good plight or good peace' he was authorized to bring with him from England in addition to the justiciar's normal retinue a further twenty men-at-arms, four of them knights, and forty mounted archers, 'the better to establish the peace of the land on his going thither'.

Rokeby does not seem to have reached Ireland till late in December, and must have begun to plan a tour through the south and west almost immediately. On 26 January 1350 he tested a writ at Kilkenny, and a month later had reached Cork; by the end of April he was back in Dublin, having apparently reached it by way of Meath. There seems to have been some military action during this tour, but its main purpose was probably to hold assizes and ensure that the peace was being kept in Desmond's lands. And the lawless English and Irish of the mountains south of Dublin were sufficiently overawed to elect in his presence captains of the Harolds, Archbolds, and O'Byrnes who swore before him to keep the peace towards the king and his people.[2]

[1] *Analecta Hibernica*, II, p. 121 and pp. 93–291 *passim*. For other references for the period up to the appointment of Lionel of Clarence as lieutenant in 1361 see J. Otway-Ruthven, 'Ireland in the 1350s: Sir Thomas de Rokeby and his successors', *Journ. R.S.A.I.*, XCVII.

[2] The Archbolds chose their captain on 23 April. There had certainly been a

In July 1350, perhaps as the result of representations made by a council held at Kilkenny in June, a series of instructions from England required Rokeby, together with the chancellor and treasurer, to undertake what was in effect a general overhaul of the Irish administration. The rolls of the exchequer and other courts were to be examined for the whole period since the death of Edward I, as the king was informed that there were errors prejudicial to him; the king was to be informed of any incompetent officials holding office by virtue of commissions under the English great seal, and such officials coming in future were to be rejected; and a commission of oyer and terminer was issued concerning ministerial oppressions since 1330. Moreover, the justiciar and chancellor were to enquire what should be done concerning certain iniquitous customs which should rather be called corruptions which removed men from the king's fealty and against which the community of Ireland had often petitioned. In addition, they were to cause absentees to provide for the defence of their lands.[3]

The execution of this programme must have occupied the government very fully, but there seems to be no trace of its results, except in so far as it must be supposed to be behind the ordinances issued at a great council at Kilkenny in November 1351. But before that, in the winter of 1350–51, Rokeby had held assizes in Wexford, the liberty being in the king's hand because of the minority of the heir of the earl of Pembroke, and in the late summer of 1351 had conducted a campaign in Upper Ossory against MacGilpatrick. Then in November he held a great council at Kilkenny which produced a set of ordinances which seem to have been partly inspired by the enquiries ordered in the summer of 1350, though they deal with many other matters, and particularly the problems of defence.[4] But the ordinances dealing with official oppression and no. 16, which laid down that disputes between Englishmen shall be decided by the common law, not by 'the law of the march and of Breawen (Brehon), which is not law and ought not to be called law', seem clearly to arise from the enquiries. Above all, however, the government seems to have been preoccupied by the problems of defence: the ordinances lay down that lords are to provide for the defence of their lands in the marches: if they do not, the king's officers are to take the revenues of those lands for their defence. They forbid the quartering of private forces on the countryside in

campaign against the O'Byrnes before September 1350 (E. Curtis, 'The Clan System among English Settlers in Ireland', *E.H.R.*, vol. 25, pp. 116–20; P.R.O., Dublin, Mem. Rolls, vol. 25, pp. 325–6).

[3] *C.C.R., 1349–54*, pp. 195, 198; *C.P.R., 1348–50*, pp. 590, 592.

[4] *Early Statutes*, pp. 374–96.

the land of peace; private agreements with rebels, whether English or Irish; alliances by marriage, fosterage or otherwise with the king's enemies, English or Irish; wanton breaches of an official truce or peace between English and Irish; the stirring up of war by Englishmen against other English. Four wardens of the peace were to be appointed in each county, who were to assess the men of the county to arms and review them regularly; captains of lineages were to be responsible for the arrest of felons from among their own lineage, adherents or retainers. Almost the only part of the ordinances that was new was the provision that the English statute of labourers, which sought to fix wages at the pre-plague level, should be proclaimed and enforced: for the most part they applied the old remedies to the old problems, and were to be re-enacted in substance by the Statutes of Kilkenny in 1366.[5]

By this time Rokeby was already preparing to devote himself to the problems of the south-west, where, though the administration of Desmond's lands seems to have been brought under control, there was evidently trouble with the Irish of west Cork. In September the bishop of Cloyne had been empowered to treat with the rebel Irish in his diocese 'to bring them back to the king's fealty and peace'. In February 1352 the government seems to have been in Cork, and in March Rokeby went to England, leaving the bishop of Limerick as his deputy. He returned in June, and in September began a full-scale campaign against 'MacDermot'— Dermot Og MacCarthy, lord of Muskerry and Duhallow, a cousin of the reigning king of Desmond. Rokeby's own force was about 1,000 men at its largest, including a number of Irish in the later stages of the campaign, and he seems to have been joined by Cormac MacCarthy of Desmond, acting independently. We know nothing of the details of the campaign, but since part of the justiciar's force seems to have been transported by boat down the Shannon from Limerick to Askeaton the attack was presumably from the north, through co. Limerick: probably there was also an attack from the south. The campaign was over by the end of January 1353 and had clearly had a complete success: the colonists were re-established in the valley of the Lee, and 'MacDermot' was driven out of Muskerry. On 1 February Cormac MacCarthy was granted extensive lands in Muskerry 'among the woods', and though MacDermot's descendants continued to hold Duhallow the later lords of Muskerry were the descendants of Cormac's second

[5] For the absentees, see above, p. 256; for the keepers of the peace, who were not, of course, new, pp. 180–1. The magnates had been made responsible for their men and kindred in the thirteenth century (above, pp. 177–8).

son.[6] Moreover, MacNamara had also submitted, and Rokeby rebuilt the castle of Bunratty in Thomond, though it seems to have
been lost again by 1355.

So far Rokeby's justiciarship had been remarkably successful: it
is not surprising that after he had been superseded in 1355 the
mayor and citizens of Cork wrote to the king praising 'the evident
usefulness of his good works' and urging his reappointment.[7] But
though the problem of the south-west had been solved, at any rate
for the time, there remained the position in Leinster, to which
Rokeby now turned his attention. In September 1353 there was a
campaign against the O'Byrnes which lasted till the middle of
October, but at some time during 1354 there seems to have been
a general confederacy among the Irish, led by 'Muryertach
McMurgh, calling himself king or prince of Leinster', who in spite
of a peace to which he had sworn was said to be organizing a
general attack on the colony. Rokeby seems to have broken this up
by negotiation, but in the autumn yet another campaign was being
prepared against O'Byrne which was based on Wicklow and lasted
from the middle of September to the end of October. And on this
occasion Rokeby seems to have been heavily defeated: we hear
only that many of his men were gravely wounded and went home,
but since early in October he sent frantic messages for reinforcements to the city of Dublin, and apparently also to the Dublin
county court and to Ormond, and the marshal was sent by sea to
Dublin to bring 'McMurgh' from Dublin castle to Wicklow, the
conclusion that he had in fact sustained a serious defeat is irresis-
tible.

The peace which concluded this campaign was soon broken. In
February 1355 the government had gone again to Munster, no
doubt to consolidate the settlement which had been made in Cork
in 1353. In April O'Byrne again rose in war: the council hurriedly
garrisoned all the strongholds in the marches of Dublin against
him, and a fresh campaign had begun by 24 April which lasted
for a fortnight and was succeeded in the second half of May by one
against the O'Nolans of co. Carlow. It is clear that O'Byrne had
not been subdued, for the guards set against him were maintained
till at least August 1357, and probably later, and it was said in
August 1355 that he and his associates daily threatened to invade
the marches of counties Dublin, Kildare, Carlow and Wexford,

[6] The published pedigrees, for which see W. F. T. Butler, *Gleanings from Irish
History*, especially pp. 137–56, are remarkably confused: the identifications of
'Macdermot' and Cormac MacCarthy are based on the unpublished Mac-
Carthy pedigree prepared by Mr K. Nicholls.

[7] P.R.O., London, S.C. 1/38/26.

a great part of which he had already destroyed. In May 1355 a local council was summoned to Naas to provide for the defence of the marches of Kildare, and we hear of guards set at a number of places in co. Kildare by order of the council. Moreover, in other parts of Ireland the opportunities provided by the preoccupation of the government with Leinster were being seized: in Tipperary O'Kennedy had risen in rebellion, and in the north Aedh O'Neill was advancing on Dundalk with a great army in April. The justiciar was in no position to take action; he could only send the archbishop of Armagh, who was conducting a visitation of the diocese of Meath, to Dundalk to treat with O'Neill. Nor was the position in Leinster being restored: in Kildare particularly the people of the county, among them conspicuously the earl of Kildare himself, were refusing to play their proper part in the guards which the council had ordered, and in July the government was reduced to requiring the bishop of Kildare to proclaim public excommunication against the O'Connors of Offaly and the O'Dempseys who, with banners displayed, daily invaded the parts of Kildare.

By this time it had already been decided to supersede Rokeby. On 8 July 1355 Maurice fitz Thomas earl of Desmond was appointed as his successor and took up office on 17 August, Rokeby having continued to act till 9 August, when he sailed for England, leaving Kildare as his deputy. It is not very easy to account for Desmond's appointment, considering his past history: it is possible that the king had not altogether believed the more dramatic allegations made against him. Moreover, it is unlikely that it was intended that he should remain justiciar for long: he was now sixty-two years of age, and may already have been in indifferent health. The attitude of Kildare in refusing to co-operate in the guards in his county earlier in the year may well have been the result of some temporary disaffection which had put him out of court; Ormond was perhaps going with the king on the expedition to Calais which took place in October, and was certainly present at the opening of the parliament held at Westminster in November. Given all this, Desmond may well have been the only obvious choice, and in England the main interest of the moment was the war with France.

Desmond was confronted by all the difficulties which had embittered Rokeby's last year, but it does not seem that he was able to take any effective action about the situation. In November he was said to be about to undertake a campaign against O'Byrne, who was still threatening co. Dublin, but he died on 25 January 1356. The Irish council appointed Kildare as justiciar, an appointment confirmed by the king on 30 March, and then on 24 July

Rokeby was reappointed, with power to bring with him from England at the king's wages three knights, seventeen squires, and sixty archers in addition to his normal retinue. He reached Ireland in October, finding the situation very much as he had left it. He turned first to Munster, where Desmond's lands were in the king's hand because his heir was a minor, and there were apparently disturbances for the counties of Cork and Limerick and the Cross of Tipperary were induced to grant a subsidy, perhaps in their county courts, for action against the rebels. But we hear of no campaign in this area; instead there was one in Leinster, against the O'Tooles, O'Byrnes and O'Nolans, in which more than 1,000 men were engaged for more than two months early in 1357. But on 23 April, four days after the campaign had ended, Rokeby died at Kilkea, co. Kildare, which seems to have been his headquarters.

The council appointed the treasurer, John de Boulton, to succeed Rokeby, and he acted till the autumn, by which time the king had appointed Amory de St Amand, an English magnate who was also a tenant-in-chief in co. Dublin and had served with distinction in the war in France, as justiciar. He was to have forty men-at-arms, ten of them knights, and one hundred archers at the king's wages in addition to the normal retinue, and took up office on 27 November. Leinster was, as usual, disturbed, but St Amand turned first to Munster, where Desmond's lands were still in wardship. About 17 February 1358 the justiciar, accompanied by the chancery, the treasurer, and other officials, began a progress which had brought him to Cork by the end of March. The government remained at Cork, Kilmallock, and Limerick till early in July, when it returned to Dublin. Though Munster too was disturbed, there had been no campaign: guards had been set on the borders of Tipperary and Limerick, and the communities of Cork, Limerick and Waterford had granted a subsidy, presumably in their county courts, 'to fight the Irish', 'to resist McBrene del Nathirlagh'[8], but we hear only of the appointment of keepers of the peace and the issue of commissions to treat for peace with the English and Irish of Munster.[9]

By the time the justiciar returned to Dublin the affairs of Leinster were becoming increasingly urgent. In April and May messengers had been sent from Munster to treat with the Irish of Leinster and with O'More of Leix 'for the good of the peace', but in July the castle of Killoughter, near Wicklow, was being besieged by the

[8] Aherlow, co. Limerick.
[9] In July the de Burgos were robbing in Limerick and Tipperary and the Cantetons, Barretts and Barrys were disturbing the peace in Cork.

Irish, and there were other clashes with O'Byrne and O'Toole 'in the parts of Wykynglo and elsewhere in the marches', while by the middle of the month a war had begun against O'More. A subsidy was granted for it by the earl of Kildare and the community of the county, but by 12 August we hear that a peace had been concluded by the assent of the communities of counties Kildare and Carlow, and the annals say that in this year 'O Morda gave a great defeat to the Galls of Dublin, killing two score and two hundred.' In September, however, we hear again of attacks by the Irish on co. Kildare, and at the end of the month the justiciar himself was engaged in parleys with O'More and MacMurrough at Athy.

After this we hear nothing more of war against O'More; emphasis shifts to the threat from the Irish of the Leinster mountains, 'Obryn, Otothill, MacMurghith, Onolan and other Irish of the parts of Leinster, felons and enemies openly at war'. Subsidies were granted by the communities of counties Dublin, Kilkenny, Wexford and Kildare, and the campaign, which seems to have been in the region of Imaal, began on 2 November and lasted till 7 February 1359. In January a parliament met at Kilkenny which granted a general subsidy for the war against 'Art Kevenagh, who, lately preferred by the king as McMurgh, has now become a traitor'. But it also sent messengers to the king to expound 'arduous and urgent business intimately concerning the land of Ireland', and licences were issued to treat, by advice of the justiciar and council, with the captains of the Irish of Leinster and to take truces with them. Evidently the war was going badly, and we need not be surprised that on 16 February the earl of Ormond was appointed to succeed St Amand as justiciar.

Ormond took up office on 18 March 1359, and immediately summoned a council to Dublin for 1 April, and another to Waterford for 8 April. On 20 March he ordered that no fencible men, except the late justiciar's retinue, should be allowed to leave the country, since there were confederacies between the Irish of Leinster and elsewhere by which each Irish captain should rise in war in his march at a certain time. The whole south-east was disturbed, and though Ormond seems to have had some success against Mac-Murrough, who had given hostages by May, the O'Byrnes and O'Tooles were still at war. And there was a continuing war in the midlands: in July 1359 Ormond led an expedition against the O'Tooles, MacMurroughs and O'Mores, 'in the parts of Leys by Athy', but in February 1360 Kildare represented that since the previous Easter O'Connor, O'More, O'Doyne, MacGeoghegan, O'Melaghlin, and O'Shinnagh, 'captains of the Irish in the parts of Leinster and Meath', had been at war, and he had fought them almost continuously at his own expense. But at least by this time there had been some successes against the O'Byrnes, for there were ten of their hostages in Dublin castle, and for a time we hear no more of troubles in Leinster. Instead, in the spring of 1360, attention was turned to Munster, where in April there was a campaign based on Kilmallock. It seems that in the same period the justiciar was active in south Connacht, but we have no evidence as to what he did there.

Meanwhile, the messages sent by the parliament of January 1359 had produced in the following summer a series of orders as to the obligation of lords to provide for the defence of their lands and castles in the marches; the removal of ministers indicted of felonies; the granting of lands at less than their true value; the illegal acquisition of lands by ministers; the revocation of pardons granted to those who had killed their indictors; and the custody of judicial records. But nothing was done to provide the military assistance for which the message may well have asked: the needs of the war in France were too pressing. When in October 1359 the king announced his departure for France he was, he told the Irish government, leaving England 'empty of armed power and destitute of lords, whereby there is no room to send men or money to Ireland at present, although it is said they are needed there'.[10]

By the summer of 1360 the colonists, after the long drawn out struggle against the Irish of the Leinster mountains which had occupied so much of the previous decade, were plainly in a mood of desperation. The great council which met at Kilkenny on 27 July sent fresh messengers to the king with a petition which set forth their position unambiguously. They were, they said, enfeebled by the plague, and by the failure of the magnates to defend their lands in the marches; they were impoverished by oppressions without payment, tallages, and the bad government of former ministers. The treasury was empty because continuous war left the justiciar no time to hold pleas or make profits, and the king's old debts could not be levied because of the poverty of the lieges. The Irish had with one consent risen in war throughout the land; they had conquered a great part of it in divers marches, and would conquer the whole if help were not speedily sent from England. They implored the king, 'as those who sorrowfully have endured and endure our life in maintenance of your land and rights to our power, and can no longer endure', to send to the relief of them and the land 'a good sufficient chieftain, stocked and strengthened with

[10] C.C.R., 1354–60, pp. 575–8, 595–6.

men and treasure, of which they can live, out of England, as a
noble and gracious prince is bound to do for his lieges'.[11]

Conditions were more favourable for the success of this petition
than they would have been a year earlier. In May 1360 a truce had
been concluded between France and England, and a draft treaty
prepared, which was ratified in October. The treaty of Brétigny
marked the end of the first stage of the Hundred Years' War, and
it was at last possible for the English king to spare time and effort
for the affairs of Ireland. During September the king seems to have
summoned the justiciar to England, and he left Ireland early in
October, having appointed Kildare as his deputy. On 1 April 1361,
Kildare was appointed as justiciar, but this was only till the 'good
sufficient chieftain . . . out of England' for whom the petition had
asked could be sent.

Edward's third son, Lionel of Clarence, was now twenty-two
years old, and since he was, as the husband of Elizabeth de Burgo,
daughter and heiress of the last earl of Ulster, the greatest of the
absentee lords of Ireland his appointment was an obvious one. In
March it was announced that he was about to proceed to Ireland:

Because our land of Ireland, by the attacks of Irish enemies, and through the
impotence of our lieges there, and because the magnates of our land of England
having lands there, take the profits thereof but do not defend them, is now subjected to such devastation and destruction that, unless God avert and succour
the same it will be plunged soon into total ruin, we have for the salvation of the
said land ordained that our dear son Lionel shall proceed thither with all dis-
patch and with a great army.

Sixty-four absentees were summoned to Westminster for Easter,
to give counsel, and were ordered to accompany Lionel in person
or by proxy; in May a king's clerk was being sent in advance to
Ireland to announce his coming; in July the sheriffs throughout
England were ordered to proclaim that all Englishmen having
lands in Ireland should go themselves with all their power to Ireland or send others in their place to be there on Lionel's arrival,
'and shall receive and dwell upon their said lands, and defend the
land of Ireland with other lieges', on pain of forfeiture of such
lands. Elaborate preparations of all kinds were being made in both
England and Ireland: the Irish government was ordered to forbid
the export of provisions of any kind; to cause all hostages and
prisoners in the custody of the king's English lieges to be brought
to Dublin castle and kept there; to cause shipping to be arrested,
manned and provisioned and sent to the ports of Chester and
Liverpool. In July hurdles were being sent to Liverpool and Bristol

[11] *Parliaments and Councils*, no. 16.

for the shipping of horses; the earl of Stafford had been having war horses purveyed in Ireland for the king's service; and not only soldiers were being recruited in England, but also stone masons and carpenters for the repair of the king's castles in Ireland.[12]

Lionel was formally appointed as the king's lieutenant in Ireland on 1 July 1361, and on 23 July an indenture between him and his father laid down that he was to be advised by the council in Ireland, and by the lords who went with him from England 'on all acts passing of favour under the great seal of Ireland or under his own', especially pardons and grants of land.[13] In September he sailed from Liverpool with his army under the command of the earl of Stafford, himself a leading absentee, lord of a third of the liberty of Kilkenny as one of the co-heirs of Gloucester. He reached Dublin on 15 September, and though a considerable part of his army had been left behind at Liverpool for lack of shipping proceeded almost immediately to a campaign against the Irish of Wicklow. We know nothing in detail about this expedition: he tested letters at Wicklow on 28 September and 13 October, and the Dublin annalist says that he 'proclaimed in his army that no native of Ireland should approach it, and 100 of his soldiers were slain'. The Irish annals say nothing of O'Byrne, but tell us that MacMurrough was treacherously arrested by Lionel and died in captivity.[14]

After this initial show of strength the new government settled down to a considerable reorganization. It was obviously realized that the major problem which must be dealt with was that presented by the constant state of war with the Irish of the Leinster mountains which had been steadily worsening throughout the century, and which threatened the very heart of the settlement. The great massif of mountains running southwards from within a few miles of Dublin itself into county Wexford effectively cut Leinster in two, and though they are not very high, Norman settlement seems to have stopped at approximately the 600-foot level. Though the coastal plain had been settled, as had Kildare, Carlow and Kilkenny to the west, the mountains remained a largely impenetrable barrier, harbouring O'Byrnes, O'Tooles, MacMurroughs and others, who periodically descended on the plains and rendered all the fringes of their country unsafe.[15] Dublin was not geographically in the best position to control this area, and it had apparently

---

[12] *Foedera*, III, pt. II, pp. 609–11; *C.C.R., 1360–64*, pp. 177, 187, 198, 253–5, 255–6, 278; *C.P.R., 1361–4*, pp. 19, 61.

[13] *C.C.R., 1360–64*, pp. 278–9.

[14] Ibid., p. 212; *Chart. St. Mary's*, II, p. 395; *AC*; *ALC*; *A. Clon.*; P.R.O., Dublin, Mem. Rolls, vol. 28, pp. 10–11, 22.

[15] Cf. *Cal. Justic. Rolls*, III, p. 244.

been decided before Lionel left England that the seat of government should be transferred to Carlow, which commanded the valley of the Barrow, and provided a centre from which he could strike eastwards at the Irish of the mountains and westwards at the O'Mores, O'Connors and others who threatened the western borders of Leinster, as well as at the O'Melaghlins and others on the western and southern borders of the lordship of Meath. The exchequer was really the only fixed centre of government, and by 30 September 1361 Robert Holywood, one of the remembrancers of the exchequer, was already sitting at Carlow, by advice of the council, with a small force for the defence of the town. On 19 October the sheriff of Dublin was ordered to provide two strong carts to bring to Carlow tables and other necessities for repairing and constructing the castle and the king's exchequer there. In the course of the next few years considerable sums were spent on the repair of the castle and the walls of the town, and it was intended to transfer the common bench there as well in Michaelmas term 1363, though this was postponed because there was then no suitable place to keep the rolls, and the town was almost totally destroyed, having been several times burnt by the Irish, and in the same term the exchequer itself had temporarily returned to Dublin. Carlow was not, indeed, an entirely convenient place: in 1364 a newly-appointed treasurer represented that 'the place of the exchequer of Ireland at Karlak, being as it were on the frontier of the Irish rebels, there is no safe access to it by the king's lieges', and exchequer officials complained that the price of provisions was unreasonably high. But in spite of all inconveniences, the exchequer was to remain at Carlow till the reign of Richard II, and the town was certainly in many ways a better military headquarters than Dublin. Kilkenny might have been better still, but Kilkenny was not in the king's hand.[16]

The lieutenant himself, however, and with him the chancery, remained at Dublin. A good deal had been done to renovate the castle before his arrival, but now he ordered other works 'for his games and pleasure': by Christmas 1361 a 'castle', and by the following Easter a fence (these must have been for tournaments); the renovation of the gardens and arbours of the castle; the construction of a barge at his wife's request.[17] But in November he

---

[16] P.R.O., Dublin, Mem. Rolls, vol. 28, pp. 346–50, 560; vol. 29, pp. 88–89, 235–9, 240–41; vol. 30, pp. 163–6; Genealogical Office, MS 192, p. 131; *C.P.R., 1364–7*, p. 23; *C.C.R., 1364–8*, pp. 150–51; *Chart. St. Mary's*, II, p. 396; below, p. 327.

[17] Gilbert, *Viceroys of Ireland*, pp. 544–6; P.R.O., Dublin, Mem. Rolls, vol. 28, pp. 341–2, 343–4, 346–50.

summoned a parliament which met at Dublin on 7 January 1362, and granted a subsidy from both clergy and laity.[18] What else it did we do not know, but it seems likely that messages were sent asking for reinforcements, for in February the king issued a fresh order to a number of persons to make ready with all their power to cross to Ireland and remain there on its defence, since the lieutenant had lost many of his men, 'so that he and the lieges with him are in peril from the increasing strength of the said enemies'. More usefully, orders were given to array one hundred Welsh archers and one hundred spearmen, to be sent to Ireland to stay there on the king's wars. The most the king could obtain from the absentees when they appeared before the council was a grant of their revenues in Ireland for the next two years, and in June it was ordered that these revenues should be paid to Walter de Dalby, the clerk of the wages of war.[19]

The war was, indeed, very expensive,[20] and it was an added difficulty that 1361 was the year of the second outbreak of the plague. We have again widespread complaints that lands are wasted by the war and the death of tenants by war and pestilence, and on 14 July 1362 after discussion by the whole council it was agreed that the rents of the king's demesne lands, as well as any others which were in his hand, should be reduced by a quarter, or even a third. The revenue was still further reduced when later it was found necessary to pardon to the people of Ireland all debts and accounts whatsoever owed to the king before 13 October 1362, because of 'the losses which they have sustained because of the wars arisen in that land to preserve the king's honour and to recover his rights, and for the salvation and defence of that land against the king's Irish enemies'. That in spite of all this the average annual revenue for which the treasurer accounted during Clarence's lieutenancy was higher than it had been since before the Bruce invasion suggests that the administration during these years was more effective than might appear on the surface.[21]

[18] The date of this parliament, which is usually described as that of a.r. 35, and was therefore assigned by Richardson and Sayles to 1361, is fixed by P.R.O., Dublin, Mem. Rolls, vol. 28, p. 473.

[19] *C.C.R., 1360–64*, p. 384; *C.P.R., 1361–4*, p. 163; *Cal. Fine Rolls, 1356–8*, p. 224. For the eventual restoration of lands, see *C.C.R., 1364–8, passim*.

[20] From 3 July 1361 to 23 August 1364, the clerk of the wages received £22,100 and paid out £22,348 on wages and shipping only. About £3,400 of this came from the Irish exchequer; and a great deal more must have been spent on provisions, on compensation for horses lost and on miscellaneous expenses (P.R.O., London, E. 101/28/22, f. 16v. I owe this reference and note to Dr J. F. Lydon).

[21] P.R.O., Dublin, Mem. Rolls, vol. 28, pp. 275–6, 679–81; H. G. Richardson and G. O. Sayles, 'Irish Revenue, 1278–1384', *Proc. R.I.A.*, LXII C, pp. 87–100.

In February 1362 the lieutenant was at Drogheda, and in May at New Ross, while at Easter Stafford was 'in the parts of Kilkenny'. It was apparently in this summer that there was said to be 'arduous war' in Munster,[22] but we hear of no campaign, though in June substantial reinforcements were being prepared in England and Wales, 'because the king has to send without delay no small number of armed men and archers for the defence of Ireland against the Irish enemies'.[23] Then, apparently in September, 'Cathal Oc O Conchobair and Feidlim O Conchobair's son, the king of Connacht' raided Westmeath, burning all before them—'they burned fourteen churches and Cell Cainnig (Kilkenny West), and it would be hard to count up or estimate the amount of damage done to Meath that time'. And though the lieutenant led an expedition there, the annals tell us that the O'Connors returned home in safety. By February 1363 further reinforcements were being sent from England, and in May the king, appointing a commission to enquire into the behaviour of ministers in Ireland, specially required information

by whom the king's war in that land is protracted and deteriorated and in what manner the reformation and safety of the land can best be ordered. He has commanded the sheriffs of Dublin, Meath, Louth and Kildare to send jurors before them, and he has the matter very much at heart.

Though the Dublin annalist asserts that after his first campaign against O'Byrne Lionel 'brought the whole people, as well of England as of Ireland, together, and prospered well, and made many wars round about with the Irish with the aid of God and the people of Ireland', it is plain that things were going badly. In November 1363 the king ordered that the whole Irish revenue should be devoted for the next year to 'retaining men of Ireland needed for the war, and for payment of wages to them'. In February and March 1364 there was a campaign in Leix, presumably against O'More, and against the O'Byrnes, and on 22 April Lionel returned to England leaving Ormond as his deputy.[24]

[22] P.R.O., Dublin, Mem. Rolls, vol. 28, pp. 64, 122–3, 394–5, 401–2.
[23] C.C.R., 1360–64, pp. 339–40; C.P.R., 1361–4, p. 227; J. F. Lydon, 'William of Windsor and the Irish Parliament', E.H.R., LXXX, p. 253, n. 4; Richardson and Sayles, The Irish Parliament in the Middle Ages, p. 80, n. 45. Windsor, later himself lieutenant, contracted to supply a force of sixty men-at-arms and sixty archers for a year, and on 8 November 1363 entered into a second indenture for a force of 120 men-at-arms and 200 archers; at the end of 1364, by order of the Irish council, he retained a similar force with 210 kernes in place of seventy of the English archers (C.C.R., 1364–8, pp. 108–9).
[24] AC; A. Clon.; P.R.O., Dublin, Mem. Rolls, vol. 28, pp. 377–8, 378–9, 394–5; C.P.R., 1361–4, pp. 309, 312, 313, 369; C.C.R., 1360–64, pp. 450, 488–9, 554; Chart. St. Mary's, II, p. 395.

On 6 June Ormond was forbidden to hold any sessions or pleas in Munster: 'for particular causes set forth before the king and council' they were to be reserved till Clarence's return. A week later he and the chancellor were ordered to appease all disputes between the king's subjects by the best means they might, and to have it proclaimed throughout Ireland that none of the English should make any disturbances among themselves on pain of two years imprisonment and the payment of ransom at the king's will, as it has been reported to the king that there are

divers dissensions and debates arisen between the English born in England and the English born in Ireland his subjects, whereby in times past hurt and peril has happened in Ireland, and worse is feared unless the same be speedily appeased.

The subject was to be returned to in the Statutes of Kilkenny, eighteen months later, which provided that no difference should be made between the English born in Ireland and the English born in England, by calling them 'English hobbe or Irish dog, but that all shall be called by one name, the English lieges of our lord the king' on pain of a year's imprisonment and to be ransomed at the king's will.[25]

We do not know what was the result of this, but it is not difficult to see how such dissensions had arisen. Many of Lionel's followers were young and inexperienced men; those who were not had learned the art of war in France in circumstances wholly different to those which existed in Ireland. All were no doubt shocked by the partial assimilation of the Anglo-Irish to the Irish which had been the subject of legislation as early as 1297, and was again returned to at Kilkenny.[26] And no doubt all, or nearly all, though wholly ignorant of local conditions and difficulties, were convinced that they knew far better than the Anglo-Irish (whose record in the last generation had not, it must be admitted, been very impressive) how they should be met. It is not in the least surprising that disputes arose, and we can well believe that they gravely hampered the successful prosecution of the war.

Ormond seems to have been active entirely in the south-east: in July he was at New Ross and Waterford; in September he appears at Tullow, co. Carlow; in October and early November at Carlow.[27] Clarence returned in December 1364 and must have

[25] *C.C.R., 1364–8*, pp. 63–64. Some time before this the earl of Kildare and three others had been chosen by 'certain of the commons of Ireland' to go to England on business affecting the state of Ireland (ibid., p. 58); their representations may be behind these orders.

[26] *Early Statutes*, pp. 210–11; below, p. 293.

[27] *Chartae, Privilegia et Immunitates*, p. 64; P.R.O., Dublin, Mem. Rolls, vol. 28, pp. 452, 467–8, 478, 487, 500, 532–5, 612–3, 614.

made piteous representations to his father, for in February 1365, in renewing the reservation of the revenue of Ireland for the war, the king speaks of Ireland as 'sunk in the greatest wretchedness through the poverty and feebleness of his people there because of the destructions and hostile attacks often made by his Irish enemies'.[28] But he seems to have been stirred to a new energy, for in the spring, for the first time as far as the records show, he began an extended progress through the country, and seems to have conducted a campaign in Leinster, where he is said to have recovered lands in co. Carlow. By 24 April he was at Cork, and was holding pleas there on the morrow of the Ascension. He was still at Cork on 20 June, and on 20 August was at Kilmallock. It was presumably during this period that the O'Briens of Thomond submitted to him, or at least so they alleged in submitting to Richard II in February 1395. In October we find the lieutenant at Carlow, Castledermot and Trim; late in November he was at Mullingar, and early in December at Drogheda.[29] Then in February 1366 he held at Kilkenny a parliament which produced the most celebrated statute of medieval Ireland.[30]

It is difficult to see why the Statutes of Kilkenny have been taken by modern writers as marking a kind of watershed in the history of the English colony in Ireland, for in fact there is very little in them that is new: they have much more the character of a codification than that of new law. Their general purpose is, indeed, expressed by the preamble:

at the conquest of the land of Ireland and long after the English of the said land used the English language, dress, and manner of riding, and they and their subjects called betaghs were governed by English law ... and now many English of the said land, forsaking the English language, fashion, manner of riding, laws and usages, live and govern themselves by the manners, fashion, and language of the Irish enemies, and have made divers marriages and alliances between themselves and the Irish enemies, by which the said land and its liege people, the English language, the allegiance due to our lord the king, and the English laws are put in subjection and decayed, and the Irish enemies raised up and relieved contrary to reason.

In this spirit the statutes forbade any alliance by marriage, gossipred, fostering of children, concubinage, *caif*, or otherwise between English and Irish; enacted that every Englishman should

---

[28] *Cal. Fine Rolls, 1356–68*, p. 308.

[29] *Cal. Ormond Deeds*, II, nos. 112–3; P.R.O., Dublin, Cal. Mem. Rolls, vol. 29, pp. 15–16, 19–20, 33–36, 72–73, 101–2, 241–3, 282, 686–9; E. Curtis, *Richard II in Ireland*, pp. 40, 136–7.

[30] *Early Statutes*, pp. 430–68. For the most recent discussion of the Statutes of Kilkenny see G. J. Hand 'The Forgotten Statutes of Kilkenny: a Brief Survey', *The Irish Jurist*, new series, I (1966), pp. 299-312.

use the English language and an English name, and English customs, fashion, manner of riding and dress, and that the Irish living among the English should speak English among themselves; forbade the use of *lei de marche ne de Breon* among the English; prohibited the admission of any Irishman 'of the nations of the Irish' to any cathedral or collegiate church, or to any ecclesiastical benefice or religious house among the English; and forbade Irish minstrels to come among the English or be received by them, 'since they spy out their secrets, whereby great evils have often happened'. But the only part of this that was new was that concerning the Irish language and Irish minstrels: in 1297 one of the earliest Irish statutes had provided that Englishmen 'should relinquish the Irish dress, at least in the head or hair'; in 1310 religious houses in 'the land of peace or English land' had been forbidden to admit any 'not of the English nation'[31]; the ordinances made under Rokeby in 1351 had forbidden alliances between English and Irish, and the use of Brehon law. In 1360 a royal writ had laid down that though it had been proclaimed that 'no mere Irishman, being of the Irish race' should be appointed to municipal office, or admitted to any ecclesiastical benefice, this was not to be understood to apply to those who had 'continually and unswervingly remained in loyalty and obedience to us' and were known to be of good character.[32]

All this, the part of the statute for which it is chiefly remembered, was in practice rather a system of control than a flat prohibition. We find licences to foster children,[33] and marriages between English and Irish continued. In 1416 an English statute, reciting the prohibition of the admission of Irishmen of 'Irish nation'—that is, members of the clans continually at war against the English— stated that licences granted by the king's lieutenants in Ireland had enabled such Irishmen to be promoted to archbishoprics and bishoprics,

and whereas they are called peers of parliament in the said land, they bring with them to the parliaments and councils held there Irish servants, whereby the secrets of the English in the said land have been and are daily discovered to the Irish people, rebels to the king, to the great peril and mischief of the loyal lieges of the king in the said land.

At this period, of course, and for long afterwards, the king could dispense individuals from observing the terms of a statute, which in its origins was simply a royal command, with exactly the same authority as any other royal command, and this provision in the

[31] This had been almost immediately revoked: see above, p. 138.
[32] *Early Statutes*, pp. 420–21.
[33] *C.C.H.*, p. 98, no. 271; p. 146, no. 187.

Statutes of Kilkenny had in fact established not an absolute prohibition, but machinery by which the admission of Irishmen to benefices could be controlled. And even if lieutenants were forbidden to grant such licences, as was done in 1416, there remained the power to grant charters of English law, which put the person to whom they were granted, and usually his issue, in exactly the same position as any Englishman, including the right to hold benefices among the English. As for the Irish language, we need only remark that it was Ormond and other Anglo-Irish magnates who acted as interpreters when Richard II came to Ireland.[34]

These were the most celebrated clauses of the statute, but they were only a small part of the whole. It was inevitably much preoccupied with defence. It provided in a clause which seems to be new in Ireland, but is practically identical with English legislation, that because of the necessities of a land at war the commons in the marches of war are not to use the games called 'hurlings, with great clubs at ball upon the ground . . . and other games which men call coitings', but are to practise archery, and the use of lances, and 'other gentle games which pertain to arms'. Once a war has been begun, which is to be done in future only by the council, with the advice of the people of the county where it begins, it is to be continued till the Irish enemies are finally destroyed or pay the cost of the war in full and make fine for contempt. When peace is made, it is to be stipulated that no Irish are to occupy the lands of the English, or the Irish being at peace, against the will of the lords of such lands. Parleys with Irish or English rebels are only to be held with the leave of the court, or in the presence of the sheriff or the keepers of the peace. Neighbouring counties are to join in a war when warned by the keepers of the peace or the sheriff. If any Englishman break a truce or peace made by the royal officials between English and Irish he is responsible for the damages resulting, and shall make fine at the king's will. No Englishman shall stir up war against others on pain of life and limb and forfeiture of lands. The prohibition of the keeping of kernes and idlemen in the land of peace is repeated. Other clauses deal with a variety of official oppressions, arrange for the fixing of prices in the towns, and other miscellaneous matters, including a repetition of the prohibition of opprobrious names between the English of England and the English of Ireland.

Hardly any of all this is new, and the statute re-enacts the bulk of Rokeby's ordinance of 1351,[35] itself largely a codification, pos-

---

[34] *Early Statutes*, pp. 560–61; above, p. 188; Curtis, *Richard II in Ireland, passim*.
[35] See the concordance in *Early Statutes*, p. 374.

sibly under the influence of the doctrine propounded in England in 1353 that 'ordinances and agreements made in councils are not of record, as if they had been made in common parliament.'[36] It was from time to time confirmed later in the middle ages, and finally in Poynings' parliament in 1494. But it is difficult to believe that it did in fact mark any new departure, or any change of policy. For more than two generations, as we have seen, and quite possibly for longer, for there may well have been enactments of Irish parliaments before 1297 which have not survived, the principles which it enunciated and the tendencies which it attacked had been developing. Nothing was in fact changed by it, and the importance which has been attached to this codification by modern historians seems misplaced. If we are looking for a watershed, for the point at which it was realized that the complete conquest of Ireland would not be achieved, or at which it became impossible, we must look earlier: perhaps before the end of the thirteenth century.

After the parliament Clarence returned to Munster, where from Michaelmas to Christmas 1365 the Irish of Tipperary, 'O Kenedies, Odures, Omolrians and McBrenes', had been making war in the marches of Limerick, so that the community of co. Limerick had had to garrison their borders. By 12 April he was at Clonmel, where he remained for some time, and on 20 May at Kilmallock. It seems that on this occasion there was a campaign, for in September he granted to Richard Og Barrett lands in Muskerry which had been wasted by the Irish of Munster, and which he had now 'perambulated with a great army, and by great war acquired', but we know nothing more of it. By 3 July he was at New Ross, where he seems to have remained throughout the month; on 6 August he was at Kilkenny, and remained there or at Castledermot till October, when he returned to Dublin.[37]

It is not easy to estimate what had been achieved by a lieutenancy on which a great deal of money, though probably not enough,[38] had been spent. It is likely that, as Windsor did later,[39] he had used his army largely to provide local garrisons instead of fighting spectacular campaigns, and there is a certain amount of evidence that the situation worsened appreciably after his departure: the

---

[36] *Rotuli Parliamentorum*, II, pp. 253 (42), 257 (16).

[37] *C.P.R., 1377–81*, p. 258; P.R.O., Dublin, Mem. Rolls, vol. 29, pp. 173–4, 202–3, 235–9, 240–41, 292–6, 297–9, 694–5, 699–700, 707–8; *Cal. Gormanston Reg.*, p. 58; *Reg. Sweteman*, no. 18; *Reg. Alen*, p. 216.

[38] See J. F. Lydon, 'William of Windsor and the Irish Parliament', *E.H.R.*, LXXX, p. 253, n. 3.

[39] See below, pp. 298–9, 303–7.

inquisition taken after his death in 1367 says that when he was in Ireland his manors in Connacht were worth £200 a year, but now nothing because they have been occupied by Sir Edmund de Burgo and other rebels, English and Irish, and no royal official dare go there, while in 1375 a jury swore that the citizens of Cork could not come to the exchequer at Carlow after his departure without 'a great posse of armed men' because of 'divers tribulations and the risks of the roads'.[40]

Clarence, whose wife, the heiress of Ulster and Connacht, had died in 1363, leaving only an infant daughter, left Ireland finally on 7 November 1366, when the council appointed Thomas de la Dale, who had been chief justice of the justiciar's bench in 1363–4, as keeper. On 20 February 1367 the king appointed Gerald fitz Maurice, earl of Desmond, as justiciar: he took up office about 23 April, and held it till 20 June 1369. Almost his first act was to summon a parliament to Kilkenny for 14 June, but there seems to be no evidence as to what was done in this assembly. Desmond showed great activity: he was holding pleas in Dublin in May; in June he was at Kilkenny for the parliament and held pleas there, and later at Clonmel; in October he held pleas at Naas and Carlow. In January 1368 he held pleas at Wexford, and in February, after he had been in Carlow and Castledermot, at New Ross; by 12 March he was at Cork, where he held pleas and summoned a parliament to Dublin for 1 May.[41]

This parliament had been ordered by the king as the result of complaints, probably coming from the parliament of 1367, that

the Irish and others our enemies rode in hostile array through every part of the said land, committing homicides, robberies and arsons, pillaging, spoiling and destroying monasteries, churches, castles, towns and fortresses, without showing reverence or respect to God, or to Holy Church, or to any person . . . so that the land was at point to be lost, if remedy and help were not immediately supplied.

In April 1368 the archbishop of Armagh had been forbidden to leave the country, though summoned to England, because wars had newly arisen in his marches and those of the archbishop of Dublin. In May the prelates, magnates and commons, having 'well and long debated' the matter, concluded that the only remedy was that the absentees should come and remain upon their lands 'in their own persons or by their strong men, sufficient and well

---

[40] *Calendar of Inquisitions Post Mortem*, XII, p. 321; *C.P.R., 1374–7*, p. 207.
[41] P.R.O., Dublin, Mem. Rolls, vol. 29, pp. 459–60, 520–54, 564, 634, 662–5, 698, 766–7; vol. 30, pp. 10–11, 79–80, 162; *Reg. Sweteman*, no. 32; *Parliaments and Councils*, no. 19.

equipped for war'. This opinion was reported to the king under the seals of the prelates and magnates, who soon afterwards wrote again reporting that the situation had further deteriorated, and that the lordship of Ireland was 'for the most part destroyed and lost'.[42] It was probably at this time that it was decided to summon the royal service to Kilkenny, and there seems to have been a campaign against the O'Tooles in the summer.[43]

Meanwhile, before the end of July the king had acted on the report of the Kilkenny parliament: an ordinance made by the English council required all who held lands in Ireland to go there in person before the next Easter, to reside continuously on their lands, or, if they could satisfy the council that this was impossible, at least to send men-at-arms in their place, on pain of forfeiture of the lands. On 28 July orders to this effect were issued to sixteen individual magnates. In December the Irish government was ordered to summon a parliament or great council to discuss the ordinance, and to certify what quotas of men should be required of the absentees and what lands they held. And by this time, though William of Windsor was not formally appointed as lieutenant till 3 March 1369, it had been decided to send him with an army to Ireland: on 1 November the Irish government had been ordered to arrest ships for his passage, and the departure of men, horses, or provisions from Ireland had been forbidden.[44]

The ordinance about the absentees did not work as was contemplated. Its immediate effect was to cause a number of magnates, who had for some ten years seen much of the revenues of their lands in Ireland appropriated by the exchequer, decide to rid themselves of property which had become merely an embarrassment. Amory de St Amand had already in 1363 sold his manor of Gormanston in cos. Dublin and Meath to the Prestons; now the heirs of Thomas de Clare disposed of their manor of Inchiquin and Youghal, co. Cork, and the de Verdon heirs hurriedly sold their lands in Louth and Meath, with the exception of Loughsewdy, which was perhaps

---

[42] C.C.R., 1364–8, pp. 353–4, 482–3; Early Statutes, pp. 470–71; P.R.O., London, S.C. 8/207/10349–50.

[43] N.L.I., MS 761, p. 297. There was a campaign against the O'Tooles when Thomas Burley was chancellor (C.C.H., p. 80, no. 5; p.88, no. 77). Richardson and Sayles omit Burley from their list of chancellors, but he was taken prisoner when chancellor by the Berminghams of Carbury, co. Kildare, in the autumn of 1368 (Grace, Annals, p. 154; C.C.H., p. 82, no. 62; p. 85, nos. 6, 16; p. 88, no. 76). He does seem to have been acting as chancellor in the summer of 1368, and the revocation of his appointment was vacated because nothing done (C.P.R., 1367–70, p. 123). But the campaign for which the royal service was proclaimed was probably in November, when a clerk of the wages was appointed (P.R.O., Dublin, Mem. Rolls, vol. 30, p. 106).

[44] C.C.R., 1364–8, pp. 448, 453, 482–3, 499–500; Early Statutes, pp. 470–71.

unsaleable.[45] We must suppose that others followed suit, and it does not seem that the number of resident lords was increased at all.

Nevertheless the English government, in spite of the rapidly worsening relations with France which led to the renewal of the Hundred Years' War at the end of 1369, was still prepared to spend considerable sums on the attempt to repair the position in Ireland, and the lieutenancy of William of Windsor was a continuation of that of Clarence. The indenture into which he entered with the king provided that he should receive the really enormous sum of £20,000 from the king for the maintenance of himself and his retinue in Ireland. It was, of course, hoped that it would be possible to obtain a further substantial contribution to his expenses in Ireland, but it cannot really have been supposed that it would be possible to return to the position of the thirteenth century, when the Irish revenue had normally produced a comfortable surplus for the king's use. Windsor's attempts to obtain enough, by way of parliamentary grants, even to carry on the war in Ireland were before long to produce a storm of protest.[46]

Windsor arrived in Ireland on 20 June 1369 and immediately summoned a parliament to Dublin for 30 July. In the interval he visited Carbury, co. Kildare, which, as we have seen, was sufficiently disturbed under the Berminghams, and dealt firmly with the marchers who had taken cattle from the Irish, presumably during a truce. Then at the parliament he showed his commission, announced the forfeiture of the lands of the absentees, and obtained a grant of customs duties. After this he seems to have turned to the war against the Irish of Leinster: the Irish annals tell us that 'Diarmait Red-hand MacMurchada, high king of Leinster' was treacherously taken prisoner by the Black Knight and eventually executed, and Gerald Kavanagh, a possible successor, killed. In October he was at Castledermot, co. Kildare, where Sir John de Bermingham of Donadea, co. Kildare, was accused in his court of certain seditions, felonies, and treasons, and condemned to be drawn and hanged on his own acknowledgement. In November he was at St Mullins, co. Carlow, to which he returned in February

---

[45] *Cal. Gormanston Reg.*, pp. 18–24; *C.C.R., 1360–64*, pp. 547–8; ibid., *1369–74*, pp. 72, 113–14; *Cal. Ormond Deeds*, II, nos. 120, 134, 145, 151, 162, 174, 179, 184, 187, 232; J. Otway-Ruthven, 'The Partition of the de Verdon Lands', *Proc. R.I.A.*, LXVI C. Except for the sale of part of Inchiquin to William of Windsor from whose heir Ormond acquired it in 1420 (*Cal. Ormond Deeds*, III, no. 37) all these sales were to persons normally resident in Ireland.

[46] *E.H.R.*, LXXX, p. 257; Richardson and Sayles, 'Irish Revenue, 1278–1384', *Proc. R.I.A.*, LXII C, pp. 87–100; below, pp. 299–300.

after holding a council at Dublin early in January at which the clergy granted a subsidy.[47]

Windsor seems to have remained engaged in the war against the Leinster Irish till the summer of 1370, when a disaster in Munster called him away: on 10 July

Gerald fitz Maurice, earl of Desmond, Sir John Nicholas and Sir Thomas fitz John, and many other nobles, were taken prisoner, and a number killed, near the monastery of Magio, to wit Maii, in co. Limerick by Obreen and Maccomar [MacNamara] of Thomond, on account of which the lieutenant went to Limerick to defend Munster, leaving off the war upon the Otothiles and other Irish in Leinster.[48]

The city of Limerick itself was burnt by 'McFinar': the destruction must have been very great, for the justiciar and council ordered payment for 1,050 ash trees for its repair. The lieutenant was at Naas on 29 July; by 8 August, and probably earlier, the government was at Adare, co. Limerick, where, according to his enemies, Windsor stayed for twenty-two weeks without taking the field: he arrested all the ships there (presumably in the Shannon estuary), but did not go to Thomond to make war, preferring to make 'a false peace', taken by himself and the bishop of Meath. The official version of this was that the bishop of Meath was in Munster with men-at-arms to make war on and bring to the peace O'Brien, MacNamara and others. MacNamara submitted on 15 December at Adare, giving hostages and undertaking inter alia to keep the peace towards the bishops of Killaloe and Limerick, to restore ecclesiastical property, and to pay a fine of 1,000 cows. It was no doubt at the same time that O'Brien also undertook to pay a fine of 1,000 cows and MacCarthy 'Karbraghe' one of 140 cows. Some at least of those from MacCarthy were paid; those due from O'Brien and MacNamara were assigned to the citizens of Limerick in aid of the restoration of the city. It was further alleged by Windsor's enemies that he had forced certain citizens of Dublin and Drogheda to go to Limerick and stay there till they had paid heavily for leave to go home, and that in September he ordered the citizens of Dublin either to lend 50 marks or to come with sixty armed men to join his retinue at Adare for three months, issuing a similar order to the men of Drogheda. Windsor seems to have remained at Adare till the end of the year; then in January 1371 he held a parliament at Kilkenny where he was granted a subsidy, and it was agreed

[47] M. V. Clarke, 'William of Windsor in Ireland', Proc. R.I.A., XLI C, pp. 83–84; Parliaments and Councils, nos. 21, 23; AC; ALC; AU; Cal. Gormanston Reg., p. 140; C.P.R., 1370–74. p. 337. Bermingham was pardoned for good service.
[48] Chart. St. Mary's, II, p. 397; Grace, Annals, pp. 154–6. The Irish annals place this in 1369, but 1370 seems to be the correct date.

that he should return to Cashel to make war on the Irish. It would seem that the trouble was now in Tipperary, and the Irish annals say that in this year 'Brian Ua Ceinneidigh, king of Ormond, fell in treachery by the Foreigners'. According to Windsor's enemies, however, 'he remained at Cashel all the winter without doing any good'. Then, in June 1371, he held a parliament at 'Balidowille' (Ballyduagh, near Cashel),

and there were all the good men of Uriel, Meath, and of the county of Dublin, archbishops, bishops, knights, burgesses, and the good men of Cork and of Kerry. in great mischief for lack of victuals

and he forced them to grant a subsidy.[49]

Since Windsor's arrival the Anglo-Irish had had a quite unprecedented burden of taxation imposed on them. Parliamentary taxation was certainly not new in Ireland, but between July 1369 and June 1371 Windsor had held six assemblies, had demanded taxation from all of them, and had obtained it from five. And quite apart from taxation on a national scale there were local levies and the burden of purveyance: it was later alleged by a jury that in December 1369 Windsor had imposed on co. Meath a tallage of half a mark on every ploughland 'without the consent and against the will of the said county', and in February 1370 had taken a crannoc of corn and a crannoc of hay from each ploughland, paying little more than half the market price, and nothing for transport. In March 1370 the sheriff of Louth, and no doubt other sheriffs, was ordered to proclaim that all tithes were to be kept for the lieutenant: ecclesiastics and religious houses with an accumulation of tithe corn were obvious marks for the purveyors. Further, there was the duty of local defence: one of the accusations against Windsor was that in July 1369 he had forced the Dubliners to maintain six men-at-arms and eighteen archers at Saggart for three weeks at their own expense.[50] When to all this we add the private losses suffered in a land continually at war, and remember that 1371 was the year of the third outbreak of the plague,[51] we need not be surprised that a growing resistance is evident, which by September 1371 had resulted in complaints to the king and council. On 10 September Windsor was

[49] C.C.H., p. 82, no. 52; p. 122, no. 24; Clarke, loc. cit., pp. 86–87, 117, 120, 121; Journal of the North Munster Archaeological Society, III, p. 254; Reg. Sweteman, no. 106; AU; Parliaments and Councils, nos. 26–28.

[50] J. F. Lydon, loc. cit.; M. V. Clarke, loc. cit., pp. 113, 115, 116, 120–21; Reg. Sweteman, no. 201.

[51] For instance, when Windsor went to Munster in 1370 O'More took the opportunity to rise and burnt Athy; in the autumn of 1369 McGuinness had plundered the marches of Louth (C.C.H., p. 87, no. 60; Dowdall Deeds, no. 257). In January 1371 Sir John Hussey's lands in Meath were wasted by pestilence (P.R.O., Dublin, Mem. Rolls, vol. 30, p. 404).

ordered to supersede the demands made by him upon the towns
of Dublin and Drogheda, and on 20 October to suspend the collection of all the taxes granted since 1369, described as 'new and unheard of imposts not to be endured'.[52]

What immediately followed we do not know, but by January
1372 it had been decided to remove Windsor. The first appointee,
Richard de Pembridge, flatly refused to serve, and was replaced
by Robert de Assheton, chancellor of Ireland in 1364–6, whose
indenture with the king is dated 8 March. Windsor was, of course,
continuing to act as lieutenant, and held a parliament at Kilkenny
in January, and a great council in Dublin in February, but on 6
March the chancellor was forbidden to seal anything, except writs
de cursu, at his command. At the same time the exchequer was forbidden to make any payments except by the king's command under
the great seal of England. When these letters were read before the
Irish council on 10 April it was decided that on account of the war
the due payments must be made. But by this time Windsor had
left the country, summoned before the council in England, and
Kildare, appointed as keeper, acted till Assheton arrived on 20
June.[53]

Even before Windsor's departure a serious situation had arisen
in Munster. On 27 March Desmond and others were ordered to
go to their lands in co. Limerick, with as many men-at-arms as
possible, to resist 'Obreen of Tothemond', who with a great multitude of Irishmen was purposing to make war anew on the county,
while the local authorities in co. Cork were ordered to array the
men of the county and cause them to stay on its defence. After
Windsor left the country we hear that 'OBreen, McKonnar, Richard Og [de Burgo] of Connaght, and almost all the Irish of Munster, Connacht, and Leinster, and many English, enemies and
rebels' had risen in war, and were allied to make a universal conquest throughout Ireland before the lieutenant's return. The main
danger was, however, clearly in Munster, and on 16 April the
sheriffs and seneschals of the province, together with Kilkenny,
Dublin, Louth, Kildare and Meath, were ordered to array all the
fencible men of their counties to go at the king's wages in the company of Kildare against O'Brien and other Irish who had risen
anew. The core of the force should have been provided by Windsor's retinue, which had been left in the country and was to be paid
by the money arising from the scutage decided on in the parliament
at Kilkenny, but in fact it seems to have been melting away, for on

[52] *C.C.R., 1369–74*, pp. 246, 256–7, 259, 265–6.
[53] *C.C.R., 1369–74*, pp. 365, 420; *C.C.H.*, p. 85, nos. 149, 155.

10 May the local authorities in counties Kilkenny, Kildare and Dublin, and the ports of Dublin and Drogheda were ordered to arrest men of the retinue absenting themselves from the king's service without leave. Their wages were probably much in arrears, for the money from the scutage would in any case come in slowly, and by 22 May such complaints had reached the king and council in England as to result in an order that it should not be exacted in respect of lands 'which are in the hands of the Irish the king's enemies'.[54]

Kildare seems to have set out for the south at the end of April. He was at Carlow from 27 April to 8 May; at Kilkenny on 9 May, and at Clonmel on the 10th. He had reached Cork by 15 May, and the government remained in the south all summer, principally at Cork, but also at Limerick and Kilmallock: on 8 June Kildare held a local council at Ballyhea. It seems that he succeeded in dividing the enemy: on 26 May a substantial payment was ordered to Richard Og, presumably the same who had earlier been said to be in alliance with O'Brien, for service against the enemy with 'his whole adherence'. In 1374 'Comar McComarre' [MacNamara] captain of his nation represented that O'Brien had made war on his late father because he and his men had become the king's faithful lieges, and had devastated most of his lands and county Limerick and the adjacent parts, and he himself, after his father's death, had assembled a retinue of four hundred men to make war on O'Brien at his own expense.[55]

Kildare's authority must have ceased with Assheton's arrival on 20 June, though it is likely that he was left to complete the campaign which he had begun, and which seems to have quietened the south for the time being. Assheton's first action on landing in Ireland was, in consultation with the council, to modify the force for which his indenture with the king had provided: he was to bring with him from England sixty men-at-arms and one hundred archers, to be paid by the English revenue, and was to engage in Ireland eighty hobelers and 200 kerns, to be paid by the Irish revenue. On 21 June he retained instead 'certain English men-at-arms and archers', and presently found that they would not remain

[54] *C.C.H.*, p. 82, no. 50; p. 84, nos. 132–4; p. 85, nos. 142–5, 147–9, 155; *C.C.R., 1369–74*, pp. 380–81; P.R.O., Dublin, Mem. Rolls, vol. 30, p. 205. On 6 March Ormond had agreed to go to England with a body of the retinue, English born in England, remained on his lands (*C.C.H.*, p. 81, no. 19; p. 84, no. 119). In June 1369 the owners of the de Verdon lands had petitioned for a reduction of scutage because a great part of the manors of Dundalk and Loughsewdy was occupied by Irish enemies and *malveis Englis* (P.R.O., Dublin, Mem. Rolls, vol. 30, pp. 110–11).

[55] *C.C.H.*, p. 83, no. 90; p. 86, no. 21; pp. 81–85, *passim*.

in Ireland unless they were paid rewards in addition to their wages like the other English of the retinue.[56] There is no further trace of his movements: presumably he went to Munster, and on 7 October he tested a writ at Kilkenny, and one at Dublin on 9 October. Then in January 1373 he held a parliament at Kilkenny, in which it was agreed to send messengers to the king and council to ask that the earl of March should be appointed as lieutenant, and that on no account should Windsor be sent back. March, the husband of Lionel of Clarence's heiress, and in his own right lord of Meath, was much the greatest of the absentees, and an obvious choice even though he was only twenty-one. But though the king promised to send him to Ireland as soon as convenient, and preparations were actually taken in hand for his departure, nothing came of it. And meanwhile, on 20 September 1373, Windsor had been reappointed, this time as governor and keeper.[57]

In Ireland, during 1373, attention seems to have shifted momentarily from Munster. In July the justiciar was active in co. Louth, testing writs at Drogheda and making a peace with McGuinness. The settlers of Meath are said to have made an attack on Annaly, co. Longford, and to have been defeated in Kinaleagh (bar. Moycashel, co. Westmeath), and a new seneschal of Meath could not go to Carlow to take oath because of the wars then imminent in Meath. In Leinster MacMurrough was at war and took the constable of Carlow castle prisoner: the council ordered a guard to be set at Carlow, and we hear of a parley between Assheton and the Irish of Leinster. But Assheton had left the country before the end of September, leaving Ralph Cheyne as his deputy, and Cheyne too was gone by 2 December, when, 'the land being left entirely without governance', the council appointed William Tany, prior of the Hospital, as justiciar. And at the time of Assheton's departure the O'Byrnes had been again at war, taking and burning the New Castle of Mackinegan and taking the constable prisoner.[58]

Windsor had sent his retinue ahead of him, and his critics of

[56] C.C.R., 1374–7, pp. 170–71; P.R.O., London, S.C. 8/217/10845; Richardson and Sayles, The Irish Parliament in the Middle Ages, pp. 81–82. The English troops Assheton retained in Ireland must have been the remains of Windsor's retinue. Kildare tested a writ as keeper at Cork as late as 28 June: presumably the news of Assheton's arrival had not reached him (Cal. Carew MSS, Book of Howth, p. 360).

[57] P.R.O., Dublin, Mem. Rolls, vol. 30, pp. 299–301; C.P.R., 1370–74, pp. 247, 337, 353, 373; Foedera, VII, p. 28; Clarke, loc. cit., pp. 99, 107–8. The messengers from the Kilkenny parliament do not seem to have appeared before the council till September.

[58] Cal. Gormanston Reg., p. 138; Reg. Sweteman, no. 10; P.R.O., Dublin, Mem. Rolls, vol. 30, pp. 197–9, 324–6, 337–43, 348–9; AC; Dowling, Annals, p. 24; C.C.H., p. 86, nos. 30, 41, 47; p. 87, no. 60; p. 88, no. 93; p. 89, no. 110.

1376 complained that they arrived in Dublin, Waterford and elsewhere about the middle of December 1373 and lived at the expense of the lieges without doing anything against the Irish. Windsor himself landed at Waterford on 18 April 1374. His indenture required him to serve for one whole year with 200 men-at-arms and 400 archers, taking for wages and reward for himself and his retinue for the year £11,213 6s. 8d. He undertook also to serve at the king's pleasure after this time, with the same retinue or a smaller one as the king and council thought necessary, with fees and wages at the same rate, 'on condition that reasonable ordinance touching the rule of the said land be made by the king and council, with consideration of his advice in this'. On 4 May he showed his patent to the council at Kilkenny. In the middle of the month he went to Dublin, where he held a great council on 27 May, and remained in Dublin till late in August, refusing, according to his enemies, to do anything till the balance of the subsidies granted at Kilkenny and Ballyduagh in 1371 had been paid. His critics alleged that when he arrived in April 'the Irish of Munster and some false English' had been at war, and that he had ignored appeals to succour the people of the country 'as a man come in the king's name': with some inconsistency they go on to say that on his arrival in the spring he sent 120 horsemen to Kilmallock, who remained for a year 'living on the poor commons and paying little or nothing', and eighty archers and eighty horsemen to the neighbourhood of Buttevant, who remained for some six months.[59]

It is not quite clear what was in fact happening in Munster in the spring of 1374. The sheriffs of Cork and Limerick excused themselves for not appearing at the exchequer at Carlow in the quindene of Easter by saying that there was 'fervent war' in their counties, and the roads were too dangerous, the sheriff of Limerick saying that 'Obren of Thomond, who calls himself king of Munster, and Richard Oge de Burgo of Connaght, and other divers nations' daily destroyed and devastated his county. But it was testified in the exchequer that there had not been any such war in those counties, and the bishop of Limerick had been able to get to Carlow on that day. But there must have been evident danger, for early in May the council sent William son of Richard de Burgo of Connacht to his father to warn him to fight O'Brien of Thomond, captain of his nation, 'who falsely and without a title claims to have the lordship

[59] Clarke, loc. cit., pp. 89–91; Devon, *Issues of the Exchequer*, p. 197; *C.P.R., 1370–74*, p. 345; *C.C.H.*, p. 86, no. 19. Commissions of array for his retinue had been issued on 24 September, and the concentration of shipping for his passage at Liverpool, Bristol, and Milford Haven was ordered in October (*C.P.R., 1370–74*, pp. 338–9, 344, 347).

of Ireland'. Certainly by the autumn there was open war: on 7 September Windsor and the council at Naas agreed that since he could not himself leave Leinster for Munster without danger of the destruction of the marches of Leinster, the bishop of Meath (Stephen de Valle, bishop of Limerick 1360–69) should go to Munster to aid 'Comarre McConmarre' and his men against O'Brien and others, English and Irish, with such a force as he considered necessary. Since the treasury was empty, and seemed likely to remain so, the bishop was to obtain a local subsidy in Munster; if he could not induce the people to grant it, then he was to have grain and cattle in every county in Munster, to be paid for by the sheriffs from the issues of their bailiwicks. In October we hear that MacNamara was in the field against O'Brien with eighty horsemen and footmen at his own expense. As for the bishop, his enemies alleged that he caused sometimes as many as 200 soldiers to live on the poor commons, paying nothing; that he came to co. Tipperary with Richard Og de Burgo and 1,000 horsemen and remained a fortnight, living on the people and paying little or nothing; that he then went to Clonmel with thirty horsemen and stayed there a week; that he took fourteen score cows in the county of Kerry, paying nothing, and daily made other great extortions, destructions and oppressions in Munster; that he imposed on the clergy of Kerry 55 marks against their will; and that he made the commons of Munster pay Richard Og de Burgo subsidies amounting to 1,400 marks.[60]

Meanwhile war continued in Leinster, and by the end of 1374 new dangers were threatening. When on 20 November Windsor summoned a parliament to Dublin for 20 January the writs spoke of dangers in various parts of Ireland, and specifically in Ulster. It seems that there had been an expedition to Ulster which had been defeated with heavy losses, but when the parliament met no subsidy was granted; all that could be obtained was a small loan from individuals, and it is clear that matters were becoming increasingly difficult. A rather uncertain peace with the Irish of Leinster had been made by the spring of 1375, but the war in Munster continued, and the English government was growing impatient. On 30 March the king wrote to Windsor that he intended to deliberate on the state of Ireland with the council, and to send its decisions before Trinity (17 June): Windsor was to summon a parliament for the morrow of Trinity to receive the message and provide for the government of the country in accordance with it. He was enjoined

[60] P.R.O., Dublin, Mem. Rolls, vol. 30, pp. 322–4; *C.C.R., 1374–7*, p. 5; *C.C.H.*, p. 86, no. 22; p. 87, nos. 59, 63–65; Clarke, loc. cit., pp. 93–94.

to remain in office, keeping his retinue together; 2,000 marks of what was due for the last half year was sent with the letter, and the rest was promised shortly, together with payment at the same rate for the future.[61]

The parliament which met at Kilkenny on 18 June granted a subsidy, but not very much: only 400 marks, and only from the counties of Munster, including Kerry, with Kilkenny and Wexford. Clearly representations that

> Breen, late O Breen of Tothemonia, Irishman, our enemy, having confederated with him O Conghir of Connacht and many others, as well English as Irish, of their adherence and covin, our enemies and rebels, to destroy the faithful people of our said land and to make a general conquest of the land, and especially of the parts of Munster,

must be resisted had had little effect on a parliament still angrily remembering Windsor's earlier subsidies. At the same time it was agreed that the bishop of Meath, in company with Windsor, should set out for Munster and Connacht as soon as the parliament was over, and remain there as long as seemed necessary, with such force as they thought good. The bishop was on this duty from 8 July till 1 September, and on 3 August Windsor and 'other magnates and peers' were said to be setting out with a great army to Thomond: the local authorities in Limerick were ordered to purvey provisions, and horses for cartage. They must have had local support, for it was evidently in this year that Turlough O'Brien was appointed captain of his nation, to wit O'Brien of Thomond, by the royal power, and undertook 'a most strenuous war' against the former O'Brien, who was threatening to destroy Munster. But in fact Turlough was driven from his country for lack of the aid promised him.[62]

By this time the English government had lost patience. The war in France was going badly, and much of the gains of its first stage had already been lost. The constant drain of money to finance fruitless wars in Ireland was beginning to seem more than could be

---

[61] *Parliaments and Councils*, nos. 32, 34; *AC*; *AU*; *C.C.H.*, p. 95, no. 200; p. 96, nos. 208, 212, 223–4; p. 97, nos. 233, 237. The annals speak of two defeats in Ulster, one in 1374 and one in 1375, but Sir James de la Hyde, who is said to have been killed in the second, was certainly killed not later than the beginning of November 1374, 'slain in the king's service', 'killed by McGynouse and other Irish of Ulster' (*C.C.H.*, p. 86, no. 30; p. 89, no. 125; *Dowdall Deeds*, no. 257, where 43rd year is a misprint for 48th). The repair of Wicklow castle, said to have been taken by the Irish early in 1374, was ordered in May 1375 (Clarke, loc. cit., p. 89; *Cal. Pembroke Deeds*, no. 64).

[62] *Parliaments and Councils*, nos. 35–38, 54; *C.C.H.*, p. 99, nos. 281–2; p. 101, no. 59; below, pp. 310–11. A sheriff of co. Clare was appointed on 12 August, but it does not seem that this came to anything (*C.C.H.*, p. 91, no. 30).

borne. On 18 June the king addressed letters patent to all in Ireland, reminding them of the great and unprofitable expenses which he had incurred in the war in Ireland: expenses which could no longer be comfortably borne. Nicholas Dagworth was being sent to them to expound the king's business, so that they might arrange to bear a reasonable share of these expenses. Dagworth left London on 23 July, and must have reached the Irish government, which was then at Limerick, some time before 28 August, when a parliament was summoned to Kilkenny for 6 October to consider 'most urgent business specially touching the safety and defence of Ireland'.[63]

Windsor was by this time in desperate straits: money was not coming in from England; he could get nothing in Ireland; his retinue was unpaid, and unwilling to remain; the king was pressing him to continue in a service in which, as he pointed out, he could do nothing without troops. But the parliament at Kilkenny, confronted with all this, simply replied that if the king and council wished Windsor to stay in Ireland with his retinue they must provide for them: they themselves could not undertake the burden because of the losses which they had sustained. All Windsor could obtain was the agreement of the council to provide for the payment of thirty-seven men-at-arms and eighty-five archers for the next quarter. An impasse had been reached, and had obviously been expected, for Dagworth now produced writs ordering the sending of two proctors from each diocese, two knights from each county, and two citizens or burgesses from each city or borough to the king and council in England, to consult about the government of Ireland and an aid for the king. Writs were accordingly issued by Windsor on 25 October: the representatives elected were to be with the king in February 1376.[64]

This unprecedented demand provoked widespread resistance. Clergy, counties and towns alike, though almost all of them elected representatives as instructed, stated roundly that 'according to the liberties, privileges, rights, laws and customs of the church and land of Ireland' they were not bound to elect representatives and send them to parliaments and councils in England, and almost all refused to empower their representatives to grant a subsidy. The majority of returns are phrased in almost the same words, suggest-

[63] *C.P.R., 1374–7*, pp. 117, 120; *Parliaments and Councils*, no. 41; Clarke, loc. cit., p. 61, n. 26.
[64] *Parliaments and Councils*, no. 46; J. F. Lydon, 'William of Windsor and the Irish Parliament', *E.H.R.*, LXXX, p. 262. Dagworth went back to England to report, probably early in December, for he reached London on 22 December (Clarke, loc. cit., p. 61, n. 26).

ing a concerted movement, perhaps arranged at Kilkenny before the parliament broke up. In at least two cases new elections were ordered, but the results were no more satisfactory than before.[65]

The representatives arrived in England at some time in the spring of 1376. Windsor was summoned to England in February, together with Robert Holywood, the chief baron of the exchequer, and William Carlisle, the second baron: the officials of whom the Anglo-Irish were particularly complaining. It is not clear when they left Ireland: Windsor seems to have acted till 20 June. But a whole series of charges against these three and the bishop of Meath had been sent to England, alleging 'extortions, oppressions and injuries inflicted upon divers persons' by them: these were sent back to Ireland by Nicholas Dagworth for investigation, but at the end of the year the commissioners were ordered to stay any process against Windsor, as he had been given a day to answer before the king and council, and we hear nothing more of it. The whole affair had coincided with, and probably been influenced by, the political excitements and factions of the Good Parliament in England. But during the summer the principal officers of the Irish administration had been dismissed, and so far at least the Anglo-Irish had won their case.[66]

We need not concern ourselves with the truth or falsehood of the charges against Windsor. Few medieval officials conformed to modern standards of official propriety, and there is certainly no difficulty in believing that he acted in a high-handed way, which the Anglo-Irish must particularly have resented from a mere upstart knight. But while he was clearly at best a tactless and heavy-handed governor, it is impossible not to feel some sympathy for him: the colonists complained in one and the same breath that he did not conduct an expedition against the Irish, and that he put garrisons in Munster, and showed themselves increasingly unwilling to pay anything towards their own defence, so that he was reduced to a position in which the emptiness of the treasury made loans totalling less than £30 a matter of importance early in 1375. In fact his policy of avoiding major campaigns, which produced no real result beyond that of a temporary truce, sure to be broken before long, and using instead a policy of stationing his professional army in comparatively small garrisons in the vulnerable areas of Munster, was probably the only useful one.[67] But it was necessarily

[65] Lydon, loc. cit., pp. 262–6.
[66] Clarke, loc. cit., p. 63, n. 38, and *passim*.
[67] This policy seems to have been a continuation of that of Clarence, under whom Windsor had first been employed in Ireland. See above, p. 294.

a policy entailing continuous expense, and not producing any immediate spectacular results: it would have taken supreme tact to induce the colonists to pay for it, and this Windsor clearly did not possess, while their taxable capacity was probably in any case less than it would have required.

CHAPTER X

Richard II and Ireland

KILDARE had been appointed on 16 February 1376 to act as caretaker till Windsor returned, or till further order: he was to be justiciar, responsible primarily for Leinster, with the bishop of Meath as his subordinate, in charge of Meath and Munster. Kildare acted from 21 June till 21 September; the bishop was already in Munster, where the war with O'Brien continued. By 24 July it had been decided not to send Windsor back, and Ormond, who was in England at the time, was appointed to succeed him. On 8 August he entered into an indenture with the king to serve for a year with 120 men-at-arms and 200 English archers, and by the end of the month shipping was being arrested for the passage of these men from the ports of Bristol and Chester, and a clerk of the wages had been appointed to pay them, and to be 'overseer of the king's retinue in Ireland'. In May 1377 Ormond was empowered to replace any of these men who left the service for lack of payment by 'suitable persons, English born in Ireland' at the same wages as the English born soldiers. He did not succeed in retaining the full number for the whole period, but the force cost the English exchequer the considerable sum of £5,080 6s. 2d., which seems actually to have been paid. Clearly, in spite of the growing impatience of the English council at the continued drain of money to Irish wars, there was no change of policy.[1]

Ormond took up office at Michaelmas: his retinue did not arrive till 4 October. In December Nicholas Dagworth was recommissioned to go to Ireland 'to survey the state of the land'. The parliament held at Dublin early in January 1377 may have been summoned with a view to this, though it seems unlikely that he arrived in time. But some important things were done in it. The war against the Irish of Leinster seems to have been the main preoccupation of the early winter: we hear that the town of Carlow

---

[1] *Parliaments and Councils*, no. 38; *C.C.H.*, p. 101, no. 59; *Cal. Ormond Deeds*, II, no. 238; *C.P.R.*, *1374–7*, pp. 336, 337; *Cal. Fine Rolls*, *1369–77*, p. 364; *C.C.R.*, *1374–7*, p. 389. In August and September 1376 a number of persons going to Ireland on the king's service had protections (*C.P.R.*, *1374–7*, pp. 336, 337, 338, 344).

had been burnt; that there were wars at Tullow 'in the marches of co. Carlow' against the MacMurroughs, O'Nolans, O'Byrnes and O'Mores; that Art Kavanagh, 'claiming to be captain of the Irish of Leinster', had made war on the Leinster counties and could only be pacified by payment of the fee of 80 marks which he alleged to be owed to him by the king. Ormond had conducted an expedition, in which he was supported by some of the Irish of Tipperary, and in the parliament at Dublin 'Art son of Dermot McMorgh of Kenseley' appeared in person before the justiciar and council and bound himself with his 'nation' and adherence to be faithful and to go to war with the king against the Irish insurgents of Leinster with all his power, and to make faithful stay with the king for a year from 2 February, receiving a fee of 40 marks. About the same time a peace was made with O'Nolan.[2]

The peace with the Irish of Leinster was not a very lasting one, but it freed the justiciar to attend to the affairs of Munster, where the war with Brian O'Brien was still raging, and the peace was further disturbed by a dispute, the causes of which do not appear, between Desmond and the de Burgos. The bishop of Meath had been governing Munster in 1376, and had had the assistance of some at least of the Irish in the war against O'Brien, for the community of co. Limerick in his presence had granted 7 marks to 'McDermot McBreen' for his wages, and those of divers footmen. But he does not seem to have had much success, and by 26 February 1377 the justiciar was about to set out for co. Limerick 'with a great company of men-at-arms, to stay there on the war'.[3]

In fact the expedition does not seem to have begun till April, but by 18 April the government was at Waterford, where news seems to have reached it that the situation had worsened, for on account of the dispute between Desmond and the de Burgos it was decided on 20 April that the chancellor and treasurer, who had been chosen by the justiciar and council to go to England to expound the state of Ireland, should remain, 'for most urgent reasons touching the state of the land, and imminent perils'. By 24 April the government was at Clonmel, by 1 May at Youghal, and by 10 May at Cork, where it seems to have remained for the greater part of the summer. The dispute between Desmond and the de Burgos seems to have been settled at the beginning of June, when Desmond, at the summons of the justiciar, came to Cork 'with a great power of men', and stayed for some days at his own expense. Tur-

---

[2] *C.P.R., 1374–7*, pp. 396, 415; *Cal. Ormond Deeds*, II, no. 238; *C.C.H.*, p. 99, nos. 1–3, 8; p. 100, nos. 12, 27, 30–34; p. 102, no. 79.
[3] Ibid., p. 102, nos. 73, 80; p. 103, no. 91.

lough O'Brien of Thomond, 'captain of his nation', also came to Cork at the justiciar's summons, 'for the reformation of the peace between the lieges of Cork and Limerick and the Irish of the said parts', but we know nothing of any campaign which followed, except that by March 1378 Turlough was a penniless wanderer, driven out of his country by Brian O'Brien for lack of the help which had been promised him.[4]

This was hardly Ormond's fault, for though the death of Edward III on 21 June 1377 made no immediate difference to the situation in Ireland since Richard II, who succeeded his grandfather, was a minor and the council which governed for him would make no dramatic changes, when the justiciar's original indenture of August 1376 expired in 1377 nothing was done to renew his retinue. He was obliged to retain nine men-at-arms and sixty-seven archers at his own expense from 7 October to 20 January. The English council seems, indeed, to have taken little interest in the situation in Ireland, except to revive the indictments of Windsor's time: Ormond, Dagworth and others were commissioned to hear and terminate them. Dagworth himself seems to have been in England in the autumn, returning to Ireland at the end of the year, and during 1378 seems to have been occupied largely in taking indictments against officials, and in investigating the rights of the king in general.[5]

Meanwhile, early in 1378, the Irish war had taken a new and more ominous turn. In January, when the justiciar held a great council at Castledermot, Art MacMurrough of Ui Cennselaigh was still at peace, according to the agreement of the previous year. But by the time the parliament which had been summoned on 22 January met at Castledermot on 8 March, the whole of Leinster seems to have been again at war. Carlow had again been burned, and 'Murgh Obreen', having assembled a great power of the king's enemies in Munster, had arrived in Leinster and was threatening to destroy it, while Art MacMurrough was threatening to burn Carlow again, and 'McMurgh', captain of his nation, O'Carroll and others had risen in war with O'Brien. Faced with this situation, the justiciar was practically powerless. A garrison could be provided for Carlow, but since the retinue had dispersed, he had no force with which to counter any general attack. It was hurriedly

[4] C.C.H., p. 101, nos. 51–53; p. 102, no. 75; p. 103, no. 91; *Parliaments and Councils*, no. 54; *Cal. Ormond Deeds*, II, no. 237; *C.P.R., 1377–81*, p. 382. For Turlough O'Brien, see above, p. 305. He was subsequently retained in the king's service for life at an annual fee (*C.C.H.*, p. 108, no. 53; p. 116, no. 6; p. 151, no. 18; *Council in Ireland*, pp. 18–19).

[5] C.C.H., p. 103, no. 13; p. 104, nos. 62, 69; p. 105, nos. 88–89, 96; *Cal. Ormond Deeds*, II, no. 237; *C.P.R., 1377–81*, pp. 52, 87; *C.C.R., 1377–81*, pp. 26, 171–2, 224, 225, 324, 383–4; *Cal. Inquisitions Miscellaneous*, IV, no. 92.

agreed that Ormond should have two men-at-arms and fourteen archers beyond those retained on his fee, and that the royal service should be summoned for May, the army of Cashel of this year. Meanwhile the only expedient that presented itself was the desperate one of buying O'Brien off: he was offered 100 marks to withdraw with his force. This sum was granted by the clergy, magnates and commons of the Leinster counties, and seems to have been advanced in cash or in kind by individual magnates: O'Brien took a corporal oath before the council to accept these terms.[6]

A dangerous precedent had been set, and the Irish of Leinster were still unappeased. In April the MacMurroughs, O'Byrnes and O'Tooles had risen in war, and by June,

McMurgh, captain of his nation, claiming to be king of Leinster, there being confederated and allied with him all the Irish of Leinster and Murgh O Brien and O Kerwyll and several others, as well Irish as English rebels of Munster, with a great number of men on horse and foot supporting him, with intent to destroy the said parts of Leinster and to make a general conquest on the lieges there, had wickedly risen in open war.

The Irish council agreed that in this emergency the justiciar should retain such a force as he considered necessary at the king's wages, but the treasury being, as usual, empty, Ormond had to advance the money himself. The English council, informed of the situation by the treasurer whom the March parliament had appointed to go to England to report the state of the country and seek a remedy, authorized the employment of these additional troops, and in September a small force, engaged in the first place for half a year, was being sent from England. In April 1379 it was arranged to retain them for a further quarter. It seems that the treasurer should have had 2,000 marks from the English exchequer (he had only had half of it), to be used, together with as much as could be spared from the Irish revenue, in financing local resistance to the Irish: the English council had promised to make further provision for Ireland, but had not done so. It had, indeed, in August 1378, in a general letter addressed to all the lieges in Ireland, reproached them for their divisions and lack of mutual good will, and any effort to provide in common for the common safety, promising to arrange at the approaching parliament for the relief of Ireland and the chastisement of the king's enemies and rebels, but nothing had come of this. In the circumstances it was decided at a council meeting at Castledermot on 30 April, at which representatives from the Lein-

[6] *C.C.H.*, p. 103, no. 17; p. 104, nos. 35, 38–45, 49, 61; p. 105, nos. 82, 90–91, 100, 104, 110; p. 106, nos. 111–12; *Early Statutes*, pp. 472–5; *Parliaments and Councils*, no. 57.

ster counties were present, that what was in hand should be spent on the retinue and the remainder, when it was available, on local resistance. When the quarter ended, on 31 July, it was agreed that since war was still raging the small balance remaining in the treasurer's hands should be employed in retaining the retinue for as long as possible, as the council had still sent nothing.[7]

By August 1379 Ormond was with the king in England, and after treaty with the council obtained provision for the payment of the very considerable sum due to him, and a release from an office becoming increasingly thankless and expensive. At last the earl of March, for whom the Anglo-Irish had asked in 1373, was to be sent, but for the time being John de Bromwych, who had been Clarence's leading retainer, and was now retained by March by a life indenture, was appointed as justiciar. On 26 August the arrest of ships for his passage with a force of sixty men-at-arms and 120 archers was ordered. Ormond had the letters releasing him from office read to the council at Naas on 13 October: Bromwych had not yet arrived, and the council vainly implored him to remain in office for the time being; Kildare too refused, and finally the treasurer, the bishop of Ossory, was induced to act till Bromwych arrived. And at least some sort of settlement had been made with the Irish of Leinster: there had been parleys with MacMurrough, O'Byrne, O'Nolan, O'Toole and other Irish at Baltinglass, and on 19 October at Moone, co. Kildare, 'Art McMurgh', captain of his nation, was admitted to the peace, swearing particularly to see to the safe-keeping of the ways between Carlow and Kilkenny. And by November Ormond was occupied in the wars in Munster.[8]

Bromwych was in Ireland by December, but meanwhile, on 22 October, Edmund Mortimer, earl of March, lord of Meath in his own right, and earl of Ulster and lord of Connacht in right of his wife, the only child of Clarence and Elizabeth de Burgo, had been appointed the king's lieutenant in Ireland. He was to have all the revenues of Ireland, and in addition 20,000 marks from England in three years: once more a serious attempt was to be made to recover the position, though Mortimer had to lend the king £1,000 for the expedition, and an ominous note was struck by the statement that the king was informed that owing to excessive grants the Irish revenue was insufficient for the maintenance of the war and other charges.[9]

[7] *C.C.H.*, p. 105, nos. 92–93, 97–99, 104; *Parliaments and Councils*, nos. 52, 60; *Cal. Ormond Deeds*, II, no. 237; *C.P.R., 1377–81*, pp. 271, 272.

[8] *C.P.R., 1377–81*, pp. 380, 382, 385; *C.C.H.*, p. 106, nos. 5, 8, 15, 26. Ormond was owed £985 12s. 5d., and had to agree to accept 1,000 marks (£666 13s. 4d.).

[9] *Chart. St. Mary's*, I, p. 10; *C.C.H.*, p. 116, no. 21; *C.P.R., 1377–81*, pp. 390, 483.

Mortimer reached Ireland in May with a considerable force, and seems to have made the lordship of Ulster his first objective. The Irish annals say that he went with a great force to Ulster and 'destroyed many townes both spirituall and temporall', naming places which are all in the north-west, so that the campaign seems to have been directed against O'Neill. The government seems to have been established at Down for at least two months, and the annals say that the Irish chiefs, headed by O'Neill, 'came into his house'—i.e. did homage to him. But, they go on,

Art Magennis, king of Iveagh, was taken prisoner by treachery in the house of Mortimer, and the Gaels of Ireland took fear of him from that out, so that they and the English of Ireland avoided him.

The expedition to Ulster seems to have occupied most of the summer, and then Mortimer returned by way of Athlone, where he recovered the castle, and his lordship of Meath. On 3 November he held a parliament at Dublin, where the Statutes of Kilkenny were confirmed, and a grant was made of new customs for three years, as well as a subsidy from the clergy. He seems to have remained in Dublin for the rest of the winter, and was unwillingly involved in December in a remarkable scene, when the bishop of Cloyne, celebrating a mass in the castle chapel for the repose of his wife's soul, introduced a new preface into the mass:

There are two in Munster who destroy us and our goods, namely the earl of Ormond and the earl of Desmond with their followers, whom in the end the Lord will destroy.

The lieutenant and his court hurriedly removed themselves, hoping, we are told, that the bishop was only out of his mind, but he persisted; a charge of heresy was sent to Rome; and Ormond proceeded against the bishop for slander in the court of the archbishop of Cashel and obtained heavy damages and costs.[10]

Meanwhile, fresh war was preparing in both Leinster and Munster. By the end of April 1381 O'Toole had again risen in war. The retinue seems to have been stationed in strategic places throughout the south, but in July the lieutenant was so occupied in Leinster that he could not attend the great council which had been summoned to Clonmel for 5 August, and appointed the treasurer and Sir Thomas Mortimer, his brother, to hold it in his place. A full scale expedition against O'Brien was being planned. The royal

[10] *A. Clon.*; *AU*; *C.C.H.*, p. 109, nos. 100–11; p. 122, no. 26; *Early Statutes*, pp. 478–9; *Cal. Ormond Deeds*, II, no. 245. The bishop had been deprived by the pope by 1394 at latest, and probably by the end of 1392 (*Cal. Papal Letters*, IV, p. 480; *Council in Ireland*, pp. 88, 89, 103, 110, 111).

service of Ireland was summoned to Cashel for the Saturday after
Michaelmas, and at Clonmel the clergy and others of the south and
west agreed to maintain fifteen men-at-arms and 150 archers for
half a year, starting on 15 August. On 23 October the lieutenant
was still at Carlow, but by 4 November he was at Clonmel, and
was in Cork when he died suddenly on the night of 26 December.[11]

A grave emergency was created by this sudden disappearance
of authority. The chancellor and the chief justice, who were in
Cork, wrote hurriedly to the treasurer and the earls of Ormond and
Desmond, asking them to come to Cork at once to provide a justiciar, but they were unable in the interval to hold the retinue together. On 2 January 1382 Mortimer's household, with the whole
retinue of men-at-arms and archers, withdrew towards Leinster
and Meath, leaving the city and county of Cork exposed to the
attacks of 'the nation of the Barrets and other Irish enemies and
rebels then at war', and the whole country in grave danger. The
chancellor issued writs summoning the local prelates and magnates, and representatives of Cork and Limerick, to a council which
met at Cork on 9 January.

In this council, which must have been attended by certain em-
barrassments, since there were present not only the earls of Ormond
and Desmond, but also the bishop of Cloyne, who took a leading
part, everyone showed an understandable reluctance to take upon
himself the office of justiciar. The chancellor having expounded
the position, the magnates and representatives discussed the situation in the absence of the officials, and decided that first of all a
governor must be found. The council, in the king's name, required
Ormond and Desmond—the obvious candidates—to decide between themselves which should undertake the responsibility. Each
replied that, on account of the war raging on his marches, he could
not take office. The bishop of Cloyne then asserted that the land
could not be so well governed by anyone born in it as by a strenuous knight of the realm of England, and the council and magnates
having accepted this proposition, he proposed Sir Thomas Mortimer, both on account of his military ability and because he believed that the retinue, which was under his command, would
more willingly serve under him than under anyone else. Asked
whether Thomas would be willing to serve, the bishop said that if
he could have a certain retinue maintained at the expense of the
country he believed that he would. He produced a schedule of the

[11] *C.C.H.*, p. 108, no. 47; p. 109, no. 81; p. 110, nos. 118–119; p. 113, nos. 166–
72; p. 114, nos. 173–83; p. 119, nos. 132–3; *Parliaments and Councils*, no. 65; *Cal.
Ormond Deeds*, II, no. 249; *Journal of the Kildare Archaeological Society*, VIII, p. 468;
N.L.I., MS 761, pp. 297–8.

numbers required, and the treasurer explained that, judging by his experience, the Irish treasury would be quite unable to produce the sum required. The council then asked the prelates and magnates present if they would undertake to supply the funds needed to retain the retinue for a year, or even part of a year, and, as it was near sunset, they asked for an adjournment.

When the meeting reassembled the next day, the whole body replied that they could not pay such a sum: if such a burden must be borne for a year, it could only be done by the whole land, which must be summoned at one time for the purpose.[12] But since this could not be done without great delay, they unanimously agreed that a justiciar must be chosen at once. Ormond and Desmond again refused to take office; the treasurer, who was next approached, excused himself on grounds of bodily infirmity; the chancellor, John Colton, dean of Dublin, was forced to take office, with great reluctance, and on condition that he should be allowed to relinquish it in the next parliament or great council. Meanwhile, the treasurer was to treat with Mortimer and the retinue to remain till a parliament could meet.[13]

The unfortunate Colton, left in Cork without any retinue, was forced to retain a small bodyguard at his own expense. Meanwhile, on 24 January the king appointed as lieutenant the new earl of March, Roger Mortimer, a child of seven years old. This absurdity was slightly mitigated when the assembly which met at Naas on 3 March, which must have received the news of the appointment with stupefied incredulity, appointed Sir Thomas Mortimer, his uncle, as his deputy, to remain constantly at his side. It was probably also at this meeting, in which only Dublin, Kildare, Louth and Meath were represented, that it was decided that none should leave the country without licence, and that Sir Hugh Cheyne should go to Ulster for the reformation of the peace. And in the south-west war was raging: we hear that, encouraged by Mortimer's death, 'Obreen of Tothemon', with an excessive power, was attempting a general conquest of Limerick, Kerry, and Cork, and it had been agreed that Desmond should go to Limerick 'to repress their malice', receiving 200 marks for a quarter. By April he had been so far successful that a commission of oyer and terminer was issued for these counties. Some action seems also to have been going on in Leinster and the midlands: we hear of prisoners taken from the O'Tooles, and hostages from O'Connor of Irth. A parliament met at Dublin on 16 June, and found the infant lieu-

---

[12] i.e. a parliament or great council must be summoned.
[13] *Parliaments and Councils*, no. 66.

tenant absent on account of illness. The assembled magnates, prelates, and commons angrily petitioned the king, representing that
such a thing had never been heard of since the conquest of Ireland:
it seemed to them that such an assembly could not be called a
parliament, though they were willing in all the circumstances that
it should be held to be one, saving their liberties. It does not, however, appear what was done in it: it had been agreed before it met
to send the treasurer to England to report on the state of the land,
while at some period during the summer another messenger was
sent for the same purpose.[14]

We may well suppose that the representations made were bitter,
but it was not till 1 July 1383 that a new lieutenant was appointed:
Philip de Courtenay, the nephew of the archbishop of Canterbury,
and a member of a great west country family. On 10 July orders
were issued to arrest ships for his passage, and he landed at Waterford on 11 September. Munster was still the chief preoccupation
of the Anglo-Irish government: on 27 January 1384 the royal service was summoned to Kilmallock for a spring campaign against
'Obreen Shamagh' and other Irish enemies, proposing to make a
general conquest of Munster. It does not seem that the campaign
was very successful: by the summer Brian O'Brien had made an
alliance with many Irish from Munster, Leinster and Connacht,
threatening both Munster and Leinster, and by the autumn there
were in addition great disputes between the earls of Ormond and
Desmond, appeased with difficulty in the early winter. And it
seems probable that from early in his career Courtenay was not
on the best of terms with the Anglo-Irish. By March 1384 the
archbishop of Dublin was, with the king's leave, going to England
'to give information touching matters which concern the king's
advantage'. On 10 September the archbishop was appointed chancellor, and seems to have returned immediately to Ireland. Between
26 November and 1 December the lieutenant left Ireland for England, leaving Ormond as justiciar. On 30 December, clearly as the
result of representations made by Courtenay, the chancellor was
ordered to desist from

calling together the council and summoning parliament in Ireland, laying imposts upon the people there, granting charters of pardon and taking great fines
for them to his own use, without special authority of the king or of Philip de
Courtenay his lieutenant in Ireland, and not to meddle under any pretence in
aught save matters which may concern his office and the needful ruling and de-

[14] *C.C.H.*, p. 112, nos. 87, 90, 93, p. 114, nos. 189–90; p. 117, nos. 65–66; p.
118, nos. 80, 92–97, 111–12, 115–16; p. 129, no. 40; *C.P.R., 1381–5*, p. 88; *C.C.R.,
1381–5*, p. 154; *Parliaments and Councils*, no. 67. March's appointment was known
in Ireland by the middle of February (*C.C.H.*, p. 115, nos. 211–15).

fence of Ireland, especially in the lieutenant's absence, as the king has heard . . .
that by colour of his office the chancellor after his last coming to Ireland has
done all those things . . .

It is not clear what underlies all this: there is no other trace of any
parliament or great council in 1384, nor of any subsidy. But Courtenay was successful in the struggle: on 1 March 1385 he was reappointed as lieutenant, and was to hold office for ten years from
the day he landed, with all the revenues of the land, while on 8
March the bishop of Ossory, the treasurer, was appointed as chancellor. Moreover, Courtenay was ordered to deal with erroneous
judgements, lands unduly given, charters improperly granted, and
other things done to the king's prejudice since his departure.[15]

Courtenay landed at Dalkey on 6 May to find trouble in the
midlands, where O'Connor Faly was at war, and also in the Leinster mountains. In July the lieutenant was so engaged in the war
against MacMurrough, O'Nolan, O'Byrne and O'Toole that he
was unable to attend a council at Kilkenny, while O'Neill, who
had had considerable successes in Ulster in the previous year, was
now threatening Louth in alliance with MacMahon. Moreover, it
does not seem that the resentments of the colonists against the lieutenant had been appeased, for when on 23 October he held a great
council at Dublin he took the remarkable step of inviting any who
felt themselves to be aggrieved by any extortions, oppressions or
imprisonments committed by him to complain. Nobody took this
opportunity, and the main business of the council was clearly the
discussion of the dangers of the land. The prelates, lords and commons, gloomily considering the great power of the 'Irish enemies
and English rebels', assisted by other enemies of Scotland and
Spain, and their own weakness and poverty, so that they feared an
imminent conquest of most of the country, could suggest no other
remedy than the coming of the king in person. The archbishop of
Dublin and the bishop of Ossory were chosen to bring the message
to the king: if he could not come himself, he should at least send the
greatest and most trustworthy lord of England.[16]

Unfortunately for the success of this embassy, Richard, now in
control of his kingdom, had already determined to give Ireland to

[15] *C.P.R., 1381–5*, pp. 288, 383, 455, 462, 532, 540; *C.C.R., 1381–5*, pp. 356,
482, 500, 532–3; *Analecta Hibernica*, II, pp. 200, 289–90; N.L.I., MS 761, pp. 297–
8; *C.C.H.*, p. 121, nos. 77, 85; p. 122, no. 28; p. 123a, no. 31 (Jan. must here be
a misprint for June); p. 128, no. 15; p. 130, nos. 72–3. Courtenay had £1,152
from the Irish revenue in the year following September 1383 (*Analecta Hibernica*,
II, p. 200).
[16] *C.C.H.*, p. 123, nos. 1–2; p. 126, no. 195; p. 127, no. 210; p. 128, nos. 8–10,
15; p. 129, no. 31; *Early Statutes*, pp. 484–7; *C.P.R., 1385–9*, p. 91.

the man who was certainly in his eyes the greatest and most trustworthy lord of England, Robert de Vere, earl of Oxford. On 12
October, because he wished shortly to give de Vere the title of
marquis of Dublin, he had made him certain grants in England,
'to hold until he has conquered Ireland and can hold it in peace'.
De Vere was formally created marquis of Dublin on 1 December,
and was given the land and lordship of Ireland with all its profits.
In future all writs in Ireland would run in his name, and he had in
effect palatine rights there. Courtenay continued as lieutenant till
Easter 1386, when he was discharged, protesting that this was contrary to his indenture with the king, by which he had been appointed for a set term, not yet expired. After him the prior of the
Hospital acted as 'justiciar of the marquis' till the arrival of Sir
John de Stanley, lieutenant of the marquis, at the end of August.[17]

It seems to have been contemplated that de Vere should come
himself to Ireland. In March and April 1386 shipping was being
provided for his passage, and on 23 March he was granted the
ransom of John of Blois for the maintenance of 500 men-at-arms
and 1,000 archers in Ireland for two years after his arrival there.
In June arrangements were being made to muster at Bristol the
retinues of the earl of Ormond and Sir Roger Drury, all of whom
were to be English, going to Ireland as part of a greater number
retained by the king's order by the marquis of Dublin. But English
political affairs were going badly: by this time there seemed to be
an imminent danger of a full-scale invasion from France, and feeling was rising high against the king's favourites. In the English
parliament of October 1386 there was a violent clash between the
king and his opponents, which resulted in the triumph of the opposition, and the putting of the royal power in commission, nominally for a year. The king left Westminster and for ten months from
February 1387 toured the midlands and the north, organizing a
new royalist party. De Vere, who had been created duke of Ireland
just before the parliament met, remained at Richard's side, and
no attempt seems to have been made to organize Ireland as a base
for royal power: instead de Vere was made justice of Chester and
north Wales, from which the king was to draw his chief military
support for the rest of the reign. The commission must have had
suspicions of Ireland, for on 2 January, 'on information that divers
Irish rebels had entered the realm as spies', their arrest was ordered

---

[17] *C.P.R., 1385-9*, pp. 112-13, 115; *C.C.R., 1385-9*, p. 232; *C.C.H.*, p. 130, nos.
1, 2, 13; p. 131, no. 31. Courtenay represented that he had been deprived of all
his goods in Ireland by de Vere's officers and had been in danger of arrest and
imprisonment: the English council agreed that he should be paid 1,000 marks in
compensation (Devon, *Issues of the Exchequer*, p. 241).

but this seems to have embarrassed only perfectly innocent students at Oxford. The archbishop of Dublin, who had been one of the messengers sent by the great council of 1385 and was in England from 14 January 1386 to 27 September 1387, was with the king, for he was one of those who witnessed the sealing of the judges' opinion, condemning the whole programme of the opposition as illegal, at Nottingham in August 1387. And the idea that de Vere might go to Ireland in person was not quite abandoned: in the winter of 1386–7 horses were to be provided for his expedition, and in the course of 1387 a number of persons obtained grants of protection because they were going to Ireland on the king's service in de Vere's company.[18] But nothing came of this, and Richard's attempt to recover power at the end of the year met with complete failure; de Vere, the only one of the favourites to take up arms to support his master, was outmanoeuvred, and at Radcot Bridge on 19 December the campaign collapsed. De Vere fled overseas and died at Louvain in 1392; the king's cause was in ruins, and most of his friends were condemned, and many executed, in the Merciless Parliament, which met in February 1388. Till May 1389, when Richard recovered power, the commission continued to govern.

Meanwhile the marquis's government in Ireland had had to function as best it could. We cannot suppose that what was happening in England was without its repercussions in Ireland, but there is no trace of this. Desmond and the sheriff of Cork had been appointed as deputies for the defence of Munster in January 1386, and by March 1387 there were renewed disputes between Ormond and Desmond: the earl of Kildare was appointed to settle them. In Leinster MacMurrough was again at war in 1386, but was again admitted to the peace on 1 November, and O'Byrne and O'Toole were certainly raiding the marches in the same year, for the commons of Fingal granted a subsidy to maintain guards against them. A good deal of attention was paid to the affairs of Ulster, Meath, and even Connacht, which were, of course, in the wardship of de Vere because of the minority of the earl of March, but the government remained in Leinster and Meath, spending some days as far west as Tristernagh, co. Westmeath, in April 1387.[19]

The condemnation of de Vere in the Merciless Parliament had of course annulled the grant of Ireland, which now reverted to the king. Stanley had returned to England in 1387 and the bishop of

[18] *C.P.R.*, *1385–9*, pp. 91, 117, 123, 131, 132, 136, 157, 248, 275, 278, 312, 322, 352; ibid., *1388–92*, p. 88.

[19] *C.C.H.*, p. 127, no. 238; p. 131, no. 42; p. 134, no. 149; p. 135, no. 160; p. 136, no. 191; p. 137, nos. 217, 220, 226.

Meath had been acting as de Vere's justiciar: on 4 April 1388 he was ordered to remove and abolish de Vere's seal, banners and pennons, which he had erroneously continued to use after de Vere's forfeiture was commonly known, and to return to the king's. On 26 April the order was repeated, and all de Vere's seals were to be destroyed in an assembly of notables summoned by writ for the purpose, and the fragments deposited in the treasury. Further, all offices granted by de Vere were to be resumed, and regranted to suitable persons, and de Vere's conviction of treason was to be notified by writ to prelates, magnates, and local authorities, and publicly proclaimed. A clean sweep was made of all the principal officers of the Irish administration by English letters patent, though since the field of choice in Ireland was necessarily limited some of those newly appointed had, like the justiciar himself, previously served de Vere. In the absence of the Irish chancery rolls for this year we cannot tell what was done about the lesser officials, but no doubt any who might be regarded as de Vere's dependants fell with him.[20]

In July a great council was held at Castledermot. It must have been in it that the archbishop of Armagh was chosen as a messenger to the king and council, and there were also present at Castledermot messengers from England. It seems to have granted a subsidy, which was being levied in October, and it must have been here that the clergy and commons of co. Dublin granted that they would find eighty armed men at their expense, and that it was agreed to adopt the English statute of that year fixing the wages of labourers. The council seems to have been adjourned to Clonmel a fortnight later, when the justiciar was unable to attend, and appointed deputies to hold it, and he also appointed a deputy in co. Louth because he was unable to go there, but no reason is given.[21]

The bishop continued to act as justiciar till the autumn of 1389. At some time in 1388–89 there seems to have been an expedition to the north: at any rate he summoned the service of Carlingford in this year, but we know nothing more of it. There is certainly no suggestion of vigorous action by the justiciar in the provinces: he appointed Ormond as 'keeper and governor' of counties Kilkenny and Tipperary, and Sir Thomas de Burgo as 'keeper of Connacht

---

[20] *C.C.R., 1385–9*, pp. 388, 411; *C.P.R., 1385–9*, pp. 436, 438, 441. The persons appointed as judges may not have taken up office: new appointments were made in Ireland in the course of the summer (*C.C.H.*, p. 137, nos. 4–6; p. 138, no. 62).

[21] *Parliaments and Councils*, no. 71; *C.C.H.*, p. 141, nos. 187–91, 200; p. 142, no. 220; *Early Statutes*, pp. 488–90.

and deputy of the justiciar', and proliferated grants of power to individuals to treat with whatsoever enemies and rebels in their own districts. None of this was new, but the bishop seems to have made appeasement into a system to an altogether new degree.[22]

Thomas de Mortimer had been appointed as justiciar on 5 March, and there were proposals to revive the duchy of Ireland for the king's uncle, the duke of Gloucester, one of the appellants. But nothing came of this; Mortimer never took office, and after Richard had re-assumed power on 3 May 1389 no more was heard of these proposals. On 1 August John de Stanley, who had been de Vere's lieutenant, was appointed justiciar for three years. He landed at Howth on 22 October, and his first action must have been to summon the parliament which met at Kilkenny on 3 December, and was adjourned to Castledermot and later to Ballymore and Naas. And probably in December Stanley was presented with an opportunity which so occupied him that he was unable to attend the session at Castledermot on 3 February and had to appoint the keeper of the rolls as his deputy. O'Neill had been steadily pressing on the colonists in Ulster, and the government had been in no position to take effective action against him: now Neill O'Neill the younger, the son of Neill Mor, had been taken prisoner, and towards the end of January 1390 Stanley was on his way north. He was at Drogheda on 21 January, and at Dundalk on 24 January, and by 20 February he had made an agreement with O'Neill by which the prisoner was released in exchange for hostages: his eldest son, and two of his nephews, with four other unnamed hostages. The children were in the castle of Trim by the first week in Lent, and the agreement was read in the parliament at Castledermot on 12 March. The hostages remained in custody till at least 1402, and were clearly a major factor in inducing O'Neill to submit to Richard II in 1395.[23]

The position in Ulster had been temporarily transformed by this success, but the rest of the country remained disturbed. In the midlands there seems to have been war early in 1390 between Kildare and the O'Dempseys, and at some time during his term of office Stanley made an expedition against the Irish in the neighbourhood of St Mullins, co. Carlow. In January and March 1391

[22] N.L.I., MS 761, pp. 297–8; *Llanthony Cartularies*, p. 169; *C.C.H.*, p. 141, nos. 184, 199, 216; p. 142, nos. 225–6.
[23] *C.P.R., 1388–92*, pp. 20, 91, 110, 134, 275, 300; ibid., *1399–1401*, pp. 327, 330; ibid., *1401–5*, p. 183; *C.C.H.*, p. 142, no. 238; p. 144, nos. 76–77; p. 145, nos. 136, 140; p. 147, nos. 222, 240; p. 151, no. 19; *Analecta Hibernica*, II, p. 214; *Council in Ireland*, pp. 191, 262–3; *AU*; *AC*; below, p. 328.

he was in Meath, and in the late summer of that year he was in Munster, testing letters at Kilmallock. He had had reinforcements from England in the spring or early summer, but there does not seem to have been any major campaign. And by this time there was an enquiry on foot into his official conduct. In February 1391 the bishop of Ossory and others were commissioned to assemble, either all together or in separate meetings, the 'better, more suffi-cient, discreet and fit prelates, lords, magnates and commons' of the whole country, and to enquire on oath concerning the state of Ireland and its causes and remedies; the capture and release of O'Neill and all other Irish prisoners since Stanley's coming; his retinue and its numbers and composition; the Irish revenue and his dealings with it; and finally the behaviour of officials in general. There seems to be no trace of these assemblies, though it is reason-able to suppose that some at least were held, and one result may have been the order of 20 May to the treasurer to pay no fees or wages to any who do not occupy their office in person, as the king is informed that many officials occupy their offices by deputies, 'who cease not and fear not day by day to inflict oppressions, grievances and excessive extortions upon the people of the land'. And whether as the result of the enquiry or not, in September the bishop of Meath was re-appointed as justiciar, and was sworn in before the council at Trim on 3 October.[24]

This was clearly intended only as a temporary measure: in May 1392 the duke of Gloucester was appointed lieutenant, with the intention that he should lead a major expedition to Ireland. He was to have a total of 34,000 marks from the English exchequer over a period of three years, and when his patent was cancelled on 23 July 1392 he had already had 9,500 marks for his own wages and those of the troops going with him on the king's service to Ireland. On 24 July Ormond was appointed as justiciar, and orders were issued to survey the muster of the force which, by advice of the council, the king had ordered to set out for Ireland. But the bishop must have continued to act till 8 October, when Ormond's patent reached him, with letters dated 25 July announcing the king's intention of sending March as soon as possible: meanwhile he was sending the chancellor, the archbishop of Dublin, with a force, and 2,000 marks to be delivered to the treasurer and used for the defence of the land. And in October one of the absentees, Philip Darcy, was setting out for Ireland by the king's command

24 *C.C.H.*, p. 147, nos. 234–5; p. 148, nos. 42–43; *Council in Ireland*, pp. 94–95; *Reg. All Hallows*, pp. 89–90; *Chartae, Privilegia et Immunitates*, p. 88; *C.P.R., 1388–92*, pp. 404–5, 479; ibid., *1391–6*, p. 10; *C.C.R., 1389–92*, p. 255. Stanley was not in disgrace: see *C.P.R., 1388–92*, p. 499.

'to recover his inheritance and the king's lordships, as well as to defend the same against the Irish rebels'.[25]

There is for this period a survival unique in Ireland: a roll of petitions to the council which vividly illustrates the state of the country at this time. We hear of a war in 1391–2 between O'Reilly and the Anglo-Irish of Meath, 'so that the commons of Westmeath in the parts of Kells were about to be lost'. The justiciar and the archbishop of Armagh, acting with the commons of Meath, could find no other remedy than to buy O'Reilly off by promising him 84 marks, and inducing one of the local gentry to give his son as a hostage. In Leinster MacMurrough, O'Nolan, O'Ryan and others had been openly at war; the town of Carlow, still the seat of the exchequer and the only fixed centre of government, had been burnt by MacMurrough, O'Carroll, and 'all the other Irish enemies of the king of the parts of Leinster and Munster', and the county, with much of co. Kildare, had gone up in flames. No official action seems to have been taken against them except by the chancellor, the archbishop of Dublin, who represented that he had come to Naas with a force of 200 at his own expense, upon which the enemy retreated. And though a number of private persons had joined him, the townsmen of Castledermot simply bought MacMurrough off by a fine of 84 marks, which they assessed among themselves. The men of Colmanstown in the royal manor of Newcastle Lyons, co. Dublin, represented that it had recently been burnt by the Irish; some of the tenants were killed, and sixteen were dead of the late pestilence there, so that only three remained. In Munster, where in the summer of 1392 the son of Murrough O'Brien, reputed 'the most dangerous and chief malefactor of all the king's enemies', had risen in war with 'an excessive power', planning, so Ormond said, to destroy the lieges of both Munster and Leinster (Ormond's remedy had been to give his father 70 marks to draw him off),[26] we hear that the cities of Cork and Limerick and the town of Youghal were in the march, and the country round them so destroyed and ruined by Irish enemies and English rebels that no one could go there without an armed escort.[27] Ormond's brother had maintained 'a great company of horse and foot for these four or five years . . . at his own costs' to

[25] Gilbert, *Viceroys*, pp. 552–7; Devon, *Issues of the Exchequer*, p. 247; *C.C.H.*, p. 149, no. 3; *C.P.R., 1391–6*, pp. 86, 126, 134, 231; *Council in Ireland*, pp. xvi–xvii, 54–55, 255–60.

[26] *C.C.H.*, p. 150, no. 21. This was so far successful that O'Brien was not among MacMurrough's allies in this year.

[27] For recent petitions from Cork and Limerick, see *C.P.R. 1388–92*, pp. 152, 495, 496; ibid., *1391–6*, p. 203; *C.C.R. 1385–9*, pp. 521–2.

defend counties Cork, Tipperary and Kilkenny, and now successfully petitioned for a grant, under a statute confirmed in the parliament held at Kilkenny in January 1393, of all the lands in the
cantred of Offa west of the Suir except the baronies of Cahir and
Dromloman, since they were destroyed and laid waste by Irish
enemies and English rebels because of the negligence of their owners.
The state of Connacht is sufficiently expressed by the fact that the
bishop of Clonmacnoise, sent as a justice there in 1390 to investi-
gate disorders in Galway, was refused an escort by the king's
sheriff.[28] In the north O'Neill had led an army against Dundalk in
1392,[29] and we hear that the whole Carlingford peninsula, with
its castles, was wasted and destroyed.[30]

All things considered, it is not surprising that on receiving his
patent of appointment on 8 October 1392 Ormond, instructing
the former justiciar to summon a council at Castledermot as soon
as possible, wrote: 'the charge seems to us very difficult, nor are we
capable of undertaking it in the state the land is in at present, nor
do we know how we can sustain it without great dishonour and
destruction of our poor and simple estate'. And the discontents of
the country were further exemplified when the archbishop of
Dublin complained that the earl of Kildare had illegally quartered
one hundred men called 'kernemen' on his lordship of Ballymore
Eustace, co. Kildare, to such destruction of him and his tenants
as had not before been seen there.[31]

The archbishop seems to have been one of the messengers to the
king chosen in the parliament of Kilkenny in January 1393, and no
doubt it was their representations which caused the confirmation
on 26 June of the ordinances made for the government of Ireland
in October 1357, and an order, dated 15 July, that they should be
proclaimed and enforced in Ireland. In July, too, reinforcements
led by Sir Thomas Mortimer were being sent to Ireland, and
the bishop of Annaghdown, on his petition alleging that the malice
and power of the king's enemies made it impossible for him to stay
in his diocese, or even to receive its revenues,[32] had leave to recruit
200 archers in England for service in Ireland. At Christmas the
justiciar was at New Ross; the parliament which had been summoned to Castledermot for 19 February 1394 was prorogued on 6
February before it met, on the grounds that Ormond would then

[28] E. Curtis, 'The Pardon of Henry Blake of Galway in 1395', *Journal of the
Galway Archaeological and Historical Society*, XVI, pp. 186–91.
[29] *AU*; *AC*; *ALC*.
[30] *Council in Ireland*, p. 208.
[31] Ibid., pp. xvi–xvii, 130–2.
[32] This was because of the schism in the church. See above, pp. 139–40.

be occupied in Munster. It seems to have been now that the royal service was summoned to Kilmallock, and there was certainly an expedition to Munster. In May we hear that a great expedition against the O'Byrnes had recently been undertaken by the justiciar, while at some time before this he had also been active in Westmeath. And in May a potentially revolutionary decision was taken by the council: the employment of one Richard Sonner (? *recte* Gonner), smith, to remain at Carlow for three months making 'gonnes' and other armaments for the defence of the town. It was, however, to be long before firearms became an effective factor in Irish wars.[33]

But now a supreme effort was about to be made. The political climate of England was settled, and external dangers had been removed by the conclusion of a truce with France, while there was a nominal peace with the Scots. The time had come for that visit of the king in person for which the Anglo-Irish had long been asking, and the death of Richard's queen, Anne of Bohemia, on 7 June may have precipitated his decision. At any rate, on 16 June he ordered a proclamation that all men born in Ireland should return there immediately, as he had taken the firm resolve shortly to go there in person, 'in certain hope . . . of better and more prosperously ruling the land and people there than heretofore used to be done'. The export of provisions from Ireland was forbidden; commissions were issued for the arrest of ships for the expedition; on 1 July all yeomen and archers of the crown were ordered to be with the king by 3 August at latest, ready to sail to Ireland. A little later the bishop of Meath, who was then in England, and with Baldwin de Redyngton, the controller of the household, and John de Stanley, was being sent ahead to prepare for the king's arrival, was empowered to receive to the king's obedience all rebels in Ireland willing to come in, and to survey his castles there. Purveyance was to be made against his arrival, while the most elaborate preparations, including the raising of loans amounting to well over £20,000, were being made in England. And the great absentee lords of Ireland, headed by the earl of March, who brought with him Sir Thomas Mortimer, as well as men with experience of Irish administration, such as Philip de Courtenay, and other magnates, of whom the duke of Gloucester was the greatest, were all preparing retinues. When Richard sailed from Haverfordwest

---

[33] *Council in Ireland*, pp. 130–2; *C.P.R., 1391–6*, pp. 298, 301, 357; *C.C.R., 1392–6*, pp. 227–8; Gilbert, *Viceroys*, pp. 566–7; Lynch, *Feudal Dignities*, p. 332; *C.C.H.*, p. 150, nos. 1, 4, 12–13; p. 151, no. 16; N.L.I., MS 761, pp. 297–8. *Les Obrynnes* of *C.C.H.*, p. 150, no. 4, may have been O'Briens, not O'Byrnes, but Ormond had certainly been active in Wicklow (ibid., p. 151, no. 17).

towards the end of September 1394, he had with him the largest army ever sent to Ireland during the middle ages. Something over 5,000 men-at-arms and archers had been engaged for the expedition, and in addition there were the Cheshire archers and other retainers who had been summoned on 1 July, at whose numbers we can only guess, as well as the forces raised in Ireland by the magnates, and by the commissions of array ordered by the king. The total may have amounted to between 8,000 and 10,000 men: as Froissart says,

it is not in memory that ever any king of England made such apparel and provision for any journey to make war against the Irishmen, nor such a number of men-at-arms nor archers.

It was comparable to the armies which were led against France during the Hundred Years' War.[34]

Richard landed at Waterford on 2 October. Not all his entourage had yet arrived—Gloucester, in particular, did not reach Ireland till near the end of the month—and in any case, it was still too early to undertake a campaign which would have to be fought largely in heavily wooded country: the leaves were still on the trees, and his archers would have lost much of their efficacy. It was not till 21 October that Richard left Waterford; on 28 October, by which time Gloucester had joined him, he attacked MacMurrough in the wood of Leighlin, 'which is his principal fortress', and drove him out; on 30 October MacMurrough and others submitted, and O'Byrne, O'Toole and O'Nolan were brought to Dublin with the king, though MacMurrough was left at large for the time being.[35]

At Dublin a parliament was held on 1 December, which must have been summoned before Richard left Waterford. Before it met it had already been decided to move the exchequer and the bench from Carlow back to Dublin, nominally for the convenience of the people, but probably because the earl of Nottingham, the marshal, who accompanied Richard, was now lord of Carlow. We have no account of the deliberations of the parliament, but they were undoubtedly in the spirit of the letter which Richard had written from Haverfordwest to the duke of Burgundy, in which he stated his purpose as 'the punishment and correction of our rebels there, and to establish good government and just rule over our faithful

34 J. F. Lydon, 'Richard II's Expeditions to Ireland', *Journ. R.S.A.I.*, XCIII, pp. 135–49; A. Steel, *The Receipt of the Exchequer*, pp. 70–71.
35 E. Curtis, 'Unpublished Letters from Richard II in Ireland', *Proc. R.I.A.*, XXXVII C, pp. 276–303; M. D. Legge, *Anglo-Norman Letters*, nos. 154, 271; Lydon, loc. cit.

lieges'. It is probable that it was in this parliament that the negotiations which were to lead to the submission of the great majority
of the Irish chieftains in the next few months were planned. The
new factor in the situation was, of course, the presence of the king
with an overwhelming armed force, much of which he was em-
ploying in a ring of garrisons round the Irish of Leinster, while
some had been sent as far afield as Cork. But it is clear that Richard's forces were employed primarily in Leinster, and that his first
objective was to restore the English position there: elsewhere the
display of armed might which this involved would act as a warning. We can take it that all, or almost all, of the magnates and
prelates were present, including the archbishop of Tuam, who was
with the king at Christmas. Gloucester was sent back to England
to inform the council and the parliament which met at Westminster
in January and made substantial grants in aid of the war in Ireland; his return to Ireland with several other magnates and a force
of about 260 men was being prepared by the beginning of February.[36]

Meanwhile, affairs in Ireland had been progressing rapidly.
Though there was activity in Leinster—we hear on 6 January that
Kildare was occupied in the king's wars in Leinster, the earl of
Rutland was taking submissions in Wexford and Nottingham was
negótiating with MacMurrough—the main centre of interest in
January was clearly in Ulster, where the archbishop of Armagh
had been conducting intensive negotiations with the Irish. The
younger O'Neill's hostages, about whom he was deeply concerned,
were still in the castle of Trim,[37] and the whole position was complicated by the fact that he was nominally the tenant of the earl of
March, as earl of Ulster, and that in the course of the expansion of
the O'Neill power which had taken place since the murder of the
Brown Earl two generations earlier much territory had been occupied, either by him or by his *irrachts*, to which the earl laid claim,
as well as by the 'bonnaght' of Ulster, which seems to have been
much in his mind.[38] Nevertheless, on 8 January 1395, the king
could write

From day to day we have, thank God, pleasant news, that is that O[neill] and
our other Irish rebels will come to surrender to us, submit, recognize their
offences, and receive for them whatever we will devise

and, though the younger O'Neill held back, on 19 or 20 January

---

[36] *C.C.H.*, p. 154, nos. 54–55; *Anglo-Norman Letters*, no. 3; Curtis, *Richard II in
Ireland*, pp. 123–4, 127–8; Lydon, loc. cit.; *Misc. Annals*, p. 153; *C.P.R., 1391–6,*
pp. 525, 586–7.
[37] See above, p. 322.   [38] See above, p. 216.

his father, both for himself and as proctor for his son, did homage and fealty to Richard in person at Drogheda, undertaking to surrender to March the bonnaght of Ulster and all other services which they or their ancestors owed to the earl's ancestors. This had been preceded by a discussion with March in the king's presence as to the position of the other Irish chiefs of Ulster, on which they were unable to agree—it was left to be decided by the king—and as to the lands which March claimed, which O'Neill agreed to give up. It remained for the younger O'Neill to appear in person, but the first step towards a settlement in Ulster had been taken.[39]

The king was back in Dublin by 1 February, and by this time action in Munster was beginning to bring results. Before the end of January the king had heard that 'our rebels who call themselves kings and captains of Munster and Connacht' were ready to do homage. This was a little premature: there was apparently to be heavy fighting in Cork in March, and none of the Connacht men, English or Irish, came in till April, but by 4 February Richard had received from Brian O'Brien of Thomond a letter in which O'Brien undertook to find pledges for his fealty to the king, and, rather surprisingly in view of the history of Munster in the last generation, asserted that

among all the English and Irish of your land of Ireland I have acquired neither lands nor possessions by conquest, nor made any profits save such as your predecessors . . . granted and gave to my predecessors.

These protestations in no way prevented him from attempting to deter O'Neill from submitting: on 26 February the younger O'Neill wrote to the archbishop of Armagh

according to your sage counsel we made to come to us all the great men of the Irish of Ulster to consult with them about my going to the king's court, and there were with me then envoys from O'Brien, O'Connor, MacCarthy, and many others from the south, urging me strongly not to go to the king.[40]

The principal activity of February was, however, in Leinster. Here Nottingham, who as lord of the liberty of Carlow had a special interest, had been negotiating with MacMurrough, and on 7 January made an indenture with him 'in a field between Tullow and Newcastle', by which at MacMurrough's petition the king received him to his grace and peace, and MacMurrough swore to give full possession to the king of everything which he or his men had lately

[39] *C.C.H.*, p. 154, no. 53; *Richard II in Ireland*, pp. 105–7, 144–6; 'Unpublished Letters from Richard II in Ireland', loc. cit. p. 287; *Anglo-Norman Letters*, nos. 143–4; below, pp. 331–2.
[40] *Richard II in Ireland*, pp. 74–75, 115–16, 143, 146–7; 'Unpublished Letters', pp. 287–8.

occupied in Leinster, and undertook that all his subjects and tenants in these places would swear fealty to the king. He swore further that before the first Sunday of Lent he would leave all Leinster to the true obedience, use and disposition of the king, and that
he would deliver his brother as a hostage by 21 January. In return
he was guaranteed an annual payment of 80 marks to him and his
heirs for ever, and his wife's inheritance in the barony of Norragh.[41]
Finally he undertook that 'all the armed men of war of his company, household or nation' should leave Leinster and go with him
at the king's wages to make war on other lands occupied by the
king's rebels, and he and his men should have all the lands they so
acquired to hold in perpetual inheritance from the king and his
successors as his true lieges and subjects. He was followed in these
undertakings by all his *irrachts*, each of whom was to be provided
with an annual fee for life, as well as wages to attack the king's
enemies elsewhere, and MacMurrough finally undertook that he
would make war on any who failed to keep the agreement. In pursuance of this agreement letters patent were issued on 12 February,
empowering Nottingham to receive the liege homage of the Irish
of Leinster, both MacMurrough and others who had already come
to the king's obedience and any who might do so in future, and to
assign lands to the captains and leaders of men of war leaving
Leinster according to his discretion. Ormond, Desmond, and all
other subjects were to counsel, aid and obey Nottingham in this.[42]

We have no means of telling who had originally proposed this
remarkable scheme, or whether it was ever really supposed that it
could be carried out. Its attractions for the English were obvious,
but it also offered advantages to the Irish, who undertook to give
up recent conquests, which they may well have feared that in the
new situation they would be unable to hold, but not apparently
the lands which they had held at the beginning of the century, and
were offered in return the chance of making conquests elsewhere
which they would hold 'in perpetual inheritance'. But in fact by
the time Richard left Ireland there was no room for this, for practically every important chief in Ireland, with the exception of
O'Donnell and the other chieftains of the north-west, had sub-

[41] MacMurrough had married, *c.* 1390, Elizabeth Calf or La Veele, widow of
Sir John Stanton of Otymy, tenant of two-thirds of the barony of Norragh (approximately the modern barony of Narragh and Reban East, co. Kildare) in her
own right. In January 1391 her lands had been taken into the king's hand because
she was adherent to 'MecMorgh', one of the king's principal enemies in Ireland
(*C.C.H.*, p. 148, no. 27). See E. Curtis, 'The Barons of Norragh, co. Kildare',
Journ. R.S.A.I., LXV, pp. 84–101, and J. Otway-Ruthven, 'Knights' Fees in
Kildare, Leix and Offaly', ibid., XCI, p. 170.
[42] *Richard II in Ireland*, pp. 76–77, 80–85. Cf. ibid., pp. 98–99.

mitted to him. It may well be that one of the factors producing these submissions had been the prospect of having the Leinster Irish added to Richard's forces in the way proposed, and this may very probably have been the real motive of the king's advisers in accepting a scheme which on the face of it seems wildly impracticable.

However this may be, on 16 February 1395 'in a certain field vulgarly called Balygory by the town of Carlow on the side of Slievemargy' there was a dramatic meeting. Nottingham, with some of his following, met Gerald O'Byrne and Donal O'Nolan, captain of his nation, coming from a wood where many armed Irishmen were assembled, and had the letters patent of 12 February read, first in Latin, and then translated into English and Irish by a Hospitaller, 'learned in the Irish tongue'. Then the principal Leinster chiefs, including MacMurrough himself, successively did homage in Irish. On the next two days, at Carlow and Castledermot, some minor personages came in. Then on 19 February in Dublin Donat O'Byrne, who had done homage there the day before, swore before the king himself to observe the agreement of 7 January. The submission of Leinster was thus complete, though on Richard's journey southwards in March a number of the Leinstermen took oath to the king in person.[43]

Meanwhile negotiations were actively in progress in Ulster; in Meath, where we hear that 'O Fearghail submitted to Mortimer at Trim and returned with honour on that occasion'; in Munster, where Ormond was negotiating with O'Brien and perhaps Desmond with MacCarthy; and in Connacht. On 12 February letters patent had empowered Nottingham to take the liege homage of 'Brien O Brien duke of Tothmond' and all others of Thomond who came to the king's faith and obedience, and on 4 March, 'in a certain field called Maghadhir by the town of Quin', the letters were read, and O'Brien, who had himself submitted to the king in Dublin on 1 March, repeated the oath of allegiance, followed by MacNamara and the rest of the Irish of Thomond. In March, with the bishops of Killaloe and Kilfenora, he went to Dundalk and did homage to the king in person for himself and the captains of Thomond.[44] And by this time the chiefs of Ulster, among whom the archbishop of Armagh and Sir Thomas Talbot had been working indefatigably, and of Meath had come in. By 5 March the king had gone north again to Drogheda, and here, and at Dundalk,

---

[43] *Richard II in Ireland*, pp. 75–85, 100–01, 103–5, 108–9, 129.
[44] *Misc. Annals*, p. 153 (*s.a.* 1394); *Richard II in Ireland*, pp. 93–94, 137; M. V. Ronan, 'Some Mediaeval Documents', *Journ. R.S.A.I.*, LXVII, pp. 229–34.

which he reached before 19 March, the captains of the Irish of
Meath and Breifne, and those of Ulster, including the greatest of
them all, Neill O'Neill the younger, appeared, doing homage and
fealty in person.[45]

By this time Richard must have had a letter from his council in
England, urging him to return as, among other things, it was reported that the Scots were about to break the truce. By 14 April
the rumour of his imminent departure had reached O'Neill, and no
doubt it had been decided on while Richard was still in co. Louth.
He was in Drogheda on 21 March, when he received a letter from
Malachy O'Kelly of Ui Maine, the first of the Connacht Irish,
among whom both Murrough O'Kelly, archbishop of Tuam, and
John of Desmond, the earl's brother, had been very active, to
show signs of submitting. He must then have gone south through
Dublin: by 28 March he was at Connell, co. Kildare, on 29 March
at Castledermot, on 30 March at Carlow and Leighlin Bridge, and
by 3 April at Kilkenny. Everywhere on this journey he received
the personal homage of the Leinstermen, who swore to observe the
agreement made in January. Some of MacMurrough's reeves swore
to exercise their office before their lord, the marshal, and a great
effort to cut passes in the woods of this area seems to have been
contemplated, for on 4 April the sheriffs and seneschals of the
Leinster counties and Waterford were ordered to be at Leighlin
Bridge, each with four men from each ploughland of his county,
with axes and provisions for eight days, 'to do what shall be enjoined on behalf of the king'.[46]

The king remained at Kilkenny throughout April, and now the
submissions from the south and west came in. Already, on 13 February, Tadhg MacCarthy, 'Prince of the Irish of Desmond', had
written professing that he and all his ancestors had been the king's
men from the time of the conquest, attempting nothing to the prejudice of him or his lieges: he could not then come to the king, but
would gladly come in when Richard approached Munster. It seems
that after this he was defeated in battle by Rutland about the
middle of March, and now, on 6 April, he appeared with Mac-
Carthy Reagh and did homage. During the rest of the month the
remaining captains of Munster submitted, as well as O'Connor
Don of Connacht. Then Richard moved to Waterford to take ship:
on 30 April O'Brien and O'Connor Don, both of whom had already
done homage, repeated it there, and the bishops of Kilfenora and

---

[45] *Richard II in Ireland*, pp. 87–90, 97–98, 101–3, 116–17.
[46] Ibid., pp. 64–65, 71–72, 100–01, 104–5, 108–11, 124–5, 137–40; *A.P.C.*, I,
pp. 57–59; *C.C.H.*, p. 155, nos. 65–67.

Kilmacduagh declared on oath that they had power to do homage for the 'names and nations' of all their *irrachts*. On the next day, when Richard had already taken ship, O'Connor Don, with William de Burgo (the Clanrickard Burke) and Walter de Bermingham of Athenry, formerly rebels against the king, came on board and were knighted. On 15 May the king sailed for England.[47]

This expedition, the greatest display of armed might ever seen in Ireland during the middle ages, had had, up to a point, a remarkable success. The Irish chiefs, with very few exceptions, had said that they were, and should be, the king's lieges; they had agreed that they held their lands of him; they had said that they were ready to defend his standard. The element that has not so far been considered is that of the Anglo-Irish.

On 1 February Richard wrote to the regent and council in England that there were in Ireland three classes

wild Irish, our enemies, Irish rebels, and obedient English . . . the said Irish rebels are rebels only because of grievances and wrongs done to them on one side, and lack of remedy on the other. If they are not wisely treated and put in good hope of grace they will probably join our enemies.

This has been generally interpreted as meaning that the three classes are the Irish in general, the 'degenerate English', and the English lieges. But it is not easy to believe that when Richard wrote Irish rebels he meant English rebels. In the seventeenth century, indeed, the distinction between the old English and the Irish had ceased to be made in many official documents, but there is no evidence that this was so in the fourteenth. All the language of the submissions suggests that it was not. Not very many English submitted, as far as the evidence goes, but those who did are nearly all described as English rebels, and certainly none as Irish rebels. In 1399 the Irish council wrote to the king of the Irish enemies and the English 'nations' which are rebels in all parts of the land. Richard himself had written in January of 'O'Neill and our other Irish rebels'. Moreover, his language in the letter of 1 February seems to echo that of the Irish chiefs themselves. On 7 January O'Connor Faly wrote: 'I know that I have transgressed against your excellency before these times, mainly because I found no one to do justice between the English and me.' At some date before 19 January Neill O'Neill the elder said

[47] *Richard II in Ireland*, pp. 62–63, 65–68, 90–95, 99–100, 107–8, 111–15; 'Unpublished Letters', loc. cit., pp. 287–8; *Anglo-Norman Letters*, no. 159. The text says that O'Brien and O'Connor Don appeared at Waterford on 20 April, but 30 April must be intended.

when I heard of your joyful coming to the land of Ireland I greatly rejoiced and now rejoice, hoping to obtain justice for many injuries done by the English marchers to me and mine, and if I have in anything offended against your majesty's subjects, I have not done it to deny your lordship, which I have ever recognized and now continually recognize, and if I could have had justice from any minister of yours for the injuries done to me, I would never have made the reprisals (*vindicacciones*) which I have made.

Again, in an undated letter written to the archbishop of Armagh, probably soon after 19 January, O'Cahan says: 'whatever evil I have done to the marchers I have done in retaliation for their wrongs against me'. Such language as this seems clearly to lie behind the phraseology of Richard's letter, and it seems a forced interpretation to suppose that here, and here alone, Irish means English.[48]

On this interpretation, Richard was distinguishing between the wild Irish, those who had never submitted to the crown—principally O'Donnell and his *irrachts*[49]; the Irish rebels, the great majority, who were prepared to call themselves the king's lieges, but said they had been driven to self-help by the failure of his ministers to do justice; and the English. It is of course true that by no means all the English of Ireland could be described as obedient, but nor could all the English born in England: the degree of disorder produced by them, except perhaps for the very spectacular misdoings of the first earl of Desmond earlier in the century, was not markedly greater than was perfectly normal in any medieval state. The chief difference in Ireland was that, particularly in Connacht, where as we have seen royal power had really ceased to operate, they inevitably allied themselves with the Irish, becoming involved in the confused pattern of warfare that went on among the rival Irish clans. The submissions do not include many of the English, but it is clear that in fact more, probably many more, obtained individual pardons from the king.[50]

Ormond had continued to act as justiciar while the king was in Ireland, but when Richard sailed March was left as lieutenant.

---

[48] *A.P.C.*, I, pp. 55–57; Curtis, *History of Mediaeval Ireland* (2nd ed.), pp. 267, 272; *Richard II in Ireland*, pp. 71, 73, 79, 129, 131–2, 142–3; *Anglo-Norman Letters*, nos. 16, 143; *Council in Ireland*, p. 264.

[49] O'Donnell does, however, seem to have been in some sort of tenurial relation to the earls of Ulster at the beginning of the century, and submitted to Talbot in 1415 and to March in 1425. See above, p. 216; below, pp. 349, 363–4.

[50] E. Curtis, 'The Pardon of Henry Blake of Galway in 1395', *Journal of the Galway Archaeological and Historical Society*, XVI, pp. 186–9; *Journal of the Kildare Archaeological Society*, VIII, p. 470; *Cal. Pembroke Deeds*, no. 84. There are more than twenty letters under the Irish great seal between December 1394 and April 1395 which do not appear in the calendar in printed sources alone, and it would seem that the roll omitted a great many of the instruments of this period.

The problems of Ireland had not, of course, been settled by the events of the last few months: at most conditions had been established in the framework of which a reasonably satisfactory solution might have been worked out. But there were endless possibilities of dispute between English and Irish as to lands occupied by the Irish and claimed, often with good legal title, by the English, and only a strong and impartial hand could have disentangled the chaos with reasonable satisfaction to each side. And March was only just twenty-one, a very young and inexperienced man, of whom impartiality could hardly be expected, since he was lord of Ulster, Trim and Connacht. It was not of much help that Sir William Scrope, the chamberlain, had been left behind as justiciar, for it was intended that they should act separately: in July it was expressly stated that it was necessary that the government of the country should consist of two persons, the lieutenant in one part of the country and the justiciar in another, and that they could rarely meet. When on 25 April 1396 March and Scrope were reappointed, March's sphere was defined as Ulster, Connacht and Meath; Scrope's as Leinster, Munster and Louth. This arrangement was repeated in September 1396, and again in January 1397, when March's infant son, Edmund, temporarily replaced his father. March was reappointed for three years in April 1397, and the arrangement seems then to have been less formal, for we hear not of a justiciar, but of an arrangement in the indentures between the king and March by which Sir Edward Perrers should govern in Munster and Leinster in the lieutenant's absence.[51]

The working out of the settlement with the Irish was thus left principally to March, though in making new arrangements for the financing of the chancery establishment in July 1395 the king laid down that though the exchequer was to meet any deficit, preference was to be given to the payment of 'all sums granted whilst the king was in Ireland to Irishmen submitting to the king's allegiance'. Quite soon after the king's departure the Irish government was asking whether such Irish captains who had subsequently risen in war with banners displayed should still be paid these annuities. In fact, wars seem to have continued as before. Before Richard had left Ireland O'Neill had written to him anxiously that he learnt that March intended to attack him as soon as the king had gone, and the annals say that in 1396 March with Ormond, Kildare, 'the Galls of Ireland and a host of Gaels' made an incursion into

---

[51] *Cal. Ormond Deeds*, III, pp. 350–51, 353–4; *C.P.R., 1391–6*, pp. 575, 607, 710–11, 715; ibid., *1396–9*, pp. 29, 58, 62, 118, 147, 185. The initial appointment of March and Scrope was no doubt made under the Irish seal and has not survived.

Ulster after March had made a treacherous raid on O'Neill. They plundered and burned Armagh, and 'took sway over Ulaidh after that'. We hear too of attacks by March on O'Farrell and O'Reilly, and it is clear that no satisfactory or permanent settlement was made. There is no evidence as to what was happening in the rest of Ireland: Rutland, created earl of Cork, probably soon after Richard's arrival, seems to have remained in Ireland for over a year, but we know nothing of his activities, nor of those of either Ormond or Desmond. In Leinster there seem to have been disturbances on both sides. And by no means all of the Irish had really accepted the settlement made by their chiefs. O'Connor Don had written on 3 April 1395 that he would come to the king 'although against the will of divers Irish of my lordship', and O'Neill on 24 March that 'I cannot trust my own people since they see me turned away (declinatum) from them to your most excellent majesty'.[52]

March was in England in the first half of 1397, and does not seem to have returned to Ireland before the end of July at the earliest. He was again in England in the spring of 1398, when his council was retaining captains to serve in the Irish war: no doubt the retinue of one hundred men-at-arms, two of them bannerets and eight knights, 200 mounted archers and 400 archers on foot with which he had come to Ireland in 1394 was much reduced. His appointment as lieutenant was repeated for two years on 24 April, the unexpired portion of the appointment of the previous year. In June he held a council at Naas in which he was granted a subsidy for the wars. But he seems to have aroused the king's suspicions, for on 26 July his brother-in-law, Thomas Holland, duke of Surrey, the king's half-brother, was appointed to replace him, his appointment dating from 1 September. But by this time March was already dead, killed in an engagement with the O'Byrnes at Kellistown near Carlow on 20 July. His son was not yet seven years old, and once again the whole Mortimer inheritance was in the king's hand. In Ireland the council chose Reginald de Grey of Ruthyn, lord of the liberty of Wexford, who had arrived in Ireland in the previous autumn, to act as justiciar: he held a council at Dunboyne on 1 August which again granted a subsidy. Surrey, the lieutenant, reached Ireland in the autumn, and was sworn in on 7 October.[53]

[52] C.P.R., 1391–6, pp. 595, 602; ibid., 1396–9, p. 2; Lambeth, Carew MSS, vol. 619, no. 207; Richard II in Ireland, pp. 113–14, 124–5, 133–4; Misc. Annals, pp. 55–7.
[53] C.P.R., 1396–9. pp. 118, 147, 185, 204, 336, 402; ibid., 1399–1401, p. 81; ibid., 1422–9, p. 34; C.C.R., 1396–9, p. 325; G. A. Holmes, The Estates of the Higher Nobility in Fourteenth Century England, pp. 76, n. 7, 129–30, 130–31; Dugdale, Baronage, I, p. 150; N.L.I., MS 761, pp. 291–2; Marlborough, Chronicle.

Meanwhile, in the autumn of 1397 the king had announced that he intended shortly to come to Ireland in person,[54] and though nothing came of this at the time, by the spring of 1399 preparations were being made for his second expedition. Since he returned to England in 1395 affairs there had seemed to go prosperously for him. A twenty-eight years truce with France, sealed in March 1396, had been crowned by his marriage to the French king's daughter, and at home serious opposition among the magnates seemed to be dead. But the French alliance aroused suspicions and uneasiness, added to by Richard's grandiose foreign schemes—he dreamed of being elected as king of the Romans, and had also projected an Italian expedition. And in the autumn of 1397 Richard, who had neither forgotten nor forgiven the proceedings of the appellants in 1388, at last took his revenge. In a new appeal of treason Gloucester, Warwick, Arundel, and Arundel's brother, the archbishop, were attacked: the archbishop was banished; Arundel was executed; Gloucester died, almost certainly murdered, in prison at Calais and was posthumously condemned; Warwick was sentenced to perpetual banishment. Some lesser persons were impeached, including Sir Thomas Mortimer, March's kinsman, who was with him in Ireland.[55] And Richard's suspicions may well have been aroused against March himself, for it is alleged that when March appeared at the second session of this parliament at Shrewsbury on 27 January the people met him joyfully, wearing his colours and hoping through him, the heir presumptive, for deliverance from the grievous evil of such a king, a demonstration which may well have had something to do with his removal from office in the summer.[56] Meanwhile, the king's friends had been rewarded with lavish grants, and it was declared that any attempt to reverse the acts of this parliament was *ipso facto* treason. Moreover, though Norfolk and Hereford, two of the original appellants, had not only been omitted from the appeals of 1397 but had themselves been appellants, a quarrel between them in which Hereford alleged that Norfolk had warned him that they were both about to be destroyed by the king gave Richard an opportunity to banish them in the autumn, Norfolk for life and Hereford for ten years. When in February 1399 Hereford's father, John of Gaunt, duke of Lancaster, the king's uncle, died, Richard extended Hereford's sentence of banishment to life and confiscated his inheritance. And meanwhile he had exacted heavy fines from all those individuals and

[54] *C.C.R.*, *1396–9*, pp. 154, 157.
[55] Ibid., pp. 60–61, 226–7, 244.
[56] Adam of Usk, *Chronicon*, ed. E. M. Thompson, pp. 18–19.

corporations who had been in any way implicated with the appellants in 1387–8, had made extensive use of the courts of the constable and marshal, and had in many ways alarmed and alienated public opinion at every level.

It would seem that Richard himself felt confident that he had adequately secured his position. The expedition to Ireland must already have been decided on before John of Gaunt died on 3 February, for writs to arrest ships for it were issued on 7 February. In January the king had received petitions from Ireland representing, no doubt among other things, that the king's revenues were gravely diminished by excessive grants of lands and offices, and these petitions may have precipitated the decision to make a second expedition. The main problem was clearly in Leinster, where March had led an expedition against 'Obren' in 1397 as well as the fatal one of 1398. In May 1399 Surrey was granted the barony of Norragh for the life of Art MacMurrough, who had forfeited to the king. But there had been plenty of trouble elsewhere: in 1398 Kildare had been taken prisoner by O'Connor Faly, and we hear of wars in both Munster and Meath.[57]

Richard landed with his army at Waterford on 1 June, and wrote soon afterwards informing the regent that Surrey had taken a great prey of cattle, and had, in an expedition against 'Macmurgh, O Brin and the others' killed 162 armed men and kerns. From Waterford he went to Kilkenny, and from there marched against MacMurrough. It seems that MacMurrough could not be brought to battle, and in a parley with Thomas le Despenser, created earl of Gloucester after the duke's death, refused to contemplate submission, claiming to be rightful king of Ireland. Richard, receiving this news at Dublin, which he had reached on 1 July, marched south again to burn MacMurrough out of his woods,[58] but before long he had messages from the council in England, informing him that Henry of Lancaster had landed in Yorkshire to claim his inheritance, and urging his immediate return. On 27 July he sailed from Waterford; by the middle of August he was a prisoner in Henry's hands, and by 30 September Henry had made himself king.

---

[57] *C.P.R., 1396–9*, pp. 511, 572; *Cal. Fine Rolls, 1391–99*, p. 293; Marlborough, *Chronicle*; *A. Clon. AC.*
[58] 'Unpublished Letters', p. 289; *Anglo-Norman Letters*, no. 286.

CHAPTER XI

Lancastrian Ireland: the Growth of Faction

WITH THE departure of Richard and his army, followed by that of Surrey, Ireland was left in a state of confusion. Surrey's brother, Edmund Holland, later earl of Kent, seems to have acted as his brother's deputy for the time being: later the bishop of Meath acted as justiciar.[1] The council had written anxiously to England, probably early in September: Mac-Murrough, who had begun the war before Richard came, had continued it after his departure and was demanding the barony of Norragh and his annuity, with the arrears. He was at open war, and had now gone to Desmond to assist the earl of Desmond to destroy the earl of Ormond[2]: afterwards he would return with all the power he could from Munster to destroy the country. O'Neill had assembled a great army to make war unless he had the release of his hostages, as he said was promised. Surrey's soldiers were out of pay and discharged: there were no troops for the defence of the country, and no money to pay them, for the money which the lieutenant had had for the purpose had been brought back to England. The Irish enemies were strong and proud and of great power, and there was nothing to resist them, for the English marchers were neither able nor willing to ride against them without a greater paramount power. As for the rebel English nations, they were nothing but sturdy robbers, and more oppressive to the poor lieges than the Irish, whose accomplices they were. The king had no profit of the revenues of the land, for the law could not be executed, and in any case much of the country had been given as liberties to others or was given over to rebellion and war, so that the king had only

---

[1] The bishop was justiciar in January 1400, and must have been acting for some time (*C.C.H.*, p. 159b, no. 11). Surrey's commission had of course lapsed with Richard's deposition.

[2] The trouble between Ormond and Desmond in this period may have been caused by rivalry over Youghal and Inchiquin. See above, pp. 296–7 and below, p. 358.

the county of Dublin and part of Kildare.[3] All the other profits of
the land had been given to others, so that little or nothing came
into the exchequer, and nonetheless many fees and annuities to
both English and Irish were charged on it; no baron of the exchequer was learned in the law, and the other exchequer officials
were illiterate and incompetent.[4]

This melancholy picture seems to have been only too true, but
Ireland was the least of the problems which faced Henry IV after
his usurpation of the throne. He may ,indeed, well have feared
that the claims of the infant earl of March, who was, strictly speaking, the right heir to the throne, might find support in Ireland, but
the problems of establishing his position in England, where the
first rebellion against him occurred in January 1400, and of providing against the external dangers from France and Scotland, besides the danger in Wales, where Owen Glendower's rebellion
began in September 1400 and was not finally suppressed till 1408,
necessarily took first place. But a list of articles drawn up by lords
and commons in the English parliament on 31 October for submission to the king includes the necessity of making provision for
the safe-keeping of Ireland, and on 10 December John de Stanley
was appointed as lieutenant for three years.[5]

Stanley took up office between 10 March and 13 March 1400,
and one of his first acts was to ratify, at the king's order, the letters
patent by which Richard II had granted MacMurrough Norragh
and the annuity. Then he left Dublin and toured Meath, Leinster,
and parts of Munster. At Skreen, co. Meath, probably on 29 April,
he held a local council, in which the community of Meath granted
a subsidy for the defence of their marches; at the end of May the
chancery was at Waterford and Clonmel, and because he was occupied in 'divers arduous business in the parts of Meath, Leinster
and Munster' deputies were appointed in Ulster and Connacht.
In July he went as far north as Dundalk, and at the end of the
month the community of co. Louth granted a subsidy to resist
'Nelanus Onell, captain of the Irish of Ulster'. In October he was
in Kilkenny, and in January 1401 the community of co. Dublin
was being assembled to grant a subsidy. And meanwhile he and
others were inquiring as to the property left in Ireland by Richard,

[3] The number of liberties had been added to by the grant of Cork to Rutland
and Louth to Surrey, while the wardship of March's lordships had been granted
to Surrey for three years without rent (*C.P.R., 1396-9*, pp. 429, 483).

[4] *Council in Ireland*, pp. 261-9. For the revenue at this period, see below, p. 343.

[5] *Anglo-Norman Letters*, no. xxiv; *C.P.R., 1399-1401*, p. 92. Stanley was to have
a retinue of ninety-nine men-at-arms and three hundred archers, and was paid
£1,000 in the autumn of 1400 (Devon, *Issues of the Exchequer*, p. 279).

selling the 'fuel of wood and coals' provided for Richard's household and left in Dublin, and arranging to ship to England the military stores (including cannons) which the keeper of Richard's privy wardrobe had left to be kept in the great hall of Dublin castle. It is clear that he was beset by financial difficulties, for by December 1400 he had complained to the king that the payments which should have been made to him from the English customs revenue were much in arrears, and on 12 July 1401, after he had been superseded, a general order was issued to respite his debts in Ireland till Christmas, when certain sums of money were due to him by the king, so that he could not pay his own debts till then.[6]

Stanley's appointment had been subject to the proviso that he might be removed at three months' notice if the king in person, one of his sons, or an earl of the blood royal came to Ireland, 'there to abide upon the wars', and on 18 May 1401 he was notified that the king's second son, Thomas of Lancaster, then aged twelve or thirteen, had been appointed as lieutenant. Ten days earlier he had been ordered to keep safe till further order all military stores and other property of Richard II now in Ireland, and to keep in custody without ransom all rebels and hostages, orders which must have been made in anticipation of Lancaster's appointment. Stanley went to England in May, leaving Sir William Stanley as his deputy. Lancaster was formally appointed on 27 June for six years from 18 July: Sir Stephen Le Scrope, his deputy, reached Ireland on 23 August, and Lancaster himself arrived in Dublin on 13 November. But in effect Le Scrope governed Ireland for the next few years, and in December, because there was war everywhere, was formally appointed as Lancaster's deputy and 'governor of the wars' in his absence. During 1402 local deputies were appointed, for Kildare and Carlow, and for Ulster.[7]

Even before Lancaster's arrival Le Scrope had been negotiating with the Irish chieftains of Leinster and the midlands. By 14 September he had induced O'Connor Faly to enter into an indenture, which was being considered by the English council in November, promising to be a faithful liege; on 8 November O'Byrne entered into a similar undertaking; on 13 December MacMahon undertook to be a faithful liege, and to be ready with all his power

[6] *C.C.H.*, pp. 155–9, *passim*; p. 155, no. 6; p. 156, no. 42; p. 157, nos. 72–74; p. 158, nos. 114–16, 119, 4–5; p. 159a, no. 7; p. 159b, nos. 8–9; p. 160, no. 19; *C.P.R., 1399–1401*, pp. 154, 214, 397, 523; *Cal. Fine Rolls, 1399–1405*, p. 50; *C.C.R., 1399–1402*, p. 79; *Anglo-Norman Letters*, no. 381.

[7] *C.C.R., 1399–1402*, pp. 338, 342; *C.P.R., 1399–1401*, p. 507; *C.C.H.*, p. 160, no. 21; p. 162, no. 84; p. 164, no. 174; p. 170, no. 67; p. 172, no. 21; Marlborough, *Chronicle*.

against the king's enemies and rebels, and was granted in return the land and lordship of Farney, co. Louth (now co. Monaghan), except the castle; on 4 February 1402 O'Reilly recognized that he and all the Irish under his rule were the king's lieges, and swore to observe this allegiance during the minority of the earl of March. There must be a background of military action to all this, but we hear only of an attack by MacMurrough on Wexford, in the course of which he seems to have been defeated, for many of his hired Munster troops were killed.[8]

But however successful Scrope had been for the time being in the east, he does not seem to have gone further afield, and in Munster we hear that in 1402 there was a great war between Ormond and Desmond,[9] in which the MacWilliam Burkes came to the assistance of Ormond, who in 1401 had made an alliance, sealed by a marriage, with Theobald fitz Walter de Burgo, by which they and their kindred undertook to aid each other with their whole power in all wars and disputes, saving only more ancient friendships. But in the spring or early summer of 1402 Scrope must have gone to England, for in August he was empowered to arrest ships in the ports of Chester and Liverpool for the passage of himself and his troops to Ireland.[10]

By this time financial difficulties were becoming acute. In August 1402 the Irish government wrote to the king that Lancaster was

so destitute of money that he has not a penny in the world, nor can he borrow a penny, for all his jewels and his plate, beyond what he must keep of necessity, are put and remain in pledge. His soldiers have departed from him, and the people of his household are about to depart . . . And the country is so weakened and impoverished by the long nonpayment, as well in the time of our said lord your son as in the time of other lieutenants before him, that it can no longer bear such a charge.

But there was little to be hoped for from England: it must have been after this letter had been received that the English treasurer wrote to the king that he had been ordered to pay in haste great sums, including £1,000 to Lancaster for Ireland, but Lancaster was still in arrears for a great part of what he should have had for the first half year, and there was not even enough in the treasury to pay the messengers sent with letters summoning a meeting of the council. At the end of the year Lancaster himself wrote from

---

[8] C.C.H., p. 165, nos. 232–3, 236–7; A.P.C., I, p. 176; AC; ALC.

[9] The fourth earl of Desmond had died in 1400; the fifth earl was only about sixteen in 1402, and was theoretically in wardship, but Desmond was now really beyond the control of the Dublin government.

[10] AC; ALC; Misc. Annals, p. 171; Cal. Ormond Deeds, II, nos. 352–3; C.P.R., 1401–5, p. 135.

Drogheda that most of his soldiers had come to their captains, demanding leave to return to England, saying that they could no longer serve unless their wages were paid, and many had already gone. And the deficit continued to rise, even though in June 1403 he was given an assignment on the customs in the port of Kingston upon Hull, by which time, of the yearly sum of £8,000 which he should have received, £9,156 was in arrears. In April 1405, because of the non-payment of what was due to him, all his jewels and plate were pledged, and by 1407 the arrears amounted to more than £20,000.[11]

While there was little to be had from England, there was less to be had from Ireland. In March 1403 the lieutenant was granted all revenues belonging to the king in Ireland, to be applied to the defence of the land and other expenses there. Unfortunately, by this time this meant almost nothing. A fragmentary statement of the Irish revenue which can be dated c. 1406 shows that the annuities charged on the king's demesne manors exceeded their total annual value; that of the two great wardships in the king's hand only £17 remained to the king out of the annual revenue of the lordship of Trim, and nothing could be received from the lands of the earl of Desmond, because of the rebellion; that the whole fee farm rents of the cities of Waterford and Cork had been granted away. We must suppose that the rest of the revenue was in much the same state. Subsidies were certainly granted from time to time in Ireland: in the parliament held at New Ross in December 1401 various counties made grants in kind for the expenses of the lieutenant's household, and similar grants seem to have been made at the parliament held at Dublin in April 1402, when a cash subsidy seems also to have been granted, and there were further grants in kind in September. There were also the usual local grants, made presumably in county courts or local councils, to maintain soldiers for the defence of a particular march for a limited time.[12] But none of this went very far, and this background of constant financial embarrassment must largely explain that acceleration in the decline of English power in Ireland which is so apparent in Henry's reign.

Lancaster returned to England on 8 November 1403, leaving Scrope as his deputy. But on 2 February 1404 Scrope suddenly left

[11] F. C. Hingeston, *Royal and Historical Letters during the Reign of Henry IV* (Rolls Series, 1860), I, pp. 73–76; *Anglo-Norman Letters*, no. 331; *C.P.R., 1401–5*, pp. 266, 269, 464; ibid., *1405–8*, pp. 18, 385, 431, 445; *C.C.R., 1402–5*, pp. 198, 446–7. Lancaster was paid £1,200 sometime in 1402 (Devon, *Issues of the Exchequer*, p. 287).

[12] *C.P.R., 1401–5*, p. 212; Trinity College, Cambridge, MS O.8. 13 (fragments of an account bound in as flyleaves); *C.C.H.*, p. 161, nos. 61–64; p. 162, no. 65; p. 165, nos. 228–9; p. 166, nos. 242–3, 249–50, 253, 14.

Ireland, having made no provision for the carrying on of the government, so that the land was left 'in great desolation', with the king's enemies and rebels preparing to seize the opportunity, and little or nothing in the treasury to hire soldiers or pay the fees of officials. In this emergency a great council at Castledermot granted Ormond, 'as their soldier and governor and not as justiciar or officer of the said land', a subsidy from the whole of Leinster and the counties of Meath, Louth, Waterford and Tipperary, while Dublin, Waterford, Drogheda and the other towns were to contribute proportionately. They undertook to make a further grant if necessary, and they emphasized that the grant was made on condition that coign and prises of victuals without payment should cease while he was justiciar, and that the grant, made in such necessity for their own protection and defence, should not be made a precedent.[13]

The crisis of the year was in Ulster, where the annals say, 'the Galls were driven from the whole province, and the North was burned . . . and the monasteries were despoiled'. This seems to have happened in the early summer, and it appears that a great council was hurriedly summoned to Castledermot in which fresh subsidies were granted—the commons of co. Dublin granted 9d. on each ploughland towards the support of 800 footmen going to recover Ulster, destroyed as well by the Scots and other enemies of the 'out isles' as by the Irish. There seems to have been an expedition, probably in July, and on 12 August another great council at Dublin considered the recovery and relief of the parts of Ulster, which had been destroyed and devastated, and from which the lieges had been expelled or had fled. Unless they were brought back before the grain sown that year was reaped Ulster would never be recovered, and the enemy would have an unimpeded way into Louth and Meath. McGuinness, O'Hanlon, MacGilmurry, MacCartan and 'McGion' were named as the principal destroyers, and held the road into Ulster strongly. It seems that a fresh expedition followed, which must have been successful, for Ormond was still gratefully remembered by the Ulster colonists some seventeen years later.[14]

By October 1404 Scrope was returning to Ireland, but in June 1405 he went again to England, this time having appointed Ormond as his deputy. When Ormond died in September, Kildare was chosen by the council to succeed him, and because Kildare was too occupied in Leinster to go to Connacht Sir William de Burgo was

---

[13] *Council in Ireland*, pp. 269–72.
[14] *Misc. Annals*, p. 173; *C.C.H.*, p. 178, no. 77 (c); *Analecta Hibernica*, II, pp. 206, 207–8; P.R.O., London, S.C. 1/57/69.

appointed keeper there. We hear that on Corpus Christi day 1406 the citizens of Dublin, with the country people, vanquished the Irish enemies, and that in the same year the prior of Connell routed an Irish force, but nothing of what the justiciar did. In the autumn Scrope returned, and in 1407, presumably in the course of a tour in Ormond's lands, which were in wardship, 'gaue an overthrow to the Irish of Mounster, by whome Teige O'Keruell, prince of the territory of Elye, was slaine'. By the end of 1407 Scrope was returning to England, and on 8 December appointed the new earl of Ormond (who was about seventeen) as his deputy during his absence. But in the spring of 1408 a fresh expedition under Lancaster, whose patent had been renewed in 1404, 1405 and 1406, and who now in July entered into fresh indentures with the king, was being prepared. He was to be paid 7,000 marks a year for three years, and the old debt of £9,000 was to be paid off within this time, elaborate assignments being made to secure payment. He was to remain with his retinue in Ireland for three years from 1 May, unless summoned to England by the king or council, when he might appoint a deputy and still receive the whole sum. If he returned to England of his own accord, there was to be no reduction for six months, but after that payment was to be at the discretion of the king and council. If after the end of three years either payment or sufficient assignments could be made for 7,000 marks a year for the remainder of the term of twelve years for which he had been reappointed in 1406 he was to be bound to remain in Ireland with his retinue for this period.[15]

Lancaster landed at Carlingford on 2 August, and at once made his way to Dublin, where his first act seems to have been to arrest Kildare, apparently for irregularities committed while he was justiciar, and imprison him till he made fine. He seems to have established himself at Kilmainham by 12 August, and here, according to Marlborough, he was presently wounded in an attack made by the Irish and hardly escaped death. Then he had the royal service proclaimed at New Ross, and on 13 September issued a safe-conduct to all coming to him in the company of Ormond, whom he had ordered to be present with him in person, with all his power of horse and foot, in the journeys to be made against certain Irish. There was a campaign in Leinster, and throughout the winter his headquarters seem to have been at Kilkenny, where in January he held a parliament 'for a tallage to be granted'. Then, in the middle

[15] C.P.R., 1401–5, pp. 456, 464, 503; ibid., 1405–8, pp. 57, 143, 237; Marlborough, Chronicle; AC; AU; A. Clon.; Grace, Annals; C.C.H., p. 179, no. 29; p. 184, no. 157; Cal. Ormond Deeds, II, no. 391; A.P.C., I, pp. 313–18.

of March 1409, he returned to England, leaving Thomas le Botiller, prior of the Hospital, as his deputy, since Scrope had died of the plague at Castledermot on 4 September.[16]

Lancaster never returned to Ireland: he was later employed in the wars in France, and was killed at Baugé in 1421. But he remained nominally lieutenant till 1413: in August 1409 the English council considered that it would be expedient that John de Stanley should be lieutenant, if the king and Lancaster agreed, and suggested an arrangement by which Lancaster should receive 2,000 marks a year from the revenues of Ireland and 1,000 marks from the king, 'so that the king be discharged of him and his people'. But it seems that either Lancaster or his father refused to accept this, and indeed there can have been little likelihood of his getting anything from the Irish revenue. In June 1410 Lancaster was petitioning the council to give him an assignment for £3,000 of the old debt and £4,666 13s. 4d. (i.e. 7,000 marks) for the custody of Ireland for the year beginning 1 May 1410, 'according to the tenor of the indentures made between the king and the petitioner'. The council replied tartly that if he would perform the covenants contained in the indentures they would do their best to secure him payment. In July they estimated that £2,656 13s. 4d. was required for Ireland—approximately the sum estimated for Carlisle and the west march of Scotland—but in April 1411 they made Lancaster a new assignment for £5,086 13s. 4d.[17]

Meanwhile the government of Lancaster's deputy in Ireland had been arousing a considerable volume of complaint. We hear that in 1410 he made an expedition against the O'Byrnes, in the course of which some of his troops deserted to the enemy; in 1411 there was trouble in Meath, where the annals say that the sheriff was taken prisoner by O'Connor Faly, and in Munster the Geraldines were warring among themselves and Desmond was driven out by his uncle. Late in the year an afforced council at Naas elected the archbishops of Dublin and Cashel to go to the king to declare to him the evils of the land. It seems likely that complaints against Botiller had already reached England, for just after the council meeting at Naas letters reached Ireland ordering the magnates to certify as to the government of the country since Lancaster's departure. But it was not till August 1412—it seems immediately after the English council had been considering the evil government

---

[16] *C.P.R., 1408–13*, p. 85; ibid., *1413–16*, p. 195; Marlborough, *Chronicle*; *A. Clon.*; *C.C.H.*, p. 190, no. 46; p. 191, nos. 75, 78–79; p. 192, nos. 123, 128, 152; *Cal. Ormond Deeds*, II, no. 396.

[17] *A.P.C.*, I, pp. 319–20, 340–1, 350; ibid., II, p. 15.

of the deputy of 'Monsieur de Clarence' (Lancaster had been created duke of Clarence in July) and had decided to discuss the problem with Clarence's council to have their advice as to a remedy—that Botiller was ordered to appear in person before the king in England 'to answer touching what shall be laid against him'. He seems simply to have ignored the summons: on 20 November the chief justice of Ireland was ordered to have it proclaimed throughout Ireland that he was to be before the king in February on pain of forfeiture. Whether he appeared or not we do not know, but on 20 March 1413 Henry IV died, and the grant to Thomas of Lancaster lapsed and was not renewed, although he remained lieutenant until the new lieutenant actually arrived in Ireland.[18]

On 8 June 1413 Sir John de Stanley, whom the council and the new king had wanted to appoint in Lancaster's place in 1409, was appointed as lieutenant. He was to hold office for six years, taking the issues of the land. For the first three years, starting at the beginning of July, he was to have such a force as seemed good, and was to receive £2,000 a year, half yearly in advance, from the English treasury. In August ships were being arrested for the passage to Ireland of Desmond and Ormond, each with a considerable force: the annals say

The earl of Ormond came to Ireland, bringing the power of the king of England with him this year. And the earl of Desmond came to Ireland, and many Englishmen came with him to devastate Munster.[19]

Stanley himself arrived in September (he was sworn on 25 September), but he died on 18 January 1414. The annals attributed this to the lampoons of the poets: he was

a man who granted no protection to cleric or layman or to the poets of Ireland, for he plundered every one of its clerics and men of skill in every art on whom he laid hands and exposed them to cold and beggary. He plundered Niall son of Aed O hUicinn in Usnagh of Meath ... After this the Ui Uicinn made lampoons on John Stanley and he lived only five weeks till he died from the venom of the lampoons.

The Anglo-Irish complained more temperately that he had paid little or nothing of his debts since he first came to Ireland under Richard II, but committed divers extortions and oppressions, against law and to the great injury of the land, and asked that his heirs and executors, whom they alleged to have been greatly

---

[18] Dowling, *Annals*; *AC*; *ALC*; *Reg. Fleming*, nos. 185–6; *A.P.C.*, II, p. 35; *C.C.R.*, *1409–13*, pp. 286–7, 401; ibid., *1413–19*, p. 38; *C.P.R.*, *1413–16*, pp. 73, 293.

[19] *AC*, quoted here, reads Meath, but *AU*, which like *AC* places this in 1414, reads Munster, which seems more probable.

enriched by the goods of the land, should be compelled to come to Ireland and make restitution.[20]

On Stanley's death the council elected Thomas Cranley, archbishop of Dublin, as justiciar, and appointed Sir Edward Perrers, Janico Dartas, and Christopher Hollywood, captains of long experience in Ireland, as 'governors of the king's wars'. In February the treasurer was setting out for England to declare the state of Ireland to the king and council and seek a remedy, and a parliament was held at Dublin which lasted for a fortnight,

In which time the Irish burned all that stood in their way, as their usuall custome was in times of other parliaments; whereuppon a tallage was demaunded but not granted.

But by this time the king must already have decided on his choice of a new lieutenant, for on 24 February he appointed Sir John Talbot of Hallamshire, Lord Furnivall, for the term of six years. Talbot, who was about twenty-nine, had already had some experience of war in Wales (he was later, as earl of Shrewsbury, to be the greatest of the English captains in France), and he was an obvious choice for Ireland, since his wife was one of the de Verdon heirs, who still retained interests in Westmeath, and the lordship of Wexford, which he eventually inherited, belonged at this time to his brother. But he did not arrive till November, and meanwhile the government had to be conducted by Cranley, who was about seventy-seven and could hardly be expected to act vigorously to check disorder. In Meath the colonists were heavily defeated by O'Connor Faly (it was alleged that the ransoms of the prisoners amounted to 1,600 marks); in Leinster a raid by the English of co. Wexford was routed by MacMurrough; only in Kildare was there a success, when the colonists defeated O'More and O'Dempsey near Kilkea, while Cranley in Castledermot prayed for them in procession with his clergy.[21]

Talbot landed at Dalkey on 9 November, and his patent was read to the council on 13 November. Three days later he ordered the arrest of all Irish enemies taking gold and silver abroad without leave, and in February 1415 there was a further order to arrest all traitors, outlaws, and felons, and to take the children of rebels, English or Irish, to be nourished among the liege English. From the beginning Talbot seems to have acted with great vigour. The Irish annals say

[20] C.P.R., *1413–16*, pp. 53–54, 117; *A.P.C.*, II, pp. 130–31; *AC*; *AU*; *C.C.H.*, p. 221, no. 111; Gilbert, *Viceroys*, pp. 568–9.

[21] C.C.H., p. 203, nos. 37, 17; Marlborough, *Chronicle*, s.a. 1413, 1414, 1417; *C.P.R.*, *1413–16*, p. 164; *AC*; *AU*; *AFM*.

he plundered Leix and Caislen na Cuilentraige, the castle, that is, of Fachtna O Morda's son, and brought slaughtered cows and horses and cattle out of Oriel. And he destroyed the sons of the Bretnachs and hanged Gerald son of Thomas Caech, a Geraldine. Moreover he plundered many of the poets of Ireland . . . in the next summer he plundered O Dalaig . . . in Machaire Cuircne.

The details of this are filled in by a report sent to the king by an afforced council which met at Naas in June 1417. First Talbot proceeded against O'More of Leix, laying his country waste, taking his castle, in which there were divers English prisoners, and defeating him in the field. O'More was forced to submit, giving his son as a hostage and entering into an indenture to serve with the lieutenant against all Irish enemies and English rebels. After this O'Farrell and O'Reilly submitted, and the lieutenant, accompanied by O'More, who brought two 'battles', one mounted and one on foot, attacked and defeated MacMahon, who surrendered on the same terms as O'More and sent his brother, 'with a great multitude of their people', to serve against O'Connor Faly. O'Hanlon had previously been forced to submit on the same terms, and had actually served with a force of more than 300 against MacMahon, but now 'disloyally rose up agayne in warres and distroyed your faythfull leiges'. It was presumably at this point that Talbot had the royal service proclaimed at Carlingford; he ordered 'divers great jorneys' against O'Hanlon, laid waste his country, and cut a great pass through a wood which was two leagues and more in breadth, 'thorow terror of which thinge he dayly made supplication to have peace' and gave hostages, followed by 'the greate O Nele pretendinge himself to bee kinge of the Irish in Ulster', O'Neill Boy, McGuinness, Maguire, O'Donnell and others, who offered to serve with Talbot against all other Irish enemies and English rebels, 'which thinge hath not beene seene by longe tyme in theise partes until the coming of your leiuetenaunt aforsayd'.[22]

All this seems to have been the work of 1415, and so far Talbot had managed a triumph, securing the borders of Meath and Louth, together with those of Ulster. But it was another matter to consolidate these successes. Talbot was a first class soldier, who had brought considerable forces with him. But the victories he had gained would rapidly melt away unless he could maintain a sufficient armed force to overawe his late enemies and new allies, and in the existing state of the Irish revenue this could only be done if he had regular payment of the sums due from England. And this was precisely what he could not secure. He had been promised

[22] C.C.H., p. 205, no. 86; p. 209, nos. 183–4; AC; Ellis, Original Letters, second series, I, no. 19; N.L.I., MS 761, pp. 297–8. According to archbishop Swayne a 'battle' consisted of 400 men (Reg. Swayne, p. 109).

4,000 marks a year, and it is clear that he did not get it. In February 1416 he appointed the archbishop of Dublin as his deputy, and took ship for England at Clontarf on 7 February. By the end of the month he was on the agenda of the English council, and late in April he was petitioning anxiously about the payment of his salary; about an increased force of soldiers; about the safe keeping of the marches; an 'increase of people'—perhaps a request for new settlers; the safe keeping of the Irish sea; the supply of bows, which he was told to supply at his own expense, and cannon, which the council thought the king should send to Ireland if he pleased. But the time was ill-chosen: the Hundred Years' War had been resumed in the summer of 1415; in October Henry had won the great victory of Agincourt, and all his interest and effort were directed towards exploiting it. By June Talbot's return to Ireland was being prepared, and it does not seem that he had gained very much by his visit.[23] And though the parliament held in his absence by his deputy had granted him a subsidy of 400 marks, this was not enough to alleviate his difficulties very materially, and he was clearly faced by a growing volume of complaint about abuses many, though not all, of which were simply the product of his financial position.

Probably in the parliament held during his absence, the Irish commons had produced a set of petitions complaining bitterly of the administration. The soldiers, they said, took prises at their will without payment, and also coign: 'divers sums of money each week, sometimes 20d. a week for each man, sometimes more, and sometimes less', and if the people cannot pay the soldiers distrain them. The lieges were often imprisoned without any indictment, contrary to the Great Charter, and held without trial till they purchased charters of pardon, and this not only by sheriffs and other ministers, but by soldiers and others who were not ministers. The land was destroyed by the extortions of the purveyors of the households of lieutenants and other governors: people had given up complaining because they could get no remedy. Kernes and idle men, as well mounted as on foot, retained by the Geraldines, Burkes, Powers and other great nations of the land, oppressed them with coign. They complained of the administration of justice, and they complained that a commission had been issued to assess 'Aghy Macmahowne, an Irishman and of Irish nation', with other Irish enemies, on co. Louth, to the destruction, they said, of the lieges, 'for the said Aghy and other Irish will not take such food and drink as

[23] *C.C.H.*, p. 212, nos. 101–2; *A.P.C.*, II, pp. 191, 198–200; *C.P.R., 1416–22*, p. 31.

the said poor commons use themselves', and they had their *caifs* and their children throughout the county, spying out its roads and fortresses.[24] Again, in the parliament which met at Dublin in January 1417, the archbishop of Dublin was chosen as messenger to the king, and a message was prepared which the chancellor refused to seal. It complained of outrageous impositions, which caused people to leave Ireland for England; and of prises of grain and cattle made by the lieutenant's officers and soldiers on churchmen, against the liberties of the church. It alleged that officials were incompetent, so that the laws were not duly kept, and asked that the chancellor, treasurer, chief baron of the exchequer and the justices should in future be appointed by English patents. Finally it asked that proclamation should be made in England that all born in Ireland should return.[25] When Talbot left Ireland in 1420 Marlborough says he went

carrying along with him the curses of many, because hee, being runne much in debt for victuall and divers other things, would pay little or nothing at all.

In 1421 the Irish parliament was still complaining that he had committed various oppressions and extortions, and took their goods, paying little or nothing: they asked that he should be compelled to send his attorneys to Ireland to pay his debts and amend his oppressions.[26] But in fact Talbot was in an impossible position: he must maintain his retinue, and if his salary was not paid it was inevitable that his unpaid soldiers should resort to the oppressions of which the Anglo-Irish complained, and which an unpaid lieutenant could not afford to put down.

The course of events after Talbot's return in 1416 is not very clear. There was war with O'Connor Faly, who seems to have had an initial success, though late in the year Talbot razed the castle of Edenderry. In the same year MacMurrough heavily defeated the English of Wexford. In 1417 Talbot was active against the O'Farrells, who had burnt Fore, co. Westmeath, and seems to have had some success. These operations probably took place late in the year, for the afforced council which met at Naas in June 1417, and was attended by clergy and laity from Dublin, Kildare, Louth and Meath, did not mention them in writing to the king. After detailing

---

[24] *A.P.C.*, II, pp. 43–52. Nicholas dated this early in the reign of Henry IV, which is clearly impossible; Richardson and Sayles put it in 1422 (*Irish Parliament in the Middle Ages*, p. 351), but the reference to MacMahon seems to put it in 1416. See above, p. 349. *Caif* seems to be the Irish *caomh*, a friend, associate, equal. In the decrees of a late fourteenth-century provincial synod of Armagh it is used as equivalent to concubine (*Reg. Swayne*, p. 11).

[25] *A.P.C.*, II, pp. 219–20; *Early Statutes*, p. 566.

[26] Marlborough, *Chronicle, s.a.* 1419; *Early Statutes*, p. 570.

his operations in 1415, they said simply that he had made 'divers other jorneis and labours' for the relief of the lieges, and at the time of writing had just repaired the bridge of Athy, co. Kildare, and erected a tower for its protection, so that they could safely leave their property in the fields, 'which hath not beene seene here by the space of these thirty yeares past'. Very recently Maurice O'Keating, chieftain of his nation, traitor and rebel, had submitted unconditionally to the lieutenant, entering into indentures and giving his son as a hostage. Talbot was about to go to the king to seek payment of the sums due to him, but they had implored him not to go

consyderinge the great destruction and disease which hath come unto this lande by his laste absence from us, and eschuinge greater that may come and are likely to falle uppon the same if he shoulde be absente at this presente tyme.

They asked that he might have a sufficient payment to make him strong enough to resist the malice of the enemy, and to enable his soldiers to pay for prises: his salary was not nearly enough to support them.[27]

One other action of Talbot's was referred to by this council. He had, they said, borne great labour and expenses about the release of the earl of Desmond

falsely and deceitfully taken and detayned in prison by his unkle to the great distruction of all the contry of Mounstre until now that he is delivered by the said leiftenant.

Talbot himself, writing on 11 July to Bedford, left as the king's lieutenant in England when Henry went to France that month, adds to this: he has had great expense for a long time about the deliverance of Desmond from the hands of his enemies. Desmond is now with him in his own household, without a penny of his own, for all his lordships, castles and towns have been destroyed and wasted since his taking, as is too melancholy to relate. Desmond, who had succeeded his brother in 1400 when he was about fourteen, had, according to the Irish annals, been expelled by his uncle, James of Desmond, in 1411. Later legend alleged that he had married the daughter of a common Irish tenant, and that his uncle had seized this opportunity. However this may have been, he had, as we saw, returned to Ireland in 1413, 'to devastate Munster', and we must suppose that wars of which we know nothing followed. He is said to have surrendered the earldom to his uncle in 1418; certainly he left Ireland and served in France, where he died in the summer of 1420 and was buried at Paris on 10 August in the pre-

[27] AC: AU; Ellis, Original Letters, second series, I, no. 19; above, p. 350.

sence of Henry V. As he seems to have left no legitimate son James of Desmond succeeded him, and in 1421 was campaigning in Munster with Ormond.[28]

The main purpose of Talbot's letter was to stress his financial necessities. The king had given him a heavy burden with too little money to maintain it, perceiving which the enemy had now risen in war again. He asked that what was due to him might be paid in haste, for his soldiers would not remain with him, nor the country-side supply them with anything, except for ready payment. The Irish enemies and English rebels regularly made war from St Patrick's day to Michaelmas. Two days earlier he had ridden against O'Connor Faly and defeated him, and broken down his castle of Croghan. He was writing because the great council's mes-sage, of which he enclosed a copy, had not yet been sent, on the news that the king had gone to France. But no payment seems to have been made, and on 25 October he wrote again: he was left as a man desolate, and the land about to be destroyed, for he had had no payment and his soldiers were leaving him from day to day, so that he could not resist the enemy without reinforcements, which he had no money to obtain. There were troubles in Munster: the lieutenant had been there before Michaelmas, had made peace with all the Irish enemies, and had made Walter Burke enter into an indenture to become the king's liege and swear to keep it in the presence of the bishop of Waterford and others, but now the prior of Kilmainham had quartered several Irish enemies and chieftains with all their power to the number of fifteen 'battles' on the coun-ties of Kilkenny and Tipperary, forcing the people to pay their wages to the amount of 1,600 marks, as well as their maintenance, while Walter Burke had done the same in Limerick and Cork.[29]

It was perhaps in January 1418 that Talbot had a letter, which seems to be from the captain of his garrison in Athy, complaining that their wages were in arrears, and reporting that MacGilpatrick of Ossory was ready to become his man, and to serve against any-one, particularly O'Connor Faly and James of Desmond, who were, he said, gathering forces against the lieutenant, though it was against McGuinness that there was action this year, and the royal service was proclaimed at Louth. But the major incident of 1418 was a conspiracy, real or imagined, among the Anglo-Irish them-selves. On 26 June at Clane Talbot arrested the earl of Kildare, Sir Christopher Preston, and Sir John Bellew, and imprisoned them

[28] B.M., MS Cotton Titus B. XI, part I, no. 31; *Complete Peerage*, IV, pp. 245–6; *AFM*; *AC*; *ALC*; above, p. 347.
[29] B.M., MS Cotton Titus B. XI, part I, nos. 31, 46.

in the castle of Trim, 'because they sought to commune with the prior of Kilmainham'.[30]

There is nothing to indicate what lay behind this, though since Ormond was Kildare's son-in-law, and the prior of Kilmainham was still Thomas le Botiller, Ormond's illegitimate half-brother, it is very likely that it was in some way connected with the growing enmity between Ormond and Talbot which was to be a dominant factor in Irish politics for nearly thirty years, and had certainly begun some time earlier.[31] But though Thomas le Botiller, whose deputyship under Lancaster will be remembered, was clearly an unsatisfactory person, there seems to be no evidence that he was in fact implicated in anything at this point. On 27 October a commission was issued for the arrest of ships for the passage of the prior of Kilmainham 'going by the king's command to the king's person', and the Irish annals say that he took to serve in France

eighteen score men with red shields and eighteen score with pure white shields; and not often has so numerous and well born a host embarked from England.

He did good service to Henry at the siege of Rouen, and died in France in 1419.[32] Of those who were arrested, we know only that Talbot was ordered on 1 November to cause them to be brought before the council at Westminster in February, certifying the cause of their arrest. It was no doubt as a result of this order that on 9 January 1419 Talbot and the council exemplified at Trim two documents found in Preston's possession when he was arrested. Meanwhile his lands were being treated as forfeit, his manor of Gormanston being granted to Sir Thomas Talbot, the lieutenant's brother, on 12 February 1419, while two of Kildare's manors were granted to the lieutenant's son on 12 March to hold in fee and inheritance in each case.[33]

The documents found on Preston had been the coronation oath and the tract known as the *Modus Tenendi Parliamentum*, about which controversy is still raging. This is not the place to discuss it:

[30] P.R.O., London, S.C. 1/43/176; N.L.I., MS 176, pp. 297–8; *Analecta Hibernica*, II, p. 266; *AFM*; *AC*; *AU*; Marlborough, *Chronicle*.

[31] See below, pp. 357–8. It was possibly connected with this that all Ormond's lands were taken into the king's hands for his debts due to the crown by a judgement in the Irish exchequer in July 1417, and do not seem to have been restored till 1420 (P.R.O., Dublin, Mem. Rolls, vol. 37, pp. 170–73; vol. 38, p. 415. I owe this reference to my pupil, Mr C. A. Empey).

[32] *C.P.R., 1416–22*, p. 202; *AC*; *Memorials of Henry V*, ed. C. A. Cole (Rolls Series, 1858), p. 52; *Archaeologia*, XXI, pp. 54, 57. The English exchequer paid for the passage of the prior from Waterford to France with two hundred horse and three hundred foot (Devon, *Issues of the Exchequer*, p. 356).

[33] *C.C.R., 1413–19*, p. 472; R. Steele, *Bibliography of Royal Proclamations*, I, pp. clxxxviii–cxcii; *Rotuli Selecti*, pp. 65–66.

it need only be said that most historians hold that it was composed in England in the reign of Edward II, and associate it with the party led by Thomas of Lancaster in opposition to that king. Mr Richardson and Professor Sayles, however, while refusing to consider it of any real significance, hold that it originated in Ireland in the reign of Richard II, and that, therefore, the form in which Preston possessed it in 1418, which differs in several respects from the English texts, represents the original version.[34] It is, for a number of reasons, difficult to accept this view, and a consideration of the history of Preston's family will suggest reasons for its having been in his possession in 1418 which are consistent with the view that it originated in England under Edward II.

The connection of the Preston family with Ireland began in the early fourteenth century, when Richard and William of Preston, the sons of a prosperous merchant of the Lancashire town, settled in Drogheda and began to build up property there. We cannot be certain that they were identical with the Richard and William of Preston who were among the adherents of Thomas of Lancaster pardoned by the king in 1318, but they very probably were. They were joined in Ireland by their younger brother, Roger, and he and his son Robert, who purchased Gormanston from Amory de St Amand in 1363, both served as royal justices in Ireland. It was Robert's eldest son, Christopher, who was arrested in 1418. Christopher had had a register of his title deeds compiled in 1397–8, and had clearly made a thorough search of all the documents in his possession, for the register includes much that had no direct connection with his own lands: there is no difficulty in supposing that he found among his father's papers a copy of a document which seems to have clear Lancastrian connections, and which may either have been already modified to suit Irish conditions, or have been subsequently modified by Preston himself.[35]

None of this helps us to discover whether there was in fact a conspiracy against Talbot in 1418. As we have seen, there was certainly widespread discontent, produced by the exactions inevitably made by a body of soldiery whose pay was always in arrears, and by the misgovernment of which successive parliaments and councils com-

---

[34] See M. V. Clarke, *Medieval Representation and Consent*, chapter v; V. H. Galbraith, 'The *Modus Tenendi Parliamentum*', *Journal of the Warburg and Courtauld Institutes*, XVI, pp. 81–99; Richardson and Sayles, *The Irish Parliament in the Middle Ages*, pp. 137, 142.

[35] For the history of the Prestons, see *Cal. Gormanston Register*, pp. iv–xi. Miss Clarke's view, accepted by Professor Curtis, that in exemplifying the *Modus* Talbot was being forced to accept 'Lancastrian constitutionalism' does not really stand up to examination: he was simply sending evidence to the council in England.

plained, while Talbot may well have been high-handed in other ways. There was a marked tendency about this time to appeal to the Great Charter, as the petitioners of 1416 had done, and as Ormond himself, or perhaps only the chancery clerks, was to do in 1427, when as justiciar he issued letters patent forbidding the oppression of the bishop and clergy of Cloyne by the support of horsemen and footmen, or by 'coignes and other undue contributions'.[36] But though the Anglo-Irish might be thinking in terms of the rights secured to them by law, and of the obligations of rulers, and though the quarrel between Ormond and Talbot had certainly begun by this time, Ormond himself was serving in France in the campaign of 1418–19, and Kildare and Preston were both men of about sixty: it is hardly likely that they were planning any sort of rising. Perhaps their offence was really that they were trying to send representations against Talbot to the king. In any case they must have been cleared, for in fact they recovered all their lands, and Preston was one of the messengers sent to the king by the parliament of 1421.

In 1419 the Irish of Leinster were again at war, but the capture by Talbot of 'Mac Morthe, chiefe Captaine of his Nation, and of all the Irish in Leinster' seems to have improved the English position for the time being. This was Donnchad, the son of Art Kavanagh who had died in 1418. When Talbot left Ireland he brought him with him, and in July 1421, as 'Donaat Macmurcoo, prisoner in your Tower of London', MacMurrough was petitioning the king, representing that he desired above all things to be his liege: he would bind himself in any way desired, and would make all his subjects do the same, and offered his son and heir as a hostage. He was still a prisoner in 1424, when he was handed over to Talbot to whom his ransom belonged, and though he was sent back to Ireland in 1427, it is of his brother Gerald that we hear, receiving the fee of 80 marks a year in Donnchad's name, and raiding the colonists from time to time.[37]

Talbot's term of office was now approaching its end: he had been appointed for six years in February 1414 and he was being more and more bitterly attacked by his enemies among the Anglo-Irish. Marlborough says he went to England on 22 July 1419, leaving his brother, Richard Talbot, archbishop of Dublin, as deputy, but he does not seem to have left Ireland finally till February 1420, after which the archbishop was appointed, presumably by

[36] Above, p. 350; *The Pipe Roll of Cloyne*, pp. 59–60.

[37] *AU*; *AFM*; Marlborough, *Chronicle*; *A.P.C.*, II, p. 301; *C.P.R.*, *1422–9*, p. 261; *C.C.H.*, p. 233, no. 7; p. 235a, no. 7; below, p. 364. *AC* places Art Kavanagh's death in 1416.

the Irish council, as justiciar.[38] Meanwhile, on 10 February Ormond had been appointed as lieutenant, and orders were issued to arrest ships for his passage, with his troops, on 20 February. He landed at Waterford early in April, having employed the interval in recruiting men for service in Ireland by indenture.[39]

Ormond's appointment seems to have been a victory for what was apparently a steadily growing faction opposed to Talbot. It is not clear how the enmity between Talbot and Ormond began, but by this time there was evidently an almost murderous hatred between the two. Ormond himself had been much out of Ireland during Talbot's lieutenancy, having accompanied the king to France in the Agincourt campaign, and again in the campaign of 1418–19. Nevertheless he said in 1422 that he had been with Talbot in five 'journeys', in which he had had heavy losses, and that during these expeditions his men had been billeted by the lieutenant's herberger, and, by the lieutenant's order, fed by the people without payment, for which Talbot had subsequently had him indicted of treason. To this he added a long list of oppressions of various kinds against his tenants and servants, which he suggested had been inspired by personal spite against him, though in fact most of them seem to have been the prises without payment of which general complaints had been made earlier. The most serious charge was that, having granted the king's peace to Walter Burke and other rebels, Talbot ordered the prior of Kilmainham, who seems to have been in charge of the defence of Ormond's lands during his absence, to discharge his soldiers, upon which, in alliance with 'Tayke O Brene the grettest rebell of all Mownester and Sir William Burke the grettest rebell of Conaght', they burnt and destroyed the earl's countries with, it was suggested, the connivance—indeed perhaps the encouragement—of the lieutenant. Talbot, on his side, alleged that Ormond, knowing that the prior of Kilmainham 'purposyd mysgovernaunce' against the lieutenant, had deliberately left the country; that he had arranged that his lordship of Oughterany, co. Kildare, should pay black-rent to O'Connor Faly's wife for its protection, and that as a result O'Connor had ridden through it unhindered to attack the king's lieges elsewhere; that he had maintained in his service the constable of his castle of Arklow, knowing him to have, in alliance with the O'Byrnes, murdered the king's constable of Wicklow castle and taken the castle; that he and the prior had received a certain rebel and traitor and kept him safe in their country; and finally that Ormond had

[38] Marlborough, *Chronicle*; attestations in *Rotuli Selecti, passim.*
[39] *C.P.R., 1416–22*, pp. 256, 260, 261, 274; *Cal. Ormond Deeds*, III, no. 38.

unlawfully arrested Thomas Talbot, the lieutenant's cousin, and handed him over to Irish kernes, who carried him off to the house of O'Connor Faly, held him to ransom, and ill-treated him.[40]

We need not enquire as to the truth or falsehood of these charges and counter-charges: that they could be made is evidence of the state of feeling which existed. Ormond's party included James of Desmond, against whom Talbot had campaigned, and who now, with his nephew's death in France, became the unquestioned earl. In 1422 the alliance was sealed when Ormond granted Desmond for life the custody of his lands in Imokilly, co. Cork, with half their profits, while in 1429 these lands became the marriage portion of Ormond's daughter in a marriage with Desmond's son and heir. Kildare was Ormond's father-in-law, and presumably supported him. The greatest of the Anglo-Irish were thus on Ormond's side. As for the prelates those of Munster seem to have supported Ormond; the archbishop of Armagh was neutral; the archbishop of Dublin, Talbot's brother, was inevitably the leader of his party. We have no evidence as to the alliances of lesser men, but the administration, after a lieutenancy of six years, was inevitably staffed largely by Talbot's partisans, and he had been conspicuously lavish in grants of lands while in the king's hand, in pardons of debts and accounts due to the king, and similar favours, which, though they diminished the revenue, no doubt won him supporters. And finally Talbot had, of course, the enormous advantage that he was now with the king, and thus in a position to influence decisions in England.[41]

One of Ormond's first actions as lieutenant was to hold a council at Dublin on 23 April 1420, where the summons of a parliament was decided on, and then he turned to remodelling the administration. Laurence Merbury, the chancellor, who had certainly been one of Talbot's supporters, had been appointed by English letters patent and so could not be removed, but new barons of the exchequer were appointed on 24 April and 26 April, and a new treasurer on 10 June. It seems that a strenuous attack was made on Merbury: in October he was going to England by the king's command, and was given leave to appoint a deputy. He was reappointed by English letters patent in the summer of 1421, with leave to remain in England till 1 September, appointing a deputy. But he seems to have failed to do so, for on 21 August the justiciar and

[40] M. C. Griffith, 'The Talbot-Ormond Struggle for Control of the Anglo-Irish Government, 1414–47', *I.H.S.*, II, pp. 376–97; *Rotuli Parliamentorum*, IV, pp. 198–9; above, p. 353.

[41] *Cal. Ormond Deeds*, III, nos. 51, 88; below, p. 361; *Rotuli Selecti, passim*.

council in Ireland declared the office vacant because of his absence without a deputy since 1 August, and appointed a successor. Meanwhile Merbury was being 'impeached in England for divers matters illicitly done against the king while he was chancellor', and on 8 April 1423 he himself complained to the Irish council that he had been most gravely slandered before the council in England by James Cornewalsh, Ormond's appointee as chief baron of the exchequer. But by this time the Talbot party was again in the ascendant.[42]

Meanwhile, Ormond had conducted vigorous campaigns against the Irish of the midlands, apparently both before and after the parliament which met at Dublin on 7 June 1420. It may be noted that this parliament still represented the greater part of the country: all the counties of Leinster; all the counties of Munster except Kerry; Meath and Louth. Connacht and Ulster were absent, though it is not unlikely that they were summoned. The lieutenant was granted a subsidy of 700 marks, and the parliament was then adjourned till December, when it granted a further 300, and had a final session in April 1421, when John Swayne, archbishop of Armagh, and Sir Christopher Preston were chosen as messengers to the king and articles highly critical of Talbot's administration were prepared. They complained in general terms of oppressions, non-payments and coigns practised by lieutenants and their deputies, and also by magnates and 'nations': the land would never have relief without the king's presence. They complained of failure to execute the laws; that former lieutenants, to whom the revenues had been granted, had spent little or nothing on the wars; that they were so burdened with intolerable charges and wars that people were fleeing the land in great numbers. They made complaints of official misconduct and incompetence; they said that the Irish Sea was dominated by the king's enemies, Castilians, Scots and others, to the particular destruction of merchants; they asked for a pardon of debts, and that all chief governors might have power to receive homages from tenants-in-chief, so that they should not have to go to England, and to present to all benefices; they complained that they were no longer allowed to go as students to the Inns of Court in England. And in particular, they complained of the oppressions of Stanley and Talbot as lieutenants; they praised Cranley; and they said that Ormond, having been required by them in this parliament to keep the laws and repel all manner of

---

[42] *Parliaments and Councils*, p. xxv; *C.P.R., 1416–22*, pp. 300, 394; ibid., *1422–9*, pp. 3, 75, 88, 103; *C.C.R., 1422–9*, p. 41; *C.C.H.*, p. 219, no. 49; p. 225, nos. 26–27, 39; p. 228, no. 74.

extortions and oppressions and make due payment, not only promised before all the estates of parliament to do so, but undertook that
if he did not receive adequate funds from the king he would assign
all the rents of certain of his own best lands for the purpose. Further, he had abolished 'an evil, most heinous, and insupportable
custom called coigne'.[43] Much of this was no doubt inspired by
Ormond's campaign against Talbot: it does not seem that any
chief governor ever had great difficulty in procuring the sort of
parliamentary message he wished for, but there can be no doubt
that there was a genuine body of support for Ormond.

The parliamentary session of April 1421 had dealt with other
contentious and difficult matters. There was a dispute between the
bishop of Cloyne and 'another prelate' (presumably the bishop of
Cork) whose see he was seeking to unite with his own: this was
referred to Rome. But far more sensational was the case of the
archbishop of Cashel, Richard O'Hedigan, who was accused by
the bishop of Waterford and Lismore of a wide variety of offences

among other, one was that he made very much of the Irish, and that he loved
none of the English nation, and that he bestowed no Benefice upon any English
man, and that he counselled other Bishops not to give the least Benefice to any
of them; that he counterfeited the Kings Seale and letters Patents; that he went
about to make himselfe King of Munster; and that hee had taken a Ring from
the image of Saint Patricke, (which the Earle of Desmond had offered) and bestowed it upon his Concubine. And he exhibited many other enormious matters
against him in writing, by whom the Lords and Commons were troubled.[44]

Meanwhile, the Irish wars continued. On 7 May 1421 O'More
defeated Ormond's men; a month later Ormond himself came
with 'a very great army' into Leix and forced O'More to sue for
peace. But it was in Ulster that danger was greatest in this year.
MacMahon 'did much hurt in Vrgile, by wasting and burning all
before him', and on 4 June the whole community of the earldom of
Ulster wrote to Ormond from Down, denouncing 'Odo McGyn-
nys, captain of his nation, . . . if all our members were turned to
tongues we could not, God knows, fully express the frauds, decep-
tions, infidelities and perjuries of the said son of perdition and
enemy of Jesus Christ', and imploring him to come to their aid,
otherwise they will depart to a safe place, saving at least their lives.
The royal service was proclaimed at Louth; in July Ormond, no
doubt on his way north, induced the community of the liberty of

[43] *Early Statutes*, pp. 562–85. Cf. *C.C.H.*, p. 217, no. 19.
[44] Marlborough, *Chronicle*. The union of Cork and Cloyne had been decreed in
1326, but was not in fact effected till 1429. Nothing else appears about the
charges against O'Hedigan: he remained archbishop of Cashel till his death in
1440.

Meath to grant him a subsidy in aid of the wars; we hear of a meeting arranged with O'Neill at Dundalk, but it does not appear whether he fought either MacMahon or McGuinness.[45]

By this time only a few months were left of Ormond's term of office—he had been appointed for two years from his arrival in Ireland in April 1420—and he was taking pains to secure his position. In March 1422 he procured testimonials from the counties of Limerick and Kildare, and no doubt from others. The bishops of Limerick and Emly, the prior of the convent of Limerick, the towns of Limerick and Kilmallock, the sheriff and community of co. Limerick formally declared that he had made war against the king's enemies in the most commendable way, receiving much assistance from Desmond, and had restored them

who through the wars and destructions of the Irish enemy and the English rebels of our lord the king, had been in great part subjugated by hostile force to their laws and customs, to English manners, the laws of the kingdom and the customs of the land of Ireland in which the liege people of our lord the king have rejoiced since the time of the conquest . . .

Ormond, they added, had made full payment for everything taken by him and his men from the king's faithful people. No doubt these testimonials were needed, for by this time Talbot was making formal charges of treason against Ormond, first in a great council before Henry V, who died in France on 31 August 1422, and then before John, duke of Bedford, constable of England, the king's brother, in the constable's court. By the summer of 1423 Ormond was in England, and had to bind himself to do no harm to Talbot's adherents, and not to withdraw from the court without special licence of the council. But in the English parliament of November 1423 it was decided that, because of the 'dissensions, commotions, litigation, scandals and other intolerable evils' which had arisen among the lieges because of these charges, they should be quashed.[46]

When Ormond's commission ended the Irish council had chosen William fitz Thomas, prior of the Hospital, as justiciar, and he acted till after the king's death, when on 4 October the council of regency appointed archbishop Talbot as justiciar during pleasure, and Merbury as chancellor. Clearly Talbot's party had won. But the position in Ireland was difficult, for Ormond's withdrawal seems to have been followed by widespread Irish risings. Gerald Kavanagh burnt and plundered the county and town of Wexford;

[45] Marlborough, *Chronicle*; P.R.O., London, S.C. 1/57/69; N.L.I., MS 761, pp. 297–8; *C.C.H.*, p. 220, nos. 96–97; *AC*.

[46] M. Griffith, loc. cit., p. 392; *C.C.R., 1422–9*, pp. 69, 132; *Rotuli Parliamentorum*, IV, pp. 198–9.

O'Reilly attacked the barony of Kells, co. Meath; O'Neill, O'Donnell and MacMahon successfully attacked Louth and Meath, 'and
all the foreigners were left under tribute'; the O'Tooles were warring on Dublin and Kildare. It must have been against the O'Tooles
that a royal service was proclaimed at Mullamast in south Kildare.
By June 1423 the position seems to have improved, for the justiciar
had received messengers from O'Byrne and Gerald Kavanagh, as
well as from O'Connor Faly and Desmond, and Gerald Kavanagh
had come to the peace and sworn to serve the king faithfully. But
O'Connor Faly, together with the Berminghams of Carbury, was
still at war, as was O'Reilly, and though Desmond had come from
Munster to Carbury with a great army of English and Irish, and
in company with the justiciar and the whole power of the men of
Meath had laid Bermingham's country waste, they had been unable to do much against O'Connor. That the danger was acute
may be judged from the size of the subsidy which the community
of Meath was prepared to grant in this emergency: a mark from
each ploughland to the justiciar, and as much to pay Desmond.
Desmond's help had indeed been very necessary, for the Irish council had not been prepared to provide the justiciar with more than
twelve men-at-arms and sixty archers.[47]

Meanwhile, the council in England had been making more permanent arrangements for the government of Ireland. Edmund
Mortimer, earl of March, though he represented the legitimist
claim to the crown, and had been a focus of intrigue ever since the
accession of Henry IV, had been more fortunate than those in a
similar position were to be under Henry VII: he had preserved
both his life and his lands. As the greatest of the Anglo-Irish landowners he was a natural choice, and he was not without military
experience, having served under Henry V in France. Moreover he
was on bad terms with Gloucester, the king's uncle and 'protector',
who governed England in the absence of his brother Bedford in
France: there was much to be said for getting March out of England. The arrangements were being discussed in the council in
March and April 1423. It was agreed that if March went to Ireland
in person he should have 4,000 marks a year; if he sent an English
baron as his deputy, 3,000 marks; if a bachelor, 2,000. Later it was
agreed that he should have 5,000 marks: he was to have the revenues of Ireland as part of this, and any deficit would be made up

[47] *C.C.H.*, p. 224, nos. 9, 14; p. 225, nos. 22, 24–25, 29, 37–38; p. 228, no. 66;
p. 230, nos. 112–15, 118, 120–22; p. 240, no. 52; *C.P.R., 1422–9*, p. 3; N.L.I.,
MS 761, pp. 297–8; *AC*; *AU*. A mark from each ploughland in Meath is estimated as either 360 or 300 marks, and the clergy granted 120 marks: the whole
parliamentary subsidy was seldom as much as the double grant.

by the English treasury. Finally on 9 May he was appointed lieutenant for nine years from the first day of his landing in Ireland. On 29 June orders were issued for the arrest of ships for the passage of his troops, and on 16 July the Irish government ordered the arrest of ships to be sent to Beaumaris in Anglesey for his passage with his army. But on 4 August at Ludlow he appointed the bishop of Meath as his deputy, and it was not till the autumn of 1424 that he came himself, 'with a great following of English and Welsh', only to die of the plague at Trim on 18 January 1425. He left no children, and his estates passed to the son of his sister Anne and Richard earl of Cambridge, the duke of York, greatgrandson of Edward III, carrying to him all the Mortimer lands and claims.[48]

March had had little time to do anything in Ireland, but O'Byrne had submitted and entered into an indenture with him, and at the time of his death the Ulster chiefs, O'Neill and his tanist, O'Donnell and O'Neill Boy, who had just submitted to him at Trim, were still in Meath and were taken prisoner. Talbot must have come to Ireland with him, and on his death was chosen as justiciar by the Irish council, which agreed that he should retain one hundred archers. It is clear that he proceeded to take vigorous action against O'Byrne and O'Connor Faly, for they both submitted in elaborate indentures. At Trim on 27 March 'Calvarius Oconchur, captain of the nation of Offaly' solemnly undertook that he and his men, from whom he had 'general power and special mandate', would be the king's faithful lieges; he undertook to restore all English lands, except those of which he claimed to have been enfeoffed, which were to be the subject of arbitration; he renounced 'the tribute called blackrent'; he undertook to release his prisoners without ransom; not to bring any accusations against the justiciar for what he had done; not to receive or favour Irish enemies or English rebels at war against the king. He was to pay a fine of 1,000 marks for his pardon and admission to the peace, and he gave hostages and took oath to observe all this. On 10 April at Dublin 'Donat Obryn, captain of his nation' entered into a similar agreement, confirming one made with March and undertaking specially to protect the lordship of Wexford and the king's lieges and Talbot's tenants in it, and to obey the archbishop of Dublin and to allow him and his ministers to exercise his jurisdiction within his territory.[49]

---

[48] *A.P.C.*, III, pp. 49, 68; *C.P.R., 1422-9*, pp. 96, 122; *C.C.H.*, p. 232, no. 1; p. 233, no. 14; *AC, s.a.* 1423. The Irish government made difficulties about admitting the bishop (above, p. 157, n. 42). Ormond was acting as deputy in the summer of 1424 (*C.C.H.*, p. 240, no. 37; p. 243, no. 26; *Cal. Pembroke Deeds*, no. 135 (ii)).

[49] *AU*; *C.C.H.*, p. 238, nos. 112-13; p. 239, no. 2.

By this time the English government had appointed Ormond as lieutenant for one year from 13 April, with a fee of £1,000 a year. Under him the submissions continued: MacMahon on 12 May; Eoghan O'Neill on 23 July, and probably O'Donnell, for in October 1426 the hostages of MacMahon, O'Donnell, captain of his nation, O'Neill, and Meiler de Bermingham were all in the justiciar's hands; O'Toole on 8 August. All were in much the same terms, O'Neill agreeing in particular to render the bonnacht of Ulster. There may well have been others which have not survived, and when on 13 September a council meeting at Dublin sent James Cornewalsh, chief baron of the exchequer, one of Ormond's supporters, to represent the state of Ireland before the English council he had striking, if impermanent, successes to report. But nothing was done to renew Ormond's commission as lieutenant, and when it expired on 13 April 1426, the Irish council seems to have reappointed him as justiciar with the customary fee of £500. At any rate it agreed that as this fee was insufficient to support the wars and burdens of the land he should have an additional twelve men-at-arms and sixty archers at the king's wages. But this force was, of course, inadequate to maintain the successes of the previous year: O'Connor Faly rose in war, and in the summer or early autumn it was necessary to resist 'Gerald Okevenagh'. Then, on 15 March 1427 Sir John de Grey was appointed by the English council as lieutenant for three years from the date of his landing, which does not seem to have been before the middle of August, though Ormond was released from office on 31 July.[50]

Grey was to come with a considerable force: the orders to arrest shipping for his passage contemplate one of 600 men with their horses. And Donnchad MacMurrough, who had been a prisoner since 1419, was sent ahead in the hope that he could bring back his people to the peace. In fact, however, as might have been expected, his brother, Gerald Kavanagh, seems to have been much too firmly established. In November the lieutenant, discussing the situation with the council, spoke of Gerald Kavanagh having a great multitude of kernes and other Irish to destroy the country: he had spent 500 marks of his own, beyond what the king paid him, to retain soldiers and support other burdens. The archbishop of Armagh, writing late in the year to some member of the English government, fills in the details. Grey arrived with few of his men, for lack of shipping, and the Irish of Leinster seized the chance to rise under

[50] *C.P.R., 1422–9*, pp. 273, 397–8; *C.C.H.*, p. 239, nos. 118–20, 3–4; p. 240, no. 59; p. 242, nos. 1–5; p. 243, nos. 16, 29; p. 244, no. 41; p. 245, nos. 12–14; *AC*; *Rotuli Selecti*, p. 99; *Reg. Swayne*, pp. 66–67; *Report of Commissioners respecting the Public Records of Ireland, 1810–15*, pp. 54–56.

MacMurrough with some 3,000 footmen. This force advanced into Kildare and burnt the town of Connell: though Grey advanced to Naas, he had too few men to attack, and the Irish were able to advance westwards into Meath till Grey came up with reinforcements, when they withdrew. Grey now turned to a successful attack on O'Connor Faly, but meanwhile MacMurrough was laying Wexford waste till the county had to pay him 213 marks to withdraw. Then he returned to Kildare, and took Castledermot, a walled town, by assault, and after this Grey made peace with him. Then the northern Irish went to war, and it does not seem that any real effort was made to resist them. The poor husbandmen who had no other living had had their corn burnt, and had nothing sown, and could buy no corn, and so they were undone for ever.

This Contre was never in so gret a Meschefe as hit ys nowe . . . the Enmyes . . . woll owre ryde all this contre and Fynaly conquere hite bot if ther be hasty remedy ordeyned . . . some tyme within thes 3 yeres a man myght have kepyne this Contre betyre with 400 bowes than now with 800.

He attributed this deterioration to the quarrel between Ormond and Talbot, in which the whole country had taken sides. If it could be ended, and both or either of them sent over with 400 archers, the country would be saved, for

the enmyes dredith hame both more than they do all the world I trow for if any of hame both were in this Lond all the enmyes in Irlond wold be ryght fayn to have peace.

In another letter written about the same time he complained of the prises and purveyance of lieutenants and their soldiers, who, it was said, owed £20,000 and more: the poor husbandmen bore all and paid for all, and were at the same time destroyed by war. If nothing were done he expected the enemy would finally conquer the land by the spring, so that only the castles and walled towns would be left, and the husbandmen in the last few years had fled the country to England and elsewhere in such numbers that 'there is mo gone out of the londe of the kyngis lege pepyll than be in'.[51]

Grey's lieutenancy was not a success, and shortly before Christmas he left Ireland, leaving the bishop of Meath as his deputy. On 23 March 1428 Sir John Sutton, Lord Dudley, was appointed as lieutenant for two years from 30 April: his indentures provided that he was to have 5,000 marks in the first year for twenty-four men-at-arms and 500 archers, and 4,000 marks in the second for 24 men-at-arms and 400 archers. By October the Irish council was writing

[51] C.P.R., 1422–9, p. 424; AU; C.C.H., p. 245, nos. 2–3; p. 246, no. 31; Reg. Swayne, pp. 107–8, 109–11.

to England of the things which he had powerfully done against the Irish enemies, by which they were so reformed to the peace that many of their captains had joined him against O'Byrne. The parliament held at Dublin in November wrote in its message to the king that in the previous year the land had been about to be lost, but Sutton had since his arrival manfully and diligently made war on the enemy. Like the council in October, they asked that he might have speedy payment of what was owed him: he had had great expense in maintaining troops 'of the gise of this land' in addition to his soldiers. They complained of the frequent changes of lieutenants, and their misgovernance and that of their deputies, and asked that while things went well such changes should not be made. They complained too of unsubstantiated allegations irresponsibly made in the past against lieutenants, justices, and 'otheres estates of your said land', and asked that those making such allegations to the king and council in England should be required to find surety to prosecute them, on which the charges should be sent to the Irish council to be examined in the next parliament or great council, which would report to the king. They spoke of the good service which Ormond had rendered since the time of Henry IV, and asked that he should be paid his arrears, so that he could pay his debts. His last long-continued absence, they said, encouraged the enemy to make war, and greatly weakened the lieges. This parliament also granted a subsidy, and a number of statutes were passed, dealing *inter alia* with the exodus of servants and labourers from the country, and the provision of financial assistance for those prepared to build towers for the defence of co. Louth.[52]

But not everyone was prepared to accept the message sent to England by this parliament. On 1 April 1429 the lieutenant showed to the council a document, produced it would seem by the Talbot faction, which he said he learned had been sent by certain people in Ireland to deny the message. It asserted that the misfortunes of recent years had been due not to misgovernment, but rather to certain magnates and gentlemen, who had incited Irish enemies and English rebels to arson and other enormities, while neither the magnates, the commons, the counties nor the boroughs had been willing to go in the lieutenant's company to resist the enemy. As to the request that the lieutenant should not be changed while things went well, they said that it was against the law thus to circumscribe the royal power, and that in any case things had never been as bad

[52] *C.P.R., 1422–9*, pp. 470, 475–6, 493; *C.C.H.*, p. 246, no. 35; p. 248, no. 19; p. 249, nos. 20, 22; Betham, *Early Parliaments*, pp. 352–9; *Reg. Swayne*, pp. 85–86; *Liber Primus Kilkenniensis*, p. 57; *Statutes, Henry VI*, pp. 10–25.

as now. As to the verification of accusations against chief governors by Irish parliaments or councils, they said that jurisdiction over such defaults belonged to the king alone, and that the truth was not to be had from such assemblies, for those who were sent to them were chosen not for the good of the king and people, but by the will of the magnates and gentlemen. As for the commendation of Ormond, what he was doing at present tended rather to the ruin and destruction of the land than its good, and they saw no need to pay him his arrears, considering the subsidies he had been granted and the sums he had taken privately. All the councillors present were asked if they knew anything of these articles, and all individually denied it: the articles were enrolled and sent to England with a statement that the council wished to have nothing to do with so great a deception of the king and his people of Ireland. But clearly there was an underground movement in being, and it would seem that open war broke out later in the year between the Ormond and Talbot factions, for in July archbishop Talbot, who as chancellor had been present at the council meeting of 1 April, was summoned to England with five others to explain why many of his subjects, armed and arrayed in warlike manner, had unlawfully assembled in great conventicles and gone from place to place, holding towns, fortalices and other places to ransom, with, it was said, his connivance, and they were also ordered to have Ormond's son, taken and detained in prison by them, before the king in chancery.[53]

Sutton left Ireland late in 1429 or early in 1430, appointing Sir Thomas Strange as his deputy. His appointment terminated at the end of April 1430, and by this time Strange had been appointed as treasurer, and the archbishop of Dublin had been appointed, apparently by the Irish council, as justiciar. The Talbot party had won for the time being, and in April Ormond was on his way to the wars in France. It is not surprising that the wars in Ireland went badly in this year. In September the council agreed that as O'Connor Faly, O'Reilly and others had assembled to lay the land waste and the justiciar's retinue was insufficient to resist them, he should have a reward of 100 marks, which was still unpaid nine years later, and the great council which met at Dublin on 30 September spoke of his great labours, 'more than any other Lieutenaunt or other Governor did in thayre time before this'. Nevertheless, they went on, the Irish enemies and English rebels had conquered in Munster almost the whole of Limerick, Tipperary, Kilkenny and Wexford (sic) as well as almost all Carlow, Kildare, Meath and Louth, so that hardly anything but co. Dublin was uncon-

[53] C.C.H., p. 248, no. 13; p. 249, nos. 27–30.

quered and out of tribute (i.e. blackrent). The enemy was assisted by 'grete multitude of Scottes sende unto thaym oute of Scottelond'. They could do nothing unless the king sent 'comforte and strength of popull in haste and a notabull and manfull chiefetayne havynge sufficeante of gode to paye his sowdiors and the trewe liege popull'. And at some time during the year there must have been a campaign against O'Byrne or MacMurrough, for the royal service was summoned to Mullamast in south Kildare, while O'Neill burnt the plain of Louth and Dundalk, and made an expedition into Westmeath and south Longford, where not only the Irish of the midlands, but also 'the foreigners of Westmeath in general' submitted to him.[54]

On 29 January 1431 Sir Thomas Stanley was appointed lieutenant for six years from 12 April, though it was not till September that he arrived. His departure seems to have been delayed by difficulties over money: the English treasurer was unable to pay him the sums stipulated in his indentures, and early in 1434 he was owed 5,000 marks, and the treasurer said that the state of the revenue was such that he dared not pay him, or even make him assignments. It is not surprising that Ormond said bitterly about this time that if what was spent on one year of the war in France were applied to Ireland over several years a final conquest could be made. Nevertheless, Stanley held his retinue together: when on 4 November 1434 they were mustered near Mellifont by the archbishop of Armagh and the treasurer, who made them shoot in their presence, there were 400 of whom only twenty-four were found to be insufficient.[55]

Stanley seems to have gone back to England before the end of 1432, appointing Sir Christopher Plunket as his deputy, and did not return till late in 1433. In the next year there was the one conspicuous success of his lieutenancy. O'Neill and O'Donnell descended on Meath (it was no doubt against them that the royal service was summoned to Louth), and O'Donnell was captured and taken to Stanley's lordship of Man. But when at the end of 1435 he went to England again to report and seek payment he was furnished with a message from the council which had only disasters to relate. The land of Ireland, it said, was well nigh destroyed; there was not left in Dublin, Meath, Louth and Kildare an area more than 30 miles in length and 20 broad not subjected to enemies and rebels. In Carlow, where sixty years before there had been 148

[54] C.C.H., p. 263, no. 9; N.L.I., Harris Collectanea, IV, p. 314; C.P.R., 1429–36, p. 72; AU; N.L.I., MS 761, pp. 297–8.

[55] C.P.R., 1429–36, p. 105; C.C.H., p. 253, no. 16; A.P.C., IV, pp. 79–80, 198–9; The Libelle of Englyshe Polycye, ed. G. Warner, p. 39; Reg. Swayne, pp. 145–9.

castles and piles, and which even thirty years before was one of the keys of the land, there were left only the castles of Carlow and Tullow. The counties of Munster, with Kilkenny and Wexford, were in such a state that the few lieges left in them were not sufficient to provision the cities of Waterford, Cork and Limerick. For thirty years no lieutenant had gone there except for 'a sodan journay or an hostyng', nor had the king's courts, parliaments, and great councils, been held there except for one parliament at Kilkenny ten years before. The provinces of Armagh and Tuam [Ulster and Connacht] are subject to enemies and rebels, except for the castles of Carrickfergus and Ardglass with part of co. Louth in Armagh and the walled towns of Galway and Athenry in Tuam, and have not been visited by any chief governor for forty years, 'but it were for acteyng, hosteyng, or a sodan journey'. The seas are infested by the king's enemies, Scots, Bretons, Spaniards and others. They asked that the king should either come himself, or send the lieutenant back in haste, with sufficience of goods and men, 'and that he se that the said land be duely keppyd and gouernyd during his terme', or else

some other grete lorde of the kynges blode, and such as the peple woll drede and be aferd of . . . and to be here before the begynyng of this somyr, or else the saide lande is like to be fynaly destrued.[56]

Stanley, who had left the archbishop of Dublin as his deputy, did not return till late in 1436, and left Ireland for good when his commission expired on 12 April 1437. Archbishop Talbot was elected as justiciar by the council, and acted till the arrival of Leo, Lord Welles, who was appointed as lieutenant on 12 February 1438. Welles seems to have been understandably reluctant to accept appointment: we hear that he had been persuaded, and his commission specifically laid down that after he had visited the country and taken order for its defence and government he might absent himself for good cause, leaving a deputy with full powers. In April Ormond was being sent over with him, and his retinue was being mustered in Cheshire. He seems to have returned to England very soon, leaving his brother, William Welles, as his deputy. But before 19 May 1440 Welles had been taken prisoner by the brothers of Thomas fitz Gerald, prior of Kilmainham, 'and many other Irish enemies and English rebels and familiars of the prior'. The prior was involved in this treason, but obtained a pardon. It was presumably this emergency that brought the lieu-

---

[56] *Cal. Ormond Deeds*, III, no. 101; *C.P.R., 1429–36*, pp. 285, 321, 325, 330–31; Betham, *Early Parliaments*, pp. 360–65; *AC*.

tenant back: Ormond acted as deputy for the time, but on 10 June the lieutenant presided at a council meeting, and he seems to have remained in Ireland till early in 1441, when Ormond was again left as deputy.[57]

It was now that the continuing quarrel between Ormond and the Talbots reached its climax. The Talbot group was well entrenched in the administration, for it included the treasurer, Giles Thorndon, the chancellor, Richard Wogan, and the chief justice of the king's bench, Christopher Bernevale. Nevertheless, the great council which met at Naas on 23 June 1441 sent a message to the king which seems to have been inspired by Ormond. It asked for an answer to the articles which had been sent by the parliament held before Lord Welles in November 1440; it said that all pleas arising in Ireland had been terminable in the king's court there; that it had not been accustomed for anyone to be summoned to England by English writs to answer for anything except treason touching the king's person or a writ of error in parliament; and it alleged that unfit persons, 'unsufficient and unconnyng', had been admitted to office by both English and Irish patents and asked that they might be refused if found incompetent on examination by the 'governour' and council. On 20 August the deputy and council gave further instructions to the messenger who was being sent with this: he was to ask that Englishmen born in Ireland might have the same rights in England as Englishmen born in England; he was to complain of the absence of the lieutenant, the non-payment of his fee (in April 1442 the sum of £2,000 and more was still owed to Welles), and the prodigal spending of such money as there was; and he was to ask that ships and merchandise going to England which had not paid customs in Ireland should be forfeited, and that since the citizens of Cork and Limerick no longer answered for their fee farm in the exchequer, ships of those towns coming to England should be arrested. Then in November a parliament at Dublin sent a message the content of which was later furiously disputed. It certainly asked that the deputy (or perhaps Welles, the lieutenant) should have sufficient payment to keep the number of soldiers required by his indentures; that people should not be summoned to England from Ireland by writ or privy seal (the king said he would do so if necessary, and not otherwise); and that as there were few temporal lords of parliament in Ireland the lieutenant or his deputy or the justiciar might have power to create them, to which the king said that this was a power he reserved to himself,

[57] *C.C.H.*, p. 261, nos. 40, 6; p. 262, no. 11; p. 263, no. 2; *C.P.R.*, *1436–41*, pp. 140–41, 200; *C.C.R.*, *1435–41*, p. 177.

but he would consider names. Then, on 27 February 1442 Ormond was appointed lieutenant.[58]

It was clearly after this that archbishop Talbot produced a document which he alleged to be the message sent by the parliament of November. The whole body, both lords spiritual and temporal and commons, had, he said, asked to have as lieutenant a mighty lord of England. Ormond was 'aged, vnweldy and vnlustie' (he was now about fifty-one), and had 'for lak of labour' lost most of his own possessions in Ireland; he had at various parliaments made Irishmen and his own household servants knights of the shire; he had allowed magnates and prelates to absent themselves from parliaments and pocketed their fines; he had caused named persons to be held prisoner by 'Irish enemies'. When Welles last left the country most of the gentlemen and commons had been anxious that Ormond should not be deputy. Not only Talbot, but also March and Grey while they were lieutenants, had impeached him of 'many grete tresons, the which stonde yet vndetermyned'. Finally the archbishop asserted that Ormond had done many other things which he might not declare because of his order: he asked that Welles, Dudley, and Stanley, former lieutenants, the treasurer and other officers should be summoned and examined as to Ormond's rule, and a commission of enquiry appointed in Ireland, Ormond being first discharged so that he could not intimidate witnesses.[59]

The English council could not ignore Talbot's representations. It seems that the articles were sent to the Irish chancellor, probably early in May, with orders to report privately whether they were true or not. Ormond, however, learnt of them, and insisted, first at a council meeting afforced by various gentlemen of county Dublin summoned by him on 26 May, and then on 5 June at a council at Trim, similarly afforced by gentlemen of Meath, that they should be produced so that he could answer them. On 5 June the articles were read, and the council having deliberated in private, apart from the lieutenant, denied that the parliament of 1441 had sent a message desiring the appointment of an English lieutenant, or that Ormond had packed parliaments as alleged, or that there had been the opposition alleged to his appointment as deputy. As for the accusation that Ormond had sent men to the prisons of Irish enemies, he was able to produce one of those named, who said flatly that it was quite untrue. Ormond himself said that the king

[58] P.R.O., London, E. 101/248/16, m. 1; N.L.I., Harris Collectanea, IV, pp. 336–9; *C.P.R.*, *1441–6*, p. 45. Wogan had been appointed chancellor on 27 February 1441 (ibid., *1436–41*, p. 514).

[59] *A.P.C.*, V, pp. 317–20; *Council in Ireland*, pp. 273–6; *Statutes, Henry VI*, pp. 50–53.

could judge for himself whether he was 'aged, unwieldy and un-lusty to labour' or not; that he had all the castles, towns and lord-ships that had been delivered to him when he came of age in 1411 in as good a state as they had been then, and better (this was cer-tainly true in substance); and that March had never made any charges of treason against him that he knew of: if anyone wished to make them in the name of Grey, or if Talbot wished to make them, he was ready to defend himself as the king ordered. A week later Wogan, the chancellor, wrote to the king that he had not caused the acts of this council to be enrolled: it had been done by the keeper of the rolls, in fear of his life. Had Ormond not been lieutenant, some of the Meath gentlemen would certainly not have excused him. He asks the king to give him leave to appoint a de-puty as chancellor as often as necessary, 'for I may not bere his [Ormond's] hevy lordship'. Later Wogan was to represent that because he had executed the king's commands concerning Ormond the latter had had him indicted of treason in Ireland, where none of the king's lieges dared acquit him for fear of the earl.[60]

It is quite clear that relations between the lieutenant and the chancellor had become impossible, and on 21 July an urgent meet-ing of the council was held to consider the latest turn in the crisis. The chancellor had withdrawn from the great council which had been summoned to Naas for 6 July, taking the great seal with him. The council had been adjourned to Dublin for 30 July; the chan-cellor had refused to appear before the lieutenant, though sum-moned; it was then discovered that he had taken ship for Wales, while nothing was known of the seal. It was, however, handed in to the treasury by a friar, who said it had been given to him in con-fession: it had been out of official custody for several days, and showed signs of recent use.[61]

By 24 August the news of these disputes had reached the English council, for it was decided that the lieutenant should be sent for, while archbishop Talbot was to remain in England (he had been appointed as chancellor of Ireland on 7 August), and Thorndon, the treasurer, who had been in England for some time, was to be sworn to advise as to impartial men in Ireland who might hold office as their deputies, and also to put in writing his views on the position. Four days later, since the quarrel between Ormond and the archbishop 'beth in grete cause of the divisions and rumoures that beth amongst the kynges poeple there', both were to be sum-moned by privy seal to be before the council in England in Febru-

[60] Council in Ireland, pp. 276–87; C.P.R., 1441–6, p. 91.
[61] Council in Ireland, pp. 288–94; P.R.O., London, E. 101/248/16, m. 2.

ary 1443. Meanwhile Thorndon seems to have produced his articles: a general and on the whole impartial statement, in which he said that because of the quarrel between the two factions it was impossible to obtain impartial justice in Ireland if the interests of either party were concerned; that the exchequer officials were afraid to levy the king's debts for fear of losing office on a change of lieutenant; that the king's revenues were greatly diminished by lavish grants of annuities, pardons of debts, and so on; and that 'the charges of the Justice of Irland and his officers this yere' exceeded the revenue by £1,456 18s. 1d.[62]

By October 1442 both Ormond and the archbishop were back in Ireland, and after an unseemly squabble in which Talbot refused to appear before the lieutenant and council to show his patent as chancellor, and Ormond refused to deliver the great seal to him unless he did, a council meeting at Trim on 21 November proceeded to make charges against the archbishop: when he was chancellor in the time of Dudley he had refused to make letters patent appointing a deputy for the lieutenant till Dudley allowed him to nominate his own candidate; he had alienated the revenue; he had received a person convicted of treason; he had ignored Ormond's warrants and letters as lieutenant. Considering all this, his office was seized into the king's hand. In March 1443 Wogan was reappointed as chancellor.[63]

A certain degree of harmony seems to have been restored to the Irish government by the removal of archbishop Talbot, and in the spring of 1443 the Irish council was writing to England asking for the payment of the arrears due to Ormond and lamenting the diminution of the revenue, which was no longer nearly sufficient for the payment of officials though annuities continued to be granted, while Cork, Limerick and Galway no longer paid their fee farm rents or customs. The English council agreed that payment should be made as stipulated in Ormond's indentures, ordered the calling of a parliament to consider what grants might be resumed, and ordered writs to the towns to pay what was due or else come to explain themselves. But it also ordered the restoration of Shrewsbury's rents in Ireland, which seem to have been taken into the king's hand by Ormond. Then, apparently early in 1444, the quarrel flared up again. Thorndon presented a further set of articles to the council in England, which this time made no pretence of impartiality. He accused Ormond of a wide range of corruptions; of having introduced on four separate occasions a bill to prevent

[62] *A.P.C.*, V, pp. 202, 206, 321–4.
[63] *Council in Ireland*, pp. 295–303; *C.P.R., 1441–6*, p. 126.

anyone from petitioning the king unless under the great seal or by act of a parliament or great council which had been rejected because some of the commons, true liegemen to the king, said such a statute would be treason; of disobeying a variety of royal commands under various seals; and of bribing the prelates to make 'his owne men of his howsehould' their proctors in parliaments and great councils.[64]

It is not surprising that after this Thorndon's position as treasurer became untenable. Ormond summoned a council meeting at Drogheda for 27 March: before that day Thorndon had secretly taken ship for England. The letters by which he had appointed Christopher Bernevale, the chief justice, his deputy were held to be invalid, and the lieutenant, moved, he said, 'by reason and the laws and ancient customs of the land', declared the office vacant, and further asserted that Thorndon had consorted with one Thomas fitz Morice, a notorious traitor, who had forcibly released from prison Thomas fitz Gerald, 'styling himself Prior of the Hospital', detained there on suspicion of felony and treason. Meanwhile, in England fitz Gerald was charging Ormond with treason before the council in England, as did Thorndon when he reached it. On 23 March privy seal letters were directed to Ormond, summoning him to appear before the king and council on 'certain grete and chargeable matteres the weill of our Reaume, Lordshipes and subgittes concerninge'.[65]

Meanwhile steps had at last been taken to end the original quarrel between Ormond and Shrewsbury. Before the summer of 1444 Ormond's daughter, Elizabeth, had married Shrewsbury's son, and the parties were now allied. The hospitaller who deposed before the lieutenant and council at Drogheda on 21 June that he had heard Thorndon promise the archbishop of Dublin to make a sedition against Ormond, and would himself be the first to cut his head off and bear it in a napkin to the king, was one Thomas Talbot, himself a later prior. And in the great council at Drogheda on 26 June a large assembly, having deliberated apart, declared that there was no one there who could complain in anything of the lieutenant, who was to be thanked for his labours in defence of the land, in which he had spent much of his own goods. Since great confederations of Irish enemies and English rebels existed, they asked urgently that he might be allowed to remain at least till Michaelmas, when the harvest would be in, and that he might return as quickly as possible, with the arrears due to him, and 'gra-

[64] *A.P.C.*, V, pp. 297, 301, 304–5, 325–34. See above, p. 371.

[65] *Cal. Ormond Deeds*, III, no. 159, pp. 152–3; *Council in Ireland*, pp. 303–13. It was probably at this time that charges were formulated against Bernevale (M. Griffith, 'The Talbot-Ormond Struggle', *I.H.S.*, II, pp. 395–7).

cious hope of future payment'. On 28 August Ormond appointed Richard Nugent, baron of Delvin, as his deputy, making elaborate assignments for his payment for six months, and providing a force of 120 archers for him. In November, however, archbishop Talbot was appointed as justiciar, and on 12 March 1445 Shrewsbury himself became once more lieutenant for a term of seven years, though he did not come to Ireland till the autumn of 1446, and left it in the summer of 1447.[66]

In England the charges made against Ormond were allowed to drop, in spite of the efforts of his enemies, Thorndon and the prior, who continued their vendetta although deserted by their principals, to improve their position by adding a charge of necromancy, apparently in 1446. In Ireland, Desmond seems to have joined Ormond's enemies, for in 1446 he was laying waste counties Kilkenny and Tipperary.[67] But there is little evidence about what was happening during this period: we may suppose that the violent quarrel of 1441–4 engaged much of the attention of the administration. Since the beginning of the century the position of the English colony had deteriorated with a frightening momentum. The main cause of this was certainly the failure to provide successive lieutenants with adequate resources from England, coupled with the steady decline of the Irish revenue, which was both a cause and a consequence of the contraction of the area effectively controlled from Dublin. As the complaints of successive parliaments and councils had shown, this was by now approximately the area later known as the pale: beyond it, though the English settlers remained, they were either obliged to pay tribute or 'blackrent' to the Irish 'nations' which threatened them, or were themselves the 'English rebels' of whom we constantly hear as confederated with the Irish. And though the Irish showed no disposition to unite, except for a passing campaign, and were perfectly ready, on the appearance of a superior force, to enter into agreements to renounce blackrent, to restore their recent conquests, to be the king's faithful lieges and follow his banner against other enemies, only the maintenance of such a force could have ensured the performance of these agreements. That this had never been done was due in the first place to financial stringency, and secondly, or at least so archbishop Swayne had thought in the 1420s,[68] to the quarrel between Talbot and Ormond. This was now ended, but the harm

[66] Cal. Ormond Deeds, III, nos. 159, 161; Council in Ireland, pp. 303–13; C.P.R., 1441–6, pp. 345, 359.
[67] Cal. Ormond Deeds, III, p. 153; Richardson and Sayles, Irish Parliament, pp. 165, 206–7; Devon, Issues of the Exchequer, pp. 459, 463.
[68] Above, p. 365.

which it had done remained, in the distortion of the administration of justice, in the embitterment of faction, and in all the evils
which existed for other reasons in England at the same period.
And neither Ormond, who died in 1452, nor Talbot were any
longer young. A new chapter in Irish history under new men was
about to begin.

CHAPTER XII

Yorkist Ireland: the Dominance of Kildare

ON 9 DECEMBER 1447 Richard duke of York, the heir of Mortimer, was appointed lieutenant for ten years. York, the son of the Richard of Cambridge who had been executed in 1415, was now thirty-six years old, and one of the greatest of the English nobles. His grandfather, Edmund of York, had been the fifth son of Edward III; his mother, Anne Mortimer, was the sister and heiress of Edmund Mortimer, earl of March, who had died childless at Trim in 1425, and her grandmother had been the daughter of Lionel of Clarence, the third son of Edward III, while her father, Roger Mortimer, had been recognized as the heir presumptive of Richard II in 1385. In spite of his father's attainder York had inherited the entailed lands of the earldom of Cambridge; from his mother he got all the accumulated lands of the Mortimers: property in England which included the lordship of Clare; a great lordship in the marches of Wales; and in Ireland the earldom of Ulster, the lordships of Meath and Connacht, and some more scattered lands.[1] His total annual income from England and Wales has been estimated at between £6,500 and £7,000.[2] What should be added to this for his Irish lands we cannot tell: probably not very much, for Ulster and Connacht were for the most part only nominally his, but Meath was still substantially intact, apart from its western extremities, and must have yielded something, though not perhaps very much above the necessary expenses of its administration and defence. Moreover, he was not only very wealthy, but his marriage to the youngest daughter of the first earl of Westmoreland had provided him with a whole network of powerful connections all over England.

In spite of his father's treason in 1415, and though his ancestry makes him appear to us an obvious danger to the Lancastrian

---

[1] For the Mortimer inheritance see G. A. Holmes, *The Estates of the Higher Nobility in Fourteenth Century England*, though it largely ignores the Irish lands.
[2] E. F. Jacob, *The Fifteenth Century*, p. 465. The net income from the crown lands had been stated as only £8,399 19s. 2d. in 1433 (ibid., p. 477).

crown, York seems to have been in fact a loyal servant of Henry
VI. In February 1436, when he was twenty-four, he had been appointed to the lieutenancy of France after Bedford's death, though
this first term of office lasted only till the autumn of 1437. In 1440
he was reappointed, and this time held office till 1445. But the
Beaufort faction which dominated the English council complicated
his whole position in France by entrusting the not very competent
Somerset with independent commands, while the payments due
to York fell heavily into arrears. After Somerset's death in 1444
Suffolk became the leader of the Beaufort faction; in the summer
of 1444 he arranged the marriage of Henry VI to Margaret,
daughter of René of Anjou, king of Sicily, and the wedding took
place in England on 23 April 1445. The intention had been to
secure a general peace with France, though in the event the only
result was a prolongation of the truce which had been a part of the
arrangements for the marriage.

The English political scene was markedly changed by the arrival
of Margaret, who easily dominated her husband, and who gave
her whole support to Suffolk. And it is clear that Suffolk and York,
who was still endeavouring vainly to secure payment of what was
owed to him, were mutually antagonistic. In the circumstances it
was natural to employ York, an experienced soldier and administrator, with great interests in Ireland, to succeed Shrewsbury there,
while he was at the moment, since all Henry's uncles were now
dead leaving no heirs, the next heir to the throne till the king should
have a child.[3] The position was clearly difficult, but it does not
seem that the motive of his appointment was really to exile him,
since his indentures provided that he might appoint a deputy and
return to England whenever he pleased, and in fact he did not go
to Ireland till July 1449.

Richard's formal appointment as lieutenant was dated 9 December 1447, but he had entered into indentures with the king on 29
September. He was to receive the entire revenue of Ireland, and
in addition 4,000 marks for the first year and £2,000 a year thereafter. He had all the usual powers, and the appointment was to
last for ten years. It was not, however, till 6 July 1449 that he
reached Ireland; in the interval first Shrewsbury's brother, the
archbishop of Dublin, and then Richard Nugent, baron of Delvin,
acted as his deputies. There is little evidence as to what was happening in Ireland for the greater part of this period, but in February
1449 Delvin held a parliament at Dublin. This body granted a
subsidy, and concerned itself with the cancellation of the fines for

[3] Henry's son was not born till 13 October 1453.

non-attendance at the great council of 1447 which had been imposed, it was alleged unjustly or unreasonably, by Shrewsbury on
a number of bishops; with arrangements for the construction of
castles in co. Meath; and with the cancellation of the commission
of oyer and terminer issued to Thomas fitz Gerald, prior of Kilmainham, and others in the counties of Dublin and Kildare and
the quashing of its proceedings. Since it had been the prior who
had accused Ormond of treason, and Ormond had appointed
Delvin as his deputy in 1443, this may well have been a last echo
of the Talbot-Ormond feud. Apart from the parliament, we hear
only that the deputy and Ormond took part in a war between the
O'Reillys, and that O'Neill and other enemy captains invaded
co. Louth, and were resisted by the archbishop of Armagh and the
sheriff of the county, who spent £100 of their own in wages, but
we must suppose that careful preparations were being made and
negotiations conducted with the Irish chieftains, particularly those
of Ulster.[4]

On 6 July 1449 Richard landed at Howth, 'with greate glory
and pomp'. On 16 July he wrote to the archbishop of Armagh to
send all the fencible men he could collect, archers and others, with
provisions for six days, to meet him at Bray, co. Wicklow, on 1
August, 'to go on hosting' with him. No doubt others were summoned on the same occasion, but the notice was very short, and in
fact the expedition against the Irish of Wicklow which was clearly
contemplated did not take place till later in the year. Instead
Richard turned to the north: by 22 August he seems to have been
at Drogheda, and before 15 August some of the Irish chiefs had
come in: McGuinness with 600 men, horse and foot; MacMahon
with 800; both O'Reillys with 700. In addition there was Mac-
Quillan, with 800 men, 'with many oon other that beth the kynges
legemen. For these other Yrysshmen beth come yn by grace to do
ye kynges service'. The total number was said to be 30,000 (3,000
is a more probable figure), and all this must have been the result
of negotiations of which we know only that the deputy and Ormond
are said to have taken a truce between English and Irish.[5]

On 27 August came the submission of the greatest of the Irish
of Ulster, Henry O'Neill, the son and eventual successor of Eoghan
O'Neill of Tir Eoghain. By an indenture, dated at Drogheda,
O'Neill, 'son and heir of Eugenius O Neel, captain of his nation',

[4] *Cal. Carew MSS, Book of Howth*, pp. 477–8; *A.P.C.*, VI, pp. 92–93; *Statutes,
Henry VI*, pp. 110–64, 206–8; *AU*; MacFirbis, *Annals*, p. 222.

[5] MacFirbis, *Annals*, p. 224; Gilbert, *Viceroys*, p. 582; Gilbert, *Facsimiles*, III,
plate xl; E. Curtis, 'Richard Duke of York as Viceroy of Ireland', *Journ. R.S.A.I.*,
LXII, pp. 165–6; *Cal. Christchurch Deeds*, no. 294.

having full power for his father, sons and brothers, and all his subjects, recognized himself to be the man of the earl of Ulster and
undertook to restore all the possessions of the de Burgo earls of
Ulster occupied by him or any of his family or subjects, as well as
the 'bonnaght' anciently owed to the earl. He promised to make
war at his own expense against any Irishman of Ulster rebelling
against the duke, and to provide him with 500 horse and 500 foot
should he have occasion to make war in Ulster. He undertook
further to restore all lands of Englishmen, especially the Fews, the
inheritance of Sir John Bellew, to pay tithes, and to restore ecclesiastical property. York promised that if the O'Neills were injured
by any of his subjects within the earldom of Ulster he would cause
justice to be done 'according to the laws and customs of the said
earldom'; if they were injured by any Irishman from outside it, he
would assist them as the case required. Henry undertook to pay
the duke 600 fat cattle for homage and fealty, submitted himself to
ecclesiastical censures for the observance of the agreement, and
took a corporal oath on the gospels and 'a certain golden cross
containing a portion of the wood of the Holy Cross'. It was probably about the same time that a number of the O'Hanlons submitted to the duke, and at some time before Michaelmas 1449
some of the Irish of the midlands came in, as well as the Berminghams of Carbury, the earl of Desmond, and some other Anglo-
Irish. There are said to have been formal indentures with all of
them, which have not survived, and most of the Irish gave the
duke a tribute of cows.[6]

York next turned south against the Irish of the Wicklow mountains, apparently accompanied by the forces of the Ulster Irish, as
well as the English of Louth, Meath and Dublin. He raided the
lands of O'Byrne, who before long submitted, swearing to be the
king's true servant, to pay a tribute, to allow the escheator to take
wreck of the sea for the king, and that he, with his children and
chief retainers, would wear English clothes and learn English. It
was probably after this that the other Irish of the south-east came
in, headed by MacMurrough. At Symondeswode (Kiltimon, co.
Wicklow) the duke knighted the chief of the Anglo-Irish who had
taken part in the campaign, and by Michaelmas his triumph
seemed to be complete. When the great council which had been
summoned for 17 October met at Dublin it must have seemed that
Ireland was in a fair way to be recovered, though experience must
have suggested that the submissions of the Irish were unlikely to be

[6] E. Curtis, 'The "Bonnaght" of Ulster', *Hermathena*, XXI, pp. 87–105; 'Richard Duke of York as Viceroy', loc. cit., pp. 167–8; MacFirbis, *Annals*, p. 224.

lasting, while the whole south-west was untouched except by the appearance of Desmond and a few other Anglo-Irish lords. It may have been about this time that the English of the city and county of Cork represented that the Irish

have now the whole country under them; but that the Lord Roche, Lord Barry, and Lord Courcy do only remain, with the best part of their ancestors' posses-sions . . . we, the king's poor subjects of this city of Cork, Kinsale and Youghal, desire your lordships to send hither two good justices to see this matter ordered and amended, and some captain with twenty Englishmen, that may be captains over us all, and we will rise with him when need is to redress these enormities all at our cost, and if you do not, then we are all cast away, and then farewell Munster for ever.[7]

The great council concerned itself with, among other things, the abuses of coign, arising from the keeping of armed forces by the marchers of co. Dublin and elsewhere; false accusations; the abuse of writs of privilege issued by the chancellor and other officials on behalf of men who were not in fact their officers or servants; 'notorious and known thieves' and those caught redhanded, who might lawfully be killed, the slayer receiving a penny from every plough and a farthing from every cottage in the barony. It pro-vided for the safe custody of certain castles erected by York in the marches of Meath, and for the walling of Thomastown, co. Kil-kenny, Fethard, co. Tipperary, and Newtownards, co. Down. Order was given for removing O'Neill and his power from the Fews—presumably detailed arrangements for carrying out the agreement with O'Neill, though there is no evidence that any-thing came of it. And a subsidy was also granted, at least by the clergy.[8]

We know little or nothing of the events of the winter, but it is clear that by the time a parliament met at Drogheda in April 1450 there was a financial emergency, arising from York's inability to obtain payment of what was due to him from England. Already in September 1449 he had had leave to sell or mortgage part of his lands held in chief of the crown so that he could meet the expenses of his office. In December the English treasurer had been ordered, in part payment of what was due to him, to make him payment or sufficient assignment of £1,200. It seems unlikely that he ever got any of this, and in May 1450 there was said to be due to him 4,700 marks of his salary, besides more than £6,000 of the annuities which he had inherited,

---

[7] 'Richard Duke of York as Viceroy', loc. cit., pp. 166–7; Gilbert, *Viceroys*, pp. 356–7.
[8] *Statutes, Henry VI*, pp. 166–77; *Reg. Swayne*, pp. 194–5.

to right greet hindering and grevous damage of ye same oure cousin, as he sayth, by cause wherof and for ye non payment of ye said wages he hath right greetly empoverisshed himself by chevysance of good and otherwise, as it is said.

It is not surprising that there was a real air of financial urgency about the session at Drogheda. After the usual formal confirmations of the liberties of church and state, its first act was one of resumption: so much has been granted away that the king's officers cannot be paid their fees and wages, nor can other charges be supported. Next, it was enacted that the statute of 1445, which had provided that no scutage should be levied during the following ten years, should be relaxed to permit the levy of one at that time, since the lieutenant

has no payment of the king for the protection of this his said land, and he is likely to bear great charges and costs in resistance of the Irish enemies, who according to appearances mean to go to war, and the lieutenant, considering the poverty of the common people, will not charge them at this time with any subsidy.

It seems, however, that the clergy at least did grant a subsidy, perhaps as the equivalent of the scutage.[9]

There is little evidence of what followed, but in June York wrote to his brother-in-law, the earl of Salisbury, that MacGeoghegan, who had submitted in the autumn, had risen with three or four Irish captains, 'associate with a great fellowship of English rebels', had burnt Rathmore and other villages in Meath and murdered and burnt the inhabitants, and 'be yet assembled in woods and forts, awaiting to do the hurt and grievance to the king's subjects that they can think or imagine'. He had, he said, written to the king to hasten his payment, so that he may engage sufficient soldiers

For doubtless, but if my payment be had in all haste, for to have men of war in defence and safe-guard of this land, my power cannot stretch to keep it in the king's obeisance: and very necessity will compel me to come into England to live there upon my poor livelihood. For I had liever be dead than any inconvenience should fall thereunto by my default: for it shall never be chronicled nor remain in scripture, by the grace of God, that Ireland was lost by my negligence.

Later York was to declare in the English parliament of 1454 that because of the non-payment of his wages for service in France and Ireland he had been compelled to sell much of his substance, to pledge his jewels and plate, and to borrow from all his friends.[10]

[9] Richardson and Sayles, *The Irish Parliament in the Middle Ages*, p. 231; *A.P.C.*, VI, pp. 89–90, 92–93; *Statutes, Henry VI*, pp. 178–248; *Reg. Swayne*, p. 196.
[10] Holinshed, *Chronicle*, ed. Sir H. Ellis, VI, pp. 267–8; *Rotuli Parliamentorum*, V, p. 255.

But in any case he might well have been thinking of returning to England, where, it must be remembered, he was still the heir presumptive, for matters there were taking an increasingly serious turn.

The war in France had been going increasingly badly for the English: Rouen had been lost at the end of October 1449, and in the parliament which met in November charges had been brought against Suffolk. In February 1450 the commons presented a formal petition accusing him of treasonable actions in relation to France, and in March a further set of charges relating to administrative action at home. The king, refusing to accept the first set of accusations, banished him for five years on the second, avoiding by this prerogative action the formal trial which, in the temper of the country, would certainly have been disastrous to Suffolk. But when on 30 April Suffolk sailed from England his ships were intercepted, whether by simple pirates or not is unknown, and on the next day his headless body was cast ashore at Dover. At the end of June the bishop of Salisbury, one of his friends, was dragged from the church in which he was saying mass and murdered: he had been a royal chaplain, and was certainly a court bishop, though it seems likely that the immediate cause of the murder was a quarrel between the people of Salisbury and their lord, the bishop.

These murders were an ominous sign of the breakdown of order, and already by the time of the bishop's death the Kentishmen had risen and were marching on Blackheath, led by Jack Cade, who called himself Mortimer,[11] denouncing oppressive officials, particularly those who were members of the royal household, and suggesting the recall of York. The rising was bloodily put down, but it was inevitable that York, who wrote to the king that he had been informed that

divers language hath been said of me to your most excellent estate that would sound to my dishonour and reproach and charge of my person . . . certain persons laboured to indict me of treason,

should return, especially since, as we have seen, he had been starved of the funds that should have reached him from England. He tested letters patent issued at Dublin on 14 August, was at Trim on the 26th, and soon afterwards landed at Beaumaris in Anglesey and marched to London at the head of a considerable force.[12] The government retaliated by recalling Edmund Beaufort,

---

[11] It is not clear who Cade was: he was alleged to be an Irishman, and may have been a cousin of York's as he claimed, but there is no evidence.

[12] *Paston Letters*, ed. J. Gairdner, Introduction, pp. 80–82; *C.P.R., 1446–52*, p. 404; R. Butler, *Notes on Trim Castle* (1861), p. 77.

created duke of Somerset in 1448, from France to make him constable of England. Beaufort, the grandson of John of Gaunt, the fourth son of Edward III, was the king's nearest kin, though the legitimation of his father and uncles in 1407 had expressly excluded them from the throne. Nevertheless, Somerset might be regarded as the counter to any claim to the succession by York. But whatever may have been in York's mind he was not now putting forward any claim, though he pressed on the king the necessity for reform.

York remained in England till 1459, when he fled to Ireland after the defeat of his forces at Ludford Bridge, but it was only between March 1454 and February 1455, and November 1455 and February 1456, when he was protector during the king's insanity, that he had any real power. Though on the whole the commons supported him, petitioning in 1451 that he should be recognized as the heir to the throne, the magnates tended to back the Lancastrian faction led by Somerset. But we need not follow the disputes of these years, which led to the outbreak of open civil war in 1455, except in so far as they affected the position in Ireland.

On 28 July 1450, by which time York's preparations for his return to England must certainly have begun, he had retained Ormond for life, to do him service as well in war as in peace, as well in England when he should happen to be there as in Ireland, against all men except the king and his heirs, at an annual fee of 100 marks, and when he left Ireland he left Ormond as his deputy. One of Ormond's first actions was to summon a great council to meet at Drogheda in November. This body was largely concerned in confirming arrangements made by Ormond for the payment of the salaries of officials, providing also that the keeper of the rolls should continue to hold office in spite of any writs under the English great or privy seal or the signet. It provided also that though the ancient custom of the land was that parliaments should not be held oftener than once a year, nevertheless 'on account of the imminent wars of the king's Irish enemies, who are accustomed to go to war immediately after Easter' one might be held before the next Easter, and a subsidy was granted, at least by the clergy, for the expenses of messengers sent to the king, and another to the deputy in the parliament which met at Dublin in March 1451.[13]

We know little or nothing about what Ormond did in 1451, but in 1452 he clearly embarked on an extensive campaign. First 'the

[13] *Cal. Ormond Deeds*, III, no. 177; *Statutes, Henry VI*, pp. 250–90; *Reg. Swayne*, pp. 197, 198. The statement that it was Ormond's son, the earl of Wiltshire, who was deputy seems to have originated with Gilbert (*Viceroys*, p. 362) and is contradicted by all the record evidence.

two earls' (apparently Ormond and Desmond) took the castle of
Owney, co. Limerick, from O'Mulrian; then he turned to the midlands, where he took the castle of Lea from O'Dempsey and rescued
one of the Berminghams of Carbury from Irry, where he was held
prisoner by O'Connor Faly. After that he went to Annaly, where
O'Farrell submitted 'and promised nine score beeues for to grant
him peace'. Then he went by way of Fore to co. Cavan, where the
O'Reillys submitted, and on to Oriel to obtain the submission of
MacMahon,

and thence to the meeting of Clanna-nell, and caused Henry O-Nell to diuorce
Mac-William Burkes daughter . . . and marched thence to Baliathafirdia mac
Daman, wherein he died afterwards, after he has don theise journeyes within
one moneth and a halfe.[14]

Ormond, who was about sixty-two at the time of his death on
23 August 1452, was succeeded by his son, who had been created
earl of Wiltshire in 1449. The whole face of Irish politics was
changed, for Wiltshire was a leading member of the English court
party of the Beauforts, and the whole Butler interest was thus removed from the Yorkist side. But Wiltshire was in England and
remained there, so the immediate difference in Ireland was not
very great, though the loss of the 'best Captaine of the English
nation that was in Irland and England in those ages' must have
been a heavy blow to the Anglo-Irish. He was succeeded as deputy
by Sir Edmund fitz Eustace, who was presumably elected by the
council and had to face renewed wars by the Irish.[15]

Meanwhile, on 11 February 1451 York's original appointment
as lieutenant, for ten years from 9 December 1447, had been repeated. But on 12 May 1453 the earl of Ormond and Wiltshire was
appointed lieutenant for ten years from 6 March, without reference to York. This was, of course, a move in the party struggle in
England, and Wiltshire remained in England, appointing John
Mey, archbishop of Armagh, as his deputy. In July 1453 preparations were being made for the transport of an army to Ireland, but
we have little evidence as to what followed. It does not seem that
Mey was an active governor, and in June 1454 the English of co.
Kildare petitioned York, who was then protector, complaining of
'mysrule and mysgovernaunce' so that the lieges dared not go to
the king's courts or to market towns for fear of attack; Kildare and
Meath had been destroyed by a dispute between Wiltshire and
'Thomas fitz Morice of the Geraldynes' over the manors of May-

[14] MacFirbis, *Annals*, pp. 232–3.
[15] MacFirbis, *Annals*, pp. 232–3.

nooth and Rathmore,[16] and repeated appeals to Mey as the earl's deputy had been without result. It was perhaps as a result of this appeal that the question of whether York or Wiltshire was the rightful lieutenant was raised in the English council on 6 February 1454 and by 15 April it had been settled in favour of York, and

it is aggreed and accorded undre certaine fourme betwix theym that claymed the right of the said lieutenaunsie so as it is no longer to be doubted whoo oweth to be lieutenaunt there.

Presumably fitz Eustace regained his authority as deputy as soon as the news reached Ireland: at any rate he was holding a parliament, the writs for which must have gone out about the middle of May, on 5 July. But on 25 October fitz Eustace died, and Thomas fitz Maurice, the seventh earl of Kildare, became justiciar, presumably elected by the council. He tested letters as justiciar till at least 13 February 1455, but by that date York, whose appointment had been confirmed on 1 December 1454, had probably already appointed him as his deputy. At any rate he held this office by 18 April, when a great council was held before him which was largely concerned with the disorders of the country, as was the parliament which he held in October.[17]

By this time the quarrels of the English factions had led to open civil war: the first battle of the Wars of the Roses, at St Albans on 22 May 1455, had resulted in the death of Somerset and the triumph of York, who was to dominate the government for some time. But the court party, now directed by the queen, was effectively in power by the autumn of 1458, and a year later the war broke out again, and the Yorkists were routed at Ludford Bridge on 12 October 1459. York escaped to Ireland, while his son, the earl of March, the future Edward IV, fled with his principal supporters to Calais. The parliament which met at Coventry in November attainted them, and on 4 December Wiltshire was reappointed as lieutenant for twelve years. He appointed Sir Thomas Bathe, Lord Louth, and John Mey, archbishop of Armagh, as his deputies,[18] but York was well entrenched in Ireland, and these appointments seem to have

[16] The fourth earl of Ormond had married Elizabeth, daughter and heiress of the fifth earl of Kildare, who died in 1432, and had succeeded to Kildare's lands in her right. The succession to the earldom of Kildare is obscure at this point, but Thomas fitz Maurice, the fifth earl's grand-nephew, was recognized in 1456 and the attainder of the earl of Ormond and Wiltshire in 1462 enabled him to recover all the Kildare inheritance (*Cal. Ormond Deeds*, III, nos. 101, 213, 242).

[17] *C.P.R., 1446–52*, p. 465; ibid., *1452–61*, pp. 82–83, 102, 202; Ellis, *Original Letters*, series 2, I, no. 39; *A.P.C.*, VI, pp. 172–3; *Cal. Ancient Records of Dublin*, I, no. LXVI; *Statutes, Henry VI*, pp. 300–437.

[18] *C.C.R., 1454–61*, p. 426.

been wholly ineffective. A parliament held before York himself at Drogheda on 8 February 1460, and subsequently adjourned to Dublin, proceeded to a frankly revolutionary programme. It expressly confirmed the patent which had renewed York's appointment as lieutenant in 1457. It enacted that, whereas the king had appointed York his lieutenant in Ireland, 'wherein he represents in the absence of our said sovereign lord out of the said land his right noble person and estate', he should be provided with the protection of the law of treason. It enacted that whereas

the land of Ireland is and at all times has been corporate of itself, by the ancient laws and customs used in the same, freed of the burden of any special law of the realm of England, save only such laws as by the lords spiritual and temporal and the commons of the said land had been in great council or parliament there held admitted, accepted, affirmed and proclaimed, according to sundry ancient statutes thereof made,[19]

and had its own seal, and also its own constable and marshal, no one in Ireland should be compelled to answer outside Ireland to any appeal of treason or any other matter, except by order under the great seal of Ireland, and that appeals of treason taken in Ireland should be determined before the constable and marshal of Ireland, within Ireland. It enacted further that for the defence of the land against the Irish enemies every subject should provide in his house one mounted archer for every £20 of his yearly rent,

arrayed defensively with bows and arrows fit for war according to the English fashion, to be ready at all times upon warning . . . so long as the most high puissant prince, the duke of York, shall remain in the said land.

It provided for the issue of a distinctive coinage; it passed an act of resumption, and revoked all licences for absence: the revenues of absentees were to be employed upon the defence of the land.[20]

York had thus secured his position in Ireland. It had been made treasonable to attack him in any way; it had been made impossible for his enemies in England to proceed against any of his supporters in Ireland; he had created a force of archers for himself, for it was clearly intended that he should take them with him when he left Ireland; and the act of resumption had done something to provide him with funds. Opposition was not, indeed, absent, as is shown by the acts against Thomas Talbot, the prior of the Hospital (but he had surrendered to York by March), against Thomas Bathe, whom Wiltshire had appointed as his deputy, against James Corne-

[19] This was the really revolutionary claim made in this parliament, and had no validity in law or custom. See above, p. 190.
[20] *Statutes, Henry VI*, pp. 638–800.

walsh, the chief baron of the exchequer, against Richard Bermingham, who was said to have gone into England to bring about an
invasion of Ireland, and to have procured writs to summon divers
persons to England, 'to the intent to embarrass them there by
untrue appeals of treason', and against four persons who were
alleged to have brought into Ireland letters under the privy seal
inciting the native Irish chieftains to make war on York. But it is
clear that the great majority of the Anglo-Irish were solid in supporting York, and the last acts of this parliament in its session at
the end of July gave all who wished to attend upon him when he
should go to England leave to absent themselves from Ireland.[21]

Meanwhile in England there had been a good deal of local disorder and a considerable persecution of Yorkist supporters. Early
in the summer York and the earl of Warwick, who was with him
in Ireland, had drafted a manifesto in which they were able to
point convincingly to oppression and misgovernment by the Lancastrian ministers, and to refer to the letters to the native Irish,
encouraging them to 'enter into the conquest of the said land'. On
26 June a force headed by March and Warwick landed at Sand-
wich from Calais; on 10 July the royal army was defeated at
Northampton. York felt that his moment had come: he landed at
Chester, probably with a force from Ireland, went southwards
through the marches to his own lands, and finally reached the
parliament which had been summoned to London for 7 October
by 10 October. Here he proceeded to claim the crown as his by
right of inheritance. But however great the resentments aroused by
Lancastrian government, the lords were not prepared to accept a
change of dynasty. Finally at the end of October a compromise
was arrived at: Henry VI was to retain the crown for life, but was
to be succeeded by York and York's heirs. The attainders made at
Coventry a year earlier were reversed, and the principality of
Wales with lands to the annual value of 10,000 marks was assigned
to York, who was proclaimed heir-apparent and protector on 8
November. Lancastrian opposition was, however, unabated, and
at Wakefield on 30 December he was defeated and killed. But this
was not the end of his party, which was now led by March and
Warwick, and in March 1461 the Londoners accepted March as
king. On 29 March, at Towton, Edward decisively defeated the
Lancastrian forces, though queen Margaret, her son, and Henry
VI escaped to Scotland, where they were hospitably received.

Meanwhile Kildare, whom York had left as his deputy, was
governing Ireland. The council had chosen him as justiciar on

21 *Statutes, Henry VI*, pp. 648–60, 740–44, 752–4, 766, 792–8.

learning of York's death, and he was subsequently appointed by Edward IV and sworn on 1 May 1461. There is little evidence as to what had been happening during the autumn and winter: we hear only of the usual wars in the marches. The English civil war can have had little or no echo in Ireland, where the Lancastrians seem to have had almost no support except from the Butlers, and the execution of Wiltshire after Towton, and his subsequent attainder and that of his brothers, which of course entailed the forfeiture of their lands, substantially altered the balance of Anglo-Irish politics. Although the sixth earl of Ormond was formally restored in 1475, the Butlers in effect vanished from the Irish political scene for the whole Yorkist period, while in 1461 the Ormond inheritance was at the disposal of the new régime. In 1462 the sixth earl made a desperate attempt, arriving in Ireland, apparently in January, 'with a great multitude of Englishmen'. The city of Waterford was taken and destroyed by them, but finally they were defeated by Desmond at Pilltown near Carrick-on-Suir. The principal result of the expedition was that the Polestown branch of the Butlers, who had joined in the rising, was also involved in the attainder.[22]

Meanwhile, on 28 February 1462, the king's brother, the duke of Clarence, who had been born in Dublin castle in 1449, had been appointed as lieutenant for seven years from 6 March. On 20 March Roland fitz Eustace entered into indentures with the king to serve as his deputy, with a force of 300 archers 'born of our Reaume of England' and paid by the English exchequer, from 19 April till Michaelmas; he was formally appointed on 16 May. But before very long he disappeared from office, and on 1 April 1463 the seventh earl of Desmond, who had succeeded his father in the previous year, was appointed as deputy. Desmond was to remain in office till 1467. He was a man described by the Irish annalists as valiant and successful in war, handsome, learned, affable, eloquent and hospitable, generous, especially to the Irish poets, and a suppressor of vice and theft. During his deputyship an act was passed authorizing the establishment of a university at Drogheda, which came to nothing, and he endowed a collegiate church at Youghal, as well as founding with Kildare and others a chantry in the parish church of Dunsany. At the same time he was the lord of an earldom in which the native Irish element was certainly predominant, and the annals say expressly that he was learned in Latin, English and Irish: a renaissance magnate with an Irish tinge.[23]

[22] *C.C.H.*, p. 268, nos. 1–3; MacFirbis, *Annals*, pp. 242–4, 247–8; *C.P.R., 1461–7*, p. 263; *Statutes, Edward IV*, pt. I, pp. 42, 176–8, 182–3, 185.

[23] *C.P.R., 1461–7*, pp. 142, 185, 201, 437; *Analecta Hibernica*, X, pp. 28, 39–41; *AFM, s.a.* 1468; *Statutes, Edward IV*, pt. I, pp. 322–30, 368, 558.

The beginning of Desmond's deputyship was marked by renewed disturbances. The commons of Meath rose against him, 'him to haue slayne at the first takyng vpon him thoffice of the depute lieutenauncie', and Ormond made another attempt in the summer: the deputy is said to have spent seventeen days with 20,000 of his own men 'brannyng, destruyng and wastyng of the said Ormond is lordships', while in Leinster the English were defeated by the O'Byrnes. But in the parliament which met at Wexford in October 1463 and was successively adjourned to Waterford, Naas and Dublin there was more attention than had been usual for many years to the problems of the south and south-west: it was, for instance, enacted that the people of Cork, Limerick, Waterford and Youghal might trade with the Irish in spite of any statutes to the contrary. And this parliament sent a message to the king testifying to Desmond's services and emphasizing that he had governed himself and the lieges according to the laws, and

by suche as ben welwillers vnto your moost preeminence profite and dignite Roial . . . the said depute havyng tendre respect vnto the lawes and custumes laudably used in the daies of your full noble progenitors within this your said land wherevnto he hath applied him to set and put tranquilite, peix and rest among your subiects and true liege people of this your said land in such wyse as by Goddis grace and his said labour, pollitique wit, reule, manhode, wisdome and streyngthe couth reche your said land resteth in reisonable peas and tranquilitie at this tyme aswel with your rebelx as Irissh enemyes.

They ask the king to ignore any accusations against Desmond, and to send 'some refresshing of goode and power' from England to resist Irish enemies and English rebels.[24]

The message makes it clear that Desmond was not without opponents among the Anglo-Irish, and indeed we learn from an act of the same parliament that one James Dokeray of Drogheda had gone to England in the summer of 1463, alleging that Desmond had extorted coign and livery from the king's lieges in Meath and was 'councilled, ruled and governed by the king's great traitors and rebels'. Nor, perhaps, was it altogether helpful to Desmond's public image that 'MacWilliam Bourke and O Donell and many of the English and Irish of Irland went to Dublin towards Thomas Earl of Desmond, Lord Deputy of Irland, and adhered to him'. An incursion of the Irish and Gaelicized English of the west must have been more alarming than reassuring to the Anglo-Irish of the east. And immediately after this, MacFirbis tells us that 'nine of the Lord Deputies men were slaine in Fingall thorough the instigation of the Bishop of Meath'.[25]

[24] *Statutes, Edward IV*, pt. I, pp. 138–40, 180–87; MacFirbis, *Annals*, p. 249.
[25] *Statutes, Edward IV*, pt. I, p. 96; MacFirbis, *Annals*, p. 253.

It seems clear that William Sherwood, bishop of Meath 1460–82, who had been deputy for a time in 1462, was one of the leading figures in the opposition to Desmond. No doubt there was much behind the quarrel which we shall never know, but when the deputy and the bishop both went to the king this year Desmond seems to have convinced Edward that he was in the right. But perhaps the king was not entirely happy about the situation, for in the summer of 1465 we hear that John Tiptoft, earl of Worcester, now mentioned for the first time in connection with Ireland, was going to Ireland with an armed force, which was to include artillery, 'for the safe custody of that land'. But though Tiptoft received £100 for the collection of soldiers to go to Ireland, nothing came of it at the time. It does not seem, however, that there was any intention of superseding Desmond, who was sent £200 by way of reward.[26]

In 1466 the deputy met with a considerable disaster. In an expedition against Offaly his forces were heavily defeated, and he and many others taken prisoner. The annals say that the defences of Meath were permanently weakened by this, and in the west the O'Briens of Thomond, apparently encouraged by this weakening of Desmond's power, invaded his territories in the summer, subjugating the Irish of Desmond and Ormond, conquering the country of the Clanwilliam Burkes, and also dominating co. Limerick and forcing the city of Limerick to pay tribute. Later in the year we hear of Desmond leading an army against the O'Byrnes, but though O'Brien died before the end of the year, we hear of no attempt to repair the disaster in the west.[27]

It is not altogether surprising that the king decided to replace Desmond. Worcester's appointment as deputy, nominally by Clarence, but really by the king, does not seem to have survived, but on 17 April 1467 arrangements were being made for his transport to Ireland 'for the repression of the rebels', and in Easter term he was paid £721 16s. 8d. and 250 marks, and seems to have had a further £2,896 16s. 8d. in Michaelmas term. On 18 August the muster of 700 archers of his retinue was ordered to be taken at Beaumaris. Meanwhile, the royal service had been summoned to Kildare in June, though we hear nothing of the expedition which must have been intended. It is not clear when Worcester arrived in Ireland, but it was presumably at latest by the end of October, when the writs for the parliament which met at Dublin on 11 December must have been issued.[28]

[26] C.P.R., 1461–7, p. 488; Analecta Hibernica, X, p. 29.
[27] MacFirbis, Annals, p. 258; AU.
[28] C.P.R., 1467–77, pp. 29, 54; Analecta Hibernica, II, p. 284; ibid., X, pp. 29, 43, 45.

The course of events at this parliament is by no means clear. In the session before Christmas everything seems to have been harmonious, and Worcester and Kildare combined to found a chantry at Dunshaughlin. But the session which began at Drogheda on 4 February 1468 was quite different in tone. Desmond is said to have gone to it against the will of his friends and advisers, having had full satisfaction and fair words from Worcester. But the first act was to attaint Desmond, Kildare and Edward Plunket of

horrible treasons and felonies contrived and done by them, as well in alliance, fosterage and alterage with the Irish enemies of the king, as in giving to them horses and harness and arms, and supporting them against the king's faithful subjects.

We do not know what lay behind this: later tradition held that Edward's queen, Elizabeth Woodville, was avenging herself on Desmond for some tactless remarks, but there is no contemporary evidence. It was probably at the same time that Sir John Gilbert accused the treasurer, Roland fitz Eustace, Lord Portlester, the former deputy, of having said to Desmond that he should take it upon himself to be king of Ireland, and that he and the whole land would obey him. Though Gilbert fled to O'Connor Faly, 'then openly at war, adhering to him as a false traitor', rather than prove his accusation, it is not impossible that there had been some plot against Worcester during January. In any case Desmond was arrested in the Dominican friary, 'in ugly treachery', and was executed on 15 February, 'slain by the swords of the wicked, or shall I rather say made a martyr of Christ', wrote an Anglo-Irish annalist, and an Irish one that he was 'beheaded without proper cause. . . . all Ireland and from Rome westwards was filled with sorrow and affliction'.[29]

All three of the Irish earldoms were now under attainder, and with Desmond dead, Kildare in prison, and Ormond in exile Worcester seems to have felt secure. But in the summer there was the reaction to Desmond's execution that might have been expected. On 28 June the lords wrote from the parliament which was again in session at Drogheda that 'Gerot of Dessemond' (the late earl's brother) with 20,000 galloglasses and some 2,000 horsemen, had come into Meath, burning, wasting and destroying, upon which Roland fitz Eustace, the treasurer, released Kildare from prison, and 'thei with suche felowship as they couthe make went

[29] *Statutes, Edward IV*, pt. I, pp. 454–62, 464–6, 572–4; *Cal. Carew MSS: Book of Howth*, pp. 186–7; Grace, *Annals*, p. 165; University College, Oxford, MS 103, f. 53d; *AC*.

in to the said Gerot to eide and supporte him'. By the time Worcester came up to attack, Garret had also been joined by O'Connor Faly and Donnell Kavanagh, for the sake of plunder, but the deputy 'putte him to rebuke', and Kildare and the treasurer were left after his retreat to make their peace with the deputy, who accepted their submission, 'consideryng that your subiectes shoulde continue in the more tranquillite and peas from the daiely sautes of your Irishe enemyes and Englishe rebelx such as was bounden in affinite to the saide Erle of Kildare'. And in the same year Garret of Desmond seems to have raided co. Tipperary, burning Fethard. Nor were these the only disasters of the year: in the early summer the seneschal of Ulster with some 500 of the men of Lecale was killed by Conn O'Neill, and O'Reilly made a great raid into Louth, though he was defeated and killed with 300 of his following by a force in which the men of Drogheda seem to have been prominent, and which followed up this success by raiding into Cavan. And the Irish of Leinster were not yet at peace: when Kildare's attainder was reversed at the end of July he had to undertake to do faithful service, and to cause the Irish of Leinster to be at peace to the best of his ability. It was inevitable that the letter of 28 June should implore the king to send Worcester soldiers and money, without which 'we can not undrestande howe your saide lande may be conserved and defendet'. But, like all such appeals, this had little effect: in March 1470 Worcester was owed £4,535, principally for soldiers' wages. Nevertheless, one major danger disappeared after this, for in Desmond almost all the Irish rose against the Geraldines, while the O'Briens raided across the Shannon. Eventually Garret's only Irish ally, Cormac son of Donough MacCarthy, tanist of MacCarthy of Carbery, succeeded in making himself chief of Carbery, and Garret then turned to an attack on his nephew, James, the new earl. The boy's mother, in alliance with 'all the Munstermen she could find', fought back, and in the next year both Murrough O'Brien and MacCarthy Mor with other lesser chiefs campaigned successfully against Garret, after which O'Brien

refused to depart till James was named earl. When the host heard that they decided to go with James to Cork in order to place him in possession of his inheritance and he then received the title of earl from the mayor of Cork and the nobles of his territory and the rest of his friends with the consent of laymen and clergy[30].

[30] P.R.O., London, S.C. 1/58/50 (printed with some omissions by I. D. Thornley, *England under the Yorkists*, pp. 256–9); *Statutes, Edward IV*, pt. I, pp. 572, 586–92; *AC*; *AU*; *C.P.R., 1467–77*, p. 193; *Analecta Hibernica*, X, p. 45; University College, Oxford, MS 103, ff. 55–56.

After 1467 we hear little of Worcester's doings. He was still high in favour with the king, who sent him a great cup for the baptism of his eldest son, born on 14 July 1469.[31] Then, early in 1470, he was recalled and was appointed lieutenant in place of Clarence on 23 March. The background to this was the breach between Edward and Warwick, once his principal supporter, which had been developing for some time. By the summer of 1469, in alliance with Clarence, who hoped for the crown, Warwick was actively plotting to raise the country against Edward; in July he invaded England from Calais, and by August had secured the king's person. But he hesitated to go further, and by the beginning of 1470 Edward was again in command of the situation; in April Warwick fled to Calais, and in September, now in alliance with France and the Lancastrians, he landed in the west country at the head of a considerable force, rapidly augmented by Lancastrian sympathizers. On 2 October Edward sailed from King's Lynn for Burgundy, and a few days later Henry VI was reinstated in London. The parliament which met on 26 November declared Henry king, and established the succession in his heirs male, and, failing them, in Clarence. But the Lancastrian party was by no means united: apart from the unreliability of Clarence, some of the greatest men were bitterly opposed to Warwick, and were not prepared to act till queen Margaret arrived, and she delayed in France till April, when it was already much too late. For in the middle of March 1471 Edward IV had landed in the Humber; on 11 April he entered London, and was now in possession of Henry VI; on Easter Sunday, 14 April, Warwick was defeated and killed at Barnet; at Tewkesbury on 4 May the forces of queen Margaret, who had landed at Weymouth on the day of Barnet, were heavily defeated. Her son, with many of the Lancastrian leaders, was killed, while others were executed after the battle. The Yorkists were firmly reestablished.

These events seem to have had little effect on the course of affairs in Ireland. Yorkist enthusiasms had no doubt been cooled by Worcester's proceedings, while a Lancastrian party hardly existed. Worcester seems to have left Sir Edward Dudley as his deputy, but at some stage, probably in the summer of 1470, Dudley left Ireland, and Kildare was elected by the council as justiciar. On 18 October 1470 Worcester, 'that object of execration to all the men of Ireland', was executed by the victorious Lancastrians, who reappointed Clarence as lieutenant on 18 February 1471. Edward pardoned Clarence, who went over to the Yorkists shortly after his

31 *Analecta Hibernica*, X, p. 30.

brother landed in March 1471, but it seems to have been the end of the year before his position in Ireland was restored, for Kildare was still justiciar at the beginning of December 1471 and first appears as deputy on 28 December. As justiciar he held a parliament at Dublin on 26 November 1470, in which the Yorkist side was firmly taken, for it was enacted that coins should be struck with the legend *Edwardus dei gratia rex Anglie et dominus Hibernie*, and it referred to Edward as 'our sovereign lord', but apart from an order to surrender all Worcester's property to the justiciar there was no reference to the events which were going on in England. Nor do we learn very much about what happened in Ireland in 1471[32]: Kildare attacked MacMahon, and O'Kelly raided Westmeath, but was defeated by the local Anglo-Irish. But it is clear that there was widespread disorder, with which the resources of the colony were no longer able to deal. In 1470 the tenants of Saggart, not ten miles from Dublin, but under the mountains, had made a separate truce with Esmond O'Toole, putting themselves into his protection: all parliament felt able to do about this was to order that either they should be obliged to abandon it, or else all their neighbours should be allowed to enter into similar truces. 'Harolds' country' in the Dublin mountains was in rebellion so that no one dared go there to levy any subsidy, 'for fear of their lives, or of being made prisoners and delivered to the Irishmen'. The county of Meath was greatly impoverished by the war of the Irish, and English rebels. The parliament of 1471 granted the justiciar a retinue of eighty archers, half to be paid by him, and half by the inhabitants of Dublin, Meath, Louth and Kildare, for whose protection they were intended, but by the early summer a great part of the town of Saggart had been lately burned by the O'Byrnes and O'Tooles. Further afield, in May 1472 MacMurrough was over-running co. Wexford, and a royal service was proclaimed at Wexford, apparently in February 1473.[33]

In the autumn or early winter of 1473 Sir Gilbert Debenham, one of the king's household, and James Norris were sent by the king to Ireland *in ambassiata*, apparently in response to a message sent by the parliament of December 1472. They must have attended the parliament held at Dublin on 18 March 1474, which established the Guild of St George, a force of 120 mounted archers, forty horsemen, and forty pages, to be paid out of a grant of cus-

[32] *AC* seem to put the events in Desmond assigned by the Munster annals to 1468–9 in 1471–2 (see above, p. 393).

[33] *Statutes, Edward IV*, pt. I, pp. 652, 654, 662–4, 666–8, 674, 714–18, 808–10, 894; ibid., pt. II, p. 766; *AC*; *C.P.R., 1467–77*, p. 243; Hore, *History of Wexford*, V, p. 132.

toms, and commanded by the deputy and twelve of the most hon-
ourable persons of Dublin, Kildare, Meath and Louth. But in
addition it prepared a message to the king to be brought back by
Debenham and his companions. The ambassadors, it said, had
discussed the situation with the three estates and the council, and
had seen for themselves 'thextreme subduyng and destrucyon of
the sayd land', caused not only by Irish enemies and English rebels,
but also by the Scots,

which ben entred and dwellen in Ullester to the nomber of XM¹ and more which
proposen and dayly conspiren to subdue al thys land to the obeysaunce of the
kyng of Scottes havyng in their mynd the grete conquest that Bruse som tyme
seuer³⁴ to the kyng of Scottes made in the same land, whos malycyous entent to
resist is inpossible to the kynges subgettes of the said land, which ben but pety
nombre in comparyson of the grete multitude of her Iryssh ennemys Englysh
reblez and Scottes.

It complained, as always, that lieutenants and deputies had not
paid their debts, because they were not paid their wages, 'for the
which nother they myght pay her dettes nor contynu still for de-
fense of the land, but lewe it wors then they fynd it'. It asked the
king either to come himself before August, or to send Clarence or
some other lord of the blood royal, with at least 1,000 archers and
cash to pay them. It asked that proclamation should be made that
all persons of Irish birth in England should return on pain of forfeiture, and it alleged that if Ireland were brought 'holy under the
kynges obeysaunce and lawes' the revenue might amount in a
short time to 100,000 marks a year.³⁵

Edward, however, had other things to think of than Ireland.
Clarence's loyalty was uncertain, and there had been a Lancastrian attack on the coast of Cornwall in the autumn of 1473. In
1474 he was largely preoccupied with negotiations for a treaty
with Burgundy, finally concluded in July, and with negotiations
with Scotland, which resulted in a marriage treaty in October. All
this was designed to lead up to a new expedition against France,
and there was little to spare in the way of time, men or money for
Ireland. But on 18 August 1474 a commission was issued to take
ships for the transport of a force which was being sent to Ireland
under Debenham, who was retained for a year from 15 September
to go to Ireland for its relief, safe-custody and defence with 400
archers, paid by the English exchequer. On 18 April 1475 Thomas

³⁴ D. Bryan, *The Great Earl of Kildare*, p. 19, makes this read 'somtyme sen' to
the Kyng of Scottes', but the original seems to be 'seuer', an adherent (P.R.O.,
London, C. 47/10/29, m. 1).
³⁵ *Analecta Hibernica*, X, p. 30; *Statutes, Edward IV*, pt. II, pp. 188–94; D.
Bryan, *The Great Earl of Kildare*, pp. 17–22.

Danyell was further retained, apparently in addition to Debenham, to do 'service of werre' in Ireland, with one hundred archers paid by the English exchequer, and a further 120 'at the wages of the inhabitants of Ireland'.[36]

By this time Kildare had been replaced as deputy by William Sherwood, bishop of Meath, Desmond's old enemy, in circumstances of which we know nothing. But the state of the country is vividly suggested by the account in the Irish annals of a circuit made by O'Donnell in Connacht, after which he proceeded through co. Longford to the barony of Kilkenny West, co. Westmeath, 'and the Dillons and the Daltons made peace with him'. He then went on to Offaly and Carbury, co. Kildare, where he was joined by O'Connor Faly, and opposed by the Anglo-Irish of Meath, 'and the lands were destroyed in the fighting. Peace was afterwards made, and O'Donnell returned home by way of Athlone.' In 1477, as a result of quarrels among the MacCarthys, 'war spread throughout Munster and all the south was destroyed, Gall and Gael'. It is not surprising that early in 1477 we find the deputy going to England 'to solicit the good grace of the king and his dearest brother of Clarence for the public good and relief of this land'. In June he was being sent back with a force of 200 archers, while the archbishop of Armagh, Edmund Connesburgh, who had been consecrated in 1475 but never got possession, was commissioned with one of the king's squires to examine and determine 'certain strifes, discords and controversies between certain magnates in Ireland'.[37]

Meanwhile in England Edward's expedition to France in 1475 had ended in a treaty by which, among other things, the king of France undertook to pay the king of England an annual pension. But Clarence had been becoming more and more troublesome: in the summer of 1477 he was involved in a Lancastrian rising in Cambridgeshire and Huntingdonshire, and was condemned on a number of charges of treason and put to death on 18 February 1478. His condemnation had, of course, ended Sherwood's powers as deputy, and when the news reached Ireland the council elected the earl of Kildare as justiciar.[38] On 10 March 1478 the duke of Suffolk was appointed as lieutenant for twenty years, but he never took office, and Kildare continued to act as justiciar, and between May and September 1478 held a parliament whose acts were afterwards annulled.

It seems that before the end of May 1478 the earl had been

[36] C.P.R., 1467–77, pp. 467, 524; Analecta Hibernica, X, pp. 30–31, 46–48.
[37] AC; Statutes, Edward IV, pt. II, pp. 464–6; Analecta Hibernica, X, p. 31; C.P.R., 1477–85, pp. 71, 79.
[38] This was Gerald, the eighth earl, his father having died in March 1478.

removed from office and forbidden to hold a parliament by letters under the English privy seal and signet. On 6 July the king's infant son, George, who died within a year, was appointed lieutenant in place of Suffolk, and Henry, Lord Grey, was appointed as deputy for the next two years. He was to have 300 archers, and was to have for the first year £2,000 from the English exchequer, and for the second £1,825, to be paid half by the English exchequer and half out of the Irish revenue, 'if so be that the same reuenues woll strecche therto'; his men were to be ready for mustering in north Wales by 19 August. But there was a strong party in Ireland which supported Kildare, who was opposed by a faction headed by the bishop of Meath, with the chief justice, Philip Bermingham, as a leading member. The bishop had been Desmond's enemy in 1463; Bermingham had been an adherent of Ormond's and had been condemned as a traitor and pardoned in 1462. It does not appear even what the quarrel was, nor have we the evidence on which to base an opinion as to its merits: it was most likely this that the archbishop of Armagh had been sent to determine in 1477. And now Kildare's party openly opposed the new deputy. Grey presumably landed in Ireland about the middle of September, for he summoned a parliament to Trim for 6 November. But the constable of Dublin castle, the prior of Kilmainham, garrisoned the castle against him, broke down its bridge, and refused him admittance; Sir Roland fitz Eustace, the chancellor, wilfully absented himself from the deputy, depriving him of the use of the great seal; the sheriffs of Dublin and Louth made no return to the writs of summons to parliament.[39]

Faced with this determined opposition, Grey seems to have returned to England early in the new year, leaving Sir Robert Preston, Lord Gormanston, who seems to have been a supporter of the bishop of Meath, as his deputy. He was soon followed by Kildare and his supporters: the archbishop of Dublin, the prior of Kilmainham, and the prior of All Hallows. On 10 February 1479 they had a safe-conduct as they were coming to the king from Ireland 'for certain causes concerning the peace of the land'. Bermingham was also in attendance on the council in England about this time, and though we know nothing about the discussions which must have gone on, the king issued 'articles' declaring his pleasure on the 'gret variances of late in our said land of Irland' which were in effect a victory for Kildare. The subsidy granted in Grey's par-

---

[39] *Statutes, Edward IV*, pt. I, pp. 24–28; ibid., pt. II, pp. 650–54, 676–8; *Analecta Hibernica*, X, pp. 48–49; *C.P.R.*, *1476–85*, p. 121. The parliament was adjourned from Trim to Drogheda.

liament at Drogheda was confirmed; the acts of resumption passed in both Grey's parliament at Drogheda and Kildare's at Naas were annulled, except that the resumption of offices made at Drogheda was to stand: the king had appointed the bishop of Meath as chancellor and Roland fitz Eustace as treasurer, and would appoint others as chief baron of the exchequer and master of the mint; Kildare was appointed deputy. A general act of resumption from 1422 was to be passed in the next parliament; any act restraining tonnage and poundage was to be repealed; so was the act forbidding the summons of men out of Ireland by English writs. At the same time, a set of directions was issued for the performance of the duties of the chancellor, and other chancery officials; the treasurer, with a particular direction that fitz Eustace should remit all ill will against the bishop of Meath, Bermingham, and all others, as the king had commanded them to do to him; the judges; and the deputy himself, who was to make sure that fitz Eustace delivered the great seal to the bishop of Meath. Finally, directions were given for the council, whose acts were to be by majority, and for the mint.[40]

In May 1479 the king's second son, Richard duke of York, then only four, was appointed to succeed his brother as lieutenant, and Lord Gormanston was continued as deputy for the time, being retained with the king with forty archers and twenty men-at-arms from 1 June till 30 September. In fact, he was still testing letters patent as deputy on 18 October. But Kildare must have arrived very soon after this, and remained deputy through all changes of lieutenant into the reign of Henry VII. On 12 August 1480, after the duke of York's original appointment for two years had been extended for a further twelve, Kildare entered into fresh indentures with the king, to run for four years from 5 May 1481. He was to have eighty archers and forty other horsemen, taking £600 a year from the Irish revenue: if this could not be paid, the deficiency was to be met by the English exchequer. Meanwhile the earl had held a parliament, which met at Dublin on 10 December 1479 and lasted, with adjournments, till January 1481; it granted a subsidy, it passed an act of resumption, as directed by the king, it re-established poundage and the guild of St George, which had been abolished by the bishop of Meath, and it renewed the old legislation against absentees.[41]

[40] Cal. Christ Church Deeds, no. 1014; Bryan, The Great Earl of Kildare, p. 40; Analecta Hibernica, X, p. 32; Statutes, Edward IV, pt. II, pp. 680–81; Gilbert, Viceroys, pp. 592–9.
[41] C.P.R., 1476–85, pp. 153, 210; Analecta Hibernica, X, pp. 18, 31–32, 50; Gilbert, Viceroys, pp. 600–01; Statutes, Edward IV, pt. II, pp. 682–831.

We have very little evidence as to the course of affairs in Ireland during this period. The royal service was proclaimed at Kildare in September 1480, and in February 1483, in a parliament held at Limerick, the earl, asserting that he had brought to the king's obedience the counties of Carlow and Kildare, but that the lands recovered remained largely waste because the persons claiming them did not come to inhabit them, had himself granted all such unoccupied lands from Calverstown to Carlow, and from Carlow to Leighlin Bridge. And we may suppose that during this period Kildare was extending and completing that network of alliances by which, in the early sixteenth century, almost all the Irish chieftains of the south-east and midlands owed him those rents which had earlier belonged to the lords of Meath and Leinster.[42]

On 9 April 1483 Edward IV died, and was succeeded by his son, Edward V. But on 25 June Edward was deposed and replaced by his uncle, the duke of Gloucester, Richard III, in circumstances which are still the subject of lively historical discussion, though they need not concern us here. But the accession of Richard III was marked by an attempt to check the power of the deputy, which seems to have been uncontrolled at the end of Edward IV's reign. The fact was, of course, that with Desmond to all intents and purposes gone over to the Irish and Ormond an absentee Kildare was left as the only really important Irish magnate, and that unless the crown were prepared to intervene either in person, or at least by a prince of the blood royal of full age and with sufficient prestige to assert his authority effectively, there was really no alternative to him. Successive parliaments and great councils had asked for such intervention, but the crown, fully engaged in the restoration of order in England, had never been in a position to provide it. But Richard was prepared to make the effort to reassert royal authority, and might perhaps have succeeded in doing so had he lived longer.

Richard was concerning himself with the affairs of Ireland within a month after his accession. On 19 July he appointed his son as lieutenant, and, probably very soon afterwards, despatched Master William Lacy, who had been in Ireland on the king's business in 1479, to negotiate with Kildare and the council. Lacy was instructed to tell them that the king hoped to attend to Ireland as soon as he had established England; Kildare had been appointed deputy for a year from 31 August, and after that during pleasure, because the king wanted to intervene in person as soon as he was free to do

---

[42] *Analecta Hibernica*, II, pp. 266, 287–9; ibid., X, pp. 132-4, 135-6; *Ninth Report of the Historical MSS Commission*, pt. II, pp. 275–8.

so. Kildare was to be spoken to apart and flattered; when he agreed to take office his commission was to be given to him, and he was then to be pressed to go to England at once to enter into indentures with the king. Lacy was to give the council a letter under the privy seal about the Irish mint, which was to be put into effect at once, and was to announce that the king wished all officers to hold during pleasure, that new seals should be made for Ireland, and that the statute of premunire should be put in execution against those obtaining benefices by provisions. The king also wanted an account of the Irish revenue.[43]

There was little in this that can have been welcome to Kildare, but he was able to evade much of it. He did not go to England, sending instead John Estrete, the king's serjeant at laws, to make his excuses and present petitions, the general drift of which appears from Richard's answers. He asked that he might be granted the deputyship for nine or ten years; he asked for wages of £1,000; and he asked for a grant to him and his heirs male of the manor of Leixlip and the custody of Wicklow castle. He asked also for a promise of safe-conduct from some of the English magnates as well as from the king. Richard in effect said that he would do nothing till the earl came to him, which he was urged to do before 1 August 1484; he sent letters of protection under the signet, saying that he would keep them and see them kept as duly as if they were 'passed undre the seales of alle the lordes of his land': he had never been known to break a promise. When the earl came, he would take him into favour as much as ever Edward IV had, and would extend the grant of office as he asked; as to his wage, when he came he was to bring a statement of the Irish revenue: if there was a balance of £1,000 he could have it, if not the king would satisfy him, and would in any case grant him Leixlip and Wicklow. It appears that Kildare did in fact go to England in the summer of 1484, and in September, perhaps as a result of discussions with Kildare, the bishop of Annaghdown, Thomas Barrett, an exile from his see who had already been employed as an envoy by Edward IV in 1467, was being sent to Ireland on an embassy to the 'English rebels' of the south-west and west, and also to endeavour to make peace in Ulster.[44]

Barrett was given a set of instructions covering negotiations with

---

[43] *Analecta Hibernica*, X, p. 32; Ellis, *Original Letters*, third series, I, no. 42; J. Gairdner, *Letters and Papers of Richard III and Henry VII*, I, pp. 43–46.

[44] Gairdner, *Letters and Papers*, I, pp. 91–93; Bryan, *The Great Earl of Kildare*, pp. 278–82; *Analecta Hibernica* X, pp. 42–43. An estimate of the revenue prepared early in 1485 shows only £185 12s. 8d. at the deputy's disposal (ibid., pp. 17–27: see above, pp. 165–6).

Kildare himself, now appointed deputy to the earl of Lincoln, who had been appointed lieutenant on 21 August, after the death of the prince of Wales, and letters to the treasurer and others. But more significant were a series of letters to the Anglo-Irish lords of Munster and Connacht, of whom Desmond was of course the chief. It seems that the bishop had already been in Ireland, for all the letters refer to the good reports made by him on the recipients. Desmond was clearly the main target of the mission; the bishop was to tell him that although his father had been

extorciously slayne and murdred by colour of the lawes within Ireland . . . ayenst alle manhode, reason, and good conscience

like things had happened in England, as for instance in the death of Clarence, and the king deplored it. The bishop was given power to take Desmond's oath of allegiance; he was to exhort him not to marry without the king's advice and knowledge, for the king intended to provide him a fitting wife; and he was to induce him to abandon the wearing of 'the Irisshe arraye' and wear English clothing instead: a wardrobe of gowns, doublets, shirts, hose, hats and tippets, and a collar of gold, was supplied, which the bishop was to give Desmond when he had promised to wear them. Finally, he was to be exhorted to maintain the rights of the church and keep good order in his country. And in addition to this mission in Munster and Connacht, Kildare was to be exhorted to bring Ulster once more into the king's possession, which it was thought he might well do, since his brother-in-law, the great O'Neill, occupied most of it, and the king would be very willing to take O'Neill into his favour, as Edward IV had his father. Moreover, it was hoped that O'Donnell would come in, 'by the meanes that the kynges grace hath committed and shewed unto the said bisshop': if he did, Kildare was to receive him.[45]

It was long since an English government had really looked beyond the boundaries of the four obedient counties, and perhaps all this scheme for extending English power once more throughout Ireland had its genesis chiefly in the imagination of the bishop, though it may well have been such a report on the revenue as that of 1485, with its lists of former revenues from lands in Ulster, Connacht and Munster, now waste or in the hands of others, which inspired it.[46] But we know nothing of how the bishop fared in Ireland, and in England the disaffection which had existed throughout Richard's reign was mounting, while Henry Tudor, the last,

[45] Gairdner, *Letters and Papers*, I, pp. 67–78; *Analecta Hibernica*, X, p. 30.
[46] Ibid., pp. 24–26.

though doubtful, heir of the Lancastrians, was preparing an invasion, supported by France. Finally, on 7 August 1485, Henry landed at Milford Haven; on 22 August Richard was killed at Bosworth, and Henry VII was on the throne.

Ireland remained strongly Yorkist in feeling, as was soon to be shown, but for the moment these events had no apparent result there. Henry had for the time being no attention to spare, but on 11 March 1486 he appointed his uncle, Jasper Tudor, duke of Bedford, lieutenant, and Kildare was continued as deputy, with the other great officers. But the return to power of the Lancastrians in England meant the return to favour of the Butlers, and Kildare found it politic to marry his second daughter to Piers Butler, the cousin and heir male of Ormond, who eventually became the ninth earl. But when, early in 1487, there was brought to Ireland a boy of ten who was alleged to be Edward earl of Warwick, the son of Clarence, he was enthusiastically accepted by the majority of the Anglo-Irish, apparently in good faith, as the true heir to the throne. In fact Warwick was a prisoner in the Tower, and was eventually executed in 1499; the boy was one Lambert, son of Thomas Simnel of Oxford. But he was accepted as Warwick at a meeting of magnates which included all the chief officers of the government; messages were sent to the duchess of Burgundy, Edward IV's sister, and on 5 May a force of 5,000 German mercenaries landed in Ireland with the earl of Lincoln. Only the archbishop of Armagh, Octavian del Palatio, and the Butler interest, with the city of Waterford, to whose recorder the English treasurer was ordered on 21 March to make a payment for the purchase of bows, bow-strings and arrows,[47] held out for Henry. On 24 May Simnel was crowned as Edward VI in Christ Church cathedral, apparently by the archbishop of Dublin, in the presence of Lincoln, Kildare, the chancellor, the treasurer, and many other magnates, lay and ecclesiastical. A parliament was summoned in his name, and the city of Waterford was ordered to provide forces to 'assist him in his voiage into his province of Mounster'. But Waterford asserted its loyalty to Henry VII, flatly denouncing Simnel and his supporters as traitors, and in alliance with the Butlers and their towns, as well as the O'Byrnes, resolutely held out.

On 4 June the German troops, together with a considerable body of the Anglo-Irish and, apparently, a native Irish force, sailed for England. At Stoke, on 16 June, they were decisively defeated, with heavy losses which included Kildare's brother, and

---

[47] *Analecta Hibernica*, X, pp. 33, 51. Other references for Henry's reign will be found in D. Bryan, *The Great Earl of Kildare*.

Simnel was captured. But in Ireland Kildare still held out; on 20 October Henry, writing to the mayor and citizens of Waterford, said that

the said earl with the supportation of the inhabitants of our said city of Dublin and others ther, to the high displeasure of almighty God, and contrary to the duty of their allegiance, will not yet know their seditious opinions, but unto this day uphold and maintain the same.[48]

It was not till near the end of the year that Kildare and his supporters submitted, and in June 1488 Sir Richard Edgecombe was sent to Ireland, equipped with power to grant pardons (they had been made out on 25 May, and were entrusted to him), take oaths of fealty, and grant safe-conducts to those coming to England to treat about the affairs of Ireland.

It has seemed surprising to many writers that Henry should have been so lenient to the rebels. But it is difficult to see what else he could have done. His position in England was still precarious, and the possibility of continental intervention in support of Yorkist plots was by no means at an end. Any course in Ireland other than the one he took would have required overwhelming military force, since apart from the Butler dominated area in the south-east the Anglo-Irish had, apparently to a man, been involved in the support of Simnel, and Kildare had a sufficient alliance among the native Irish to have made it reasonably certain that, as far as they involved themselves at all, it would have been in support of Kildare rather than Henry. Had Kildare and his party been driven to desperation, it might well have meant simply the loss of a country which the Tudors were not yet in a position to hold by force. And Henry had done what he could to secure himself support independent of Kildare in Munster. On 7 December 1487 Desmond had been murdered at the instigation of his brother John; his heir was his brother Maurice. On 8 April Maurice was given licence to enter on his lands without sueing out livery, and was granted the office of constable of Limerick castle for life; on 17 April he was commissioned to arrest rebels, enquire of them by juries, and deliver the gaols of them throughout Munster. Maurice, Lord Roche, was commissioned to keep the county of Cork, and Cormac MacCarthy of Muskerry and Florence MacCarthy of Carbery and their heirs were given grants of English law and liberty, with a general pardon of all offences.[49] A bull against disturbances concerning

---

[48] C. Smith, *Antient and Present State of the County and City of Waterford*, p. 133.

[49] *Cal. Ormond Deeds*, III, no. 273; W. Campbell, *Materials for the Reign of Henry VII*, II, pp. 309, 313, 496. Florence MacCarthy was also granted the customs, cokets and prise wines west of the Old Head of Kinsale.

the right of succession, in which Ireland was specifically included, was also procured from pope Innocent VIII.

Edgecombe landed at Kinsale on 27 June and took the oaths of the Lords Barry and Courcy, and of the town authorities. Then he sailed along the coast to Waterford, where he was received with enthusiasm, though the citizens were distressed to learn that he had a pardon for Kildare, whose continued rule would, they asserted, mean the ruin of the city. Finally, on 3 July, he reached Lambay, and sent a messenger to Dublin to find the bishop of Clogher, Thomas Dartas, or 'Richard the king's porter', who must have been conducting the preliminary negotiations.[50] Dartas appeared in Lambay the next day, bringing news that Kildare was out of Dublin, and on 5 July Edgecombe landed at Malahide and reached Dublin that afternoon. In Dublin he waited at the Black Friars, with mounting irritation, till 12 July, when Kildare at last arrived, with a body of 200 horsemen, and established himself in state at Thomas Court.

Negotiations now began, and lasted for more than a week. It seems that Edgecombe had been instructed to ensure that Kildare and the Yorkists entered into bonds by which their lands should be automatically forfeited if they ever rebelled against Henry, and this they flatly refused to do, telling Edgecombe on 18 July that rather than do so 'they wold become Irish every of them'. And Edgecombe's hand was gravely weakened since it was now common knowledge that James III of Scotland, who had been in alliance with Henry VII, was dead—he had been murdered on 11 June— and, probably, that the alliance was unlikely to be continued under his successor. Finally, on 20 July, it was agreed that Kildare and the others should take oaths of allegiance to Henry, and should further swear that they would never assist his rebels or traitors and would resist and disclose any plots against him that might come to their knowledge; they would cause any messengers bringing letters or messages from the duchess of Burgundy or anyone else to pervert them from their allegiance or cause rebellion, or anyone using seditious language against Henry to be taken and punished; and they would not hinder the execution of the papal bull against those troubling Henry's title or rebelling against him. On 21 July first Kildare and then the other lords did homage, and then Kildare and the bishops and other lords took the oath during mass, after which a solemn Te Deum was sung, and the ceremonies concluded with a dinner. Little remained to be done: the next day, after long discussion with Kildare and the council, Edgecombe went to

See *Analecta Hibernica*, X, pp. 33–34, 53.

Drogheda and granted pardons to the towns of Drogheda and Trim. On 30 July he took ship from Dalkey.

The Irish Yorkists had thus submitted, but were by no means converted, and their tempers can hardly have been improved by the famous banquet of 1489, when Henry, having summoned the temporal lords to England, caused them to be waited on by Simnel. In July 1490 Kildare was summoned to England, to appear within the next ten months. But he did not come: nearly a year later, in June 1491, he wrote that he had intended to come as ordered, but had been asked by the lieges, and especially Desmond and 'the lord Bourk of Connaght', to remain for their defence, and to settle a quarrel between Desmond and Burke. If the king would send a messenger, he would cause Desmond and Burke, with all the lords spiritual and temporal of Munster and Connacht, to enter into the same engagements as he himself had entered into before Edge-combe. On 4 June the lords spiritual and temporal, writing 'in playne parlement', asked that Kildare might remain: when he had lately been ill the Irish had been planning to divide the country between them if he died. A month later Desmond, Piers Butler (Ormond's agent), Lord Roche and Lord Courcy wrote from Limerick confirming what Kildare had said and adding that he had faithfully kept his oath.

In spite of these protestations, another Yorkist pretender was about to appear in Ireland, and it is not impossible that there had already been some correspondence with Margaret of Burgundy. In November 1491 there landed in Cork Perkin Warbeck, who was put forward as Richard duke of York, Edward IV's second son, one of the princes murdered in the Tower. He certainly asked support from both Kildare and Desmond: it is not certain whether he got it from Kildare, but he did from Desmond and from Munster in general. But Warbeck did not remain long in Ireland, and nothing very much seems to have come of his visit, though in December Henry appointed Sir James of Ormond, an illegitimate son of the sixth earl, and Thomas Garth captains of an army being sent to Ireland to repress rebels and enemies in Kilkenny and Tipperary, and granted Sir James the lands of the earldom of March in Leinster, Meath and Munster for two years, and afterwards during pleasure. It does not, however, seem that a very important force was sent, but in February 1492 a ship was further provided to cruise on the coasts of Ireland, 'for to haue an herkenyng always to the state and condicion of our rebelles there', with a crew of 110, armed with bows, bills, and a barrel of gunpowder.[51] Mean-

[51] *Analecta Hibernica*, X, pp. 34–35, 55–56.

while James of Ormond, whose mother had been an O'Brien, had allied himself to the O'Briens and the Clanrickard Burkes, and at some time in the first half of 1492 attacked the Butler country and obtained its submission. On 10 June Kildare, who was still deputy, wrote to Ormond that James had brought into counties Kilkenny and Tipperary

the O Brenes with diverse others Irishe enemys, and theretwo destroyed the kyngs subgettes, and spareth no churches ne religious places, but hath spoyled them,

alleging that he had not only the king's authority, but also Ormond's.[52] But on 11 June Kildare was replaced as deputy by the archbishop of Dublin, while James of Ormond became treasurer, and Sir Alexander Plunket chancellor.

A bitter struggle between Kildare and James of Ormond followed, and Kildare's enemies seem to have been active in England, for in February 1493 he wrote to Ormond that he understood he had been accused to the king of having supported Warbeck, which was untrue, as the 'lordes of this land' had certified the king. He adds

this land was never distrued till nowe, whate by reason of the comyng downe of your bace cosyn [James of Ormond] with the kyng is Irish enemyes to set his moost noble auctorite in hure, and promysed them grete godes with all their gettyng on the kyng is English subjectis, that all is lost. Your said cosyn pubblisheth and name hymself erle of Ormound, and because he cannot have the better over your kynnesmen he provoketh and styrreth Irishmen ther aboute the countes of Kylkenny and Typperary to destrue the said countees, which bene in substance destrued all redy; and whether this be your pleasyre or no I knowe not.

Sir James and the archbishop had, he said, agreed that at the next parliament Sir James should be legitimated and recognized as earl of Ormond.[53]

The immediate result of Kildare's representations was a general pardon, issued to him on 30 March 1493, on condition that he sent his eldest son and heir to the king within six months. On 10 April pardons were issued to Desmond and his brother and others. But by this time it must have become plain to the king that the archbishop was not the man to control the warring factions, and on 6 September 1493 Sir Robert Preston, Lord Gormanston, was appointed deputy in his stead. On 12 September Preston held a council at Trim which was concerned principally with the keeping of the peace: it was attended by Kildare and the other principal magnates of the pale, and Henry Wyatt and Thomas Garth, 'the kyngs commissioners', and it required that 'every lord and gentleman the kyngs subjects of this said land' should give the deputy

[52] Gairdner, *Letters and Papers*, II, p. xxxviii.
[53] Gairdner, *Letters and Papers*, II, pp. 55–56.

'their sufficient plegge saufly to be kept in the kyngs castelles of Dublin and Trym', and be bound by recognizances in chancery to observe its articles.[54] In late October Preston held a parliament at Drogheda, but this was afterwards invalidated because Bedford, whose deputy he was, had resigned before the parliament was summoned. And immediately afterwards all the contending parties, the archbishop, Kildare, Preston, and James of Ormond, went to England. Kildare was there till the middle of May 1494, and by this time an oath of fealty had been obtained from Desmond, who had undertaken to put his son and heir in Kildare's hands. On 14 May Kildare entered into an indenture with the king by which he undertook that he would make every effort to get the boy into his hands, and would send him to the king if Desmond failed to be a faithful subject and true liegeman. But nothing came of this, and by the summer the king was clearly contemplating a complete reconstruction of the Irish government. In September his second son, Henry, was appointed lieutenant, with Sir Edward Poynings as his deputy, while Charles VIII of France had already been informed that, at the request of the principal English-speaking clergy and magnates of Ireland, including Kildare, the king was sending to Ireland 'a good and sufficient army accompanied by good and great personnages, as well for war as for justice'. Poynings landed at Howth on 13 October with a force of something under 700 men, summoned a parliament, and then embarked on an expedition against the north, probably against O'Donnell, who seems to have been supporting the claims of Warbeck. But the expedition seems to have come to grief in O'Hanlon's country when James of Ormond alleged that Kildare was conspiring with O'Hanlon to assassinate Poynings. When the parliament met at Drogheda on 1 December it proceeded to attaint Kildare 'for his greate and manifold treasons'. He was arrested in Dublin on 27 February 1495, and on 5 March he was sent to England and lodged in the Tower. Meanwhile Poynings' parliament had passed a variety of acts, of which the most important and lasting were those which explicitly subordinated the parliament of Ireland to the English council. In future no parliament was to meet in Ireland without express licence under the great seal of England, and no act was to be passed in any such parliament unless it had first been sanctioned by the deputy and council and approved by the king and council in England. Though the disorders of Ireland made it necessary to send Kildare back as deputy in 1496, Poynings' acts mark a clear watershed between medieval Ireland and the Tudor period.

[54] *Analecta Hibernica*, X, pp. 88–91.

Bibliography

I HAVE NOT attempted to give a complete bibliography, since in the near future the source material will be surveyed by the *Guide to the Sources of Hiberno-Norman History* which is being prepared for the Irish Manuscripts Commission under the editorship of Dr J. F. Lydon, while my former pupil, Mr P. W. A. Asplin, now of the Glasgow University library, is preparing a critical bibliography of the secondary material. Moreover, there is already in print *Manuscript Sources for the History of Irish Civilisation*, ed. R. J. Hayes (11 vols., Boston, 1965). I have therefore confined my bibliography to the works cited in foot notes, omitting books concerned with English or continental history which have been cited only once or twice, and have made no attempt at a critical bibliography. But it seems proper to draw particular attention to some works of reference, which provide indispensable tools for the historian.

The first of these is H. G. Richardson and G. O. Sayles, *The Administration of Ireland, 1172–1377*, which provides detailed lists of all the principal officers of the Anglo-Irish administration during this period. For the rest of the middle ages there is nothing comparable, but there are lists of chancery officials in my article on 'The Medieval Irish Chancery', and of the judges in Elrington Ball, *The Judges in Ireland*, while the latest list of chief governors is that in *The Handbook of British Chronology* (2nd edition), which also contains invaluable lists of the Irish bishops. There is a list of medieval Irish parliaments in H. G. Richardson and G. O. Sayles, *The Irish Parliament in the Middle Ages*. The lists of Irish peers in the *Handbook* have only a limited usefulness for the middle ages, since there were few Irish earls, but a number of barons will be found in the *Complete Peerage*, which is in any case much more detailed. The pedigrees of certain families—e.g. the earls of Ormond—are usefully supplemented by Burke's *Peerage*. The *Dictionary of National Biography* is valuable for many lesser men. There is no really satisfactory work on the pedigrees of Irish rulers.

Historical maps of Ireland hardly exist. Lewis's *Atlas Comprising the Counties of Ireland* (London, 1837), which shows the baronies as they existed before the rationalizations of the nineteenth century, is extremely useful. The *Map of Monastic Ireland* compiled by R. N. Hadcock (Ordnance Survey, Dublin, 1959) is, however, the only specifically historical map to have been separately published. The volumes of the *Civil Survey*, ed. R. C. Simington (Irish MSS Commission, 1931–61), though they describe the conditions of the seventeenth century, often throw light on the middle ag .. There has been little strictly historical study of Irish place names, but reference may be made to P. Walsh, *The Place Names of Westmeath* (Dublin Institute for Advanced Studies, 1957), and to the late Dr Liam Price's model study of the place names of co. Wicklow, published in parts by the Royal Irish Academy and the Dublin Institute for Advanced Studies between 1938 and 1958. The older names are surveyed in E. Hogan, S.J., *Onomasticon Goedelicum* (Dublin, London, 1910).

For the introductory chapter, though J. F. Kenney, *The Sources for the Early History of Ireland: an introduction and guide* (Columbia, 1929), deals comprehensively with the ecclesiastical sources, no such comprehensive guide to the secular sources exists.

Manuscript Sources cited in Footnotes

Public Record Office, Dublin.
> Record Commissioners' Transcripts of Memoranda Rolls. See
> J. F. Lydon, 'Survey of the Memoranda Rolls of the Irish
> Exchequer, 1294–1509', *Analecta Hibernica* XXIII (1966), pp.
> 49–134.

Public Record Office, London.
> S.C. 1   Ancient Correspondence.
> S.C. 8   Ancient Petitions.
> C. 47   Miscellanea of the Chancery.
> E. 101   Exchequer, King's Remembrancer's Accounts.

British Museum.
> MS Cotton Titus B XI.
> Additional MS 4790.
>   „ „ 6041.
> MS Lansdowne 229.

National Library of Ireland.
> MS 761.

Trinity College, Dublin.
> MS E.3.4.
> MS E.3.20.

Genealogical Office, Dublin.
> MS 192.

University College, Oxford.
> MS 103.

Trinity College, Cambridge.
> MS 0.8.13.

Lambeth.
> Carew MSS, vol. 619.

Printed Works cited in Footnotes

Account Roll of the Priory of the Holy Trinity, Dublin, 1337–1346, ed. J. Mills, Royal Society of Antiquaries of Ireland, 1891.

Acts of Archbishop Colton in his Metropolitan Visitation of the Diocese of Derry, ed. W. Reeves, Irish Archaeological Society, 1850.

Adomnan's Life of Columba, ed. and transl. A. O. and M. O. Anderson, Edinburgh, London, 1961. The notes and apparatus in the edition by W. Reeves, Dublin, 1857, are still of value.

Analecta Hibernica, Irish MSS Commission, 1930–.

Ancient Laws of Ireland, 6 vols., Dublin, 1865–1901.

Anglo-Norman Letters and Petitions from All Souls MS 182, ed. M. D. Legge, Oxford, Anglo-Norman Text Society, 1941.

The Annals of Clonmacnoise, ed. D. Murphy, S.J., Royal Society of Antiquaries of Ireland, 1896.

The Annals of Connacht, ed. A. Martin Freeman, Dublin Institute for Advanced Studies, 1944.

The Annals of Innisfallen, ed. S. Mac Airt, Dublin Institute for Advanced Studies, 1951.

The Annals of Ireland by Friar John Clyn and Thady Dowling, ed. R. Butler, Irish Archaeological Society, 1849.

'The Annals of Ireland, from the Year 1443 to 1468, translated from the Irish by Dudley Firbisse, or, as he is more usually called, Duald Mac Firbis, for Sir James Ware, in the year 1666', ed. J. O'Donovan, *The Miscellany of the Irish Archaeological Society*, I (1846), pp. 198–302.

Annals of the Kingdom of Ireland by the Four Masters, 7 vols., Dublin, 1848–51.

The Annals of Loch Cé, ed. W. M. Hennessy, 2 vols., Rolls Series, 1871.

'The Annals of Tigernach', ed. W. Stokes, *Revue Celtique*, vols. xvi–xviii (1895–7).

Annals of Ulster, ed. W. M. Hennessy and B. MacCarthy, 4 vols, Dublin, 1887–1901.

Archaeological Survey of Northern Ireland: County Down, Belfast, 1966.

Archivium Hibernicum, Maynooth and Dublin, 1912– .

Armstrong, O., *Edward Bruce's Invasion of Ireland*, London, 1923.

Ball, F. Elrington, *The Judges in Ireland*, 2 vols., London, 1926.

Barrow, G. W. S., *Robert Bruce*, London, 1965.

Betham, Sir William, *The Origin and History of the Constitution of England, and of the Early Parliaments of Ireland*, Dublin, 1834.

The Black Book of Limerick, ed. J. MacCaffrey, Dublin, 1907.

The Book of Armagh, ed. with introduction and appendices by J. Gwynn, Dublin, London, 1913.

Brooks, E. St J., *Knights' Fees in Counties Wexford, Carlow and Kilkenny*, Irish MSS Commission, 1950.

Bryan, D., *Gerald Fitzgerald, the Great Earl of Kildare, 1456–1513*, Dublin, 1933.

Butler, W. F. T., *Gleanings from Irish History*, London, 1925.

Calendar of Ancient Deeds and Muniments Preserved in the Pembroke Estate Office, Dublin, Dublin, 1891 (privately printed).

Calendar of the Ancient Records of Dublin, vol. I, ed. J. T. Gilbert, Dublin, 1889.

Calendar of Archbishop Alen's Register, c. 1172–1534, ed. C. McNeill, Royal Society of Antiquaries of Ireland, 1950.

Calendar of the Carew MSS, ed. J. S. Brewer and W. Bullen, 5 vols., Rolls Series, 1871.

Calendar of Chancery Warrants, London, 1927.

Calendar of Charter Rolls, London, 1903–27.

Calendar of Christchurch Deeds, in the *20th, 23rd* and *24th Reports of the Deputy Keeper of the Public Records of Ireland.* (Index in *27th Report.*)

Calendar of Close Rolls, London, 1892–1963.

Calendar of Documents Relating to Ireland, ed. H. S. Sweetman, 5 vols., London, 1875–86. Cf. G. J. Hand, 'Material used in *Calendar of Documents relating to Ireland*', *I.H.S.*, XII (1960), pp. 99–104.

Calendar of Documents relating to Scotland, ed. J. Bain, Edinburgh, 1881–8.

Calendar of Fine Rolls, London, 1911–62.

Calendar of the Gormanston Register, ed. J. Mills and M. J. McEnery, Royal Society of Antiquaries of Ireland, 1916.

Calendar of Inquisitions Post Mortem, London, 1904– .

Calendar of the Justiciary Rolls, Ireland. Vols. I (1295–1303) and II (1305–7) ed. J. Mills, Dublin, 1905–14; vol. III (1308–14) ed. M. C. Griffith, Dublin [1956].

Calendar of Inquisitions Miscellaneous, London, 1916– .

Calendar of Ormond Deeds, ed. E. Curtis, 6 vols., Irish MSS Commission, 1932–43.

Calendar of Papal Letters, ed. W. H. Bliss, J. A. Twemlow, and C. Johnson, London, 1893– .

Calendar of Patent Rolls, London, 1891– .

Canons of the 'First Synod of St Patrick' and of the 'Second Synod of St Patrick', ed. and transl. L. Bieler, *The Irish Penitentials*, Dublin, 1963.

Catalogue of Pipe Rolls, in the *35th–39th, 42nd–45th, 47th, 53rd* and *54th Reports of the Deputy Keeper of the Public Records of Ireland*.

Chartae, Privilegia et Immunitates, Dublin-London-Edinburgh, 1889.

Chartularies of St. Mary's Abbey, Dublin, ed. J. T. Gilbert. 2 vols., Rolls Series, 1884.

Chronicle of Ireland by Henry Marlborough, Dublin, 1633, and many other editions.

Chronicon Scotorum, ed. W. M. Hennessy, Rolls Series, 1866.

Clarke, M. V., 'William of Windsor in Ireland, 1369–1376', *Proc. R.I.A.*, XLI C (1932), pp. 55–130.

——, *Medieval Representation and Consent*, London, 1936.

Close Rolls of the Reign of Henry III, London, 1902–38.

Collectio Canonum Hibernensis, ed. H. Wasserschleben, *Die irische Kanonensammlung*, Leipzig, 1885.

Colmcille, Fr., O.C.S.O., *The Story of Mellifont*, Dublin, 1958. (See also Ó Conbhuí.)

Complete Peerage of England, Scotland, Ireland, Great Britain and the United Kingdom, ed. Vicary Gibbs, London, 1910–59.

Confession of St Patrick, ed. L. Bieler, *Libri Epistolarum Sancti Patricii Episcopi*, Dublin, 1952. Trsl. L. Bieler, *The Works of St. Patrick*, London, 1953.

County Louth Archaeological Journal, Dundalk, 1904– .

Crede Mihi: the most ancient register book of the archbishops of Dublin before the reformation, ed. J. T. Gilbert, Dublin, 1897.

Crith Gablach, ed. D. Binchy, Dublin, 1941.

Curtis, E., 'The Clan System among English Settlers in Ireland', *E.H.R.*, XXV (1910), pp. 116–20.

——, *Richard II in Ireland, 1394–5, and Submissions of the Irish Chiefs*, Oxford, 1927.

——, 'Unpublished Letters from Richard II in Ireland, 1394–5', *Proc. R.I.A.*, XXXVII C (1927), pp. 276–303.

——, 'Sheriffs' Accounts of the Honor of Dungarvan, of Twescard in Ulster, and of County Waterford', *Proc. R.I.A.*, XXXIX C (1929), pp. 1–17.

——, 'The "Bonnaght" of Ulster', *Hermathena*, XXI (1931), pp. 87–105.

——, 'Richard Duke of York as Viceroy of Ireland, 1447–1460', *Journ. R.S.A.I.*, LXII (1932), pp. 158–86.

——, 'Rental of the Manor of Lisronagh, 1333, and Notes on "Betagh" Tenure in Medieval Ireland', *Proc. R.I.A.*, XLIII C (1934), pp. 41–76.

——, 'The Barons of Norragh, Co. Kildare', *Journ. R.S.A.I.*, LXV (1935), pp. 84–101.

——, 'The Pardon of Henry Blake of Galway in 1395', *Journal of the Galway Archaeological and Historical Society*, XVI (1935), pp. 186–9.

——, 'The MacQuillan or Mandeville Lords of the Route', *Proc. R.I.A.*, XLIV C (1938), pp. 99–113.

——, *History of Mediaeval Ireland from 1086 to 1513*, 2nd edition, London, 1938.

Davies, Sir John, *Discovery of the True Causes Why Ireland was never Entirely Subdued*, London, 1747 (first edition, London, 1612).

Devitt, M., 'The Barony of Okethy', *Kildare Archaeological Society Journal*, VIII (1915–17), pp. 276–301, 388–98, 464–88.

Devon, F., *Issues of the Exchequer*, London, 1837.

Dowdall Deeds, ed. C. McNeill and J. Otway-Ruthven, Irish MSS Commission, 1960.

Dunning, P. J., 'The Arroasian Order in Medieval Ireland', *I.H.S.*, IV (1945), pp. 297–315.

——, 'Letters of Pope Innocent III to Ireland', *Archivium Hibernicum*, XIII (1947), pp. 27–44.

——, 'Irish Representatives and Irish Ecclesiastical Affairs at the Fourth Lateran Council', *Medieval Studies Presented to Aubrey Gwynn, S.J.*, pp. 90–113.

Edwards, R. D., 'Papal Provisions in Fifteenth Century Ireland', *Medieval Studies Presented to Aubrey Gwynn, S.J.*, pp. 265–80.

Éigse: a journal of Irish studies, Dublin, 1939– .

Ellis, Sir H., *Original Letters Illustrative of English History*, second series, London, 1827.

——, third series, London, 1846.

English Historical Review, London and New York, 1886– .

Ériu: the journal of the School of Irish Learning, Dublin, 1904– .

Expugnatio Hibernica, Giraldi Cambrensis Opera, V, ed. J. F. Dimock. (Rolls Series, 1867), pp. 207–411.

Extents of Irish Monastic Possessions, 1540–1541, ed. N. B. White, Irish MSS Commission, 1943.

Feil-Sgríbhinn Éoin Mhic Néill, ed. J. Ryan, Dublin, 1940.

FitzMaurice, E. B. and Little, A. G., *Materials for the History of the Franciscan Province of Ireland*, British Society of Franciscan Studies, IX, Manchester, 1920.

Foedera, Conventiones, Litterae, et Cujuscunque Generis Acta Publica, ed. T. Rymer. 4 vols. in 7, Record Commission, 1816–69.

Galbraith, V. H. 'The *Modus Tenendi Parliamentum*', *Journal of the Warburg and Courtauld Institutes*, XVI, pp. 81–99.

Gilbert, Sir J. T., *Facsimiles of the National MSS of Ireland*, 4 parts in 8, Ordnance Survey Office, Southampton, 1874.

——, *History of the Viceroys of Ireland*, Dublin, 1865.

Gleeson, D. F., 'The Coarbs of Killaloe Diocese', *Journ. R.S.A.I.*, LXXIX (1949), pp. 160–69.

——, *A History of the Diocese of Killaloe*, Dublin, 1962.

Griffith, M. C., 'The Talbot-Ormond Struggle for Control of the Anglo-Irish Government, 1414–47', *I.H.S.*, II (1941), pp. 376–97.

Gwynn, A., S.J., 'The Black Death in Ireland', *Studies*, XXIV (1935), pp. 25–42.

——, 'Ireland and the English Nation at the Council of Constance', *Proc. R.I.A.*, XLV C (1940), pp. 183–233.

——, 'Nicholas Mac Maol Íosa, Archbishop of Armagh, 1272–1303', *Feil-Sgríbhinn Éoin Mhic Néill* (1940), pp. 394–405.

——, *The Medieval Province of Armagh*, Dundalk, 1946.

——, 'The Origins of St. Mary's Abbey, Dublin', *Journ. R.S.A.I.*, LXXIX (1949), pp. 110–25.

——, 'Henry of London, Archbishop of Dublin', *Studies*, XXXVIII (1949), pp. 295–306, 389–402.

——, 'Edward I and the Proposed Purchase of English Law for the Irish', *Trans. R. Hist. Soc.*, 5th series, 10 (1960), pp. 117–27.

Hadcock, R. N., 'The Order of the Holy Cross in Ireland', *Medieval Studies Presented to Aubrey Gwynn, S.J.*, pp. 44–53.

Hand, G. J., 'The Dating of the Early Fourteenth-Century Ecclesiastical Valuations of Ireland', *Irish Theological Quarterly*, XXIV (1957), pp. 271–4.

——, 'The Medieval Chapter of St. Mary's Cathedral, Limerick', *Medieval Studies Presented to Aubrey Gwynn, S.J.*, pp. 74–89.

——, 'The Status of the Native Irish in the Lordship of Ireland, 1272–1331', *The Irish Jurist*, new series, I (1966), pp. 93–115.

——, 'The Forgotten Statutes of Kilkenny: a brief Survey', *The Irish Jurist*, new series, I (1966), pp. 299–312.

——, *English Law in Ireland, 1290–1324*, Cambridge, 1967.

Handbook of British Chronology, 2nd edition, ed. Sir F. M. Powicke and E. B. Fryde, Royal Historical Society, 1961.

Historic and Municipal Documents of Ireland, ed. J. T. Gilbert, Rolls Series, 1870.

Historical Studies: IV, ed. G. A. Hayes-McCoy, London, 1963.

——, V, ed. J. L. McCracken, London, 1965.

History of the Church of Ireland, ed. W. Alison Phillips, Vol. II, Oxford, 1934.

Hogan, J., 'The Tricha Cét and Related Land Measures', *Proc. R.I.A.*, XXXVIII C (1929), pp. 148–235.

Hore, P. H., *History of the Town and County of Wexford*, 6 vols., London, 1900–11.

Hughes, K., 'The Offices of S. Finnian of Clonard and S. Cíanán of Duleek', *Analecta Bollandiana*, LXXIII (1955), pp. 342–72.

——, 'Additional Note on the Office of St. Finnian of Clonard', *Analecta Bollandiana*, LXXV (1957), pp. 337–9.

——, *The Church in Early Irish Society*, London, 1966.

The Irish Cartularies of Llanthony Prima and Secunda, ed. E. St. J. Brooks, Irish MSS Commission, 1953.

The Irish Ecclesiastical Record, Dublin, 1864– .

Irish Historical Studies, Dublin, 1938– .

Irish Monastic and Episcopal Deeds, A.D. 1200–1600, ed. N. B. White, Irish MSS Commission, 1936.

The Irish Pipe Roll of 14 John, ed. O. Davies and D. B. Quinn, *Ulster Journal of Archaeology*, 3rd series, IV (1941), supplement.

Jacobi Grace, Kilkenniensis, Annales Hiberniae, ed. R. Butler, Irish Archaeological Society, 1842.

Journal of the Cork Historical and Archaeological Society, Cork, 1892– .

The Journal of the Royal Society of Antiquaries of Ireland, Dublin, 1849–

Lawlor, H. J., 'A Calendar of the Register of Archbishop Sweteman', *Proc. R.I.A.*, XXIX C (1911), pp. 213–310.

——, 'A Calendar of the Register of Archbishop Fleming', *Proc. R.I.A.*, XXX C (1912), pp. 94–190.

——, 'Fragments of a Lost Register of the Diocese of Clogher,' *County Louth Archaeological Journal*, IV (1916–20), pp. 226–57.

Leask, H. G., *Irish Castles and Castellated Houses*, Dundalk, 1941.

Leland, T., *History of Ireland*. 3 vols., London, 1773.

Letters and Papers Illustrative of the Reigns of Richard III and Henry VII, ed. J. Gairdner, 2 vols., Rolls Series, 1861–3.

Liber Primus Kilkenniensis, ed. C. McNeill, Irish MSS Commission, 1931.

Lydon, J. F., 'An Irish Army in Scotland, 1296', *The Irish Sword*, V (1962), pp. 184–90.

——, 'Irish Levies in the Scottish Wars, 1296–1302', *The Irish Sword*, V (1962), pp. 205–17.

——, 'Richard II's Expeditions to Ireland', *Journ. R.S.A.I.*, XCIII (1963), pp. 135–49.

——, 'The Bruce Invasion of Ireland', *Historical Studies* IV (1963), pp. 111–25.

——, 'Edward II and the Revenues of Ireland in 1311–12', *I.H.S.*, XIV (1964), pp. 39–57.

——, 'William of Windsor and the Irish Parliament', *E.H.R.*, LXXX (1965), pp. 252–67.

——, 'The Irish Church and Taxation in the Fourteenth Century', *I.E.R.*, CIII (1965), pp. 158–65.

——, 'Three Exchequer Documents from the Reign of Henry III', *Proc. R.I.A.*, LXV C (1966), pp. 1–27.

Lynch, W., *A View of the Legal Institutions, Honorary Hereditary Offices, and Feudal Baronies, Established in Ireland During the Reign of Henry the Second*, London, 1830.

McCracken, E., 'The Woodlands of Ireland circa 1600', *I.H.S.*, XI (1959), pp. 271–96.

MacIomhair, D., 'The Boundaries of Fir Rois', *County Louth Archaeological Journal*, XV (1962), pp. 144–79.

McKerral, A., 'West Highland Mercenaries in Ireland', *Scottish Historical Review*, XXX (1951), pp. 1–14.

MacNiocaill, G., *Na Buirgéisí XII–XV Aois*, 2 vols., Dublin, 1964.

——, 'The origins of the *Betagh*', *The Irish Jurist*, new series, I (1966), pp. 292-8.

Martin, F. X., 'The Irish Augustinian Reform Movement in the Fifteenth Century', *Medieval Studies Presented to Aubrey Gwynn, S.J.*, pp. 230–64.

Materials for a History of the Reign of Henry VII, ed. W. Campbell, 2 vols., Rolls Series, 1873–7.

Medieval Studies Presented to Aubrey Gwynn, S.J., ed. J. A. Watt, J. B. Morrall, F. X. Martin, O.S.A., Dublin, 1961.

Mills, J., 'Notices of the Manor of St. Sepulchre, Dublin, in the Fourteenth Century', *Journ. R.S.A.I.*, fourth series, IX (1889), pp. 31–41, 119–26.

——, 'Norman Settlement in Leinster: the Cantreds near Dublin', *Journ. R.S.A.I.*, XXIV (1894), pp. 160–75.

Miscellaneous Irish Annals (A.D. 1114–1437), ed. S. Ó hInnse, Dublin Institute for Advanced Studies, 1947.

Nicholson, R., 'A Sequel to Edward Bruce's Invasion of Ireland', *Scottish Historical Review*, XLII (1963), pp. 30–40.

——, 'An Irish Expedition to Scotland in 1335', *I.H.S.*, XIII (1963), pp. 197–211.

Nugent, W. F., 'Carlow in the Middle Ages', *Journ. R.S.A.I.*, LXXXV (1955), pp. 62–76.

Ó Conbhuí, C., 'The Lands of St. Mary's Abbey, Dublin', *Proc. R.I.A.*, LXII C (1962), pp. 21–86. (See also Colmcille.)

O'Doherty, J. F., 'Rome and the Anglo-Norman Invasion of Ireland', *I.E.R.*, XLII (1933), pp. 131–45.

——, 'St. Laurence O'Toole and the Anglo-Norman Invasion', *I.E.R.*, L (1937), pp. 449–77, 600–25; LI (1938), pp. 131–46.

——, 'Historical Criticism of the Song of Dermot and the Earl', *I.H.S.*, I (1938), pp. 4–20.

Orpen, G. H., *Ireland under the Normans, 1169–1333*, 4 vols., Oxford, 1911–20.

Otway-Ruthven, [A.] J., 'Anglo-Irish Shire Government in the Thirteenth Century', *I.H.S.*, V (1946), pp. 1–28.

——, 'The Dower Charter of John de Courcy's wife', *U.J.A.*, 3rd series, XII (1949), pp. 77–81.

——, 'The Request of the Irish for English Law, 1277–80', *I.H.S.*, VI (1949), pp. 261–9.

——, 'The Native Irish and English Law in Medieval Ireland', *I.H.S.*, VII (1950), pp. 1–16.

——, 'The Organization of Anglo-Irish Agriculture in the Middle Ages', *Journ. R.S.A.I.*, LXXXI (1951), pp. 1–13.

——, 'The Constitutional Position of the Great Lordships of South Wales', *Trans. R. Hist. Soc.*, 5th series, 8 (1958), pp. 1–20.

——, 'The Medieval County of Kildare', *I.H.S.*, XI (1959), pp. 181–99.

——, 'Knight Service in Ireland', *Journ. R.S.A.I.*, LXXXIX (1959), pp. 1–15.

——, 'Knights' Fees in Kildare, Leix and Offaly', *Journ. R.S.A.I.*, XCI (1961), pp. 163–81.

——, 'The Mediaeval Irish Chancery', *Album Helen Maud Cam*, II (Louvain-Paris, 1961), pp. 119–38.

——, 'The Medieval Church Lands of County Dublin', *Medieval Studies Presented to Aubrey Gwynn, S.J.* (1961), pp. 54–73.

——, 'Parochial Development in the Rural Deanery of Skreen', *Journ. R.S.A.I.*, XCIV (1964), pp. 111–22.

——, 'The Chief Governors of Mediaeval Ireland', *Journ. R.S.A.I.*, XCV (1965), pp. 227–36.

——, 'The Character of Norman Settlement in Ireland', *Historical Studies* V (1965), pp. 75–84.

——, 'Ireland in the 1350's: Sir Thomas de Rokeby and his Successors', *Journ. R.S.A.I.*, XCVII (1967).

——, 'The Partition of the de Verdon Lands in Ireland in 1332', *Proc. R.I.A.*, LXVI C (1967).

Parliaments and Councils of Mediaeval Ireland, ed. H. G. Richardson and G. O. Sayles, Irish MSS Commission, 1947.

Patrologia Latina, ed. J. P. Migne, 221 vols., Paris, 1844–64.

Pontificia Hibernica: Medieval Papal Chancery Documents concerning Ireland, ed. M. P. Sheehy, 2 vols., Dublin, 1962–5.

Proceedings of the International Congress of Celtic Studies, 1959, Dublin, 1962.

Proceedings and Ordinances of the Privy Council of England, ed. N. Harris Nicolas, 7 vols., Record Commission, 1834–7.

Proceedings of the Royal Irish Academy, Section C. Dublin, 1902– .

The Red Book of the Earls of Kildare, ed. G. MacNiocaill, Irish MSS Commission, 1964.

The Red Book of Ormond, ed. N. B. White, Irish MSS Commission, 1932.

The Register of John Swayne, ed. D. A. Chart, Belfast, 1935.

Registrum Prioratus Omnium Sanctorum juxta Dublin, ed. R. Butler, Irish Archaeological Society, 1845.

Report of Commissioners Respecting the Public Records of Ireland, 1810–15.

Reports of the Deputy Keeper of the Public Records of Ireland. See *Calendar of Christchurch Deeds* and *Catalogue of Pipe Rolls*.

Richardson, H. G., 'Norman Ireland in 1212', *I.H.S.*, III (1942), pp. 144–58.

——, 'Some Norman Monastic Foundations in Ireland', *Medieval Studies Presented to Aubrey Gwynn, S.J.*, pp. 29–43.

——, and Sayles, G. O., *The Irish Parliament in the Middle Ages*, Philadelphia, 1952.

——, 'Irish Revenue, 1278–1384', *Proc. R.I.A.*, LXII C (1962), pp. 87–100.

——, *The Administration of Ireland, 1172–1377*, Irish MSS Commission, 1963.

——, *Parliament in Medieval Ireland*, Dundalk, 1964.

A Roll of the Proceedings of the King's Council in Ireland, ed. J. Graves, Rolls Series, 1877.

Ronan, M. V., 'Some Mediaeval Documents', *Journ. R.S.A.I.*, LXVII (1937), pp. 229–41.

Rotuli Chartarum, 1199–1216, ed. T. D. Hardy, Record Commission, 1835.

Rotuli Litterarum Patentium, ed. T. D. Hardy, Record Commission, 1835.

Rotuli Parliamentorum, 7 vols., London, 1783.

Rotuli Selecti ad Res Anglicas et Hibernicas Spectantes, ed. J. Hunter, Record Commissioners, 1834.

Rotulorum Patentium et Clausorum Cancellarie Hibernie Calendarium, ed. E. Tresham, Irish Record Commission, 1828.

Rotulus Pipae Clonensis, ed. R. Caulfield, Cork, 1859.

Russell, J. C., 'Late-Thirteenth-Century Ireland as a Region', *Demography*, III (1966), pp. 500–12.

Sayles, G. O., 'The Siege of Carrickfergus Castle', *I.H.S.*, X (1956), pp. 94–100.

——, 'The Rebellious First Earl of Desmond', *Medieval Studies Presented to Aubrey Gwynn, S.J.*, pp. 203–29.

——, 'The Legal Proceedings against the First Earl of Desmond', *Analecta Hibernica*, XXIII (1966), pp. 3–47.

See also Richardson, H. G., and Sayles, G. O.

Sheehy, M. P., 'The Bull *Laudabiliter*: A Problem in Medieval *Diplomatique* and History', *Journal of the Galway Archaeological and Historical Society*, XXIX (1961), pp. 45–70.

The Song of Dermot and the Earl, ed. G. H. Orpen, Oxford, 1892.

Statutes and Ordinances and Acts of the Parliament of Ireland, King John to Henry V, ed. H. F. Berry, Dublin, 1907.

Statute Rolls of the Parliament of Ireland, Reign of King Henry the Sixth, ed. H. F. Berry, Dublin, 1910.

Statute Rolls of the Parliament of Ireland, First to the Twelfth Years of the Reign of King Edward the Fourth, ed. H. F. Berry, Dublin, 1914.

——, *Twelfth and Thirteenth to the Twenty-first and Twenty-second Years of the Reign of King Edward the Fourth*, ed. J. F. Morrissey, Dublin, 1939.

Studia Hibernica, Dublin, 1961– .

Studies: an Irish quarterly review, Dublin, 1912– .

Topographia Hibernica, Geraldi Cambrensis Opera, V, ed. J. F. Dimock (Rolls Series, 1867), pp. 3–204.

Thesaurus Palaeohibernicus, ed. W. Stokes and J. Strachan, 2 vols., Cambridge, 1901–3. Supplement, Halle, 1910.

Transactions of the Royal Historical Society, London, 1872– .

Ulster Journal of Archaeology, Belfast, 1853– .

Ussher's Works, ed. C. R. Elrington, 17 vols., Dublin, 1847–64.

Vetera Monumenta Hibernorum et Scotorum Historiam Illustrantia, ed. A. Theiner, Rome, 1864.

Watt, J. A., 'Laudabiliter in Medieval Diplomacy and Propaganda', *I.E.R.*, LXXXVII (1957), pp. 420–32.

——, 'English Law and the Irish Church: the Reign of Edward I', *Medieval Studies Presented to Aubrey Gwynn, S.J.*, pp. 133–67.

Wood, H., 'Letter from Domnal O'Neill to Fineen MacCarthy, 1317', *Proc. R.I.A.*, XXXVII C (1926), pp. 141–8.

——, 'The Muniments of Edmund de Mortimer, Third Earl of March, Concerning his Liberty of Trim', *Proc. R.I.A.*, XL C (1932), pp. 312–55.

Zeitschrift für celtische Philologie, Halle, 1896– .

Index

Abbeylara (Longford), 119, 121
Aberteivi: *see* Cardigan
Achonry, bishop of, 140
Adamnán, abbot of Iona, 19; Life of Columcille by, 18, 20
Adare (Limerick), 298
Aghabo (Leix), 264
Agincourt, battle of, 350, 357
Ahascragh (Galway), 217
Aherlow (Limerick), 282
Ailill Molt, king, 12
Airgialla (cos. Louth, Armagh and Monaghan), 20, 32 *n* 94
All Hallows, Dublin, priory of, 50, 112; prior of, 398
Allen, battle of, 11, 13
Amiens, the Mise of, 196
Amounderness (Lancashire), Hervey Walter of, 67
Anglesey: *see* Beaumaris
Angulos, the de, 90, 266. *See also* MacCostello *and* Nangle
Anjou, Margaret of, wife of Henry VI of England, 378, 388, 394
Annaghdown, bishop of, 325; Thomas Barrett, bishop of, 401–2
Annaly, Muinter Anghaile (south Longford), 53, 91, 200, 302, 385. *See also* O'Farrell
Antrim, modern co., 50, 59, 65, 72, 203, 224; the Glens of, 82, 224
Any (Hospital, Limerick), 250
Aquitaine, 42
Archbolds, the, 277
Ardagh (Longford), 53; diocese of, 126; the Ardagh Chalice, 27
Ardee (Louth), 222–3, 226; barony of, 70, 212, 222, 272
Ardfert (Kerry), diocese of, 131
Ardfinnan (Tipperary), 67
Ardglass (Down), 369
Ardmail (Tipperary), 112
Ardnurcher (Westmeath), 78, 97; rural deanery of, 127

Ardrahan (Galway), 205
Ardscull (Kildare), 228–9
Arezzo, 37 *n* 5
Argentan, 48
Arklow (Wicklow), 35, 235, 250, 357
Armagh, 26 *n* 76, 32, 336; Franciscans at, 143; modern county, 25, 70
Armagh, Book of, 20, 32; church of, 17, 20–21, 22; abbots of, 14, 18, 20–21, 22; bishops of, 20; St Malachy of, 40; archbishops of, 39, 130, 141, 145, 235 *n* 38; (Nicholas Mac Maol Íosa), 38; (Gelasius), 51, 56; (Luke Netterville), 131 (Stephen Segrave), 215; (Richard fitz Ralph), 281; (Milo Sweetman), 295; (John Colton), 321, 324, 328, 329, 331, 334; (John Swayne), 358, 364, 368; (John Mey), 379. *See also* John Colton, Edmund Connesburgh, Richard fitz Ralph, Walter Jorz, Nicholas Mac Maol Íosa, John Mey, Thomas O'Colman Octavian del Palatio, John Swayne
Armagh, dean of, 141; diocese of, 141; registers of, 136, 141; province of, 39, 130, 133, 140, 369
Arra, Aros (Tipperary), 67, 267, 273 *n* 71; barony of Owney and Arra, 67
Arroasian canons, 40, 129
Arundel, earl of, 337
Art, Sheyn son of, 274
Asgall, king of Dublin, 46, 47
Askeaton (Limerick), 262, 279
Assaroe (Donegal), 82; abbot of, 136 *n* 47
Assheton, Robert de, 300, 301–2
Athassel (Tipperary), 247
Athenry (Galway), 193, 201 *n* 25, 203, 227, 369; lords of: *see* Bermingham
Athleague (Lanesborough, co. Longford), 90, 94
Athleague (Roscommon), 255